Time for My Soul

Time for My Soul

*A Treasury of Jewish Stories
for Our Holy Days*

Annette Labovitz
Eugene Labovitz

Jason Aronson Inc.
Northvale, New Jersey
London

First Jason Aronson Inc. softcover edition—1996

Copyright © 1987 by Annette Labovitz and Eugene Labovitz

10 9 8 7 6 5 4 3 2 1

Library of Congress Cataloging-in-Publication Data

Time for my soul.

    Includes bibliographical references.
    1. Fasts and feasts—Judaism—Meditations. 2. Fasts
and feasts—Judaism—Literary collections. 3. Hasidim—
Legends. I. Labovitz, Annette. II. Labovitz, Eugene.
BM690.T55   1987   296.4'3   86-32243
ISBN 0-87668-954-3 (hardcover)
ISBN 1-56821-924-5 (softcover)

Manufactured in the United States of America. Jason Aronson Inc. offers books and cassettes. For information and catalog write to Jason Aronson Inc., 230 Livingston Street, Northvale, New Jersey 07647.

Behold, days are coming, and I will send
          a famine in the land,
But the famine will not be for bread,
And the thirst will not be for water,
But to hear the word of God.

Amos 8:11

Contents

Foreword

Civilization has half destroyed the world with its soullessness.

We Jewish people lost a whole generation by making Judaism so shallow that our young people all over the world refuse to make anything so meaningless part of their lives. The saddest moments in my life are when I meet Jews who don't have the faintest idea how deep, how beautiful, and how heavenly our *Torah* and the holidays are. God, in His infinite mercy, is again rebuilding the world, again rebuilding the holiness of us Jewish people.

Annette and Eugene Labovitz are in the forefront of this great rebuilding. Their book is not just a book. It is one of the stones with which God is rebuilding Jerusalem.

This book will give so many people a chance, not only to understand with their head but to taste with their very tongue the sweetness of our festivals.

Blessings and love,
Shlomo Carlebach

Preface

Once, Rebbe Yisachar Ber of Radishitz, a disciple of Rebbe Yaacov Yitzchak, Hachozeh (the Seer of Lublin), passed through a village and arranged to stay in the inn for the night. The innkeeper made his guest comfortable and then retired.

That night Rebbe Yisachar Ber could not sleep; he paced and sprinted, sometimes with a brisk gait, sometimes nimble-footedly skipping a beat. He paced to an invisible rhythm.

The innkeeper was trying to sleep in the room below, but he was restless. He listened to the dance steps pounding on the ceiling overhead all night.

In the morning, the innkeeper asked his guest why he could not sleep, why he danced all night, why he paced the floor.

Rebbe Yisachar Ber replied, "Before I answer your question, let me ask you one. Tell me, where did you buy the clock that is hanging on the wall of my room?"

"I did not buy that clock," said the innkeeper. "It was given to me by a lodger in payment for room and board. Let me tell you what happened." The innkeeper spoke rapidly.

Once, Rebbe Yosef of Torchyn was on the road between Lublin and Torchyn. Without warning, the sky on that unusually warm, sunny day turned into a mass of rumbling clouds. Lightning blazed across the heavens. Rebbe Yosef sought shelter in this inn. I made him comfortable. He remained for a few days, until the stormy weather subsided and the roads were passable. When he approached to thank me for my hospitality, I asked payment for room and board. He was not prepared to pay for his lodging, so he said, "I have no money with me, but I do have a few precious possessions that I inherited from my father, the Seer of Lublin. I carry them with me wherever I travel. I will let you choose whatever you think is equal to the price of room and board."

He opened his backpack and spread out a long black coat, a belt, and a clock. I looked over the three items, hesitated, but couldn't decide what I wanted, so I ran to call my wife. We examined the three items and whispered to each other. Finally, my wife said, "The coat and the belt are of absolutely no value to us, but we could use the clock, since it will chime the hour we are supposed to milk our cow."

Lowering my voice, I whispered, "We will accept the clock in payment for your room and board."

Excitedly, Rebbe Yisachar Ber shrieked, "I knew this clock once belonged to my teacher, the Seer of Lublin. You see, normally a clock ticks away the minutes and hours. It ticks away: One day, another day gone, *oy vey*, another day gone, *oy vey*." He paused and scowled. "But this clock—this clock that once belonged to my rebbe—sings: One day closer, one day closer, one day closer. When I heard the chimes of my rebbe's clock, I could not sleep. How could anyone who really hears the message of my rebbe's clock ever sleep?"

Acknowledgments

The Torah thoughts and stories in *Time for My Soul* were taken from the writings and lives of the following holy masters:

Rebbe Klonimous Kalman Epstein, Cracow
Rebbe Sholom Rokeach, Belz
Rebbe Avraham ben Rebbe Yitzchak Mattisyahu Weinberg, Slonim
Rebbi Elyahu ben Shlomo, Vilna Gaon
Rebbe Zusia, Anipoli
Rebbe Nachum, Tzernoble
Rebbe Mayer Halayve, Apt
Rebbe Mordechai, Neschiz
Rebbe Elimelech, Lizensk
Rebbe Yisrael Friedman, Rizhin
Rebbe Areleh Roth, Me'ah She'arim, Israel
Rebbe Moshe David Friedman, Putik
The *maggid* of Koshnitz
Rebbi Yitzchak Luria, Arizal
Rebbe Pinchas Shapiro, Koretz
Rebbe Aharon Hagadol, Karlin-Stolin
Rebbe Yisachar Ber, Radishitz
Rebbe Yaakov Yitzchak Horowitz, Hachozeh, Lublin
Rebbe Mordechai Yosef, Izbitzia
Rebbe Chanoch Henich Hakohen, Aleksander

Rebbe Nachman, Bratzlav
Rabbi Yehuda Lev Ben Bezalel Loew, Maharal, Prague
Rebbe Yechezkel Shraga Halberstam, Shinova
Rebbe Shlomo Hakohen, Radomsk
Rebbe Shmuel, Kaminka
Rebbe Tzvee Hirsh, Nadverna
Rebbe Yisrael ben Eliezer, Baal Shem Tov, Medziboz
Rebbe Yehuda Layb Ayger, Lublin
Rebbe Yaakov Yitzchak, Bialy
Rebbe Chaim Halberstam, Sanz
Rebbe Yosef Mayer, S'finka
Rebbe Layve Yitzchak, Berditchev
Rebbe Moshe Shabosker
Rebbe Gershon Chanoch, Izbitizia, Radzhin
Rabbi Yechezkel ben Yehuda Landau, Prague
Rebbe Avraham Yehoshua Heschel, Apt
Rebbe Tzvee Elimelech Shapiro, Diniv
Rebbe Mendele, Sokolov
Rebbe Mayer Kvaller
Rebbe Yechiel Mayer, Gustinin

Many of these stories were first brought to our attention by our friend Rabbi Shlomo Carlebach, an inimitable storyteller. He was also responsible for directing us to material which is not commonly known.

Our special thanks to Arthur Kurzweil, who envisioned *Time for My Soul* when it was but a small collection of stories, to Muriel Jorgensen, whose meticulous editing and guidance through every stage created a book from a manuscript, and to the staff at Jason Aronson.

Annette Labovitz
Eugene Labovitz

Introduction

As we travel around this country, we are consciously aware of the spiritual loneliness that is affecting so many people. It seems to us that this generation is searching for something. The questions we are most often asked are: If we were born Jewish, what does being Jewish mean? What does living Jewishly mean? How is Judaism relevant to our lives?

Our book, *Time for My Soul: A Treasury of Jewish Stories for Our Holy Days*, provides a few clues about living Jewishly. Through the *Torah* thoughts and stories spanning the Jewish calendar year, the reader will be introduced to Jewish living. The essences of the *Torah* thoughts describe not only how and why we observe Jewish holidays, but they also provide a deeper spiritual meaning for the symbols of our holy days. The stories depict the role models, the patterns, the glimpses of the past that are part of our magnificent heritage. They show how our people lived, coped with the ever-changing vicissitudes of their Diaspora experience, persevered through difficulties, yet always incorporated everyday living with spiritual moments.

We have met people who, because of their loneliness or lack of knowledge of their own heritage, are running away from Juda-

ism. To those of you who may be feeling alienated, we hope that
you will keep an open mind and avoid discarding what is right-
fully your tradition. To those of you who are fortunate enough to
have been born into an observant, knowledgeable environment,
we hope that the thoughts and stories in this book will give you
an even deeper insight into the spirituality of our religion.

This book is a tool to help begin the search or to continue the
search for a rich Jewish tradition. We hope it will be the spade
with which you dig into your past and uncover is roots. We hope
it will help you discover where you come from, so you will have a
clearer idea of the direction you are headed.

The following story is symbolic of our hopes and dreams to
instill in you a desire to keep our tradition alive, to transmit these
thoughts and stories to your children, grandchildren, and
great-grandchildren.

Rebbe Aharon Hagadol of Karlin-Stolin lived approximately one
hundred years after Rebbe Yisrael ben Eliezer, the Baal Shem
Tov, founder of the chasidic movement. The Karliner taught his
disciples to *daven* fervently, loudly, with great enthusiasm.
They screamed and yelled at the top of their lungs. They did this
to remove all alien thoughts from their minds during prayer.[1]

In Karlin-Stolin, it was the custom to *daven minchah*[2] very
late. The Karliner explained, "When I come up to the Heavenly
court, I will be asked why I *daven minchah* so late. This is what I
will answer. Master of the Universe! Why are You so late in
sending the Messiah to redeem Your people?"

One afternoon, the Karliner said to a few of his *chasidim*,
"Harness the horses to the wagon. We have to travel to a distant
shtetl before we can *daven minchah*."

They looked at each other in amazement, for even they
knew that the time was rapidly approaching when it would be
too late for the afternoon prayer.

They traveled long past dark. Finally, one of the *chasidim*

---

[1]The Karlin-Stolin *chasidim* still *daven* in the same manner today.

[2]According to Jewish law, the afternoon service should be completed before sunset.

said assertively, "Rebbe, it is getting so late. We really have to stop along the way to *daven*."

The rebbe pointed in the direction they were traveling and answered reflectively, "See that little inn on the top of the hill, at the edge of this *shtetl*? One of the few Jews in this *shtetl* lives in that inn. That's where we will *daven minchah*."

The wagon stopped at the inn. The rebbe and his *chasidim* alighted, walked up the path, and knocked at the door. A very old man responded to their knock. He stood in the doorway, startled.

The *chasidim* asked the old man, "We have arrived with our rebbe from far away. We need to *daven minchah*. May we come in?"

The old man moved away from the doorway, and the rebbe and his *chasidim* entered one by one. They knew that there must be a special reason for their rebbe to have taken them to this inn in order to *daven minchah*. The reason was not apparent to them yet, but they screamed and yelled the *minchah* prayer, as was their custom.

A few peasants were still roaming the street. When they heard the screaming and the shouting, they thought there was a fire in the inn. They ran to their homes to fetch buckets of water to extinguish the fire.

When they returned with their buckets, they saw that the fire was from the prayers of the Karliner. They put down their buckets and joined the rebbe. After the service, the peasants wanted to show how much they loved the rebbe and his *chasidim*, how grateful they were for having been allowed to share in holy praying. They ran home again. This time they returned with apples, grapes, and oranges.

Together they arranged a feast. They sang and studied with the rebbe until very late. Then the rebbe stood up. He wanted to bless each one of the peasants before he returned home. Afterwards, he bid farewell to them and motioned his *chasidim* out of the inn. They piled into the wagon. The rebbe was the last one to emerge. When he was seated in his place in the wagon, he called the old man out of the inn and said to him, "*Nu!* Tell me already!"

The old man said hesitatingly, "I want you to know that my grandfather lived in this house. Exactly one hundred years ago, when I was a lad of seven, the Baal Shem Tov was here. I remember the occasion so clearly. It was exactly like tonight. He arrived late, with a group of his followers. He asked my grandfather if he could *daven minchah* in this inn. When the peasants heard that the Baal Shem Tov was here, they came running from the surrounding area. They joined him in prayer, pouring out their hearts for the coming of the Messiah. Then they ran back to their homes and brought apples, oranges, and grapes. They made a feast. They studied and sang. Afterwards, the Baal Shem Tov blessed each one of them. Before the Baal Shem Tov left, he put his hands on my head and said, 'My dear little boy, remember what I am telling you. I want you to know that one hundred years from now, someone will come here. He will do the same thing I did. Tell him I was here. Tell him I was here.' "

To all of you, we hope this book will provide the cement between you and yet unborn generations, so you will be blessed to retell to your heirs the *Torah* thoughts and stories in *Time for My Soul.*

ANNALS OF COMMUNISM

Each volume in the series Annals of Communism will publish selected and previously inaccessible documents from former Soviet state and party archives in a narrative that develops a particular topic in the history of Soviet and international communism. Separate English and Russian editions will be prepared. Russian and Western scholars work together to prepare the documents for each volume. Documents are chosen not for their support of any single interpretation but for their particular historical importance or their general value in deepening understanding and facilitating discussion. The volumes are designed to be useful to students, scholars, and interested general readers.

Stalin's Secret Pogrom

The Postwar Inquisition of the
Jewish Anti-Fascist Committee

ABRIDGED EDITION

Edited and with introductions by
Joshua Rubenstein and
Vladimir P. Naumov

Translated by Laura Esther Wolfson

Published in association with the
United States Holocaust Memorial Museum

Yale University Press
New Haven and London

Published with assistance from the Kingsley Trust Association Publication Fund established by the Scroll and Key Society of Yale College.

This volume has been prepared with the cooperation of the Presidential Commission of the Russian Federation on the Rehabilitation of Victims of Political Repression.

The assertions, arguments, and conclusions contained herein are those of the volume editors. They do not necessarily reflect the opinions of the United States Holocaust Memorial Council or the United States Holocaust Memorial Museum.

Abridged edition published in 2005.

Designed by James J. Johnson and set in Sabon type by The Composing Room of Michigan, Inc., Grand Rapids, Michigan.
Printed in the United States of America by Vail-Ballou Press, Binghamton, New York.

Library of Congress Cataloging-in-Publication Data

Nepravednyi sud. English.
Stalin's secret pogrom : the postwar inquisition of the Jewish Anti-Fascist Committee / edited and with introductions by Joshua Rubenstein and Vladimir P. Naumov ; translated by Laura Esther Wolfson.—Abridged ed.
p.   cm. — (Annals of Communism)
Includes bibliographical references and index.
ISBN 0-300-10452-9 (pbk. : alk. paper)

1. Lozovskii, .A., 1878–1952—Trials, litigation, etc.   2. Evreiskii antifashistskii komitet v SSSR—Trials, litigation, etc.   3. Trials (Political crimes and offenses)—Russia (Federation)—Moscow.   4. Courts-martial and courts of inquiry—Soviet Union.   5. Judicial error—Soviet Union.   6. Jews—Persecutions—Soviet Union.   7. World War, 1939–1945—Jews.   I. Rubenstein, Joshua.   II. Naumov, Vladimir Pavlovich.   III. Title. IV. Series.
KLA41.L69N4713   2005
345.47′0231—dc22

2005041774

A catalogue record for this book is available from the British Library.

The paper in this book meets the guidelines for permanence and durability of the Committee on Production Guidelines for Book Longevity of the Council on Library Resources.

10   9   8   7   6   5   4   3   2   1

Yale University Press gratefully acknowledges the financial support given for this publication by the John M. Olin Foundation, the Lynde and Harry Bradley Foundation, the Historical Research Foundation, Roger Milliken, Lloyd H. Smith, Keith Young, the William H. Donner Foundation, Joseph W. Donner, Jeremiah Milbank, the David Woods Kemper Memorial Foundation, the Daphne Seybolt Culpeper Foundation, the Milton V. Brown Foundation, and the Lucius N. Littauer Foundation.

For Jill and Benjamin

Contents

Illustrations follow page 64

Preface

IN the spring and summer of 1952, a secret trial was held of a large group of Jewish figures who were connected, in one degree or another, with the activities of the Jewish Anti-Fascist Committee (JAC). In the press there was no hint that the trial was taking place, even though some of the defendants were well-known scholars, political and social figures, poets, and writers. In the indictment they were accused of grave crimes against the state, including hostile, antigovernment activities and espionage. Their names vanished from the pages of newspapers and journals and from all historical, literary, and other publications. It was as if these people had never existed. In those rare instances in which any of them were mentioned by scholars or journalists, it was never without derogatory epithets.

After Stalin's death, on March 5, 1953, the material in the case of the Jewish Anti-Fascist Committee was reviewed. In the summer of 1953 the security agencies, the prosecutor's office, and the political leaders of the country possessed irrefutable evidence of the complete innocence of all the defendants. Investigation showed that the case of the Jewish Anti-Fascist Committee was a gross fabrication by the investigative agencies and that the "confessions" of the defendants had been obtained through torture and refined mistreatment. In those years, however, the final decision on rehabilitation was made by the highest party organs. They took that step in 1955, but in secret. Open publication of the decision was forbidden. Knowledgeable people could only guess what happened from the fact that the names of several convicted in the JAC case began to appear in the press without the usual denunciations. The censors ensured that no information leaked out about their fate. The rehabilitation of the victims in the JAC case was not spoken of openly and directly until late 1988, thirty-six years after their unjust trial; it took several more years for the documents associated with the case to see the light of day. In the late 1930s, publication was undertaken of the transcript of the trial of the "Rightist-Trotskyite Bloc," including Nikolai Bukharin, but there are sound reasons for believing that the text is unreliable, indeed, fabricated (*The Case of the Anti-Soviet "Bloc of Rights and Trotskyites" Heard Before the Military Collegium of the Supreme Court of the U.S.S.R.* [Moscow, 1938]).

In the overwhelming majority of cases, sentences within the walls of the Lubyanka prison were passed by the Special Council of the Ministry of State Security. This extra-judicial agency had an extremely simplified procedure for examining cases. On occasion, more than two hundred cases were examined in a single session. In essence, the council formally confirmed a sentence decided on before the session began.

Political trials occupied a special place in the Soviet system as one of the means of maintaining power and as a method of shaping public opinion. These trials were like the apexes of gigantic pyramids of repression, the sizes of which today seem monstrous. The trial of the JAC was the last trial held in Stalin's time and under his direction. It reveals little-known aspects of the internal policies of the Soviet government in the 1940s and 1950s, and specifically the anti-Semitism that had far-reaching consequences for both the domestic and the foreign policies of the country.

Direct supervision of the case against the JAC case was initially assigned to Vladimir Komarov, deputy chief of the investigative unit for especially important cases of the secret police (MGB). The essence of this man, his morality and his style of thinking, are revealed in a letter that he wrote to Stalin in February 1953, when he himself was enjoying all the luxuries of Lefortovo's internal prison. He bragged:

> Members of the investigative unit know well enough how much I hate our enemies. I had no pity for them and, so to speak, squeezed the spirit out of them and made them reveal their enemy contacts and deeds.

Defendants literally trembled before me. They feared me like the plague, feared me more than they did the other investigators. Even the minister did not evoke the terror that they showed when I personally interrogated them. Enemies under arrest fully knew and sensed my hatred of them. They saw me as an investigator who had a harsh punitive attitude toward them and therefore, as other investigators told me, they tried in every way to avoid meeting me or having me interrogate them. . . . I especially hated and was pitiless toward Jewish nationalists, whom I saw as the most dangerous and evil enemies. Because of my hatred of them I was considered an anti-Semite not only by the defendants but by former employees of the MGB who were of Jewish nationality.

Undoubtedly, Komarov's anti-Semitism was why he was assigned to head the investigation of the JAC. In the hands of this monster, the case of the so-called Jewish nationalists was to have been quickly closed and sent to the judicial agencies.

The investigation bogged down, even though the qualities of torturer and butcher of which Komarov was so proud were fully displayed to those arrested in the case. We cannot completely envisage the torments to which these people were subjected once they were inside the Lubyanka, but there is evidence from the victims themselves and admissions by their interrogators that give us an idea of how so-called confessions were obtained and how the judicial farce was prepared.

In a letter to the chairman of the Military Collegium of the USSR Supreme Court dated June 6, 1952, Boris Shimeliovich wrote that on the first day of his arrest, on the orders of Minister of State Security Viktor Abakumov, one investigator and several other personnel had beaten him right in the minister's reception room. Each of them tried to hit Shimeliovich in the face. They beat him with a rubber truncheon and kicked him in the legs. The beatings continued during his subsequent time in prison, becoming more intense when he refused to sign a confession. After a month of interrogation Shimeliovich was brought to the investigator's office on a stretcher. Even after that, the torture and beatings did not stop.

Soon after their arrests, the other prisoners also underwent interrogations every night or endured freezing cells and solitary confinement.

The testimony that the investigators obtained from the defendants during interrogation underwent special processing in the secretariat of the Ministry of State Security, the MGB. Jacob Broverman, deputy chief of the secretariat, embellished the testimonies so that they turned into self-accusations and confessions to criminal activities. The investigators understood the role that Broverman was assuming and called his office "Broverman's kitchen" because it was there that the defendants' testimonies were "cooked" according to the needs of the investigation.

The MGB leadership hastened to inform Stalin of the successful course of the investigation and sent him special reports, memorandums, and interrogation records on the principal defendants. In the first two months of the investigation Stalin was sent about twenty such interrogation records.

A short time after the intensive interrogations had ended, some of the defendants retracted their confessions, and the investigation came to a halt. Facts were insufficient, and documents were lacking. Opposition from the defendants was disrupting the schedule for preparing the trial. More and more months went by without results. This was without precedent in MGB practice of that time.

Then, in March 1950, all the defendants in the JAC case were informed that the investigation was over—all except Itsik Fefer. He was therefore given to understand that he would not be among the defendants in the case.

The JAC case was ready for review by the Special Council. But the organizers had prepared for other scenarios, and these plainly indicate the special importance that was accorded to the forthcoming trial. Confessions of the defendants were needed not in the office of the investigators but by the Military Collegium of the USSR Supreme Court. To some degree there had to be public evidence of the charges. The MGB leadership was uncertain that it could bring about a trial with the available testimony. Nearly another year and a half went by, and the trial had still not started. This is how the first stage in the JAC case ended.

During the many years of investigation the conception of the trial had changed. Initially a broader-scale trial had been planned. In the indictment drawn up on March 25, 1950, others had figured in the role of defendant, including Polina Zhemchuzhina (the wife of Vyacheslav Molotov), the poet Shmuel Halkin, along with eleven others. This broader trial did not take place. The reasons for its cancellation call for further study. It is known, however, that in 1950 several principal participants in the future trial of the JAC—Solomon Lozovsky, Joseph Yuzefovich, and Benjamin Zuskin—retracted confessions that had been obtained through threats, blackmail, and torture. Boris Shimeliovich, moreover, never admitted that he was guilty of anything.

Meanwhile, events developed in the top echelons of the government and in the MGB leadership that were of genuine consequence for the fate of the JAC members under arrest.

In July 1951, Minister of State Security Viktor Abakumov was removed from his post and arrested. Right after that, the leaders of the investigative unit for especially important cases turned up in the cells of Lefortovo prison. Many investigators who had been involved in the JAC case were dismissed from the MGB. Direction of the investigation fell to Mikhail Ryumin, the new chief of the investigative unit for especially important cases.

Ryumin renewed investigation of the JAC case, initiating another round of interrogations, document analysis, and special examinations. Through Semyon Ignatiev, the new minister of state security, Ryumin obtained questions that had been prepared by Stalin himself for use in the interrogations. Ryumin supervised all the work of the investigative group and evidently had special authority from the highest level to complete the JAC case. Ryumin proudly boasted that he was the "plenipotentiary of the Central Committee to uncover the Jewish nationalistic center."

The investigation took new turns. Attempts were made to present the JAC as "the center" that directed the activities of Jewish nationalistic organizations in all government structures, including the MGB. The case was far from complete, but the Special Council still decided on grave measures of punishment, up to the death penalty. At that time, arrests and trials were taking place of the members of "the organization of Jewish bourgeois nationalists in industry" (for example, the Stalin Automobile Plant in Moscow and the Kuznetsk Metallurgical Combine), in the mass media, and in public health agencies. A trial was held of the leaders of the Jewish Autonomous Region (Birobidzhan), and Jewish employees of the Ministries of Foreign Affairs and State Security were arrested.

Ryumin pursued a harder prosecutorial line toward the defendants than had been followed by his predecessors, and he concealed the gross violations of legality and means by which the chief confessions had been obtained—by extortion, beatings, and threats.

Instructions were issued that former MGB personnel of Jewish nationality were to be considered members of a bourgeois nationalistic underground. Those who had worked abroad were interrogated as spies. The investigators were particularly tireless in attempting to uncover the connections that allegedly existed in the MGB between Jewish bourgeois nationalistic organizations and the JAC.

An especially important orientation of the investigation was the attempt to uncover a bourgeois nationalistic organization inside the party apparat. This was obviously not easy, for no Jews were left, but Ryumin nonetheless personally interrogated former MGB personnel along those lines.

The JAC case was also artificially linked to other cases that were handled by the MGB or the Military Collegium of the USSR Supreme Court. In all, there were about seventy such cases. The conception of the JAC case by its fabricators required them to prove the existence of an anti-Soviet bourgeois nationalistic center that directed a ramified Jewish bourgeois nationalistic organization throughout the entire Soviet Union. Ignatiev and Ryumin believed that they had to show the involvement of major figures in the activities of this organization, and therefore the investigators attempted to obtain testimony that Ilya Ehrenburg, perhaps the most highly regarded journalist in the country, was criminally involved in JAC activities. They even attempted to link the JAC to Kaganovich, Molotov, and other leading figures in the government.

In this stage of the investigation the organizers of the fabrication markedly stepped up their attempts to obtain from the defendants some evidence of their espionage activities. Ryumin later acknowledged that he had received from Stalin a questionnaire for interrogating the defendants in the JAC case that was largely devoted to the defendants' links to foreign intelligence services. The investigators made urgent attempts to find any documents that could show any links between JAC members and foreign intelligence personnel. But there were no such documents.

The leaders had high hopes for the archives of the JAC, which were in the possession of the investigators. To substantiate the fabricated conclusions reached in the investigation, a group of experts was set up to study and evaluate individual documents. It was the idea of Ignatiev and Ryumin to use these documents to establish a convincing scenario showing the guilt of the JAC leaders. Ryumin's suggestion seemed to provide a way out of the existing impasse.

Even before seeing the documents or dealing with the archives, Ignatiev and Ryumin informed Stalin that these documents fully revealed the committee's nefarious activities. In their letter to Stalin, Ignatiev and Ryumin stated that "these documents are of considerable operational interest from the standpoint of documenting the espionage and nationalistic activities of the defendants. Instructions have now been given to put these documents in order and to study them thoroughly. We cannot rule out that as a result of this work new instances will be disclosed of hostile activities of the defendants and it may become necessary to reopen the investigation into this case."

This task did not appear difficult to the MGB leadership. It was only necessary to gather "expert witnesses" who would provide what the MGB needed if placed in such conditions that they would be compelled to take up the position desired by the MGB and yield the results promised to Stalin. But despite all the subtlety, trickery, embellishments, outright inventions, and crudely overt pressure on the expert witnesses, the MGB was not able to obtain convincing documents testifying to either espionage or nationalistic activities by the JAC leadership.

Not all the expert witnesses sacrificed their consciences to accommodate the MGB. Solomon Lozovsky and Joseph Yuzefovich, for example, were accused of transmitting to American intelligence agencies highly secret information that had been prepared by a special unit of the Central Committee. The director of that unit, Nikolai Pukhlov, refuted all such claims in the indictment and convincingly showed that the document was nothing but material reprinted from the English press. Nonetheless, this document figured in the official indictment. It was the documentary foundation of the accusation against the JAC leaders.

The case was falling apart. The defendants retracted their confessions. The investigators hurriedly tried to revive them. The investigation had lasted more than three years, and even at the third and final stage it required another eight months to hammer out the indictments presented to the arrested members of the committee.

At the final stage of formulating the case, a group of investigators suggested removing Benjamin Zuskin, Leon Talmy, and Khayke Vatenberg-Ostrovskaya from among the accused, because they had not had any connection with the committee leadership and because the accusations against them were weak. Ryumin categorically turned down the suggestion out of fear that the case would collapse altogether.

By the spring of 1952 the investigation was complete. On March 5, Lieutenant Colonel Pavel Grishaev, assistant chief of the investigative unit for especially important cases of the MGB, carried out the decision to unite the investigative cases against Solomon Lozovsky, Itsik Fefer, Solomon Bregman, Joseph Yuzefovich, Boris Shimeliovich, Lina Shtern, Leyb Kvitko, David Hofshteyn, Peretz Markish, David Bergelson, Ilya

Vatenberg, Leon Talmy, Benjamin Zuskin, Emilia Teumin, and Khayke Vatenberg-Ostrovskaya into a single case and assign it the number 2354. All were accused of having committed crimes covered by articles 58-1a; 58-10, parts 1 and 2; and 58-11 of the RSFSR Criminal Code. Colonel Konyakhin, deputy chief of the investigative unit, approved that decision.

On March 22, 1952, Lieutenant Colonel Kuzmin, senior investigator of the investigative unit for especially important cases of the MGB, and Lieutenant Colonel of Justice Prikhodko of the Military Prosecutor's Office of MGB Troops, stated that the preliminary investigation on the case was complete and that the data obtained was sufficient for handing the defendants over for trial. They informed the defendants of this decision and allowed them to examine the entire case file. The defendants had eight days to read through forty-two massive volumes. It is hard to imagine how these tormented people, worn down by incarceration and endless interrogations, could read forty-two volumes in eight days when the investigators had had difficulty mastering the material in several months. But the course of the trial shows that they did study all the material that dealt not only with them personally but also with other participants in the trial.

In March 1952, on Ryumin's orders, Grishaev drew up the indictment in the JAC case. On March 31, Ryumin, as deputy minister of state security, approved the official indictment. On April 3, Semyon Ignatiev, minister of state security, sent the text of the official indictment to Stalin. His cover letter follows:

> Comrade Stalin:
> I hereby submit to you a copy of the official indictment in the case of the Jewish nationalists and American spies Lozovsky, Fefer et al. The investigative file has been sent for review by the Military Collegium of the USSR Supreme Court with the proposal that Lozovsky, Fefer, and all their accomplices, with the exception of Shtern, be shot.
> Shtern is to be exiled to a remote area for ten years.
>
> S. Ignatiev
> April 3, 1952

The following day the MGB was informed that the Politburo had approved the official indictment and had reached the decision to have all the defendants shot, with the exception of Lina Shtern. Her term of exile was reduced to five years. On April 5, 1952, Major General Kitaev, deputy chief prosecutor of the Soviet Army, drew up the following resolution: "Official indictment approved. Case to be submitted for review by the Military Collegium of the USSR Supreme Court without presence of prosecutors or defense."

On April 7, 1952, the case was submitted to the Military Collegium of the USSR Supreme Court. The Supreme Court specified that the Military Collegium reviewing the case would consist of the chairman, Lieutenant General of Justice Alexander Cheptsov, and the members Major General of Justice Ivan Zaryanov and Major General of Justice Jacob Dmitriev.

On April 21, 1952, the Military Collegium of the USSR Supreme Court held a preliminary session with the participation of the prosecutor, Kitaev, who reported on the circumstances of the case and the nature of the accusations and proposed that the official indictment be approved and submitted to the Military Collegium of the USSR Supreme Court and that all the defendants be tried on the charges in the indictment. The case was to be reviewed in secret judicial proceedings without participation by members of the state prosecutor's office or of defense counsel and without calling witnesses. Lieutenant General of Justice Cheptsov, the co-reporter, concurred in the opinion of Kitaev.

On May 8, 1952, the Military Collegium of the USSR Supreme Court began to review the JAC case. The judicial farce had begun. At the same time, the MGB's investigative unit for especially important cases launched a new round of repression. On March 13, 1952, a resolution was drawn up to begin an investigation into all the individuals whose names had been mentioned during the interrogations in the JAC case. This list included 213 people. Those involved were faced with loss of liberty, suffering, torment, and torture. Among them were many well-known figures, including Ilya Ehrenburg, Vasily Grossman, Samuil Marshak, and Matvei Blanter. Drawing on the large number of people designated for "arrest or already under arrest," Ignatiev set to work forming a group for future trials. The organizers of repression were already thinking of further steps. It was at that time that the "Doctors' Plot" began to unfold. From the very beginning it took on a sinister cast: it was to be a concluding chapter in Stalin's diabolical scheme to broaden repression against the Jews and to carry out massive repressions in the country as a whole.

The transcript of this trial was intended for official use only. The MGB leadership was dissatisfied with the course of the judicial proceedings and threatened Lieutenant General Cheptsov of the Military Collegium with punishment. It was very important to him to portray the judicial proceedings precisely, which probably explains the painstaking nature of the transcript. Under the document-handling rules of the punitive agencies, this published transcript of the trial in the JAC case was kept top-secret for many years, although it contains no state secrets whatsoever. The transcript shows the entire course of the judicial examination by the Military Collegium of the USSR Supreme Court between May 8 and July 18, 1952.

The text of the original transcript is divided into eight separate volumes. Two secret sessions of the Military Collegium are represented by minutes of those sessions signed by M. Afanasiev, judicial secretary of the collegium.

The transcript generally indicates the day and time of the judicial sessions of the Military Collegium. In all cases the hour and minute of the start and finish of the sessions are indicated. The dates on which the sessions were held are not always indicated, however. To determine these, special research had to be done based on analysis of various types of documents.

The secret sessions of the judicial collegium were not recorded by established procedures. They represent the minutes of meetings of sessions, signed by the secretary of the Military Collegium and were added separately to the transcript. To more fully present the entire picture of the judicial proceedings these minutes are inserted in the text of the transcript for the day of the secret session and are designated as such.

Vladimir P. Naumov
Translated by Francis M. McNulty

Acknowledgments

NUMEROUS colleagues and friends helped me to bring this volume to completion. I would like first to thank my Russian colleague Vladimir Pavlovich Naumov for his gracious hospitality and assistance during my two trips to Moscow in 1996 and 1997. Vladimir Pavlovich, who is executive secretary of the Presidential Commission of the Russian Federation on the Rehabilitation of Victims of Political Repression, responded to my numerous questions with patient authority. Other people in Russia deserve special mention for lending me their time and energy: Oleg Naumov of the Russian State Archive of Social and Political History (RGASPI) and his colleagues helped me in my research efforts, as did staff members of the State Archive of the Russian Federation (GARF) and the Russian State Archive of Literature and Art (RGALI). Boris Frezinsky has also been a constant source of information and judgment.

Relatives of several defendants, in Russia, Israel, and the United States, were generous with their time and permitted me to talk with them about their loved ones in spite of the emotional difficulty of recalling their tragic fates: Vladimir Shamberg; Dora Fefer; Vladimir Talmy; Levia Hofshteyn; Lev Bergelson, his wife Noya Lvovna, and their daughter Marina Raskina; Marina Yuzefovich; Tamara Zuskin-Platt and her sister Alla Zuskin-Perelman. I am also grateful to Nadezhda

Aizenshtadt Bergelson, Raya Kulbak, Fedor Lyass, Jessica Platner, and Anna Stonov and her son, Leonid, for speaking with me about their relatives who were also arrested and in some cases executed. Elisheva Bezverkhnaya shared many memories of the State Jewish Theater and the work and personalities of Solomon Mikhoels and Benjamin Zuskin.

I am particularly grateful to the Lucius N. Littauer Foundation for its support of my research efforts. The Forward Foundation honored me with the Lucy Dawidowicz Prize in History while I was still in the midst of my research and writing; hopefully, they will find this volume meets their highest standards.

I would also like to acknowledge the long-standing support of my colleagues at the Davis Center for Russian Studies at Harvard and the patient assistance of Anna Arthur of Widener Library. The assistance I received from the following archives was essential to my work: the Center for Judaic Studies at the University of Pennsylvania; the archive and library of the YIVO Institute in New York; the Library of Congress; the Andrei Sakharov Archives at Brandeis University, now at Harvard University; the Jewish Public Library of Montreal; the archive of the American Jewish Joint Distribution Committee in New York; the World Jewish Congress Collection of the Jacob Rader Marcus Center of American Jewish Archives in Cincinnati, Ohio; and the Reference Center for Marxist Studies in New York. Russ Taylor of the Special Collections and Manuscripts Division of the Harold B. Lee Library of Brigham Young University and Janet Jensen, the granddaughter of Franklin S. Harris, provided essential assistance.

Among the many scholars I consulted let me mention in particular Ruth Wisse, David Fishman, David Roskies, Thomas Bird, Avram Nowershtern, Shimon Redlich, Robert Conquest, Leonid Smilovitsky, Itche Goldberg, Zvi Gitelman, Eugene Orenstein, Omry Ronen, Harold J. Berman, Gennadi Kostyrchenko, Benjamin Harshav, David Brandenberger, Jeffrey Veidlinger, Henry Srebnik, Robert Weinberg, and Robert Tucker. Shirley Novick, Morris U. Schappes, Paul Robeson, Jr., Moisey Loyev, and Sidney J. Gluck, of New York, also gave me their time and assistance.

Martin Peretz and Leon Wieseltier of the *New Republic* took a strong interest in this project and published an essay of mine about the case when I was still in the early stages of my research. Working on this initial draft helped me to orient the direction of my research and thinking about the fate of the Jewish Anti-Fascist Committee.

My research assistant Edward Portnoy, of New York, proved to be an invaluable asset, translating Yiddish documents and answering innumerable questions about Yiddish literary and cultural history. Mark Kuchment helped me decipher the ins and outs of Soviet cultural and political history, as well as polish the translation of the trial transcript. Boris and Natalia Katz helped me handle subtle points of Russian language and generally offered their encouragement as the work progressed.

I would also like to thank my agent, Robin Straus, for her unerring counsel and Clodene Anderson for her patient help with computer software. My colleagues at Amnesty International USA understood the significance of this project, not least because of our determined opposition to the death penalty. My editor Jonathan Brent was always encouraging, and I feel honored and grateful to him for having offered me this project. Benton Arnovitz of the United States Holocaust Memorial Museum was also instrumental in bringing the project to my attention. And I want especially to recognize and thank Laura E. Wolfson for her arduous work of translation.

Finally, I want to express special gratitude to my wife, Jill Janows, who patiently accompanied me on another, prolonged scholarly adventure at the very time our lives were joyously complicated by the arrival of our son, Benjamin.

Joshua Rubenstein

Note on the Translation

THE transcript of the secret 1952 Moscow trial of fifteen Jewish figures associated with the Jewish Anti-Fascist Committee was first published in Moscow under the title *Nepravedny Sud: Posledny Stalinsky Rasstrel* (An Unjust Trial: Stalin's Last Execution) in 1994. This volume was based on the eight-volume stenographic record of the trial, which was kept for over forty years in a closed archive of the Soviet-era Committee for State Security, or the KGB—now the Federal Security Service, or the FSB—following the collapse of the Soviet Union. The editors of the Moscow edition cut some sections of the transcript that were not directly germane to the charges against the defendants. Additional sections in the Moscow volume that were redundant or that touched on questions only remotely relevant to the story of this case were also removed by the American editor before the material was translated for the original English-language hardcover edition, which appeared in 2001. Several brief exchanges in court that were not included in *Nepravedny Sud* were taken from the stenographic record and included in that edition as well.

For this paperback edition, the American editor removed a good deal of material from the version of the trial transcript that first appeared in 2001. These sections, like material that was cut from the published Russian text, exceeded what was necessary to grasp the full drama of what took place. The editor also took advantage of this new edition to correct a handful of errors that other students of the period graciously brought to his attention.

In the course of the trial, the judges frequently question the defendants about statements they had made during their prolonged pre-trial detention. These interrogation records became part of a forty-two-volume set of investigation materials that are often cited in the original stenographic record, particularly when the presiding officer reads from these earlier statements in order to challenge a defendant in court. For the sake of clarity, the translation generally refers to the "interrogation" of the defendants during the preliminary investigation (in effect, when they were held between the time of their arrest and the opening of the trial) and their "testimony" during the trial itself.

It was also necessary to provide extensive notes, to identify individuals and explain events referred to in the transcript, and to clarify numerous mistakes in the testimony of the defendants and in the assertions of court officials; these notes, as well as the biographical portrait of each defendant, were prepared by Joshua Rubenstein. All translations in the notes are by him as well. Within the notes there are references to material in Russian archives. Documents in these archives are cited and numbered by collection (*fond,* or *f.*), inventory (*opis,* or *op.*), file (*delo,* or *d.*), and page (*list,* or *l.,* or, in plural, *ll.*): thus, for example, RGASPI, f. 17, op. 125, d. 35, ll. 62–65.

The guide used in transliterating Russian words and proper names was J. Thomas Shaw's standard work, *The Transliteration of Modern Russian for English-Language Publications,* published by the University of Wisconsin Press in 1967. With few exceptions, his System I was followed throughout the text and notes. In transliterating Yiddish words and proper names, YIVO orthography was used wherever possible, with the exception of names that have become commonly familiar in the English language. As all scholars of Russian and of Yiddish culture know, there is no single method for rendering either Russian or Yiddish words into English.

Chronology

August–September 1939	Nazi Germany and the Soviet Union sign a Non-Aggression Pact. Germany invades Poland. The Soviet Union occupies the Baltic states and eastern Poland.
June 22, 1941	Germany invades the Soviet Union.
August 24, 1941	Famous Soviet Jewish figures appeal by radio to Jews in the West to support the war effort against Nazi Germany.
September 1941	The German invaders massacre tens of thousands of Jews at Babi Yar, outside Kiev. Similar open-air massacres are carried out throughout Ukraine, Belorussia, and the Baltic states during the German occupation.
March 1942	The Soviet government creates five anti-fascist committees, including the Jewish Anti-Fascist Committee, to win support from the West.
June 1942	The first issue of the Yiddish newspaper *Eynikayt* is published.
February 1943	The Red Army defeats the Wehrmacht at Stalingrad.
May 1943	Solomon Mikhoels and Itsik Fefer leave for a seven-month tour of North America and England.
June 1944	The Western Allies invade Western Europe on D-Day.

May 1945	Nazi Germany surrenders.
January 1946	B. Z. Goldberg visits the Soviet Union.
March 1946	Winston Churchill delivers his famous "Iron Curtain" speech in Fulton, Missouri.
September 1946	Paul Novick visits the Soviet Union.
January 1948	Solomon Mikhoels is murdered in Minsk.
May 1948	The State of Israel is established. The Soviet Union and the United States immediately recognize the new Jewish state.
September 1948	Golda Meyerson (Meir) arrives in Moscow as head of the first Israeli diplomatic legation.
November 1948	The Jewish Anti-Fascist Committee is disbanded.
January 1949	The Soviet press begins an "anti-cosmopolitan" campaign.
May 1952	The Soviet government opens a secret trial of fifteen Jewish figures associated with the Jewish Anti-Fascist Committee.
August 1952	Thirteen of the defendants are executed.
January 1953	The Soviet press unmasks a group of doctors, most of whom are Jewish, who are said to be plotting the deaths of Soviet leaders.
March 1953	Joseph Stalin dies.
April 1953	The new Soviet leaders disavow the "Doctors' Plot."
November 1955	The case of the Jewish Anti-Fascist Committee is officially closed; relatives are informed of the deaths of the defendants.
February 1956	Nikita Khrushchev denounces Stalin in a "secret speech" before the Twentieth Party Congress.
March–April 1956	Two Yiddish newspapers, the *Forverts* (New York) and *Folks-shtime* (Warsaw), carry the first credible reports about the fate of the defendants.

Stalin's Secret Pogrom

Night of the Murdered Poets

L ATE ON THE NIGHT OF JANUARY 12, 1948, the renowned Yiddish actor and theater director Solomon Mikhoels was murdered in Minsk on the direct orders of Joseph Stalin. This was not an ordinary operation. As director of Moscow's State Jewish Theater and chairman of the Jewish Anti-Fascist Committee (JAC), which played a prominent role in Soviet propaganda efforts against Hitler during World War II, Mikhoels had earned an international reputation. But with the onset of the Cold War and the impending creation of Israel, Stalin came to suspect Mikhoels's loyalties. Dispatched to Minsk ostensibly to review a play for the Stalin Prize, Mikhoels was lured from his hotel and taken to the country house of Lavrenti Tsanava, head of the Belorussian security services, where he was summarily killed. His body was left in the snow along a quiet street, where, in the morning, workers discovered him. Mikhoels's death was declared the result of a traffic accident. To complete the camouflage, he was honored with a state funeral.

Many people suspected that Mikhoels's death was not a mishap. During the funeral, when the body lay in state for a full day in the State Jewish Theater, the Yiddish poet Peretz Markish observed that "the flow of people" did not stop, and "along with them, raised from stinking ditches and pits, came six million victims, tortured and innocent."[1] Markish, in other words, understood that Mikhoels was killed because he was a Jew. But Markish tried to be careful; he showed his verse to only a handful of people and allowed only two politically innocuous verses to be printed on January 17 in *Eynikayt* (Unity), the Yiddish-language newspaper associated with the JAC. Publicly, the Kremlin continued to treat Mikhoels as a revered figure. But two weeks after his death, his murderer, Lavrenti Tsanava, was secretly given the Order of Lenin "for exemplary execution of a special assignment from the government."[2]

This was the beginning of Stalin's assault on the Jewish Anti-Fascist Committee and the leading figures of Soviet Yiddish culture, who were the primary vehicle for Jewish identity in the country. Barely three years after the Holocaust and the defeat of Nazi Germany, Stalin now embarked on his own solution to the Jewish problem. As Peretz Markish remarked to a friend, "Hitler wanted to destroy us physically. Stalin wants to do it spiritually."[3] This campaign culminated on August 12, 1952, with multiple executions in the basement of Moscow's Lubyanka prison.

Jewish communities have increasingly commemorated this event as the Night of the Murdered Poets. Convicted at a secret trial in the spring and summer of 1952, the last significant political trial of the Stalin years, all the defendants, except for the biologist Lina Shtern, were executed on a single night—twenty-four writers and poets (so it was believed), all men (so it was said)—in one of the most vicious episodes of anti-Semitism in Russian history.

But because the regime refused to confirm for many years what actually happened, myriad rumors obscured the nature of the case and the identity and number of the defendants. Today, years after the collapse of the Soviet Union, with the availability of previously closed archival material, including the trial transcript (which was published in Moscow in 1994 and forms the central document of this volume) and because of the tireless research of several Russian and Israeli scholars, the details of Stalin's anti-Semitic star-chamber can be plainly and accurately described.[4]

The trial did not involve twenty-five defendants. There were fifteen defendants, all falsely charged with a range of capital offenses, from treason and espionage to bourgeois nationalism. Although five prominent literary figures were among those indicted—the Yiddish poets Peretz Markish, Leyb Kvitko, David Hofshteyn, and Itsik Fefer and the novelist David Bergelson—the remaining ten defendants were not writers at all but were connected in various ways to the Jewish Anti-Fascist Committee, a group that the regime had created during World War II to encourage Western Jewish support for the alliance with the Soviet Union.

Several defendants were famous Soviet personalities. Solomon Lozovsky, who turned out to be the principal defendant, had been a longtime member of the Central Committee of the Communist Party and was deputy people's commissar for foreign affairs of the USSR throughout the war. Boris Shimeliovich had been the medical director of one of Moscow's most prestigious hospitals. Lina Shtern, renowned for her pathbreaking work in biochemistry and medicine, was the first woman member of the Soviet Academy of Sciences. And Benjamin Zuskin was the premier actor at the State Jewish Theater in Moscow, where he and Solomon Mikhoels had created a world-renowned Yiddish repertory; after the death of Mikhoels in January 1948, Zuskin became the theater's artistic director.

The investigators also roped in six little-known functionaries, some of whom had virtually nothing to do with the work of the Jewish Anti-Fascist Committee, but whose alleged involvement in various crimes served to demonstrate the breadth of JAC treachery: the trade-union activist Joseph Yuzefovich; the journalist and translator Leon Talmy; the lawyer Ilya Vatenberg and his wife, Khayke Vatenberg-Ostrovskaya, who worked as a translator for the JAC; the editor Emilia Teumin; and the party bureaucrat Solomon Bregman, who joined the JAC in 1944 and quickly became an informer, sending denunciations about Jewish "nationalism" within the committee to party officials. Talmy and the Vatenbergs had lived for many years in the United States before deciding to move to Russia in the 1930s out of loyalty to communism; their years in America made them vulnerable to charges of espionage.

But only the martyred Yiddish writers are mentioned at August 12 commemorations. The other defendants who lost their lives, as well as the sole survivor, Lina Shtern, are rarely, if ever, remembered, perhaps because their connection to the case has only recently been divulged and they were hardly known in the West to begin with, or perhaps because careers as loyal Soviet citizens do not fit comfortably into an easy category for Westerners to honor.

The five Yiddish writers also had complicated biographies. With the exception of Itsik Fefer, each had left the Soviet Union in the 1920s for extended stays abroad. Markish lived in Poland and France; Kvitko, in Germany; Hofshteyn, in Palestine; Bergelson, in Germany, Denmark, and the United States. And each had returned, unable to find a place for himself abroad as a Yiddish writer.

At the same time, Yiddish culture was increasingly fragile, with few prospects, whether in an open democracy like the United States, where millions of Yiddish speakers had recently immigrated; in a country like Poland, where a large Jewish community was free to practice its religion but still faced anti-Semitic restrictions in the broader society; or in the developing Jewish homeland in Palestine, where the revival of Hebrew as an everyday, modern language was a primary goal of the Zionist movement.

Leyb Kvitko, for example, was barely able to support himself in Germany; at one point he had to accept work as a porter in Hamburg. David Hofshteyn lived for a year in Palestine, but as a Yiddish poet he had few professional opportunities. Although Zionist leaders were promoting the use of Hebrew, Yiddish—which was associated with "European ghetto culture"—was actively discouraged. The Language Defense Corps patrolled the streets, burning kiosks where Yiddish newspapers were sold and throwing stink bombs during lectures and performances in Yiddish.[5] Faced with this kind of hostility and given family pressures to return to Kiev, Hofshteyn, too, made the fateful decision to go back. Peretz Markish restlessly searched for a haven, living in Poland and France, traveling to Germany, even to Palestine. But despite his wide recognition and literary acclaim, a career as a Yiddish writer could not provide him with an adequate livelihood. Most Yiddish literary figures were also proofreaders and copy editors, jobs that Markish, by temperament, could not be expected to pursue. After five years in Europe, he returned to Moscow in 1926.

David Bergelson was the most reluctant to move back. Although he visited the Soviet Union on several occasions, he stayed in Europe and America from 1921 until 1934. The regime, however, recognizing Bergelson's stature as a novelist, cultivated his loyalty. Other Yiddish writers encouraged him to return, and the regime made promises to support his work. The Kremlin was subsidizing the arts, including Yiddish literature, and each of these writers—Markish, Kvitko, Hofshteyn, and Bergelson—came to regard the Soviet Union as the only country where they could still find a large enough readership to make a living.

Once inside Stalin's kingdom, they were all compelled to accept the regime's ideological demands, engage in Stalinist propaganda, and lend their names to ugly denunciations of condemned political figures. Markish, Kvitko, and Hofshteyn, who had spent time in Europe, found it unnerving to be in such an ideological cauldron and to know they would never be able to escape it. As Markish wrote to a friend, the writer Joseph Opatoshu,* in New York in November 1929, the situation was "very strained and aggravated. . . . In general, we don't know what world we're in. In this atmosphere of trying to be terribly proletarian and one hundred percent kosher, much falseness, cowardice, and vacillation have manifested themselves and it is becoming somewhat impossible to work."[6]

By the late 1920s, a whole traditional way of life was under assault. The Jewish section of the Communist Party (the notorious Yevsektsiya) was the driving force behind the broader party directives for the Jewish minority. It was at the initiative of the Yevsektsiya that Hebrew was prohibited, making the Yiddish press the principal medium for propaganda among the poor, rural masses in their shtetls. Religious observance came in for ridicule from secular, communist Jews who initiated campaigns to make it difficult to observe Jewish holidays and the Sabbath.

It was in this atmosphere that Yiddish writers were expected to help create a secular Yiddish culture that was a fundamental part of the Kremlin's plan to wean the Jews from their religious and cultural ties. Knowing that the regime was determined to cleanse their writings of biblical and religious imagery, as well as of nostalgia for the shtetl and traditional Jewish life, they accepted severe censorship of their work. The Yiddish alphabet, which is written in Hebrew characters, was adjusted for ideological reasons. There was even an attempt to screen Yiddish for words of Hebrew origin and, where possible, replace them with words from German or Russian roots. Such measures were part of a concerted effort to make Soviet Yiddish literature conform to Stalin's classic dictum for all minority cultures: "national in form, socialist in

*Joseph Opatoshu (1887–1954) was born in Poland and emigrated to New York in 1907. He was a prolific prose writer in Yiddish.

content." As the writer Der Nister wrote to his brother in Paris, "Here one has to turn one's soul upside down."[7]

Legally, Yiddish remained the officially recognized language of the Jewish minority, but the very books and newspapers that were being produced in Yiddish were helping to turn its native speakers away from the new Soviet Yiddish culture. The regime's manipulation and control were having a devastating effect. Increasingly assimilated into the general economy, Yiddish-speaking Jews were faced with a language that was like an artificial version of the Russian they encountered all around them; the language they once knew was no longer their own.[8] By the late 1930s, fewer parents were sending their children to Yiddish-language schools. Yiddish books were removed from libraries, and Yiddish scholarly institutes shut down, along with many schools and newspapers. All the Yiddish writers understood that future generations would have little, if any, access to genuine Yiddish culture. As Bergelson acknowledged during the trial, they were becoming "superfluous."

The German invasion of Poland in September 1939 reinforced the isolation of Yiddish writers within Soviet borders. Following the Non-Aggression Pact in August, Stalin was now an ally of Hitler, which led to the suppression of information about Nazi atrocities in the Soviet press. At the same time, the Red Army took over the Baltic states and initiated a new purge of Yiddish culture within local Jewish communities. When the poet Zelig Akselrod protested the closing of Jewish schools and newspapers in Vilna (Vilnius), he was arrested and executed by the Soviet security police.[9]

Around the same time, Peretz Markish traveled to newly occupied areas of eastern Poland as a member of the Writers' Brigades, whose job it was to indoctrinate Polish Yiddish writers into the new Soviet reality. In Bialystok, Markish came upon the actor David Lederman, whom he had known in Warsaw in the early 1920s. Asking to see him in private, Markish showed Lederman an article by the writer Moyshe Nadir* in which Nadir explained why he had broken his long-standing ties with the American Communist Party and the Yiddish-language communist newspaper the *Morgen Freiheit* (Morning Freedom) following the Hitler-Stalin pact. "Moyshe Nadir has revealed that he raised a snake around his neck," Markish reported to Lederman. "Only he nourished

---

*Moyshe Nadir was the pen name of Isaac Reiss (1885–1943).

this snake around his neck? Only he alone? And maybe all of us weaned the snake? And a time may come when this full-grown snake will choke all of us. . . . Yes, if it keeps going like it's been going, the time will come that the snake wrapped around our necks will choke us."

Markish urged Lederman to keep their conversation to himself. Lederman said later that Markish's "eyes filled with tears. He fell into a spasmodic wail. It was very difficult for me to calm him. He prepared himself to part with me, embraced me, and said that he believed that the conversation with me should not be made known to anyone until the time comes when it can be told."[10] Markish, however, like all Soviet writers, recognized the need for more than silence. He also understood the necessity of praising the snake; in 1940, after seeing Lederman in Bialystok, Markish published a lengthy, obsequious poem glorifying Stalin.[11] As for David Lederman, he did not recount his conversation with Markish until 1960, long after Markish and his colleagues had succumbed to the Kremlin python.

The Jewish Anti-Fascist Committee

The investigation and subsequent trial in 1952 were directed as much against the Jewish Anti-Fascist Committee as against the remnants of Jewish culture in the country. The JAC, led by Solomon Mikhoels, had been established in 1942 along with four other anti-fascist committees—for women, youth, scientists, and Slavs—each designed to appeal to a different segment of foreign public opinion in support of the alliance against Nazi Germany. All operated under the direct supervision of Solomon Lozovsky, who was deputy chairman of the Soviet Information Bureau (Sovinformburo), as well as deputy people's commissar for foreign affairs. The JAC played a significant role in the Soviet war effort, raising money in the West and encouraging support for the alliance between the Soviet Union and its democratic allies. Indeed, the JAC's success and the renown of its chairman. Solomon Mikhoels, made the committee all the more visible a target for Stalin.

The history of the JAC remains among the most complex and dramatic chapters of Soviet Jewish history. Adolf Hitler's armies invaded the Soviet Union early in the morning of June 22, 1941. Six weeks later, eight prominent Jewish cultural figures—including Mikhoels, Bergelson, Kvitko, and Zuskin—sent a letter to Lozovsky proposing "to organize a Jewish rally aimed at the Jews of the USA and Great Britain, and also at Jews in other countries." The letter concluded, "In our opinion, a rally with the participation of Jewish academicians, writers, artists, and Red Army fighters will have a great impact abroad."

The list of speakers they suggested revealed the political innocence that would later plague the committee. On the one hand, it seemed reasonable to put forward figures like the historian and philosopher Abram Deborin, the ophthalmologist Mikhail Averbakh, and the violinist David Oistrakh. All were Jewish and seemed prominent enough in their fields, at least inside the country, to appear alongside Mikhoels, Markish, and the others. But the proposal also listed General Yakov Smushkevich—a renowned air force officer who had earlier, under the pseudonym General Douglas, been sent to Spain to assist Republican forces and who was appointed chief commander of the Soviet Air Force in 1939 following his heroic conduct at the battle of Khalkin Gol, where Soviet troops fought Japanese forces in Mongolia. Smushkevich had been wounded and was twice awarded the medal Hero of the Soviet Union). The eight Jews who put forward his name did not know that Smushkevich had been arrested in early June 1941 as part of Stalin's ongoing, massive purge of the armed forces. (Smushkevich was executed in October.) Lozovsky was far better informed. As he remarked to his superior, Alexander Shcherbakov, a Central Committee secretary, deputy commissar for defense, and director of the Sovinformburo, in a handwritten note across the letter, "If [the rally] is approved in principle, several changes may be made in the list of speakers."[12]

The regime, in fact, accepted the proposal and organized both an international broadcast and a mass rally in Moscow's Park of Culture, an event that was attended by thousands of people on August 24, 1941. Led by Solomon Mikhoels, speaker after speaker emphasized Jewish unity and the terror of Nazi persecution. Mikhoels warned that the Nazis planned "the total annihilation of the Jewish people." Markish invoked the image of "the biblical Job, stunned by everything that passed in front of his eyes." Bergelson asked, Is it possible that "this people will give up and perish? A people which, over the course of thousands of years, suffered unheard of humiliations, bloodshed and slaughter at the hands of its enemies?" The writer Ilya Ehrenburg spoke in the most personal terms. "I grew up in a Russian city. My mother tongue is Russian. I am a Russian writer. Like all Russians, I am now defending my homeland. But the Nazis have reminded me of something else; my mother's name was Hannah. I am a Jew. I say this proudly. Hitler hates us more than anything, and this makes us proud."[13]

Such remarks contradicted two decades of Soviet propaganda and censorship that prohibited any talk of Jewish unity or a concern for Jewish suffering. But Hitler's swift advance loosened many constraints. Encouraged by the Sovinformburo, which had examined their speeches in August 1941, these men and their colleagues spent the next four years writing poems, stories, plays, and articles, all with the same persistent emphasis on Jewish suffering and heroism and on the need for Jews throughout the world to work together, "as brothers and sisters," to vanquish Hitler. No one could have guessed in the grim summer of 1941, with the Red Army reeling before the Nazi onslaught, that such sentiments would be held against the JAC and form the basis of capital charges against its leadership.

Stalin also received concrete proposals for a Jewish committee against fascism from Henryk Erlich and Viktor Alter, the leaders of the Bund in Poland, a popular Jewish socialist movement. Once the Bolsheviks had taken control of Russia after the revolution, the Bund, like all the other socialist parties, had been suppressed. But it continued to thrive in Poland as one of the principal opposition parties to that country's authoritarian (and anti-Semitic) regime.

Although Henryk Erlich and Viktor Alter had escaped the Germans after the invasion of Poland, Stalin's secret police arrested them in the fall of 1939. Denounced to Soviet officials by a Polish Jewish communist, Erlich was detained at the train station in Brest-Litovsk. Alter was arrested in Kowel in western Volhynia. But Stalin released them two years later in the wake of Hitler's advance. By the early fall of 1941, with the Red Army in full retreat, Stalin had no choice but to improve relations with the Western powers. Erlich and Alter enjoyed excellent contacts with labor groups in the West. With their release, Stalin hoped to reassure their supporters and enlist both men in Soviet plans against Hitler. At the behest of the Kremlin, Erlich and Alter proposed a committee that would involve Soviet Jews and refugees from German-occupied countries. They even suggested the formation of a Jewish Legion in the Red Army to be made up of American volunteers.[14]

But their proposals were rejected. They were initially submitted to Lavrenti Beria, head of the secret police, who passed them along to

Stalin for final approval. Stalin was not about to establish a genuinely independent Jewish organization, let alone one with international pretensions. Moreover, by December 1941 the Red Army had undertaken its first full-scale counteroffensive, relieving the pressure on Moscow, where the Wehrmacht had reached the suburbs, and forcing the Germans out of Rostov. This temporary success restored Stalin's confidence, leaving Erlich and Alter expendable. For decades it was assumed they had been summarily executed in early December, but in fact they were kept in solitary confinement in Kuibyshev. Erlich committed suicide in his cell in May 1942; Alter was shot in February 1943.[15]

The idea of a Jewish committee against Hitler remained on the table, however, and one was formally accepted by the spring of 1942. In February, Mikhoels and the journalist Shakhno Epshteyn, who would become executive secretary,[16] submitted a list of fifteen goals for the JAC. They included producing publications about Jewish suffering and heroism in the war effort, developing a strong "anti-fascist campaign among the Jewish population abroad," and organizing "a campaign for financial contributions especially in the United States, to bring medicine and warm clothing for the Red Army and people evacuated from regions occupied by the Germans." Lozovsky was especially impressed by this final goal. In a cover note to Shcherbakov, Lozovsky noted that "we could receive millions of dollars in medicine and warm clothing for the Red Army and the evacuated population, for very little work indeed."[17]

From the outset, the JAC's goal was clear: to help the war effort by soliciting money and political support for the Soviet Union, principally from wealthy Jews in the West. It would not operate independently, but rather, like all Soviet institutions, be closely supervised by party officials. The committee was not supposed to breathe without proper permission.

But the war, and, specifically, reports of horrific Nazi atrocities, created a passion among many members of the JAC that could not be easily restrained. As Ilya Vatenberg told his judges in 1952, the war created "nationalistic germs" because the "cruel and bestial policy which Hitler carried out . . . reminded many Jews that they were Jews." Whatever the degree of their loyalty to the regime, whether it was voluntary, coerced, or the result of circumstances that would overwhelm an ordinary human conscience, people like Mikhoels, Ehrenburg, Markish, Shimeliovich, and Lina Shtern did not efface their identity as Jews. The regime had itself to blame for this tension, for Kremlin officials granted the committee members an extraordinary dispensation, encouraging them to speak and write as Jews, to describe Jewish suffering, and to appeal to fellow Jews in other countries on the assumption, long denied, that there was something real about the concept of Jewish unity that in the context of the war could be useful for the Soviet Union. To this task, they all, even Itsik Fefer and Shakhno Epshteyn, the most committed communists among them, applied themselves without restraint.

Within weeks after the German invasion, on July 18, a group of Yiddish writers, among them Markish, Bergelson, and Kvitko, appealed directly to the Sovinformburo "to establish a Yiddish newspaper." At the time, the only Yiddish newspaper in the entire country was being published in Birobidzhan—the Jewish Autonomous Region that Stalin had established along the Chinese Manchurian border five thousand miles east of Moscow—but it had only a nominal readership in a region where fewer than twenty thousand Jews resided. (The region had never attracted enough Jewish settlers to become a genuine Jewish territory within the Soviet Union and was increasingly regarded as nothing more than a vehicle for propaganda among gullible, left-wing Jews abroad.) Markish and his colleagues understood the "urgent need" for such a newspaper both as a way to help organize the "Jewish masses" and as a moral gesture toward the country's Jewish minority. But Shcherbakov dismissed the idea out of hand. "Inadvisable at this present time," he wrote across the page. "Let the Jewish writers work for Moscow newspapers."[18] But the Jewish writers did not give up. In September, Mikhoels added his name to an appeal, and this time Shcherbakov accepted the proposal. But in October, with Moscow under threat by the German advance, the idea of a Yiddish newspaper was lost in the turmoil that engulfed the capital.

The idea was not revived until March 1942, when Mikhoels and Epshteyn appealed again to their political masters. Their letter to Shcherbakov made note of "evacuated Jews" who needed a "political education" in Yiddish. Then they added a decisive argument: the lack of a Yiddish newspaper "plays into the hands of insidious hostile elements—clerics, Zionists, and Bundists—trying to expand their influence on significant sectors of the Jewish population. On the other hand, this is used by the Jewish bourgeois press abroad, especially in the USA, to sow distrust among the Jewish masses toward the USSR."[19]

This time their proposal reached its goal. Within a month of receiving their letter, Lozovsky confirmed that the newspaper would be entitled *Eynikayt,* that Shakhno Epshteyn would be the chief editor, that Mikhoels, Bergelson, Fefer, and Kvitko, among others, would be on the editorial staff, and that initially, it was to be published once every ten days. These questions settled, *Eynikayt* came out for the first time on June 17, 1942. The newspaper was a milestone in Soviet Jewish history, but it lasted for less than seven years. Within months after the last issue in 1948, almost all the people responsible for producing it would begin to disappear.

But the successful effort to launch *Eynikayt* was only a portent of more ambitious projects to come. The war created surprising opportunities. Itsik Fefer composed one of the most outspoken tributes to Jewish endurance during the conflict. Entitled "I Am a Jew," the poem expressed a defiant pride in Jewish heroism and history in the face of Nazi atrocities. Invoking the images of Solomon and Samson, Rabbi Akiba, Judah Ha-Levi, and Spinoza, Fefer reached back to biblical times before inevitably concluding with references to Yakov Sverdlov—a Jew, the main party organizer from 1913 to 1918, and the first titular head of the Soviet state (from November 1918 to his sudden death of Spanish influenza in March 1919)—and to Lazar Kaganovich, people's commissar for transport and the only Jewish member of Stalin's Politburo. As a work of literature, "I Am a Jew" is little more than a mediocre exercise in propaganda, as the following stanzas illustrate. But as a document, it testifies to the broad latitude Jewish writers enjoyed during the war.

> I am a Jew.
> The wine of enduring generations
> Strengthened me on my wanderer's way.
> The evil sword of pain and lamentations
> Nothing that I hold dear could slay—
> My people, my faith, and my head unbowed.
> It could not stop me being free and true.
> Under the sword I cried aloud:
> "I am a Jew!"
>
> Pharaoh and Titus, Haman made their aim
> To slay me in their times and lands,
> Eternity still bears my name
> Upon its hands.

And I survived in Spain the rack,
The Inquisition Fires, too.
My horn sounded this message back:
"I am a Jew!"
. . . .
I am a Jew who has drunk up
Happiness from Stalin's cup.
To those who would let Moscow go
Under the ground, I call out—"No."
The Slavs are my brothers, too,
"I am a Jew!"

I am a ship against both shores.
Into eternity my blood pours.
On my pride in Sverdlov I depend,
And on Kaganovich, Stalin's friend.
My young go speeding over the snows,
My heart bombs and dynamite throws,
And everywhere the call comes through:
"I am a Jew!"
. . . .
Despite the foe who comes destroying
Under the Red Flag I shall live,
I shall plant vineyards for my enjoying,
And on this soil I will thrive.
Whatever the enemy may do
The liberty of the world we shall save.
I shall dance on Hitler's grave.
"I am a Jew!"[20]

Itsik Fefer stands at the center of the JAC tragedy. Born to a poor Hebrew teacher, Fefer gained enormously from the opportunities offered by the revolution. He remained grateful to the party for the prestige he enjoyed and was among the most loyal and conformist Yiddish poets. He also helped to enforce strict ideological control over other Yiddish writers, often denouncing colleagues for their "nationalistic hysteria."[21] Mikhoels did not trust him and was disturbed when he learned that Fefer would accompany him on their famous trip to North America and England in 1943 to raise money and political support for the Soviet war effort. On the eve of their departure, Mikhoels expressed misgivings. Fefer "can hardly be counted on for support and assistance," Mikhoels confided to his family.[22] Peretz Markish expected to accompany Mikhoels (in New York, the writer Sholem Asch wanted to invite David Bergelson), but the regime decided to dispatch Fefer instead, knowing it could count on him to watch over Mikhoels and make regular reports to a Soviet "handler."[23]

Mikhoels was in Tashkent, where the State Jewish Theater had been evacuated to in 1941, when he received word that he would be going to America. Mikhoels stopped by Benjamin Zuskin's apartment before departing, hoping to see Zuskin's daughter Tamara, to whom he was especially close. Not finding her at home, he left her the following note: "I will be taking an examination in political grammar. Cross your fingers! I am going to America."[24] Mikhoels no doubt thought of his message as a clever way to describe his trip. But he was embarking on a political mission that would require more than luck to survive.

The timing of the trip reflected Soviet sensitivities on several matters. With the victory at Stalingrad in February, Soviet prestige was restored; hopes for victory over the Nazis on the Eastern Front became much more realistic. But Soviet losses continued to be enormous, compelling Stalin to sustain good relations with his Western allies. Word of Erlich's and Alter's deaths, which Soviet ambassador to the United States Maxim Litvinov acknowledged in February after months of heavy pressure (he claimed they had been "convicted [and executed] as spies and subversive agents" because they had appealed to the Red Army not to fight the Germans), provoked consternation in England and the United States.[25] Stalin must have sensed the need to counter such a troublesome admission. Soviet planning for the Mikhoels-Fefer trip began in March 1, and they were on their way by early May.

The sojourn of Mikhoels and Fefer in the West was one of those astonishing events that at first appears to be so hopeful and promising and yet, in hindsight, carries nothing but the seeds of destruction. Lasting over a seven-month period, the trip was unprecedented in its scope and ambition. Vyacheslav Molotov, people's commissar for foreign affairs,* briefed them on the eve of their departure, and Soviet President Mikhail Kalinin saw them off from the Kremlin. Even Stalin stepped out of his office to bid them farewell. Once Mikhoels and Fefer left Moscow, it

---

*Vyacheslav Molotov (Skryabin) (1890–1986) served as Soviet prime minister from 1930 to 1941 and as foreign minister from 1939 to 1949.

took them forty days to reach America, traveling on U.S. military aircraft through the Middle East and parts of Africa. From June to December 1943, they visited major American cities, spent a few days in Mexico and Canada, and then concluded their mission with a visit to England.

Jewish organizations in America lent their names and resources to making the visit a success. A National Reception Committee was organized, headed by Albert Einstein and B. Z. Goldberg, who were both sympathetic to the Soviet Union. Goldberg in particular was an articulate fellow traveler, an adept and prolific Yiddish journalist whose professional visibility was enhanced by his marriage to the daughter of the famous Yiddish writer Sholem Aleichem.

Mainstream Jewish organizations like Hadassah, the Jewish National Fund, the Zionist Organization of America, and B'nai Brith also welcomed Mikhoels and Fefer, as did James Rosenberg of the American Jewish Joint Distribution Committee.* The American Jewish Committee, however, kept its distance, not wanting to be associated with B. Z. Goldberg, while socialist groups, like the Jewish Labor Committee, the Bund, and the social-democratic *Forverts* (Forward) newspaper, voiced outspoken criticism of the visit.

Such controversy was inevitable, but the heartfelt enthusiasm that greeted the visitors was more than the result of Soviet propaganda or a blind faith in Stalin. Mikhoels and Fefer were the first official representatives of Soviet Jewry to visit the West, and they came in the midst of the Nazi genocide of the Jews and while the wartime alliance was in place. The Red Army had just inflicted a mortal blow to the Wehrmacht, so it was altogether natural for American Jewry and sections of the broader American public to greet them with profound enthusiasm. Wherever they visited—Philadelphia, Chicago, Pittsburgh, Detroit, Boston—they were welcomed with fund-raising dinners and testimonials. Mass rallies were organized in Los Angeles and San Francisco. In Hollywood they met Thomas Mann, Theodore Dreiser, Upton Sinclair, Charlie Chaplin, and Edward G. Robinson. In New York, Jewish furriers presented them with three specially made, luxurious fur hats and coats, one of each for Stalin himself, Mikhoels, and Fefer.[26] B. Z. Goldberg brought them to

---

*James Rosenberg (1874–1970) was a leading member of the Joint Distribution Committee. A lawyer by profession, he was also an artist, writer, and philanthropist. In 1947–1948, he headed the U.S. delegation to the United Nations when the Convention Against Genocide was adopted.

Sholem Aleichem's grave in Queens. They also visited Marc Chagall, who had once worked with Mikhoels to help establish Moscow's State Jewish Theater. Chagall was thrilled to see them and encouraged his friends in America to greet the visitors warmly and put aside misgivings about their Soviet allegiance. "Several times I saw my 'pupil'—Mikhoels (and Fefer)," he wrote to Joseph Opatoshu in July 1943. "From up close, they are very good Jews. . . . In any case, I think it is not necessary to 'criticize' them—they are our kind of Jews."[27] There were awkward moments, too. The writer Alexander Pomerantz, who had known the poet Izi Kharik, asked Fefer about Kharik's whereabouts. Fefer told him that Kharik had been killed by the Nazis, a deliberate lie, for, as Fefer well knew, Kharik—a faithful communist and an accomplished Yiddish poet "with a wry affection for the shtetl traditionalism he saw declining"—had disappeared during the Great Purge in 1937.[28]

The FBI was also interested in Mikhoels and Fefer. Nine years after their visit, in a confidential report on Marc Chagall, the FBI noted that its "investigation reflected that Michoels [sic] was interested in a scientific report in Russian prepared by a Russian physicist concerning the theory of the atom structure."[29] Mikhoels was unsuited for any kind of espionage assignment, making it difficult to understand what the FBI believed it knew about him or what kind of clandestine assignment Mikhoels could have pursued, given the high visibility of his travels in America.

Without question, the most impressive public event of the visit was the mass rally in the Polo Grounds in New York on July 8. Fifty thousand people jammed the stadium, which was decorated with American, Soviet, and blue and white flags in recognition of the Allied effort against Hitler and of Jewish national aspirations. Mayor Fiorello La Guardia welcomed the crowd. Mikhoels and Fefer, speaking in Yiddish, repeatedly urged support for the Red Army. American speakers engaged in unprecedented pro-Soviet rhetoric. Sholem Asch claimed that the Soviet Union was the first state to abolish anti-Semitism, an indirect rebuke of American society, which still tolerated limits on Jews in industry and higher education. Rabbi Stephen Wise denounced "Jewish Trotskyites" for their attacks on Mikhoels and Fefer. B. Z. Goldberg praised "the great leader Marshal Stalin," and James Rosenberg proclaimed that "Russia has given life, asylum, bread and shelter to a vast Jewish population." Paul Robeson, the famous African-American singer and actor, concluded the program with Russian and Yiddish songs.

The Soviet press was euphoric. *Eynikayt* used its report of the Polo Grounds rally to issue a special appeal to American Jews. The response in *Pravda* was equally enthusiastic. Reports on the rally appeared in two successive issues. *Pravda* quoted the belief of Nahum Goldmann, the leader of the World Jewish Congress, that the visit by Mikhoels and Fefer would reinforce ties between Soviet and world Jewry. The newspaper also made clear that the Polo Grounds rally had been the largest pro-Soviet rally ever held in the United States and that, for the most part, it had been organized by well-known American Jewish organizations.[30] Years later, Fefer claimed that during their stay in America, he and Mikhoels had been "like two parachutists within an encirclement," as if they had landed in enemy territory.[31] But Fefer wrote this in February 1948, within weeks after Mikhoels's death, when it was no longer useful to recall how warmly they had been received.

Public rallies like the one at the Polo Grounds were accompanied by more discreet events. Within a few years, these meetings and discussions would weigh heavily on the fate of the JAC, particularly those concerning *The Black Book* and the proposal to resettle displaced Soviet Jewish Holocaust survivors in the Crimea.

The idea of publishing a *Black Book* about Nazi persecution of Jews on Soviet territory originated both in the West and at the initiative of Ilya Ehrenburg. Throughout the war, Ehrenburg—who was the most influential journalist in the Soviet Union—collected documents and testimonies about Jewish suffering. His readers, in particular Red Army soldiers, were a constant source of information. His ultimate goal was to create a comprehensive documentary account that would describe Nazi persecution in every region under occupation and serve to rally protest against domestic Soviet anti-Semitism.

The fate of *The Black Book* was tied to the shifting aims of Soviet propaganda. A similar idea had been proposed near the end of 1942 by Albert Einstein, Sholem Asch, and B. Z. Goldberg in a telegram to the JAC. As representatives of the pro-Soviet American Committee of Jewish Writers, Artists, and Scientists, they invited the JAC to participate in a joint volume about the mass murder of the Jews. Mikhoels wanted to endorse the project, but the JAC could not reach a decision on its own.

Only after Mikhoels and Fefer met with Einstein in the summer of 1943 were they able to secure permission from the Sovinformburo. By the end of their visit, they had reached an agreement with the World Jewish Congress, the National Council in Jerusalem, and the American Committee. Each was to collect documents for a joint publication in various languages. Once the JAC could go ahead with its efforts, *Eynikayt* issued a public appeal, on July 27, for eyewitness testimonies and other information on the annihilation of Jews.

By the time Mikhoels and Fefer were back in Moscow, the JAC and a special literary commission headed by Ehrenburg had begun the work. Under Ehrenburg's direction, more than two dozen writers produced vivid accounts of Nazi atrocities. The Yiddish poet Abraham Sutzkever* prepared more than two hundred pages on Nazi persecution in Lithuania. The Russian-Jewish poet Margarita Aliger edited testimonies from the Brest area of Belorussia. Vasily Grossman, who after Ehrenburg was the most widely recognized Soviet war correspondent, visited Maidanek and Treblinka after their liberation in the summer of 1944 and was among the first to interview survivors and confirm how the Germans carried out mass exterminations. One survivor, learning about *The Black Book*, wrote to Ehrenburg that it would serve as a new book of *Lamentations* for the Jewish people, "a monument . . . , a cold stone on which every Jew will be able to shed bitter tears over his wounded friends and relatives."[32]

Mikhoels and Fefer also began to consider a second project during their stay in New York: the possible resettlement of Jews in the Crimea. By that time, there was already a long history of Jewish settlement in the peninsula. By 1795, when Catherine the Great had acquired almost a million Jewish subjects after the successive partitions of Poland, she hoped to turn the Jews into agricultural workers by encouraging migration to the Crimea. Throughout the nineteenth century as well, there were repeated attempts to set up Jewish agricultural colonies on the peninsula. The Bolsheviks, too, using the Society for the Settlement of Jewish Toilers on the Land (OZET), pursued several proposals in the 1920s to turn parts of the northern Crimea into a Jewish agrarian region. The Joint Distribution Committee, in full cooperation with the So-

---

*Abraham Sutzkever (1913–), Yiddish poet and partisan fighter, survived the liquidation of the Vilna ghetto by the Nazis. He was brought by special airlift to Moscow in 1944. He testified at the Nuremberg trials on February 24, 1946, and later emigrated to Palestine.

viet government, had helped to support these colonies through a sub-
sidiary organization called Agro-Joint, which lasted from the early
1920s until 1938. At the height of the project, as many as twenty thousand Jews inhabited these colonies. Several colonies even had Hebrew
names and were regarded as training centers for emigration to Palestine.[33]

With Mikhoels and Fefer in New York, the JDC hoped to renew its
work inside the Soviet Union. James Rosenberg, a leading supporter
of the Agro-Joint project, was able to arrange several meetings with
Mikhoels and Fefer with the support of the Soviet consul Eugene Kisselev, who also attended at least two of these discussions. The JDC proposed to send packages to individual Jewish survivors and to distribute
relief supplies on a nonsectarian basis in predominantly Jewish regions
of the country. Rosenberg also recalled the JDC's work in the Crimea,
but the Nazis had already devastated the region, killing tens of thousands of its Jewish residents; the Red Army would not liberate the
Crimea until the following spring. As one JDC executive reported in a
"highly confidential" memorandum immediately after a meeting in
New York in September 1943, "So far as the Crimea was concerned, so
much havoc and ruin had been worked on the population and on the resources of that area that, at least in the immediate future, it did not seem
to lend itself to the kind of program that was intended by us."[34]
Mikhoels and Fefer, however, came away from their meetings with
wealthy American Jews with a far grander plan for the future than the
discussions warranted. Whereas the JDC leadership believed that it
would be premature even to consider sending relief shipments to the
Crimea, Mikhoels and Fefer left America with genuine hopes that support from the West could lead to a substantial and ambitious project, far
beyond anything JDC leaders had either promised or proposed. For
Mikhoels, Fefer, and their colleagues on the Jewish Anti-Fascist Committee, such hopes turned into a tragic miscalculation.

The Crimea Proposal

Soon after their return from the West, Mikhoels and Fefer, together with
Shakhno Epshteyn, visited Vyacheslav Molotov and, according to Fefer's testimony in court, raised the question of creating a Jewish republic
in the Crimea or in the area of the Volga Germans' republic. "At the time

we liked the sound of it. 'Where there used to be a republic of Germans, there should now be a Jewish republic.' Molotov said that this sounded good demographically, but that there was no point in raising the question and creating a Jewish republic on this land, as the Jews were an urban people and you couldn't simply plunk Jews down on a tractor. In addition, Molotov said, 'As to the Crimea, you write the letter and we will have a look at it.'"

If Fefer's account is correct, the JAC leadership was acting with suitable caution, not directing a written appeal to the Kremlin until after it had received a signal "from above" that a proposal about the Crimea would be seriously considered.[35] Lozovsky himself reviewed their letters to Stalin and Molotov. It is unlikely that an experienced and cautious party veteran like Lozovsky would have helped Mikhoels draft the letters if he had not had sufficient reason of his own to believe that such an appeal would be considered on its merits. As the letter concluded, "The creation of a Soviet Jewish republic would solve once and for all in a Bolshevik manner, in the spirit of the Leninist-Stalinist nationalities policy, the problem of the state and legal position of the Jewish people and the further development of its long-lived culture. Such a problem, which was impossible to solve for many centuries, can be solved only in our Great Socialist country."[36]

Outside the JAC, too, there was widespread interest in resettling displaced Jews in the Crimea. The JAC received appeals from individuals and groups of Jews across the country who were anxious to relocate there. Letters such as these reflected a commonly held belief that the government was considering an alternative to Birobidzhan as an autonomous Jewish region. The JAC, meanwhile, continued to carry out research on its own. Leyb Kvitko was sent to the Crimea to assess Jewish losses and gauge the possibility of resurrecting the Jewish colonies. (The vast majority of Jews who once lived in the Crimea had been killed by the Nazis, and Stalin had deported the Crimean Tatars in the spring of 1944. Kvitko was visiting a near wasteland.) All of this activity surrounding the "Crimea question" was carried out openly, under the full supervision of the Sovinformburo.[37] The worst that was said to them at the time came from Lazar Kaganovich, of the Politburo. He summoned Mikhoels, Fefer, and Epshteyn to his office and rebuked them for advancing the notion of a Jewish republic in the Crimea. "Only actors and poets could come up with such an idea," he told them, at least according to Fefer's testimony in court. Even when Mikhoels and his colleagues understood that the regime was not about to accept their proposal, no recriminations or threats were forthcoming. But Stalin and his secret police had long memories.

Mikhoels and Fefer returned to a country that was different from the one they had left. The tide of war had turned decisively in favor of the Soviet Union and its allies. At the same time, people in Moscow had grown more aware of the scale of German atrocities, particularly against the Jews. This information was having a profound impact on the mood of the JAC, compelling many members to seek to broaden its functions. Proposals were made to resettle Jewish refugees, to reestablish Jewish collective farms, to revive Jewish cultural life, and to collect eyewitness testimonies about the extermination of Jews on occupied Soviet territory.

Many JAC members were also learning about the fate of their relatives. In 1944, Joseph Yuzefovich heard from a cousin who had survived the war by posing as a gentile. This man informed Yuzefovich that he had taken in a four-year-old Jewish orphan whose parents had been killed by the Nazis; Yuzefovich was an uncle to this little girl's mother. The man could no longer care for her and wanted to know if Yuzefovich and his wife would be willing to adopt her. They were childless and immediately accepted the proposal. Soon after, Lozovsky arranged for an airplane to be dispatched with three nurses aboard to bring the girl from eastern Poland to Moscow.[38]

Other JAC members had more devastating news. The Nazis killed Fefer's father, Grossman's mother, Shimeliovich's brother, Zuskin's first wife, Rachel Holland—the mother of his daughter, Tamara. They murdered Hofshteyn's mother and a younger brother in Babi Yar, a ravine outside Kiev. Lieutenant Colonel David Dragunsky, who was associated with the committee, lost his parents and two sisters.*

In a book published in 1944, David Hofshteyn described his dread

---

*David Dragunsky (1910–1992) commanded tank units during World War II and participated in the capture of Berlin; he twice received the Hero of the Soviet Union award. After the war, when he reached the rank of major general, he participated in a number of events to honor the memory of Holocaust victims and advocated the construction of memorials; see Redlich, *War, Holocaust and Stalinism*, p. 231, for his letter to Mikhoels asking the committee to set up "monuments for the executed children, old people and women. . . . We must erect fences, monuments and inscriptions everywhere and show dates." By the late 1960s, Dragunsky was notorious for his activity in Soviet anti-Zionist propaganda and became chairman of the Soviet Anti-Zionist Committee in 1983.

knowing he would shortly be returning to Kiev, after its liberation by the Red Army. "For months I made preparations," Hofshteyn wrote. "I prepared myself for the shock, for the anguish. For months I have been stifling the first scream that will erupt the moment I see there everything I already know—our disaster, our catastrophe in its full dimension."[39]
Ilya Ehrenburg shared Hofshteyn's anguish and was the first to write a poem about the massacre at Babi Yar. "My countless relatives!" he cried. "As if from every pit, I hear you calling me."[40]

Mikhoels summarized the feelings of all the surviving Jews in November 1944 in a handwritten letter (in Yiddish) to B. Z. Goldberg in New York: "Everything here would be good if not for the horrifying news and images of the liberated cities and shtetls, if not for the image of the ghastly holocaust that the German, may his name be erased, brought upon our people. Words, descriptions, stories, and eyewitness testimony pale against that which was lost and against what happened in reality."[41]

In 1944, it was still possible to convey such feelings without restraint or apology.

The newspaper *Eynikayt* exemplified the "liberal" atmosphere of wartime Russia and the greater latitude that Jewish writers enjoyed. In an initial issue, Peretz Markish detailed Nazi atrocities in Poland and in occupied Soviet territory. David Bergelson wrote about conditions in France, where thousands of Jews were rounded up and deported by "fascist gendarmes."[42] The JAC also sent a call to the Jews of Palestine in which unmistakably Jewish national and historical themes were highlighted: "On the Palestinian earth the immortal heroes of the Jewish people Judah Maccabee and Bar Kochba raised the flag of rebellion against the predecessors of Mussolini and Hitler. On the Palestinian earth, our brilliant poet Judah Ha-Levi sang his swan song about undying love for the homeland and the immortality of the people."[43]

At times, *Eynikayt* went still further, publishing explicit endorsements of Zionism and the gathering of Jewish exiles in Palestine. Stalin wanted to undermine the British Mandate in Palestine, which made it easier for *Eynikayt* to encourage Zionist longings. No less a figure than Shakhno Epshteyn wrote that "it should be understood that no normal, thoughtful, and freedom-loving person could be opposed to the settlement and development of their home by Jews in Palestine. . . . That is their absolute right as a collective."[44] Even with the close of the war, *Eynikayt* continued to publish articles that challenged typical Soviet constraints. There were continuing reports about the Holocaust and efforts to rebuild Jewish life in Poland and France; articles about developments in Palestine, diplomatic maneuvering over Jewish refugees, and U.N. debates over the future of the British Mandate. In April 1948, the final year of its publication, *Eynikayt* marked the fifth anniversary of the Warsaw Ghetto Uprising; in May, the establishment of Israel; and later, the fighting that broke out as Israel's Arab neighbors attempted to invade the reborn Jewish state. In an ordinary country, it would be routine for a Yiddish-language newspaper to highlight Jewish concerns from a sympathetic and "national" perspective. But once *Eynikayt* was closed and its editors and writers arrested, what had once been permitted was now used against them.

During the war the regime tolerated the committee's initiatives, although several informers from within the JAC denounced it for taking on "politically harmful" functions and for "intervening in matters in which it should not interfere." Shakhno Epshteyn complained that some JAC members wanted to transform the committee "into a commissariat for Jewish affairs."[45] But the JAC could not ignore Jewish suffering. The committee received mountains of appeals from Jews whose lives had been devastated by the Nazis. "As much as we would like to keep within narrow bounds, we are unable to do so," Mikhoels explained to his colleagues. "Hundreds of letters are being received every day, and hundreds of people . . . are turning [to us]. Life is persistently knocking at our door. . . . We cannot escape the multitude of Jewish problems. . . . No matter how much we drive them away, they return all the same."[46] So, under Mikhoels's leadership the JAC approached Kremlin officials, requesting assistance in one case after another.

In April 1943, for example, Mikhoels and Epshteyn appealed to Shcherbakov to help Yiddish writers who had been evacuated from western regions of the Ukraine and Belorussia, as well as from Moldavia and the Baltic republics. "Taking into account that questions of assistance to writers is not one of the committee's functions, while the flow of letters, complaints, and appeals . . . continues unabated, we consider it our duty to bring this problem to your attention," they wrote to Shcherbakov. They appended a list of thirty Yiddish literary figures, among them Der Nister, Rokhl Korn, Isaac Platner, and Chaim Grade. On this occasion, their appeal was honored. Instructions were issued to provide work for the writers in Uzbekistan and Kazakhstan (where they were residing), and the Literary Fund gave each one a "onetime monetary advance."[47]

Such appeals might seem unremarkable, but in Stalin's kingdom the committee was crossing a dangerous boundary between what was permitted and what was forbidden. When Peretz Markish expressed concern over the mistreatment of Jews who had survived the war and then returned to hometowns in the Ukraine only to face discrimination and hostility from neighbors and officials, he was denounced for making "damaging speeches" and "an anti-Soviet declaration."[48] In August 1944, committee leaders wrote to Lozovsky asking permission to work with Western Jewish organizations in helping Jews who had survived the Nazi occupation. This was particularly urgent because "assistance which Jewish organizations abroad sent through the Red Cross" was not reaching individual Jews. Two months later, Mikhoels and Epshteyn repeated similar concerns to Molotov himself: "The neglect of the Jewish population . . . is continuing and is taking on the character of a gross violation of Soviet principles." The very next day, Molotov ordered an investigation into their charges but added, in a note to the Commissariat of State Control (with copies to the JAC), that the JAC "was not created to handle such matters and the committee apparently does not have a completely accurate understanding of its functions."[49]

Complaints like these became a common occurrence. After the defeat of Nazi Germany, Shakhno Epshteyn bitterly claimed that Ilya Ehrenburg had asserted that "there is nothing for the JAC to do as far as propaganda against fascism among foreign Jews is concerned, since the Jews least of all need anti-fascist propaganda. The main task of the JAC must consist of fighting anti-Semitism in our country."[50] The committee was also criticized for highlighting the participation of Jewish soldiers in the Allied victory. Mikhoels himself could barely constrain his impatience. "No one is going to think that it was two Jewish brothers who took Berlin."[51] With the war over, the regime grew increasingly suspicious of the JAC and the role its leaders had assumed as representatives of Soviet Jewry, a role the Kremlin had never intended to encourage. Much of what the JAC had been instructed to do during the war—

exploit contacts with Jews in the West and document Nazi atrocities—would now turn into the basis for a criminal indictment.

The Postwar Years

With the end of the war, it would have been natural for the JAC, along with the other four anti-fascist committees, to be honored for its work and then dutifully and formally closed. Except for the scientists' committee, which was disbanded in 1948—no doubt because Stalin did not want to permit scientists to have direct contact with foreign colleagues—the other committees continued to function and evolve. Except for members of the JAC, no one from the other anti-fascist committees suffered reprisals for their wartime efforts, including the opera singer Valeria Barsova, who while representing the women's committee traveled with a large delegation to Yugoslavia, Bulgaria, and Romania in early 1945, where she gave more than sixty recitals.[52]

But reprisals were delayed. For the moment, the regime recognized the usefulness of further efforts among the Jews. At the same time, the JAC leaders were struggling to define new goals for the committee. This transition exacerbated long-standing tensions. Shakhno Epshteyn died in July 1945. Fefer was assigned to take his place as executive secretary and editor of *Eynikayt*. Not surprisingly, the JAC now found itself in frequent conflict with elements of the Soviet leadership and bureaucracy. Ehrenburg and Grossman continued to press for publication of *The Black Book*. But once the war was over, attempts to document Jewish suffering were dismissed as expressions of Jewish particularism. Itsik Fefer also understood that the atmosphere was changing. In 1946, when he published an anthology of his verse in Russian translation, he removed the poem "I Am a Jew"; such sentiments were no longer acceptable.[53]

Other developments reinforced the JAC's isolation and vulnerability. After the trip by Mikhoels and Fefer to the West, several Western Jewish organizations invited the JAC to send representatives to conferences in Europe. On each occasion, the invitation was forwarded to the Central Committee with a request for permission to attend. The World Jewish Congress in particular was eager to maintain ties with Soviet Jewry and sent repeated invitations, only to see their overtures rebuffed by party bureaucrats. For Mikhoels, these constant rejections underscored the renewal of isolation that followed the victory over Germany and were a disheartening reminder that the trip in 1943 was a miraculous anomaly.[54] It must have been some consolation when both B. Z. Goldberg (in January 1946) and Paul Novick (in September) were permitted to visit from New York. Both were veteran Yiddish journalists with impeccable pro-Soviet credentials. No one could have imagined how their visits would later be used against the committee.

In 1946, B. Z. Goldberg was already a practiced apologist for the Soviet Union. Born near Vilna in 1895, Goldberg came from an Orthodox Jewish family. His father was a rabbi and a *shohet* (ritual slaughterer). The family was part of the massive emigration of Jews from Eastern Europe to the United States in the decades before and after the turn of the century. Goldberg (his real name was Benjamin Waife) joined his father in America in 1908. He studied in a New York yeshivah before moving with his parents to Michigan and then Iowa. Goldberg later returned to New York to study at Columbia University, where he completed his bachelor's and master's degrees in psychology. In December 1914, he met the renowned Sholem Aleichem and soon began teaching English to his youngest daughter, Marie; they were married in 1917.

Starting in high school, Goldberg showed deftness as a writer, contributing articles in English and Yiddish to various newspapers. In New York, he became associated with *Der Tog* (The Day), an independent liberal newspaper, where he eventually worked as managing editor for fifteen years and contributed a daily column on foreign affairs. Goldberg was also an indefatigable lecturer and traveler; by the end of his life, he had visited every country in Europe, Latin America, and the Middle East, as well as China and Japan.

In 1932, Goldberg agreed to contribute a daily column on world affairs to the *Brooklyn Daily Eagle*. The following year he began a tour of Europe and the Middle East, filing articles in English and in Yiddish. For readers of *Der Tog*, Goldberg's four-month trip to the Soviet Union in 1934 was a signal event. His dispatches from Birobidzhan in particular attracted thousands of new readers and established Goldberg's reputation in the Yiddish press. He expressed nothing but praise for what he found there. In a telegram to New York, Goldberg emphasized how hearty outdoor work was transforming Russian Jews. His tone and words echo the frequently invoked prescription of farming for Jews, whether in Palestine, the Crimea, the Argentine pampas, or the Soviet Far East.

AS A NATIONAL EXPERIENCE BUILDING UP OF AN UNCULTIVATED COUNTRY
LIKE BIRODIDJAN IS WONDERFUL TONIC PEOPLE WHO NEVER HAD FRESH AIR
NEVER HAD PHYSICAL EXERCISE WHO WERE AFRAID TO VENTURE OUTSIDE
HOUSE ARE GETTING OUT ... MANY ARE BOUND TO FAIL MANY MORE TO
COMPLAIN BUT AFTER HAVING LIVED AND SUFFERED AS RUSSIAN JEWS HAVE
IT IS GOOD CURE TO UNDERTAKE THIS HEALTHY TASK PHYSICALLY AND SPIR-
ITUALLY[55]

Goldberg remained an enthusiastic admirer of the Soviet Union and of
Birobidzhan for two more decades. After his visit in 1934, he joined pro-
Soviet organizations in New York: the American Committee for Birobidzhan and the National Council of American-Soviet Friendship. Dur-
ing the war, he also assumed a leadership role in the Jewish Division of
American Russian War Relief and served as president of the American
Committee of Jewish Writers, Artists, and Scientists, an organization
with strong pro-Soviet sympathies. In 1943, he helped to host the visit of
Mikhoels and Fefer to the United States and actually served as chairman
of the Polo Grounds rally. During the JAC trial in 1952, Emilia Teumin
testified that Fefer had told her that Goldberg "was not a Communist
Party member out of tactical considerations, but on his own he played a
prominent role." Fefer could have been overstating the degree of Goldberg's loyalty to impress Teumin. But at a minimum, Goldberg was a reliable fellow traveler. There were also rumors that Goldberg was a foreign agent of the MGB working abroad.[56] At one point in 1948, when
Goldberg was heavily involved in the presidential campaign of Henry
Wallace, both the FBI and the Immigration Service considered the possibility of revoking Goldberg's American citizenship, although nothing
came of it.[57] Given his background, it is hardly surprising that he was
the first Western Jewish journalist to visit the Soviet Union after the war.

Goldberg arrived on January 11, 1946, and stayed until June 8, except
for several weeks when he traveled in Finland, Sweden, and Denmark.[58]
He spent most of his time in Moscow, where he was impressed by the
scope of the JAC. "It occupied the entire ground floor of a sizable building and parts of the floor above" at 10 Kropotkin Street, Goldberg recalled many years later. "There was a considerable staff of workers—re-
ceptionists, stenographers, secretaries, messengers, researchers, writers,
specialists, heads of departments." For Goldberg, the JAC had become
"the focal point of the entire spiritual life of the Soviet Jews." He soon

visited Lozovsky and told him that "the committee seemed to be developing into a sort of Soviet Jewish Congress . . . and it might as well assume this function formally . . . now that the war was over."[59] But Lozovsky ignored Goldberg's observation, recognizing the potential heresy it represented.

Goldberg had other prestigious appointments. He saw President Kalinin, and while he was still in Moscow the Kremlin granted him an extraordinary dispensation, paying him sixty thousand dollars in hard currency as royalties for books by Sholem Aleichem that had been published in the country. Goldberg was also interested in writing about British foreign policy and asked Lozovsky for help. Lozovsky instructed a special Moscow institute to turn over to him a review of British policies based on material published in the British press.

Outside Moscow, Goldberg was allowed to visit several cities in the Ukraine and the Baltic republics, where he traveled with Itsik Fefer, and to see Stalingrad, where the Red Army had stopped the German advance. In Kiev he addressed Jews during a Passover service in a synagogue. He also met with important government and party leaders, including an assistant to Nikita Khrushchev, who was in charge of the Ukraine. During his stay, Goldberg dispatched thirty-three articles to the United States, Canada, Great Britain, Palestine, and Poland; all his writing was friendly to the Soviet Union, as Mikhoels and Fefer reported to the Central Committee.

Goldberg, however, experienced at least two things that should have opened his eyes to the true situation in the country. Both concerned Itsik Fefer. At one point, another writer told Goldberg that Fefer "wants to resign as secretary of the JAC, but they won't let him." Goldberg was confused and asked why. The answer was equally startling. "Itsik Fefer knows that the day of punishment will come, and he does not want to be around when it happens." At the time, Goldberg dismissed such concerns "as a joke."[60] The second incident must have been harder to ignore. When he was walking with Fefer one day in Moscow, they were both arrested by the police and taken to the Lubyanka. Goldberg never understood the real reason for their arrest. Years later, he could only recall that he and Fefer had been conversing in Yiddish and that the police had noted how well dressed he (Goldberg) was. Fefer was terrified when he showed his credentials and pled that it was all a mistake of some kind. They were detained for several hours before being released.[61]

Goldberg wanted very much to visit Birobidzhan, but permission never came through. After two months in the Soviet Union, he was ready to leave, but Mikhoels prevailed on him to stay, holding out the possibility that Molotov would finally approve a trip to the Far East. Mikhoels was still hoping—as late as 1946—for a favorable response from the Kremlin about the Crimea becoming a Jewish republic, and he wanted Goldberg to be able to dispatch the news from Moscow to the world, just as he had in May 1934, when Birobidzhan was officially designated the Jewish Autonomous Region.

Goldberg left the Soviet Union without a visit to Birobidzhan. But he kept any disappointment to himself and remained steadfastly loyal to the Kremlin. In a letter to Mikhoels and Fefer, however, Goldberg made clear that his inability to see Birobidzhan aroused questions within the AMBIJAN movement—American Birobidjan Committee, a communist front organization which actively raised funds and recruited settlers)—whose members were anxious to hear a firsthand account of how the region was faring. Goldberg reassured the AMBIJAN members as best he could, not hesitating to overstate the number of Jews who had settled there or the general conditions they faced. And he continued to correspond with Mikhoels and Fefer, sending them reports about his travels in Eastern Europe, Turkey, and Palestine and holding out hope that one or both of them would be able to travel again and "make a tour of Latin America."[62]

As late as February 1948, a month after the murder of Solomon Mikhoels in Minsk, Goldberg was still prepared to defend Soviet interests. The *New York Times* published articles that February contending that anti-Semitism was increasing in Russia and questioning the viability of Birobidzhan. Goldberg quickly responded. In a statement issued by the National Council of American-Soviet Friendship, Goldberg cited his recent extended stay in the Soviet Union as the basis for denying any allegations of anti-Semitism in the Soviet Union. He also made exaggerated claims about conditions in Birobidzhan and even asserted that plans were afoot "for the establishment of a full-fledged Yiddish State University" there, repeating a baseless official claim that was never seriously considered by Soviet authorities.[63]

At the end of July, seven weeks after Goldberg left the country, Paul Novick was waiting in Warsaw to secure a visa for the Soviet Union. Mikhoels sent a letter asking Andrei Zhdanov, secretary of the Central

Committee and chief ideologist for literature and culture, to expedite permission. But it was not until September 11 that Mikhail Suslov, a leading Central Committee member and head of its Foreign Relations Department, wrote a note to Zhdanov expressing his and Molotov's agreement to allow Novick into the country.[64]

Novick made no secret of his commitment to communism and the Soviet Union. Born in Brest-Litovsk in 1891, he emigrated to the United States and by the early 1920s had begun a long association with the Communist Party of the USA, serving as assistant editor and then editor of the *Morgen Freiheit* for more than half a century. During that time, he traveled to the Soviet Union at least six times, including a visit to Birobidzhan in 1936. Novick was thrilled by what he saw there. "Birobidzhan. A word that is now on the lips of Jews all over the world," he sighed in New York the following year. "An expression of workers' strength for the full solution to the Jewish question."[65] The Kremlin was engaged at that time in a concerted campaign to promote Birobidzhan. In 1936, Benjamin Zuskin starred in a famous film called *Seekers of Happiness* in which Jewish refugees who had earlier fled tsarist Russia for the West now decide to escape the Great Depression. They find their way to Birobidzhan and settle on a flourishing Jewish collective farm. This soon-to-be-forgotten film was a centerpiece of the regime's propaganda efforts.

Well before Novick's last visit to Moscow under Stalin in 1946, he had come to know several people who would soon disappear. David Bergelson, Leon Talmy, and Ilya Vatenberg had all lived in New York and worked for the *Morgen Freiheit* in the 1920s. Novick knew their wives as well, among them Khayke Vatenberg-Ostrovskaya, who would join her husband in the dock. When Mikhoels and Fefer visited New York in 1943, Novick saw them "almost every day."[66] His four-month trip to the Soviet Union, coming soon after Goldberg's visit, reinforced a wistful feeling among JAC members that they would be able to maintain ties with Western Jews.

But Novick's trip was not as extensive as he had hoped it would be. Mikhoels and Fefer informed Suslov of Novick's impending arrival and asked that he be greeted as warmly as Goldberg had been.[67] But even Mikhoels and Fefer, in a discreet note to Suslov, make clear that they did not support a visit to Birobidzhan by Novick, "because no American journalist has gotten permission" to visit there, including Goldberg.[68]

Novick spent time with numerous Yiddish writers and saw the devastation of Jewish communities in the Ukraine and Lithuania. In Vilna, he "sensed that there would be revival of the Yiddish theater, museum, synagogue, and a children's Yiddish school, which soldiers from the Red Army had helped to clean up."[69] As a loyal communist, Novick was ready to share nothing but positive impressions of his trip.

But Novick, like Goldberg before him, must have left with a feeling of some anxiety for his friends. He was not given permission to see Birobidzhan, either. Bergelson told him "that Jews are not needed as before," confirming that anti-Semitic quotas and restrictions were now keeping them out of various positions and institutions.[70] Peretz Markish was hardly more hopeful. Two years later, he inscribed a book for Novick with the phrase "Everything will be all right," hoping against hope that it would prove to be true.[71]

By 1946, the regime, in fact, was considering disbanding the JAC. In August, supervision was transferred from the Sovinformburo to the Foreign Relations Department of the Central Committee. Instead of Lozovsky, the JAC would now be supervised by Mikhail Suslov. Neither change boded well for the committee. Lozovsky and the Sovinformburo had been oriented to interacting with the West. Suslov was far more the orthodox Marxist—meaning Stalinist—than Lozovsky, and the Central Committee was far less open-minded than the Sovinformburo. Suslov began to collect reviews of the committee's work, looking for reasons to close it altogether.

His own secret report that November was damning. Copies were sent to Stalin and other members of the Politburo. Suslov was a cautious, subservient tool; he would never have initiated such an action without direction from Stalin himself. Suslov began his report by acknowledging that the JAC had "played a certain positive role [during the war], furthering . . . the mobilization of Jews abroad in the struggle against German fascism." But now its work was "politically damaging." The committee had taken on "an increasingly nationalistic, Zionist character" and was "strengthening the Jewish reactionary bourgeois-nationalistic movement abroad." After citing dozens of examples of correspondence, requests, and articles from *Eynikayt,* all of which were said to reflect the JAC's determination to fight "for the reactionary idea of a single Jewish nation," Suslov called for the committee's "liquidation."[72] But Stalin was not ready. With the coming crisis over Palestine, the Kremlin believed that the JAC could still prove to be useful as a conduit of information about events in the Middle East and as a "face," however shrouded, for Soviet Jewry.

Still, Suslov identified the very terms that would later be invoked to destroy the committee. His evaluation and the fate of the JAC could not be separated from an anti-Semitic campaign that was growing more explicit, a campaign that ironically had begun after the victory at Stalingrad in February 1943.

Anti-Semitism and the Murder of Solomon Mikhoels

The so-called Jewish problem had always vexed Bolshevik leaders. Long before seizing power in Russia, Vladimir Lenin developed his own solution for the fate of the Jews. He firmly believed in their complete assimilation and opposed any nationalist alternative. In those years, two decades before the revolution, Lenin was engaged in a fierce debate with the Bund, which was attracting tens of thousands of Jewish followers in large parts of the Russian Empire and competing effectively for their allegiance against Lenin's Bolshevik underground. Hoping to undercut the Bund's appeal, Lenin denounced its overt call for cultural and national autonomy. As Lenin explained in one of his most extreme formulations, "Only a Jewish reactionary middle class strongly interested in turning back the wheel of history can rail against 'assimilation activities.'"[73] That the Jews did not inhabit a specific territory and that they were abandoning "Yiddish for the language of the people among whom they lived" meant they were ready to relinquish their separate identity.[74]

The revolution, according to Lenin, would lead to their disappearance. Freed of discrimination and racist violence, the Jews would abandon their religious traditions. Without a territory or a language to call their own, they would adopt the Russian language and culture more quickly than would other non-Russian or at least non-Slavic minorities.

Joseph Stalin wanted to accelerate the process. He expected that the Jews would disappear as the regime offered the carrot of modernization, with a stick for those who refused to assimilate.[75] It was one thing, though, for Bolshevik leaders to formulate an ideological approach before the revolution; it was another when they could exercise power and apply their doctrine against real people.

The Bolshevik leadership contained many activists of Jewish origin.

Although they were thoroughly assimilated and had no interest in religion, they were also acutely aware of the tsar's anti-Semitic policies and regarded any expression of anti-Semitism as a mark of reactionary prejudice. So Stalin had to be careful. "As a leader and a theoretician," Nikita Khrushchev once noted, Stalin "took care never to hint at his anti-Semitism in his written works or in his speeches."[76] Nevertheless, many of Stalin's most important rivals in the party—Leon Trotsky, Grigory Zinoviev, and Lev Kamenev—were Jews. As Stalin consolidated control, he was intent on eliminating them and their supporters, many of whom were also of Jewish origin.

On the other hand, Stalin was not the kind of anti-Semite who could not abide working with even a single Jew. Lazar Kaganovich and Lev Mekhlis* were close associates for many years. The Hungarian Jew Karl Pauker commanded Stalin's personal security detail for a time in the 1930s and used to shave the dictator with an open razor, before his own execution during the Great Purge in 1937. Their Jewish origins were incidental to Stalin so long as they were useful to him and he could rely on their absolute loyalty.

Once in power, Stalin initially proved to be flexible about the Jewish problem. He found it opportune to denounce anti-Semitism, as in his famous statement to the Jewish Telegraphic Agency in January 1931: "Anti-Semitism is an extreme expression of racial chauvinism and as such is the most dangerous survival of cannibalism."[77] In the 1920s and 1930s, Stalin permitted Jewish settlements to flourish in the Crimea, supported the creation of a secular Yiddish culture, and established a Jewish autonomous region in Birobidzhan to rival Palestine for the allegiance of Jewish masses inside and outside the country. He was once reported saying, "The Czar gave the Jews no land. Kerensky gave the Jews no land. But we will give it."[78†] Stalin, it seemed, was ready to help the Jews become a "normal" national minority with a territory of their own.

---

*Lazar Kaganovich (1893–1991) was a veteran Bolshevik leader. From 1925 to 1928 he was first secretary of the Ukrainian party committee. He served as head of the Moscow party committee from 1930 to 1935, joining the Politburo in 1930. In 1935 he supervised the construction of the Moscow subway, and during World War II he served on the State Defense Committee. He was expelled from the party in 1957, following Stalin's death and a subsequent confrontation with Nikita Khrushchev. Lev Mekhlis (1889–1953) served in the Red Army from 1918 to 1921. He headed the Red Army political administration in the late 1930s and served as people's commissar for state control after the war.

†Alexander Kerensky (1881–1970) became head of the Provisional Government that assumed power in Russia after the abdication of the tsar in February 1917.

For two decades following the Bolshevik takeover, new laws against anti-Semitism helped to prevent overt attacks on Jews. The regime was well aware that the abdication of the tsar and the subsequent October Revolution had undermined traditional Jewish life. Within the space of a few years, Jews fled the Pale of Settlement* and flocked to the country's major cities, seeking education and professional advancement. By the end of the 1930s, Jews had assumed prominent roles throughout Soviet society, particularly as party activists, editors, and journalists and as leaders of industrial enterprises and cultural institutions.

The visibility of Jews was noticeable enough to complicate relations between Nazi Germany and the Soviet Union. Stalin assured Hitler's foreign minister, Joachim von Ribbentrop, in 1939 that "as soon as he had adequate cadres of gentiles, he would remove all Jews from leading positions."[79] But the German invasion compelled Stalin to adjust his domestic policies. The regime granted all the national minorities much greater latitude, allowing them to celebrate their contributions to the war effort as Jews, say, or as Kazakhs.

The victory at Stalingrad, however, marked a turning point. With this decisive defeat of the Wehrmacht, the Red Army began the arduous task of driving the Germans back into Europe. Stalin could foresee his greatest triumph and soon adopted a more nationalistic posture in favor of the Great Russian people and at the expense of all the national minorities. Between October 1943 and June 1944, several small nationalities were expelled from border areas to Central Asia or Siberia after being unjustly accused of treason and collaboration with the enemy: the Chechens, Ingush, Karachays, Balkars, Kalmyks, and Crimean Tatars among them. (Earlier, in 1941, the Volga Germans and the Leningrad Finns had been deported from their lands after the German invasion, even though there was no evidence of their collaboration against the Kremlin.) Russian chauvinism also went hand in hand with anti-Semitism. Individual Jews were vulnerable because many had achieved visible positions in cultural, scientific, and academic realms; the time had now come to replace them. Virtually every institution in Soviet society was affected; newspapers, university faculties, the Bolshoi Theater—all

*Under the tsars, Russian Jews were confined to the Pale of Settlement by laws of 1795 and 1835. The Pale covered much of present-day Ukraine, Belarus, Poland, Latvia, and Lithuania. By 1897 more than five million Jews lived there. Jews needed special permission to live outside the Pale.

underwent purges to significantly reduce the number of Jews in leading positions.

Just months after the victory at Stalingrad, in the spring of 1943, David Ortenberg, editor of *Krasnaya Zvezda* (Red Star), was summoned to the office of Alexander Shcherbakov and told he had too many Jews on his staff; he would have to let some go. "It has already happened," Ortenberg assured Shcherbakov, and he proceeded to list the names of nine correspondents, all Jews, who had fallen at the front. "I can add one more . . . myself," Ortenberg told him, then walked out without saying good-bye. By August, he had been relieved of his duties at *Krasnaya Zvezda*.[80]

Things were no better in the army. In 1943, Ehrenburg's daughter Irina lost her job with the frontline newspaper *Unichtozhim Vraga* (We Will Destroy the Enemy). A Soviet colonel stormed into the newspaper office and began to curse the staff. Too many were Jews. "Is this a synagogue?" he shouted. The newspaper was shut down, and the journalists assigned to other posts.[81]

Stalin's personal animus against the Jews cannot be ignored. In her memoirs, his daughter, Svetlana, recalled Stalin's frequent anti-Semitic remarks. When she was still in high school and embarked on a romantic friendship with Alexei Kapler—a Jew, a war correspondent, and a film writer in his early forties—Stalin abruptly accused him of being a British spy and ordered his arrest. When Svetlana protested, Stalin cut her off. "She couldn't even find herself a Russian," he muttered to himself.[82] A year later, Svetlana married Grigory Morozov, a Jew who had been her classmate. Unhappy about her choice of husband, Stalin refused to meet Morozov, but he did not prevent the marriage from taking place. Nonetheless, Stalin liked to tell Svetlana that "the Zionists put him over on you."[83]

With the onset of the Cold War and the establishment of Israel in 1948, Stalin linked the threat of war with the United States to his suspicion that Soviet Jews had other loyalties. Although the Jews had demonstrated their reliability in the struggle against Hitler, if a conflict with America and the West flared up, Stalin believed they would betray him.

The JAC could not survive these tensions. Mikhoels was murdered on Stalin's personal orders in January 1948, the assassination disguised as a traffic accident. Stalin's paranoia about Jews and Zionism was now turning deadly.

Mikhoels had long felt vulnerable. As far back as 1934, he had told his daughters not to believe any accusations that might be leveled against him.[84] When he returned from his trip to the West in 1943, Mikhoels told Bergelson that he would soon be killed, and from that time on, he feared for his life.[85] In 1946, Mikhoels began receiving death threats at home, telephone calls that in Stalin's Moscow could have originated only within security circles. When he walked his dog at night, he would call Peretz Markish, who lived nearby, and ask to meet him on the street. Within the JAC, he kept up appearances. At one presidium meeting in the fall of 1947, just three months before his death, Mikhoels proclaimed that "Jews feel more physically secure in the Soviet Union than in any other country in the world."[86] To an inexperienced observer, such a statement could be taken to reflect Mikhoels's unswerving loyalty to Stalin. But the presidium was peppered with informers—at least Itsik Fefer, Solomon Bregman, and Grigory Kheifets (a former security agent) were all reporting to the authorities—and presidium minutes were examined by the Central Committee.[87] Mikhoels would never have uttered a subversive thought in such company.

Mikhoels, in fact, exhibited the rare quality of retaining profoundly Jewish loyalties even as he served the regime and was a Soviet patriot. He was born Solomon Vovsi in Dvinsk (Daugavpils), Latvia, in 1890 and received a traditional Jewish education, with studies in Hebrew and Talmud. His first wife was the daughter of a rabbi who founded the first Hebrew-language daily newspaper in tsarist Russia. Although Mikhoels was always drawn to the theater, he pursued a professional education in the law, not abandoning such ambitions until 1919, when he joined a Yiddish theater studio in Petrograd, then followed it to Moscow, where it grew into the State Jewish Theater. Mikhoels quickly established himself as a premier actor and as a director whose productions attracted the attention of a broad audience. The regime also trusted Mikhoels enough to have him urge David Bergelson on two occasions to move permanently to Moscow.[88]

Mikhoels flourished within official Soviet culture even as he insisted on preserving the Jewish character of his theater. "If we turn ourselves into a theater of translation," Mikhoels warned his colleagues in December 1933, "then to us, as a Jewish theater, there is nothing more to be done. Our path is unique—it is only compatible with the creative growth of Jewish theater and Jewish drama."[89] Mikhoels persevered and was richly rewarded. He was first honored by the regime in 1926, when he was named an Honorary Artist of the Russian Federation. In March 1935, he was given the title People's Artist of the Russian Federation for his performance of King Lear.[90] Four years later, in honor of the State Jewish Theater's twentieth anniversary, Mikhoels was awarded the Order of Lenin and named People's Artist of the Soviet Union—becoming one of hardly a dozen individuals with that honor in the country. That year, in 1939, he was "elected" to serve on the Moscow City Council. As late as 1946, when he and the JAC were already under substantial pressure, Mikhoels was awarded the Stalin Prize in honor of the play *Freylekhs* (Rejoicing). Mikhoels understood that the regime had ulterior reasons for honoring him. He once explained to his daughter that the regime used him and Ilya Ehrenburg as a *shirma*, a decoy: it could point to them whenever someone raised a troubling question about anti-Jewish measures.

Mikhoels was not thoroughly seduced by official rewards. In the 1930s, he befriended the poet Osip Mandelstam and his wife, Nadezhda. Mandelstam was arrested in 1934 for a poem denouncing Stalin, and although he was soon released, he faced several years of poverty and internal exile before dying in a labor camp in 1938. Mikhoels was among a handful of people to give the Mandelstams money, an act of rare civic courage in Stalin's Moscow.[91]

Mikhoels remained sensitive to anti-Semitism and often expressed his alarm. In April 1942, within months of his appointment to the JAC, Mikhoels, joined by Shakhno Epshteyn, sent a note to Shcherbakov objecting to a prominent article in the party journal *Bolshevik*, which maliciously understated the number of medals that individual Jewish soldiers had received for valor during the first six months of the war. Although the Jews constituted a tiny minority within the Soviet population, they had received the fourth highest number (after the Russians, Ukrainians, and Belorussians) and would soon surpass the Belorussians. Shcherbakov ignored their appeal. Two years later, the JAC sent memorandums to various Soviet officials, this time complaining about the treatment of Jews who had survived the Nazi onslaught and wanted to reestablish themselves in their old communities. In many towns they were being refused residence and work permits. After a government commission dismissed their concerns, Mikhoels could barely restrain his anger. "After such an answer things will only get worse," he observed.

"The anti-Semitic bureaucrats will see that they can get away with any-thing."[92]

At one point, Mikhoels visited Shcherbakov and personally appealed on behalf of Jews who remained in liberated regions. According to Mikhoels's account, Shcherbakov "listened to the terrible details of the suffering of these people who had passed through all the tortures of hell, with the ice-cold, calm, and impassive face of an absolutely indifferent person. With a cold tone he rebuked us, saying that if the Jewish Anti-Fascist Committee took up the appeals of those who had suffered during the war, then it would drown in this material and would stop dealing with its real political work—the struggle with fascism. . . . Not a muscle in his calm, smug face even moved."[93]

With the war over, Mikhoels was one of the few prominent Jews who dared to express his mourning over Jewish losses publicly and explicitly. On a visit to Kiev in September 1945, Mikhoels was invited to speak at the Kiev State Jewish Theater (whose building had miraculously sur-vived the war). Mikhoels carried a crystal vase to the rostrum, "but there were no flowers in the vase—it was filled with a yellow and black substance," one observer reported. "Before I came," Mikhoels began, speaking in Yiddish, "some friends from the Moscow Theater and I went to a store to buy this crystal vase. We then went directly to Babi Yar and filled the vase with earth, which held the screams of mothers and fa-thers, from the young boys and girls who did not live to grow up, screams from all who were sent there by the fascist beasts." Holding up the vase, Mikhoels continued. "Look at this. You will see laces from a child's shoes, tied by little Sara who fell with her mother. Look carefully and you will see the tears of an old Jewish woman. . . . Look closely and you will see your fathers who are crying 'Sh'ma Israel' and looking with beseeching eyes to heaven, hoping for an angel to rescue them. . . . Lis-ten, and you will hear the Jews deported to the death camps singing the song 'We do not go the last way.' . . . I have brought you a little earth from Babi Yar. Throw into it some of your flowers so they will grow symbolically for our people. . . . In spite of our enemies, we shall live."[94]

Upon his return to Moscow, Mikhoels insisted that the JAC presidium support "a movement to create monuments to the victims of fascism," in particular at Babi Yar, where the ravine "had not been fenced off. This is a neglected, disgraceful place," he told his colleagues.[95] Such heartfelt displays of identity could not have endeared Mikhoels to Soviet officials.

Mikhoels was also perceived as too sympathetic to Zionism. He did not conceal his interest in a Jewish homeland. As Mikhoels told the poet Abraham Sutzkever when they first met in Moscow in 1944, "When I flew to America, . . . I kissed the air when we passed over Palestine."[96] Three years later, in December 1947, he and Benjamin Zuskin held an evening in honor of the founder of modern Yiddish literature, Mendele Mocher Sforim, in Moscow's Polytechnic Museum, one of the largest and most prestigious halls in the capital. Before performing scenes from Mendele's play *The Travels of Benjamin III*, Mikhoels explained that it concerned a man searching for the road to the Promised Land. He asks a peasant he meets along the way, "Where is the road to Eretz Yisroel [the land of Israel]?" Mikhoels responded himself. "Recently Comrade Gromyko gave us the answer to this question from a rostrum at the United Nations." (On May 14, 1947, Gromyko forcefully endorsed the partition of Palestine into Jewish and Arab-controlled areas, repeating Soviet support for partition on November 26.) The audience erupted with applause. Mikhoels's daughter remembers that it lasted for ten minutes, leaving her father "pale, motionless, and shocked." The next day, just before New Year's, Mikhoels went to the central radio office to listen to a tape of the performance. But the tape had been "inadvertently erased"; Mikhoels knew it was a bad sign.[97]

He was a marked man, too outspoken a person, too much the actor, for Stalin to safely presume that if he was "prepared" for a show trial, he could be trusted to perform a role produced by the secret police. Better to kill him outright. Within a week, he was assigned to evaluate a play in Minsk; he did not return alive from the trip. Stalin's daughter overheard her father on the telephone when he received word of Mikhoels's death and recalls him approving the official story that it was the result of an automobile accident.[98] What she did not know was that her father and the security police had begun to conspire against Mikhoels months before.

In 1947, Stalin had been disturbed by reports in the Western press about his daughter's private life. He ordered Viktor Abakumov, minister of state security (the MGB), to investigate, but Abakumov was not able to uncover their source. In the meantime, Stalin had initiated a series of reprisals against his late wife's relatives (the Alliluyeva family), whom he no longer protected. In the course of the ensuing investigation, Abakumov learned that an acquaintance of Mikhoels named Isaac Goldshtein was also friendly with the Alliluyevas and that Mikhoels had asked Goldshtein for information about Svetlana Alliluyeva and her husband, Grigory Morozov. Mikhoels, it seems, was hoping to see if Morozov, who had also been a classmate of Svetlana's older brother Vasily, could be persuaded to approach his father-in-law in order to seek a softening in the anti-Semitic atmosphere emanating from the Kremlin. According to Goldshtein's testimony to the MGB, which may well be completely unreliable, Mikhoels did meet Svetlana and her husband, but nothing came of their contact. (The couple separated in 1947.) But Mikhoels's vain attempt to influence Stalin through a personal avenue reflected both desperation on his part and a severe lack of understanding of how to gain access to Stalin or influence his thinking.

Once Abakumov learned from Goldshtein about Mikhoels's undesirable interest in Svetlana and her Jewish husband, he employed torture against Goldshtein to help turn this otherwise innocent information into a plot in which Mikhoels conspired with American and Zionist intelligence circles to gather information about the leader of the Soviet government. Abakumov then showed Goldshtein's "confession" to Stalin, which reinforced Stalin's resolve to eliminate Mikhoels.[99] As we shall see, Stalin was growing more and more disturbed about expressions of interest in Palestine and, later, Israel among Soviet Jews; JAC leaders and other prominent individuals were to pay for any indiscretion.

Moscow, 1948

After the murder of Mikhoels, the JAC continued to function, but under an ominous cloud. It could not withstand the events of 1948. In May, the State of Israel was proclaimed, gaining the immediate recognition of the Soviet and American governments. Stalin was anxious to see the British out of the Middle East and even harbored a fugitive belief that the new Jewish state would join the Soviet bloc. As Israel defended itself against an invasion by five Arab armies, Stalin authorized arms supplies through Czechoslovakia, an infusion of substantial support that proved essential to Israel's success in the war. Soviet Jews, like their brothers and sisters around the world, followed developments in the Middle East with a passionate concern. Many wrote letters to the JAC, accusing it of moral cowardice and urging its leaders to be more outspoken in defense of Israel. Many combat veterans sought to volunteer in Israel's army.

Still others insisted on going to Israel as an expression of Zionist long-ing. One letter addressed to *Pravda* in May asked that "all Jewish resi-dents of the town of Zhmerinka [in the Ukraine] be permitted to go."[100] The JAC reacted nervously. Fefer saw the need for *Eynikayt* to "publish a series of articles instilling patriotism in order to rebuff harmful atti-tudes of residents of the town of Zhmerinka and people like them."[101] Both Fefer and Grigory Kheifets forwarded detailed information about "volunteers for Israel" to the Central Committee, many of whom were arrested. But Fefer and Kheifets could not suppress spontaneous support for the new Jewish state.[102]

This upsurge of emotion was reinforced in September by the arrival of Golda Meyerson (Meir), who headed the first Israeli legation to the Krem-lin. Enormous crowds greeted her in front of Moscow's main synagogue on Saturday, September 11, when she attended Sabbath morning services with members of her staff. The Israelis were not prepared for such an overt and emotional display of support. "Exhausted from the tension, we returned to our rooms with mixed feelings," Mordechai Namir, the lega-tion's first secretary, recalled in his memoirs, *Mission to Moscow*. "With all of our joy that fortune had granted us such a reunion with our broth-ers, there was also a sinking feeling in our hearts because of the suspicion that the blatant conduct of the congregation had crossed the acceptable limits of the city and that we had participated in a very tragic event."[103] But Moscow's Jews were not finished. Several weeks later, even larger crowds assembled on Rosh Hashana and again on Yom Kippur. They waited for hours in front of the synagogue, then escorted Golda Meyerson through the streets, shouting, "Next Year in Jerusalem." Stalin had had enough. On November 20, the party leadership approved the immediate disbanding of the Jewish Anti-Fascist Committee, "since, as the facts show, this committee is a center of anti-Soviet propaganda and regularly submits anti-Soviet information to organs of foreign intelligence."[104] *Eynikayt* was closed, as was Der emes, the Yiddish publishing house.

Once again, Svetlana heard her father express suspicions about the Jews. Her former father-in-law, Joseph Morozov, was arrested. (At the time he was working in Lina Shtern's institute, a fact soon used against her.) When Svetlana appealed to her father, he reacted with anger. "No, you don't understand," Stalin told his daughter. "The entire older gener-ation is contaminated with Zionism and now they're teaching the young people, too."[105]

The crackdown was broad and deep. In Birobidzhan, Jewish members of the party leadership were carried off in a series of arrests between 1948 and 1951, including Alexander Bakhmutsky, the secretary of the regional party committee, and several Yiddish writers who had taken up residence there. They were accused of disseminating pro-American sentiments by accepting relief packages from the West, thereby encouraging "the impression that the United States and not the Soviet people was responsible for the achievements" of Birobidzhan.[106] In February 1949, Georgy Malenkov presided over a meeting of Central Committee members to discuss cultural affairs. Among its 150 decisions that day—to observe the 125th anniversary of the birth of the Czech composer Bedrich Smetana, to send a Soviet orchestra to East Germany, and to increase the circulation of several sports magazines, for example—the Central Committee voted to "dissolve" societies for Yiddish writers in Moscow, Kiev, and Minsk and to close Yiddish-language journals in Moscow and Kiev.[107]

It was in the midst of this comprehensive assault on Jewish cultural life that fifteen people associated with the Jewish Anti-Fascist Committee were arrested. Their case was just beginning.

David Hofshteyn, who lived in Kiev, was the first to be taken. He had long been under surveillance; earlier that year Abakumov had reported to Stalin that Hofshteyn headed a "Jewish nationalistic group" in the Ukraine that was coordinating anti-Soviet activity with the JAC presidium in Moscow.[108] He was arrested on the night of September 16, 1948. Hofshteyn was kept in Kiev for six weeks before being transferred to Moscow. Once a month Feige Hofshteyn traveled to Lefortovo prison to hand over two hundred rubles for her husband to buy food. Years later, she understood how naive she had been. As long as money or a parcel was accepted, a prisoner was presumed to be alive. But after Hofshteyn's death was officially confirmed in 1955, more than half the money she had delivered for him was returned.[109]

Itsik Fefer's arrest on December 24, 1948, marked a crucial stage in the case. By that time, he was already cooperating with the investigation. Earlier that month, Fefer had stopped by Mikhoels's apartment "accompanied by two unknown men in traditional felt hats," Natalia Vovsi-Mikhoels later recalled. "Give me all your father's foreign correspondence," Fefer asked of her.[110] But Natalia and her sister knew of no archive at home. A day or two before his arrest, Fefer was seen with no less a figure than Viktor Abakumov in Mikhoels's former office at the State Jewish Theater. They spent several hours going through files and papers, presumably looking for documents that would compromise Mikhoels and the work of the JAC.

The secret police came for Fefer himself at two in the morning. After several hours, they left, taking Fefer, a number of papers, and several photographs. "I am not guilty of anything," Fefer told his daughter as they led him away. Fefer's wife and his younger sister Darya appealed for help from Ilya Ehrenburg, who told them he was equally afraid. They called on the novelist and cultural bureaucrat Alexander Fadeyev,* but he refused to receive them; standing on the stairs at the Writers' Union, he chased them away.[111] Peretz Markish learned of Fefer's arrest within days. "This son of a bitch will not go to his grave alone," Markish predicted.[112]

The actor Benjamin Zuskin was arrested on the same night as Fefer was. MGB agents came to his apartment and began a search, only to learn that Zuskin had been admitted to a hospital the day before for treatment of severe insomnia. Ever since Mikhoels's death, Zuskin had been living under relentless stress. He was the natural successor to Mikhoels; Zuskin, though, was not an administrator by temperament, and the responsibilities aggravated his chronic insomnia. Zuskin also sensed that he was being followed. That December, the State Jewish Theater was scheduled to go on tour, but to everyone's surprise, Zuskin announced he could not go owing to health concerns. In reality, the regime was denying him a routine travel permit. His family learned years later that he had been making telephone calls from the apartment of Mikhoels's daughters a floor below, where he could converse in a closed-off room; he did not want his wife to know about the denial or his appeals. She, too, was an actor in the State Jewish Theater, but unlike her husband, she had to go to Leningrad to perform.

The MGB agents found Zuskin heavily sedated and asleep in his hospital room. The duty physician intervened, insisting Zuskin was ill, under medical care, and should not be awakened or moved. But the agents ignored such pleas. They carried Zuskin out to a car and drove him to

---

*Alexander Fadeyev (1901–1956) was a Soviet novelist and leading figure in the Union of Soviet Writers for many years, serving as general secretary from 1946 to 1954. In that capacity he was often called on to sign arrest orders for members of the union. Fadeyev committed suicide following Khrushchev's secret speech in 1956.

Lefortovo prison where he awoke the next day in his cell still wearing his hospital gown.[113]

The next arrests did not take place until a month later, on January 13, 1949, a year after the murder of Mikhoels, when Boris Shimeliovich and Joseph Yuzefovich were taken away. Shimeliovich had been especially close to Mikhoels and consistently supported his attempts to broaden the functions of the JAC. Yuzefovich had worked with Lozovsky for decades; Abakumov needed him to incriminate Lozovsky. That night, agents also came for Fefer's wife and sister. No relatives of any of the other defendants were arrested or exiled until January 1953, when the regime—five months after the execution of thirteen defendants— abruptly began exiling their relatives to remote areas of Siberia and Kazakhstan. Fefer's wife and sister were treated differently. Under severe threats, his wife signed a confession, while his sister, who initially re-sisted, was forced to stand for twenty-four hours until she, too, gave in and confessed to knowing Itsik Fefer's crimes. They spent seven years in labor camps, the only relatives to receive such harsh treatment. It is hard to know exactly why they were singled out. Perhaps it was a means to in-timidate Fefer even further, or perhaps the MGB believed, rightly or wrongly, that they knew too much about Fefer's role at the JAC and so had to be removed from Moscow.

Nine more defendants were arrested between January 24 and January 28: Ilya and Khayke Vatenberg, David Bergelson, Leyb Kvitko, Solomon Lozovsky, Solomon Bregman, Emilia Teumin, Peretz Markish, and Lina Shtern.

The arrest of Solomon Lozovsky required unusual measures. His grandson Vladimir Shamberg was married to Georgy Malenkov's daugh-ter, and Malenkov, the deputy prime minister and Central Committee secretary, was the closest aide to Stalin himself. In late January, Sham-berg was informed that his wife, Volya, wanted a divorce. This news came as an absolute shock to him. But the timing and the speed of the di-vorce made it clear that it was her father who needed this divorce. At the time, there was a two-stage procedure for obtaining a divorce: an appli-cation would be made to a district court, then a month later the couple would be divorced in Moscow City Court. But not in this case. Sham-berg was taken directly to the city court by a KGB colonel, the comman-der of Malenkov's personal guard, and the divorce was granted almost immediately.[114] Malenkov obviously wanted to be free of any connec-

tion with a future "enemy of the people" and with a "relative of an enemy of the people." The very day after the divorce, Lozovsky was summoned to appear before Malenkov and another important party leader,
Matvei Shkiryatov, who interrogated him about how he had helped
Fefer, Mikhoels, and Epshteyn edit their "Crimea letter" in February
1944. The fact that he had not discouraged them or informed on them to
the Central Committee was now held against him.[115] Malenkov told
Lozovsky that he was being expelled from the Central Committee and
from the Communist party. In a last-ditch attempt to save himself, Lozovsky appealed directly to Stalin. "For the last time, I beg you to listen
to me, and take into consideration that I have never betrayed either the
Party or the Central Committee."[116] But Stalin ignored his appeal. A
few days later, on January 26, Lozovsky was arrested on Stalin's personal order while walking with his daughter in the courtyard of his
apartment building.

The regime also took unusual care with Lina Shtern, trying to discredit her before her arrest with a clumsy and transparent maneuver.
Shtern normally delivered her weekly lecture on physiology at Moscow's
Second Medical Institute at nine in the morning. But on one late January
afternoon she was instructed to begin at eight the next morning. The ad-
justment in schedule was not officially announced. Nonetheless, a small
number of students learned of the change; several tried to contact classmates, taking care to alert only people they were confident were not informers. The next day, a small number of students, fewer than twenty of
the nearly two hundred who regularly attended, were on hand; they all
understood that the regime was planning a provocation. As Shtern began to speak, an institute official—in reality, he was the "resident" security officer—interrupted her and asked for an intermission. Shtern was
then told that her students had stopped attending her class because they
no longer respected her. With that, she was summarily fired; her arrest
followed soon after.[117] Her arrest, too, was handled in a special way. A
military officer came to her apartment and announced that the minister
of state security wanted to speak with her. She was taken to Abakumov's
office, where her arrest took place, and was already in prison when her
belongings were searched.

The final arrest, that of Leon Talmy, came more than six months later.
By then, Talmy had other things on his mind. His American-born son,
Vladimir, had enlisted in the Red Army in 1942 at the age of seventeen

and become the commander of a sapper platoon. He was severely wounded by a mine in February 1944 and spent six months in the hospital. Upon his recovery, Vladimir was assigned to the Military Institute of Foreign Languages (his first language was English, which he spoke with his parents until his enlistment). From there he was sent to Berlin in 1945 to work as a translator for the Soviet Military Administration and the Economic Directorate of the Allied Control Council. But his contacts with Americans got him into trouble: on December 5, 1947, Soviet secret police carried out a search of his room and found a copy of the defector Victor Kravchenko's famous book *I Chose Freedom*. Convicted of anti-Soviet agitation, Vladimir was sentenced to twenty-five years in the camps. In the spring of 1949, Leon and Sonia Talmy were planning to visit their son in Siberia. But Leon was arrested on July 3, 1949, the day before they were to leave. Sonia traveled alone and told Vladimir that his father had suffered a stroke.[118]

At least one other arrest took place that had a direct bearing on the JAC case: Polina Zhemchuzhina, the wife of Foreign Minister Vyacheslav Molotov, was taken prisoner on January 21, 1949. A Jew, she was born in 1897 (her real name was Perl Karpovskaya) and joined the Bolshevik party in 1918. She married Molotov in 1921 and soon became a close friend to Stalin's wife Nadezhda Alliluyeva, who committed suicide in 1932. Zhemchuzhina was among the last people to speak with Alliluyeva before her death, a fact that provoked Stalin's resentment and suspicion. Nonetheless, Zhemchuzhina was able to forge a political career. She played a leading role in Soviet perfume production and then in the food industry before becoming people's commissar for the fishing industry in 1939. That year she was elected a candidate member of the Central Committee. But already in 1939, Stalin was making her life difficult. She was held responsible for the presence of "vandals" and "saboteurs" in her commissariat, removed from her position in the fishing industry by a vote of the Politburo, and transferred to a lesser position elsewhere.

A precipitating incident took place in November 1948. Zhemchuzhina met members of the Israeli legation at a diplomatic reception on November 7. She hardly restrained herself. "I've heard that you attend the synagogue," she told Golda Meyerson, speaking in Yiddish. "Very good. Keep going. The Jews want to see you." When Meyerson asked how Zhemchuzhina knew Yiddish so well, she proudly responded, "Ikh bin a yidishe tokhter" (I am a daughter of the Jewish people).[119] Her enthusiasm for Israel came to Stalin's attention. By December, Abakumov was gathering "information" about her "nationalistic" activities and her ties (real and concocted) with Mikhoels, Lozovsky, and the JAC. Stalin was informed of her "politically unworthy behavior," and in January she was arrested. For a time, the investigators considered making Zhemchuzhina the central figure in the JAC case; all the defendants were questioned about her. Her brother, Sam Karp, was a businessman in the United States and had met with Mikhoels at Zhemchuzhina's request in 1943, which also made her vulnerable. Fefer and Zuskin were both compelled to have personal confrontations with her soon after their arrests (while she was still at liberty). But Zhemchuzhina held firm and denied all the accusations. After her arrest, the investigators attempted one last ploy to break her spirit. Several of her assistants were also arrested, and at least one was compelled to testify that Zhemchuzhina had used her position to seduce him. Still she did not relent. In the end, it was decided to separate her fate from the JAC case and send her into exile in Kazakhstan. During the JAC trial, there were only faint echoes of her one-time connection to the case.[120]

Reactions in the West

The disappearance of the Yiddish writers aroused anxiety in the West, where they were well-known figures with numerous personal and professional contacts. But Soviet spokesmen and their allies knew how to deflect troublesome questions. Alexander Fadeyev, for one, visited New York in March 1949 to attend the Scientific and Cultural Conference for World Peace, commonly called the Waldorf Conference because it was held at the Waldorf-Astoria Hotel. Hundreds of famous Americans participated, including Arthur Miller, Norman Mailer, the Harvard astronomer Harlow Shapley, and Howard Fast, who helped to organize the conference as an active member of the American Communist Party. Publicly and privately, Fadeyev was confronted with questions on the whereabouts of several writers; in response he lied, assuring anyone who asked that he had recently seen them and knew their work.[121]

The following month, Fadeyev led a large delegation of Soviet figures to the World Peace Congress in Paris. According to Howard Fast, leading Jewish members of the American Communist Party, including Paul

Novick and Chaim Suller of the *Morgen Freiheit,* had grown sufficiently alarmed over rumors out of Moscow that they asked Fast, who was planning to attend the Paris congress, to seek out the Soviet delegates and charge "the leadership of the Soviet Union with anti-Semitism." Once in Paris, Fast arranged to meet privately with Fadeyev, who listened carefully to Fast's concerns and then dismissed his charges with a flat-out denial that anti-Semitism would be tolerated in the Soviet Union, although he did claim that a broad conspiracy existed involving Zionist circles and the Joint. Fast shared this information with Novick upon his return to New York.[122] But Fast, Novick, and Suller kept their fears to themselves; they were not prepared to express their anxieties publicly.

Novick, in fact, steadfastly defended the Soviet Union even as he tried to clarify the fate of his friends. In July 1949, he learned that Sholem Asch had written a sharp letter to the IKUF (a left-wing Yiddish cultural organization in New York) in which he denounced the disappearance of the Soviet Yiddish writers. Novick immediately responded, attacking Asch for taking "a step that plays into the hands of the war-mongers." Novick assured Asch that such "reports not yet verified" were lies. "Honest people, when they hear the current reports about the Yiddish writers, and the incitement on this score, must say to themselves: in over thirty years there were many incitements, and every time it turned out that the inciters—were inciters."[123] Within Jewish communist circles, Novick's attitude was tragically typical.

Paul Robeson had a more complicated response to the case. He had met Mikhoels and Fefer in New York in 1943 and was aware in 1949 of rumors concerning Fefer's disappearance. Robeson, moreover, could read Russian and followed the Soviet press as it embarked on a harsh "anti-cosmopolitan" campaign. On January 28, 1949, *Pravda* let forth a stream of venom against "an unpatriotic group of theater critics": almost all were Jews. Numerous articles followed, emphasizing the alienation of Jews from Russian culture and often referring to them as "rootless cosmopolitans," "persons without identity," and "passportless wanderers."

Robeson traveled to Moscow that June to help mark the 150th anniversary of the birth of Alexander Pushkin. He saw Jewish friends who explained how bad things were. When Robeson asked to see Fefer, he was told that Fefer was away on vacation. But Robeson insisted on see-

ing him. The authorities were in a bind; they understood that Robeson
was prepared to call their bluff. So, in a remarkable turn of events, it was
arranged for Fefer to see Robeson in Robeson's hotel room. Secret police
went to Fefer's apartment to retrieve a clean suit and shirt for him to
wear.

A rumor is attached to this incident: that Fefer had been tortured, his
fingernails torn out, leaving him with bandaged hands that he at first attempted to conceal only to display as a silent, horrifying signal. There is
no truth to this. Fefer was not physically mistreated in prison, at least according to Vladimir Naumov, who has had access to the case files. In
fact, Robeson understood from Fefer that he was a prisoner, along with
other prominent cultural figures, but Fefer implored him to keep silent
about his fate in order not to jeopardize his family.

Soon thereafter, Robeson delivered his last Moscow concert (which
was also broadcast on national radio). Before his encore, he asked the
audience for quiet and made a few remarks. "He expressed with emotion the sense he had of the deep cultural ties between the Jews of the
United States and the Soviet Union and of how that tradition was being
continued by the present generation of Russian-Jewish writers and actors." He regretted the untimely death of Solomon Mikhoels but expressed his satisfaction over having just seen Itsik Fefer, who appeared
"pale and sickly." Fefer, at that moment, was a "disappeared person,"
making Robeson's gesture on his behalf an unheard-of event in Soviet
public life. Robeson concluded by singing the famous Jewish partisan
song inspired by the Warsaw Ghetto Uprising, "Zog nit keyn mol" (We
do not go the last way), as his only encore, stirring the heavily Jewish audience.[124]

Back in America, Robeson denied reports of anti-Semitism, telling a
reporter from *Soviet Russia Today* that he had "met Jewish people all
over the place. . . . I heard no word about it." Robeson justified his silence on the grounds that any public criticism of the USSR would reinforce the authority of America's right wing, which, he believed, wanted
to see a preemptive war against the Soviet Union.[125] But by all accounts,
he did not even alert his friends in the party to what he knew, or search
for other, discreet ways to help Fefer once he decided not to make a public appeal. As one party comrade said in rebuke of Howard Fast in January 1957, "If you and Paul Robeson had raised your voices in 1949,
Itsik Fefer would be alive today."[126]

Ilya Ehrenburg would not speak up, either. In Paris in April 1949, just months after the principal arrests, he attended the World Peace Congress and, though asked by friends about the "anti-cosmopolitan campaign," avoided sharing any information. Ehrenburg had a harder time in London the following year. At a press conference attended by nearly two hundred journalists, he endured a barrage of tough questions. The Korean War had recently broken out, and the reporters were in no mood for relaxed give-and-take. One asked Ehrenburg about the fate of David Bergelson and Itsik Fefer. Ehrenburg responded that he had not seen either of them for two years, and before that, he had seen them only rarely, an answer that was more or less factually true. But then Ehrenburg diverted his audience with a further remark. "If anything unpleasant had happened to them," he claimed, "I would have known about it." Ehrenburg knew that Fefer and Bergelson had been arrested, but unless he was prepared to seek political asylum in England and abandon his wife and daughter to Stalin's revenge, he had no choice but to reassure the assembled journalists about their fate and cover up the secret pogrom of JAC members.[127]

In 1950 as well, when the *American Jewish Yearbook* carried the alarming news that "leaders of the [Anti-Fascist] Committee and most of the well-known Yiddish writers were arrested and deported" (a claim that was only partially true), there was no concerted effort to save them by Jewish organizations in the West, Israeli officials, or the Western democracies.[128] The prisoners were on their own.

Under Interrogation

With one exception—Itsik Fefer—all the defendants were brutally interrogated; some were beaten and tortured, placed in grim punishment cells, or subjected to endless nocturnal interrogations. The interrogators turned everything they did or said into evidence of "nationalism." "Giving a lecture, writing verse, literary evenings, meetings with young students, language lessons, the study of history, studio exercises, the theatrical repertoire"—any activity that writers, poets, and people of culture routinely pursue became an example of "nationalistic" subversion.[129]

Within months, investigators worked out confessions to four crimes: (1) bourgeois nationalism; (2) the creation of an anti-Soviet nationalistic underground; (3) treason against the Soviet Union; and (4) espionage on behalf of U.S. intelligence. There was no trick to their methods. Boris Shimeliovich was beaten mercilessly; he told his judges that he counted more than two thousand blows to his buttocks and heels. He had to be brought to interrogations on a stretcher. But Shimeliovich did not give in and alone among all the defendants refused to confess to any crime. Joseph Yuzefovich initially resisted as well, refusing to implicate Lozovsky or himself. But after a savage beating, Yuzefovich relented. As he told the court, "I was ready to confess that I was the pope's own nephew and that I was acting on his direct personal orders." Khayke Vatenberg-Ostrovskaya was the only woman among these defendants to be placed in a punishment cell, in March 1949 and then again in June, each time for a handful of days. The experience of sitting alone in a cold cement cell, with nothing to eat but bread and water, overwhelmed her with fear and exhaustion. "I was interrogated with a rubber cudgel lying on the table," she told the court, and "driven to such a psychological state that I started looking for crimes." Her interrogators even threatened to "make a cripple" out of her. Several months after David Hofshteyn was moved from Kiev to Moscow, he grew so desperate in Lefortovo prison that he feigned insanity, hoping to avoid further mistreatment and interrogations. For a time, whenever the corridor guard approached or food was being served, Hofshteyn would suddenly begin speaking strangely or throw himself around the cell. But his jailers had so much experience with recalcitrant prisoners that they simply ignored his behavior until he tired of the charade.[130]

Peretz Markish was among the most brutally treated. After his arrest, he was subjected to interrogations two or three times a day. In the daytime, he was questioned from late morning to about five in the afternoon and was called out again for interrogation in the investigator's office at 11:30 that night and was generally there until five the next morning. This went on until April 19. By then he had been interrogated ninety-six times, bringing him to complete exhaustion. Markish was put in solitary confinement three times and spent a total of sixteen days there. But not until July 1949, after Mikhail Ryumin, a deputy to Abakumov and one of the most feared security officers, took over his case, was Markish compelled under torture to sign a confession.[131]

Lina Shtern, in spite of her recognition as a scientist, was not exempt from the interrogators' brutality. She was taken to see Abakumov after her arrest. She had hardly stepped into his office when he shouted at her.

> "We know everything! Come clean! You're a Zionist agent, you were bent on detaching the Crimea from Russia and establishing a Jewish state there."
>   That's the first I've heard of it," she said in a strong Jewish accent.
> "Why you old whore!" Abakumov roared.
>   "So that's the way a minister speaks to an academician." Lina Shtern shook her head in dismay.[132]

Shtern sustained her dignity throughout her ordeal. A series of interrogators tried to break her will; one summoned her eighty-seven times for interrogation. Shtern, too, ultimately gave in and signed a confession.

The interrogators often indulged in crude anti-Semitic invective. Emilia Teumin was forced to admit that "under Lozovsky the Sovinformburo had been turned into a synagogue."[133] Colonel Vladimir Komarov, who conducted much of the case, screamed at Lozovsky that "Jews are low, dirty people, that all Jews are lousy bastards, that all opposition to the party consisted of Jews, that Jews all over the Soviet Union are conducting an anti-Soviet whisper campaign, and that the Jews want to annihilate all of the Russians."[134] Even a Jewish interior police official who must have brought about his own share of human misery was offended by the tenor of such interrogations and complained to his superior that "the investigators are interrogating these prisoners as Jews and not as criminals."[135]

Only one defendant, Itsik Fefer, immediately cooperated with the investigation, detailing a host of baseless accusations against the JAC and helping to embroider an ugly and elaborate quilt of lies and fabrications that would hold the indictment together in 1952. As a result of his betrayal, more than one hundred people were arrested, many of whom were also executed or perished in camps. On the eve of the trial, Fefer was reassured that if he continued to cooperate, his life would be spared.

The regime, it is now believed, originally intended to conduct an open "show trial" reminiscent of the infamous proceedings against leading Bolsheviks in the 1930s. Beaten, intimidated, utterly humiliated, the defendants were being turned into compliant actors for another Stalinist charade. In March 1950 they were informed that the investigation of their case was complete; normally a trial could be expected to follow in short order. But the security organs were distracted by other urgent matters. Stalin was organizing a trial for Leningrad party leaders whom he had decided to eliminate. Several had been arrested in late 1949 after they had already been dismissed from official positions and expelled from the party. Then, on January 13, 1950, *Pravda* announced that the Presidium of the Supreme Soviet had reinstated the death penalty. Abolished in 1947, perhaps to reassure the public that the terror of the Great Purge would not be repeated, it was now to apply to crimes of treason. By September the former party leaders of Leningrad were tried and executed. In Moscow the same year, other Jewish figures who had also been arrested were either executed or died in prison: the Yiddish writer Der Nister perished in a labor camp; the literary critic Yitzhak Nusinov died in Lefortovo prison; and the journalists Shmuel Persov and Miriam Zheleznova were shot.

The case of Persov and Zheleznova involved the arrest of another 250 people and engaged the security organs for months. They were both veteran journalists who had contributed numerous articles to *Eynikayt*. In one prominent series, Persov and Zheleznova wrote about Jewish workers from two prestigious Moscow enterprises: the Dynamo Machine Tool Plant and the Stalin Automobile Factory. They reported on cultural programs that the workers were organizing, particularly art and theater studios, and amateur literary efforts. Four years later, these articles were held against them. Both Persov and Zheleznova were arrested on April 4, 1950, accused of heading a "terrorist center," compelled to confess, then brought before a summary military court—presided over by Lieutenant General Alexander Cheptsov—and condemned to death. The executions took place on November 23, 1950; Zheleznova was forty-three years old at the time of her death.[136]

The poet and playwright Shmuel Halkin was among the lucky ones. He, too, had been arrested and at one point faced a personal confrontation with Fefer, who pressed him to confess. But then Halkin was separated from the JAC case, and he received ten years in the camps. Halkin survived and returned to Moscow, where he reported on the crude nature of his treatment. "How could you be a Soviet patriot," one investigator had asked him, "with relatives all over the world?"[137]

By the time the trial took place in the spring of 1952 several of the defendants' tormentors were themselves in jail, among them one of Stalin's chief henchmen, former Minister of State Security Viktor Abakumov.

Abakumov had been useful to Stalin for a number of years; after the war, it was Abakumov who spearheaded the anti-Semitic campaign and prepared material to incriminate Mikhoels. But Abakumov was mistrusted by others in the party leadership, particularly Beria and Malenkov, who were anxious to see him removed. Mikhail Ryumin sensed Abakumov's vulnerability and decided to outflank him as an even more brazen anti-Semite.[138] In November 1950 the prominent Kremlin doctor Yakov Etinger had been arrested for critical remarks he was making about Stalin on the telephone. According to Mikhail Ryumin, who wrote to Stalin in June 1951, Abakumov was refusing to allow Etinger to be interrogated about terrorism or involvement in the death of Alexander Shcherbakov, who, everyone believed, had died of natural causes in 1945. Ryumin also denounced Abakumov for deliberately placing Etinger in such difficult conditions that he died in prison before investigators could learn all they could from him. Finally, Ryumin claimed that the JAC case was dragging on with no definite word when the trial would take place. Abakumov was soon arrested, as were other investigators associated with him.[139]

Ryumin took over the JAC case, insisting that the defendants be interrogated about terrorism, a charge that had not been raised previously. Ryumin, it seems, believed there was no better way to ingratiate himself with Stalin, who was increasingly paranoid about plots against his life. It was here that the Doctors' Plot emerged, along with its discreet and soon to be visible connections to the JAC case. Beginning in the fall of 1951, Ryumin and his new team of investigators raised questions about the behavior of several Kremlin doctors. Ryumin focused on Shimeliovich. On December 19, 1951, Shimeliovich was asked about Dr. Yevgeniya Lifshitz, a prominent pediatrician who was treating the children and grandchildren of Kremlin officials. Shimeliovich also directly supervised Dr. Miron Vovsi, a first cousin to Mikhoels who had served as chief physician of the Red Army during the war. Lifshitz, Vovsi, and Stalin's personal physician (the non-Jewish) Vladimir Vinogradov, among others, would be arrested in 1952.

In the meantime, the JAC case required greater attention. As the defendants languished in prison, several began to retract their confessions. In 1950 alone, Lozovsky, Zuskin, and Yuzefovich disavowed their testimony. In an unusual admission, the new Minister of State Security Semyon Ignatiev wrote to Malenkov and Beria—who at that time was still a member of the Politburo but was no longer formally involved in matters of internal security—that "there are almost no documents to substantiate the evidence given by the arrested about the espionage and nationalistic activity they carried out under the concealment of the JAC."[140] In spite of all the interrogations, the torture, and the coerced confessions, the case was still not ready. Not until January 1952 was the investigation officially resumed. "Experts" were called in to examine *Eynikayt* and other material deemed relevant to the prosecutor's case. Finally, on March 5, a definitive list of fifteen defendants was drawn up based on an alleged Zionist and American-inspired plot against the Soviet Union. Ignatiev approved the indictment on March 31 and urged in a note to the Politburo that all the defendants be executed, except for Lina Shtern, who was to receive ten years of exile. In other words, over a month before the trial even began, the fate of the defendants was sealed.

The Trial

The conduct of the proceedings was completely unprecedented. The trial opened at noon on May 8 in the Dzherzhinsky club hall of the Ministry of State Security—literally within the walls of the Lubyanka—and lasted until July 18. Three military judges presided, led by the chairman of the Military Collegium of the Supreme Court, Lieutenant General Alexander Cheptsov, who had been appointed to this august position in 1948 after more than two decades of work within the official bureaucracy. There were no prosecutors or defense attorneys. In this regard, the tribunal was proceeding within the framework of applicable Stalinist laws. On July 10, 1934, jurisdiction over serious counterrevolutionary crimes, including espionage, had been given to the Military Collegium of the Supreme Court. Other laws could be invoked to exclude prosecutors and defense counsel. This was, of course, nothing less than terror masquerading as law.[141]

From the outset, however, the judges must have sensed that this would not be a routine Stalinist charade. Only Fefer and Teumin fully admitted their guilt, whereas Lozovsky, Markish, Shimeliovich, and Bregman refused to plead guilty to anything; the others pled guilty "in part." Once the testimonies began, the defendants were permitted to make lengthy statements and to cross-examine each other, an aspect of the trial that re-

sulted in moments of high drama, particularly when outspoken defendants like Solomon Lozovsky and Boris Shimeliovich challenged Itsik
Fefer. Because the trial was not a public one, there was no need to constrain the defendants from expressing themselves. And as the trial progressed, the judges grew more respectful of them, while the presiding
judge, Alexander Cheptsov, soon understood that the entire case was a
fabrication and tried to stop the proceedings. Under his direction,
stenographers recorded every word of judges and defendants alike, creating a reliable account of the proceedings.

To the judges, the defendants must have seemed as if they came from
another world; several had been born to rabbis, ritual slaughterers, or
Hebrew teachers in small Jewish towns in remote regions of the Russian
Empire. The judges could not help but expose their prejudices and igno-
rance. They often asked about the significance of kosher meat, wonder-
ing what it meant for Jews and how it differed from ordinary food. Leyb
Kvitko was asked if he believed in God and if leaders of the JAC attended services in the Moscow synagogue. During the war the Jewish
Anti-Fascist Committee had been assigned the explicit responsibility of
appealing to Jews around the world. Now the same committee was
charged with advocating "the uniqueness of the Jewish people" and
with "using biblical images in a positive manner." As one judge asked
Yuzefovich with regard to *Eynikayt,* "You saw that articles were exclusively about Jews. What did you make of the fact that it was all about
Jews, Jews, Jews, and there was nothing about Soviet Man?" At one
point, Bergelson grew so frustrated by the judges' aggressive questions
that he spontaneously blurted out: "There cannot be anything criminal
in the phrase 'I am a Jew' [referring to Fefer's poem]. If I approach
someone and say 'I am a Jew,' what could be bad about that?"

The transcript often makes for painful reading. During the trial most
of the defendants could not avoid abasing themselves. Fefer, the principal accuser, began his testimony by incriminating several codefendants,
claiming that he had recognized "nationalistic views" in the work of
Bergelson, Hofshteyn, and Kvitko as early as 1920, when he first met
them in Kiev. He added that Shimeliovich was "an aggressive Jew,"
while Lina Shtern did not regard the Soviet Union as her "true fatherland." Fefer also accused Vatenberg-Ostrovskaya of comparing conditions in Moscow with better material conditions in the United States.
Kvitko claimed that Hofshteyn and Shtern had Zionist tendencies.

Markish testified that the "very fact" that the Jewish Anti-Fascist Committee collected information on Jewish suffering was an act of nationalism. Fefer admitted that the JAC separated Jewish heroism from the general heroism of the Soviet people. Kvitko went even further, telling the judges that "if the committee, in organizing Jews, was not preparing them for assimilation, if we were making nearly assimilated Jews back into Jews again, then that meant that we were acting against Comrade Lenin's directives and against the party line." Kvitko confirmed that the demonstrations that accompanied the death of Mikhoels and the arrival of Golda Meyerson—that "lady from Palestine"—showed the "destructive" and "harmful" effect of the JAC on the country. Bergelson confessed that his religious upbringing was tantamount to nationalism. Kvitko denied believing in God and declared that "the only god I have is the power of the Bolsheviks." Talmy agreed with Bergelson that "the Jewish religion is a crudely nationalistic religion." Markish accused other writers of artificially tearing "Soviet Yiddish literature out of the healthy flow of Soviet culture and [herding] it into the cattle car." Bergelson said that Hofshteyn had encouraged the study of Hebrew. Hofshteyn regretted that he continued to write in Yiddish, and Kvitko admitted that "by continuing to write in Yiddish, we unwittingly became a brake on the process of assimilation." Lozovsky could not restrain his impatience with such denunciations. "To write for a Yiddish newspaper, a writer had to write in Yiddish," he reminded the court. "What is on trial here is the Yiddish language."

The principal accusation revolved around the "Crimea question": whether during their visit to New York in 1943, Fefer and Mikhoels, in league with James Rosenberg of the Joint Distribution Committee, offered to establish a Jewish republic in the Crimea so that Zionists and American imperialists could use it as a "beachhead" to dismember the Soviet Union. Several defendants were also accused of passing state secrets to two American Jewish figures—Paul Novick, the communist editor of New York's *Morgen Freiheit,* and the Yiddish journalist (and fellow traveler) B. Z. Goldberg.

Other accusations were equally far-fetched. Four of the Yiddish writers had left the country in the 1920s; their time abroad, too, was used against them—evidence of long-standing disloyalty. Emilia Teumin was condemned for failing to contradict Mikhoels and Fefer when they supposedly uttered "nationalistic" remarks in her presence. "I was poisoned with bourgeois nationalism," she admitted in a final plea for her life. Leon Talmy had accompanied American agronomists, including Franklin Harris, president of Brigham Young University, to Birobidzhan in 1929, then written a book about the expedition. "Experts" testified that the book contained "state secrets"; in reality, the regime needed to connect Talmy, along with Ilya Vatenberg and Khayke Vatenberg-Ostrovskaya, to the case because they had lived for years in the United States. The Cold War was on, and America was the enemy.

But if the regime expected the defendants to cooperate fully in their own destruction, it was sorely disappointed. Lozovsky in particular demolished the indictment and Fefer's testimony. Lozovsky, too, had signed a confession after Komarov subjected him to eight nights of non-stop interrogation. As Lozovsky explained to the court, he understood that it was hopeless to resist, and decided to wait until his trial, when he hoped to speak his mind to a broad public audience or at least to party leaders. In this he was frustrated, for Lozovsky's only listeners at the time were three judges, his fellow defendants, and a stenographer. Lozovsky's testimony lasted for six days and was the emotional high point of the trial. His words deserve to be remembered, especially his opening statement:

> As you know, my family name is Dridzo. This name cannot be translated into any language. When we asked our father what it meant, he told us that, according to a story passed down from father to son, a distant ancestor of ours was among the eight hundred thousand Jews who fled from Spain in 1492, when the chief inquisitor, Tomás de Torquemada, issued a decree compelling Jews to convert to Catholicism or leave the country. Anyone who refused was required to leave Spain within two months. I became Lozovsky in 1905 at a conference of Bolsheviks in Tammerfors, where I first met Comrade Lenin and also Comrade Stalin. My father was a Hebrew teacher. He knew the Talmud, he knew Hebrew well, and wrote poetry in Hebrew. My mother was illiterate. My father taught me to read Hebrew, to pray, and to read Russian. The very fact that a teacher of Hebrew taught his son Russian shows that he was not a fanatic. I was religious until the age of about thirteen.

After three and a half years of complete isolation, during which he was subjected to brutal threats and torture, Lozovsky preserved his dignity, suggesting that this Soviet military tribunal was comparable to the Spanish Inquisition and that his judges were no different from Torquemada.

Lozovsky then proceeded to take apart the indictment as no defendant in a Soviet political case had ever done before. Could the JAC hand over the Crimea to American imperialism? Lozovsky reminded the judges that in 1945 "Roosevelt flew to the Crimea [for the Yalta conference] with a large group of intelligence agents in numerous airplanes. He did not fly in to see either Fefer or Mikhoels, or to worry about settling Jews in the Crimea, but to see about more serious matters. . . . What could Hofshteyn, Vatenberg-Ostrovskaya, or Zuskin . . . pass along?" As for charges of espionage, Lozovsky made it clear that the committee saved copies of all correspondence, making it hard to believe that it had something to conceal. Moreover, as Lozovsky told the judges, "Would I have gotten in touch with a poet and an actor if I had wanted to engage in espionage? The doorman at the People's Commissariat of Finances would not do such a thing, let alone the deputy minister of foreign affairs, an old revolutionary, and a veteran of the underground. All of this is nonsense." Were Goldberg and Novick really espionage agents? Lozovsky pointed out that the Soviet press had nothing but praise for each of them; the JAC could hardly be expected to know they were spies when the security organs who arranged for their trip did not know, either. But none of those functionaries were in the dock! Cheptsov grew skeptical of this charge and asked security personnel for confirmation that Goldberg and Novick were American agents. The answer must have astounded him: Cheptsov was informed that they were Soviet agents, not American ones, but that he was obliged to proceed as things stood.

The trial wore on. Cheptsov was under increasing pressure to conclude it and condemn the defendants. Ignatiev sent him threatening notes; Ryumin arranged listening devices in the judges' chambers. Cheptsov held firm. The entire case was such an obvious fabrication that Cheptsov even interrupted the trial for a week on two occasions and appealed to judicial and party officials to renew the investigation. Such an action by a Stalinist judge was unheard-of. But Cheptsov was not acting out of purely idealistic motives. A veteran jurist, he had condemned other Jewish figures at earlier trials that were no less contrived. But there is reason to believe that Lozovsky's eloquence and bearing impressed the judges—as did the fact that Fefer began to back away from his accusations during the questioning of Lozovsky, then admitted in a closed session that he had been an informer and was now repudiating his testimony altogether. Cheptsov, moreover, sensed the continuing disarray within security circles, and he wanted to be sure that his severe instructions—to condemn obviously innocent people, including Solomon Lozovsky, who was an Old Bolshevik with a distinguished party and government career—still applied.

Furthermore, and this may have been the deciding factor in Cheptsov's thinking, the defendants were disavowing their confessions, and there was no credible, material evidence of their guilt. As a professional Stalinist judge, Cheptsov may well have believed in Andrei Vyshinsky's* judicial philosophy: that in a Soviet court, a confession represented the highest form of justice. But now there was neither evidence nor confessions; the investigation was incomplete and therefore a failure.[142]

Still, Cheptsov's behavior was unprecedented. He asked party and government leaders to reopen the investigation, a request that, if it had been accepted, could have spared the lives of the defendants. But the final decision could come only from the highest officials. In the end, Cheptsov appealed to Malenkov himself. Their meeting took place in the presence of Ignatiev and Ryumin, who had become the driving force behind the case. Malenkov abruptly rebuffed Cheptsov's appeal. "Do you want us to kneel before these criminals?" he told him. "The Politburo has investigated this case three times. Carry out the Politburo's resolution."[143] Even then, Cheptsov drew out the process further. After announcing the verdict on July 18, he ignored Ryumin's demand to immediately carry out the executions and instead forwarded requests for clemency to his superiors. Cheptsov also sent Stalin a personal statement from Lozovsky. Nothing helped. Except for Lina Shtern, who was sentenced to five years of exile, and Solomon Bregman, who collapsed into a coma during the trial and died in prison in January 1953, the remaining thirteen defendants, including two women, were convicted and sentenced to death; the executions were carried out on August 12, 1952, David Bergelson's sixty-eighth birthday.

From the time of Hofshteyn's arrest in September 1948 until the executions in August 1952, nearly four years had passed. A combination of factors, including the outspoken resolve of some of the defendants, had

---

*Andrei Vyshinsky (1883–1954) was prosecuting attorney during the show trials of the 1930s. He was appointed deputy commissar for foreign affairs in 1940 and foreign minister in 1949. After Stalin's death, he became ambassador to the United Nations.

prolonged the process and complicated Stalin's plans. Although the case unfolded in the midst of a terrible public campaign of anti-Semitic invective, none of the defendants were even mentioned in the official press. Their arrests, years of pretrial detention, the trial itself, and the executions all passed without a single reference in Soviet newspapers. Without a show trial to culminate the process and help mobilize the country for a broader anti-Semitic campaign, the case failed to fulfill its broader purposes. Yiddish culture was further degraded, and JAC leaders were punished for their wartime pretensions. But this was not enough.

Stalin pushed ahead once again. That spring a new round of arrests took place, this time of Jewish doctors. Among the first to be arrested was Yevgeniya Lifshitz, the physician about whom Shimeliovich was interrogated in December 1951; her arrest took place on June 4, 1952, in the midst of the JAC trial. Her interrogators insisted that she confess to trying to harm her young patients; they also wanted her to incriminate other doctors, including Miron Vovsi. But she refused and, in despair, attempted to hang herself. She was then taken to the Serbsky Forensic Psychiatry Institute—which gained notoriety in the Brezhnev period for its "treatment" of healthy political dissidents. But even here, in spite of the effects of psychotropic drugs, she held out against her tormentors. Other doctors were more easily broken. Using threats and beatings, Ryumin secured confessions that Kremlin doctors had deliberately harmed Alexander Shcherbakov and Andrei Zhdanov, thereby causing their demise.

In Eastern Europe, too, Stalin was beginning to expose "Zionist conspiracies." At least two MGB investigators with experience in the JAC case, Vladimir Komarov and Mikhail Likhachev, were dispatched to Prague and other capitals to facilitate the investigations. In November 1952, fourteen leaders of the Czech Communist Party, among them eleven Jews, were brought to trial, accused of plotting to undermine communist rule. The most prominent defendant was Rudolf Slansky, former head of the party. The prosecutors emphasized the Jewish origins of most of the defendants and repeatedly denounced them as "Zionist adventurers." Newspapers and radio broadcasts throughout Eastern Europe and the Soviet Union attacked Slansky and his codefendants. In one typical statement, Radio Bucharest proclaimed: "We also have criminals among us, Zionist agents and agents of international Jewish capital. We shall expose them, and it is our duty to exterminate them."[144] A week after their conviction, Slansky and ten others were hanged, their bodies cremated, and the ashes dumped along the side of a highway.

By the end of 1952, Stalin's paranoid anxiety about Jews and Americans was in plain view within Kremlin circles. On December 1, 1952, he declared during a Presidium meeting that "every Jew is a nationalist and an agent of American intelligence. Jewish nationalists believe that the U.S.A. saved their people (there you can become rich, bourgeois, and so forth). They believe they are indebted to the Americans."[145]

In December and January families of the JAC defendants were summoned to police stations and notified that they were being stripped of permission to reside in the country's major cities. They were charged with being relatives of traitors to the motherland and summarily exiled for ten years to remote areas of Siberia and Kazakhstan. Elderly parents, spouses, brothers and sisters, and at least two young children—Bergelson's granddaughter and Yuzefovich's daughter—were transported with political prisoners and ordinary criminals. They were still not informed of what had become of their loved ones.

It was during those weeks, on January 13, 1953, that the world first learned of the Doctors' Plot: *Pravda* announced the arrests of several physicians, linking them to an American and Zionist plot led by the "Joint" (the American Jewish Joint Distribution Committee) and to the late Solomon Mikhoels, who now, for the first time publicly, was exposed as a "bourgeois Jewish nationalist" who had worked with agents of American intelligence. The same article also claimed that Miron Vovsi had accused Boris Shimeliovich of giving orders "to wipe out the leading cadres of the USSR." This was the first public mention of a defendant in the JAC case and an indication that the regime may have been preparing to make an announcement about the executions and connect the JAC case with the new and more ominous Doctors' Plot.[146]

While full details remain elusive, there are many indications that Stalin was planning to turn the Doctors' Plot into an occasion for a show trial, execute the defendants, and then deport the Jewish population of the Soviet Union's major cities to Central Asia and Birobidzhan. Signatures on a petition addressed to Stalin affirming the guilt of the doctors were even collected among Jewish cultural figures. Ilya Ehrenburg was among a handful of individuals who refused to sign such a statement. And only Ehrenburg then took the additional step of writing to Stalin himself, explaining how such an action would harm Soviet prestige in the West.[147] Stalin hesitated. His health was ebbing away, and he died at the beginning of March. His death was announced on March 5. Within a month the Doctors' Plot was disavowed by the new leadership, and the terror was over.

Almost immediately, Soviet spokesmen came under tremendous pressure to explain the whereabouts of some of the Yiddish writers, but they denied that anything was amiss and deliberately misled American communists like Howard Fast with lies about the writers' well-being.[148] Not until November 1955 were the families of the JAC defendants told that their relatives had been executed. Lina Shtern, alone among the defendants, returned to Moscow, yet she was so frightened by what she had experienced that she spoke to very few people about the interrogations or the trial that followed.

Finally, in March 1956, within weeks of Khrushchev's "secret speech" denouncing Stalin, Leon Kristal, the U.N. correspondent for the *Forverts*, broke the news about multiple executions of Jews taking place on August 12, 1952; Kristal was able to name at least six of the martyrs—Markish, Bergelson, Kvitko, Hofshteyn, Fefer, and Lozovsky.[149] The communist press could no longer sustain its silence. A month later, the Warsaw Yiddish newspaper *Folks-shtime* (The People's Voice) became the first quasi-official source from within the communist bloc to confirm Kristal's account. It acknowledged that numerous Yiddish writers had been victims of "Beria's gangs" and even referred to the liquidation of the JAC with the phrase "its leaders sentenced to death," a vague but unmistakable admission that some kind of trial had taken place.[151] After Stalin's death and particularly after Khrushchev's secret speech, loyal communists continued to blame things on the malicious influence of Lavrenti Beria, Stalin's former security chief. Beria, in fact, was not connected to repression of the JAC.

Well before these announcements, Paul Novick knew that something terrible had happened to his Moscow friends, but his loyalty to the Soviet Union and steadfast belief in communism compromised his judgment. He did everything he could to cushion the news and reassure his readers that Yiddish culture would be revived to its previous glory now that Stalin's "cult of personality" had been exposed and Leninist principles restored. Novick's long-standing loyalty was tragically typical of many in his generation. As his widow, Shirley Novick, observed after learning about the fate of the Yiddish writers, "It was unbelievable to us. We believed in the party like religious Hasidim."[151]

Paul Novick carried a heavy sense of guilt over the fate of his friends. David Bergelson had come to New York in 1929 hoping to find a job, but he could not arrange a reliable means to support his family. He had to return to Europe and eventually moved to the Soviet Union. Novick was deputy editor of the *Morgen Freiheit* in those years and may have felt that he could have done more to help Bergelson establish himself in America. When Novick traveled to Moscow in 1959, he immediately visited Bergelson's widow. Entering her room, he fell on his knees, burst into tears, and begged for forgiveness.[152]

As for the defendants at the trial, it is not clear what they believed about the system they each served. Their lives darkly embodied the tragedy of Soviet Jewry. A combination of revolutionary commitment and naive idealism had tied them to a system they could not renounce. Whatever doubts or misgivings they had, they kept to themselves, and served the Kremlin with the required enthusiasm. They were not dissidents. They were Jewish martyrs. They were also Soviet patriots. Stalin repaid their loyalty by destroying them.

Joshua Rubenstein

Jewish artists in Kiev, with two visitors from the American Jewish Joint Distribu-
tion Committee, 1919. *Standing, left to right:* Isidore Eliashev (Bal makhshoves),
Elias Tcherikover, unidentified visitor, Nokhem Shtif, Dr. H. Spivak, Zelig
Kalmanovitch, David Bergelson, Volf Latzky-Bertoldi. *Sitting, left to right:* sculptor
Jacob Epstein, Leyb Kvitko, Issachar Ber Rybak, unidentified visitor, Joseph
Tchaikov. (From the Archives of the YIVO Institute for Jewish Research, New
York.)

A portrait of the famous Yiddish literary group Di khaliastre (The Gang)—Mendl
Elkin, Peretz Hirschbein, Uri Zvi Greenberg, Peretz Markish, Melekh Ravitch, and
I. J. Singer—at the villa of Alter Kacyzne, in the suburb of Swider, nineteen miles
from Warsaw, 1924. Kacyzne was a famous photographer of Jewish life in Poland;
he was killed in July 1941 during a Nazi pogrom in Tarnopol. (From the Archives
of the YIVO Institute for Jewish Research, New York.)

Leon Talmy, protecting himself from mosquitoes, at Ashikan gold-working camp
in Birobidzhan, August 21, 1929. From a scrapbook of photographs taken by
Franklin S. Harris during the scientific expedition to Birobidzhan. (L. Tom Perry
Special Collections, Harold B. Lee Library, Brigham Young University, Provo,
Utah.)

Benjamin Zuskin in *Seekers of Happiness,* a Soviet film that romanticized life
in Birobidzhan to lure Jews from around the world to settle there, 1936. (Archive of
his daughter Ala Zuskin-Perelman.)

Portrait of the poet
David Hofshteyn.
(Archive of his daughter
Levia Hofshteyn.)

Solomon Mikhoels and other actors of the State Jewish Theater in Moscow shortly
after Soviet President Mikhail Kalinin (*lower left*) gave them medals to mark the
twentieth anniversary of the theater, April 8, 1939. (Sovfoto/Eastfoto.)

Peretz Markish visiting Jewish cultural figures in Soviet-occupied Lwow (L'viv),
Poland, as a member of the Writers' Brigade dispatched there to acclimate Polish
Yiddish writers to the reality of life under the Soviet regime, 1941. *Outer circle, left
to right:* Nahum Bomze, Yehoshua Perle, Israel Ashendorf, Barukh Shnaper, Sanya
Friedman, Shmuel J. Imber, Hertsog, Hersch Weber. *In front, left to right:* Alter Ka-
cyzne (with glasses), Markish, Niusia Imber, Tanya Fuks. (From the Archives of the
YIVO Institute for Jewish Research, New York.)

Prominent Jewish cultural figures, Moscow, August 24, 1941. *Front row, left to
right:* writer Samuil Marshak, poet Peretz Markish, novelist David Bergelson,
architect Boris Iofan, writer Ilya Ehrenburg. *Back row, left to right:* pianist Yakov
Flier, violinist David Oistrakh, critic Isaac Nusinov, actor Solomon Mikhoels,
pianist Yakov Zak, actor Benjamin Zuskin, painter Alexander Tishler, journalist
Shakhno Epshteyn. They are making a worldwide appeal to their fellow Jews to
support the Soviet war effort against Nazi Germany. (Archive of the late Irina
Ehrenburg.)

Press conference at the Soviet foreign office, Moscow, summer 1941. *Left to right:*
two men from Reuters News Agency, a Czech correspondent, the American novelist
Erskine Caldwell (husband of the photographer, Margaret Bourke-White),
Solomon Lozovsky, Nikolai Palgunov of the Soviet press agency TASS, and Henry
Shapiro of United Press. (Photo: Margaret Bourke-White, *Life Magazine* © Time
Warner Inc.)

Membership card for Boris Shimeliovich in a trade union for medical personnel. (GARF.)

Itsik Fefer and Solomon Mikhoels with Albert Einstein in Princeton, New Jersey, during their five-month visit to America, June 1943. (Central Archive of the Federal Security Service, Moscow.)

Fefer and Mikhoels in the WEVD broadcast studio in New York, June 22, 1943. (U.S. Holocaust Memorial Museum Photo Archives.)

Fefer and Mikhoels backstage at the Henry Miller Theater in New York, with Helen Hayes and Rhys Williams, stars of the play *Harriet*, in 1943. (Sovfoto/Eastfoto.)

Mikhoels and Fefer with New York Mayor Fiorello La Guardia.
(Jewish Public Library Archives, Montreal.)

Rally in the Polo Grounds, New York, where fifty thousand people gathered to welcome
Mikhoels and Fefer and to support the war effort against Nazi Germany, July 8, 1943.
Left to right in front row: writer Sholem Asch, unidentified woman, Fefer, Mikhoels,
Nahum Goldmann of the World Jewish Congress, Rabbi Stephen Wise, and James
Rosenberg of the American Jewish Joint Distribution Committee. Sitting in the second
row, visible between Mikhoels and Goldmann, is Marc Chagall. (Jewish Public Library
Archives, Montreal.)

Fefer and Mikhoels with the actor Eddie Cantor, Polo Grounds.
(Jewish Public Library Archives, Montreal.)

Fefer and Mikhoels with Paul Robeson, Soviet Consulate in New York, summer
1943. (Jewish Public Library Archives, Montreal.)

Fefer and Mikhoels with the labor leader Sidney Hillman, Soviet Consulate
in New York, 1943. (Jewish Public Library Archives, Montreal.)

Mikhoels and Fefer with the violinist Yehudi Menuhin (*far left*), Hollywood Bowl,
Los Angeles, 1943. (Jewish Public Library Archives, Montreal.)

Fefer, Charlie Chaplin (*center*), and Mikhoels with two unidentified men
in Los Angeles, 1943. (GARF.)

Presentation of three fur coats and hats to Mikhoels and Fefer by the International
Fur and Leather Workers Union in New York, 1943. Irving Potash is modeling the
coat and hat. The communist writer Ben Gold appears on the right. (From the collection of the late Abraham [Avrum] Orenstein, activist in the union and in the field
of Yiddish culture.)

The Yiddish journalist B. Z. Goldberg, Mikhoels, Fefer, Marie Waife Goldberg (the daughter of Sholem Aleichem), and Mitchell Waife at the grave of Sholem Aleichem, Jamaica, Queens, 1943. (Annenberg Rare Book and Manuscript Library, Van Pelt–Dietrich Library Center, University of Pennsylvania.)

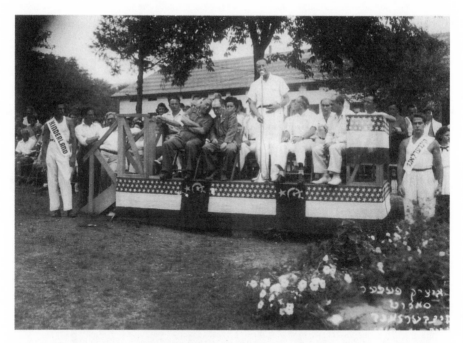

Fefer at Camp Kinderland, Hopewell Junction, New York, August 8, 1943. Kinderland was a left-wing summer camp with a strong emphasis on Yiddish culture. (Photo by Benjamin Itzkowitz. From the Archives of the YIVO Institute for Jewish Research, New York.)

Fefer and Mikhoels in Mexico, 1943. (GARF.)

Farewell dinner given to Mikhoels and Fefer by the administrative committee of the Jewish Council for Russian War Relief, Hotel Commodore, New York, October 15, 1943. (GARF.)

Boris Shimeliovich, medical director of the Botkin Hospital in Moscow and a leader of the Jewish Anti-Fascist Committee. (Central Archive of the Federal Security Service, Moscow.)

Plenum of the Jewish Anti-Fascist Committee, April 1944. Ilya Ehrenburg, David Bergelson, Solomon Mikhoels, Shakhno Epshteyn, and Lina Shtern are in the front row. (GARF.)

General Jacob Kreizer, Epshteyn, and Bergelson during the war. (GARF.)

Holocaust Memorial Service at the Choral Synagogue, Moscow, March 15, 1945.
From right: Fefer, actor Benjamin Zuskin, musician Leonid Utesov. Stalin gave his
approval for the memorial service, which took place twice, in 1945 and 1946. (U.S.
Holocaust Memorial Museum Photo Archives.)

Holocaust Memorial Service at the Choral Synagogue, 1945. The banner, in Hebrew, reads: "The Jewish People Lives." (U.S. Holocaust Memorial Museum Photo Archives.)

The physiologist Lina Shtern with other prominent Soviet women. *From left to right:* the highly decorated fighter pilot Polina Gelman, the mathematician Pelegeya Kochina, Shtern, and the opera singer Deborah Pantofel-Nechetskaya. Shtern was the first woman to become a full member of the Soviet Academy of Sciences. She was associated with the Jewish Anti-Fascist Committee, as well as with the anti-fascist committees of scientists and women. (GARF.)

B. Z. Goldberg sitting next to Lina Shtern. Goldberg spent the first half of 1946 in the Soviet Union, a visit later held against the Jewish Anti-Fascist Committee. *Left to right:* poet Abraham Sutzkever, unidentified man, Goldberg, Shtern, General A. Katz, poet Shmuel Halkin. (Annenberg Rare Book and Manuscript Library, Van Pelt–Dietrich Library Center, University of Pennsylvania.)

B. Z. Goldberg with members of the Jewish Anti-Fascist Committee, Moscow, 1946. *Standing on the left:* Leyb Kvitko and David Bergelson. *Sitting, left to right:* Itsik Fefer, Joseph Yuzefovich, Peretz Markish, Goldberg, Solomon Mikhoels, Leyb Strongin, Aron Kushnirov, Shmuel Halkin. (Central Archive of the Federal Security Service, Moscow.)

Sutzkever (*standing*), Markish, Halkin, Fefer, Goldberg, Bergelson, Kushnirov, novelist Chaim Grade, and journalist Shmuel Persov. (Central Archive of the Federal Security Service, Moscow.)

The Yiddish communist journalist Paul Novick sitting between Bergelson and
Mikhoels, with other members of the Jewish Anti-Fascist Committee, Moscow,
1946. Novick visited the Soviet Union in the final months of 1946. His visit, too,
was later held against the committee. (GARF.)

The American Paul Novick (*center*) with Soviet Jewish war heroes, Moscow, 1946.
(GARF.)

The last known photograph of Solomon Mikhoels, taken on the day before his assassination, Minsk, January 1948. Mikhoels is sitting between two unidentified men. *Standing, left to right:* Goldshvartz, Misha Rivin, Gaydarin, Vladimir Golubov-Potapov (who was killed with Mikhoels). (From the Archives of the YIVO Institute for Jewish Research, New York.)

Peretz Markish speaking at the memorial for Solomon Mikhoels, May 24, 1948. (Central Archive of the Federal Security Service, Moscow.)

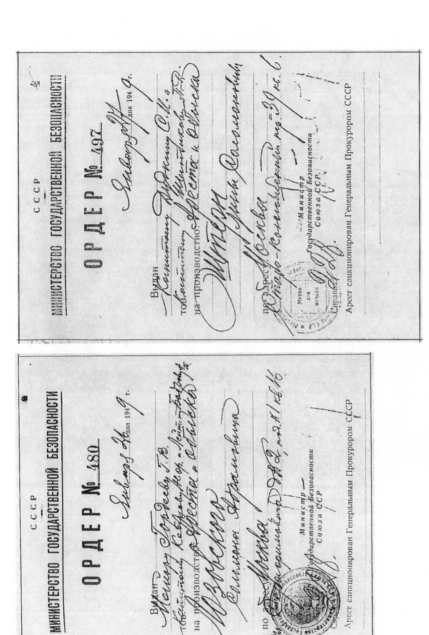

Orders to arrest Solomon Lozovsky and Lina Shtern and search their apartments, Moscow, January 1949. (Central Archive of the Federal Security Service, Moscow.)

Memorial to Mikhoels, Novodevichy Cemetery, Moscow, 1948. (GARF.)

Solomon
Lozovsky

Joseph
Yuzefovich

Benjamin
Zuskin

13108   № 8.

11515. ЮЗЕФОВИЧ-ШПИНАК.ИОСИФ СИГИЗМУНДОВИЧ 1890.

11455 ЗУСКИ   ЕНИАМИН ЛЬВОВИЧ 1899

Photographs of the defendants taken during their interrogations; some of the effects of torture and mistreatment are evident on their faces. (Shtern: U.S. Holocaust Memorial Museum Photo Archives; the rest: Central Archive of the Federal Security Service, Moscow.)

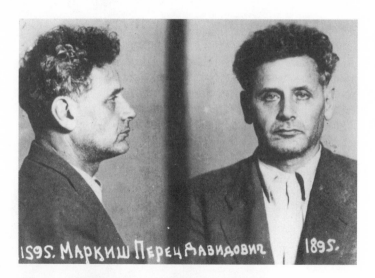

Peretz Markish

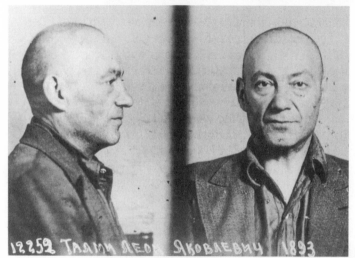

Leon Talmy

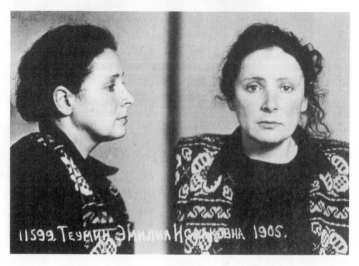

Emilia Teumin

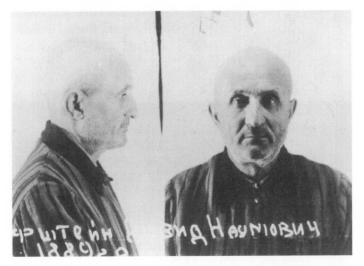

David Hofshteyn

Lina Shtern

Ilya Vatenberg

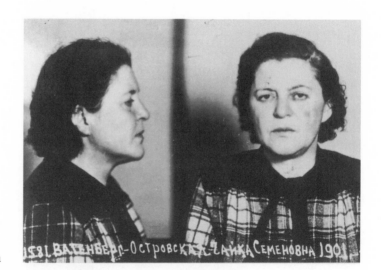

Khayke
Vatenberg-
Ostrovskaya

Solomon
Bregman

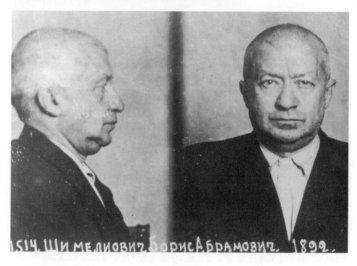

Boris
Shimeliovich

Cover for the original transcript of the Jewish Anti-Fascist Committee trial. Instructions at the top read "to be preserved forever" and "top secret." (Central Archive of the Federal Security Service, Moscow.)

The Yiddish journalist Mirra Aizenshtadt Zheleznova, arrested in connection with her reports on Jewish cultural activities at two prestigious factories in Moscow; around 250 workers were also arrested. She was executed along with her colleague Shmuel Persov on November 23, 1950. (Archive of her daughter Nadezhda Bergelson.)

Военная Коллегия
Верховного Суда
Союза ССР

Форма № 30

С П Р А В К А

5 января 195 6.

№ 4н 014764/55

Москва, ул. Воровского, д. 13.

Дело по обвинению АЙЗЕНШТАДТ /ЖЕЛЕЗНОВОЙ/
Мариам Соломоновны пересмотрено Военной Коллегией
Верховного Суда СССР 28 декабря 1955 года.

Приговор Военной Коллегии от 22 ноября 1950
года в отношении АЙЗЕНШТАДТ /ЖЕЛЕЗНОВОЙ/ М.С.
по вновь открывшимся обстоятельствам отменен и дело за отсутствием состава преступления прекращено.

ПРЕДСЕДАТЕЛЬ ВОЕННОЙ КОЛЛЕГИИ ВЕРХОВНОГО СУДА
СОЮЗА ССР
ГЕНЕРАЛ-ЛЕЙТЕНАНТ ЮСТИЦИИ

/А.ЧЕПЦОВ/

П Л

ЦТ МО 7549—55.

Certificate of rehabilitation for Mirra Aizenshtadt Zheleznova, issued on January 5, 1956. It was signed by Alexander Cheptsov, who presided over her trial in 1950 and over the trial of the Jewish Anti-Fascist Committee members in 1952. (Archive of her daughter Nadezhda Bergelson.)

PART ONE

Court Record of the Military Collegium of the USSR Supreme Court

Judicial Proceedings Against Members of the Jewish Anti-Fascist Committee

May 8–July 18, 1952   Moscow

COURT CONSISTING OF:

PRESIDING OFFICER Lieutenant General of Justice Cheptsov
MEMBERS   Major General of Justice Dmitriev and
                   Major General of Justice Zaryanov
SECRETARY   Senior Lieutenant M. Afanasiev

Conducted without a government prosecution or defense team participating.

Noon, May 8, 1952

Presiding Officer: I declare this session of the Military Collegium of the USSR Supreme Court open. The case to be heard involves accusations of treason against Lozovsky, Fefer, Bregman, and others.

[The secretary reported that the accused: Lozovsky, Fefer, Bregman, Yuzefovich, Shimeliovich, Kvitko, Markish, Bergelson, Hofshteyn, Zuskin, Shtern,

Talmy, Vatenberg, Teumin, and Vatenberg-Ostrovskaya were brought to the court session under guard.

The Presiding Officer confirmed the identity of the defendants, who gave the following testimony about themselves:]

Lozovsky: I, Solomon Abramovich Lozovsky, was born in 1878. I am originally from Danilovka, Dnepropetrovsk region. I am the son of a teacher. I
am Jewish by nationality. I first joined the party in 1901, was expelled from
the party in 1914 and in 1917, and I was a member of the Russian Socialist
Democratic Revolutionary Party (Internationalist) from 1917 to 1919. I
have had no party penalties assessed and was removed from the party most
recently on January 20, 1949. I have the following government awards: the
Order of Lenin, Order of the Great Patriotic War, First Degree, and Order
of the Mongolian People's Republic and the medals For the Defense of
Moscow, For Valiant Labor During the Great Patriotic War, 1941–1945,
and In Memory of Moscow's Eight-hundredth Anniversary. I was brought
to trial in a Kharkov court during the tsarist period in 1908 and found
guilty of affiliation with the Social-Democratic Party. I have not been tried
under the Soviet government. I am married, with three daughters, several
grandchildren, and one great-grandchild. Prior to my arrest I was the head
of the Sovinformburo until July 1947. I have been writing a book for the
last year and a half, was one of the chief editors of the *Diplomatic Dictionary,* and headed the department of international relations at the Higher
Party School of the Central Committee of the Communist Party. I was arrested on January 26, 1949. I received a copy of the indictment on May 3,
1952.

Fefer: I, Isaac Solomonovich Fefer, was born in 1900. I am originally from the
shtetl of Shpola, Kiev region. I am the son of a village schoolteacher, I am
Jewish, and did not complete my higher education. I have been in the party
since 1919, have not been expelled from the party, and had a party penalty
assessed in 1947. I was a member of the Bund from 1917 to 1919. Until I
was arrested, I wrote poetry all of my life. I am married. I have an adult
daughter. I have the following awards: the Badge of Honor received in
1948 and two medals For Valiant Labor During the Great Patriotic War,
1941–1945. I was arrested on December 24, 1948. I received a copy of the
indictment on May 3, 1952.

Bregman: I, Solomon Leontevich Bregman, was born in 1895. I am originally
from Bryansk region. My father engaged in trade. I am Jewish. I have a
high school education. I have been a party member since 1912, was never
expelled from the party, and have never had any penalties assessed. My last
position was Deputy Minister of State Control of the Russian Federation. I
am married and have one son. I have been awarded the medals For the Defense of Moscow, In Memory of Moscow's Eight-hundredth Anniversary,
and For Valiant Labor During the Great Patriotic War, 1941–1945. I was

arrested on January 28, 1949. I received a copy of the indictment on May 3, 1952.

Yuzefovich: I, Joseph Sigizmundovich Yuzefovich, was born in 1890. I am originally from Warsaw. I am from a white-collar family. My mother was a housewife. I have been a member of the Communist Party since May 1917. I am a research fellow at the Institute of History of the Soviet Academy of Sciences. I am married and adopted a daughter born in 1940 to parents who were executed by the Germans. I have the following awards: the medals For Valiant Labor During the Great Patriotic War, 1941–1945, and In Memory of Moscow's Eight-hundredth Anniversary. I was arrested on January 13, 1949. I received a copy of the indictment on May 3, 1952.

Shimeliovich: I, Boris Abramovich Shimeliovich, was born in 1892. I am originally from Riga. I am Jewish. I have been in the Communist Party since April 1920. Prior to that I was in the Bund for five months. I have the following awards: the Order of the Red Banner of Labor and the Order of the Great Patriotic War, 1941–1945, First Degree, and the medals For the Defense of Moscow, For Victory over Germany During the Great Patriotic War, 1941–1945, For Valiant Labor During the Great Patriotic War, 1941–1945, and In Memory of Moscow's Eight-hundredth Anniversary. I also have a certificate confirming that I was awarded the honorary degree of Distinguished Doctor of Russia. I am married and have a son and a daughter. I have an advanced degree in medicine. My most recent position was that of medical director at the Botkin Clinical Hospital, a position that I held for eighteen years. I was arrested on January 13, 1949. I received a copy of the indictment on May 3, 1952.

Kvitko: I, Leyb Moiseyevich Kvitko, was born in 1890. I am originally from the village of Goloskovo, Odessa region. I am Jewish. I have been in the party since 1941. Prior to that I was not a member of any party. I am a professional poet. I am married and have an adult daughter. I was educated at home. I have the following awards: the Order of the Red Banner of Labor and the medal For Valiant Labor During the Great Patriotic War, 1941–1945. I was arrested on January 25, 1949. I received a copy of the indictment on May 3, 1952.

Markish: I, Peretz Davidovich Markish, was born in 1895. I am originally from the city of Polonnoye, formerly of Volynsk province, currently Zhitomir region. I am Jewish. I am married and have three children.* I was educated at home. I am a poet by profession and have been a member of the Communist Party since 1939. I have engaged exclusively in literary pursuits. I have the following awards: the Order of Lenin and the medals For Victory over Germany During the Great Patriotic War, 1941–1945, and

---

*Markish is referring to two sons, Shimon and David, by his wife, Esther. He also had a daughter from a previous relationship. She lives in Ukraine today.

For Valiant Labor During the Great Patriotic War, 1941–1945. I was arrested on January 28, 1949. I received a copy of the indictment on May 3, 1952.

Bergelson: I, David Rafailovich Bergelson, was born in 1884.* I am originally from the shtetl of Sarna, Kiev province. I am Jewish, from the family of a merchant with a sizable business. I was schooled at home, in addition to which I studied at a Jewish religious school. I am married and have one son. I received the medal For Valiant Labor During the Great Patriotic War, 1941–1945. I am a writer. I was arrested on January 24, 1949. I received a copy of the indictment on May 3, 1952.

Hofshteyn: I, David Naumovich Hofshteyn, was born in 1889. I am originally from the shtetl of Korostyshev, Kiev region. I am Jewish, from the family of an office worker, and then my father had a small shop. I am married and have three children. I am self-taught. I received my high school diploma before the revolution, and under Soviet rule I received a college equivalency degree. I completed my graduate studies in 1929. I have been in the party since 1940. I am a poet. I received the Badge of Honor and the medal For Valiant Labor During the Great Patriotic War, 1941–1945. I was arrested on September 16, 1948. I received a copy of the indictment on May 3, 1952.

Zuskin: I, Benjamin Lvovich Zuskin, was born in 1899. I am originally from Lithuania, from the city of Panevezhis, Lithuanian Soviet Socialist Republic. My father was a tailor. I am Jewish. I first studied at the Academy of Mining and then at an applied military high school in 1915. After that I went to college. I am married, with a young daughter.† I was awarded the Order of the Red Banner, received the medal For Valiant Labor During the Great Patriotic War, 1941–1945, and am a laureate of the Stalin Prize, Second Degree. I have never been a party member. I am a People's Artist of the Russian Federation and the Uzbek Soviet Socialist Republic. Before my arrest I was the artistic director of the Moscow State Jewish Theater. I was arrested on December 24, 1948. I received a copy of the indictment on May 3, 1952.

Shtern: I, Lina Solomonovna Shtern, was born in 1878. I am originally from the Baltic region, from the city of Liepaya (formerly Kurland).‡ I am Jew-

---

*Bergelson was born in 1884. Throughout the trial transcript, including when he is being directly quoted, the year of his birth is given as 1882.

†Zuskin is referring to his daughter Alla, by his second wife. He also had a daughter named Tamara, by his first wife. At the time of the trial, Tamara, a medical doctor, was living in Poland.

‡Lina Shtern was actually born near Kaunas, Lithuania, in 1875. The court transcript and standard encyclopedias list her birth as having occurred in the Latvian city of Liepaya in 1878. Recent scholarship by the St. Petersburg historian Vladimir Didulin has now corrected the historical record. See *Pervy Syezd Konfederatsii istorikov meditsiny—mezhdunarodnaya* (First Congress of the Confederation of Historians of Medicine—international) (Moscow, 1998), pp. 18–219.

ish. I am from a merchant family. I am single. I have been a party member since 1938. Prior to that I was not a member of any party. Before my arrest I pursued scientific research. I have an advanced degree. I graduated from a university in Vienna* with a dual degree in medicine and chemistry and did scientific work and teaching. I was director of the Institute of Physiology of the Academy of Sciences and head of the physiology department of the Second Moscow Medical Institute. I am a full member of the Soviet Academy of Sciences and of the Soviet Academy of Medical Sciences. I was awarded the Order of the Red Star and the Order of the Red Banner of Labor, the medals For Valiant Labor During the Great Patriotic War, 1941–1945, and In Memory of Moscow's Eight-hundredth Anniversary, and badges for Outstanding Work in Health Care. I am a Stalin Prize laureate. I was arrested on January 28, 1949. I received a copy of the indictment on May 3, 1952.

Member of the Court: What scholarly works have you published?

Shtern: I have published about four hundred scholarly works on physiology and biochemistry.

Presiding Officer: For what did you receive the Stalin Prize?

Shtern: For my publication "The Hemato-Encephalic Barrier."†

Talmy: I, Leon Yakovlevich Talmy, was born in 1893. I am originally from the shtetl of Lyakhovichi, Baranovichi region. I am Jewish. I am from a merchant family. I am not a party member. While I was in America from 1914 through 1917, I was a member of the Socialist Party. Then I was a member of the Communist Party before being transferred here by the Soviet Communist Party. I withstood a purge, but my transfer into the party was not authorized, as I could not find people who had been members of the party before the revolution to provide recommendations for me. I am married and have a son. I did not complete my higher education; that is to say, I studied at the university for one year. I was awarded the medal For Valiant Labor During the Great Patriotic War, 1941–1945. I am a journalist and translator. Most recently I worked at the Sovinformburo. I was arrested on July 3, 1949. I received a copy of the indictment on May 3, 1952.

Vatenberg: I, Ilya Semyonovich Vatenberg, was born in 1887. I am originally from the city of Stanislav. I am Jewish. My father was first a white-collar worker, then a manual laborer, and finally he worked as a broker. He sold real estate in New York. I am not a party member. I am a former member of the American Communist Party. I am married. I have a law degree. I graduated from law school in New York. Before my arrest I was senior control editor at the State Publishing House of Literature in Foreign Languages. I

---

*The transcript is mistaken here. Lina Shtern graduated from the University of Geneva in 1903.

†The Hemato-Encephalic barrier is the frontier between the blood and the cerebrospinal fluid.

was arrested on January 24, 1949. I received a copy of the indictment on May 3, 1952.

Teumin: I, Emilia Isaacovna Teumin, was born in 1905 in Bern, Switzerland. I am Jewish. My father and mother were émigrés. My father was a white-collar worker, my mother a housewife. While in Switzerland, my father was a member of the Central Committee of the Bund. I have been a member of the Communist Party since 1927 and have not been expelled from the party. I am married. I am an editor by profession. Most recently I was deputy editor of the *Diplomatic Dictionary*. I was awarded the Badge of Honor and the medals In Memory of Moscow's Eight-hundredth Anniversary and For Valiant Labor During the Great Patriotic War, 1941–1945. I was arrested on January 28, 1949. I received a copy of the indictment on May 3, 1952.

Vatenberg-Ostrovskaya: I, Khayke Semyonovna Vatenberg-Ostrovskaya, was born in 1901. I am originally from the village of Zvenigorodka, Kiev region. My father was a butcher in a slaughterhouse. I did not complete my higher education. I graduated from high school in New York and then studied in college. I am married. Defendant Ilya Vatenberg is my husband. We have no children. I received the medal For Valiant Labor During the Great Patriotic War, 1941–1945. I was a translator at the Anti-Fascist Committee and, most recently, a translator at the State Publishing House of Literature in Foreign Languages. I was arrested on January 24, 1949. I received a copy of the indictment on May 3, 1952.

Presiding Officer: The case will be considered by the Military Collegium, consisting of the Presiding Officer Lieutenant General of Justice Cheptsov and members Major General of Justice Dmitriev and Major General of Justice Zaryanov. The secretary is Senior Lieutenant M. Afanasiev.

According to law, you the defendants are granted the right, should you have a basis to do so, to challenge the makeup of the entire court or individual members of it, as well as the secretary.

[Each of the defendants responded that they did not object to any of the members of the court.

The Presiding Officer explained the rights of the defendants during a court session:]

During the trial you have the right to ask each other questions and to give the court explanations of any issue as you feel necessary, and in addition you have the right to petition the court.

Defendant Lozovsky, do you understand your rights? Do you have any petitions?

Lozovsky: I understand my rights. I do have petitions regarding the inclusion of certain materials. The investigation team has these materials, but did not deem it necessary to include them in the forty-two volumes. I am referring to the materials that I gave to Fefer and Mikhoels to take to America. I ask that they be included in the case because they contain nothing secret. This is precisely why they have not been included in the case.

The text of the materials given by defendant Teumin to [B. Z.] Goldberg. The investigation team has these materials and has not included them in the case, apparently because they contain nothing secret.

I am accused of being in contact with Goldberg. Well, in the materials removed from the Jewish Anti-Fascist Committee, there was a book of Goldberg's in defense of Soviet policy and against American government policy, which he wrote when he returned from the USSR. This book was not included in the forty-two volumes. It could serve as proof that the materials that Goldberg was given were used in the interests of the Soviet Union, and not to cause the country harm.

My response to foreign journalists on the goals of the Anti-Fascist Committees, including the Jewish Anti-Fascist Committee, was published in April 1942. This response was edited by Molotov and Shcherbakov. I ask that these materials as well be included in the case.

Presiding Officer: Defendant Fefer, do you understand your rights during the court session?

Fefer: Yes, I do.

Presiding Officer: Do you have any petitions to make to the court?

Fefer: I filed my petitions when I was served with the indictment. I would like the court to study the collection of my selected poems. Investigator Lieutenant Colonel Kuzmin has this collection in Russian.

Presiding Officer: Defendant Teumin, do you understand your rights in court? Have you any petitions to make to the court?

Teumin: I understand my rights and I have a petition to make. In the indictment it says that I edited materials for the Jewish Anti-Fascist Committee. Not only did I never edit such materials, but I never even read them. This was proven during the investigation, specifically in one of the last interrogation records for 1952, which emphasizes that I never saw these materials. I ask that the investigation material be checked and compared against the indictment. I have no other petitions.

Presiding Officer: Defendant Markish, do you understand your rights in court? Do you have any petitions for the court?

Markish: I understand my rights. I have one petition—if possible, to append to the case materials a book published in Warsaw by Soviet Ambassador Voykov.* It is directly related to the accusation against me. This book is not in the case materials. It can be obtained at any library or from my home. In addition, the investigation team has a review of my speeches in Warsaw during the period 1920–1923. I ask that the review be included in the case materials, for it contains an appraisal of my speeches.

*Pyotr Voykov (1888–1927) served as Soviet ambassador to Poland in the 1920s. He was assassinated by White émigrés in Warsaw in 1927 and thereafter canonized by the regime. Markish may have been trying to curry favor with the court by citing a friendship with Voykov.

Presiding Officer: Defendant Yuzefovich, do you understand your rights in court? Do you have any petitions?

Yuzefovich: I understand my rights and I have a petition. A promise was made by an investigator and a prosecutor to provide the court with a copy of the materials from Institute 205 entitled "On England's Colonial Policy" that I gave to Goldberg according to Lozovsky's instructions. So I ask that the court receive these materials for examination.

Presiding Officer: Defendant Bregman, do you understand your rights in court? What petitions do you have before this court?

Bregman: I understand my rights and I have no petitions to make.

Presiding Officer: Defendant Kvitko, do you understand your rights? Do you have any petitions?

Kvitko: I understand my rights and I do have petitions to make. I ask that the letter that I sent to the attention of MGB investigator Colonel Grishaev be included in the case materials. This letter contains facts relating to the case. I am asking for this because I have difficulty speaking in public and this statement of mine covers the facts more specifically and in greater detail. I wrote this statement about three weeks ago.

In the case materials there are two documents where my name is signed in Fefer's handwriting. I ask that these documents be removed from my materials because I did not sign them.

I request that the court study or include in my case materials my book *1919,* published in Berlin in 1920. This book is about the pogroms committed by Petlura* and his followers in the Ukraine. This book has been represented to me as anti-Soviet when it is in fact anti-Petlura. The book was written in Yiddish. It is available at the Lenin Library or from my private collection.

I ask that a book of mine published in 1948–1949, before my arrest, by the publishing house Sovietsky Pisatel (Soviet Writer) be included in the case.

Presiding Officer: Defendant Bergelson, do you understand your rights in court? What petitions do you have?

Bergelson: I understand my rights. I have some petitions for the court.

I ask that the testimony that I wrote out by hand, which I gave during the preliminary investigation right after I was arrested, be included in the case materials.

---

*Simon Petlura (1879–1926) was a Ukrainian nationalist and opponent of the Bolsheviks who has long been accused, particularly within Jewish circles, of directing a series of devastating pogroms against Jewish communities in the Ukraine during the Russian Civil War. Petlura was assassinated in Paris on May 25, 1926. For a balanced look at the historical record on this controversy, see Henry Abramson, *A Prayer for the Government: Ukrainians and Jews in Revolutionary Times, 1917–1920* (Cambridge, Mass., 1999).

I ask that my *Selected Works* be included in the case materials because in the indictment it says that when I lived abroad I wrote constantly against the Soviet Union. It is apparent from that collection of stories that I did not always write against the Soviet Union, but only at one time. I also ask you to include in the case materials the stories that later appeared in the magazines *Krasnoye Znamya* (Red Banner) and *Novy Mir* (New World) under the title "Days of Upheaval."

Presiding Officer: Defendant Hofshteyn, do you understand your rights in court? Do you have any petitions to make to the court?

Hofshteyn: I understand my rights and have no petitions.

Presiding Officer: Defendant Vatenberg, do you understand your rights? Do you have any petitions?

Vatenberg: I understand my rights. I ask to withdraw the petitions that I made on May 3 of this year when I was served the indictment. I have no new petitions.

Presiding Officer: Defendant Shimeliovich, do you understand your rights? Do you have any petitions to make to the court?

Shimeliovich: I understand my rights. I have petitions.

The document certifying to the completion of the investigation in March 1950 contained my request to include in the case materials my statement sent to the attention of special investigator Lieutenant Colonel Ryumin, dated May 15, 1949. I request that this statement be included in the case. That is my first request. I kept insisting on having it included, and when I signed a second statement in March 1952, I asked to have my declaration about this included in the statement and to record that I have never pled guilty and do not plead guilty now.

Presiding Officer: This explanation relates to the nature of the case, whereas what we are asking is whether you have any petitions regarding documents to be included in the case materials.

Shimeliovich: In March 1952, I requested that a number of statements that I had previously signed be included in the case materials. A list of these documents was included in the second statement certifying the end of the investigation. Several days later I was informed that this list of documents, including the February 11 statement about the investigator's improper actions, had been rejected. I ask that the documents on that list, which were in the second statement, be included in the case materials. I have no other petitions.

Presiding Officer: Defendant Zuskin, do you understand your rights?

Zuskin: I understand my rights.

Presiding Officer: What petitions do you have for the court?

Zuskin: I have some petitions. The indictment states that I sent a number of articles to the American press about the state of art in the Soviet Union. I

have already said that I wrote about the work of the Moscow Jewish Theater. I wrote no more than three or four articles about the artists. I ask that
these materials be appended to the case materials so that the court has an
idea what was in these articles of mine.

Presiding Officer: Defendant Talmy, do you understand your rights?

Talmy: I understand my rights.

Presiding Officer: Do you have any petitions for the court?

Talmy: I have one petition, that the testimony which I wrote out by hand and
which served as the basis for the examination record written by Lieutenant
Colonel Artemov in September 1949 be included in the case materials.

Presiding Officer: Why is that necessary? You will be granted the right to respond to the accusations against you, and there you can say what you like.
It will be recorded in the transcript.

Talmy: The thing is that my testimony in the examination records was summarized and changed to the point of unrecognizability. Also, in connection
with what I stated during the interrogation, I believe that the experts' conclusion about my book *On Virgin Soil* is erroneous and incorrect. I petition
the court to summon these experts into court so that everything can be
made clear and so that I can simply prove that their conclusion is wrong. A
translation of my book exists. The case materials contain only excerpts
from the book in Russian, selected very tendentiously. In order to make a
judgment about my book, a full and accurate translation must be available.
I would also request that my articles from the newspaper *Naye tsayt* (New
Times)* be included in the case materials.

When I signed the statement confirming that the investigation was over,
I told the prosecutor and the investigator that the investigation materials
demonstrate that it was wrong to connect my case with those of the other
defendants. I have no other petitions.

Presiding Officer: This is an explanation about the nature of the case and not
a petition. Defendant Shtern, do you understand your rights in court?
What petitions do you have?

Shtern: I understand my rights. I have several petitions.

It says here that I gathered some sort of classified information, and as evidence it is stated that I established contact with three Americans who came
to the USSR and that I gave them a collection of scientific papers (published
by the Academy of Medical Sciences). How can I prove that this is all
wrong? These are scientific problems that Soviet and foreign scientists were
working to solve, and I am accused of passing on a collection of scientific
papers in exchange for money. The collection is called *The Problems of Bi-*

**Naye tsayt was a Yiddish-language newspaper of the Fareynikte Party (United Jewish Socialist Workers' Party); it was published in Kiev.

ology in Medicine. This book came out in 1944 to coincide with my jubilee celebration. This is how festschrifts are put together—scientists submit their works. I request that this collection be included in the case materials. It was written in 1944 and it contains nothing secret.

Presiding Officer: Defendant Vatenberg-Ostrovskaya, do you understand your rights in court? Do you have any petitions for the court?

Vatenberg-Ostrovskaya: I understand my rights. I have no petitions to make.

Presiding Officer: The Military Collegium of the USSR Supreme Court, having heard the defendants' petitions and conducted an immediate deliberation, has determined that the petitions will be decided during the course of the trial.

Testimony by the Defendants

[At the instruction of the presiding officer, the secretary reads out the indictment.]*

Presiding Officer: In a preparatory session on April 21, 1952, the Military Collegium of the USSR Supreme Court confirmed the indictment for this case, putting Lozovsky and the others on trial based on the conclusions in the indictment. The case is set for hearing in a closed court session without a defense or prosecution team and without witnesses being called to testify.

Presiding Officer: Defendant Fefer, do you understand the indictment as it has been presented to you?

Fefer: I do.

Presiding Officer: Do you plead guilty?

Fefer: I do.

Presiding Officer: Defendant Teumin, do you understand the indictment?

Teumin: Yes, I do.

Presiding Officer: Do you plead guilty?

Teumin: Yes, I plead guilty.

Presiding Officer: Defendant Markish, do you understand the indictment?

Markish: I do.

Presiding Officer: Do you plead guilty?

---

*The indictment was forty-five pages long and recounted a full list of crimes ascribed to the JAC as a whole and to individuals in particular. The sentence of the court, presented by the judges on July 18, 1952, summarizes the major points of the indictment; it is reproduced at the end of the trial transcript. The text of the indictment, dated March 31, 1952, can be found in the archives of General Dmitry Volkogonov in the Manuscript Division of the Library of Congress, Washington, D.C.

Markish: I do not plead guilty.

Presiding Officer: Defendant Yuzefovich, do you understand the indictment?

Yuzefovich: Yes, I do.

Presiding Officer: Do you plead guilty?

Yuzefovich: I plead guilty in part.

Presiding Officer: Defendant Lozovsky, do you understand the indictment?

Lozovsky: I do.

Presiding Officer: Do you plead guilty?

Lozovsky: No, I do not plead guilty to anything.

Presiding Officer: Defendant Bregman, do you understand the indictment presented to you?

Bregman: Yes, I do.

Presiding Officer: Do you plead guilty?

Bregman: I do not.

Presiding Officer: Defendant Kvitko, do you understand the indictment? Do you plead guilty?

Kvitko: I understand the indictment and plead guilty in part.

Presiding Officer: Defendant Bergelson, do you understand the indictment?

Bergelson: I do.

Presiding Officer: Do you plead guilty?

Bergelson: In part.

Presiding Officer: Defendant Hofshteyn, do you understand the indictment?

Hofshteyn: Yes.

Presiding Officer: Do you plead guilty?

Hofshteyn: In part.

Presiding Officer: Defendant Vatenberg, do you understand the indictment?

Vatenberg: Yes, I understand it.

Presiding Officer: Do you plead guilty?

Vatenberg: I plead guilty in part.

Presiding Officer: Defendant Shimeliovich, do you understand the indictment?

Shimeliovich: Yes, I understand it.

Presiding Officer: Do you plead guilty?

Shimeliovich: I have never pled guilty and I do not do so now.

Presiding Officer: Defendant Zuskin, do you understand the indictment?

Zuskin: Yes, I understand it.

Presiding Officer: Do you plead guilty?

Zuskin: In part.

Presiding Officer: Defendant Talmy, do you understand the indictment?

Talmy: Yes, I understand it.

Presiding Officer: Do you plead guilty?

Talmy: In part.

Presiding Officer: Defendant Shtern, do you understand the indictment?

Shtern: Yes, I do.

Presiding Officer: Do you plead guilty?

Shtern: I plead guilty only to having been a member of the presidium of the Jewish Anti-Fascist Committee and, as a Party member, of not probing at all into the committee's activities. I have never engaged in espionage or in anti-Soviet activities. I am guilty of the fact that as a Party member of whom a certain level of vigilance is required, I did not exercise any vigilance whatsoever. I am guilty of not showing any interest in the work being done while I was on the committee and a member of the presidium. I think that this is all that I am guilty of.

Presiding Officer: Defendant Vatenberg-Ostrovskaya, do you understand the indictment?

Vatenberg-Ostrovskaya: Yes, I do.

Presiding Officer: Do you plead guilty?

Vatenberg-Ostrovskaya: In part.

ISAAC FEFER

Itsik Fefer was the most loyal and committed communist of the five writers on trial. Born to a Hebrew teacher in the small Ukrainian town of Shpola, Fefer was drawn to politics and literature at an early age. After the Bolshevik takeover in 1917, Fefer volunteered for the Red Army and fought in the ensuing Civil War. For a time, he was also a member of the Bund. Fefer was best known for his satirical verses. Born and raised in the center of the Hasidic movement in the Ukraine, Fefer once recalled how his grandfather gave him the name Isaac after the revered Isaac Twersky, or Reb Itsikl, of the Chernobyl Hasidic dynasty. As Fefer wrote in an oft-quoted poem,

> In all my short, happy life, I've never
> Been lost, nor forgotten the way I came.

I laugh to myself when I remember
That I carry some famous rabbi's name.*

But Fefer was equally notorious for his willingness to employ harsh political rhetoric against his fellow Yiddish writers. There are myriad examples of his demagogic attacks on them for "political deviation" and "nationalism." In the 1920s and 1930s, Fefer engaged in sharp public confrontations with several poets and writers who would later stand accused with him. Writing in the Yiddish journal *Farmest* in 1934, Fefer openly denounced colleagues in terms that a decade later could easily have been used in the indictments against them:

> Mikhoels complained that the party pays little attention to Jewish culture . . . and Markish began to shout that the reader is going away, that Yiddish literature is ill, that Jewish writers sit in local stations while the express trains pass without stopping. With all the differences in manner of appearance and mood of the speakers at the conference, one basic note was struck by all: the lack of a perspective for Yiddish culture and literature. . . . Let us take the harps and sit down to mourn the fate of the Jewish people! Notes of nationalistic hysteria were heard ("We are the last poets"), of nationalistic pride ("We have almost the best literature"), of national panic ("We have no literature"), of nationalistic maximalism ("We do not want to be a minority!"). Some comrades did not give sufficient weight to the harmful nature of such basically nationalistic utterances. And strange indeed was the conduct of those comrades who for many years had themselves been affected by the disease of nationalism, and who now kept their peace and expressed no opposition to the prevailing mood.†

At the First Congress of Soviet Writers that year, Fefer stated that Yiddish literature had been "the poor literature of a poor tribe, without a country, history, or a great literary tradition of its own."‡ Unwilling to defend his own cultural heritage, Fefer began to promote the translation of Yiddish literary works into Russian and Ukrainian in place of issuing them in their original Yiddish. His capitulation appeared to be complete.

---

*Itsik Fefer, "I've Never Been Lost," in Irving Howe, Ruth R. Wisse, and Khone Shmeruk, eds., *The Penguin Book of Modern Yiddish Verse* (New York, 1987), pp. 548–550; the translation is by John Hollander.

†Cited in Chone Shmeruk, "Yiddish Literature in the U.S.S.R.," in Lionel Kochan, ed., *The Jews in Soviet Russia Since 1917*, 3d ed. (Oxford, 1978), p. 267.

‡Yehuda Slutsky, "Jews at the First Congress of Soviet Writers," *Soviet Jewish Affairs*, vol. 2, no. 2, 1972, p. 67.

Still, Fefer remained attached to Yiddish. In the late 1930s, when the regime began to close Jewish schools, newspapers, and other institutions, all the Yiddish writers understood that future generations would have little, if any, access to Yiddish culture. Fefer opposed the closing of so many schools, which led to his dismissal as editor of the Yiddish literary journal *Sovetishe literatur* (Soviet Literature) in 1938 "for displaying nationalistic tendencies."* It was not the last time that he would face such a charge.

It is easy to condemn Fefer for cooperating with the investigation of the JAC case. His testimony led to scores of arrests and helped to construct the case against the committee. But Fefer did not abandon all feelings of loyalty to his fellow Jews. He was profoundly affected by the Holocaust; his poem "I Am a Jew" and several exchanges in court vividly displayed his heartfelt identification with Jewish victims, his father among them. Fefer, for example, appealed to Soviet officials in February 1948 to permit a small printing of *The Black Book* "in view of [its] impending cancellation." He asked for copies to be deposited in "closed sections of libraries" and other government offices in order to preserve this record of Nazi persecution in occupied Soviet territory.† Later that year, Fefer wrote appeals in defense of Israel, urging Soviet leaders to support a proposal in the United Nations to partition Palestine and create a Jewish state. He did not retract such views during the trial and on several occasions spoke up for the right of Jews to mourn their dead, to be proud of their resistance to Hitler, and to welcome the creation of Israel.

Shmuel Halkin was one of the few arrested Yiddish writers to survive. At one point during the investigation, he was taken to see Fefer for a "witness confrontation." Without raising his eyes from the floor, Fefer urged Halkin to confess to engaging in "Zionism" and "bourgeois nationalism." Halkin remained silent but, before being led away, kissed Fefer on the forehead in a sign of forgiveness.‡

*Gennadi Kostyrchenko, *Out of the Red Shadows: Anti-Semitism in Stalin's Russia* (Amherst, N.Y., 1995), p. 41.

†Shimon Redlich, *War, Holocaust and Stalinism: A Documented History of the Jewish Anti-Fascist Committee in the USSR* (Luxembourg, 1995), p. 370. Fefer's appeal, addressed to Dmitry Shepilov of the Central Committee, was dated February 13, 1948, a month after the death of Mikhoels.

‡Alexander Borshchagovsky, *Obvinyaetsa Krov* (Moscow, 1994), p. 313. Bergelson's widow also found it in her heart not to condemn Fefer. In the late 1950s she was already

Fefer: I was born in the shtetl of Shpola into the family of a schoolteacher. My
father could not afford to teach me, so I was self-educated. I lived in this
shtetl until 1922, when I moved to Kiev and started pursuing literature. I
did not engage in anti-Soviet activities in Kiev. To the contrary, I consider
myself one of the first Yiddish poets to begin writing about the Red Army,
the Party, and the Komsomol.

I confirm that I joined the Bund in 1917 and spent a year and a half in the
organization. It was a small group whose activities were confined to the
distribution of Yiddish literature. Of course I did not take part in more important matters. You see, I worked in a printer's shop as a typesetter and
there was a Jewish group there. At that time the Communist Party's attitude toward the national question suited me and so I joined the Party when
I was nineteen years old.

I started writing in mid-1918. In 1920 I met the Jewish nationalists
Bergelson, Hofshteyn, and Kvitko. They expressed their nationalistic views
in poetry. At the time I felt that Soviet reality should be written about more,
so in 1922 I published my poems about Russia.

[The presiding officer reads out testimony (vol. 2, p. 46).]

Fefer: Yes, the thing is that nationalistic sentiments are anti-Soviet sentiments
as well. Bergelson and Hofshteyn expressed their nationalistic views in
their works. In my first collection of poetry I did not express any nationalistic sentiments. I wrote a cycle of poems entitled *Russia.* My nationalism
was expressed for the most part in my frame of mind and in conversations
about my unhappiness with assimilation. I was already a Party member.
The facts of assimilation were that there were mass closings of Yiddish
schools. During the thirties many Yiddish newspapers, organizations, and
schools were eliminated. This greatly disturbed me and aroused nationalistic sentiments in me that I expressed in conversations with Bergelson and
Hofshteyn.

I stood up for Jewish organizations with all the strength that was in me.
When the Institute of Jewish Culture was shut down, Hofshteyn and I
raised the issue of founding an Office of Jewish Culture within the Ukrainian Academy of Sciences. And I did everything I could to reestablish those
Jewish organizations that had been shut down. I should also say that I often had occasion to speak out against harmful features of Yiddish literature. I wrote several articles in which I took issue with Trotskyism.

[The presiding officer reads out testimony (vol. 2, p. 52).]

Fefer: I have been in a synagogue several times because I very much love Jewish traditions. I would not say that I attended regularly, but we did have ties
to the Jewish religious community.

---

aware of rumors concerning Fefer's betrayal of the others. As she observed to a journalist in
Israel, "Have we, those who survived, the right to judge a man who went through Beria's in-
quisition cells and might have been driven mad?" See Yehoshua Gilboa, *The Black Years of
Soviet Jewry* (Boston, 1971), p. 372.

My attitudes involved some tendencies toward nationalism before the committee was created. In 1942 I was called upon to work at the Jewish Anti-Fascist Committee. Epshteyn summoned me in a telegram signed by Lozovsky. I arrived in Moscow in April 1942 and was appointed deputy editor of the newspaper *Eynikayt*. It is fair to say that from its very first issues the newspaper had a nationalistic cast to it. I consider myself guilty when it comes to the work of this newspaper. We published material about the heroism of Jews. This material should have been published, but we separated it from the heroism of the Soviet people as a whole; that is to say, we kept our own accounts. We said that we needed to know how many Jews were heroes during the war, so that we could then come to the government with our request and point to the fact that the Jews had played a prominent role in the struggle against fascism. And from the very beginning the Jewish Anti-Fascist Committee kept a running count of the victims. This then served as the basis for *The Black Book*. I knew that when the Jewish Anti-Fascist Committee was still in Kuibyshev, it had established contact with foreign press outlets at the direction of the Sovinformburo. It was sending materials—articles, feature stories, and information—for the foreign Jewish press about Soviet Jews, Jewish heroism, about their role in the defense industry, and about Yiddish culture in general.

I should add here that around 1942 there started to be talk at the Jewish Anti-Fascist Committee about how all Jewish institutions had been shut down, and that this was happening even in Jewish districts, liquidating all that had been created over the course of thirty years. It was then that the Crimea issue came up, and I do not mean the Crimean health resorts, but rather northern Crimea, where there had been three Jewish national districts before the war. At the time, we talked among ourselves about how it would be a good thing to create a Jewish republic in the Crimea, and how at Epshteyn's initiative we distributed cabinet positions among ourselves for a future Jewish republic.

In early 1943, Mikhoels and I were invited to America. Before we left we had a series of conversations with Epshteyn, Lozovsky, and Shcherbakov. The leadership of the Sovinformburo insisted that we place as much material as possible in the foreign press, material not only about Jews, but about industry, agriculture, and culture in the USSR. Lozovsky insisted that while we were in America we make arrangements not only with the progressive press, but with the bourgeois press as well, and that we try to place this material in the bourgeois press. Then we were supposed to contact Jewish bourgeois organizations in order to pump them for material assistance.

Presiding Officer: Why should they give you money?

Fefer: Since Hitler was aiming to annihilate the entire Jewish people, many Jewish capitalists contributed large amounts to a fund to aid Jews fighting fascism out of fear, even though they were opposed to socialism.

At the witness confrontation with Lozovsky, I spoke in great detail about

Lozovsky as the moving force behind the Jewish Anti-Fascist Committee and said that he was aware of all its activity and was, for all intents and purposes, the leader. There was not a single document that Lozovsky did not approve. We did not respond to anything from abroad without Lozovsky's consent and stamp of approval.

Presiding Officer: Is it really the case that your committee's task was to send material only about Jews and not about the Soviet people?

Fefer: The committee was assigned the fundamental task of uniting Jews the world over to combat fascism.

Upon our arrival in America, we met with Weizmann,* now the president of the State of Israel. We had been instructed to meet only with leaders of the press and civic organizations and not to meet with leaders of political parties. But Weizmann was the leader of a Zionist political party, so we immediately turned to Gromyko[†] for advice. Gromyko summoned Mikhoels to Washington and said that an order had been received to meet with Weizmann, although in fact, permission from Moscow did not arrive until two weeks after the meeting with Weizmann.

Our conversation with Weizmann was not very long. We met with him once. He was interested in the attitudes of Jews in the Soviet Union toward Zionists. We said that Soviet Jews would not go to Palestine, and in answer to a question about the state of Jewish culture, we replied that it was in a bad way. Then we told him about fascist atrocities. Weizmann had one request for us: that if we met with a representative of the Soviet government, we should report that if a Jewish state was created in Palestine rather than an Arab one, it would never permit any hostile statements to be made against the Soviet Union.

Later on we met with [James] Rosenberg. We had only one conversation with him and it was brief, as he spoke only English and we did not. Rosenberg is one of the directors of the Joint—a millionaire lawyer. The Joint is a bourgeois Zionist organization. The meeting with Rosenberg was not at our initiative. The Joint had sent a letter to Mikhoels's attention containing an offer of aid to Jewish war victims. Mikhoels was authorized to conduct negotiations with the Joint on behalf of the Soviet government about assistance to the Soviet population through the Red Cross without regard to nationality and without representatives of the Joint being allowed into the Soviet Union. During the negotiations, Rosenberg announced, "You demand

---

*Chaim Weizmann (1874–1952), a distinguished chemist, was president of the World Zionist Organization from 1920 to 1931 and again from 1935 to 1946. He became the first president of Israel in 1948.

[†]Andrei Gromyko (1909–1989) was a leading Soviet diplomat. He began his diplomatic career as a counselor at the Soviet Embassy in Washington, D.C., from 1939 to 1943 and then became ambassador to the United States from 1943 to 1946. He was also permanent Soviet representative to the U.N. Security Council from 1946 to 1948 and deputy foreign minister during those same years.

everything, but you aren't doing anything yourselves. But if you are able to raise the issue of settling Jews in the Crimea, then we will provide material assistance." He said, "The Crimea interests us not only as Jews, but as Americans, because the Crimea also means the Black Sea, the Balkan peninsula, and Turkey." There was no direct conversation about turning the Crimea into a beachhead.

After the war, Lozovsky convened the committee leaders and instructed them to send more material about the rebuilding of Soviet industry and agriculture.

I should say that in addition to all of this, we virtually turned the committee into a nationalistic organization and broadened its functions.

Presiding Officer: We being who?

Fefer: Mikhoels, Epshteyn, and I. Shimeliovich spoke about broadening its functions. Markish presented a proposal to provide aid to evacuees. Shimeliovich spoke about aiding the Jews who had returned to their old homes after evacuation. But this was not our business.

We arranged with American nationalists to publish *The Black Book*. We got permission to publish *The Black Book* from Lozovsky as well.

So I believe that nationalistic work was carried out in the committee and that the committee leaders sent out materials that represented state secrets. I assisted Goldberg in gathering information that was of interest to him. Goldberg came to Moscow in late 1945 [actually, in January 1946]. A reception was held for him at the committee, attended by representatives of the Jewish nationality. He met with Lozovsky. Mikhoels received him, too. He asked to have a trip around the Soviet Union, specifically to the Ukraine and to the Baltic region. Lozovsky promised to arrange this trip for him. Then Goldberg met with Shimeliovich, Markish, and Teumin.

Presiding Office: What materials did he collect at the committee and at the Sovinformburo?

Fefer: At the Sovinformburo he got materials on foreign policy, on the situation in the new democracies, and about the Soviet government's attitude toward these countries. At the committee he got material about the rebuilding of industry.

Presiding Officer: Are you familiar with the testimony of witness Gordienko, who named Goldberg, saying that he gave her an espionage assignment to gather a variety of classified information? She is Ukrainian, not Jewish.

Fefer: I have not met with her.

Presiding Officer: But you have read her testimony, which makes it clear that she received an espionage assignment.

Fefer: What surprises me is why he made this arrangement with her, when he knew so many Jews.

Presiding Officer: But you know that she was romantically involved with Goldberg, and that is why he made use of her. And from that it follows that Goldberg traveled around the Ukraine and the Baltic region, gathering classified information in the USSR.

Fefer: Yes, from the standpoint of the Register of 1945* he was gathering classified material about industry and agriculture and information about Yiddish literature.

Presiding Officer: Didn't you testify that Goldberg asked the Jewish Anti-Fascist Committee to increase its information-gathering activities about our national economy?

Fefer: Yes, he did make such a proposal, and we sent him the materials he asked for. During the entire period of the committee's existence we sent abroad about twenty thousand articles and feature stories.

Presiding Officer: When you received these instructions to broaden information-gathering in the USSR, how did you handle the organizational side of things within the committee?

Fefer: We dispatched a number of correspondents to various places, and they wrote features and articles on industry, agriculture, and culture in the USSR. This material came to the committee's editorial board for processing; then it was sent to the control editor to be checked, and then to American press outlets. Up until 1946, these materials went through the embassy, and then they were sent by mail and telegraph. No other approval, apart from our own, was required to send the materials, until 1945. This was while Epshteyn was alive. When I came to work there, I announced that no material could be sent without the approval of Glavlit.† Up till then, Epshteyn approved the materials, and there was also a military censor at the Sovinformburo. In any case, when I was there, all materials went out only after Glavlit had examined them.

Presiding Officer: Regarding the Crimea issue: When you came back from America, how did you raise this question, when, and where?

Fefer: When we came back from America, the Crimea issue was raised in the following way. I told several presidium members about how during our talk with Rosenberg, he had promised material assistance from the Joint if a Jewish republic were organized in the Crimea. We already knew that part of the population of the Crimea had been moved out and that the issue of resettling the area would come up. We decided not to write a letter until we had spoken with one or two Politburo members, as this was a very serious issue, and before we wrote the letter, we asked for an audience with Molotov. He received us (Mikhoels, Epshteyn, and me). There, among other is-

---

*The Register of 1945 was a secret set of instructions about topics that were prohibited from being mentioned in the Soviet press.

†Glavlit refers to the office of Soviet censors. Its actual existence was long denied.

sues, we raised the question of creating a Jewish republic in the Crimea or in the area of the Volga Germans' republic. At the time we liked the sound of it: "Where there used to be a republic of Germans, there should now be a Jewish republic." Molotov said that this sounded good demographically, but that there was no point in raising the question and creating a Jewish republic on this land, as the Jews were an urban people and you couldn't simply plunk Jews down on a tractor. In addition, Molotov said, "As to the Crimea, you write the letter and we will have a look at it." After that we consulted with Lozovsky. We also consulted with Yuzefovich and Shimeliovich and showed a draft of the letter to Markish. As you see, the text of the letter did not come out well. It was essentially a nationalistic venture, and to this I plead guilty.

Presiding Officer: Defendant Fefer, tell us who Levin* is.

Fefer: Levin is the former chairman of a Jewish council of organizations in the United States that organized aid to Russia during the war. He is himself a landlord and owns twenty buildings in a Negro neighborhood in New York. I met with him twice in America. But this is a repetition of what I already said during the investigation.

Presiding Officer: Speak about the circumstances of Novick's visit to Moscow. When did the visit take place?

Fefer: Novick arrived in Moscow at the end of September 1946.

Presiding Officer: Why did he come here?

Fefer: He is the editor of the daily newspaper the *Morgen Freiheit,* an organ of the American Communist Party. He came here as the editor of the newspaper and as its correspondent. I did not know that Novick was a spy, but since he was gathering material about industry, agriculture, and culture and since he met with many different people, I judged his activity to be espionage-related, based on situations that I had not known about before. I had the most conventional notions about classified information. I realize now that I had poor judgment and that I improperly understood things. Besides, I knew that Novick had published a long book in which he used all the material he had collected in the Soviet Union and in which he showed the Soviet Union in a very favorable light.

Presiding Officer: Let's get back to the work of the committee itself. Judging from your testimony, after you came back from America the Jewish Anti-Fascist Committee's hostile activity intensified by means of sending all sorts of economic information from around the Soviet Union to America. And it also, through discussions by various committee members of nationalistic activities, went beyond the scope of the committee's mandate. Tell us about that.

*Louis Levin of New York was the national chairman of the Jewish Council of Russian War Relief.

Fefer: Our return from America coincided with the committee's move from Kuibyshev to Moscow. In Moscow the committee broadened the scope of its activity. First of all, the Crimea issue was brought up—a nationalistic venture. Then a committee meeting was held. At this plenum and in the reports that Epshteyn, Mikhoels, and I gave, nationalistic themes were clearly sounded. A great deal was said about the heroism of the Jews. Then the committee received a large number of letters from various parts of the country containing complaints about discrimination by local authorities. We collected all of this material and summarized it.

Presiding Officer: What material?

Fefer: About Jews coming back after evacuation and not getting jobs. Kvitko went to the Crimea on assignment from the Jewish Anti-Fascist Committee to see what was going on there. There had been three Jewish districts there before the war. After this trip, Kvitko reported that there was evidence in various places that local authorities were taking measures to oppose the return of Jews, that many Jewish collective farm workers were in a deplorable state and not getting any assistance. This question was discussed at the Jewish Anti-Fascist Committee, and it was decided that a delegation would be sent to Benediktov,* the people's commissar of agriculture. The delegation included Shimeliovich, Mikhoels, Gubelman,† and Kvitko. Benediktov received them and he promised to look into it and to help.

We received a series of letters about how American gifts were being improperly distributed in various places, and saying that many Jews were returning from the ghettoes and not getting any help. A letter to this effect went to the people's commissar of state control, and an answer came back from Popov saying that everything in the letter had been checked and that the information that the committee had did not match the facts.

None of this was the committee's responsibility. Acting like this was a broadening of its mandate. In fact, it was not so much the committee that was dealing with these questions as Mikhoels personally. He dealt with residency permit problems for individual Jews, wrote letters to get them jobs, and so on. In this way, the committee was transformed into a unique kind of governmental department.

Presiding Officer: At your committee did you discuss only the internal Soviet situation, or were foreign affairs discussed as well? You discussed questions involving not only the lives of Jews in the Soviet Union, but questions relating to the lives of Jews abroad as well—wasn't that so?

---

*Ivan Benediktov (1902–1983) was appointed first deputy people's commissar for agriculture in December 1943. In March 1946 he became people's commissar for agriculture.

†Moisey Gubelman (1882–1968) was a longtime Communist Party member. He directed the Union of Commercial Employees between 1933 and 1947. He was also a member of the JAC presidium.

Fefer: When Mosley,* the leader of the English fascists, was released, he organized pogroms against Jews in Jewish areas of England, and the authorities did nothing. This took place when there was a Labor government in power, and we felt we must speak out in protest and show the British that their government was doing nothing. We wrote a letter to the British trade unions.

Presiding Officer: And what did Shtern have to say about this? Supposedly she refused to sign the letter?

Fefer: No, she signed it, but she said that we should check the facts and see if they were actually true.

Member of the Panel: Did the Jewish Anti-Fascist Committee send greetings to Weizmann?

Fefer: Yes, in the summer of 1948.

Member of the Panel: In connection with what?

Fefer: We sent congratulations on the founding of the Jewish state of Israel. And, I should add as well, we drafted this letter and sent it to Deputy Minister of Foreign Affairs Zorin, who looked it over and said, "I will consult with the leadership." When I called him back on the phone, he said that we could send the congratulations, and he changed only one sentence.

Member of the Panel: The case materials contain testimony that Mikhoels allegedly took a Bible with him when he went to America. What was this for?

Fefer: Not only believers read the Bible. We had to deal with backward audiences who did not always understand our anti-fascist statements, and at times it was necessary to rely on biblical language. This is why he took the Bible with him, and I have to say that it proved to be quite useful. The Bible is one of the greatest monuments of Jewish culture.

Member of the Panel: During one of the interrogations you testified that Shtern supposedly urged people to actively struggle against the nationality policy of the Party and the Soviet government, and she said that the Soviet Union was not her Motherland.

Fefer: There was an incident when I asked Shtern to write an article about the anniversary of the October Revolution. She asked what it should be about, to which I replied, about our Motherland, the Soviet Union. She said that it was not her Motherland, that she had been born in the Baltic region when it was not part of the Soviet Union. In addition, Shtern often spoke at the presidium about discrimination against Jews in the Soviet Union.

Presiding Officer: Further on you testify that during the report at the Jewish Anti-Fascist Committee presidium on Jewish participation in the partisan

*Sir Oswald Mosley (1896–1980) was a British politician and founder of the British Union of Fascists in 1932.

movement Shtern said, "Why do you all keep talking about the Germans, when you should talk about how the Belorussians helped the Germans destroy Jews." Did she say such a thing?

Fefer: Such a statement by Shtern was recorded in the transcript of a Jewish Anti-Fascist Committee session.

Presiding Officer: Further on you testify that during discussion of a brochure entitled "What Soviet Power Has Given the Jews," she proposed writing instead about what Jews had done for Soviet power.

Fefer: There was such a proposal, but it was met with objections from all members of the committee.

[Next the court clarified the way employees of the Jewish Anti-Fascist Committee transmitted articles to foreign press agencies and the degree to which the published materials contained classified information.]

Member of the Collegium: How were the materials for *The Black Book* collected? You were not allowed to publish this book, but the book came out in America nonetheless.*

Fefer: Epshteyn was still alive then.

Member of the Collegium: You say that everything was done according to law and sent through official institutions. How was this material selected to be sent?

Fefer: Everything was sent in 1944, before the prohibition, and was sent through the People's Commissariat of Foreign Affairs. There was a telegram from Gromyko saying that *The Black Book* was going to come out in the United States without any material from us. The telegram was sent via the People's Commissariat of Foreign Affairs. Based on this, Epshteyn sent all the material to the United States in 1944.

Member of the Collegium: Lozovsky was privy to all the details of the Jewish Anti-Fascist Committee's everyday activities?

Fefer: I think that would be putting it a bit strongly, because he had all sorts of things he had to do. I would say rather that Lozovsky guided and managed the committee's work. We did not have a single request that he did not know about, and there was not a single piece of correspondence that was sent without a copy going to him. We did not send out a single reply without Lozovsky signing off on it. He knew that the Jewish Anti-Fascist Committee had become a center of nationalistic activity and that the committee was carrying out nationalistic work.

The Black Book was published in New York (Duell, Sloan, and Pearce, 1946) under the auspices of the Jewish *Black Book* commission, consisting of the World Jewish Congress in New York, the Jewish Anti-Fascist Committee in Moscow, the Vaad Leumi (Jewish National Council of Palestine) in Jerusalem, and the American Committee of Jewish Writers, Artists, and Scientists in New York.

Presiding Officer: You say that the Jewish Anti-Fascist Committee was a center of nationalistic propaganda. Along with the committee, what other Jewish organizations also collaborated in this area?

Fefer: In addition to the committee, there were: the Jewish Theater, which was a kind of platform for nationalistic propaganda. The repertoire of the Jewish theater contained a large number of plays with nationalistic themes.

Presiding Officer: Which plays were included in the theater's repertoire?

Fefer: Classic Yiddish plays, including works by Sholem Aleichem; Shakespeare's *King Lear;* as well as contemporary works—Broderzon's *On the Eve of a Holiday* and my play, *The Sun Does Not Set,* about partisans. In that play I let some nationalistic mistakes slip in, contrasting Jews with Germans. Then there was Belenkovich's play *The Submarine Captain.* Also the play *Freylekhs* (Happy Tunes), which is a variety show of folk themes. This is a play depicting old rituals and customs, focusing on days gone by as the golden days of the past. Mikhoels was the theater's artistic director.

The newspaper *Eynikayt,* which published nationalistic materials. I personally published about one hundred and fifty columns there, targeted mostly at reactionary circles and warmongers.

The Yiddish Section of the Soviet Writers' Union, which organized evening programs at which nationalistic works were read and recited.

Presiding Officer: Defendant Fefer, are you familiar with the documents produced by the expert commission about the committee's nationalistic propaganda? That biblical images were exalted? That Jews should be treated as a separate class based on blood? All this was disguised with Soviet slogans, but in fact, proletarian internationalism was replaced with cosmopolitanism.

Fefer: There were no conversations about cosmopolitanism.

Member of the Collegium: Tell about your activity, about your articles, and about how you glorified nationalism.

Fefer: I have to say before the court that while there may have been times when my public activity was contaminated with nationalistic ideas, this affected my creative work least of all. My literary work is not besmirched in this way. There were individual cases of nationalistic errors. For example, the poem "I Am a Jew," cited here, and to that could be added another two or three poems that are nationalistic in tone.

Presiding Officer: Why do you consider these errors? You said earlier that you were raised in a spirit of nationalism, and especially after the 1930s the leitmotif of your work was the struggle against Jewish assimilation. This is not an error; this is a consistent line.

Is it possible to be a nationalist and write Soviet works?

Fefer: No, in poetry that cannot be done. A sage once said that poetry is the mirror of the soul. I wrote as my soul prompted me. I published around thirty books. My nationalistic tendencies came out in the following ways: I said that I love my people. Is there anyone who does not love his people? I wanted my people to have what all others had. And when I saw that everything was being closed down, everything was being eliminated, this pained me and made me rise up against Soviet power. This was what motivated my interest in the Crimea and Birobidzhan. It seemed to me that only Stalin could correct the historical injustice committed by the Roman kings.* It seemed to me that only the Soviet government could correct this injustice by giving the Jews back their nationhood. I had nothing against the Soviet system. I am the son of a poor schoolteacher. Soviet power made a human being out of me and a fairly well known poet as well.

Presiding Officer: In your poetry you make various ancient allusions, like "Samson's hair," "Bar Kochba's appeal," "the wise wrinkles of Rabbi Akiba," "the wisdom of the Biblical Isaiah," and "the thoughts of our splendid Solomon the Wise." Where is the culture of Soviet people to be found in all of this?

Fefer: There is much wisdom in the heritage of any people. I see no reason to repudiate Solomon. But I have said already that we drank our ideals from the goblet of Stalinism, and we confirmed that the Slavs were our friends. My poems were focused on the idea that we would still dance on Hitler's grave. Let me remind you of my talk at the rally in New York. In my speech I held up Pokryshkin† as an example of someone who represents all peoples.

Presiding Officer: You still keep on spreading the exceptionally nationalistic idea that the Jews suffered more than anyone, don't you?

Fefer: Yes, I feel that the suffering of the Jewish people has been exceptionally great.

Presiding Officer: Were the Jews really the only ones to suffer during the Great Patriotic War?

Fefer: Yes, you will not find another people that has suffered as much as the Jewish people. Six million Jews were destroyed out of a total of eighteen million—one-third. This was a great sacrifice. We had a right to our tears, and we fought against fascism.

[Next, the presiding officer of the court asked Fefer to describe Shimeliovich and reminded him that during the preliminary investigation Fefer had said that "Shimeliovich is one of the most aggressive members of the committee."]

---

*The Roman emperors Vespasian and Titus commanded the troops who destroyed Jerusalem in 70 C.E. and dispersed its Jewish inhabitants throughout the Roman world. This was the beginning of the Jewish diaspora.

†Alexander Pokryshkin (1913–1985) was Stalin's favorite pilot. He was named Hero of the Soviet Union three times during the war.

Fefer: That is all correct. I meant mainly the Crimea question, for Shimeliovich drew up one of the drafts of the letter to the government. When this draft was shown to Lozovsky, he rejected it, saying that it was nationalistic.

When our message to Weizmann was published—congratulations upon the occasion of the founding of the State of Israel—Shimeliovich expressed dissatisfaction that it was published only in a Yiddish newspaper. He often expressed this kind of dissatisfaction.

Presiding Officer: Is the testimony you give on page 53 of volume 2 correct?

Fefer: I said that based on the words of Mikhoels. Mikhoels had told me that at the Botkin Hospital, known as Botchina, most of the staff were Jewish, thanks to Shimeliovich.

Presiding Officer: Later, on page 144 of volume 2, you testify that Shimeliovich did a great deal to plant anti-Soviet attitudes among Jews, that he harped on the topic of anti-Semitism in the USSR, and that he spoke insultingly about certain people in the leadership of the Central Committee of the Party. Is this testimony of yours correct?

Fefer: When I spoke of sowing anti-Soviet attitudes, I meant Shimeliovich's nationalistic attitude. He said that there was anti-Semitism among certain groups, among doctors as well. Shtern spoke about this, too.

Presiding Officer: Shimeliovich was a friend of Mikhoels. Is it true, as you assert, that he was Mikhoels's number one consultant on issues having to do with nationalistic work at the committee?

Fefer: I have already said that I hardly ever met with Shimeliovich, but I do know that Mikhoels frequently said, "I must consult with Boris Abramovich," and when the letter about the Crimea had to be drafted, he asked Shimeliovich to do it.

[The next session of the Military Collegium of the USSR Supreme Court began at 12:25 P.M.]

Presiding Officer: So the issue of forming an army came up that long ago?

Fefer: The issue was not raised at the committee. We received a statement from Rogachevsky, who proposed forming a division that could be sent to Palestine to fight Arab domination.

Presiding Officer: But there were others who came to you with similar questions. Dragunsky also talked about this.

Fefer: Yes, Dragunsky talked about this. But it was not only Jews who were talking about it. Colonel Ivanov also came to us and said that he too wanted to go to Palestine. I told him that we did not handle these questions. Hofshteyn was among those people who were not happy with our passive stance on this issue. Hofshteyn had nationalistic sentiments. I should say that he was criticized more than anything else for nationalistic sentiments in his poetry. He was criticized for this in the Soviet Writers' Union of the Ukraine. Hofshteyn raised the issue of studying Hebrew.

Presiding Officer: Is the study of Hebrew one of the activities that is part of the struggle against assimilation of the Jews?

Fefer: Hebrew is hardly used today. It is a return to old values, the language of the Bible. People speak it in Palestine. And Hofshteyn did have pro-Zionist sentiments.

Presiding Officer: Did you ever have occasion to discuss nationalistic issues with him?

Fefer: We did not talk about nationalistic issues. We talked about the closing of schools. But in the summer of 1948, Hofshteyn was at the committee. He was very worked up and he attacked me, reproaching me that I was a coward, that I lacked courage. He was very unhappy that the committee was not involved in the founding of the State of Israel and the fight against the Arab countries. At the time, a lot of Jewish students were coming to us and expressing their dissatisfaction with our passive stance. But we could really do nothing without the approval of the organs that were above us. Hofshteyn, having the sentiments that he did, joined with these people and said that we were passive, that we weren't doing anything. At that time, he published a small volume of his poems in which he wrote an inscription expressing his displeasure at our passive stance and the fact that we were not helping the fighting Jewish army.

Presiding Officer: Let's go back once again to the Jewish Theater. It seems that during his last years Mikhoels produced many nationalistic plays.

Fefer: He produced a number of plays.

Presiding Officer: He told you that the theater was a platform that could be used for nonstop nationalistic propaganda, did he not?

Fefer: He did. He said that the theater is one of the main tools for drawing Jews closer to Yiddish culture.

Presiding Officer: Testify about the committee's ties with the rabbinate in Moscow and in America.

Fefer: When we were in America, representatives of the rabbinate paid a call on us. Rabbi Einstein and two other people. They asked to be in touch with the Moscow community. At the time, they were speaking at rallies. We promised to help them establish ties with the Moscow religious community. In Moscow we talked with Shlifer and Chobrutsky,* representatives of the rabbinate, and brought them a letter from America. Chobrutsky said that he would raise the issue of establishing ties with the Moscow City Council.

---

*Solomon Shlifer (1889–1957) was appointed Rabbi of Moscow during the war and became a member of the JAC. He was then appointed head of the Jewish religious community in Moscow in 1946 and served in this capacity until his death. Samuil Chobrutsky was a rabbi and head of the Moscow Jewish community.

Presiding Officer: What was the purpose of getting mixed up in that? Did they come to you at the committee about these issues?

Fefer: Chobrutsky and Shlifer were in particularly close touch with Mikhoels. Shlifer contacted Mikhoels, and the latter helped him edit the text of a speech he gave at a rally, which was subsequently published in *Pravda.*

Presiding Officer: Did Shlifer ask you for anything?

Fefer: Yes, he came to us about the literature we were receiving in large quantities from countries all over the world. And we ourselves often contacted Shlifer and other rabbis.

Presiding Officer: And did you visit the rabbi's office yourselves?

Fefer: I was in the synagogue three or four times. The first time was on March 14, 1945,* and the second time was with Novick. Then Bergelson and I went to a concert at which Alexandrovich† sang religious songs. And I was also in a synagogue in connection with a play I was writing about 1917.

Presiding Officer: Shlifer came to see you about other issues. Didn't he consult the committee about holding a reception for Meyerson's delegation at the synagogue?

Fefer: He came to me about that, but I referred him to Molotov at the Foreign Ministry.

[Fefer's testimony, during which he pled guilty in full to all of the accusations presented to him by the investigators, began on the first day of the trial, May 8, and continued through the entire morning session of May 9. Fefer was the primary figure in the prosecution's case, and therefore the trial organizers wanted his testimony to set the tone for the entire proceedings and break the will of the other defendants. But once Fefer's testimony came to an end, the others had the opportunity to ask him questions.]

Presiding Officer: Which of the defendants has questions for Fefer?

Lozovsky: I do. On August 1, 1946, all of the anti-fascist committees were removed from the supervision of the Sovinformburo system. During the twenty-nine months until the Jewish Anti-Fascist Committee was shut down, who directed the committee?

Fefer: After the committee was removed from the Sovinformburo, the com-

---

*The memorial meeting for victims of the Holocaust was held at Moscow's Choral Synagogue on March 14, 1945, in response to a call by rabbis in Jerusalem for such services to be held by Jewish communities around the world. Stalin permitted the service and publicity about it for propagandistic purposes. A similar service was permitted in 1946, but in following years, the service was prohibited.

†Mikhail Alexandrovich (1914–2002) was a popular singer who also performed as a cantor in the Soviet Union. He emigrated from the Soviet Union in 1971. See his memoirs *Ya Pomnyu* (I Remember) (Moscow, 1992), pp. 138–140, for his description of the 1945 service.

mittee was run by the Foreign Relations Department of the Central Committee of the Party.

Lozovsky: There is no such department. There is a Foreign Policy Department.

Fefer: That may well be. Suslov supervised the committee directly, and then Baranov.

Lozovsky: And not Ponomarev?

Fefer: No, he was earlier. Then Panyushkin* ran it.

Lozovsky: Who gave you permission to spend forty thousand rubles on the banquet for Novick?

Fefer: Well, I wasn't involved in any of that. Nikitin was the one who oversaw the administrative side of things for all the committees. He drew up the estimates and wrote the reports on those things and coordinated all of it with the Foreign Policy Department of the Central Committee of the Party.

Lozovsky: The investigation materials state that Suslov gave his permission. Is this true?

Fefer: I don't know whether he gave permission or not, but Suslov did give permission for Novick's trip to the Ukraine.

Lozovsky: Who gave the money, confirmed the staff, appointed the editors, and ran the newspaper *Eynikayt?* Did the Sovinformburo and I personally have anything to do with it?

Fefer: No, the newspaper was managed independently. It was the committee organ—formally speaking, that is—but in fact it was under the Central Committee Press Department. The outline for each issue of the newspaper was sent to the Central Committee department. The staff was confirmed there, and expenditures were approved. In everything having to do with control, it was run on the one hand by Glavlit and on the other by the Press Department of the Central Committee of the Party.

Lozovsky: Did I have anything to do with this newspaper?

Fefer: No, you did not.

Lozovsky: Did you and Mikhoels ever mention to me that the U.S. government was interested in a plan to settle Jews in the Crimea and that it was promising to provide aid to Jews in order to create a beachhead there?

---

*Leonid Baranov (1909–1953) was a party official who served as deputy head of the Foreign Policy Department of the Central Committee in the late 1940s. Boris Ponomarev (b. 1905) was a veteran party official who served within the Foreign Policy Department in 1944–1946 and again in 1948; he was also a leader of the Sovinformburo from 1947 to 1949. Alexander Panyushkin (1905–1974) served as deputy head of the Foreign Policy Department between 1944 and 1947, then as ambassador to Washington from 1947 to 1952. Members of the JAC were receiving directions from these party bureaucrats.

Fefer: I have given very detailed testimony about that question. If I had said such a thing to Lozovsky, then I would have testified to that effect during the preliminary investigation and in court.

Lozovsky: In his testimony Fefer stated that before his trip to the United States, he and Mikhoels visited Shcherbakov in Moscow and he gave them instructions. I would ask him to repeat the instructions they received from Shcherbakov, and I would ask if there were any contradictions between Shcherbakov's instructions and mine. And second, did I not tell them that when they addressed large audiences in the United States, they should emphasize that the Soviet Union had saved hundreds of thousands of people from the Hitlerite thugs and that they should insist on the need to open a second front, which was not being opened?

Fefer: I did not want to recall that . . .

Presiding Officer (interrupting Fefer): Lozovsky is asking whether there were inconsistencies between his directives and those given by Shcherbakov, and if there were, what were they.

Fefer: I remember now. I remember that Shcherbakov spoke of the need to place materials in the American Jewish press to broaden the audience for our services. Shcherbakov's and Lozovsky's instructions about material aid were consistent with each other. Shcherbakov focused more on the need to carry out propaganda about heroic actions performed by the people of the Soviet Union and about the Soviet Union's role in the war against fascist Germany. Lozovsky told us that we should emphasize this because in America even at that late date people did not believe that fascist atrocities had really taken place. He said that we must definitely talk about that and that we should also talk about how the Soviet Union had saved many Jews. I don't remember anything about a second front. To the contrary, Shcherbakov told us that we shouldn't say anything about a second front, because we might be deported from America.

[There followed a series of questions about Mikhoels and Fefer's trip to the United States and the visit made to the Soviet Union by the prominent American journalist B. Z. Goldberg in 1946. From Fefer's responses, it became clear that the instructions that Shcherbakov had given the Jewish Anti-Fascist Committee delegation coincided for the most part with Lozovsky's guidelines on the same subject. Fefer was unable to point to any facts indicating Lozovsky's alleged special relationship with Goldberg.]

Lozovsky: I heard that in his testimony Fefer spoke of how, after their return from the United States, they visited Molotov and discussed the Volga Germans' territory or the Crimea as possible sites for relocating Jews. Molotov supposedly replied that nothing would come of the Volga Germans' territory, but as for the Crimea, [he said] write something and we will discuss it. Is this correct?

Fefer: Yes, that's correct.

Lozovsky: Did you inform the investigation of this?

Fefer: No.

Member of the Collegium: On page 286 of volume 2, you testify that "In 1948, in connection with the founding of the State of Israel, the committee was faced with new problems. The committee was now besieged with endless phone calls and visits. Lozovsky called me several times, wanting to clarify what was happening." And further on: "For me, the founding of the Jewish state was an important, joyful occasion." What is the connection between your personal joy and Lozovsky's phone calls?

Fefer: Everything was as I have testified. In the summer of 1948 people came to us and wanted to know about this question. Lozovsky called me at home. Presidium members were in an uproar at the Jewish Anti-Fascist Committee over this. Several of them reproached us for cowardice when it came to our dealings with the State of Israel. Lozovsky asked me what was going on, and I explained it to him.

The Jewish Anti-Fascist Committee had evaluated this event just as Gromyko did. We were in complete agreement with Gromyko. There were no Zionists among us. Kheifets kept a list of everyone who came to the committee; he was assigned to do that. People really did come with various proposals—for example, there was a proposal to create a Jewish division, and we referred everyone to the Foreign Ministry.

Member of the Court: You said that the founding of the Jewish state was a joyous occasion for you. Is that correct?

Fefer: Yes, that is correct. I rejoiced at this event, that the Jews, exiled from Palestine by Mussolini's ancestors, had created a Jewish state there once again.

Shimeliovich: You testified to the effect that the nearest point of support that we had was the newspaper *Eynikayt,* which became a nationalistic platform. Tell us, during the entire period of the newspaper's existence, about seven to eight years, can you say whether even a single article of mine was published there?

Fefer: No, Shimeliovich's articles were not published in the newspaper.

Shimeliovich: In your testimony about the Crimea you say that upon your return, you and Mikhoels put together a memorandum about the Crimea, and after consulting and getting Lozovsky's approval, you sent this memorandum to Molotov. You said this at the witness confrontation. Is this correct?

Fefer: Yes, we sent the report not only to Molotov but to Stalin as well.

Shimeliovich: At the witness confrontation you said that Mikhoels was supposed to have informed me about what was in this memorandum. In the second part of your testimony you say that you, Mikhoels, and Epshteyn drew up a memorandum about the Crimea and discussed it at Nusinov's* apartment, with Shimeliovich present, and after that you sent it to the government. Did we ever discuss the Crimea memorandum that was sent to the government?

Fefer: We never met in any private apartments. We had a perfectly good committee building where we discussed everything. At the same time as our memorandum, Shimeliovich was also assigned by Mikhoels to draft a memorandum about settling Jews in the Crimea. He presented this memorandum. This question was not discussed at the presidium, but the presidium members knew what was going on in this regard.

Shimeliovich: In your testimony it says that Zhemchuzhina was at Mikhoels's funeral for six hours. And she allegedly expressed her ideas about his death, which you shared with me. I would like to ask you whether you ever told me anything about this and whether you pointed her out to me at the funeral?

Fefer: I don't remember giving such testimony. I have no recollection of that.

Shimeliovich: Yesterday in answer to the presiding officer's question about your testimony concerning Botkin Hospital, which I had the honor of managing for eighteen years, you said that among its more than three thousand employees, there were almost no non-Jews, and you said that Mikhoels told you this. In another part of your testimony it says that 50 percent of the employees at Botkin Hospital were Jews. Fifty percent and almost no non-Jewish employees whatsoever are completely different things. What are you basing your comments on, and which version do you stick to?

Fefer: I do not know whether it was 99 percent or 48.5 percent. It's hard for me to say. But yesterday I said that Mikhoels told a small group of people whom he knew well that there were quite a fair number of Jews at the hospital and that Shimeliovich made sure that this was the case and that he had a well-known hiring bias.

Shimeliovich: When you spoke of me yesterday as a nationalist, in answer to a question from the presiding officer, you said that I had verbally attacked Party and government leaders for anti-Semitism. You noted that you could recall only one case of this. That was in late 1947, when Mikhoels was not nominated to the Moscow City Council and I allegedly said that Popov was responsible and that it was a manifestation of anti-Semitism. I would like to ask if you heard this from me. Was I the one who said this to you, or was it someone else?

Fefer: I remember that Shimeliovich spoke of this at the committee some time

---

*Yitzhak Nusinov (1889–1950) was a Yiddish and Russian literary scholar. A member of the JAC during and after the war, he died in prison in the fall of 1950.

after it happened. He said that this was Popov's doing and that he apparently was not amicably disposed toward Mikhoels.

[Bregman raised the issue of the publication of *The Black Book*.]

Bregman: On page 29 in paragraph 1 of the indictment it says that Bregman participated with you on the editorial board of *The Black Book*. Was I involved in compiling *The Black Book*?

Fefer: Well, Bregman did not collect materials. There were staff members who did that. And when the material had been collected and Lozovsky requested that it be sent to the Sovinformburo, an editorial board was assembled, with Bregman as the chairman, while Grossman, Ehrenburg, Borodin,* and others were members. After the material was looked over, Bregman had some objections based purely on considerations of quality, but there was no objection to publishing *The Black Book*.

Kvitko: I have a question for Fefer. Did he brief me personally about his conversation with Rosenberg and Levin regarding the Crimea?

Fefer: I did not personally brief Kvitko about conversations with Rosenberg and Levin. But there were many discussions about it at the committee. There were discussions about how the Joint had promised to provide material support if Jews were settled in the Crimea, but I personally did not talk to Kvitko about it.

Kvitko (to Fefer): You testified that you used materials from Nusinov and Kvitko's trip to draft the letters to the government. What trip and what letters were you referring to?

Fefer: I was referring to the trip that Kvitko made to the Crimea to study the situation of Jewish collective farm workers and their reevacuation. And then after Kvitko gave his report, a letter was drafted at a meeting of the presidium for Andreyev's attention. Nusinov did not go to the Crimea. He went to the Ukraine, and he also brought back material about the difficult conditions in which Jews were living in the Ukraine. The question of job placement for Jews came up, as did questions of getting residency permits after they returned from reevacuation and the economic difficulties that Jews returning from the ghetto faced. These materials went into the letter that Mikhoels and Epshteyn sent to the government.

Presiding Officer (to Fefer): Wasn't this trip linked to the problem that had been raised, as an opportunity to gather preliminary materials to frame the question of settling the Crimea?

---

*Mikhail (Grunzenberg) Borodin (1884–1951), a Soviet diplomat and editor, was a member of the Bund before joining the Bolsheviks in 1903. He lived in the United States from 1907 to 1918. After the Bolshevik takeover, Borodin became an important figure in the Commissariat of Foreign Affairs. He served as ambassador to Mexico and then, from 1923 to 1927, served as Soviet adviser to the Guomindang in China. He was chief editor at the Sovinformburo from 1941 to 1949. Arrested in 1949, he died in prison in 1951.

Fefer: Epshteyn said that since the letter had been delivered to the government, it would be good to know what was actually taking place there.

Presiding Officer: But when Kvitko came back, did he not say that there was in fact a possibility of settling Jews in the Crimea?

Fefer: Yes, he said that there was a lot of land lying empty and that there were many letters from which it was clear that Jews who had previously lived in the Crimea wanted to return there from evacuation.

Kvitko: Why did Fefer testify that since we were unable to sell the Americans on the idea of a Jewish republic, we decided to replace that with information about the Crimea? And that I was sent there for that purpose? In the transcripts of one of the Jewish Anti-Fascist Committee sessions, it says that after the Crimea and other places (the Ukraine) were liberated from the fascists, it was decided to send a team of writers, including Dobruzhsky [Dobrushin],* Kvitko, Nusinov, and others, to the Ukraine to study the state of affairs after the fascist invasion.

Fefer: Epshteyn spoke about Kvitko's trip at the Jewish Anti-Fascist Committee presidium. Kvitko went in order to write some articles that would tell American readers about the return of evacuated Jewish collective farm workers to the Crimea, as there had been requests from American newspapers wanting to know about this. I don't know whether Epshteyn told Kvitko about this or not, but either way, this material was intended for dispatch to America, since the Americans were interested in it.

Presiding Officer: Do you have any more questions?

Kvitko: Yes. Who helped Goldberg come to the USSR and insisted on his coming? Who apart from Jewish Anti-Fascist Committee presidium members Fefer and Mikhoels helped this lowlife come here completely at the people's expense? Who of all the Jewish writers and activists knew Goldberg best and was closest to him? Who was it who was constantly praising him to the skies and extolling him as the best friend of the Soviet Union?

Fefer: Goldberg did not come to the Soviet Union at the invitation of the Jewish Anti-Fascist Committee. He came to the Soviet Union on a trip organized by his newspaper, not the Jewish Anti-Fascist Committee. While we were in America, Kisselev, the Soviet consul, recommended him as a friend of the Soviet Union and helped him get a visa. He gave Goldberg the right to enter the Soviet Union.

Kvitko (to Fefer): Why didn't you tell the presidium members that the committee supported the idea of publishing *The Black Book,* and why didn't you tell them about the book's publication abroad? What was your purpose in hiding this?

---

*Yekhezkel Dobrushin (1883–1953) was a prominent Yiddish literary critic and playwright. He was on the editorial board of *Eynikayt* and was arrested in 1949.

Fefer: All of the presidium members knew what was going on, as this question had been discussed several times. Everyone knew that such a book was supposed to come out.

Presiding Officer: How many copies were sent to the Jewish Anti-Fascist Committee?

Fefer: As far as I can remember, one of the Jewish Anti-Fascist Committee responsibilities was to collect materials for *The Black Book* about fascist atrocities committed against the civilian population. All of the correspondents who traveled to the former occupied areas were assigned to do this. Everyone knew that *The Black Book* was coming out. Then we received ten copies. I remember there were copies for Lozovsky, Shtern, Shimeliovich, Yuzefovich, Mikhoels, and Bergelson.

Presiding Officer: Did these books come straight from America?

Fefer: Yes. The books were in English, and they were sent to the Jewish Anti-Fascist Committee to the attention of these people. It may be that none was sent to Kvitko. That is why he says that he did not know the book had been printed.

Vatenberg (to Fefer): You testified that Novick was interested in information about Botkin Hospital. Are you aware that his interest in Botkin Hospital stemmed from the fact that he had had pneumonia and was treated at that hospital?

Fefer: Yes.

Vatenberg (to Fefer): Did you say that Vatenberg-Ostrovskaya glorified American living standards and slandered Soviet reality?

Fefer: She said that the clothing there was better and that there were more amenities there.

Vatenberg: And what did she say about Soviet life?

Fefer: She said that things were poorer here.

Presiding Officer: Did Vatenberg-Ostrovskaya condemn the existing order and the political structure of the USSR, or did she just say that the clothing was better in America?

Fefer: She didn't say anything against the Soviet form of government. She did not tell me what her attitudes were.

Presiding Officer: (reads out testimony, vol. 2, p. 307): Fefer, you testify that Markish stated his nationalistic views openly at the Jewish Anti-Fascist Committee plenums and in conversations with Mikhoels, Epshteyn, and you. Is this testimony of yours correct, and what specifically did Markish say?

Fefer: The testimony is correct. Markish spoke about the difficult situation in which the Jews found themselves; he said that they needed help and that the committee should fight the oppression of the Jews that was allegedly taking place. These statements of his outraged people, and Bregman responded, stating that he (Markish) would not succeed in transforming the Jewish Anti-Fascist Committee into a hotbed of anti-Soviet attitudes.

Markish (to Fefer): What does a Western orientation mean?

Fefer: A Western orientation means friendship with foreign writers and poets. It means leaving the Soviet Union for the West, where Markish spent several years. It means a yearning to learn from bourgeois writers and poets.

Markish: Did Fefer read two things that I wrote in the twenties in which I say that we Soviet writers have nothing to learn from Western European literature because it has gotten stranded in the bedroom?

Fefer: I don't remember that.

Presiding Officer: Shtern, do you have a question?

Shtern (to Fefer): I wanted to ask, what was the basis for considering me an active nationalist?

Fefer: She was not considered an active nationalist, and I did not say that. I said that Shtern made nationalistic remarks and speeches at the presidium. All of this was covered in detail at our witness confrontation. All that I could say about her I already said yesterday. I have no new information whatsoever.

Shtern (to Fefer): What were the grounds for making me a member of the Jewish Anti-Fascist Committee presidium in 1942?

Fefer: I don't know. Mikhoels and Epshteyn did that; they were the ones who invited Shtern to join.

Shtern (to Fefer): The indictment says that I was made a member of the Jewish Anti-Fascist Committee because I was a nationalist, but the case materials contain no specific information about that.

Fefer: I never gave testimony about that. The investigative agencies drew these conclusions. I did not.

[At the end of the second day of the trial, on May 9 at 8:45 P.M., Teumin's testimony began. It lasted until 2:10 P.M. the next day.]

EMILIA TEUMIN

Emilia Teumin was the youngest of the defendants. She was born in Bern, Switzerland, in 1905. Her parents had fled tsarist Russia as political émigrés—her father was an active leader of the Bund until he joined the Communist Party in 1920, whereas her mother had always been more oriented toward the Bolsheviks. In 1905, following the birth of Emilia, they all returned to Russia. Teumin herself joined the Communist Party in 1927 and worked as an editor.

Teumin's role at the committee was extremely limited. She was formally an employee of the Sovinformburo, working with Lozovsky as a contact to all five anti-fascist committees, helping them with organizational matters. She was also responsible for following developments in the Baltic region, which led to her contact with B. Z. Goldberg in 1946; Lozovsky asked her to prepare material for Goldberg about the situation in the region. In addition, Teumin helped Lozovsky edit the *Diplomatic Dictionary,* working closely with him for eight years, from 1941 until her arrest in 1949.

Presiding Officer: Defendant Teumin, in answer to the court's question about whether you understood the accusation presented to you, and whether you plead guilty, you stated that you plead guilty. Testify to the court about your crimes.

Teumin: I was born in 1905 in Switzerland, where my parents had emigrated. I have said that my father was a Bundist and a victim of repressions. After this he left for Switzerland, where he studied at a university. My mother was a seamstress and an orphan. In her youth she was an "Iskrovka."* She was arrested during a May Day demonstration, did time in prison, and became seriously ill while there, going through the early stages of tuberculosis. Her relatives gave her some money, and she went to Switzerland for treatment, where she met my father and they got married. I was born there in 1905, and in the same year my parents returned to Russia, and I went with them. I have not been abroad since then. My father died in 1936. In 1920 he joined the Communist Party. He was a chemist and director of a concern called Gazoochistka. While a member of the Communist Party, he continued to associate with Bundists, specifically with Weinstein, Frumkin, and Levin. I feel that my father retained something from his Bundist period until the very end. I once spoke with Weinstein. I told him that he had been, was, and would remain a Menshevik and a social democrat. He made a fuss and told my father he would not come to see us any more until my father set me straight. My father was a passionate chess player and would latch onto anyone who could play chess with him. Once Mikhoels visited us, and he played with my father. Then I saw him perform at the Jewish Theater, and then I met him in 1941, when he came to Kuibyshev.

Presiding Officer: You testified during the preliminary investigation that Mikhoels expressed his thoughts to you, did you not?

Teumin: In 1941 I worked at the Sovinformburo, and one of my responsibili-

---

*Iskrovka was a Bolshevik (woman) volunteer who helped to distribute copies of Lenin's newspaper *Iskra* (The Spark).

ties was to help set up all of the anti-fascist committees, including the Jewish one. Lozovsky summoned Mikhoels to Kuibyshev to chair the committee. I spoke to him several times there, then I left for Moscow and had nothing more to do with the Jewish Anti-Fascist Committee until they came to Moscow to plan their second rally. Then I was assigned to handle organizational matters for the event. I was not allowed to edit materials for the rally; Mikhoels took care of that. I was responsible for providing typists, keeping track of the agenda, and making sure that there were hotel rooms for the participants.

During the preparation for the rally Mikhoels happened to express his nationalistic views to me. He talked about the difficult situation the Jews faced in the USSR, about ongoing discrimination in hiring, and said that in Tashkent many Jewish evacuees were in very difficult straits and that the government was not doing enough to fight anti-Semitism. Instead of responding to him, I kept silent. I am guilty of that.

Presiding Officer: But did he implicate the Soviet government in this?

Teumin: He said that the Soviet government was not paying enough attention to the issue, and I neither agreed nor disagreed, but just kept silent. This was the first example of nationalism on my part.

Presiding Officer: As for creating a territory for the Jews, did he say that the Jews should be together?

Teumin: Yes, he did say that. I feel that the second example of nationalism on my part came in 1942–1943, when Fefer expressed to me approximately the same views as Mikhoels had and again I did not respond. I kept silent.

Presiding Officer: During the preliminary investigation, you, Teumin, testified (vol. 24, p. 52): "In conversations with me Fefer spoke of the supposedly unfair treatment Jews were receiving in the Soviet Union and accused the Soviet government of supposedly encouraging anti-Semitism. He spoke of the need for Jews to unite to struggle for their independence. I supported Fefer, and thus, a criminal tie grew up between us."

Is this testimony correct?

Teumin: I feel that I supported Fefer because I was silent instead of rebuking him. I was poisoned with bourgeois nationalism, and since I responded to these conversations with silence, that means that I supported him. Once, Fefer told me that the committee was planning to raise with the government the question of founding a republic in the Crimea. I asked him why in the Crimea of all places, and he answered jokingly that the climate there was good. Then I ran into him and Mikhoels in Lozovsky's office on one occasion. They were very excited, and when I asked them what was going on, they told me that their Crimea plan was being studied by "higher-ups," that it seemed to be getting support, and that things were going well. This was after they got back from America. When they got back from America, they gave a report at the Sovinformburo at which they told about the success of their speeches over there. The table was covered with piles of newspaper clippings.

Presiding Officer: Did someone go through the other committees' mail?

Teumin: We did not really have any censorship per se until the decision in 1946. During the first years that the committees were operating, the materials were looked through and checked over in Moscow by the Sovinformburo senior secretary—first Kruzhkov, then Kondakov, and then Kalmykov.

Presiding Officer: How could Kruzhkov look through all the mail himself?

Teumin: We actually had two committees, in effect—the women's committee and the youth committee—that sent articles abroad, and at that time the articles were sent in very small numbers, five or six a month.

Presiding Officer: Are you saying that you had nothing to do with correcting Jewish Anti-Fascist Committee articles?

Teumin: I think that this is apparent from the case materials as well. There are Jewish Anti-Fascist Committee employees here in this room who can tell you what my connection was to them.

Second question. In the fourth count of the accusation there is a list of names, including mine, and it says that I was actively involved in nationalistic propaganda. I never engaged in any propaganda work and was myself the target of such propaganda. This was the manifestation of my nationalism, and for this I should be punished. I subsequently rid myself of these nationalistic sentiments, but the fact that I did not rebuke him for these nationalistic remarks means that I became a co-conspirator of nationalists. I am guilty.

It was easy for me to convey information about the Baltic republics to Goldberg. Fefer rose to my defense and stated that I had given him no more than three or four articles. This is not true. I gave some information in two or three pages. But the point is not whether it was three pages or thirty. What matters is that I gave it at all. The information contained a short description of each of the three republics; that is, the main cities of these republics were listed, as well as the damage the Germans had caused, and there was information about how the economy and industry were being restored. This was in late 1945. It indicated how much land the peasants had received owing to land reform, along with information about the cultural and scientific achievements of these republics.

One fine day Fefer came to me, all excited, and said that a great friend of the Soviet Union had arrived—the American journalist Goldberg. He emphasized to me that this journalist and friend wanted to help expose the slanders about the Baltic republics that were being spread in the foreign press. I was interested in the Baltic republics, and I was concerned about the fact that there were a number of issues on which we could not present convincing responses to American reactionaries. Baltic legions were being formed in the United States, and those republics' gold reserves were being expended to support reactionary elements. Baltic reactionaries were now being repatriated to the United States from Germany. All of these circumstances reinforced reactionary activity. Then, as is well known, the U.S. government did not recognize these republics as part of the Soviet Union. These circumstances made me think about finding opportunities to tell the truth about these republics, but our opportunities were very limited. The only contacts we had were with communist newspapers, so I leapt at the chance to meet with a prominent American journalist who was a friend of the Soviet Union. Fefer told me that he was not a Communist Party member out of tactical considerations, but on his own he played a prominent role. I kept thinking that through him we could expose the reactionaries. Fefer said to me, "Let's go see Lozovsky. They'll tell you everything there."

Presiding Officer: Did you work at the Jewish Anti-Fascist Committee?

Teumin: No, except for during the preparations for one rally. My job was supposed to involve providing organizational help in Kuibyshev to all of the committees—the Slavic committee, the women's committee, the youth committee, and the Jewish committee. My responsibilities included all of them. I did this from November 1941 through April 1942. I was supposed to make sure that the rally participants were fed and housed in hotel rooms. Mikhoels edited the speeches for the rally and coordinated all of this with Lozovsky.

Presiding Officer: And through your work you were involved with the speeches given at the rallies.

Teumin: Not at all.

Member of the Court: But you were an editor, weren't you?

Teumin: This was the only committee where I didn't carry out editorial functions. Mikhoels was a good editor. He said that he could do a fine job himself and he didn't need any help.

Presiding Officer: During the preliminary investigation you described the Jewish Anti-Fascist Committee's activity as nationalistic and anti-Soviet, and you said that Lozovsky and Mikhoels had created this atmosphere at the committee.

Teumin: Here are some facts about nationalistic activity at the Jewish Anti-Fascist Committee. At one editorial meeting Epshteyn taught us how to prepare an article for the United States. For example, he said that if we were writing about an American company that had sent a gift of rubber heating pads to military hospitals, then it should be written in the following way. We should write about the heroism of a wounded Red Army soldier who was using an American heating pad and how the heating pad eased his suffering. And by all means we were to mention the name of the company that had sent the heating pads. So American businessmen were going to make deals over the blood of the Soviet people and we were supposed to thank them for it, bowing deeply as we did so.

Presiding Officer: Let's get back to the question of the description of the Anti-Fascist Committee and how Americans dealt in the blood of our fighting men.

Teumin: Here is what I heard from my former boss Severin, who was a member of the editorial commission for *The Black Book*. Supposedly there was a big argument between Ehrenburg and members of the Jewish Anti-Fascist Committee about *The Black Book*. I don't know whether Ehrenburg was a member of the Jewish Anti-Fascist Committee or not, but it seems that first they asked Ehrenburg to work on the book, and then the Jewish Anti-Fascist Committee began handling it on its own, even though Ehrenburg had been doing it. Ehrenburg felt that a different approach to the publication of *The Black Book* was required. He felt that the material gathered had to be serious and factual, that there should be Russian writers as well as Jewish ones involved, and that it must not be done carelessly. When he found out that the Jewish Anti-Fascist Committee was not only putting together its own *Black Book* but had also sent part of the materials to the United States, including his (Ehrenburg's) materials, an enormous brouhaha broke out. A commission was created to make sense of this conflict and decide whose material was better. I remember Severin telling me that he didn't like the Jewish Anti-Fascist Committee materials, and he talked to Lozovsky about it, but Lozovsky told him that the book had to be done and that the material had already been sent. But Severin didn't stand up for his point of view. And it was only here, during the investigation (I don't think that Severin knew this, either), that I found out that *The Black Book* was part of a larger *Black Book* that had been released in America. Those of us who were working at the Sovinformburo had, of course, heard of *The Black Book*, but we thought it was only about Soviet Jews.

Presiding Officer: What else have you to say to the court?

Teumin: I want to direct the court's attention to matters not yet covered here. On the day Kalinin died,* a banquet in Goldberg's honor was held at the Jewish Anti-Fascist Committee. I thought it was disgraceful to hold a banquet on such a day. When I found out about it, I went to Lozovsky and said that it was a disgrace—how could a banquet with drinking be held on a day of mourning?! Lozovsky said that everything had already been prepared at the committee and it would be hard to cancel now. On top of that, Goldberg was leaving the next day, so if there was no banquet today, then there wouldn't be any at all. The banquet was held, and people drank.

[This is the end of Teumin's testimony. On the same day, Saturday, May 10, at 2:35 P.M., the court started Markish's testimony. This session lasted until the end of the day on Saturday; court was recessed at 9:50 P.M.]

*Soviet President Mikhail Kalinin died on June 3, 1946.

PERETZ MARKISH

Born in the Ukrainian town of Polonnoye, Peretz Markish was raised in a strict religious home; his father was a Hebrew teacher, and Markish himself, who was blessed with a rich voice, sang in a synagogue choir until the age of thirteen. He served in the Russian army during World War I and in 1917 suffered so severe a concussion that at least one report circulated that he had been killed. Markish began writing poetry in Russian in 1910, but he did not publish his first poems in Yiddish until 1917, following his demobilization from the army. From then on, he was a vivid, often tempestuous presence in Yiddish cultural circles. With the end of the war and the Bolshevik takeover, Markish settled in Kiev. Ilya Ehrenburg met him there and decades later recalled "a handsome youth, with a great shock of hair that always stood on end and eyes that were both sarcastic and sad. Everyone called him a 'rebel,' and said that he was out to destroy the classics, to overthrow idols. But at our first meeting, I was reminded above all of an itinerant Jewish fiddler who plays melancholy songs at other men's weddings."[*]

Within Yiddish circles, Markish and David Bergelson were regarded as polar opposites, representing different styles of literature. Bergelson was the realist novelist, famous for his nuanced portrayals of life in small Jewish communities as they experienced the wrenching influences of modern life and severe social change. Markish, who made a name for himself as a poet, critic, and playwright, was the foremost representative of literary expressionism. In subsequent years, he was particularly famous for his long epic poems.

Markish left Soviet Russia in 1921 and for a time was associated with an unusual group of Yiddish writers in Warsaw who saw themselves as rebels. They bore the name Di khalyastre, or "The Gang." In their manifesto, which was written by Markish, they declared: "We measure [the quality of our literature], not by beauty, but by horror." Markish was "a young prophet" in the eyes of his Warsaw friends, "full of energy, . . . full of fears and sorrow over the pogroms" that had overwhelmed small Jewish towns throughout the Ukraine during the Russian Civil War. "He felt obliged to organize something all the time, to initiate something," his friend Melech Ravitch recalled.[†] Journals, public readings, literary conferences, sprang up around him.

[*]Ilya Ehrenburg, *People and Life, 1891–1921* (Cleveland, 1964), p. 321.
[†]Melech Ravitch, *Sefer Ha-Ma'asiyot Shel Chayai* (The Storybook of My Life) (Tel Aviv, 1976), pp. 422, 418–419.

The writer Zusman Segalovitsh thought of Markish as "the most popular poet in Poland, . . . sought after in the provinces with letters, telegrams, and special messengers." No other poet could rival Markish's appeal. "He was more passionate than all of us, he was handsome, and could he speak! The audience would be bewildered by this young poet and the girls all dreamed of this handsome young man. They listened to him with bated breath. His arrival in a shtetl was a holiday and a surprise, although after he left, a dispute used to break out among the listeners. One would ask the other. 'You understood something?' 'Nothing.' But it didn't matter. Markish was invited back two and three times."*

In spite of his fame in Poland, Markish could not restrain his restlessness, and over the next few years he traveled to Berlin, Paris, London, Vienna, Naples, and Palestine. "Still, I could not find a haven for myself," he explained to his interrogator a month after his arrest in 1949.†

Markish renewed his polemic with David Bergelson in 1926 following the publication of Bergelson's essay "Three Centers." This time they argued over politics and literature, Whereas Bergelson regarded the Soviet Union as the country with the broadest prospects for Yiddish culture, Markish publicly disagreed, in an article published in the Warsaw journal *Literarishe bleter* (Literary Pages). Markish's response was sarcastic and unrelenting. "Art does not grow out of political regrets," he asserted. "Kindly and intimately pinching the Comintern on the cheek does not count." As far as Markish was concerned, Bergelson was trying to atone for his years outside the country and outline "a metaphysical return route to Russia." The journal *In shpan* (In Step), Markish concluded, which was edited by Bergelson (and subsidized by the Comintern, according to rumor), "carries the distinct stamp of the new ideological dowry that Bergelson, it seems, has pledged to give to the Soviet Union."‡ But then Markish abruptly rejected his own arguments and made his way back, traveling through Kiev to Moscow. As the Yiddish literary scholar David Roskies explains it, Markish "was lured by the promise of a Yiddish cultural renaissance supported and funded by the government"§—an explanation eerily similar to Bergelson's conclusion in his essay "Three Centers."

---

*Zusman Segalovitsh, *Tlomackie 13* (Buenos Aires, 1946), p. 219.

†Interrogation record of Markish, February 21, 1949.

‡Peretz Markish, "Shpan-tsedek" (Step-Justice), *Literarishe bleter* (Literary Pages), no. 106, May 14, 1926, p. 317.

§David Roskies, foreword to Esther Markish, *The Long Return* (New York, 1978), p. x.

Markish's decision to return was influenced by several factors. His friends knew that he was drawn to Russian culture. "Pushkin and Mayakovsky raged within [his] throat," Melech Ravitch once remarked. Even after Markish reached Warsaw in 1921, he used to recklessly make frequent illegal trips across the Soviet border.* His travels and public renown notwithstanding, Markish could not break his ties to the Soviet Union.

In a memoir, Esther Markish portrays her husband as a sincere, enthusiastic supporter of the Bolsheviks. He "exalted the Soviet regime, not for personal gain or out of opportunism, but because it was his unshakable conviction that the regime had emancipated his people, had torn down the walls of the ghetto so that they, his people, could blossom anew and flourish in an atmosphere of freedom."† This may well have been his attitude when they first met in 1929. But Markish believed that he had received a hateful reception in the country in 1926, that "a whole wall" had grown between him and the leaders of Soviet Yiddish literature. "They nearly put me outside the camp of the organized Yiddish literary society of the Soviet Union," he said in a letter to Moshe Litvakov, who served as a kind of commissar for Yiddish culture. When Markish expressed a desire to leave again. Litvakov published a reply in *Der emes*, warning Markish that "you can go abroad, but be careful that at the end of your travels you don't come to us completely drained, because then you will find not a wall between us, but an abyss."‡

Within months after his return, Markish was already expressing disdain for Soviet attitudes. As he wrote to the Yiddish writer Joseph Opatoshu (whom Markish was encouraging to visit Moscow), "You don't have to wear a hat, red shoes, nor a red coat to come to us, because there already exists a word here, *khomchantsvo*, that means communist bragging, and we hate it here."§

By 1929, Markish was writing to another friend about his disappointment and his desire to leave the country if "they will let me go."** He tried to gain permission to visit Berlin and Danzig, to see friends in America. But he could not leave. Meanwhile, his work and his ability to

---

*Ravitch, *Sefer Ha-Ma'asiyot Shel Chayai*, pp. 425, 524.

†Markish, *Long Return*, p. 2.

‡Markish's letter to Litvakov and the latter's response can both be found in *Der emes*, December 23, 1926, p. 3.

§Mordechai Altshuler, ed., *Briv fun yidishe sovetishe shrayber* (Letters of Soviet Yiddish Writers) (Jerusalem, 1979), pp. 255–257. The letter is dated June 4, 1927.

**Ibid., p. 263. The letter is presumed to have been written in early 1929.

publish outside the country got him into trouble. Itsik Fefer, for one, roundly denounced Markish, calling his work "an attack on our Soviet reality." When Markish published a chapter of his epic poem "Not to Worry" in a Yiddish literary journal in Warsaw, under tremendous pressure for the "sin" of publishing in Poland, he had to write a letter of regret.* As Stalin consolidated control of the country, censorship and access to Central and Western Europe were tightening considerably. In 1929, three major Soviet writers—Boris Pilnyak, Yevgeny Zamyatin, and Ilya Ehrenburg—were castigated for publishing different versions of their novels in Soviet and Western editions. Yiddish writers like Markish, who had an enthusiastic following in the West, would now be able to reach their readers only through Soviet editions of their work.

From the early 1930s until his arrest in January 1949, Peretz Markish assumed the role of an honored and obedient Soviet writer. His plays were produced by the State Jewish Theater; he wrote a screenplay for the movie *The Return of Nathan Becker,* in which Mikhoels starred. He could even insist to Melech Ravitch—in a letter on January 18, 1932— that Ravitch should "come to us, to the Soviet Union, to warm your bones and to refresh our 'aleph-bet.' Here, in any event, it is better than any other place on earth! Better, better, better—Ravitch." But when Ravitch had the unexpected chance to visit Moscow for two days in 1935, he saw for himself how careful Markish was not to be alone with him, a foreign Jew from Poland. Ravitch felt uneasy for his friend. "Each additional moment that I spent with Markish shortens his life by a day" was how Ravitch imagined their time together.[†]

Outwardly, Markish enjoyed the regime's favor throughout the 1930s. In 1934, at the conclusion of the first Soviet Writers' Congress, he was elected head of the Inspection Committee of the union's Yiddish section, a special section for Yiddish writers (Jewish writers who wrote in Russian, like Ehrenburg and Babel, were members of the general union itself).

The same year, Markish visited Birobidzhan. Esther Markish recalls that her husband was always skeptical about Birobidzhan and any pros-

---

*Itsik Fefer, *Di royte velt,* nos. 8–9, November–December 1928, pp. 116–117; Altshuler, *Briv fun yidishe sovetishe shrayber,* p. 244; *Literaturnaya Gazeta,* August 26, 1929, p. 1. A chapter of Markish's long poem *Nit gedayget* (Not to Worry) appeared in the Warsaw journal *Literarishe bleter* on May, 11, 1928. He was then rebuked in *Prolit* (Proletarian Literature), no. 3, June 1928, p. 42.

†Ravitch, *Sefer Ha-Ma'asiyot Shel Chayai,* pp. 545, 538.

pect that it could serve as a legitimate region for Jewish settlement. According to her account, his trip there in 1934 with a group of Jewish writers confirmed his beliefs. "He came back disheartened and disillusioned."* This may well have been true, but publicly Markish lauded Birobidzhan, as in these verses from a poem in 1935:

> The houses are going up
> On the first little streets, on the sprouting alleyways,
> And a struggle with ancient times for every stride.
> But when the call goes out
> To build and to make a republic,
> The Name is proudly proclaimed—Biro-bidzhan.†

Three years later, Markish repeated these sentiments in an essay for the New York journal *Nailebn* (New Life), published by ICOR, the Association for Jewish Colonization in the Soviet Union: "And the Jewish people, which had dreamed for centuries of the "promised land," of the cherished fatherland, have found their fatherland within the borders of the great Soviet Union. Perhaps the brightest chapter in the life of the Jews residing in the Land of the Soviets has been the formation of the Birobidjan Jewish Autonomous Province on the vast expanses of rich Far Eastern Territory."‡

Markish knew what was expected of him. In January 1937, during the second famous purge trial, in which Karl Radek and Gregory Pyatakov were the star defendants, Markish contributed a short poem to *Literaturnaya Gazeta* (Literary Gazette) denouncing the accused. Markish's poem appeared on the same page as similar brief statements by Fefer and Bergelson and contained the kind of rhetoric that was standard fare for those years.

> the obscurity of night will not
> conceal their shame
> because their faces are blacker
> than darkness itself.

---

*Markish, *Long Return*, p. 34.

†Peretz Markish, "A People Is Coming to You, Taiga, to Become Young," *Nailebn* (New Life), June 1935, pp. 14–15.

‡Peretz Markish, "Jewish People Have Found Their Fatherland," *Nailebn*, December 1938, p. 11.

It concludes:

> Not a drop of mercy to this rabid
> pack of wolves;
> Let them die! Not one should be spared!*

What are we to make of this? Was Markish simply giving the regime what it expected, knowing that Radek and the others were innocent? Or did he believe, as a sincere and convinced Soviet patriot, that Stalin and the party were always right, that if the defendants were accused of terrible crimes in a Soviet court (including the preposterous charges of terrorism, wrecking, and espionage on behalf of Germany and Japan) and then offered public confessions, they must in fact be guilty and deserved the punishment in store for them? Of course, Markish, Bergelson, and Fefer—and hundreds of others who participated in such denunciations—never imagined that they would someday be in the dock facing an indictment no less absurd and a fate no less terrible. Or perhaps they did, but their obedience did not save them.

The regime, in turn, knew how to reward and manipulate its loyal servants. The Markish family lived in a spacious apartment in a building where other writers and foreign journalists resided. And in 1939, just two years after a massive purge of party figures, intellectuals, military officers, and others (including many Yiddish writers), Markish was awarded the prestigious Order of Lenin, the only Yiddish writer to be so honored.

But at least some of his colleagues sensed a profound tension in Markish's life and work. In 1944 he saw the poet Abraham Sutzkever in Vilna shortly after its liberation. Sutzkever observed that for Markish and the other Yiddish writers, "deep in their hearts . . . they knew that the time did not belong to them." Government policies kept changing, and "fear of an unclear tomorrow continually compelled Markish to erase the uncertain and write in a manner that would please the rulers."†

Markish, however, could not entirely constrain his heartfelt feelings as a Jew. At a memorial gathering held by Polish Jews in Moscow after the war, Itsik Fefer observed that the occasion demonstrated "the friendship of the Jewish peoples." Markish immediately rebuked him. "There are

---

*Literaturnaya Gazeta, February 1, 1937, p. 5.

†Nora Levin, The Jews in the Soviet Union Since 1917, vol. 2 (New York, 1988), p. 906 n. 86.

not two Jewish peoples," Markish declared. "The Jewish nation is one. Just as a heart cannot be cut up and divided, so one cannot split up the Jewish people into Polish Jews and Russian Jews. Everywhere we are, and shall remain, one entity."*

Such pronouncements were rare. Markish dared not forget where he was living or what was required of him. As late as February 1946, when anti-Semitic restrictions were growing ever more pronounced, Markish wrote the following about Stalin: "Every word of Comrade Stalin's speech breathed with wisdom and tranquility. All over again, we saw how he furthered science, labor, the people's enthusiasm in the prewar years and during the war; how he made fate itself serve the interests of the nation; how he commanded fronts on the vast spaces of the earth."†

Such obsequious phrases did not save Markish.

Presiding Officer: Defendant Markish, testify to the court as to your guilt.

Markish: I do not plead guilty to anything, but I acknowledge certain mistakes.

[After that statement Markish told the court about his childhood and adolescence, about his family, about the difficulties that he had encountered when he embarked on his creative path, and about the complicated relationships he had at that time with Bergelson, Hofshteyn, and Kvitko. The court, in turn, had an understanding of Markish's biography and tried to establish the accuracy of the investigative conclusions that Markish was dedicated to Jewish nationalism from an early age and hated Soviet power. From this the goals of Markish's foreign trips in the twenties and the time he spent living abroad became clear. The court studied in detail the activity of the Yiddish Section of the Soviet Writers' Union, in large part because of Markish's extensive remarks. The chairman and presiding officer, Cheptsov, took him to task, declaring, "Much of what you are saying is superfluous." Markish strove to emphasize that the writers seated with him on the defendants' bench were his longtime opponents who had spoken out against him on every issue that arose. Markish stated, "Whenever there was any kind of skirmish at the Jewish Anti-Fascist Committee, they did everything they could to discredit me in the eyes of the party bureau, just as Fefer is now doing before the court" (vol. 1, p. 146). Not until the second day of Markish's questioning, Monday, May 12, at 12:25 P.M., did the court move on to matters related to the Jewish Anti-Fas-

---

*Yitzhak Yanasovich, *Mit yidishe shrayber in rusland* (With Jewish Writers in Russia) (Buenos Aires, 1959), p. 316, cited in Gilboa, *Black Years,* p. 130.

†*Literaturnaya Gazeta,* February 10, 1946, p. 3.

cist Committee. The chairman read out Markish's testimony from the preliminary investigation, and Markish confirmed it publicly.]

Presiding Officer: In your testimony you indicated that in recent years you were working for the Jewish Anti-Fascist Committee, where old friends gathered, friends closely bound by ties of anti-Soviet activity dating all the way back to the early days of Soviet power. In answer to the question of how this could have happened, you say it happened because Lozovsky was the guiding spirit in all that went on there. Did the Anti-Fascist Committee really carry out hostile work under Lozovsky's leadership?

Markish: All committee activity was run past Lozovsky. Lozovsky was the inspiration, and he glorified this committee. He trusted Fefer very much. When Fefer read to him his banal piece of poetry "I Am a Jew," he said, "I liked the poem."

Presiding Officer: Further on you say (reads out testimony): "The following people were brought on to the committee: Spivak,* Hofshteyn, Bergelson, Halkin, Nusinov, Dobrushin, Shimeliovich, Lina Shtern, Strongin,† Kvitko, and I." Is this correct?

Markish: This is a general statement. I did not know Shtern at all, and I do not know her now, either.

[During the testimony, the issue of relations between Markish and Mikhoels arose. Markish gave Mikhoels extremely low marks as a theater director, as a political activist, and as a person. But during the questioning, it came out that Markish's attitude toward Mikhoels was to a significant degree the result of Mikhoels having refused to produce plays by Markish. According to Markish, everything Mikhoels did was steeped in nationalism; this attitude of Mikhoels left its mark on the artistic face of the theater that he had directed.]

Markish: In 1937 things at the theater had reached a point where Mikhoels was told, "We will close down the theater because you have saturated it with such half-mystical things that it is shameful for a Moscow theater, a theater that stands alongside the Moscow Art Theater and the Vakhtangov Theater, to serve the public such indecent fodder."

Presiding Officer: So in 1937 the theater's activity took on an acutely nationalistic character?

Markish: It was already just decaying because too much attention was being

---

*Elye Spivak (1890–1950), a philologist and Yiddish literary scholar, headed the Institute of Jewish Culture of the Ukrainian Academy of Sciences. He was a member of the JAC during the war. Arrested in January 1949, he died in prison on April 4, 1950.

†Leyb Strongin (1896–1968) was a longtime Bolshevik activist in the newspaper industry in Belorussia. He directed Der emes publishing house from 1939 to 1948 and was a member of the JAC and on the editorial board of *Eynikayt*. He was arrested in 1949 and released from exile after Stalin's death.

paid to things that were already a part of the past. In 1937, Kaganovich paid a visit to the theater. Afterward, he summoned Mikhoels and asked him, "Why are you discrediting the Jewish people?" And then he said to him, "Come see me." I remember this very well because Kaganovich said to Mikhoels, "And when you come see me, bring Markish with you." I prepared anxiously for this visit, but Mikhoels didn't go to see Kaganovich, and several days later he left on tour with the theater.

Presiding Officer: From this it is possible to conclude that Mikhoels was directing the theater more and more toward nationalism.

Markish: Mikhoels was a great actor. Although I do not know his place within international artistic circles, he was famous in the Yiddish theater. He regarded *The Travels of Benjamin III* as the theater's greatest prize, and the entire dubious legacy left by Granovsky.* And really, what did Granovsky have to do with the people? He was a person of alien sensibilities who did not want to see how the people were being liberated from that filth and were surging ahead. Mikhoels had no interest in presenting works that would propagandize socialist society. By 1937 the theater had fallen so low that no amount of patience made the situation tolerable. Mikhoels thought that no one would lay a finger on him because that would look like anti-Semitism and opposition to the party's national policy. Mikhoels was ideologically alien to me, and I to him.

Presiding Officer: Nonetheless, he headed the committee. How did he allow you to join the committee and even become a member of the presidium?

Markish: He was two-faced. He could be seductive in conversations with people. When he was named chairman of the Anti-Fascist Committee, I said that [having him as chairman] would be like having a jester on the throne. But once the government found it necessary to appoint him to lead such an important project during the war, then it had to be that way. Then I started having the feeling that Mikhoels was pretending to be an important person. And this was really true. Lozovsky presented him to everyone as someone important, a major figure, and I started having doubts. Perhaps I had been wrong to think he was a bad person.

Presiding Officer: How can this be? You described Mikhoels as a nationalist, and at the same time you were writing poetry in which you described him in different terms (reads out the verse), portraying him as a "messiah" who had suffered for his people. This does not correspond to reality. You sang paeans of praise to him, so how can you now tell the court that you didn't like him?[†]

---

*Alexander Granovsky (Abram Azarkh) (1890–1937) was the founder and first director of the State Jewish Theater. He defected in January 1929 during the group's visit to Western Europe.

[†]Following Mikhoels's death, Markish wrote a long poem praising him. Several stanzas were published in *Eynikayt,* January 17, 1948, p. 4.

Markish: There is laughter in the hall. It seems Lozovsky is laughing. I have to say, Citizen Chairman of the Court, that there is nothing funny here. Lozovsky got along exceptionally well with Mikhoels, and this made me think that perhaps I was wrong. This was how I understood it—that if the government sent someone abroad, then that person must be deserving of such treatment. Who sent Mikhoels to America? Lozovsky, a member of the government. In our country, people who are sent abroad are regarded as worthy individuals. This is a very important point.

Presiding Officer: Yes, it really is important.

Markish: I was not very interested in what went on behind the scenes at the committee. I attended only two presidium sessions. But when Mikhoels died and I read the splendid obituaries in *Pravda* and *Izvestia,* I began to reconsider.

Presiding Officer: That does not fit with your characterization of him. You described him as a nationalist.

Markish: I began to think that perhaps I thought Mikhoels was a bad person simply because we were on bad terms with each other.

Presiding Officer: He was not progressive. He was a nationalist who dragged the theater and the arts down into the swamp of Zionism. At the very least, you should have remained silent instead of writing such verses about him.

Markish: What could I do when Fadeyev himself said that people like Mikhoels are born once in a hundred years? During his funeral, all of the theater companies with whom he had been on bad terms came to honor his memory and praised him to the skies. I began to think about how Russians were coming and exalting his name, and here I was, the only person saying anything bad about him. Perhaps I was wrong and would have had a different kind of relationship with him if we hadn't had professional differences.

Presiding Officer: And you explain your poems by saying that you were going along with the situation that arose during his funeral?

Markish: The government held such a magnificent funeral for him that it made me think that perhaps I really had made a mistake. After all, I also have regrettable qualities. I'm a person, too, and maybe I misunderstood him.

Presiding Officer: What makes you think that Mikhoels was murdered?

Markish: The day after he died, the situation was vague and confusing, while someone at the committee said that Mikhoels had been murdered. A person can be murdered in a car accident, after all. For two days the thought that he had been a victim did not leave me. Then people said that he had been drunk, but then it came out that he was not drunk. In the days following his death the reasons for his death were not clearly established. He knew Trofimenko, the commander of the Belorussian Military District.

Their wives were friendly, but the Trofimenkos didn't know the details surrounding his death. A situation in which even people close to him didn't know how he had died gave me a feeling of uncertainty. I kept thinking that maybe I was wrong, and I wrote that poem in a rush of all those feelings. But I didn't publish the poem. I just did a rough outline.

Presiding Officer: Instead of paying no heed to rumors, you made use of them, and you portrayed his death as a murder, placing him side by side with the victims of anti-Semitic reprisals (reads the verse).

Markish: When rumors started circulating about his death, it was well known that there were fascists operating in Belorussia, sent there on a mission by Mikolajczyk's people.* It was possible that some fascist had killed him. This was one of the more widely disseminated versions of how he died.

Presiding Officer: Let's get back to the trip. How did you find out that Fefer and Mikhoels had gone to America?

Markish: Fefer called me on the phone a day or two before they left. He asked me to give him some poem or other and added that finally he was due for some bliss; that meant a visit to America. This grated on me when I heard it. But because this trip came right after a malicious speech against me by the leaders of the Jewish Anti-Fascist Committee and although the Central Committee looked favorably on me . . .

Presiding Officer (interrupting Markish): What do you mean exactly, "looked favorably on you?"

Markish: I mean that my works were published, and at *Pravda* I was one of the staff writers. In 1942, when my book was set in press prior to publication, a courier came from the Kremlin and asked that the press plates be handed over. And finally, as I've already said, that book was nominated for the Stalin Prize. By the party Central Committee, not by the Writers' Union. It seems to me that all of this gives me the right to say that the Central Committee was well disposed toward me. But I was removed from the editorial board of the radio.

Presiding Officer: But you didn't ask Fefer, did you? You didn't say to him, What is so wonderful about going to America? How are we to understand this?

Markish: No, I didn't say that to him, because I wasn't in the habit of having that informal a conversation with him. I am not saying that I would have gone, although I now have the right to confirm that I wouldn't have gone to America. There was a big battle going on with the Jewish Anti-Fascist

*Stanislaw Mikolajczyk (1901–1966) was a onetime leader of the Polish government-in-exile. Roosevelt admired him, but Stalin prevented him from assuming a position of power in Poland after the war. There was never any evidence that Mikolajczyk or any people around him were connected to the death of Mikhoels or to underground activity against the Soviet government.

Committee. I thought, It means the Central Committee is unhappy with me *again*. Being removed from the editorial staff list made me feel that way. And here was the victor on the phone telling me he was going to paradise. I told my wife and children about it. The war is going on, and he retreats to paradise. But if I had said anything to him, that would have given him more of a chance to scoff at me. Having slandered me at the Central Committee, he wanted to have the pleasure of making me endure yet another triumph of his—the fact that he was going to the United States.

[Further on, Markish gave his assessment of the outcome of Mikhoels and Fefer's trip to the United States and the delegation's report to the Writers' Union.]

Presiding Officer: So what did they talk about?

Markish: The writers weren't there yet. I was alone in Moscow. All the writers had been evacuated. Fefer and Mikhoels shared their impressions of the trip. When the talk was over, Fefer pulled a piece of paper out of his pocket as he was walking past me, gave it to me, and said, "Read this." It was one of the drafts of the Crimea letter. It did not yet contain that swipe at the Jews that if they didn't get the Crimea, they would leave for Poland. I said, "This is slander against the people." If they were going to write to the government on behalf of the people, at the very least they should have had some contact with the people, but what did they have? They had contact with the synagogue. What right did they have to make a statement like that?

Presiding Officer: Who was involved in drafting the letter?

Markish: Fefer, Mikhoels, and Epshteyn. And on top of that, they spread a rumor that Molotov had inspired them to compose this thing. You know, when Fefer passed this gossip to one of the writers, it began to spread quickly. And I'll tell you something else that's interesting. In 1948, Fadeyev called us, the writers, in to see him. Bergelson was there, as were Fefer, Halkin, and I. I was sitting off to the side. It was after Ehrenburg's article "Regarding a Certain Letter" was published in *Pravda.** Now, whose business is it, really, how that letter came to be? So Fefer turned to Fadeyev and said, "You know, Alexander Alexandrovich, how that letter came about, don't you? I was at the Central Committee, and the secretary said to me that actually no one had sent a letter to Ehrenburg. It was a political step." Fadeyev is a very tactful person, so perhaps he knew more than Fefer did, but that fact speaks for itself.

[A later part of the session was devoted to proving that almost all the literature—articles and features sent abroad by the Jewish Anti-Fascist Committee—contained classified information and was nationalistic in tone.

---

*The article appeared in *Pravda* on September 21, 1948, p. 3. For a full discussion of its significance, see Joshua Rubenstein, *Tangled Loyalties: The Life and Times of Ilya Ehrenburg* (Tuscaloosa, Ala., 1999), pp. 257–260.

The session that began after the break was dedicated to Goldberg's visit to the Soviet Union.]

Presiding Officer: You said that Goldberg was not only an editor, but a hardened American intelligence agent as well, and that when Fefer and Epshteyn mentioned him, they spoke of him in reverential tones.

Markish: I didn't know that he was an intelligence agent; and strangely enough, even a year and a half after that bastard dishonored our country, the State Security Ministry did not take note of this, either. A year and a half later, Simonov and Galaktionov* were in America, spent some time with him, and gave him an interview. When did my direct relationship with him begin? I did not associate with the committee. A young woman called me and said that Sholem Aleichem's son-in-law, who was the chairman of a committee of anti-fascist scientists, had arrived, and she asked me to come over, too. I came. This person had arrived; he was very important. There was no presidium session. I was there for just half an hour. There was a photographer there. I was photographed once near him.

Presiding Officer: And prior to this you never met with him anywhere?

Markish: No, we did not have a meeting. A week later I got a call from the Soviet Writers' Union asking me to come to a banquet in Goldberg's honor. I don't think that Fadeyev was acting out of any personal considerations, so that means that the people lower down in the hierarchy had been deceived, and then the deception touched higher-ups. The Soviet Writers' Union had been deceived. Goldberg is a very cunning person. He was from Russia himself and had spent several years at hard labor as a prisoner.[†] The speech he made at the banquet began with the following words: "Comrades, allow me to raise the first toast to the best writer in the Soviet Union, the man who wrote that immortal creation the Soviet Constitution." Everyone was delighted over this.

[Then Markish told the court about a meeting he had had with Goldberg in his hotel room at the National Hotel.]

Markish: He (Goldberg) asked: "Why didn't the Birobidzhan plan work out?" I said, "What stupid Jew would give up Moscow for Birobidzhan?" And I said in addition that when one of Sholem Aleichem's books comes out in

---

*The writer Konstantin Simonov (1915–1979) and General Mikhail Galaktionov (1897–1948), who was a military correspondent for *Pravda,* traveled to America for two months in the spring of 1946, together with Ilya Ehrenburg. Their visit constituted the first official cultural exchange with the United States after the war. In his testimony, Markish is confused about the timing of their trips. Simonov and Galaktionov were in America at the same time that Goldberg was in the USSR. They left New York at the end of June 1946; Goldberg did not return to America until October. So it is highly unlikely that Goldberg had a chance to interview them. For a discussion of the trip by Simonov, Galaktionov, and Ehrenburg, see Rubenstein, *Tangled Loyalties,* pp. 231–240.

†B. Z. Goldberg came to the United States in 1908. He was never a political prisoner in Russia.

Russian, hundreds of thousands of copies are published so people can derive some sustenance from it. But when the same book comes out in Yiddish, it doesn't get such wide distribution, because Jews here have closer ties to Russian culture. They want to be part of a great culture; they don't have any nationalistic enthusiasm. They don't speak Yiddish, and what would they do if they went to Birobidzhan? Ten years from now their children aren't going to be speaking Yiddish.

Presiding Officer: So you told him about your anti-Birobidzhan convictions?

Markish: I was in Birobidzhan in 1934, when I wrote a play about border guards. I remembered Birobidzhan not as Birobidzhan per se, but as people who live on the border. What was my attitude toward Birobidzhan in 1934? I looked on it as a place for Jews who wanted to till the soil and fish. I didn't think that a smart Jew would go live in Birobidzhan when he already had everything here.

Presiding Officer: What did Goldberg mean when he said (vol. 15, p. 166), "Send Mikhoels and Fefer abroad again, and we will turn the whole world on its ear?"

Markish: At one of the banquets, he said something like "Give me Mikhoels and Fefer in America, and we will turn the world on its ear," meaning that they had been in America once and worked miracles there. If they were sent over a second time, they would work even more miracles.

[On May 12 at 2:45 P.M. the judicial session continued. The questioning of Markish by the presiding officer was soon over, and the defendants had the right to ask questions.]

Presiding Officer: Which of the defendants has questions for Markish?

Lozovsky: I do. How many times and with whom did Markish come to see me and what were the issues that he, his colleagues, and I talked about?

Markish: We met rarely. In 1938 I did not know Lozovsky, and someone told me that he was the new editor of a government literary publishing house. I went to the publishing house and told him I wanted to reissue one of my books on the Civil War in a Russian-language version. He received me with a rather perfunctory air and gave me no encouragement. The book was not accepted for reissue. This was my first meeting with Lozovsky. The second meeting took place in July 1940, when there was discussion about aiding the families of Yiddish writers who had stayed in Warsaw. At the time I said that if the families of these writers could be saved, then we should do so. Then I met with Lozovsky in 1941, when I was summoned to the Central Committee along with other writers, some of whom are seated here. Lozovsky received us and said that we had to go gather information about atrocities so that later we could bear witness about how the Jews had suffered.

Lozovsky: What for?

Markish: To send this information abroad. It was not for a domestic audience. Then Kvitko and Nusinov went. I did not go.

Fefer (to Markish): You told the court that the poem about Mikhoels was not published, but it was published in *Eynikayt.*

Markish: The poem that was read out here had ninety lines. That poem was a collaboration by several poets, and it was published in *Eynikayt* on the day of his funeral. It contained twelve lines of mine.

Fefer (to Markish): Here Markish has described Mikhoels in negative terms and accused him of nationalism. I would like to ask whether Markish has spoken out against Mikhoels in print.

Markish: In print? I don't remember, but I do remember that I spoke against Mikhoels because I felt that he had made mistakes in his selection of repertoire. We had run-ins about that.

Presiding Officer: At the Writers' Union?

Markish: At production meetings at the theater.

Fefer (to Markish): Didn't Markish write a book about Mikhoels in which he spoke of him as a figure of major importance in the theatrical world and said not a word about nationalism?

Markish: I wrote a polemical article about Mikhoels, but when I said that he was a great artist, I committed no transgression; he was indeed a great artist.

Fefer: Tell us which plays of yours were produced at the Jewish Theater.

Markish: The Earth.

Fefer: In what year?

Markish: 1930.

Presiding Officer: Name the plays that were produced.

Markish: The Earth, The Family Ovadis, The Feast, and then, during the evacuation, the play *An Eye for an Eye.*

Presiding Officer: Four plays?

Markish: Yes, four plays. In 1947 I wrote the tragedy *The Ghetto Uprising,* which was very well received.

Fefer: Markish said that the Central Committee of the party recommended his book for the Stalin Prize. Did this book receive the Stalin Prize?

Markish: No. The book was nominated by the Central Committee. Fadeyev told me about it. Alexandrov* of the propaganda department of the Cen-

---

*Georgy Alexandrov (1908–1961) was an important party official. He directed the Department of Agitation and Propaganda of the Central Committee from 1940 to 1947 and the Institute of Philosophy of the Soviet Academy of Sciences from 1947 to 1954. On April 14, 1945, in a famous incident, Alexandrov criticized Ilya Ehrenburg in *Pravda* for writing too harshly about the Germans in his wartime articles.

tral Committee called in Myasnikov, the editor in chief of the State Publishing House, and said, "Give me materials on Markish right away because we are nominating him for the Stalin Prize." Then Fadeyev said at a meeting, "Markish was nominated, but he didn't get the Stalin Prize because he had so many competitors from the national republics."

Fefer (to Markish): Do you remember when Fadeyev accused you of having nationalistic material in your book?

Markish: That's nonsense. One evening he said to me, "You have a poem about a mirror falling and breaking into pieces and how you tried to put the pieces back together. But you still couldn't see your reflection in it." Fadeyev said that this poem was pessimistic. If Fefer had a shred of conscience, he would not slander Fadeyev this way.

Fefer (to Markish): Don't you remember what Fadeyev said about a shattered people and about lying in fragments?

Markish: No. He said to me, "I can tell that you were feeling sorrowful when you wrote that poem."

Fefer (to Markish): Have I ever been in your home?

Markish: No.

Fefer: After I spoke at a session of the presidium in 1944, I came to your home, where we spent two hours together. I spoke in general terms about our trip. Your wife witnessed it. I can even describe your room. I told you there that Opatoshu had boycotted our rally in America.

Markish: This is such impudence, such an unheard-of attempt to save his own skin. Think about it: how can he still talk, and what can my wife say about this? After all that happened before the trip, when he dragged my name through the mud, he now wants to say that he was in my home. That is a total lie. He doesn't even know where I lived.

Presiding Officer: Where did Markish live?

Fefer: I took the subway to the Belorussian Station, but I cannot say exactly where he lived.

Presiding Officer: Fefer, do you confirm that you were at Markish's apartment?

Fefer: I was there once. That was in 1944. After my speech at the presidium, I shared my impressions about the trip. Markish approached me and invited me to his home. I can't say that our conversation was criminal in nature, but it is a fact that it took place.

Presiding Officer: Do you recall the furniture in Markish's room?

Fefer: The room we were in was quite small. There was a narrow hallway. There was no furniture, just trestle beds covered with rugs. Markish was interested in literary people most of all. I told him that Opatoshu had boycotted our rally. He was quite surprised.

Markish: I would like to ask the people from the State Security Ministry who were in my home to say whether Fefer's description of my apartment corresponds to what they saw. He was there in 1944. I have not renovated the apartment since then. I live in a prominent building; Alexei Tolstoy* lives upstairs from me, Deputy Leonov lives downstairs from me, and so do Lebedev-Kumach† and General Nikolsky. It is an eleven-story building. Do you think an apartment in a building like that would be furnished cheaply?

Fefer: I would like to add that there were periods when Markish dropped by my apartment in Kiev a couple of times and I would give him little gifts for his wife.

Markish: It's true. I was in his apartment when my play about the liberation of the western Ukraine was being produced. After the Franko Theater produced my play, Fefer and I had dinner together at the Actors' Club.

Fefer: It was important for me to establish that Markish was a guest in my home. This is now established. I say this because there was a period when relations between us were normal. Markish could read his poems, and I would praise him when I spoke publicly.

[Almost the entire evening session of May 12 was dedicated to clarifying the nature of Markish's relationship with Fefer and Kvitko. The long-standing dislike between Markish and Fefer became obvious. They had exchanged accusations of nationalism and unseemly behavior. The judicial session was continued on May 13. Lozovsky, Fefer, Kvitko, Shimeliovich, Talmy, Bergelson, Bregman, and Yuzefovich asked Markish questions. These defendants clarified Markish's testimony and actually overturned part of it, invoking concrete facts that Markish could not deny. Specifically, contrary to Markish's testimony, Fefer confirmed that "the friendship between Mikhoels and Markish was well known. They were friends for many years, and Mikhoels produced Markish's plays with great pleasure. Apart from a brief interlude, they were close friends, and Markish never spoke out against Mikhoels."]

Presiding Officer: I would like to summarize the interrogation briefly. Please give specific answers to the questions. You have given very broad and even excessively detailed explanations. I am asking you, do you plead guilty to participating in the nationalistic activity of the Jewish Anti-Fascist Committee?

Markish: No.

Presiding Officer: So why did you confess to this during the investigation? You

---

*The writer Alexei Tolstoy (1883–1945), a distant relative of Leo Tolstoy's, was regarded as a genuinely talented but conformist literary figure. He greeted the revolution with revulsion, but returned to the Soviet Union from France in 1923. He was a close friend of Mikhoels's.

†Leonid Leonov (1899–1994) was a prominent Soviet novelist and playwright. Vasily Lebedev-Kumach (Lebedev) (1898–1949) was a poet, playwright, and screenwriter; he was particularly famous for his songs.

were asked if you pled guilty. You said, "Yes, I plead guilty. I was a member of the committee, as were other nationalists, including Bergelson, Fefer, and Hofshteyn." And then you said that a list of names was enough to indicate that the Jewish Anti-Fascist Committee was a nest of nationalists.

Markish: I was not involved in this anti-fascist committee's activity.

Presiding Officer: Perhaps what happened was that you pled guilty to acting in concert with people who were a part of the Jewish Anti-Fascist Committee and to being a nationalist up until you were arrested?

Markish: No, that phrasing does not do justice to the truth.

Presiding Officer: But during the preliminary investigation (vol. 15, pp.126–30) you testified that from childhood you were raised and educated in a spirit of nationalism. The influence of your father, Bergelson, Hofshteyn, and Kvitko helped to make you a nationalistic writer.

Markish: During this trial you have had opportunity to see to what extent I have been under the influence of these people.

Presiding Officer: Why did you give such testimony?

Markish: Very often during the investigation there was mention of what constitutes a nation and nationalism. Nationalistic narrow-mindedness is one thing. I may have written poems within a narrow context of nationalistic ideas, but the concept of nationalism is something completely different. When I gave this testimony, I was like an abnormal person. I think that each prisoner who is guilty would do his best to confess. But now, standing here, I shudder to think about it. When my play *The Family Ovadis* was being critically discussed, I said that I had written a nationalistic bias into the play. I was searching myself for blemishes so that I would fit into the category of the guilty.

Presiding Officer: You are a person of principle. How is it that you confirmed all of this during the preliminary investigation and now are denying it? Answer this for me. Do you believe that the Jewish Anti-Fascist Committee genuinely became a center of Jewish nationalistic activity, as the expert commission concluded?

Markish: Assessing the Jewish Anti-Fascist Committee's activity now, I state in the strongest possible terms that the committee did become a preserve of nationalism, and when I read through these forty-two volumes, I grew ashamed of my life. I believe that the Jewish Anti-Fascist Committee was turned into a tavern where delicate espionage dishes were prepared for intelligence agents.

Presiding Officer: The committee started sending its agents to gather material, and people started appealing to the committee about all sorts of issues. That means that it was a center.

Markish: I agree with you. There is no way that Fefer could not have understood the significance of such words as "the Crimea," "the Black Sea,"

"Turkey," "the Balkan peninsula," when hearing them from the lips of an American. But if this weren't enough to open someone's eyes to what these hints really meant, an undisguised hostile word was used as well—*beachhead*. And in court he confirmed that their every step was coordinated and approved. How, after a conversation with the fascists and their accomplices, after colluding with these reactionaries about separating the Crimea from the USSR for the American government, how, after that, did he dare to appear on the threshold of the Soviet Embassy, how did dare he look into the eyes of the Soviet government, into the eyes of the Soviet justice system!

Presiding Officer (to Markish): So what you are saying is that the committee became a nationalistic center inside the country, did things that were not its business, and, in addition to that, became a nest of espionage. But it could not have changed like that all by itself. Who specifically turned it into a nationalistic center?

Markish: When I read the forty-two volumes summarizing the Jewish disgrace, I saw that it was led by Epshteyn, Fefer, and Mikhoels and I wondered, How did they get together? Then Lozovsky's role became clear to me. Regardless of their status in the committee, they would all say, Go to Lozovsky, he'll take care of whatever it is. That was the sort of relationship they found themselves in with Lozovsky. It takes only one plague bacillus to contaminate the entire body. And I should add here that Lozovsky cherished this committee. He held it up as an example for the others, and in the end he cast his lot with them and did not disband them, a very regrettable thing for all the members of the Anti-Fascist Committee.

Presiding Officer: And the rest, like Hofshteyn, Shimeliovich, Bergelson, and the others, what role did they play in all of this?

Markish: Bergelson was the most avid supporter of Jewish national cultural traditions on the committee. The other members venerated him. He was famous in America, first of all; he is an old writer who writes about the traditions of the old world; and he represented all of that culture, which was what the Anti-Fascist Committee was looking for.

Presiding Officer: An appropriate person for criminal activity, which the committee then directed?

Markish: This can only be explained by relating it to the committee's nationalistic activity. I thought, Can I accept the idea that they were spies? I could think that of Fefer, but I cannot believe that Bergelson could be a spy. It is difficult for me to accuse these people of espionage. Let me tell you about Hofshteyn. He is a person who is, to some degree, inferior. He was slandered for his third poem, which he wrote in Kiev in 1918, and he never got over it. He grew up in a very protected environment. I remember people would say, "Hofshteyn went for supper. Let's hope nothing happens to him."

Presiding Officer: When the committee was founded, he joined it as an old nationalist?

Markish: Yes. There are Zionist elements in his makeup. He wrote a letter about Hebrew, and this was something that he nurtured in himself over the decades. When Meyerson arrived, he gave her a telegram about the need to renew Hebrew as a spoken language. Such actions are not the product of a healthy intellect.*

Presiding Officer: Could it be a political tendency?

Markish: No, it is a kind of inflammation of nationalistic passions. I read in the testimony that he once earned a living by selling prayer books. Now, is that a normal thing to do, for a communist who, as a poet, lays claim to being a scholar—to make a living selling prayer books?

Presiding Officer: So he supplied prayer books to a synagogue when he was not a communist?

Markish: This was toward the end of his time in Kiev. He had ties with a rabbi, so his conduct was in general outside the bounds of a normal person. When I look back over his career, I consider his initial verses the product of a nationalistic intellectual. His trip to Palestine, then his first book, which was merely a claim to being poetry. During the years when the most intense construction of socialism was taking place, he did not take upon himself the heavy burden that the age required of the first generation of writers. The less he succeeded in reflecting reality, the more he turned back to things of old. He had no great creative successes, but he was considered an indisputably Jewish lyric poet. By nature he is a convinced nationalist.

Presiding Officer: Was Kvitko an active committee member?

Markish: Yes, Kvitko was an active committee member. At first he was a deputy to one of the heads. This gives an idea of his activity. Kvitko is the sort of person who, if he does something, throws himself into it body and soul. He was active in two different ways. At one time he occupied a little desk in the committee offices and did something there—what exactly, I don't know. Nor do I know what he did as deputy senior secretary. Then there was his trip to the Crimea, which led to that preposterous appeal. I cannot say that Kvitko was involved in espionage, but he was a nationalist.

[Markish's testimony lasted almost three entire days—May 10, 12, and 13. After a brief break, Bergelson's testimony began, at 9:05 P.M.]

DAVID BERGELSON

Born in the Ukrainian town of Sarna, David Bergelson came from a prosperous family. His father was a lumber and grain merchant who

---

*Markish was mistaken; Hofshteyn did not send a telegram or any other communication to Golda Meyerson about the Hebrew language. He did, however, defend Hebrew in 1924, when it came under severe attack by Jewish communists.

died when Bergelson was nine years old. His mother passed away four years later. Following her death, Bergelson stayed with older brothers in Kiev, Odessa, and Warsaw. In Kiev he studied dentistry for a time but soon quit his formal education to devote himself to literature. He wrote in Hebrew and Russian before finding his true voice in Yiddish. By 1909 his first full-length work, *By the Depot,* was published in Warsaw at his own expense, and it was hailed by serious critics. Four years later, his novel *When All Is Said and Done,* which he originally wrote in Hebrew, confirmed his stature as a major prose writer. Before the age of thirty, David Bergelson was recognized as the fourth classic writer of Yiddish literature, after Mendele Mocher Sforim, Sholem Aleichem, and Y. L. Peretz.

With the Bolshevik triumph, it was difficult for Bergelson to separate his fate from the ideological and cultural pressures generated by the October Revolution. The great Hebrew poet and thinker Chaim Nachman Bialik knew Bergelson well and offered a fateful toast at his wedding to Tsipora Kutzenogaya in 1917. "Tsipeleh," Bialik urged her, "don't give him to the Bolsheviks." *

In 1919 and 1920, David and Tsipora Bergelson lived in Kiev, where he participated in the Yiddish organization Kultur lige (The Culture League) and helped to edit two literary almanacs *Oyfgang* (Ascent) and *Eygns* (Our Own), which remain milestones in the history of Soviet Yiddish culture. Bergelson disliked the Revolution and he longed to travel. He took his family to Berlin in 1921—their only child, Lev, had been born in 1918—using a Lithuanian passport provided by the poet Jurgis Baltrushaitis, who was serving as Lithuania's ambassador to Moscow, where he befriended leading literary figures. Having a Lithuanian passport made life easier for Bergelson, permitting him to visit Moscow and other parts of the country with sufficient confidence that he would be able to leave.

Throughout the 1920s, while Bergelson lived primarily in Berlin, he continued to travel frequently: to Romania in 1924; to the Soviet Union in 1926; and to America for at least six months in 1929, where he stayed in New York and gave lectures in several other cities. He also tried, without success, to find work at various newspapers. After his trip to the United States, Bergelson went on a lecture and reading tour in Poland.

---

*Lev Bergelson (son of David Bergelson), interview with author, Jerusalem, 1998.

Wherever he lived, Bergelson wrote and edited. There was a family rule that no one could enter his study before 2 P.M. In Berlin he edited two journals, *Milgroym* (Pomegranate) with Der Nister, and *In Shpan*. For a time, he wrote for the New York socialist daily the *Forverts* before becoming a correspondent for two communist newspapers, *Der emes,* in Moscow, and the *Morgen Freiheit,* in New York. In spite of his literary output, the family still relied on Tsipora's work as a secretary for financial support.*

As the decade wore on, Bergelson became caught up in ideological and cultural arguments. Like all Yiddish writers, he had to decide how to sustain a connection to his readers at a time when pressures to assimilate were becoming ever more intense. Yiddish-speaking communities were dwindling in size as the younger generation adopted Russian or English, Polish or Hebrew, as a primary language. Faced with this dilemma, Bergelson published his controversial essay "Three Centers" in 1926, in which he explored the prospects for Yiddish culture in the principal communities where it continued to flourish: New York, Warsaw, and Moscow.† Although Bergelson had yet to visit America, he understood how its open and democratic society both welcomed Jews as individuals and enticed them to relinquish many of their ethnic customs, particularly the use of Yiddish. Polish society posed another kind of challenge. There, Jews were free to practice their religion, to live together, and to maintain Yiddish cultural institutions. But Polish society still attracted younger Jews—Warsaw itself was 30 percent Jewish— and many of these Jews, like their counterparts in New York, London, Berlin, and Paris, had begun to adopt the language of the gentile majority. At the same time, the Polish government imposed severe restrictions on Jewish participation in civic life: quotas were in effect in both government and universities; businesses and factories were required to close on Sundays, putting observant Jewish business owners and workers at a disadvantage; and non-ethnic Poles born outside the 1918 borders were denied citizenship. In short, Jewish life in 1920s Poland was not a simple or easy affair.

For Bergelson, the USSR offered the broadest prospects. About two million Jews lived there whose mother tongue was Yiddish. Cultural in-

---

*They had married soon after she graduated, cum laude, from the prestigious Odessa Gymnasium for Girls.

†*In shpan* (In Step), no. 1, April 1926, pp. 84–96.

stitutions, including schools, theaters, university courses, journals, and newspapers all received generous government support, and Yiddish writers enjoyed seeing their work published in large editions. Bergelson, in fact, wrote "Three Centers" at a propitious moment, when the regime had initiated a new policy of "nativization" of cultural and political institutions; national minorities like the Jews, Ukrainians, and Belorussians were encouraged to conduct official business in their own language. One consequence was a tremendous growth in the Yiddish press. The number of Yiddish books and brochures published annually rose from 76 to 531 between 1924 and 1930; the number of Yiddish newspapers appearing on a regular basis increased from 21 earlier in the decade to 40 in 1927.* The Kremlin also instituted laws banning anti-Semitism, and numerous Jews—or at least people of Jewish origin—were prominent members of the Soviet government. Bergelson could not help but be impressed by this development.

According to Lev Bergelson, Bergelson's son, "Three Centers" marked the beginning, not the conclusion, of his father's drawn-out decision of where to live. Yiddish would inevitably die. It was suffering a prolonged terminal illness, but its decline would be more prolonged in the Soviet Union, where a sizable community of readers seemed likely to remain for at least a couple of generations. Nonetheless, Bergelson was not ready to return altogether. By writing favorably about the Soviet Union in "Three Centers" and by connecting himself to avowedly communist newspapers like *Der emes* and the *Morgen Freiheit,* Bergelson maintained his connection to the regime even as he continued to live outside Russia. He was not ready to throw in his lot with the Soviets.

Political developments forced his hand. During his stay in America in 1929, a deadly riot broke out in Hebron, a major city in Palestine with a large Arab majority and a small but vibrant Jewish minority. One hundred thirty-three Jews were killed, and the survivors fled the city.

After some vacillation, the communist *Morgen Freiheit,* although it was an anti-Zionist newspaper, condemned the massacre as an outburst of brutal religious and nationalistic fanaticism. But then the editors, under instructions from Moscow, completely changed their coverage,

---

*For further information on the policy of "nativization," see Zvi Y. Gitelman, *Jewish Nationality and Soviet Politics: The Jewish Sections of the CPSU, 1917–1930* (Princeton, N.J., 1972), p. 351. For further information on the state of Yiddish publishing in the 1920s, see ibid., pp. 332–333.

calling the riots a revolt against Zionism and British imperialism. This reversal provoked a good deal of consternation among readers and contributors. Several prominent writers resigned, among them H. Leivick and Joseph Opatoshu, both of whom were close to Bergelson. Anyone who disagreed with the Party line was thereafter considered an enemy of the communist movement and could no longer work at the paper. This development constrained Bergelson's career in New York. Bergelson was also being goaded by relatives who were communist sympathizers; "they lectured him on the collapse of capitalism in the Great Depression," as his granddaughter remembered hearing from Tsipora, "and the moral obligation he had to return to the first Socialist land in the world."* Unable to withstand the pressure and unable to elicit a firm job offer, Bergelson soon returned to Germany.

Meanwhile, the Kremlin was dispatching other Yiddish writers and even Solomon Mikhoels to encourage him to move to Moscow. And Bergelson was writing plays for Moscow's State Jewish Theater. In 1930, his play *The Deaf Man* was performed, starring Mikhoels; two years later, *A Stern Judgment* reached the stage. In the early 1930s he was promised the opportunity to buy an apartment in Moscow, a publishing house to preside over, and a literary monthly to edit. Although Bergelson continued to resist temptation, his options were growing narrower. In Berlin his son Lev was harassed by Hitler Yugend, and he was beaten once. Bergelson was visiting Moscow in 1933 when his Berlin apartment was searched by the Nazis. His wife and son fled to Denmark, where he joined them and where they remained for another year. Bergelson loved Denmark, but as a Yiddish writer, he had no professional prospects in the country. It was time to reach a decision. His wife opposed moving to Moscow. But Lev was eager to join the Komsomol, "to be like everyone else, . . . to be a part of something. . . . Also, his parents worried about his education, and only [the Soviet Union] held a firm promise of a university education to a Jewish boy at the time."† Bergelson was left with little choice and took his family to Moscow.

He quickly adapted to the regime's expectations. In August 1934, Bergelson was one of four Yiddish writers to address the First Congress of Soviet Writers. This was a signal event in the history of Soviet cultural

---

*Marina Raskin (granddaughter of David Bergelson), paper presented at the annual meeting of the Modern Language Association in Chicago, December 28, 1999.
†Ibid.

life. Although the congress celebrated Stalin's official policy of "socialist realism," a diversity of voices still addressed the delegates—Nikolai Bukharin, Isaac Babel, Boris Pasternak, and Ilya Ehrenburg expressed respect for a writer's autonomy—while a number of foreign delegates, most notably André Malraux, vigorously defended an artist's right to experiment. The Yiddish writers struck no dissonant chords. In his brief remarks, David Bergelson referred to Yiddish literature as the "vanguard" of Soviet literature, which was the "guiding" literature of the entire world. He praised Stalin for defining writers as "engineers of the human soul" and concluded with a call to "persecuted Jewish worker masses" who needed to understand that "only in close unity with surrounding vanguards, the revolutionary working class of the countries in which they live, could they achieve a genuinely great freedom, that freedom which we feel here throughout this country, which we always feel in this hall, and which reaches us from this stage."[*] This was all standard rhetoric for Soviet writers; nothing else would have been acceptable for him to say.

For several years, Bergelson was closely associated with Birobidzhan. He wrote stories and pamphlets, lending his name and rhetorical skills to attracting Soviet Jews and foreigners to support Stalin's idea of a Jewish autonomous region. And like many Soviet writers, Bergelson was directed to endorse the purge trials, sending an article from Birobidzhan to Moscow with a ringing denunciation of the defendants.[†] Bergelson, in contrast to other figures, had done his best to avoid such degrading rituals. But the circumstances of life in Stalin's Russia made it virtually impossible to avoid behavior of this kind altogether.

Did Bergelson know he had miscalculated when he decided to return to Russia? We have only anecdotal evidence to suggest his true feelings. According to one family story, upon their arrival in Moscow in 1934, Tsipora Bergelson took one look around the train station and exclaimed, "We have perished." Bergelson himself had a rude shock when he visited Birobidzhan for the first time. He had been told of its prosperity, but he was "in absolute shock" once he got there. He spent that night walking through muddy streets and over dirty wooden pavements, returning to his hotel in the morning "ashen-faced and covered in mud."

---

[*]*Pervy Vsesoyuzny Sezd Sovietskikh Pisately* (The First All-Union Congress of Soviet Writers) (Moscow, 1934), p. 271.
[†]*Literaturnaya Gazeta,* February 1, 1937, p. 5.

"This is a cursed place," he told a friend.* But it was too late to turn back. A decade later, during World War II, Bergelson befriended the Yiddish poet Rokhl Korn, who had fled Poland and sought refuge in Moscow. One afternoon, while she was visiting Bergelson's apartment, he pointed to his image in a mirror and blurted out, "See that man? I hate him."†

At the time of his arrest, the police confiscated three large bags of manuscripts. His family believes that much of this work, written strictly "for the drawer," included stories that he could never hope to publish in Stalin's time. Ilya Ehrenburg once described the compromise made by artists and intellectuals under Stalin as a "conspiracy of silence." Bergelson, too, learned to live with clenched teeth.

Presiding Officer: Defendant Bergelson, to what do you plead guilty?

Bergelson: To what specifically? I will give specific testimony on every issue.

Presiding Officer: First, tell us, to what do you plead guilty? We'll get to the details later.

Bergelson: To running away from the Soviet Union and toward nationalism.

Presiding Officer: All right. Let's hear your testimony, beginning with biographical information starting from 1918.

[Bergelson, however, began his account from a much earlier period. He recalled his youth and his first steps as a writer early in the century.]

Bergelson: I was raised and educated in a spirit of strict nationalism. I was completely surrounded by this until I was seventeen years old. When I was a child, I did not have a single Russian book. I was eleven or twelve years old when I somehow read syllables in Russian, working from the title pages of the Talmud, which, as required by law, contained the names of each book spelled phonetically in Russian. Most Jews, artisans included, studied the Talmud. Some knew more than others. I remember one saddlemaker who would explain quite intricate matters each Saturday when the Jews gathered in the synagogue. Those who didn't know or could not make sense of them on their own would gather in the synagogue, and between the two prayers, the one before evening and the evening prayer, he would read from the Talmud and explain passages.

There is a day that falls in August when the Temple of Solomon was

---

*Marina Raskin, interview with author by telephone, 1999.

†Irene Kupferschmidt (daughter of Rokhl Korn), interview with author by telephone, 1998.

burned.* On this day all Jews fast for twenty-four hours, even the children. They go to the cemetery for an entire day and pray there "together with the dead." I was so immersed in the atmosphere of that temple being burned— people talked about it a great deal in the community—that when I was six or seven years old it seemed to me that I could smell the fumes and the fire. I tell you this to indicate the extent to which this nationalism was engraved in my mind.

[The presiding officer went into all the circumstances surrounding Bergelson's and Kvitko's illegal crossing of the Soviet-Polish border in the spring of 1921. Bergelson's activity in Lithuania, Denmark, and Germany, his arrival in Moscow, and his connections with various literary and political associations were covered in no less detail, taking several hours. The presiding officer did this because the investigation materials contained admissions by Bergelson that all of his activity abroad had been nationalistic and hostile to Soviet power.]

Presiding Officer: But you speak of your ties to Zionists and nationalists, and you say that these nationalists, which would include Kvitko as well, held vicious anti-Soviet discussions and invented lies against the Soviet Union.

Bergelson: I will dwell on the interrogation record at greater length. One interrogation record that I signed was written by the investigator in advance, and for about a week I refused to sign it. There is a correction in the record added in my handwriting, which says, "This is how it came out." That was in May, I believe.

Presiding Officer: What does it mean?

Bergelson: I felt I could not deny it.

Presiding Officer: And why do you feel you can deny it here?

Bergelson: As I signed it, I was thinking that in court I would tell everything as it had happened, and the court would believe me.

Presiding Officer: And why not tell the prosecutor the truth?

Bergelson: I believed that the prosecutor would not believe me.

Presiding Officer: So, a representative of the office of the prosecutor of the Union of Soviet Socialist Republics conducts your interrogation, and you conceal the truth because you do not trust him.

Bergelson: But while that was going on, there was an investigator sitting there dictating my replies from the previous interrogation records. I should have stopped him, but I could not bring myself to do it. There was nothing else I could do.

---

*The Jewish holiday Tisha B'Av (Ninth of Av) commemorates the destruction of both Temples, in 586 B.C.E. by the Babylonians and in 70 C.E. by the Romans. The Hebrew date generally falls in early August.

[Bergelson had returned to the Soviet Union in 1934. At the next session on May 14, the court pursued the issue of what activity the Society for the Settlement of Jewish Toilers on the Land, or OZET, was engaging in. During the preliminary investigation Bergelson had signed an interrogation record in which he referred to his activity as "hostile." At the court session Bergelson significantly softened the language recorded by the investigator. The work of setting up the Jewish Autonomous Region was evaluated in exactly the same way.

The critic Moshe Litvakov and the Yiddish Section of the Soviet Writers' Union were termed organizers of nationalistic activity hostile to Soviet power.]

Presiding Officer: In regard to the Yiddish Section of the Soviet Writers' Union, you said during the preliminary investigation that Jewish nationalists smoothed your way into the section bureau, and that there you joined forces with your old acquaintances from Kiev, active enemies of Soviet power—Kvitko, Dobrushin, and Markish (vol. 17, p. 176). Is this testimony correct?

Bergelson: If you look at it through a magnifying glass.

Presiding Officer: And if you look with your own eyes, without a magnifying glass?

Bergelson: The closing of Yiddish schools alarmed us a great deal. This was an open acknowledgment that we would become superfluous. And second, we felt that this order had not come from the Central Committee.

On the other hand we knew that the number of students in the Yiddish schools was dwindling, but for me personally, it was a question of Yiddish culture in general. I saw that the parents themselves were not placing their children in Yiddish schools. I wondered what would become of Yiddish culture. Kalinin believed that Yiddish culture could develop in Birobidzhan. I read this in a pamphlet of his, and I heard him say it himself. It became clear to me that this literature had to hold out until it reached a developed stage in Birobidzhan.

Presiding Officer: Did the problem of assimilation trouble you?

Bergelson: It wasn't that I did not believe in assimilation, but rather I felt that it would be a drawn-out process, which meant prolonged agony. It could be worse than death.

Presiding Officer: And do you still consider the assimilation of the Jewish people within the Soviet people to be agony?

Bergelson: I am not speaking of the people, but of the culture.

Presiding Officer: But doesn't the culture mean the people?

Bergelson: I was so completely imbued with Soviet principles that in the end I could comfort myself with the thought that the Jewish people were living among other peoples.

Presiding Officer: Then you spoke about how you criticized the party and the government, how, as fierce opponents of assimilation, you protested the closing of Yiddish schools and sent Yiddish writers to various Soviet cities, where they gave reports and lectures and read nationalistic literature, thereby stirring up nationalistic feelings and popularizing the Bundist theory about the special nature of the Jewish people. "However," you said, "we nationalists who had planted ourselves in the Yiddish Section of the Soviet Writers' Union were not the only ones doing this type of work." There were other people, and you specifically mention Mikhoels, who joined you in this activity in 1937–1938.

Bergelson: That is from the interrogation records, about which I have already testified that everything there was seen through a magnifying glass.

Presiding Officer: And when were you interrogated with the prosecutor present?

Bergelson: It was the same thing when the prosecutor was there. There is one place where the investigator says to me, "Goldberg is an American spy." I was astonished and said, "Yes?" This "yes" is in the record, but without a question mark, and when I told that to the investigator, he said that that was not important for the record.

Presiding Officer: How could it not have significance? You were put on trial in connection with that testimony?

Bergelson: He said that it was just not done to write words with both a question mark and an exclamation point.

Presiding Officer: About Mikhoels you testified that "During the period 1937–1938, Mikhoels began to display his nationalism in an especially active way. He began to give frequent public lectures and established close ties with the Yiddish Section of the Soviet Writers' Union, so that not a single gathering devoted to Yiddish literature took place without a speech by Mikhoels. These speeches of Mikhoels were always saturated with nationalism, and although he disguised them with pro-Soviet phrases, he knew his audiences well and played effectively on their feelings. At the Jewish Theater, Mikhoels selected plays with the aim of convincing the viewer of the inevitably cyclical nature of history, the reoccurrence of Jewish suffering, directed only against them, and their isolation. Over time, all of this led to Jews from various walks of life coming to see Mikhoels at the theater for the sole purpose of pouring out their feelings to him" (vol. 17, p. 179). Is this correct? Mikhoels did an excellent job of disguising his nationalistic views, did he not?

Bergelson: Above all, he was a great actor. He was always on stage, wherever he was, and he did a wonderful job of playing the role of chairman of the Jewish Anti-Fascist Committee. In addition, he was the director of the theater. He played the role of patriot with equal success. I wrote in my testimony that every great actor plays positive and negative roles with equal artistry.

Presiding Officer: Mikhoels played the role of a Soviet patriot, and at the same time he was a nationalist?

Bergelson: Yes, he was a nationalist and played the role of a Jew and Soviet patriot as well, but he played the nationalist with greater sincerity. In this role, hints of something more sincere slipped through. When he began to play the nationalist, he became himself. And he became himself when committing crimes. When all of his crimes came to light, I came to see him with great clarity. There was nationalism in every aspect of his character. His mission was to struggle for the perpetuation of Yiddish culture.

Presiding Officer: Was your testimony about his theatrical activity accurate?

Bergelson: It was, because if you take a show like *Tevye the Dairyman* and combine it with other things, then nationalism is plain to see.

Presiding Officer: Further on, you say (vol. 17, p. 179), "Along with Mikhoels, Lozovsky and the hardy Yuzefovich played an active role in the consolidation of Jewish nationalists in 1937–1938." Is this testimony correct?

Bergelson: Correct.

[It comes out later that Lozovsky's nationalism was expressed in his attendance at a meeting to honor Sholem Aleichem in 1939,* in his initiative to create the Jewish Anti-Fascist Committee, where he played a leading role, and in his recruitment of people like Mikhoels, Bergelson, Kvitko, Epshteyn, Yuzefovich, and Markish to be involved with the committee.]

---

*At several points during the trial, there are references to an evening in honor of the Yiddish writer Sholem Aleichem, which Lozovsky was said to have attended. On March 3, 1939, Sholem Aleichem would have celebrated his eightieth birthday. That spring, the anniversary was widely marked in the Soviet Union with the appearance of "books, journal essays, newspapers, newspaper articles, public gatherings, dramatic performances, literary evenings, and museum exhibits," as the Yiddish literary scholar Zachary Baker documents in a recent study. Perhaps the most impressive event of all was held in Moscow's prestigious and imposing Hall of Columns in the House of Trade Unions on April 19, 1939. This gala literary evening was broadcast on the radio and covered in both the Yiddish-language and Russian-language Soviet press. Eight Jewish and non-Jewish Soviet authors spoke, among them Peretz Markish, David Bergelson, and Yekhezkel Dobrushin. Another group of Yiddish poets recited poems dedicated to Sholem Aleichem; they included Leyb Kvitko, Itsik Fefer, David Hofshteyn, Shmuel Halkin, Aron Kushnirov, and Zelig Akselrod. The evening concluded with a performance at which Solomon Mikhoels and other actors from the State Jewish Theater performed selections from a play by Sholem Aleichem. As Baker makes clear, "the evening brought together the cream of the Soviet Yiddish literary establishment—individuals who, almost without exception, eventually fell victim to Stalin's postwar campaign." Zachary M. Baker, "Sholem Aleichem's Eightieth Birthday Observances and the Cultural Mobilization of Soviet Jewry: A Case Study," in *YIVO Annual*, vol. 23 (Evanston, Ill., 1996), pp. 209–231.

Presiding Officer: But here in your testimony (vol. 18, p. 269) you say: "In statements by the committee directors, in various features, accounts, and articles sent, for the most part, to the United States and published as well in *Eynikayt,* the achievements of Jews in all areas of the country's economic and cultural life were shown, isolated from the achievements of people of other nationalities." The contributions of Jews in routing fascist Germany and in postwar reconstruction were acclaimed, whereas the leading role of other nationalities, including Russians, was downplayed. All of this led to diminishing the role of other nationalities and the stirring-up of nationalism. Does this match reality?

Bergelson: Yes, it matches reality. But I would like to explain how it came about that only Jews were praised, what the reason for this was, and how it began. I was summoned to the propaganda division of the Central Committee even before the Anti-Fascist Committee was set up, and they proposed that I write an appeal to Jews urging them to resist fascism. This was the first step.

Then Alexandrov called us in. He instructed me to write an appeal that was supposed to be broadcast on the radio. This appeal was directed exclusively to Jews. And that's bad, to appeal only to Jews. But because the propaganda department of the Central Committee paid no attention to that, then that was how it was supposed to be. The first rally took place. The Anti-Fascist Committee came into existence. It was a Jewish committee, so that meant its appeals were supposed to be addressed to Jews. Epshteyn, who worked at the committee, knew America well, and I also know a thing or two. And what happened was that if you wrote something that was not about Jews, it would not get published.

Certain people intended to emphasize the exceptional nature of the Jewish people. The fact is that rumors were circulating that there were no Jews at the front. I heard this later, when I was already in prison, and there were three of us sharing a cell, a Belorussian, an Armenian, and I. I heard it from them.

Presiding Officer: But you heard these rumors later. When you were writing, there were no such rumors, were there?

Bergelson: I heard this in Kuibyshev as well. I remember an incident on the tram in Kuibyshev when people were saying that all the Jews were here, and there were none at the front, and then a Jew stood up and showed that his leg had been amputated.

[The next part of Bergelson's testimony was spent clarifying all of the circumstances surrounding the preparation and sending of the letter to the government about creating a Jewish autonomous republic in the Crimea. A large period of time also went to clarify all the details of Goldberg's and Novick's visits to the Soviet Union and all of their meetings with Bergelson and other members of the Jewish Anti-Fascist Committee.

Further on, the court touched on Bergelson's testimony during the preliminary investigation about "the propaganda of nationalistic ideas" conducted
by the Jewish Anti-Fascist Committee. Some excerpts from this part of Bergelson's testimony during the judicial session of May 15, 1952, provide an understanding of the accusations brought against all of the accused and of the
testimony beaten out of them by the investigators.]

Presiding Officer: Let us now move on to your testimony about the propaganda of nationalistic ideas conducted by the Anti-Fascist Committee. (He
reads out the expert commission's general conclusions regarding nationalistic propaganda.) Do you agree with the commission's conclusions?

Bergelson: I agree with the commission's conclusions.

Presiding Officer: So, in spoken propaganda as well as in print, the Jewish
Anti-Fascist Committee celebrated biblical images and advocated the unity
of Jews the world over based on bloodlines alone, without regard to class
distinctions. Is that so?

Bergelson: The celebration of biblical images slipped by just about everyone—in their work, in conversations, and in their poetry. I see nothing
criminal in that. There are certain images that are quite appropriate to celebrate. In some cases, celebrating certain images gives rise to very useful
thoughts.

Presiding Officer (reads out appeal to world Jewry): The appeal calls upon
every Jew to take the following oath: "I am a child of the Jewish people."
This is a call to unity based on bloodlines alone, is it not?

Bergelson: The appeal speaks of unity in the struggle against fascism.

Presiding Officer: Do you feel that the Jewish people alone are struggling
against fascism?

Bergelson: Well, this was a call from the anti-fascist Jews of the Soviet Union,
who were appealing to Jews of all countries during the war, when the Soviet Union was under fascist attack. This was at a time when people with
nationalistic feelings were included in the struggle. There are many such
expressions in literature, which were permitted at the time and were appropriate then, whereas now they would be considered highly nationalistic. There was an expression: "Brother Jews." I don't see anything wrong
with this expression.

Presiding Officer: Well, for example, in his poem "I Am a Jew," Fefer constantly emphasizes that he belongs to the Jewish people, and throughout
the whole poem he keeps yelling, "I am a Jew."

Bergelson: There cannot be anything criminal in the phrase "I am a Jew." If I
approach someone and say, "I am a Jew," what could be bad about that?

[The judicial session was continued on May 15, 1952. At 8:20 P.M. the presiding officer announced a recess. At 8:45 P.M., the judicial session continued.]

LEYB KVITKO

Among the Yiddish writers on trial, Leyb Kvitko was the most widely known inside the Soviet Union. Born in the village of Goloskovo, near Odessa, in 1890, Kvitko experienced deep tragedy as a child: his parents and each of his five older siblings died of tuberculosis before he reached the age of nine. Raised by his grandmother, he taught himself to read and on the eve of the revolution made his way to Kiev, where he earned a living as a Yiddish teacher. He also began writing poetry.

His friends urged him to visit David Bergelson in order to show him his poems and seek advice and encouragement. Filled with anxiety, Kvitko introduced himself to the older, more established writer, and Bergelson responded generously. This was the outset of Kvitko's remarkable career. By 1918 his first poems were appearing in *Eygns,* and he quickly made a name for himself as one of the leading lyric poets in Yiddish, alongside David Hofshteyn and Peretz Markish. He also wrote enthusiastically about the revolution, most notably in his collections of verse *Step* and *Red Storm,* both of which appeared in 1919. A Kiev publisher offered him a contract for translations that he was also preparing, then asked Kvitko to travel in two years' time to Germany, where the publishing house was hoping to broaden its business. Kvitko agreed, leaving Soviet Russia in 1921 and remaining in Germany for five years.

In Berlin, among various projects, Kvitko collaborated with the artist and designer El Lissitzky. They produced two lovely, illustrated volumes—*Ukrainian Folk Tales* (1922) and *Belorussian Folk Tales* (1923), with the texts translated into Yiddish by Kvitko.

In spite of this success, Kvitko was hardly able to earn a living. He moved for a time to Hamburg, where he worked as a porter, and returned to the Soviet Union in 1925. The following year, he produced a poem called "Before a Portrait of Lenin," in which he expressed a steadfast faith in the country's founder.* But if Kvitko was trying to establish his credentials as a patriotic and ideologically reliable servant of the regime—hardly a surprising gesture after five years outside the country—he soon demonstrated reckless disregard for his status. In 1929, Kvitko published a series of satirical poetic sketches. In one, he criticized an unnamed writer in the following uncompromising terms:

*Leyb Kvitko, *Izbrannoye* (Selected Works) (Moscow, 1990), pp. 24–26.

> You've got ideology.
> You've got demagoguery.
> You're missing one thing:
> Talentology.*

In another, "Moyli, the Stink Bird," Kvitko issued a direct attack on Moshe Litvakov, the most powerful, vitriolic, and feared critic, "a dogmatic, fanatical Communist," in the words of Esther Markish. There were few exceptions to Litvakov's targets. When he heard that mice had eaten the manuscripts of fellow Moscow Yiddish writers, he exclaimed with a laugh, "Good. Now we will finally be rid of the mice. There is no better poison for them."†

So Kvitko's sketches were an audacious gesture, particularly for a writer whose years in Germany left him vulnerable to an ideological counterattack. It was not long in coming. In Moscow, Minsk, Kharkov, and Kiev, Yiddish writers held meetings to protest Kvitko's "counter-revolutionary act" and to call for "ethical conduct" in Soviet Yiddish literature.‡ Expelled from the editorial board of *Di royte velt* (The Red World), he was compelled to find a job in a tractor factory for a couple of years.

David Hofshteyn, who had his own ambivalent and vulnerable relationship with the regime, displayed unusual courage in this affair. According to the late Chone Shmeruk, the foremost scholar of Soviet Yiddish literature, "Hofshteyn sent out a personal letter to dozens of writers and cultural functionaries entitled 'Against the degradation,' in which he listed Litvakov's deeds as a justification for Kvitko's poem."§

Kvitko soon began to write more and more for children and was able to find first-rate translators to turn his verses and stories into Russian. By the late 1930s he was among the most popular children's writers in the country. Kvitko's books were published in enormous editions, reaching millions of readers. Generations of Soviet schoolchildren studied his verses. Perhaps the most widely known was "A Letter to Voroshilov." Written in 1937, this patriotic poem was addressed to the

---

*Cited in an article by Y. Nusinov, "Nit derlozbar" (Not Permitted), *Royte velt*, no. 9, 1929, pp. 13–14.

†Markish, *Long Return*, p. 80; Gitelman, *Jewish Nationality and Soviet Politics*, p. 279.

‡Shmeruk, "Yiddish Literature in the U.S.S.R.," p. 261.

§Ibid., p. 262. Litvakov then attacked Hofshteyn; both letters can be found in *Der emes*, October 22, 1929, pp. 2–3.

People's Commissar for Defense Klement Voroshilov in the form of a letter in verse from a young schoolboy whose older brother is about to join the army. The boy has heard that "the fascists are thinking of war / they want to destroy the Soviet land." If his brother falls in battle, the boy pledges "to grow up fast" and take his brother's place at the front.* It is no exaggeration to say that every Soviet child in school between 1937 and Kvitko's arrest in 1949 knew this poem by heart.

Presiding Officer: Defendant Kvitko, to what do you plead guilty?

Kvitko: I plead guilty before the party and the Soviet people to working on a committee that brought great harm to the Motherland. I also plead guilty to not raising the issue of closing the Yiddish Section of the Soviet Writers' Union when I was the director of that section for a time after the war, and to not raising the issue of helping to speed up the assimilation of the Jews.

Presiding Officer: Do you deny that you are guilty of engaging in nationalistic activity in the past?

Kvitko: Yes. I deny that. I do not feel that I am guilty of that. I feel that I wished for happiness for the land where I was born, with all my heart and with every thought that was in me. I consider this land my homeland, in spite of all the case materials and the testimony against me.

Presiding Officer: Begin your testimony to the court from the moment when, as you embarked on your path as a writer, you made contact with the nationalists Dobrushin, Mayzl,† Hofshteyn, Markish, and Bergelson back in Kiev, telling how you worked with these nationalists and how under their influence you ran away from the Soviet Union. Start your testimony there.

Kvitko: Before the revolution I lived the life of a beaten, stray dog. My life was worth next to nothing. Since the Great October Revolution, I have lived thirty wonderful, inspiring years, filled with happiness in my beloved native land, where every blade of grass smiles on me. And you see before you now the end of my life. If my life requires any interpretation, I can do that, but if the court has already heard enough, then I will start with whatever you suggest.

Presiding Officer: Go ahead.

Kvitko: I didn't know anyone in Kiev except Bergelson. As a person, he leaves much to be desired, but he is genuinely a very good artist. So around 1915

---

*Leyb Kvitko, *K Solntsu* (Toward the Sun) (Moscow, 1948), pp. 32–33. This volume was printed in an edition of seventy-five thousand copies, a vivid indication of Kvitko's status as a poet.

†Nakhmen Mayzl (1887–1966) was a famous Yiddish literary critic and historian of Yiddish literature.

or 1916, people told me that Bergelson had come to town. At that time I was a complete ignoramus when it came to literature; I read very little, and I had never been to school. At the age of ten I went to work in a slaughter-house. And so I had a meeting with him, and although I was writing, no one knew except the people I worked with. Our whole family consisted of eight people—six children—and all of them died of tuberculosis as adults. I was the only one left. I lost my parents at a tender age, when I was very small. I lived with my grandmother, whom I supported by working at the slaughter-house and for a leather tanner. I could not devote myself exclusively to literature then, and I was semiliterate. I taught myself to read. And so when I went to see this well-known writer, Bergelson, to show him the little things I had written, some verses, I was very much afraid. I stood outside his house for a long time and could not summon the resolve to go in, for I was very poorly dressed, and he was at that time a very rich man. His brother owned a sugar factory, and Bergelson had come to visit him. For a long while I stood in thought at the threshold of his home, unable to enter, and finally I went in. I read him my poems. He liked them very much, and he praised me. This was how I met Bergelson.

He was the first writer whom I met and who received me warmly. At that time I wrote only in Yiddish and in a very illiterate style. I didn't write in Russian. I knew Ukrainian, since I had grown up in the Ukraine. My neighbors and childhood friends were Ukrainians, and so I knew Ukrainian.

Presiding Officer: Now let us talk about how you fled abroad. During the preliminary investigation (vol. 11, p. 38) in answer to the question "Why did you flee?" you replied, "I believed that the Soviet government was mishandling the Jewish national issue. The Jews were not recognized as a nation, which led, in my view, to their being deprived of any kind of independence and the infringement of their legal rights compared to other nationalities." Testify about your motives for fleeing the country.

Kvitko: I don't know how to put it so that you will believe me. When a religious defendant stands before the court and believes that he has been wrongly condemned or found guilty, he can comfort himself with the thought, They don't believe me, I have been condemned, but at least God knows the truth. Of course, I have no god, and I have never believed in God. The only god I have is the power of the Bolsheviks. That is my god, and I say before that faith that I did the hardest work imaginable when I was a child and an adolescent. What work was that? I don't want to talk about what I did when I was twelve years old. But facing a court is the hardest work in the world. I will tell you about my flight and about the reasons for it if you give me a chance.

I have been in a cell alone for two years by my own wishes. I have a reason for this. There is not a living soul of whom I can ask advice; there is no one who is more experienced in judicial matters. I meditate and suffer alone, in my own company. In 1950 the investigator summoned me and said, "Your case is done." He pressured me to read it quickly. I sat down and rushed through the first volume, which consisted of my interrogation records, and the second volume, consisting of testimony that the other defendants had given about me. I stopped and said, "If you are going to rush me, then I won't read it. I haven't been told why I've been given this to read, nor is anyone telling me what my rights are." I asked, "Do I have the right to protest? There are deliberate lies here, and fabrications." Wherever there was dirt, there was Kvitko's name; wherever there was any kind of nastiness, there was my name; wherever there was a crime against Soviet power, there I was—I was everywhere. I said, "If I were reading these two volumes about someone I didn't know, I would say, 'Kill this bastard if that's what it takes to keep him from contaminating Soviet soil. Chase him out of here.' But I am not the thug the investigation portrayed. I am not like what is described here. That is not me. So I ask you to appoint a defense attorney for me because I can fight this. I feel I have the strength to fight against my enemy; if the party, the government, or the people will send me to smother the enemy, I will choke him without mercy—I do not value my life so highly, I value something else more. But I confess that I am very weak when it comes to those who are close to me; anyone whom I consider close to me—a Soviet person—can destroy me. You tell me: "You've done such-and-such and such-and-such, and do you know what that is? That is treason.' And if I believe that you are a true Soviet person, I'll say, 'Of course, if that is what you say, then it's true, and if it's one, three, five people saying it, then it must be all the more true, and that means I am a traitor.'"

I asked the investigator whether he would allow me to have a defense attorney. He told me, "When we send your case to court, we will also give them our conclusions and our opinion of you and all the materials about your life." During the witness confrontation with Strongin, the director of the witness confrontation asked Strongin, "Why did you publish this collection of works by the nationalist Kvitko in Russian with a print run of seventy thousand copies?" He said, "Kvitko is not a nationalist, and his book was published with an even greater print run because it sells out very quickly." The investigator interrupted him and said, "Be quiet; don't defend Kvitko; he already has his defenders." What is this? I thought. And now I see that everything that was said about me has come into play here in court. Please forgive me for these details, but this is a human being standing before you.

Presiding Officer: How did you testify about your nationalistic motivations for fleeing?

Kvitko: That is a lie.

Presiding Officer: Why? Whose lie?

Kvitko: Mine.

Presiding Officer: Why did you lie?

Kvitko: It was very hard for me to fight the investigator. If you could only imagine how they dragged me through the mud. On the eve of my arrest, a month before, the presidium of the Soviet Writers' Union planned a celebration to mark my thirtieth year as a writer. The Soviet Writers' Union, not the Yiddish Section, but the union itself, held an event in my honor. The very best writers spoke; Valentin Kataev, Marshak, Chukovsky, Bezymensky, came and sat at the presidium. There were a lot of writers, and so many wonderful speeches in my honor. Vera Vasilievna Smirnova* spoke, and she said that I knew how to present pressing current issues in a way accessible to children and do it like a true communist. And after an event like this, after such a celebration, I was arrested, and at the very first interrogation I was called a nationalist. I went mad. I didn't consider all the others nationalists at that time, either. What can I say? It was very hard for me. I fought every evening, I tell you (you can believe me or not, as you choose). Go ahead, you can cut off my head. I'm not afraid of that. I am not afraid for my life, but I assure you that I didn't want anything bad. To the contrary, all my life I have wanted to give my work to the people.

Presiding Officer: And why did you sign the interrogation record?

Kvitko: Because it would have been hard not to sign it.

Presiding Officer: So you repudiate your testimony?

Kvitko: I deny it completely.

Presiding Officer: Bergelson confessed that he fled from Moscow, and you heard his testimony where he describes this as treason. How did you meet him?

Kvitko: Is it wrong to travel together? Don't an archimandrite and a worker ever find themselves in the same train car together?

Presiding Officer: But how do you explain the fact that you tried to cross the border together with him? When did you meet up with Bergelson in Minsk?

Kvitko: I left for Minsk earlier.

Presiding Officer: How did Bergelson find you?

---

*Valentin Kataev (1897–1986) was a well-known Soviet writer. During World War II, he was a correspondent for *Pravda* and *Krasnaya Zvezda* (Red Star). Samuil Marshak (1887–1964), Soviet poet, children's writer, and translator from English of the works of Shakespeare, Blake, and Burns, was regarded by Maxim Gorky as the founder of Soviet children's literature. He wrote on Jewish themes and had lived in Palestine before the October Revolution. During World War II he was a member of the JAC. Kornei Chukovsky (Nikolai Korneichukov) (1882–1969) was a revered Soviet children's writer, as well as a poet, literary scholar, and critic. He translated many books from English, including works by Mark Twain, Walt Whitman, Oscar Wilde, O. Henry, and Sir Arthur Conan Doyle. He was the first Soviet writer to receive an honorary degree from Oxford, in 1962. Later in the 1960s, he befriended Alexander Solzhenitsyn. Vera Smirnova (1898–1977) was a children's writer and literary critic. She translated works by Kvitko into Russian.

Kvitko: I was one of the first young poets of the revolution, and I was known in Minsk.

Presiding Officer: So, in a word, you are repudiating this testimony.

Kvitko: I repudiate it. Listen to me. The revolution made a person out of me, and everything that I have I acquired thanks to the October Revolution. The day of the October Revolution will always remain in my memory as the most joyful, as the happiest holiday in my life. So the revolution could not be the reason why I left. This can be verified by looking at my poems that were published at the time in the communist press in Kiev.

Presiding Officer: When did you become a candidate for party membership?

Kvitko: In 1940, and in January 1941 I became a party member. Everyone had left, and I didn't know what to do. When writers started being evacuated from Moscow, I was evacuated, too. I didn't want to be evacuated to Tashkent with the Yiddish collective that was involved in the theater because they wrote plays. Thank God, I do not write plays, and God himself protected me from involvement with the theater and with Mikhoels.

Presiding Officer: Do you believe in God?

Kvitko: No.

Presiding Officer: So why are you talking about him?

Kvitko: I left with the Kukryniki.* We headed for Alma-Ata in order to do a new book there that would be in the spirit of the times. That didn't work out, because there were no new publications coming out there. Several months went by, and nothing came of it. Then I wrote a letter to the Propaganda Department of the Central Committee asking for a job, any job, so that I wouldn't be sitting around with nothing to do. Suddenly I get a telegram signed by Lozovsky, saying that I am being summoned for great work in Kuibyshev. So I came to Kuibyshev, and Epshteyn tells me that Mikhoels has been appointed to be chairman of the Jewish Anti-Fascist Committee, but that he, Epshteyn, will be in charge.

Presiding Officer: And you knew Epshteyn?

Kvitko: Yes, I knew Epshteyn back in Kharkov. In addition, Epshteyn told me that he was appointing me to be his assistant.

[Kvitko's testimony began on the evening of May 15 and was interrupted at 10:10 P.M. The next court session did not take place until a week later, on Thursday, May 22. The documents have yet to provide an answer to the question of what caused the unexpected break in the court proceedings. It is possible to conclude that Kvitko's total and decisive repudiation of his testimony from the preliminary investigation and the convincing nature of the facts that he marshaled in his defense put the Military Collegium in a difficult position.

*The Kukryniki was a group of three Soviet caricaturists who created famous political cartoons; their sobriquet was based on their names: Kuprianov, Krylov, and Sokolov.

We still do not know what happened during this week. But on May 22 at 12:15 P.M. the court continued the questioning of Kvitko.]

Presiding Officer: Now testify about the work of the committee itself. We have established here that the committee's mission was propaganda, and you said in this regard (vol. 11, p. 48): "In a highly nationalistic spirit we spread propaganda abroad that was supposed to serve the interests of the Soviet Union. The achievements of Jews in every area of the national economy and cultural life were shown, and the leading role of other nationalities, including Russians, was downplayed. Consequently an impression was created that the Jews were the people who counted in the USSR." Is this accurate?

Kvitko: For the most part it is accurate. Why? First of all, this is confirmed by what happened at Mikhoels's funeral, and by what I saw when Meyerson, "the lady from Palestine," arrived. All this gives me a full understanding of the fact that what the committee did was destructive and harmful to the Soviet Union.

Presiding Officer: How exactly?

Kvitko: How exactly? The nationalism that was so obvious at Mikhoels's funeral and at Meyerson's reception indicate that in conducting activities that were specifically Jewish, that is, that dealt only with Jewish matters, the Jewish Anti-Fascist Committee encouraged the intensification of nationalistic attitudes among the Jewish masses in the Soviet Union.

Presiding Officer: And what about Lozovsky?

Kvitko: This is a very complicated matter. I accuse Lozovsky of more than mere leadership.

Presiding Officer: Meaning what, specifically?

Kvitko: This is someone who knew Comrade Lenin personally. Who knew how Comrade Lenin thought about assimilation. (I've grown more familiar with this issue in prison.) Who knew how Comrade Lenin framed the issue of Jewish assimilation, where Comrade Lenin says, "Can it really be the case that under Soviet power, under conditions of freedom, the assimilation process will be slowed down, if assimilation is taking place even in bourgeois countries?" And he talks about what the assimilation process will look like. Knowing all this, what did Lozovsky do? I can understand a Yiddish writer, I understand Bergelson, I understand Markish. I understand myself.

Presiding Officer: In what sense?

Kvitko: We are writers, and our instrument is language. Whether you want to or not, you cannot go along with the assimilated segment of the Jewish population, but you can prepare people for assimilation. I feel that Yiddish literature prepared the masses for assimilation, and I am sure of that, sure because the content of this literature indicates as much. Bergelson and

Markish wrote very purposefully. We are not talking here about their errors. There were errors as well, certainly, but they were writing in favor of Soviet power, agitating in favor of all undertakings for a new life. This was how they prepared the reading public, which still hung on to Yiddish literature, for assimilation. The masses went, but that was easy for the masses, because it is easier to work at a large factory than as an artisan in a small workshop, better and easier, and more interesting. A Yiddish writer who is attached to his language has a harder time changing his instrument than the masses do; it is impossible for him to leave the culture behind, as the masses can.

Presiding Officer: And do you, Kvitko, feel that the Jewish Theater did work against assimilation?

Kvitko: Of course it was against assimilation. I saw that it was a branch of the Jewish Anti-Fascist Committee. There were ten to twelve Jews sitting in Mikhoels's waiting room waiting to get in and see him.

Presiding Officer: What did they want to see him about? Were they artists who wanted to see him about matters relating to the theater?

Kvitko: No, judging from their appearance, I would say they were there to see him about various things having nothing to do with the theater. I spent a good hour there before his lordship would receive me.

Presiding Officer: And what connection did the committee have with the synagogue?

Kvitko: It is simply shameful to speak about the relationship that Mikhoels and Fefer had with the leadership of the Jewish religious community. It was just a disgrace for a modern person, not to mention a Soviet person. Mikhoels and Fefer went to see them on holidays.

Presiding Officer: They went to pray in the synagogue?

Kvitko: No, they went to Chobrutsky's apartment. He was chairman of the community, real scum, a shady fellow, and they were friends with him. I feel that this is unforgivable. At one time I talked with Halkin a lot about how this was going to end very badly. Shlifer is a good person. I think that he was more honorable in these matters than these people were.

Presiding Officer: And was he a cleric or a secular person?

Kvitko: Apparently, he had been selected for entrance into the religious community.

Presiding Officer: And what did Chobrutsky do?

Kvitko: I've heard that he was speculating on the black market; he certainly created that impression.

Presiding Officer: Tell about how Goldberg came. Who is Goldberg, and what do you know about the circumstances of his visit? Did you meet with him? What conversations did you have? Do you know him, and how did you come to know him?

Kvitko: I know Goldberg. I didn't know him before he came here, and he did not know me. His visit here was well known and highly publicized.

Presiding Officer: Who publicized it?

Kvitko: The committee.

Presiding Officer: Including you? You were a presidium member, and no doubt the committee discussed the question, didn't it? During the investigation the investigator asked you a question about espionage contact with Goldberg, to which you answered, "I do not deny that my contact with Goldberg was criminal in nature."

[Later, the presiding officer clarified the relationship. Kvitko noted that the conversation had concerned the exchange of materials, articles, and publications about scientific, cultural, and artistic achievements. There was a plan to publish a magazine together, to be called *Moscow–New York*.]

Presiding Officer: And what was the criminal nature of your contact?

Kvitko: There was nothing criminal.

Presiding Officer: So why did you give this testimony? Who made you do it?

Kvitko: Circumstances.

Fefer: Why did you decide that assimilation was Communist Party policy?

Kvitko: In Lenin's works ("A Discussion with the Bundists")* it says that when the revolution comes, when Russia is free, it will be a favorable time for assimilation. He considered assimilation as a very progressive process and in the interests of the masses and the country. And if the committee, in organizing Jews, was not preparing them for assimilation, if we were making nearly assimilated Jews back into Jews again, then that meant that we were acting against Comrade Lenin's directives and against the party line.

Fefer: Are you aware that when Jews came to Comrades Lenin and Stalin to discuss the issue of developing their culture in their own language, they were always met with support, and that most of the Jewish organizations were created under Lenin? When Comrade Stalin was told that the Moscow Yiddish writers did not have their own literary journal, he asked, "What about the Yiddish writers of the Ukraine and Belorussia? Do they have literary journals?" Why are the Yiddish writers of Moscow the only ones who need one? If this was a policy of assimilation, then it was party policy as well, and so there would have been no Birobidzhan.

Kvitko: The very way you posed the question contains within it the whole problem. Here's why Yiddish culture was needed, just as the literature of all

---

*Kvitko is probably referring to Lenin's piece "The Position of the Bund in the Party," which appeared in *Iskra* (The Spark), no. 51, October 22, 1903. It can also be found in V. I. Lenin, *Collected Works*, vol. 7: *October 1903–December 1904* (Moscow, 1961), pp. 92–103.

the national minorities was needed, in order to prepare the masses in their native languages for assimilation by a certain time.

[On May 23, 1952, at 12:20 P.M., the court session continued.]

Fefer: As far as I know, you wrote a piece about fascist atrocities against Jews in the Crimea. Is this the case?

Kvitko: Yes, it is.

Fefer: And what did you do with it?

Kvitko: I don't remember. Please refresh my memory.

Fefer: You said that you didn't know anything about *The Black Book* and found out about it only during the investigation. I would like to remind you that you wrote that piece for *The Black Book.*

Kvitko: But it wasn't for the American edition; it was for the Soviet one.* At that time there was no talk of publishing *The Black Book* in America. That article was published in 1943 in the Ukrainian magazine *The Ukraine,* which was coming out at that time in Moscow. This was before your trip to America. So the question of creating *The Black Book* in 1942 could hardly have come up. Perhaps I proposed that piece for *The Black Book* a year after it was written, when there was talk of publishing *The Black Book* in the Soviet Union.

Fefer: In late 1942 a telegram had already arrived from Albert Einstein, the famous American scientist, with a proposal to the Jewish Anti-Fascist Committee to jointly publish *The Black Book.* There were many conversations about this. Since you were sharing an office with Epshteyn, you must have known about it. After all, we didn't get many telegrams from Albert Einstein. It was an event. So that is why I think that piece was offered to *The Black Book.* After all, it contained material about the Crimea. And the possibility of publishing a Russian-language edition of *The Black Book* was raised later by Ehrenburg.

Kvitko (speaking to Fefer): You're very smart, very careful, in the way you are testifying, always to your own advantage, and as a result you're presenting the case in a false light. For example, here is how things were when we were called in to the party Control Commission. All of the board members were there. I didn't know them. The only one I knew was Shkiryatov.† He asked me whether I had seen the letter and whether I had signed the letter that had been sent to Malenkov on behalf of the committee.

---

*Kvitko wrote at least two pieces about atrocities in the Crimea for the Soviet *Black Book* project. Ehrenburg referred to Kvitko's contribution during a meeting of the *Black Book* Literary Commission on October 13, 1944; a transcript of this meeting can be found in the Andrei Sakharov Archive at Harvard University, Grossman file, number G18. Kvitko's two contributions can be found in Ilya Ehrenburg and Vasily Grossman, *The Black Book* (New York, 1980), pp. 273–277, 285–288.

†Matvei Shkiryatov (1883–1954), a prominent party leader, was vice chairman of the party Control Commission from 1939 to 1952.

Presiding Officer: About what?

Kvitko: A letter was written saying that the committee found it vitally important to send Mikhoels and Fefer as delegates to Poland, where they would work with Polish committees (what committees, I don't know), and then from there go on to some other peoples' democracies. I don't remember this now in detail. But Fefer signed the letter with my name.

Lozovsky: When was this?

Kvitko: This was in 1947, I think. So Shkiryatov asks me whether I've seen this letter. I say no. Did I sign the letter? I say no. He is very annoyed, and he turns to Fefer and says, "Where did you learn to play these games?" He says to Fefer, "Why did you decide that you and Mikhoels should go to Poland? That you are the ones who should be sent there? Why not someone else, even Zuskin? And who are you to send letters saying that you should be the one to go, hiding behind a counterfeit signature?" That was when Shkiryatov swore at Lozovsky, too.

Fefer: You are lying.

Kvitko: Why would I lie about Lozovsky?

Lozovsky: What for?

Kvitko: For the committee.

Lozovsky: At the time, I had no involvement with the committee.

Kvitko: Perhaps you didn't, but he swore at you in connection with the committee, although you weren't involved with it. I don't know, and of course it's hard for the court to figure this all out when faced with such people, but I assure you that Shkiryatov did swear at Lozovsky. Apparently Fefer arranged this all with Lozovsky. And afterward, when we were outside by the Central Committee building, Fefer, all worked up after the rather stormy session, said to me that I would now rush off to tell "the old man" about it. And if this is not true, then you have my permission to execute me for that alone. He probably called Lozovsky on the phone before heading off to the Central Committee.

Presiding Officer: Was Lozovsky involved with the committee at this time?

Kvitko: I don't know.

Presiding Officer: Defendant Kvitko, what other testimony can you give the court that relates directly to the accusation against you?

Kvitko: Allow me to respond separately to each charge.

Charge number one—"was an active Jewish nationalist; over the course of many years carried out work hostile to the Communist Party and the Soviet government."

I cannot consider myself a nationalist. Not in my thoughts, my words, or my actions. I never spoke out or did any sort of work against the Communist Party or the Soviet government at any time in my entire life. There are no facts or documents on which to base such an accusation. I believe that from the time of the October Revolution until I was arrested, all of my activity was devoted exclusively to the Soviet people and the Soviet Motherland. Numerous irrefutable facts, my writings, and existing people, a list of whom I can present, all testify to this.

Second charge—"as deputy senior secretary of the Jewish Anti-Fascist Committee, entered into a criminal conspiracy with active enemies of the Soviet people, Mikhoels, Fefer, and Epshteyn, together with whom he used the committee for criminal purposes, transforming it into an organization hostile to Soviet power."

My answer is as follows. My secretarial position was for show, a fiction. That is apparent from Epshteyn's comments about my being useless for serious ideological and political activity and from his unwillingness to entrust me with editing materials that were sent abroad. There is no way that there could have been any conspiracy. The fact that I ran away from Kuibyshev during my third month of work shows clearly that there was no such conspiracy with them.

The third point says that I gave assignments to my accomplices to collect materials to send to the United States.

I signed only one letter for circulation, which was sent to the writer Kagan, about sending materials to the Jewish Anti-Fascist Committee. The Jewish Anti-Fascist Committee sent similar letters to every writer. How is it evident—and why do I face such an accusation—that the material which I requested should be considered classified material? Didn't the Jewish Anti-Fascist Committee send thousands of items abroad that were honest propaganda materials and that served the interests of the Soviet Union? There were many similar materials, and the letter that I signed was referring precisely to this sort of Soviet material.

The fourth charge says that in 1944 I went to the Crimea to gather information about the economic situation in the region and the size of the Jewish population there, all of which was subsequently forwarded by the committee to the United States.

Yesterday I testified that I did not go to the Crimea to gather information about the economic situation in the region. Anyone who knows me in the slightest understands that I am far from being an economist, especially one who specializes in the economy of an entire region. I, the freshly minted economist Kvitko, looked over only a few Jewish settlements. I did not gather any information, and no materials about my trip to the Crimea were sent to the United States or to other countries. I believe that my trip to the Crimea was not criminal in nature. Perhaps it was reproachable in some way, perhaps looking at how people lived there was not my concern, but it was not criminal. My intentions were correct Soviet intentions. Otherwise, there would have been people on the presidium who would have reined me in, and they would not have put together a four-person delegation to deliver the letter to the People's Commissariat of Land Use and Distribution. And finally, if there had been anything criminal or unworthy of a Soviet person in that letter, People's Commissar Andreyev or his deputy Benediktov would not have hesitated to scold me and the other delegates severely. But nothing like that happened.

The fifth charge says that in 1946 I established a personal contact with American intelligence officer Goldberg for the purpose of espionage, informed him about the state of affairs in the Soviet Writers' Union, and consented to a joint annual publication through which the Americans intended to receive intelligence information about the Soviet Union.

Yesterday I gave detailed testimony about my meetings with Goldberg. I had no espionage contact with him, nor were there any conversations or talks on forbidden topics. I did not have close contact with him. I did not answer questions having to do with politics, nor did he ask me such questions. He was not interested in asking me such questions, and I did not talk with him about such things. We made small talk about poetry, about books that were just out, about whether Sholem Aleichem was accessible to children. We talked for all of several minutes.

What do I accuse myself of? What do I feel guilty of? First of all, of not seeing and not understanding that the committee's activity was bringing the Soviet state great harm, and of the fact that I also worked on that committee. The second thing of which I consider myself guilty is this: Feeling that Soviet Yiddish literature was ideologically healthy and Soviet, we Yiddish writers, myself included (perhaps I am more guilty of this than the others), did not pose the question of how we could promote the process of assimilation. I am talking about the assimilation of the Jewish masses. By continuing to write in Yiddish, we unwittingly became a brake on the process of assimilation. The work of Soviet writers is ideologically and politically firm, and this content—the Soviet content—served in no insignificant way to promote the assimilation of large masses of the Jewish population. But in recent years the language has ceased to serve the masses, because they—the masses—have left the Yiddish language behind. So it started to stand in the way. As the director of the Yiddish Section of the Soviet Writers' Union, I did not raise the question of closing down the section. Herein lies my guilt. To use a language that the masses have left behind, that has outlived its time, and that sets us apart not only from the larger life of the Soviet Union but from Jews at large, Jews who are already assimilated, to use such a language, in my opinion, is, in its own way, a manifestation of nationalism. Apart from that, I do not feel that I am guilty.

Presiding Officer: Is that all?

Kvitko: That's all.

DAVID HOFSHTEYN

David Hofshteyn was an established and widely recognized Yiddish poet by the time of the revolution. He welcomed the Bolsheviks' triumph, hoping it would improve conditions for Jews in the country where they had long faced severe persecution. Hofshteyn wrote several patriotic poems at that time, like "October," which were sincere statements of his faith. But the violence of the ensuing Civil War tempered his hopes; one poem, "Snow," expressed such deep chagrin over pogroms that his interrogators asked him about it in 1948 soon after his arrest. Hofshteyn was well known for his generous nature, offering himself as a mentor to many younger poets, including Shmuel Halkin, Itsik Kipnis, and Itsik Fefer, whose first volume of poetry, in 1922, carried an introduction by Hofshteyn. That year he also published a book with Marc Chagall entitled *Tristia*.

Hofshteyn first left Soviet Russia for several months in 1921, traveling with David Bergelson to Berlin. But he did not stay long before returning to Kiev. It was in 1924 that he initially crossed swords with Soviet cultural officials. That year, a memorandum addressed to Soviet officials circulated within the artistic community protesting restrictions on the status of Hebrew and the arrest of Hebrew writers. Hofshteyn added his name as editor of the Yiddish journal *Shtrom* (Stream) and as a member of the Central Committee of the Kultur lige (Culture League). He then faced immediate reprisals. Other leaders of the Kultur lige called a special meeting on January 17, 1924, during which Hofshteyn backed down and offered to recant his involvement in the protest. But on February 3, at a second meeting, Hofshteyn refused to repeat his earlier recantation. This infuriated his more subservient colleagues. As a result, twenty-seven Yiddish writers declared publicly that Hofshteyn had "excluded himself from the family of Jewish activists who work among the Jewish working masses," an awkward-sounding but, in Soviet terms, sinister accusation;* a similar resolution against him circulated in Belorussia and the Ukraine. Hofshteyn was removed as editor of *Shtrom* and excluded from the Association of Writers.

All this influenced his decision to leave the country. In early 1925, Hofshteyn and his second wife, Feige, traveled to Berlin, where they saw David Bergelson and Leyb Kvitko. But Hofshteyn was not happy in

---

*Cited in Altshuler, *Briv fun yidishe sovetishe shrayber*, p. 79.

Germany. Although he was contributing poems to a New York Yiddish journal, he was barely able to support himself and his wife. As he wrote to a friend in New York, he "did not know where to go."* In April he and Feige left Berlin by train for Trieste, where they boarded a boat bound for Alexandria, Egypt.

Many of their fellow tourists were headed for Palestine to witness the opening of the Hebrew University. From Alexandria it was an easy train ride through the Sinai Desert to Jerusalem. They stayed with Feige's brothers, who were employed as construction workers on Mount Scopus, where the university was taking shape. Hofshteyn was widely known, at least in literary circles. As he, his wife, and their baggage made their way through Jerusalem, the poet Uri Zvi Greenberg recognized Hofshteyn—they had never met—and accompanied them to the university's opening ceremony. Hofshteyn could not have been happier. After only one day in Jerusalem, he wrote to a friend in New York, "I am in the land of Israel. On the one hand, this means so much to me that I am ready to repeat these words a thousand times. I have no other words, and for now I am not looking for them to fully express my astonishment."†

Nonetheless, Hofshteyn had difficulty finding a place for himself as a Yiddish poet. He barely earned a living. For a time, he joined a group of workers assigned to agricultural projects and road construction near Rehovot, just south of Tel Aviv.‡ At one point he found work in the statistics department of the Tel Aviv city government. He did publish a number of poems in Palestine, including several in Hebrew that appeared in the first issue of the newspaper *Davar* (The Word), a socialist daily published by the kibbutz movement. Looking back, we can imagine Hofshteyn staying in the country; he had an established reputation, he loved being in Palestine, his wife's brothers were already there, and six weeks before he returned to the Ukraine, his daughter, Levia, was born in Tel Aviv. So why did he leave?

In Hofshteyn's case, family pressures forced his hand. Hofshteyn had two young sons from his first marriage, Hillel and Shammai; their

*From a letter to Abraham Liessen, cited in David Hofshteyn and Feige Hofshteyn, *Izbranniye. Stikhotvoreniya. Pisma. S Lyubovyu i Bolyu o Davidye Hofshteyne* [(David Hofshteyn,] Selected Poems. Letters. [Feige Hofshteyn,] With Love and Pain About David Hofshteyn) (Jerusalem, 1997), p. 96.

†From a letter to Liessen, in ibid, p. 46.

‡Eliahu Eilat, letter to the editor, *Davar*, August 31, 1971, p. 8.

mother had died in 1920. When Hofshteyn left Kiev in 1925, his sons remained in the care of his father and sister. The children missed their father and needed material and emotional support. In addition, with their father living in Palestine, the boys were being taunted by classmates for having a "traitor" for a father. Already, it seems, with the regime not even a decade old, the Soviet mindset of mistrust for the outside world was taking hold within the population.

Being abroad also posed a practical dilemma for Hofshteyn; he had been granted a one-year visa, and it was about to expire. He was not in a position to disregard it and thereby abandon his sons and the rest of his family in Kiev. Just before he left Palestine, two fellow writers, Berl Katznelson and Moshe Beilinson, tried to convince him to remain, promising "to guarantee work."* Hofshteyn did not heed their counsel. He returned to Kiev. Feige and Levia would have to rejoin him later.

Once back, Hofshteyn immediately succumbed to pressure and submitted an open letter to *Der emes* in which he repented for his earlier mistakes. "My words during that argument [referring to the controversy over Hebrew] have been definitively liquidated, and I again want to take my place among those who are building this new life of the Jewish toiling masses in the Soviet Union."† That April, Hofshteyn also added his name to a public appeal signed by forty-eight Soviet Yiddish writers who were calling on the regime to settle half a million Jews on the land, an appeal meant to deflect attention from Zionist longings. Hofshteyn understood what he had to do. "I have just returned from Palestine," he wrote in *Der emes*. "I saw what came out of all the promises and declarations of the English mandate. . . . To get a man settled on the soil of Israel is an enormously difficult and expensive task. Every honest Jew should help the Soviet government in its great task [to settle half a million Jews on land in the USSR]."‡

Feige and Levia could not join Hofshteyn in Kiev until 1929, when Feige's personal appeal to Maxim Litvinov, the deputy people's commissar for foreign affairs§—after repeated attempts to gain permission to return—resulted in the long-sought visa. Feige and Levia would not re-

---

*Hofshteyn, *S Lyubovyu i Bolyu o Davidye Hofshteynye*, p. 49.

†*Der emes*, April 20, 1926, as cited in Altshuler, *Briv fun yidishe sovetishe shrayber*, p. 80.

‡*Der emes*, April 23, 1926, cited in Altshuler, *Briv fun yidishe sovetishe shrayber*, pp. 99–100.

§Maxim Litvinov (Wallach) (1876–1951) was people's commissar for foreign affairs from 1930 to 1939 and ambassador to the United States from 1941 to 1943.

sume their lives in Tel Aviv until 1973; David Hofshteyn, by then, was dead.

Presiding Officer: Defendant Hofshteyn, to what do you plead guilty before the court?

Hofshteyn: I will start with what has been touched upon here. I am guilty of, in 1944—when, as a thinking person, I could have written poems in which I bade farewell to the Yiddish language and read these poems in the auditorium of the Jewish Anti-Fascist Committee in the presence of all the writers (Markish, Nusinov, and others)—stating that we needed this language. I was unable to force myself and others to cease political activity in this language. Nusinov then spoke and said that it was impossible to talk so decisively about such issues as repudiating one's native language.

Second, in 1942, when I came to Kuibyshev from Ufa, Epshteyn received me, said that there was a job that would involve writing articles for American newspapers, and started giving me instructions about what these press outlets needed. I was outraged and said that we were qualified writers (he knew me very well) and that it would be a tremendous honor for them if we were to send them things that we had written, as we all knew the cultural level of that press. He started to argue with me, and I went to a superior to complain, to Lozovsky. Yuzefovich was there, and he would not let me into the office. I was very angry. Finally Lozovsky received me, and he calmed me down, and I said that I would write. And I did in fact write a small piece (a copy of it exists). I was offended that an old writer was being asked to become a reporter to provide news to what we all knew was the yellow press.

But my greatest guilt lies in the fact that when the Red Army came to Kiev, I did not follow the example of my cousin Asher Schwartzman, who went to the front.* I stayed in Kiev, giving myself over to literary dreams, and instead of taking up arms and fighting against the followers of Petlura, I busied myself with kindergartens, with schools, and with children who had been orphaned in Petlura's pogroms. I was a math and physics teacher. I started publishing textbooks and a children's magazine and also worked as a proofreader at the newspaper *Naye tsayt,* which was an organ of the Fareynikte Party.

Presiding Officer: You say, "At the same time I published my poem "Snow" in *Naye tsayt,* in which I tried to frighten ordinary Jews by portraying the horrors of socialist revolution and the 'violence' the Bolsheviks wreaked against the civilian population." Did you write this poem?

Hofshteyn: Such a poem does exist. It is a poem about snow falling and about

---

*During the Civil War, the Red Army reached Kiev in February 1919.

how on the white snow there are drops of blood, which are too red. I came from a small town, and that poem was written under the influence of a pogrom. When Soviet power came, *Naye tsayt,* which had by then been renamed *Komfon* (Communist Flag), printed verses of mine that had been lying on someone's desk for six months unpublished. This was my first revolutionary poetry.

Presiding Officer: You testified during the investigation that this poem contained slander against the Bolsheviks, saying they humiliated civilians, and this testimony is over your signature.

Hofshteyn: I was unable to think straight then.

Presiding Officer: And later you say, "In 1918 I published a slanderous article about the Red Army."

Hofshteyn: My first article about the Red Army was printed in the first Yiddish publication, which was called *Di royte armey.* This was an obituary for my cousin Asher Schwartzman.

Presiding Officer: But this testimony is over your signature. Where are you telling the truth, there or here?

Hofshteyn: I think that my memory is working at its best right now. I can recollect my whole life and remember what I have published. But then, during the investigation, I was in such a state that I could not comprehend what I was signing or what I was doing.

Presiding Officer: Are you a religious man?

Hofshteyn: No, I have never been a religious man. I lived in a small town for several years, and all of my relatives were peasants. I was one of the first Jews in those parts who pulled up trees, plowed, and mowed on Saturdays.

Presiding Officer: One does not preclude the other. A person can be religious and engage in physical labor.

Hofshteyn: But I never had any religious tendencies. The Jews have a law forbidding any work on Saturdays, and no religious Jew would desecrate the Sabbath. But I, as I've already said, did physical labor on the Sabbath.

[The next day, on May 24, 1952, at 12:15 P.M., Hofshteyn's testimony resumed.]

Presiding Officer: The session of the Collegium will resume. Do you confirm that you never talked previously with anyone about the Crimea question?

Hofshteyn: There was only one single conversation with Mikhoels in Kuibyshev. When he was a little drunk, he talked to me about that, but I did not take it seriously.

Presiding Officer: And did you say anything to him about the Crimea?

Hofshteyn: No. He said to me, "Pay no attention to what I'm telling you about Birobidzhan."

Presiding Officer: Why do you connect this conversation with the discussion between you and Mikhoels about the Crimea?

Hofshteyn: Because after Mikhoels got back from America and after I arrived from Kiev, I ran into Mikhoels when I was walking down Tverskoy Boulevard. He stopped me and asked, "Do you know who's working in the Crimea now?" I said I didn't know. He told me that Jacob Kreizer* was working there. It was said in such a way that one might have thought that the committee members had assigned him to study the Crimea. Mikhoels said that now Jacob Kreizer would do everything there. What he was doing there, I don't know.

Presiding Officer: And what did you say to him in response to this? What made you conclude that Mikhoels was constantly dealing with the Crimea question?

Hofshteyn: Suchkov told me that both Pasternak and Asmus† knew this, that Mikhoels had told them that there would be a unit established in the Crimea.

[Later the presiding officer returned to the question of Hofshteyn's espionage activity and, specifically, to the testimony he had given during the preliminary investigation about how in 1944 he had received an assignment from the Jewish Anti-Fascist Committee to gather classified information.]

Presiding Officer: You said that Mikhoels was displeased with the information being sent to him and demanded much broader information and more active nationalistic work in Kiev.

Hofshteyn: He did all that himself.

Presiding Officer: And you saw that he was doing this and decided to be the committee's representative in Kiev?

Hofshteyn: Yes, that's how it turned out. I was in the Moscow synagogue during a memorial service for the victims of fascism when even old Party members were there.

Presiding Officer: Who?

Hofshteyn: Fefer was there, and someone else as well.

Presiding Officer: And everyone there was praying?

Hofshteyn: It was a day in memory of the dead. I noted that suddenly a woman arrived. I had no idea what went on behind the scenes at the com-

*Jacob Kreizer (1905–1969) was a high-ranking Jewish military officer who commanded troops in the liberation of the Crimea and the Baltic region during World War II. In 1941 he received the Hero of the Soviet Union award. He was a member of the JAC presidium.

†Boris Suchkov (1917–1974) was a literary critic in Moscow. He wrote widely on German and French literature in particular. Boris Pasternak (1890–1960), the renowned poet, novelist, and translator, was a close friend of Valentin Asmus (1894–1975), who was a professor of philosophy at Moscow State University.

mittee. I was surprised that this woman went where she wasn't supposed to be (the women's area is in the gallery above). I turned to the people standing next to me, Halkin and Kvitko, and they told me that this was Zhemchuzhina.

Presiding Officer: Who else was there?

Hofshteyn: Fefer, Halkin, Weizmann,* and Katsovel [Katsovitsh].†

Presiding Officer: What were they praying for?

Hofshteyn: They were reading the usual prayer for the dead. Someone pointed out Academician Tarle‡ to me as well.

Presiding Officer: In your testimony you say that your home became a gathering place for Jewish nationalists. So, your home became a gathering place for anti-Soviet people, with whom you discussed your affairs. Is this testimony of yours correct?

Hofshteyn: Well, clearly all of these people were interested in Yiddish, and a lot of people came to me asking me to read them the letters that they were receiving from their relatives. Since I knew the language perfectly and was one of the only people who did, people asked me to read to them. These letters came from Palestine and elsewhere.

Presiding Officer: Did anti-Soviet people gather in your apartment in Kiev and discuss the aim of struggling against Soviet power? This is the gist of your testimony. Was your home a gathering place for Jewish nationalists?

Hofshteyn: That was not the sort of home I had.

Presiding Officer: Why did you say so in your testimony?

Hofshteyn: When I was given that to sign, I was certain that that was what I needed to do, but for what, I didn't know.

Presiding Officer: And Mikhoels and Fefer gave you anti-Soviet assignments to carry out? This is what I'm asking you. Answer my questions.

Hofshteyn: To me personally, none whatsoever.

Presiding Officer: You don't want to answer my questions. I am asking you, what anti-Soviet assignment did Mikhoels and Fefer give you in Kiev?

Hofshteyn: None.

Presiding Officer: But why did you say that they came to Kiev and reproached you for your slowness and sluggishness and pointed out the need to get in

---

*Samuel Weizmann (1882–?) was a brother of Chaim Weizmann's. He was active in the Socialist Zionist Party, which became a non-Palestine territorialist party under the tsar. He later entered the Yevsektsiya and directed industrial plants in the Soviet Union. He was arrested some time after World War II and is believed to have died in a labor camp.

†Leyzer Katsovitsh (1903–1953) was a Yiddish poet, writer, artist, and cinematographer.

‡Yevgeny Tarle (1875–1955) was a prominent Soviet historian, famous for his work on French military history and his biographies of Napoleon and Talleyrand.

touch with associations of Ukrainian émigrés in America to send information about the state of things in the Ukraine? Did you give such testimony or not?

Hofshteyn: They didn't have this kind of conversation with me personally.

Presiding Officer: You said that such instructions from Mikhoels and Fefer were given to you, Spivak, Loitsker, Polyanker, Kagan, and others. Apparently you would gather at various times, at one time with Mikhoels, at another with Fefer, and they would give you instructions on activating the work.

Hofshteyn: They said that we needed to work, but no one would have dared to say directly, "Wage battle against Soviet power."

Presiding Officer: You are demonstrating an unwillingness to answer my direct questions. How was it that Fefer sent you a special telegram telling you to receive the visitors in proper style, saying, "Receive Goldberg and get in touch with Intourist." Did you know who Goldberg was?

Hofshteyn: I could have already known who Goldberg was. Before that I had seen documents from which it was clear that he was chairman of a Jewish Union of Writers and Scientists in New York and had something to do with the campaign to aid Russia. But I didn't know anything specific about him, nor did I know anything about his relatives.

Presiding Officer: You said that you met with Goldberg in a smaller group at the Hotel Intourist, and that those present included you, Kagan, Loitsker, and a few other people as well, that questions having to do with the need to activate nationalistic projects among Jews in the Ukraine were raised, and Goldberg asked for fuller information for America.

Hofshteyn: He repeated the same thing, that he was ready to help Jews and that we should work more actively to develop Yiddish culture. For the most part, he spoke in vague phrases that meant little or nothing, sort of saying, "Don't lose heart; everything will be fine." It was nauseating to listen to him.

Presiding Officer: Is your testimony correct in which you state that he gave instructions on how to activate nationalistic work?

Hofshteyn: I believed that in and of itself this was activating nationalistic work. "If you need to have any books sent, please let us know, and we will send them to you." That was the spirit in which Goldberg conducted himself. He was playing the role of the rich uncle who was apparently well disposed to us.

Presiding Officer: Now, in regard to the question of gathering classified information: you provided assistance to Goldberg in gathering classified information in Kiev and intended to put together detailed information about the situation of Jews in the Ukraine, did you not?

Hofshteyn: A week after Goldberg arrived, Kotlyar called me in and said, "Go to the synagogue together with Goldberg. I kept him here later on purpose." This was during Passover. Kotlyar told me that we should behave diplomatically with the American visitor. He wanted Goldberg to see people dressed up for the holiday. We came to the synagogue. The entire courtyard was indeed filled with people dressed up for the holiday. We barely squeezed in there. It was clear that the rabbi had been to see Kotlyar beforehand. Goldberg looked everything over, looked at the building, saw the people, and the rabbi asked him if he would perhaps say a few words. Goldberg agreed to. He spoke in Yiddish. He said that he was not the right person to urge those present to be devout, and that he brought greetings from their relatives and friends, in a word, from American Jewry, and that he hoped that things would continue in this vein. He said that he could not give any serious commissions, as that was not his area, but that everyone should believe that American Jews would do whatever they could, and then he wished everyone good health. At this point the service started, and he could not stay any longer. We walked out and rode away. Then I said to Kotlyar that everything had turned out nicely. The courtyard had been full of people, there were new furnishings in the synagogue, and so on.

Presiding Officer: Why would a communist, a writer, a Marxist, a progressive Jewish intellectual, get involved with priests, rabbis, and obscurantists and consult with them about sermons, matzoh, prayer books, and kosher meat?

Hofshteyn: The butcher is a religious official.

Presiding Officer: Does this mean that prayers were said as cattle were slaughtered?

Hofshteyn: Yes.

Presiding Officer: So in carrying out this operation the butcher was performing a religious ritual?

Hofshteyn: Yes, without a doubt.

Collegium Member: So consequently you were not in agreement with the Soviets' ethnic policy?

Hofshteyn: I would never have dared to think that an unimportant person like myself could disagree with Soviet power on anything, especially on such an important issue.

Presiding Officer: Answer concretely. Did you agree or not with Soviet nationality policy?

Hofshteyn: I was always in agreement with the government's nationality policy. It was only Soviet power that gave us . . .

Member of the Court (interrupts): Get to the point. Why did you give this testimony? This is your testimony, and you signed it. You gave this testimony in Kagan's presence. You said that you didn't agree with the Soviet government's nationality policy, and now you're saying that you always agreed with it. So when are you to be believed? When were you telling the truth, then or now?

Hofshteyn: Now.

Member of the Court: Then why did you say the opposite before?

Hofshteyn: The things that were going on around me and the condition I was in made me agree with whatever the investigator said to me. Such a catastrophe had happened to me that I felt that, willingly or unwillingly, I was being drawn into some kind of case, and once I was drawn into it, I gave this testimony. I realized that we had become dependents of some sort, that my work was not as useful as it could have been, and when the investigator started describing me, I agreed with what he said. When Lozovsky spoke here about the death penalty, it dawned on me how important the issue was considered here. I had never thought about it before. Now I understand the full seriousness of the situation.

Member of the Court: The court is checking your testimony.

Hofshteyn: The minister told me that I needed to turn myself inside out and tell the whole truth.

Member of the Court: Why are you not turning yourself inside out now and telling the whole truth?

Hofshteyn: Only now is everything becoming clear to me. Now I understand what lies at the heart of all the accusations. Something has happened such that a Soviet citizen who was an honored person yesterday stands outside the law today.

Member of the Court: We judge a person by his deeds and not by what he thinks and says.

Hofshteyn: What were my deeds? My deeds are my written works. There is no dissent in my works.

Member of the Court: But you signed the testimony. Why did you sign it?

Hofshteyn: I was in a condition of madness.

[During Hofshteyn's testimony, other defendants gave testimony as well, specifically Bergelson.]

Bergelson: You said that you had come to Berlin because there was no work for you in Russia. Incidentally, at the time you brought me books by Kushnirovich [Kushnirov], Rossin, Khashtshevatsky, and Finenberg* with fore-

---

*Aron Kushnirov (1891–1949) was a widely known Yiddish poet and writer who was influenced by Hofshteyn and the Soviet poet Sergei Esenin. Shmuel Rossin (1890–1941) a poet and writer, contributed articles to numerous Yiddish-language journals. He died fighting the Nazis. M. Khashtshevatsky (1897–1943) wrote children's poetry and plays. He died fighting the Nazis. Ezra Finenberg (1899–1946) was a frequent contributor of poetry and prose to Yiddish-language journals.

words that you had written. So that means that there was work, wasn't there?

Hofshteyn: I did not write a foreword to Rossin's book or Finenberg's. Kushnirovich [Kushnirov] and Khashtshevatsky are both comrades of mine, and I wrote forewords for their books.

Bergelson: But that means that some books were being published then, doesn't it? Why did you say that nothing was being published?

Hofshteyn: Well, you could ask how they were published and what sort of work this is for a person when he writes two forewords in two years.

Bergelson: You said that Yuzefovich and Fefer lived in the same building—that is recorded in your testimony. Actually, Yuzefovich and I lived in the same building. He lived on the floor above me. Fefer lived on another street.

Hofshteyn: So my memory is poor.

Member of the Court (to Hofshteyn): You told us that you were not a Zionist, but Bergelson describes you as an active Zionist.

Hofshteyn: What is he basing that on?

Member of the Court: In his testimony (vol. 17, p. 170), Bergelson testified as follows: "Later, my old acquaintance from Kiev, the active Zionist David Hofshteyn, came to Berlin, as well as Samuel Weizmann, the brother of the leader of world Zionism and the current president of the State of Israel, Chaim Weizmann." And here is the signature—"Bergelson."

Bergelson: I believed when I gave this testimony that it was better to exaggerate than to underplay, and then the court would sort it out.

Member of the Court: You were warned that you must testify to the truth, were you not? And you testified that he was a Zionist, an active Zionist, and that he did not conceal his hostile activity from you, didn't you?

Bergelson: How did I see his hostility? The fact that he was going to Palestine was in itself a hostile act—a Palestinian Zionist Jew could not be friendly.

Member of the Court: So he was a Zionist?

Bergelson: Definitely. He was constantly fighting on behalf of Hebrew. This was because contemporary Zionists considered Yiddish a surrogate that didn't give Jews the opportunity to fully express their nationalistic feelings. But they needed this feeling of national pride to be transformed into nationalism. They saw that most Jews who immigrated to Palestine were assimilated; that is, they didn't know Hebrew. Hofshteyn doubtless received an assignment in Palestine. He returned with this assignment and tried to turn me against Yiddish.

His goal was the furtherance of Hebrew; clearly, that was the assignment he had received there. He argued with me about Palestine. I told him that age-old mold was gathering there. There everything was like when I was a child and an adolescent—everything shut down on Saturdays, you weren't allowed to smoke, you couldn't ride a hired carriage down the street. He tried to convince me that nothing would come of Birobidzhan. I was in love with Birobidzhan. I said that there was not a single undertaking in the Soviet Union that had not succeeded. Sooner or later it would happen. I presented him with my arguments. How we understood the support that the Soviet government had rendered to the State of Israel. We understood that the Soviet government would have provided exactly the same assistance to any colonial people to rid itself of such dependency as it had provided to help Israel rid itself of Great Britain, but no more. And he tried to convince me that it would be more, saying, "See, I was right; see how our government is handling it." As if our government had become Zionist. I have a lot of proof of this; I just have to remember it. For example, he told me how he was making efforts on behalf of Hebrew and how he had been with a delegation that met with Kamenev,* and supposedly Kamenev had expressed his liking for Hebrew. "And you," Hofshteyn said to me, "are against this."

[At 4:30 P.M., the presiding officer announced a recess. At 7:00 P.M., the court session resumed.]

Hofshteyn: I want to respond to Bergelson's questions. Bergelson has said here a lot about my feelings, and said that I am "lingering over the grave of the Hebrew language."

Presiding Officer: He stated that you were a Zionist in your worldview, a firm and ardent Zionist, and that for that reason, it was no accident that you went to Palestine.

Hofshteyn: He made a connection between that trip and Weizmann, but that is completely unthinkable, because I was invited for the opening of the university. I traveled on the same ship with relatives of Bergelson.

Presiding Officer: You have already told us about that. But Bergelson said that you were working to get Hebrew into wider use. Apparently you did have such an assignment. He said that you consulted with him about Palestine and pointed to facts such as that on Saturdays the people were not allowed to ride in a cab or smoke, that basically people weren't allowed to do anything. This was after you returned from Palestine. Apparently, when you left Palestine, you were given the assignment to defend Hebrew.

Hofshteyn: There could not have been any mention of defending Hebrew. That question was begun long before my trip to Palestine. That was back in Moscow when I signed the memorandum. As to whether or not I was a supporter of Hebrew, Bergelson should recall how he translated his novels into Hebrew. Many years ago, he had already begun printing his novels in Hebrew.

*Lev Kamenev (Rosenfeld) (1883–1936) was a close associate of Lenin's and a member of the first Soviet Politburo after the revolution. He was executed in August 1936, following the first purge trial.

Bergelson: When was that?

Hofshteyn: It was in 1914–1915 or in 1917.

Bergelson: That was in 1912.

Hofshteyn: You yourself translated your works into Hebrew.

Presiding Officer: But who speaks and reads Hebrew at all, anyway?

Hofshteyn: There is no one here who does. Where is there such a person at all?

Presiding Officer: Then what is the point of translating books into Hebrew?

Hofshteyn: At that time there were still works published in that language, only Zionist ones. A very small number of Zionists knew the language, and a small number of books were published for them. Bergelson published his works in Hebrew. I do not understand the entire point of his testimony. He points to my feelings, but I do not trust his sentiments. What language is he talking about? The language that should be spoken in Birobidzhan? A house was built for Bergelson in Birobidzhan, but he didn't live there. So what language could be at issue here?

Presiding Officer: Who built him a home in Birobidzhan?

Hofshteyn: The authorities. He went there and said that he wanted to settle in Birobidzhan, and the authorities built him a house there, but then he didn't go to live there. Furthermore, how do I know that he went to the Zionist congress and wrote about it? Someone told me that he had gone, but I don't remember who it was. He talked about it here himself.

[Then Kvitko asked Hofshteyn questions.]

Kvitko: There is an interrogation record of your testimony that the court is reading and that it believes, where you say that we agreed to carry out nationalistic activity.

Hofshteyn: I read your testimony and saw how you characterized this activity.

Kvitko: So you gave this testimony based on my testimony. In my first collection of poetry, which came out in 1918, I dedicated some poetry to you. When a poet dedicates verses to another poet, that generally reflects a certain spiritual kinship or very great respect. But by 1927, the book that contained these poems had been published in Kharkov, and the dedication was removed. As a person of considerable and substantial knowledge who has a good understanding of ethics, you probably understand what happened.

Hofshteyn: This is a trivial matter.

Kvitko: Is it really trivial when a dedication is removed from poems?

Presiding Officer: What do you ascribe this to, Kvitko? Why did you remove the dedication when the poems were republished?

Kvitko: Because in 1927 I already considered Hofshteyn a Zionist, a person with Zionist tendencies.

Presiding Officer (to Kvitko): You removed the dedication out of political considerations?

Kvitko: Out of ideological considerations. In my eyes he was a Zionist.

Presiding Officer: And when you made the dedication, he wasn't a Zionist?

Kvitko: No. That was in early 1918, when we had just met. Perhaps he was a Zionist, but he wasn't a member of a Zionist party. At that time he was already in Moscow, and I was in Kiev. But in Kiev we were already hearing that he was a very good poet. There was one small book that was wonderful, although Markish has been poking fun at it here. It contained wonderful poems of subtle lyricism. At that time he was held in very high regard. He was the first true lyric poet. And then we started to hear that he had developed connections and friends in Moscow who were not the kind of people a Soviet person should have. Engel is a Zionist, Shor is a Zionist, and you were friends with them. And there were dozens like them.

Citizen Chairman, will you permit me to ask Fefer a question?

Presiding Officer: Please do.

Kvitko: Why is Fefer questioning Hofshteyn so zealously, someone he's been very close to since 1922 and perhaps even earlier? Asking for everything that he needs and that would be useful for him. I understand that he has to defend himself, but Fefer should also remember that Hofshteyn is the person he is the closest to. Fefer has been close to Hofshteyn for twenty to twenty-five years. Hofshteyn brought Fefer into the literary world, and Fefer brought him into the Party. Why among all of these questions has there not been a single one about whether Hofshteyn had nationalistic and Zionist tendencies and whether Fefer knew about that?

Fefer: First of all, Hofshteyn and I were never personal friends. We were not on first-name terms, and often our relationship was quite tense. Why didn't I ask him about his activity? Because it seemed clear to me from his testimony about himself and his answers to others' questions. Of course, our relationship was perfectly normal. It would be wrong to say that Hofshteyn is an out-and-out Zionist. He had bursts [of Zionism]. He and I had an argument about the memorandum, and he was removed from the bureau. I myself raised the question of removing him from the bureau. When Hofshteyn drew closer to Soviet reality, when he published several books on Soviet themes, that was genuine poetry.

Presiding Officer: Defendant Fefer, testify about Hofshteyn's political activity as a member of the Jewish Anti-Fascist Committee. Did he champion the committee's nationalistic ideas in Kiev?

Fefer: The thing is that Hofshteyn did not attend a single presidium session, and he did not speak at rallies, but he did have nationalistic tendencies. I have spoken about his nationalistic poems and testified to what I know about him.

JOSEPH YUZEFOVICH

Born in Warsaw, Joseph Yuzefovich (his real name was Shpinak) joined the revolutionary movement at the age of fifteen and was active in the Bund from 1905 to 1917. Poland was part of the Russian Empire, and activists like Yuzefovich were drawn to underground work, advocating Polish independence and socialist revolution. His leadership skills earned him the attention of both the Bolsheviks and the tsarist police. In 1911 he became the Warsaw correspondent of the Bolshevik newspaper *Zvezda* (The Star) and in 1912 of *Pravda* itself. But in March 1912 the tsarist police arrested thirty-five young revolutionaries, including Yuzefovich, and he was jailed for four years, in Poland and then in a Russian prison in Kaluga, 150 miles south of Moscow.

Upon his release in 1916, Yuzefovich could not return to Warsaw because the Germans occupied the city. He moved to Moscow instead, where he lived with a false passport, all the while agitating against the tsarist regime. In the fall of 1917 he was elected to the executive committee of the Moscow Soviet of Workers' Deputies. He became closely associated with Solomon Lozovsky in that year and together with him organized an "internationalist" group of social-democrats, becoming chairman of its Moscow party organization until 1919, when he and Lozovsky were welcomed back into the Bolshevik party. The following year, during the Civil War, when the Red Army advanced into Poland, Yuzefovich was sent to the Polish front as part of a group headed by no less a figure than Felix Dzherzhinsky, who was also of Polish origin and served as the first chairman of the Cheka, the Bolsheviks' dreaded secret police. It was up to Yuzefovich to help organize worker support for the Bolshevik offensive.

For the next three decades, Yuzefovich served the party and its trade union movement as one of its most experienced organizers, particularly among the leather workers. He also worked as an assistant to Lozovsky. In March 1923 a group of leatherworkers in the city of Ostashkov named their factory for Yuzefovich. By 1931 he was a prominent enough functionary to merit an entry in the *Great Soviet Encyclopedia.** For two years, from 1931 to 1933, Yuzefovich disappeared from Moscow and carried out underground activities in the United States. In 1938 he be-

---

Bolshaya Sovietskaya Entsiklopediya (Great Soviet Encyclopedia), vol. 65 (Moscow, 1931), p. 164.

came an informer for the MGB, assigned to monitor the activity of Jewish cultural figures. Such party work aside, Yuzefovich pursued scholarly interests as well. Between 1938 and 1944 he worked as an editor of the *Great Soviet Encyclopedia,* with responsibility for its sections on workers' and professional movements. Between 1939 and 1941 he was associated with the Institute of History of the Soviet Academy of Sciences, where he wrote an ambitious paper entitled "The Origins of the Communist International." And in 1941 his book *George Washington and the Struggle for American Independence* was published in Moscow. Yuzefovich was not forgotten after his execution. In 1965 former comrades organized a memorial meeting on the occasion of his seventy-fifth birthday in the Party museum in Moscow.*

Presiding Officer: Defendant Yuzefovich, what do you plead guilty to before the court?

Yuzefovich: I reject the accusation of treason and nationalistic espionage activity, as I do that of slandering the Central Committee and the trade unions. If I am guilty, then I am guilty of carrying out Lozovsky's instructions. I passed on to Goldberg through Kotlyar a survey of England's colonial policy that was supposed to serve as source material for Goldberg for a book he was writing exposing British imperialist policy. I did not secure written approval for this from the Foreign Policy Department of the Central Committee or from any other body.

I confirm now in court as well that in my presence Lozovsky truly did arrange this with Pukhlov.† He explained to him that this survey was for an American journalist, prominent in the United States, and was supposed to simplify the task of writing a book, to be published under his name, which would show that British policy was not intended to foster peace, but was directed against peace. I now confirm, as I did during the preliminary investigation and the witness confrontation in the presence of prosecutor Kozhura, that Lozovsky instructed me to remind Pukhlov about this, an instruction that I carried out in Lozovsky's presence.

Presiding Officer: You will testify about this further, but now I am asking you a general question. To what do you plead guilty, and what charges do you deny?

*Marina Yuzefovich (daughter of Joseph Yuzefovich), interview with author, Rehovot, Israel, 1998.

†Nikolai Pukhlov (1912–1980) lectured at the Directorate of Propaganda and Agitation of the Central Committee. Between 1945 and 1948 he served as deputy director and then director of Scientific Research Institute 205 of the Foreign Policy Department of the Central Committee.

Yuzefovich: I believe that I was negligent, that I committed a great blunder in not securing anything in writing about that. I feel that I am guilty of an oversight in having trusted Grossman (the well-known Soviet writer) when he stated that the materials he had put together with Ehrenburg for *The Black Book* that was supposed to be published in the United States were approved by Glavlit. Having received Lozovsky's instructions and relying on Grossman's statement, I signed a telegram saying that materials for the book were being sent out. Prior to that I called Lozovsky and asked what I should do (because I didn't take any independent steps). Lozovsky said, "What, you mean you haven't sent the material?" After that I signed the telegram and felt that everything was as it should be.

Then I should point out that during the entire Soviet period I didn't have the slightest, remotest relationship to Jewish organizations—not to OZET, not to KOMZET,* not to the Jewish section of the Russian Communist Party or to the newspaper *Emes.* I was completely uninterested in these questions. In 1941 I started working at the Sovinformburo, and in 1942, after the evacuation to Kuibyshev, I was appointed head of the workers' and trade union press division at the Sovinformburo. I worked there until the summer of 1946, and after long appeals and insistence on my part I was finally able to return to the Institute of History and plunge into work on my doctoral dissertation on the topic of Pilsudski's May fascist putsch.† The thesis was 560 pages long, and I was supposed to give my defense in 1949 and receive my doctoral degree. Arrest interfered with that.

After I left the Sovinformburo, I didn't see Lozovsky for about two years. It was only when the Institute of History of the Academy of Sciences was preparing to publish a special scholarly collection entitled *Against Right-Wing Socialists,* which Lozovsky was appointed to edit, and I was writing a scholarly paper entitled "William Green and His Reactionary Clique in the American Federation of Labor,"‡ that Lozovsky summoned me to see him twice.

Presiding Officer: You're done with the biographical details. Now would you please answer my questions. During the preliminary investigation you confessed your guilt completely and testified that you were one of the Jewish

---

*OZET was a supposedly public organization formed by the Soviet government to publicize the settlement of Soviet Jews on agricultural lands in the Ukraine, Belorussia, and the Crimea. It was controlled by members of KOMZET (Committee for the Settlement of Jewish Toilers on the Land), who were government employees and Communist Party officials. After 1928 both organizations focused their efforts on Birobidzhan.

†Josef Pilsudski (1867–1935) was a Polish revolutionary leader and politician. He was the first head of state of independent Poland, 1918–1922. In May 1926 he led a revolt against the government and subsequently became minister of defense and the country's most powerful political figure until his death.

‡William Green (1873–1952) was a prominent American labor leader. As president of the American Federation of Labor (1924–1952), he led the struggle with the Congress of Industrial Organizations after the two labor unions split in 1936.

nationalists who carried out hostile work at the Jewish Anti-Fascist Committee. What can you tell the court in regard to this testimony?

Yuzefovich: First of all, my condition, my turmoil, was so profound, and even
now I am not over this turmoil, that for a long time I couldn't remember the
last name of the director of the Institute of History of the Academy of Sciences, Grekov. For four months I couldn't remember my sister's married
name. I couldn't remember the name of Rytikov, my deputy at the Sovinformburo.

Second, I would like to point out that the investigators understood that
testimony is like a distorting mirror, and it was no accident that I was told,
"You're so tricky, you've outsmarted yourself." But I was not being tricky.
When I signed, I believed that if the investigators did not clarify what I was
guilty of and what I wasn't guilty of, then the party, Comrade Stalin, and
the Soviet government would figure out everything in any case. I was absolutely certain that after the court made its decision, no matter what decision it made, I would be able to appeal by making a statement to Comrades
Stalin and Molotov and that I would get my case reviewed. I didn't want to
fight with the investigators, the prosecutor's office, and the State Security
Ministry. Of course, I understand and understood everything from the day
of my arrest, and I'm not playing the fool now, either.

Furthermore, I should add that after I signed the interrogation record,
the investigators began treating me with care and concern, but when I argued, things were not made easy for me. One thing I will say, though, and
I think that this will go into the court transcript, and that is this: I was
ready to confess that I was the pope's own nephew and that I was acting on
his direct personal orders. That is all I want to say. My emotional turmoil
was so great that I could not [have acted otherwise]. Maybe it was opportunism on my part, and maybe for that I should be the first to get a good
beating.

Presiding Officer: So what are you denying now?

Yuzefovich: I will answer that question, but I would like permission to say
what is true and what is not true in reality. First, upon reading the indictment, on page 24, one has the impression that I received instructions from
Lozovsky and made my way to the American press attaché myself through
the service entrance and passed secret materials to American intelligence
officer Eagan.* This is a crude distortion of reality. Here is what happened
in reality. Senior Sovinformburo staffer Balashov called me and said that I
should get dressed up, that a car had been sent for me, and I had to come
over to the Sovinformburo. When I arrived, there was already a whole

---

*Elizabeth Eagan was appointed assistant cultural officer at the U.S. Embassy in Moscow
on November 13, 1946. She was helpful to the Soviet movie director Sergei Eisenstein, supplying him with copies of American films and books. See Ronald Bergan, *Sergei Eisenstein:
A Life in Conflict* (Woodstock, N.Y., 1999), pp. 334–335.

group of people there, and we all set out together. I didn't know that we were going to a private apartment to see the press attaché. The group included a prominent writer who worked at *Pravda*, Marshak, Colonel Gurov, Borodin, Kalmykov, Balashov, Rubinin, and someone else as well.

While we were there, Eagan addressed herself to Kalmykov, the senior secretary at the Sovinformburo, and asked a question about the trade union press. Kalmykov asked me to respond. Eagan said that the Sovinformburo articles about the workers' trade union movement were being published only in the press of the Congress of Industrial Unions and by its press agency. But there were a number of local AFL [American Federation of Labor] organizations that appeared to be actively working to draw closer to the Soviet trade unions because they were sympathetic to the Soviet struggle with German fascism, and they would print our materials. I responded that we had no intention of sending our articles to *The American Federationist*. She said, "Give me a few articles, and I will send them to some of the local AFL groups. I know some people, and of course they'll print them." A few days later she called the Sovinformburo and asked for a meeting there. I told her that I was busy and suggested that she call back in a few days. I reported on this to the head of the Sovinformburo, Lozovsky, who said, "Well, take a few copies of articles that have already been published or approved by the censors, and give them to her." My deputy for workers' and trade union press affairs, Nikolai Rytikov, assembled these articles. They were copies of articles about the principles of organization building in Soviet trade unions, about insurance, about workers' compensation, and about Soviet trade unions' cultural and educational programs.

I did not give Eagan [sensitive] material but copies of articles, and I said this again when Colonel Kozhura was present. When the investigator gave me the record of the witness confrontation to sign, I indicated that there, and then I just threw up my hands and signed that testimony. I repeat, what is being referred to is not classified material, for there was no such material and I did not give it to anyone.

When representatives came from Romanian, Bulgarian, and other trade union organizations, we gave them those same articles. There could not have been anything secret in these articles. Moreover, I gave Eagan these copies of articles in the presence of people who worked in my department; that is, it was all completely official.

Presiding Officer: Do you deny that when Goldberg spoke about the Crimea, he said that if a Jewish republic was created there, the Americans would support it?

Yuzefovich: I have not heard about that.

Presiding Officer: So now the only thing you confess to is having signed the interrogation record.

[After this, the court asked Yuzefovich about the roles that Hofshteyn and

Shtern played in the activity of the Jewish Anti-Fascist Committee and about their relations with Lozovsky.]

Yuzefovich: Allow me to answer directly. The minister of state security called me in twice and asked me a question. "Tell me straight," he said, "what do you know about the criminal anti-state activity of Lozovsky and others?"

Presiding Officer: Which minister?

Yuzefovich: Abakumov. Both times I responded that I didn't know about any crimes against the state by Lozovsky, nor was I aware that I had committed any crimes against the state. After I had signed all of the interrogation records, the minister called me in a third time and very politely asked, "Do tell us straightforwardly about Lozovsky—what Lozovsky's attitude was toward the party and toward the Soviet government and what he said about Comrades Stalin and Molotov and the party Central Committee." I ask that you check what I am saying now with the minister to see that I'm not making it up. I told the minister that I was telling the truth when I said that Lozovsky always spoke of both Comrade Stalin and Comrade Molotov with the greatest veneration. I added that when I once asked Lozovsky, "How does Comrade Molotov know you?"—at the time Lozovsky had been appointed deputy minister of foreign affairs—he said, "He probably knows me from Kazan, where I was involved in underground work at one time, and Comrade Molotov was the director of a student organization."

Lozovsky: Comrade Molotov was a student at that time.

Yuzefovich: Yes, a student. I told the minister about his family situation; specifically, I said that Lozovsky was going through a period of great unhappiness because his daughter's fiancé, the son of Minister Parshin, had been run over by a train and cut into pieces.*

Presiding Officer: As to Lozovsky being removed from his post, you said in your testimony (vol. 7, p. 39) that until recently he had been hostile to the party, and sometimes in intimate conversations with you this attitude abruptly came to light.

Further on, you testified that Lozovsky had expressed his disagreement with the party's nationality policy and said that the situation of Jews in the Soviet Union had become difficult.

Yuzefovich: In reference to his expectation of an appointment, I asked him, "Won't you receive another appointment soon?" He said to me, "It's not so

---

*Yuzefovich is referring to a genuine tragedy in Lozovsky's family. His daughter and her fiancé—the son of Colonel General Pyotr Ivanovich Parshin, an engineer who had been in charge of mortar production during World War II—took a train from Moscow to visit Lozovsky at his dacha. The young man was killed in a freakish accident at the suburban train station. After Lozovsky's arrest, his wife and this daughter were sent into exile in Kazakhstan.

easy for me to get a job. I'm already seventy-two years old. When I worked at the Foreign Ministry, I was also working at the Sovinformburo, plus I was doing work on the *Diplomatic Dictionary*. I had to work until five in the morning. Then I realized what age meant," said Lozovsky, "and besides, the party Central Committee is doing the right thing to move young people forward, nurture them, and move them into senior positions." He really did say this. As for anti-Semitism, it was not by chance that I asked the question I did when Teumin was addressing the Military Collegium. I just got Volkov's and Mikhailov's last names confused. When I was asked whether Lozovsky had talked about anti-Semitism and Jews, I told the investigator that there was a senior person in the English department at the Sovinformburo, a party bureau secretary. And at a New Year's party at Faikina's—she worked in the publishing division—he behaved in an unheard-of fashion, got drunk, and started yelling that all kikes are bastards, that Lozovsky was a bastard, a Trotskyite, a Menshevik, and a kike, and that all kikes are merchants.

Presiding Officer: What was this person's name?

Yuzefovich: Volkov. A short while later, I noticed that Volkov was not around. So one day I asked Lozovsky about it. "I see that the party bureau secretary Volkov is gone. What happened?" Lozovsky told me that I should ask Faikina, and added that Volkov had a history of unpleasant incidents in Japan prior to that, and that was why he had been removed. He had worked in the Soviet Embassy there, or in the Office of the Trade Representative—I can't remember which. And second, that this same Volkov had been involved in anti-Soviet, anti-Semitic incidents that had outraged Faikina's husband, who was Russian, and he had said to his wife that if she didn't go to Lozovsky about it, he would go elsewhere himself and report the incident. So that was why I asked Teumin about this. Lozovsky also said to me, "It would be interesting to know who his drinking buddies are and where he picked up such attitudes." But did Lozovsky ever say anything to me about anti-Semitism? Absolutely not. That is rubbish. Lozovsky never made any nationalistic remarks to me, nor I to him.

Presiding Officer: More about the committee. Lozovsky nonetheless was the director of that committee, and the committee's activity was nationalistic. People have confessed their guilt and confirmed that the committee was doing things it shouldn't have; that has already been mentioned here. So how was it that Lozovsky, as the director of this committee, did not notice this hostile activity?

Yuzefovich: Lozovsky may have committed an error, but to act directly to harm the country and consciously commit a crime—he could not have done that.

I cannot imagine that Lozovsky would hear a conversation about any criminal conspiracy and not have reported to the State Security Ministry

about it. May I recall one specific fact? I figure here as one of the nationalists and betrayers of the Motherland, a spy, and a slanderer of party and
government policy. I would like to remind Lozovsky, let him say whether or
not I am right, that when I heard Goldberg say at the National Hotel (only
now I don't remember to whom he said it) that Ambassador Smith* and his
close associates took an extremely hostile and vicious stance toward the
Soviet Union, I, a slanderer, spy, and traitor, immediately wrote a note to
Lozovsky telling him that Smith took a vicious position vis-à-vis the Soviet
Union and that he was no doubt turning the American government in that
direction, too.

Member of the Court: What were the assignments facing the committee? Testify about that specifically.

Yuzefovich: I will not pretend to be young and naive. I will tell what I know.
The way I see it, the Jewish Anti-Fascist Committee existed, it was engaged
in serious work, it dealt with serious issues. The party Central Committee
knew about the committee's existence; Shcherbakov and Alexandrov gave
all the directives. None of the speeches at the rallies were secret. Everyone
knew that. When Ehrenburg declared from the podium, "I am a Jew, and
my mother's name is Hannah," that went through Alexandrov and Shcherbakov. I know that there is a Slavic committee, where work is done on
Slavic problems exclusively. The Slavic committee dealt only with Slavic affairs and wrote about Slavs, so why shouldn't the Jewish Anti-Fascist Committee deal only with Jewish problems?

Member of the Court: So at that time you believed that the committee was doing everything it should be doing, and that it was doing what it was supposed to.

Yuzefovich: There is really only one thing for me to say: that everything that
was done at the Jewish Anti-Fascist Committee was done with approval
from on high. That's what I was told. Kheifets always said that supposedly
this was coordinated with the Foreign Policy Department of the Central
Committee, and there is nothing to add. He told me this when I expressed
a desire to make some corrections. The entire policy and the practical activity of the Jewish Anti-Fascist Committee were correct at that time, in my
view. I was completely in accord with its direction. I wasn't going to become suicidal or become a murderer of my child by committing crimes.
This was never the case, and those sitting here can confirm that.

Member of the Court: How did you feel about creating a Jewish republic in
the Crimea?

Yuzefovich: Mikhoels told me that Comrade Molotov had given instructions
about that, and because this was what he told me, I felt that this was quite

---

*Walter Bedell Smith (1895–1961), a U.S. army general, was ambassador to the Soviet
Union from 1946 to 1949. See his book *My Three Years in Moscow* (Philadelphia, 1950).

possible, and I didn't doubt it for a single second. I thought that since the Jewish Autonomous Region of Birobidzhan existed, then why couldn't there be a similar republic in the Crimea? All the Jews ran away from Birobidzhan because things were bad there, and besides, it was close to the Japanese border, and in the Crimea they could really settle in. I saw nothing special in that. Personally, I had no interest in either Birobidzhan or the Crimea. Those present can confirm that.

Member of the Court: And what were your feelings about a Jewish state generally and about the idea of Jews from all over the world uniting?

Yuzefovich: At the committee the question was not posed in terms of uniting Jews from all over. Here Fefer was right in saying that that was not how the question was framed. How could there be, for example, ideological unification between citizens of the Soviet Union and citizens of Argentina or America? Second, as to creating a Jewish state in Palestine, when I was a lecturer at the Kiev regional party committee, not only Jews but Russians as well asked me about that. I told them that it was a bourgeois state and indicated that among the members of its government was a certain Greenberg [Gruenbaum]* who had previously been a member of the lower house of the Polish parliament, where he groveled before Pilsudski. I said that this was a bourgeois state, and this was mentioned not only in the case materials, but in the expert commission's conclusions as well. I am referring to my speech against sending such a huge number of articles to Palestine. I believed that sending such a mass of articles and displaying such interest in a Jewish state in Palestine in general could generate undesirable talk.

Member of the Court: Did you receive and read *Eynikayt*?

Yuzefovich: Please take my word for it when I say that I subscribed to that paper but used it for household purposes. I couldn't read it myself because my Yiddish is poor.

Member of the Court: So, although you received the paper, you didn't read it?

Yuzefovich: Yes, and everyone knows that. I wrote a number of articles for that paper, but they were about trade union issues or counterpropaganda to American reaction.

Member of the Court: You were involved in discussions about topics for the paper, and you saw that articles were exclusively about Jews. What did you make of the fact that it was all about Jews, Jews, Jews, and there was nothing about Soviet Man?

Yuzefovich: The Jewish press gleaned information about the Soviet Union from the general press. That's first. Second, there were lots of articles planned

---

*Isaac Gruenbaum (1879–1970) was an active Zionist and leader of Polish Jewry. He was a member of the Polish Sejm from 1918 until 1933, when he moved to Palestine as an executive in the Jewish Agency. He was the first minister of internal affairs in the temporary government of David Ben-Gurion and helped to organize the country's first elections.

which had nothing to do with Jews, about the thirtieth anniversary of the October Revolution, about the Soviet Union's peaceful foreign policy, or about the Stalinist Constitution. I pointed out that when mention was made of Jews, other Soviet peoples should be mentioned, too. I always emphasized this in my speeches. Everyone who has heard me speak knows that that was what I said, and not "what the October Revolution gave just to the Jews." That was not how I framed the question. I would like for not only the Military Collegium, but the party and the Soviet government as well to know what is correct and what isn't.

[As with the testimony of all of the defendants, much of Yuzefovich's questioning was taken up with the subject of Lozovsky. The preliminary investigation tried to make Lozovsky into the leader of an anti-Soviet nationalistic center. Almost all those under investigation had signed interrogation records giving testimony to this effect. None of the negative descriptions of Lozovsky recorded by the investigators in Yuzefovich's interrogation records were confirmed by the latter during the judicial session. In fact, he repudiated them completely.

Once again, and not for the first time, Lozovsky's attendance at the evening honoring Sholem Aleichem in 1939 was discussed. During the first days of the trial his attendance was unequivocally seen as a manifestation of his nationalistic position. During the session, Bergelson's testimony was cited about how Yuzefovich had said in connection with Lozovsky's attendance at this event that "Lozovsky has long sympathized with our nationalistic activity."]

Bergelson: I have to make a correction here. I said that Lozovsky is interested in Yiddish literature and that he is sympathetic toward that, not toward nationalistic activity.

Presiding Officer: And why didn't you make these corrections when you were correcting the interrogation record in your own hand?

Bergelson: If they had given me the opportunity to make all of the corrections, the interrogation record would have looked altogether different. At times I put my signature in places where I was ready to place my head.

Shimeliovich (to Yuzefovich): Yesterday you were read testimony signed by you which said that Mikhoels, Fefer, and others—at the end I, Shimeliovich, was mentioned, too—turned the Jewish Anti-Fascist Committee into a center for nationalistic and espionage activity. You have repudiated this testimony. May I consider, then, judging from your statement yesterday in court, when you said you would not ever believe that Shimeliovich is a criminal, can I conclude from that that the testimony you signed which says that Shimeliovich turned the Jewish Anti-Fascist Committee into a center for nationalism is not really true?

Yuzefovich: I stated that I do not believe that such a center existed. I stated that I do not know of such a center or underground, that I did not participate in any such underground, and in saying so I also stated that neither you nor Bregman participated in that, either.

Presiding Officer (to Fefer): And what is the testimony about Yuzefovich based on?

Fefer: My testimony in regard to Yuzefovich is based on two facts: *The Black Book* and the traveling exhibit. And also on his speeches in support of erecting memorials. There was a proposal to erect a memorial in Maidanek to Jewish victims.

Presiding Officer: Answer specifically about the testimony which you gave, that Yuzefovich expressed the view that the Jews must unite, transcending class differences, and he also talked about discrimination against Jews allegedly occurring in the Soviet Union.

Fefer: I don't recall.

Yuzefovich: There is only one thing I want to say. I never slandered anybody in my entire life, and I am sixty-two years old. During the investigation I signed everything about myself. Let Bregman take a look and see whether or not I slandered him.

I am astonished that he doesn't understand all of this. How is it that he doesn't understand the situation that's arisen? I confess that to my sorrow I lacked iron fortitude during the investigation, and I was faint of heart when I signed those interrogation records. I say "to my sorrow" because at one time I was Lozovsky's assistant. I knew him over a thirty-year period, and it was particularly hard for me during the investigation. It is terribly painful for me to talk about that.

Presiding Officer: What else can you tell the court?

Yuzefovich: I am not an enemy of the party and Soviet power. I state that until my last breath I will consider myself an honorable Soviet man and a communist.

[On May 27, at 8:35 P.M., the presiding officer announced a recess in the proceedings. At 9:05 P.M., the court session resumed.]

SOLOMON LOZOVSKY

Solomon Lozovsky was the principal defendant in the trial. Born in 1878, Lozovsky joined the Marxist underground in 1901. His real name was Solomon Dridzo, but he adopted the party pseudonym Lozovsky from a small town near Kharkov in the Ukraine. He was physically imposing, tall and broad-shouldered, and once worked as a blacksmith in Lozovaya; the town railroad station still carries an iron pole that he forged.

Lozovsky became a prominent member of the Bolsheviks. He met

Lenin and Stalin at a party conference in Finland in 1905 and was visible enough to tsarist police to warrant arrest and exile to Siberia. He and his first wife were in the same tsarist prison, along with their three-year-old daughter, who was passed between them from one cell to another. Like many exiled revolutionaries, Lozovsky escaped from Siberia and made his way to France. There he studied at the Sorbonne and picked grapes in the countryside; for a time he was also leader of the French hatmakers' union. Following the October Revolution, Lozovsky so impressed the radical American journalist John Reed that he appeared in Reed's famous book *Ten Days That Shook the World* giving a speech at a party conference.* (Stalin is not mentioned in the book, which is why it was banned for decades in the Soviet Union.) Lozovsky was not afraid to speak his mind. He was actually expelled from the party twice, in 1914 and then again in 1918–1919 on Lenin's personal orders for saying that the dictatorship of the proletariat was a foolish idea. Lenin, however, soon regained confidence in him; when the British philosopher Bertrand Russell visited Soviet Russia in 1920, Lozovsky was assigned to accompany him, then report to Lenin every night.†

Once the Bolsheviks consolidated power, Lozovsky assumed responsibilities as secretary general of the Profintern, the international communist-controlled trade union movement. By the 1930s, he was also a leading figure in the Communist International (Comintern), the principal vehicle of the party for exporting the message of revolution to the bourgeois world. (His daughter, Vera Dridzo, also assumed significant duties, serving as secretary and confidante to Lenin's widow Nadezhda Krupskaya from 1919 to 1939.) Like many veteran Bolsheviks, Lozovsky faced a personal crisis during the Great Purge. He was unemployed for a time in 1937 and 1938 and must have feared for his life. But he survived and resumed his political career, becoming director of the government printing house Goslitizdat. He remained in contact with Stalin, who once summoned him to a meeting to discuss reprinting old tsarist history textbooks.‡ Then, in 1939, Lozovsky was chosen by Vyacheslav Molo-

---

*John Reed, *Ten Days That Shook the World* (New York, 1992), p. 66.

†Vladimir Shamberg (grandson of Solomon Lozovsky), interview with author, Cambridge, Mass., 1997.

‡Russian State Archive of Social and Political History (hereafter RGASPI), f. 17, op. 120, d. 360, l. 140. Lozovsky noted his meeting with Stalin in a letter to Andrei Zhdanov dated April 17, 1937. I am indebted to David Brandenberger for bringing this document to my attention.

tov, who had replaced Maxim Litvinov as commissar for foreign affairs, to be one of three deputy commissars. (The other two were Andrei Vyshinsky, Stalin's dreaded prosecutor, and Vladimir Dekanozov, a former secret police executive close to Lavrenti Beria who served as Soviet ambassador to Germany from 1939 to 1941, the years of the Non-Aggression Pact. Dekanozov was later executed in 1953 because of his ties to Beria.)

Here again, Lozovsky distinguished himself. Already fluent in French and German, he decided that with his new position he should also master English. Each morning he came to his office an hour early to study English with a tutor. Within a year he could talk and negotiate without the help of an interpreter. During the war, Lozovsky was assigned additional responsibilities as vice chairman of the Soviet Information Bureau (Sovinformburo), which was charged with dealing with the foreign press. Virtually all news from the front was passed through Lozovsky. Such a sensitive position could have been assigned only to someone with steady judgment and with the confidence of the Kremlin that its political and strategic interests would be respected. Lozovsky matched these requirements. The legendary American photographer Margaret Bourke-White, who hurried to Moscow in 1941, vividly remembered Lozovsky. "His pale-blue eyes twinkled at us above a luxuriant chestnut-colored beard," she recalled: "Witty, clever, he was always ready with a joke when the questions of the press got too explicit. The bigger the news was and the more eager the correspondents were to hear about it, the more time Lozovsky would spend telling us about German propaganda. His favorite pastime was to disprove German claims and call them 'just some more lies out of the gossip factory.' Of German claims and boasts that they would conquer Moscow he said, 'The only way Hitler will ever see the Kremlin is in a photograph.'"* Lozovsky and Nazi propaganda chief Joseph Goebbels, in fact, monitored each other's statements. Goebbels repeatedly made note of Lozovsky in his wartime diaries. At the height of the German offensive on Moscow in October 1941, Goebbels remarked how "the jew Solomon Lozovsky exerts every conceivable effort, to save psychologically, that which, on the whole, is not to be saved."† Years later, no less a figure

*Margaret Bourke-White, *Shooting the Russian War* (New York, 1943), p. 69.

†*Die Tagebücher von Joseph Goebbels* (The Diary of Joseph Goebbels), ed. Elke Fröhlich, volume 2, *October–December 1941* (Munich, 1996), p. 105. I would like to acknowledge

than Nikita Khrushchev warmly remembered Lozovsky and his supervision of the anti-fascist committees: how he "was an energetic person and sometimes almost annoyingly persistent. . . . He used to virtually extort material from me" about Nazi atrocities in the Ukraine and then arrange for articles abroad.

As Khrushchev himself acknowledged, "The Sovinformbureau and its Jewish Anti-Fascist Committee were considered indispensable to the interests of our State, our policies, and our Communist Party." But once the war was over, it all "counted for nothing."*

Presiding Officer: Defendant Lozovsky, tell the court, to what are you pleading guilty?

Lozovsky: I plead guilty to nothing. Allow me to explain in detail.

Presiding Officer: You pled guilty during the preliminary investigation.

Lozovsky: I am not going to hide anything.

Presiding Officer: Start with biographical information.

Lozovsky: I turned seventy-four at the end of March. This is not a mitigating circumstance, but rather an aggravating one. That is item number one. The second aggravating circumstance is that in politics allowances must not be made on account of age, contrary to what Bergelson believes.

In 1927, at the Fifteenth Party Congress, I was nominated to be a candidate for membership of the Central Committee. At the Sixteenth Congress I was again a candidate. In late 1936 I became a member of the Central Committee, and at the Eighteenth Congress I was also elected a member of the Central Committee. I was on the committee for thirteen years.

The third aggravating circumstance is that starting from the time of the October Revolution, I was a member of all the Central Executive Committees of Soldiers' and Peasants' Deputies until Comrade Stalin's Constitution was adopted. On the basis of Comrade Stalin's Constitution I was twice elected deputy of the Supreme Soviet from Kyrgyzia.

The fourth aggravating circumstance is that for seventeen years I was general secretary of the Red Trade Union International and was one of the leaders of the trade union movement. In addition, I was a member of the presidium of the All-Union Central Council of Soviet Trade Unions.

The fifth aggravating circumstance is that for twenty years I was a member of the presidium of the Communist International.

The sixth aggravating circumstance is that for seven years and two months I was deputy foreign minister of the USSR and for five years I was

---

the assistance of Marc Rubenstein, who read portions of Goebbels's diaries for me and provided this translation.

*Nikita Khrushchev, *Khrushchev Remembers* (Boston, 1970), pp. 259–261.

assistant director of the Sovinformburo, then director of the Sovinformburo for a year.

I am obligated to the Communist Party for my high position and for the
path that I have traveled, which I shall recount in brief. The party raised me
up high.

If, in my testimony, I do not prove to the court that everything collected
in all of these forty-two volumes and in the indictment and all that has been
said about me is worlds away from the reality of the situation, then I deserve the death penalty not only once, but six times over.

As you know, my family name is Dridzo. This name cannot be translated
into any language. When we asked our father what it meant, he told us
that, according to a story passed down from father to son, a distant ances-
tor of ours was among the eight hundred thousand Jews who fled from
Spain in 1492, when the chief inquisitor, Tomás de Torquemada, issued a
decree compelling Jews to convert to Catholicism or leave the country.
Anyone who refused was required to leave Spain within two months. I became Lozovsky in 1905 at a conference of Bolsheviks in Tammerfors,
where I first met Comrade Lenin and also Comrade Stalin.

My father was a Hebrew teacher. He knew the Talmud; he knew Hebrew
well and wrote poetry in Hebrew. My mother was illiterate. My father
taught me to read Hebrew, to pray, and to read Russian. The very fact that
a teacher of Hebrew taught his son Russian shows that he was not a fa-
natic. I was religious until the age of about thirteen. I was made to attend
synagogue and to pray. Our generation, the generation that came of age at
the turn of the century, was generally a religious one in its youth. Even
Kalinin told me in Sochi that he would run to church as a child.

[During the entire evening session Lozovsky told about his life as a revolutionary, about important historical events in which he had been directly involved, and about his work with Lenin for Russian social democracy.

At 10:25 P.M. the presiding officer announced a break in the proceedings.
The next day, May 28, 1952, at 12:25 P.M., the judicial session continued.]

Presiding Officer: Defendant Lozovsky, continue your testimony. I ask you to
deal with those questions indicated in the indictment. You are accused of
doing work against the party in 1918–1919 and also of doing nationalistic
work through the committee. If you feel it is necessary to add anything to
what has already been said for the purposes of your defense, then I have
nothing against this.

Lozovsky: Yes. I agonized over the question of whether it is possible to hold
on to power. I had a good relationship with Ilyich [Lenin], and we talked
often during that period. After Krasnov* surrendered, Ilyich said once,

*Pyotr Krasnov (1869–1947) was an anti-Bolshevik White Cossack general during the
Russian Civil War. After World War II, he was captured and sent back to the Soviet Union,
where he was hanged in 1947 because of his military activity alongside the Nazis during the
war.

"Now we'll hang in there for two years, anyway." He could predict the future far in advance. After Ilyich gave Kamenev and Zinoviev a tongue-lashing in the press, they stopped speaking and writing openly and again became members of the Politburo. I was involved in the trade union movement.

One day Ilyich told me that he had drafted an article about worker control. He gave me his "eight points." After Ilyich died I sent the original to *Pravda*.

When Ilyich sent me his draft, he said, "Discuss it among yourselves and think about it." I discussed the issue with Tsiperovich, who at the time was working in the trade union movement. We added several points to these theses—specifically, the point about the All-Russian Workers' Control Council. A day later I returned Ilyich's draft to him with our additional points. Ilyich said that he had no objections, but that the main point was not to centralize worker control, but for workers to take control of the plants and factories into their own hands, and then later we would be able to centralize.

On November 14, 1917, the Decree on Workers' Control was published with our amendments. As executive secretary of the Central Council of Soviet Trade Unions, I started preparing for the first All-Russian Congress of Trade Unions. And here I had serious differences with the party line about bringing the trade unions under the control of the state. Comrade Lenin felt that the trade unions were very important as a link in the system of the dictatorship of the proletariat, as a school of Communism. At the time, I feared that the trade unions would be turned into a department or ministry of labor and would lose the opportunity to choose their leaders and build their organization from the bottom up, so I opposed state control of the trade unions. Later I realized that I had been mistaken. I was expelled from the party for my errors.

Presiding Officer: In what year?

Lozovsky: In December 1917.

Presiding Officer: You testified during the investigation (vol. 1, p. 37) as follows: "In December 1917 I was expelled from the Russian Communist Party for the second time because of my opposition to party policy during the October Revolution and on trade union issues. Zinoviev announced the decision to expel me from the party, adding, as he read out the resolution, 'Promise that you will renounce your views as I have done, and you can continue to carry out the same line as you did before, and the party will retain you.'" Is this correct?

Lozovsky: Absolutely correct. Zinoviev really did say this to me, but his advice was monstrous to me. I didn't understand how a person could stay in the party and continue working underground against it. I said that I would not do that.

I believe that what it says in the indictment about my expulsion from the party for double-dealing is wrong both politically and legally. What does double-dealing mean? It means to remain a party member and conduct subversive underground activity against the party. But if a person speaks out openly, can you really say that he has been removed for double-dealing? But there is a difference between being removed for double-dealing and being removed for wrong behavior, for openly stating one's opposition to the party line. So this language has nothing to do with me. I have never been a double-dealer.

In January 1918 the First Trade Unions Congress was convened, and as the secretary of the Central Council of Soviet Trade Unions, I announced the start of the Congress. Tomsky* was the first to speak. In my talk about the tasks facing the labor unions, I proposed the notion of independent trade unions, which was a political error and could not withstand the slightest criticism, but this was my point of view. Is this really double-dealing if I said in print myself that I talked about this and if the party knew about it?

The presidium of the Central Council of Soviet Trade Unions was elected, with Tomsky as chairman. I don't recall who was the secretary. I appeared to have been kept on as a presidium member.

My position in the party was unclear. I was some sort of outrageous figure. I was expelled from the party, and I remained all alone. Incidentally, in Moscow, Petrograd, and other cities, there were groups called internationalists, which brought together Mensheviks who had left Martov† and right Bolsheviks. They were in-between groups. After the government was moved to Moscow, I went there as well. Here I familiarized myself with the relevant organizations, convened a conference, and became the chairman of the Central Committee of the Social-Democratic "Internationalists."

Presiding Officer: At whose initiative was this conference arranged?

Lozovsky: It was at the initiative of certain "internationalists," and I was involved.

Presiding Officer: Why are you telling about your trade union activity? That is not what you are accused of.

Lozovsky: You'll see in a moment. It has to do with the false accusation against me.

[Lozovsky returned several times to his life story, and in response to the presiding officer's remarks about why he was doing this, Lozovsky said that in the indictment it said that he had been hostile to Soviet power since the October Revolution.]

*Mikhail Tomsky (1880–1936) was a veteran Bolshevik revolutionary and leader of the trade union movement. He committed suicide rather than allow himself to be arrested.

†Yuli Martov (Tsederbaum) (1873–1923) was a leader of the Mensheviks.

Lozovsky: But supposedly I was an enemy starting back in 1919.

Presiding Officer: This has nothing to do with the case.

Lozovsky: It has to do with my head.

Presiding Officer: You have been arraigned under a specific accusation. The indictment reads as follows: "Engaged in espionage and led the Jewish nationalistic underground in the USSR, was the moving force and organizer of the transformation of the Jewish Anti-Fascist Committee into a center of nationalistic activity, in 1943 assigned Mikhoels and Fefer the task of establishing contact with reactionary circles in the United States."

What does the story you have told us about the revolutionary workers' trade union movement have to do with this activity?

Lozovsky: But in the indictment it says that I have been an enemy since 1919.

Presiding Officer: If you would like to enumerate what party tasks you have carried out, then tell us briefly about that.

Lozovsky: So, over the whole period, until I started working at Goslitizdat, I always held party jobs that entailed great trust, for I knew the opinions of the party leadership. And this is why it is absolutely unbearable for me to read lines such as these which say that I was an enemy of the party starting in 1919.

Presiding Officer: This follows from the accusation presented to you.

Lozovsky: So, we are done with Goslitizdat. Everything has been straightened out, and all fabrications have been swept away.

On May 12, 1939, Comrade Molotov called me in and said that there were thoughts of appointing me deputy people's commissar for foreign affairs, and he asked me how I felt about this. I answered that it would all depend on who the people's commissar for foreign affairs would be. Comrade Molotov told me that he would be the people's commissar, and I needed to give my answer no later than that evening. I thought about it and accepted. I was given three days to get all my affairs in order, and I became deputy people's commissar for foreign affairs on May 15, 1939. My portfolio included the Far East and Scandinavia. In the beginning, our major headache in the Far East was Japan. I was one of those who knew all the countries well. I knew the workers' movements and the policies of all the countries. After all, I had been involved in foreign affairs for thirty years. I knew the Far East better than anyone, and even so, this was a very difficult assignment, and I did it for several years. I did it not too badly, and I know how the party leadership regarded it.

Presiding Officer: What does this have to do with the case? Details about operations in the Foreign Ministry are hardly needed here. Tell us, did you receive any reprimands or penalties at this time? Tell us about that.

Lozovsky: At the Foreign Ministry, where I worked for seven years and two months, I did not receive any reprimands. I had three conflicts during my period of trade union activity. Shall I tell you about that?

Presiding Officer: These conflicts are not part of the case. Why should we broaden the accusation? Why were you relieved of your position at the Foreign Ministry?

Lozovsky: In July 1946, after Shcherbakov died, I was appointed head of the Sovinformburo. This was why I was relieved of my position at the Foreign Ministry.

You know about the beginning of the war. On June 24, 1941, I received an excerpt from a decree that said the following. The Sovinformburo has been created and will include the following staff members: Shcherbakov, chairman, and Lozovsky, deputy. Then we added Polikarpov, chairman of the radio committee; Khavinson, senior director of TASS; Kemenov, the VOKS chairman; Alexandrov, head of the Central Committee Propaganda and Agitation Department; and Saksin, deputy general secretary of the Foreign Ministry.

Space was set aside for us at the Central Committee, and we got two or three people (Shcherbakov gave us people from his staff), and Afinogenov and Fadeyev were called in to give us some help at first. Afinogenov worked on literary matters.*

I had two responsibilities: press conferences and supplying all the international bourgeois capitalist press with information about the Soviet Union. We needed to hire people. Shcherbakov said, "I won't give you people from the front. Look for people yourself, people who can work—old people and women who aren't at the front." I started putting together a staff of people who were available, including even Renshtein, who was seventy-six years old. He knew foreign languages, and he started working with us.

The difficulty was that the materials that we took from the newspapers had to be translated into excellent English. When a newspaper editorial office abroad receives an article in bad English or French, it goes right into the wastepaper basket. The challenge was to penetrate major capitalist press outlets with information about the Soviet Union, to fight against fascism, to carry out counterpropaganda. I am accused of hiring people for the Sovinformburo who had lived abroad. But we needed people who

---

*Dmitri Polikarpov (1905–1965), a longtime party official, was active in the Department of Agitation and Propaganda of the Central Committee from 1939 to 1944 and the Soviet Radio Committee from 1944 to 1946. Jacob Khavinson (1901–1992), a prominent Soviet journalist, was a leading figure at the Soviet news agency TASS from 1939 to 1943 and an editor at *Pravda* from 1943 to 1953. His articles appeared under the name Marinin. Vladimir Kemenov (1908–1988) served as chairman of VOKS from 1940 to 1948. Saksin was an official within the Sovinformburo. Alexander Afinogenov (1904–1941) was a prominent Soviet playwright, theater director, and editor; he was killed during the bombing of Moscow on October 29, 1941.

knew foreign languages perfectly, and so I hired people who fit this criterion, even though their pasts were not altogether pure.

Do you know what the situation was at that time? The secretary of the Central Committee would give me instructions to put together a radio broadcast immediately in Yiddish for propaganda in America. We had to arouse millions of people against the Hitlerites because of their brutality. And here you're saying that there was a nationalistic rally, and Lozovsky did it all. It's like some kind of fairy tale—there was no Central Committee, no government, just Lozovsky and a couple of Jews who did everything. It's astonishing. I organized a rally according to party directives. Every speaker received instructions from the Central Committee. I read every speech, as did Alexandrov and Shcherbakov. Is it really possible to imagine that the radio committee, which was not subordinate to me, would broadcast appeals and speeches on the air without Central Committee approval?

So the rally took place. Tell me, is Academician Kapitsa* a subordinate of mine? Is the writer Ehrenburg a subordinate of mine? Do they speak according to my instructions? Recall the list of speakers. Ehrenburg says that his mother's name is Hannah, throwing that in the fascists' faces. And suddenly someone says that this means a return to being Jewish. My mother's name was Hannah, too. Am I supposed to be ashamed of that? What kind of strange psychology is this? Why is this considered nationalism?

Our task was to show the whole world that we were robust and confident in battle. In September 1941, when one of the correspondents said that there was an item in the German press saying that the Germans could already see Moscow through their binoculars, I answered with a laugh that the Germans would undoubtedly see Moscow, but as prisoners of war. In September 1941 that response made its way around the world. I laughed at Goebbels, and this went around the world in hundreds of millions of copies thanks to the capitalist newspapers and capitalist trusts. Goebbels wrote that when he reached Moscow, he would skin me alive.

I did not have an easy job, but I dare to think that I handled it pretty well. I have never talked about it, never credited myself for it, but I think that I was doing work that was truly Soviet, and it was in the interests of the party.

On October 15, 1941, at two o'clock in the afternoon I was informed

---

*Pyotr Kapitsa (1894–1984) was a Soviet physicist and Nobel laureate in 1978; he was not Jewish, although some Western reference books refer to his mother as Jewish. On one occasion, when he was asked if he was Jewish, Kapitsa is known to have responded: "No, but I expect to be soon." At the direction of the regime, Kapitsa spoke at the first Jewish wartime rally in Moscow, on August 24, 1941; he was subsequently a member of the JAC. The famous film director Sergei Eisenstein also participated in the August 24 radio broadcast. Eisenstein had an assimilated Jewish father and did not consider himself a Jew. During the August 24 meeting, he turned to Ilya Ehrenburg and asked, "Does it hurt to be circumcised when you're forty years old?"

that we would be leaving for Kuibyshev that night.* Once we got there, everything would have to be started up from the beginning. We would have to gather our people and find space to set up operations. Press conferences also continued in Kuibyshev. Comrade Molotov was in Moscow, but I got the questions and answers to him by a specially protected government line and then got them back with corrections and proposals; that is to say, that coordination and approval took place that seemed so suspicious to Yuzefovich. In late 1941, in conversation with Shcherbakov by this same line, we got the idea of creating several anti-fascist committees. We created several right away: Slavic, Jewish, women's, and youth committees, and a committee for scientists. From the name alone it is apparent that these were not class-based organizations for propaganda among the workers exclusively, but organizations meant to appeal to everyone who wanted to and could do anything in the struggle against fascism.

Where did the idea of creating committees come from? Was I the one who came up with the whole idea? Can you really imagine that here in the Soviet Union five committees could be created with the Central Committee providing money, as well as people and space, then officials would not be interested in what they were actually doing? Why am I being accused of creating the Jewish Anti-Fascist Committee and not all five committees? Why is a meeting with someone named Rosenberg better than a meeting with Mikolajczyk? Why could the Slavic committee have a visit from Anders† with my permission? Was he really a friend of the Soviet Union? Why was Beneš‡ received here? Why did the Youth committee write letters to American organizations headed by Eleanor Roosevelt herself?

And so I began hiring people, translators. The party bureau commission finds me guilty of hiring Feinberg and others. And who is Feinberg? Feinberg is the son of a communist, an old workingman who lived many years in England. Feinberg translated Lenin's works into English. Why shouldn't I hire him? Because he is a Jew?

Tell me, where is the common sense in that? Can't someone who translates Lenin translate an article by Fadeyev or Zaslavsky?§

*On October 15, 1941, prominent cultural and political figures, along with the diplomatic corps, were evacuated by train from Moscow to Kuibyshev, 530 miles southeast of the capital.

†General Wladyslaw Anders (1892–1970) was taken into custody by the Soviet regime in September 1939, then released in August 1941. He organized a Polish army on Soviet territory; it was encamped in Buzuluk, near Kuibyshev. The army was allowed to leave the Soviet Union in 1942; later it fought in Italy against the Nazis.

‡Eduard Beneš (1884–1948) was president of Czechoslovakia from 1935 to 1938 and from 1946 to 1948.

§David Zaslavsky (1880–1965) was a prominent journalist. He was a member of the JAC and contributed articles to *Eynikayt*. In 1958 he played a significant role in denouncing Boris Pasternak after Pasternak was awarded the Nobel Prize in literature for *Doctor Zhivago*.

In late 1941 five committees were created. These were not special organizations. Their mission was to get in touch with all organizations—democratic ones, progressive ones, even bourgeois ones—that wanted to aid in
the fight against fascism and help the Soviet Union. This was how it was
phrased at a press conference and then printed in the newspapers. I asked
to have this material included in the case materials, but for some reason it
wasn't done. Five committees were created. Then the issue of leadership
came up. After all, someone had to run them. There had to be a secretary
and a chairman. There were a lot of conversations with Shcherbakov about
this. He nominated Mikhoels for the chairmanship of the Jewish Anti-Fascist Committee. Shcherbakov asked me whether I knew anything about
Epshteyn, whom a lot of people knew from the Soviet Writers' Union. I
said that Epshteyn was a former Bundist.

Presiding Officer: And how was the question of Mikhoels posed?

Lozovsky: Shcherbakov wanted the chairman to be someone who was not a
party member, and Mikhoels fit this requirement. So Shcherbakov nominated him.

Presiding Officer: Had you met with Mikhoels before?

Lozovsky: I had met Mikhoels in August at a rally. Prior to that I had never
met him and didn't know him.

Presiding Officer: What about Fefer?

Lozovsky: I didn't know him before he came to Kuibyshev. I had not published him, and I didn't know his name. I had heard Markish's name.

Presiding Officer: Had you heard of Kvitko?

Lozovsky: I had heard Kvitko's name, for he was well known in the field of
children's literature.

Presiding Officer: What about Hofshteyn?

Lozovsky: I did not.

Markish: Allow me to make one very important clarification. In 1938, at the
Conservatory building in Moscow, there was an anti-fascist rally of members of the Soviet intelligentsia, which was broadcast all over the world.
Mikhoels was one of four people who spoke at that rally. Alexei Tolstoy
spoke, as did an academician and someone else. Three or four days after
Mikhoels spoke at the rally, Zaitsev, who was the party bureau secretary at
the Soviet Writers' Union, called and said, "Who is this Mikhoels character?" So even then, Mikhoels was getting attention. It is no secret that
Mikhoels's speech was enormously successful, and his name was known at
the Central Committee.

Presiding Officer: And Epshteyn?

Lozovsky: I can say only one thing about Epshteyn—that I knew him through
his literary activity. I said of Epshteyn that I knew him to be a former

Bundist. During the period of frenzied anti-Soviet agitation in the United States he spoke to the Communist Party and addressed the editorial staff of the *Morgen Freiheit*. He spent several years doing editorial work. And an editorial job in the United States is no sinecure, let me tell you.

I am also aware that for several years Epshteyn worked in the foreign division of the NKVD (secret police). And when Bergelson hinted here that Epshteyn was an agent for some foreign power, I said that he was an agent of the power known as the USSR; that is, he was an agent of the NKVD.

Presiding Officer: People consulted with you during the nomination process, and yet you did not make a single nomination yourself?

Lozovsky: I also nominated people. But there was not a single person who was appointed by me alone. That's impossible.

Presiding Officer: What, did the committee confirm the members' nominations?

Lozovsky: Absolutely. When I read the collected works of fifty prisoners and twenty investigators, I was simply stunned. How could it happen in our party, during the war, that suddenly and without the knowledge of the Central Committee a new person becomes the head of an organization? Every candidate for committee membership was checked by the Propaganda and Agitation Department through Alexandrov, and I checked what sort of people the nominees were as well. Then the nominations went to Shcherbakov for approval. That was how the candidate selection worked.

When the committees, including the Jewish Anti-Fascist Committee, began their work, I would go to the Sovinformburo for an hour or two every day. In Kuibyshev and also in Moscow, I was swamped with work for the Foreign Ministry. There were months when I was alone at the ministry; the other people were away on various matters, but the committees' work got launched anyway.

What was the work that all the committees were doing, in particular the Jewish committee, that it merited forty-two volumes' worth of attention? If you look at the testimony and the indictment, it appears that the Jewish Anti-Fascist Committee arose because of Lozovsky's initiative, with nationalistic and hostile intent, in order to establish contact with bourgeois organizations to pursue subversive work. This is sheer fiction.

We were told at the beginning not to write to communist newspapers, because then we might be called a second Comintern publisher. So that meant we had to make it into the larger press. We started gathering information about newspapers and organizations in every country. The Jewish Anti-Fascist Committee did this. All the committees did. Each committee put together a list of all the newspapers to which they might send materials and which might publish something favorable about the Soviet Union. They could be bourgeois, democratic, or farming papers, even Zionist. Why Zionist? Because Zionist bourgeois reactionaries, when it came to wiping out the Jews, could not be anything but against fascists, and they printed material about fascist brutalities.

When Fefer testified to the court, he said that Goldberg ran things at the newspaper *Der Tog,* but apparently the Jewish Anti-Fascist Committee had placed only two or three articles there. This is hypocrisy and nonsense; there were many more articles published there. Citizen Judges, tell me, is the *New York Times,* which is owned by the millionaire Sulzburger, a newspaper for the laboring masses? This newspaper has capital amounting to twenty million dollars. There the publisher is the boss, not the editor; the editor is a hired man. Sulzburger has invested over fifteen million rubles in this undertaking. This capitalist is a fervent defender of the pope, Cardinal Spellman,* and others. And we tried to penetrate that paper as well. The mission was to get into all foreign press outlets.

There was a war on, they were our allies, we had to print things about the Soviet Union. We wormed our way into the papers, each committee in its own way—the Slavic committee in its own way, the Jewish, Women's, and Youth committees each in their own ways.

If the word "information" implies "espionage," then all of the Sovinformburo's activity was espionage activity.

In addition to general information that went through the Sovinformburo departments, the anti-fascist committees sent their own particular information. From the very start, *Eynikayt* was in a separate category, because in our country newspapers have a particular look and form of control. *Eynikayt,* like all newspapers published in the Soviet Union, was under the press section of the party Central Committee. I did not appoint the department heads or the editor to *Eynikayt,* nor did I give them money. This was handled by the press section of the Propaganda Department of the Central Committee.

Presiding Officer: But this was the press organ of the Jewish Anti-Fascist Committee, was it not?

Lozovsky: What of it? I didn't give it money—it wasn't on our books. I didn't hire the editors, I did not appoint the staff, and I didn't read the paper, since I haven't read Yiddish in sixty years. Can I really bear responsibility for the fact that a newspaper that came out under the direct control of the Department of Agitation and Propaganda of the Central Committee printed nationalistic articles?

I am stating here that nothing that was written in *Eynikayt* had anything to do with me directly or indirectly. When I was told that they needed a Yiddish writer, I would help them, and that was it. To write for a Yiddish newspaper, a writer had to write in Yiddish. But when Bergelson suddenly

---

*Cardinal Francis Joseph Spellman (1889–1967) was appointed archbishop of New York in 1939 and cardinal in 1946. He was famous for advocating conservative political positions.

says that if someone writes in Yiddish, that is nationalism, that means that what is on trial here is the Yiddish language. This is beyond my capacity to grasp. Write in the language of the Negroes if that's what you want. That's your business. The point is not what language someone writes in, but how they write. There are times when national feelings shift to nationalistic feelings, and a communist ought to know that.

So the anti-fascist committees, on the one hand, and the Sovinformburo, on the other, started to send a steady flow of information about the Soviet Union, about our people, about the heroic struggle against fascism. A small stream in this flow came from the Jewish Anti-Fascist Committee, which served a particular group of newspapers. During the six years that I worked at the Sovinformburo we sent about four hundred thousand articles abroad, if one counts each article as four pages (there were longer ones, and shorter ones, but on average, they were four pages long). Of these four hundred thousand articles, about fifteen to sixteen thousand came from the Jewish Anti-Fascist Committee during those four years and two months (on August 1, 1946, the Jewish Anti-Fascist Committee was removed from the Sovinformburo) while I supervised that committee. This is basically what the work was all about.

When the committees were still in the embryonic stage, Epshteyn raised the subject of a second rally with Shcherbakov, and in connection with this he made several special trips to Moscow.

Presiding Officer: Was the first rally in 1941?

Lozovsky: Yes, it was in August 1941.

Presiding Officer: Fefer, when was the second rally?

Fefer: In early May 1942, and the third rally was in April 1944.

Lozovsky: The issue of the second rally was raised in connection with the fact that the struggle for and against the USSR had become more intense. Everyone saw that although Soviet troops were retreating, they had not been destroyed and were bravely withstanding enemy onslaughts. This led to a major turnaround at the top levels of U.S. leadership.

What was this large committee created for? You think that it was to gather together, to act, to discuss various problems? Nothing of the kind. Seventy to eighty people with the necessary qualifications were brought together to send things to America and England and all over the world so that people there would see that not only Mikhoels and Epshteyn were urging them to fight fascism, but also academicians, writers, poets, and government officials, and that they were all appealing to the broad masses to fight against fascism.

There were nine or ten committee members who had nothing directly to do with the Jewish Anti-Fascist Committee's work. I don't know who included Lina Shtern, but I do know that people like her were included because their names carried weight. Names were included "for export"—

Academician Lina Shtern, a woman; Academician Frumkin,* who never appeared at the committee offices, although his name was used. The party had the right to do that. In the testimony that I signed (I will explain later why I signed it), it says that I knew about Lina Shtern's bourgeois views. That's not true. I slandered her, and I would like to take the opportunity here to apologize to her. I cannot look her in the eye because of the slander, which was coerced out of me. I didn't know her at all. I knew that there was such a person as Academician Lina Shtern, but I didn't know her personally.

Presiding Officer: Have you finished your testimony about how the members of the committee were selected?

Lozovsky: No.

Presiding Officer: Let's finish with that question.

Lozovsky: I can't remember now what year the third plenum took place.

Presiding Officer: In April 1944.

Lozovsky: And prior to that there was one more radio broadcast.

Presiding Officer: The third radio broadcast was also in 1944.

Lozovsky: That broadcast had the same procedure as the other ones: each person wrote his own speech, then their texts were read through, translated, and checked by Alexandrov and me before going to our boss, Shcherbakov, for final approval. Every aspect of the broadcast was checked by Central Committee staff, the Sovinformburo, and Shcherbakov. At the time I expressed the thought that this was my initiative, that the committee was a sort of formless organization, that is, that it had a chairman, a secretary, some staff members, and that was it. There was no group to keep the chairman and secretary of the committee in check. Shcherbakov and I talked about this, and we decided that a presidium ought to be formed. I don't remember how many people were supposed to be on the presidium: ten, fifteen, twenty, more, fewer—I can't remember. Writers, poets, and others like that are the most disorganized people in the world. All they think about is their poetry, their books, how they can publish as many lines as possible. Who was in charge at the time? Mikhoels, Epshteyn, and Fefer. It needs to be said that Epshteyn died while he was in this position.

They drew up a preliminary list of presidium members, including Shimeliovich, Shtern, and others, totaling fifteen people in all, I think. As to Bregman, I will speak about him separately, since there was a special conversation about him and a separate decision. Did I know them all? No, not all of them. I knew that Shimeliovich worked at Botkin Hospital. I had heard Shimeliovich's name, but had never spoken with him, never met him, had

---

*Alexander Frumkin (1895–1976) was a physical chemist. He became a member of the Academy of Sciences in 1932.

not even talked to him on the phone. I looked through this list and passed it on to Shcherbakov, who was my supervisor.

I would like the court to take a long and careful look at the serious situation in which I found myself. I had two supervisors: Comrade Molotov was my boss at the People's Commissariat of Foreign Affairs, and Shcherbakov was my boss at the Sovinformburo, and from what it says here and the way it is described, it's as if I did everything on my own. All I can say is that this is not one of the more politically inspired parts, or at any rate, it is poetic slander.

In this way the presidium of the Jewish Anti-Fascist Committee was approved. And I think the list of names was even approved as proposed. I, for one, don't recall there being any changes. I think you know that this is the way the party does things: people are checked on before they are approved. Presidium members did not have to work directly at the Jewish Anti-Fascist Committee. There were supposed to be three to four editors working there, and the others did not have to be there on a regular basis.

Presiding Officer: Let's talk for a moment about how the committee staff was selected. Defendant Fefer, during the preliminary investigation you stated that it was no accident that from the very start, when the committee became active, people were brought on board who were, politically speaking, ardent nationalists, and that this happened as a result of Lozovsky's will and initiative. I am drawing this conclusion from your testimony.

Fefer: I ask to have my testimony read out.

Presiding Officer: What, are you denying it? I am simply calling things by their proper names. This is precisely the conclusion that follows from your testimony.

Fefer: That is a very harsh conclusion to draw.

Presiding Officer: You testified: "At our first meeting, Epshteyn informed Mikhoels and me about the creation of the Anti-Fascist Committee and stated that much of the credit for this should go to Lozovsky, whom he called our father" (vol. 2, p. 48).

In answer to a question about the conclusions drawn by the expert commission, you say: "As I have already testified, the nationalistic line began to go into effect at the committee from the very first days of its existence. This can be explained by the fact that active Jewish nationalists were its leaders: Lozovsky, Mikhoels, Epshteyn, and I, Fefer." Is this testimony of yours correct?

Fefer: This is the result of further reflection.

Presiding Officer: What do you mean, "the result of further reflection"?

Fefer: Let me explain what I mean. After the committee was formed I didn't look upon Lozovsky as a nationalist, and we did not talk about nationalistic questions. But during the investigation, when I began to draw conclusions about the committee's activity and thought about all of the most important parts—such as the memorandums to the Central Committee, *The Black Book,* the two memorandums about mistreatment of Jews and the materials sent abroad focusing on Jewish heroes on the front lines and at the rear—then when I summarized all of this, I understood that all this activity was the basis for accusing the committee of nationalism. And since Lozovsky followed what was going on at the committee, I called Lozovsky a nationalist. This is how I understand the words "the result of further reflection."

Presiding Officer: But you do say that you presented all important questions before Lozovsky and got his approval to implement them. So how could he not have known about all of that?

Fefer: I personally did not inform Lozovsky about who was on the committee. Mikhoels and Epshteyn let him know.

Presiding Officer: Lozovsky, at the witness confrontation with Fefer you confirmed his testimony.

Lozovsky: As regards my testimony in all of the interrogation records, it is wrong, starting from February 3, 1949, all the way to the end, and this was conscious on my part. Later I will explain why. Fefer keeps talking as if he is a witness for the prosecution. I will comment later on what Fefer's aim was in writing three volumes of fiction that reveal certain of his features. But allow me to go to the heart of the matter. The following conclusion results from Fefer's testimony: Lozovsky dealt only with the Jewish Anti-Fascist Committee. He was there day and night and thought of nothing else.

Has the court failed to consider that there was not one committee, but five? Five committees were formed with the Central Committee's approval. For what do I bear responsibility, as Shcherbakov's former deputy and a member of the Communist Party Central Committee? If you want to judge me for the Jewish committee, then I ask that you try me for all of the committees. Didn't the Slavic committee send appeals and articles abroad as well?

The witness for the prosecution keeps alluding to Epshteyn, who is dead. He said that I was the "father," that I was moved to tears. Maybe they did indeed call me "father," but in Kirgizia, people called me "Aksakal."* and in China, "Chinese elder," because I had done a lot of work involving China, and in Latin America they called me "a second Columbus." One photojournalist sent me a book and her photograph with the inscription "To Solomon the Wise." So there were quite a few people who referred to me in various ways. What does that have to do with my political activity?

Presiding Officer: But they saw you not simply as a father, but as the leader of

---

*In Central Asia, the term "Aksakal" refers to a wise, respected elder.

a nationalistic organization. When they used the word "father," they invested it with a particular meaning.

Lozovsky: The meaning that Fefer invests in it and the meaning that the late Epshteyn invested in it are not one and the same. I will testify about the activities that Fefer pursued behind my back. And he shouldn't think that just because he wrote three volumes, he can testify as a witness for the prosecution against everyone. Citizen Judges, with your experience you know how people try to evade responsibility by accusing others.

Presiding Officer: He is not a witness, but a defendant, and he is giving testimony that he considers it necessary to give.

Lozovsky: It says in the indictment that I was working to send a delegation to America, that I selected it. Let us allow for one minute that this is true. The People's Commissariat of Foreign Affairs was right next door. What would it have cost to ask, Who wrote about this delegation, and who gave permission for Mikhoels and Fefer's trip? This is an extremely simple matter, after all. I don't understand why such a simple thing was not done. This is how the matter developed: Our consul and our ambassador to America sent an encoded message to the People's Commissariat of Foreign Affairs, and then there was an open telegram addressed to the Jewish Anti-Fascist Committee stating that an anti-fascist committee of artists and writers had been formed in the United States, headed by Einstein. They got in touch with the Jewish Anti-Fascist Committee. Their mission was to rally those elements in U.S. society that would speak out against fascism. I personally believed, and still believe, that the creation of such an organization in the United States, whose activity encompassed scientists, artists, and poets and which was headed by such a world-renowned scientist as Einstein, was to the advantage of the Soviet Union. The proposal to send the delegation also came from two different sources: from the People's Commissariat of Foreign Affairs and then, openly, from the Jewish Anti-Fascist Committee. I don't remember exactly, but it seems to me that names were actually mentioned in the telegram of those who were being requested to go as part of the delegation: some army general, then Ehrenburg, Markish, Mikhoels, and others.

Fefer: In 1943 an invitation addressed to Mikhoels was received from the American Anti-Fascist Committee of Scientists and Writers.

Presiding Officer: But in 1942 you had a conversation with Mikhoels about contacting these organizations? Fefer testifies (vol. 2, p. 59): "Work to establish contact with various organizations, especially with anti-fascist ones, began back in 1942. In answer to our appeal, two organizations were formed in New York in 1942. The second organization was the Anti-Fascist Committee of Writers and Scientists headed by Einstein. We rejoiced at the formation of these two organizations. This circumstance made a strong impression on Lozovsky. Before we left for America, Lozovsky instructed us to foster closer relations with wealthy Americans."

Fefer: During the investigation I spoke about how this happened in 1942 in Kuibyshev. Mikhoels, Epshteyn, and I did indeed go in to see Lozovsky. And we had a conversation about how the first Jewish radio broadcast had resulted in the formation of two organizations in the United States: the committee of scientists and writers and the Jewish Council of Russian Relief, and that these organizations were headed by prominent people like Einstein. Lozovsky said that this was good, and proposed using these committees to get in touch with prosperous Jews in the United States in order to wring out as much as we could for the Soviet defense budget.

Presiding Officer: You confirmed that Lozovsky gave instructions to foster closer ties with rich American Jews. What was the purpose of establishing this goal?

Fefer: Shcherbakov established this goal in order to get more money for the Soviet defense budget.

Presiding Officer: Further on (vol. 2, p. 60), in answer to the question "What guided Lozovsky when he gave these instructions?" you answered, "The same nationalism that Mikhoels and I had. Lozovsky's purpose in sending extensive information to America was to gain sympathy in wealthy Jewish circles in America and enlist their support in resolving the Jewish question in the USSR."

Fefer: I deny that.

Presiding Officer: Where did you get that from?

Fefer: I simply slandered Lozovsky when I said that.

Presiding Officer: And what was the situation in actual fact?

Fefer: When Lozovsky gave us instructions to make connections with wealthy Jews through these committees, he said that this was necessary in order to get as many dollars as we could for the Soviet defense budget.

Presiding Officer: Why are you now denying Lozovsky's nationalistic motives when he gave these instructions?

Fefer: I am not denying his nationalistic motives.

Presiding Officer: When you started working on the Jewish Anti-Fascist Committee in 1941–1942 together with Epshteyn and Mikhoels, you say that not only were there goals in the organization, set by the state, having to do with anti-fascist propaganda, but there was also an opportunity to disseminate ideas about certain peculiarities of the Jewish nationality. So you had nationalistic sentiments even earlier, did you not?

Fefer: I have already said that I had nationalistic sentiments.

Presiding Officer: But when you joined the Jewish Anti-Fascist Committee, you intended to act not only on those official problems that the state had set before you, but also to carry out a mission that went beyond the committee's mandate, one having to do with the problems of Jews in the USSR, did you not?

Fefer: I had in mind the problem of preserving and developing Jewish culture.

Presiding Officer: But the struggle against assimilation is in fact a nonexistent Jewish problem, which the Jewish Anti-Fascist Committee was trying to resolve. Is that correct?

Fefer; Yes, that's right.

Presiding Officer (to Fefer): We have agreed here that you joined the work of the committee as a person who already had nationalistic sentiments.

Fefer: At that time there were some things that I did not consider to be nationalistic work. For example, I did not think that working to counter assimilation was nationalistic activity.

Presiding Officer: In response to my questions you answered that in 1941, when you started working for *Eynikayt,* you pushed your intention of struggling against assimilation.

Fefer: Yes, because an organic assimilation process was taking place.

Presiding Officer: What was the point of your struggling against this if the party hadn't set that task before us? We are stating a fact: that in 1941 you started working at *Eynikayt* with the goal not only of carrying out the tasks put to you by the party, but of struggling against assimilation and for the cultural autonomy of Jews.

Fefer: No, for the growth of Jewish culture.

Presiding Officer: All right, but that is also a nationalistic mission.

Fefer: At the time I did not consider it a nationalistic mission.

Presiding Officer: Fefer, five minutes ago you confessed that you are a nationalist, and now you are saying something different. Fefer, how are we supposed to understand you?

Fefer: On what issue? Regarding the nationalistic work at the committee and Lozovsky's nationalistic activity?

Presiding Officer: Yes, you were guided by the same nationalistic motives that Lozovsky had. You said, "He was the force behind all of our nationalistic activity."

Fefer: I have stated in my testimony throughout these judicial proceedings that I consider the Jewish Anti-Fascist Committee's work to be nationalistic. As a matter of fact, what I said to the court was that I conducted nationalistic activity and that Lozovsky did the same. The court will establish the degree of Lozovsky's guilt. But I did not say that Lozovsky directed all of our nationalistic work. I said that I drew that conclusion during the investigation, but I personally had no conversations about that with Lozovsky.

Lozovsky (to Fefer): When did you arrive in Kuibyshev?

Fefer: I came to Kuibyshev at the beginning of 1942, in April, approximately.

Lozovsky: And where did you work?

Fefer: At the newspaper *Eynikayt.*

Lozovsky: For how long?

Fefer: Until Epshteyn died, that is, until July 1945.

Lozovsky: You say that you came to me in 1942 with some questions about the committee's work. But you were working at *Eynikayt* at the time, so how could you have come to me with a question about the committee's activity?

Fefer: I came to see Lozovsky sometimes with Epshteyn and sometimes with Mikhoels.

Lozovsky: And what about contacts with rich Jews?

Fefer: This mission was given to the committee not only by Lozovsky, but also by Shcherbakov and Kalinin. You said that we needed to make contacts through American anti-fascist organizations with rich Jews and through them raise funds for the Soviet defense budget.

Lozovsky: Do you know of any document originating in the committee that went abroad (appeals and so forth), apart from articles leaving the Anti-Fascist Committee by radio or telegraph, that was not approved by Shcherbakov? Was there even a single such document that was not approved by the head of the Sovinformburo?

Fefer: If what you have in mind are speeches and appeals from the rallies, or the speeches that we made at the third plenum of the Jewish Anti-Fascist Committee, all of the most important documents crossed Shcherbakov's desk. As for daily correspondence, including questions having to do with material assistance and AMBIJAN's orders for materials for Birobidzhan, which the expert commission described as confidential, then I confirm that this correspondence was approved by Solomon Abramovich Lozovsky.

Presiding Officer: Defendant Bergelson, in your testimony during the investigation (vol. 17, pp. 57, 180, and 181) you said that for a long time prior to the establishment of the committee Lozovsky revealed himself to be a nationalist. Repeat this to the court.

Bergelson: I have to say that I began signing interrogation records of my testimony about Lozovsky saying that he was a nationalist after I was shown testimony signed in his hand that said that he was a nationalist, and after it became clear to me that the very greatest manifestation of nationalism at the committee was the Crimea memorandum, which would not have been sent had Lozovsky not lent his authority to it.

Presiding Officer: Lozovsky was arrested on January 26, 1949. Up until January 28, 1949, there was no testimony from Lozovsky about his nationalistic activity. His interrogation starts on February 3, but on January 28, 1949, you testified that "before the creation of the Jewish Anti-Fascist Committee, Lozovsky organized a series of events that were nationalistic in character and that determined or influenced the orientation of the committee's activity to a certain degree" (vol. 17, p. 58).

Bergelson: Speaking of Lozovsky's nationalism, I cited one other motif as well. After it became clear to me that the Crimea memorandum was the greatest manifestation of nationalism at the committee—and Lozovsky knew of that memorandum without a doubt—he could have used his authority to influence Mikhoels, Fefer, and Epshteyn to make them renounce the whole idea. But he didn't do that. After that it was easy for me to sign testimony saying that he was a nationalist. And the second thing is that after I learned that according to Lozovsky's testimony, Goldberg had been given documents which had not been published in the Soviet Union—that is, they were secret—I began to believe that nationalism was only part of his activity, and that was why I began to sign all of the other testimony about Lozovsky.

Presiding Officer: You also testified that before the creation of the Jewish Anti-Fascist Committee, Lozovsky brought together Jewish writers at the Sovinformburo and instructed them to get materials about the sufferings of the Jewish population connected to the Soviet-German war. This directive of Lozovsky's degenerated into nationalistic activity on the part of the Jewish writers, because materials about the Jewish population were submitted to the Sovinformburo in isolation from the sufferings and disasters that the war brought to all of the Soviet people (vol. 17, p. 57).

Bergelson: It's not true that Lozovsky brought Jewish writers together. He personally didn't bring them together; rather, Jewish writers came there themselves.

Presiding Officer: Defendant Lozovsky, what can you say regarding Fefer's and Bergelson's testimony? Both Fefer and Bergelson confirm that you formed the Anti-Fascist Committee with nationalistic goals in mind and were the ideological leader of all the committee's subsequent anti-Soviet activity.

Lozovsky: As to Bergelson, I think that the court's awareness and his own are getting mixed up here, and it is even hard to understand all that he has said. So, a person writes in Yiddish that the October Revolution gave the Jews equal rights! What is nationalistic about that?

As regards the creation of the committee for nationalistic purposes, I have to say that the Slavic committee was created for Slavic purposes, the Youth committee for the purpose of advancing the interests of youth, and the Women's committee for the purpose of advancing the interests of women. If you look at the question this way, then everything that was done was sheer nationalism.

I categorically assert that the statement that the Jewish Anti-Fascist Committee was created for nationalistic purposes is a total fabrication. The committee was created not by me, but by the Central Committee of the party. There was not one committee, but five. In this case, then, I should be held responsible for the other committees as well. Why make an allowance for the other committees? Once again I assert that the committee was created in order to rouse people against fascism. There were slogans that went like this: "Jews of the world united against fascism, scientists united against fascism, youth against fascism." These slogans came from the Central Committee of the party. You are asking why, on what basis? Here is the basis. Let the Jews, women, young people, scientists of England and America, say that they are opposed to this anti-fascist slogan; let them speak out and say that they are against this slogan. None of them could speak out against such a slogan. It was a great slogan for exposing fascist sympathizers. I assert that Bergelson is getting things mixed up. I think that the court can see that he is.

Fefer's testimony about how I became concerned . . .

Presiding Officer (interrupts Lozovsky): At the beginning he testified that in 1942 he had a conversation with you about anti-fascist organizations coming into existence in the United States and about contacts with rich Jews.

Lozovsky: I declare all of this to be poetic fabrication. An organization came into being that raised funds for the Soviet Union. This was a positive event. If we had been opposed to fund-raising, then why would we do it? And Russian Relief raised ninety-three million dollars for the USSR. Even Fefer says that I set the goal: to raise funds to assist the USSR. Not for Jews, not for the Jewish Anti-Fascist Committee, but for the Red Army aid fund. What is nationalistic about a proposal to raise money?

Was I delighted? I don't know. I am not the sort of person who goes into raptures, and in general, it is not recommended for a diplomat to go into raptures. I am a restrained person, though a passionate orator. And here every word is being transformed into evidence of nationalistic, criminal behavior.

Presiding Officer: Defendant Kvitko, you confirmed to the court that Lozovsky directed the committee's criminal activity, hired people for the committee, and guided them. You stated in your testimony (vol. 11, p. 46), "It is painful for me to talk about that, but I have to admit that we nationalists made the committee into an anti-Soviet organization. An evil hand brought us together." Is this testimony correct?

Kvitko: Only one thing is correct. During my three months in Kuibyshev with the committee, I got the impression that nothing got done at the Jewish Anti-Fascist Committee without Lozovsky's approval, but at the time I knew nothing about hostile activity.

Presiding Officer: Bregman, during the preliminary investigation you also confirmed that Lozovsky was the leader of the committee's nationalistic activity. Do you recall your testimony?

Bregman: No, I do not remember.

Presiding Officer: Let me remind you. This is from volume 5, page 53: "Selection of people for the committee, as well as the running of the committee, was overseen by Lozovsky, who was the head of the Sovinformburo and who stated repeatedly that the committee was his brainchild and that he, Lozovsky, considered its existence extremely necessary." Is this testimony correct?

Bregman: Yes, it is.

Presiding Officer: When did he say that the committee was his brainchild and that he considered its existence extremely necessary?

Bregman: I was there pretty often. I was in Lozovsky's office, and I would brief him on trouble at the committee and tell him that the committee required more active attention. Lozovsky would respond that that was in fact what he was doing, because it was his brainchild. I could not see in this statement elements of nationalism or counterrevolution.

Presiding Officer: Here is your testimony: "I knew Lozovsky from the time he worked at the Profintern, and we stayed in touch. Then I was invited to work at the Jewish Anti-Fascist Committee." You were asked, "As a Jewish nationalist?" You responded, "Lozovsky had reason to count on me because sometimes in conversation with him I expressed my views openly. Talking with Lozovsky in the summer of 1943, I informed Lozovsky that I had been relieved of my duties as a high-level trade union bureaucrat, and stated that I took this as having to do with my national background. Lozovsky expressed his sympathy to me."

Bregman: There are misstatements and distortions here. I said that I had had occasion to hear conversations at the committee about how Jews, even those who had been awarded gold medals when they graduated from high school, were not being accepted into colleges; that is, admissions decisions were being made on the basis of nationality. Conversations like this took place in the hallways. I told Lozovsky about this and asked whether the party line or a party directive had anything to do with this question. Lozovsky then told me straight out that there was nothing in the party line about that, that these were sentiments sown by Hitler and still being felt.

Presiding Officer: Who held these conversations?

Bregman: Nusinov. There was one other case, when a Jewish girl came to me with a grievance that she had not been accepted into college because she was Jewish. I told her that this affected not only Jews and that probably there was some other basis for it. I didn't do anything or take any measures to see that people like this who came with such requests got hired or accepted at a college. I told the investigator that in the Ukraine it was the general practice to consider nationality when people were hired or admitted to college. The investigator then said to me, "So you were removed from your job out of national considerations, and you are accusing the Central Committee of anti-Semitism?" In response I told him that maybe this was all happening out of a desire to achieve a balance of different nationalities, as was the case in the Ukraine. In addition, I was displeased with the fact that the party organization of the All-Union Central Committee of Trade Unions had decided to let me go without talking to me first. I expressed my dissatisfaction to two members of the Politburo. Actually I was glad to change jobs.

Presiding Officer: During the preliminary investigation you said that you had anti-Soviet conversations with Lozovsky.

Bregman: The investigators tried to convince me that my transfer to the committee was coordinated with Lozovsky based on our shared nationalistic views. The investigation team also tried to convince me that there was a conspiracy between Lozovsky and me to conduct nationalistic work at the committee. I stated that this was not the case. Lozovsky talked with me personally and said that Shcherbakov had approved bringing me onto the Jewish Anti-Fascist Committee. I was of the opinion then that there was no unity at the Jewish Anti-Fascist Committee, that there was squabbling, backbiting, and internecine rivalry, as I described it. Lozovsky will not deny that I reported to him on manifestations of nationalism and trouble at the committee. I doubt that Lozovsky, had he truly been a nationalist, would have started indicating that things were amiss at the committee. I myself was at the Central Committee twice in that connection.

Presiding Officer: Defendant Markish, do you confirm your testimony during the preliminary investigation that Lozovsky's activity in running the committee was nationalistic?

Markish: As to whether it was directly related to nationalistic activity carried out by the committee, I cannot confirm that the work in question was carried out by Lozovsky.

Presiding Officer: But you met with Lozovsky. In your testimony (vol. 15, p. 148) you said that Lozovsky taught you to emphasize Jewish national sorrow in your speeches. Did you receive such instructions from Lozovsky?

Markish: On the question of a trip and the gathering of materials about fascist brutalities, Lozovsky told writers that they must gather materials about atrocities committed against the Jews.

Presiding Officer: Did he close his eyes to the sufferings of other peoples? You testified that Lozovsky told you that you should write only about the Jews, and closed his eyes to the suffering of other peoples.

Markish: He did not say that. The very fact that these materials were being gathered qualifies as nationalism, but there were no instructions from Lozovsky to "close your eyes to the suffering of other peoples." What I want to say is this: There is no doubt that Lozovsky made clear to the writers who were in his office at that time that they should gather material exclusively about brutalities against the Jews. But as to any nationalistic motives behind such a directive, that was a conclusion drawn later during the investigation.

Presiding Officer: Is the conclusion yours?

Markish: Well, what it comes down to is that Lozovsky did not exhort writers to go and commit a crime against the Soviet people. The only thing he said was, "Go gather material about atrocities against the Jews." I deny that there were any directly nationalistic conversations.

Presiding Officer: Lozovsky, what testimony can you give regarding yesterday's testimony by Bregman, Markish, Fefer, Kvitko, and Bergelson?

Lozovsky: Above all, the conclusion that emerges from the testimony which Fefer, Kvitko, Bregman, Markish, and Bergelson gave is that when they came here, to this "house of enlightenment," they saw the light and realized that Lozovsky was the main perpetrator of all evil. I will briefly direct the court's attention to certain circumstances. Seeing the light, they signed testimony that they themselves had not given. Kvitko firmly asserts that he never thought about any evil hand of Lozovsky. So that means that there was no evil hand of Lozovsky, but rather someone's evil pen which wrote that and which Kvitko hurriedly signed.

Presiding Officer (to Bregman): Did you tell Lozovsky that supposedly there were not many Jews left in the party?

Bregman: No, I did not say that.

Presiding Officer: Did you say that there were limits on how many Jews were accepted into colleges?

Bregman: No, I did not say that.

Presiding Officer: Did you say that Jews were being let go from the civil service?

Bregman: No, I did not keep track of that sort of thing, and I did not have anti-Soviet conversations with Lozovsky.

Lozovsky: In July 1941—that would have been two to three weeks after the Sovinformburo was set up—I called in several Jewish writers, according to Shcherbakov's instructions, and told them that we needed to gather materials about fascist atrocities against the Jews to shove in the faces of those who denied that it was happening. At the time, there were assertions appearing in the American press that no atrocities were being committed. The statement that I required such information to be gathered while we closed our eyes to the atrocities against other peoples was inserted into Markish's testimony. Markish's explanations explain nothing. He even said that it was later, after he ended up here, that he concluded that I could have thought this way in 1941.

Judge for yourselves. A total of two to three weeks had passed since the organization was set up. Yuzefovich and Afinogenov were already working there by this time, handling literary affairs. Shcherbakov gave us administrator Stepanov. We started working on the premises of the Central Committee. The Central Committee gave us money and assigned us people from its staff. And suddenly a person who has been engaged in the workers' movement for forty years, the deputy minister of foreign affairs, calls people together and says, "Gather materials only about the sufferings of the Jews and close your eyes to the sufferings of other peoples."

Let's say that I am a hidden enemy, "a villain," as some here have said; still, no one thought I was an idiot, after all, to gather together people I hardly knew and say, "Hide the Hitlerites' crimes." Tell me, what sort of moral and political profile would a person need to have to say, "Hide the crimes committed by Hitler against other peoples"? Let us suppose that I said to them, "Gather material about atrocities against the Jews" in order to send that material abroad. Let us say that this is nationalism, then I ask the court to take the following circumstances into account: Did the Nuremberg trials take place under my supervision? No, there were six prosecutors who spoke at the Nuremberg trials, and the main one was Rudenko.* In order to prepare material for the Nuremberg trials, the Ministry of Justice asked the Sovinformburo for information about Hitlerite atrocities. After Rudenko and four other prosecutors had spoken, prosecutor Sheinin† spoke, and he talked about the Hitlerites' atrocities against the Jews. What, was this a nationalistic speech? The writer Sutzkever was flown over there. He, too, spoke about atrocities committed against the Jews. Why did the Soviet government arrange such speeches? Was this really nationalism?

Everything that is written here is coming down on my head, and every word here is fabricated.

Presiding Officer: During the investigation you testified: "I confess that I had nationalistic sentiments that had overwhelming influence over me" (vol. 1, p. 47).

Lozovsky: I was fully conscious when I signed that, and I will tell you why I did that, and you will see that it is all slander about me.

Presiding Officer: What, are you denying this testimony?

Lozovsky: Yes, I deny it categorically for the simple reason that it is not true.

Presiding Officer: But further on you said: "My nationalistic machinations were exposed by the Communist Party Central Committee commission

---

*Roman Rudenko (1907–1981) led the Soviet prosecution team during the Nuremberg trial of Nazi leaders. He became general prosecutor of the Soviet Union in 1953. In 1960 he presided over the trial of the American U-2 pilot Francis Gary Powers.

†Lev Sheinin (1906–1967), a veteran prosecutor, was sent to Minsk after the death of Mikhoels, then withdrawn from the case.

that at the beginning of 1947 reviewed the Sovinformburo's work" (vol. 1, p. 48).

Lozovsky: I was also fully conscious when I signed that. I wanted to explain later why I had done so. And now, about the question of filling the presidium seats.

   After the Jewish Anti-Fascist Committee delegation returned from America (of which, more later) in, I believe, early 1944, the question of convoking a plenum of the Jewish Anti-Fascist Committee was raised. Speeches and appeals were prepared for the plenum and reviewed at the Central Committee. During the plenum I told Shcherbakov that there was an unhealthy atmosphere at the committee. He had information about this through other channels as well. He said then that the people at the Jewish Anti-Fascist Committee were all writers, poets, journalists, and scientists, and that other people should be sent there who were not writers and had never worked in specifically Jewish organizations. And that it would be good to put together a group of four to five people. Epshteyn and Mikhoels put together a list of possible presidium members. As to who was on the list, I don't remember that right now, but I do know that the list was sent to Shcherbakov. After these people were confirmed, Shcherbakov told me that it would still be a good idea to send a group of trade union workers to the Jewish Anti-Fascist Committee, and he asked who I would recommend for that purpose. I said that I knew Bregman as an old Bolshevik, but the thing was that he had been removed from the All-Union Central Committee of Trade Unions. To this Shcherbakov replied, "Well, what of it? He was removed from one job; now he is doing good work in another position. Why don't you ask him to come in and see you? Have a chat with him, and ask him who he thinks you should send to the Jewish Anti-Fascist Committee to introduce a party spirit into the place and get rid of all the backbiting." I called in Bregman—this was in May or June 1944—and talked with him at length.

Presiding Officer: Did you use to meet with him before that, or did you have only occasional meetings?

Lozovsky: During the war up until 1944 we had no meetings. You have studied those forty-two volumes more thoroughly than I have, and I think that, being people of experience, you took note of the fact that all of the accused testify using one and the same phrasing, even though the people who are brought together in this case are people with different levels of culture, different positions in society. So this means that someone conspired to come up with this language. Who—those under arrest? I don't think so. That means that it was the investigators who conspired; otherwise, they could not have gotten identical phrases from various people. I state categorically that I did not talk about nationalism or about concealing our conspiratorial activity. This is rubbish.

Around the end of 1944 or the beginning of 1945, Shcherbakov fell quite ill; he had a heart attack. By this time I had come to a distinct realization that all of the committees had to be eliminated. I needed to talk to Shcherbakov about this. In late 1944 I was unable to reach Shcherbakov by telephone. He was not feeling well. In March 1945, virtually on the eve of our victory, I heard that Shcherbakov was feeling pretty well and that I could go out to his dacha and see him. So I went. When I arrived, his wife and the doctor came out and said that Shcherbakov could discuss only those subjects that would not disturb him at all. It was a complicated request, of course; he was awaiting news about the end of the war. What could we talk about that would not disturb him? Of course I promised, but nonetheless I said to him, "You know, Alexander Sergeyevich, I have the feeling that once the war is over, we need to eliminate the five anti-fascist committees. They were created during wartime. Good or bad, they have played their role." I said that the work of the Anti-Fascist Committee of Youth should be transferred to the Komsomol Central Committee, and that of the Scientists' Committee should be transferred to the Academy of Sciences. As for contacts that these committees had with various anti-fascist organizations abroad, they could be maintained through the Sovinformburo. Shcherbakov told me that it was not worth talking about this now, but when the war was over, that question would be decided. Then he asked me how our people were behaving, the ones whom we had brought onto the Jewish Anti-Fascist Committee. I told him what Bregman had reported to me. We decided that after the war we would introduce a proposal at the Central Committee to eliminate all the committees. But on May 9, the day of the great victory celebration, Shcherbakov died, and this issue remained undecided. It was necessary to talk to Zhdanov about this question, but he was in Finland for a prolonged period. We could talk to him only on a special government line, but there is not a lot you can say on the phone. My relationship with Alexandrov was strained, and I didn't want to go to him. Later I will explain what was going on in our relationship. All I want to say is that the presidium membership was confirmed by Shcherbakov, with my help. So I bore complete responsibility for this, because I was his deputy.

Presiding Officer: What testimony can you give regarding the trip to America?

Lozovsky: I have already said that I was pleased with the fact that in the United States, thanks to our propaganda campaign, an anti-fascist committee of artists, writers, and scientists and a Jewish committee, part of the America-wide organization Russian Relief, had come into being. The head of the committee of artists, writers, and scientists was the world-renowned scientist Einstein. He was a convinced Zionist, but, like many academics, he was more engaged in mathematical problems than in political ones. Russian Relief was run by some large landlord whose name escapes me now. They began fund-raising for the USSR aid fund. I approved of this state of affairs.

In 1942 our embassy in the United States sent several encoded messages stating that these organizations were approaching the Soviet Consulate in New York to discuss sending a delegation to the United States. Because these encoded messages were addressed to the People's Commissariat of Foreign Affairs, I would read and then discuss them with Shcherbakov. He said that we would have to wait for now. This was during the Stalingrad offensive, and of course it would not have made sense for us to send a delegation before the victory at Stalingrad. After the battle of Stalingrad, the international situation became clearer, and there was a great wave of pro-Soviet feeling.

Before the battle of Stalingrad the Jewish Anti-Fascist Committee received an invitation from the United States to send a delegation made up of particular individuals. Shcherbakov phoned me about the names on the list after the battle of Stalingrad (the situation was different now). I was in Kuibyshev at the time, and he and Comrade Molotov were in Moscow. This was in early 1943. Shcherbakov said, "I have the list in front of me," and he continued, "Mekhlis is coming off the list. He's a general; let him go on fighting. Ehrenburg is coming off the list. He writes well and writes every day. Impossible to send him. Markish is coming off the list. He's muddle-headed and hysterical; he doesn't know what's going to come out of his mouth two minutes from now. And then there is Epshteyn." I said that I was opposed. Shcherbakov asked, "Why do you want to reject Epshteyn?" I answered that he had been an editor at a communist newspaper in the United States for several years. If we sent him, then before he arrived, there would be a tremendous wave of propaganda against us all over America, with people yelling and screaming about how we were sending a communist to carry out agitation and propaganda. Shcherbakov agreed and then asked me: "What do you have to say about Mikhoels?" I said that I hardly knew him, and that since the first rally in August 1941 I had met with him only rarely. Shcherbakov said, "Mikhoels is a reasonable person, he is politically knowledgeable, and, incidentally, he's an excellent speaker and a first-class actor." I said that I didn't know his past. Shcherbakov said, "All right, I will find out. We absolutely have to have one person in the delegation who isn't a party member." Then Fefer's candidacy for the delegation was gone over in the same way.

Several days went by. Shcherbakov called me and said that the Central Committee had made its choice and selected two candidates, Mikhoels and Fefer, and he asked me to send a memorandum addressed to him and to Comrade Molotov proposing that Fefer and Mikhoels be sent as delegates. I wrote, saying that I proposed that so-and-so and so-and-so be sent. The office of the People's Commissariat of Foreign Affairs sent telegrams to

New York and Washington, and the Jewish Anti-Fascist Committee sent an open telegram to the two organizations that the delegation was being dispatched. Then there was the question of who the delegates were in fact going to see. It says in the indictment that they went with criminal intent and that in the United States they got involved with Jewish nationalistic organizations. So, were they going to meet with the Communist Party? Of course not. If they had been going to meet with people from the Communist Party, we would not have sent an actor, especially one who was not a party member.

Maybe they were going to meet with Jewish workers? There are four large Jewish workers' organizations in the United States. They are the Ladies' Garment Workers Union, headed by convinced enemies of the USSR; the Men's Garment Workers Union, headed by the self-styled left-winger Sidney Hillman,* who had come to the Soviet Union in Comrade Lenin's time and brought a gift from Jewish workers for a garment factory in the USSR. The third workers' organization was Workmen's Circle, a mutual aid society uniting about one hundred thousand Jewish workers, including Mensheviks, Bundists, and left-wingers. And the fourth organization was a small but tightly knit furriers' union, which brought together about fifteen to twenty thousand workers.

So perhaps the Jewish Anti-Fascist Committee delegation was going to meet with these organizations? But then the All-Union Central Committee of Trade Unions would have sent different people as members of the delegation. Who were they going to see? They were invited by two organizations—the Committee of Writers, Artists, and Scientists, and Russian Relief, whose name in English means "aid to Russia" or "military assistance to Russia." Within this organization a Jewish council had formed—I don't know who was on it—but it consisted of bourgeois elements, and it was headed by a real estate landlord named Levin or something like that. It needs to be said that there are millions of Jews in the United States who are of Russian origin. The bourgeois elements among them were well disposed toward the Soviet Union, not because they sympathized with communism, but because the Soviet army was saving millions of Jews from Hitler, and this made a tremendous impression on all Jews. This was why they raised funds to help Russia, and they raised funds from absolutely everyone, wherever they could find them. The bourgeoisie made a business out of this, but there were hundreds of thousands of ordinary people who sympathized with the USSR and gave help from the depths of their souls. So the

*Sidney Hillman (1887–1946) was a prominent American labor leader. Born in Lithuania, he joined the Bund, then fled to the United States after the failed revolution of 1905. He headed the Amalgamated Clothing Workers of America—Lozovsky referred to it with an incorrect name—and helped to found the Congress of Industrial Organizations. He was widely known for his support of the New Deal and Franklin Delano Roosevelt. See Steven Fraser, *Labor Will Rule: Sidney Hillman and the Rise of American Labor* (New York, 1992).

delegates from the Jewish Anti-Fascist Committee went to see those people who wanted to do something to help in the struggle against fascism.

Presiding Officer: Before Mikhoels and Fefer left for America, did you give them any instructions?

Lozovsky: Especially during the war, we couldn't send people abroad unless their trip was going to be of use. Everyone knows that without the Central Committee's permission and without the NKVD's approval it was impossible to go abroad. No one received an exit visa from the Soviet Union without the necessary permission, and to talk about how I sought to obtain the opportunity for them to go is just ridiculous. Let us suppose for just one minute that I did have to pull strings for them to go. There were two candidates—Mikhoels and Fefer, who are now considered nationalists. I am being asked whether the NKVD knew that Mikhoels and Fefer were nationalists. No, otherwise it would not have given permission for these people to go. Did the Central Committee know that these people were nationalists? No.

In the indictment it says that before the U.S. trip, Mikhoels and Fefer, in accordance with an order from Lozovsky, established contact with Jewish nationalistic circles and organizations in the United States and began preparing information about the internal situation in the Soviet Union. This is a horrifying crime! Why did they do this? They did it to gain the sympathy of the Jewish bourgeoisie in America and enlist its support for subversive activity within the Soviet Union.

Naturally, before their departure to the United States it was necessary to talk with these people. Because they were in Kuibyshev, they went to Moscow, where they met with Shcherbakov. Fefer said here that the instructions which Shcherbakov and I gave them were inconsistent on the issue of the second front. This is rubbish. We're politicians, after all. How could there be different points of view about a second front between the deputy people's commissar for foreign affairs and the secretary of the Central Committee? Logically this just doesn't add up. I knew our government's policy, and I knew what had to be done and why. I didn't take a single step without coordinating it with Comrade Molotov or Shcherbakov.

Prior to Mikhoels and Fefer's departure I talked to them, maybe even more than once. And here Fefer's memory failed him when it came to the substance of our conversations. I will remind him, and maybe he will recall now. I told them the following: "Above all, you are Soviet citizens, and then Jews. When you arrive in America, people will view you not only as Jews, but as Soviet citizens. Not only will the Jewish community and its press be following you; all of the American press will be scrutinizing you because you are Soviet citizens, regardless of your nationality. So, for that reason, your behavior will determine whether the Soviet Union will be discredited or whether, as the products of Soviet culture, you will conduct yourselves as befits a Soviet man." And then I said, "Keep in mind that the Americans and the American press know how to flatter when it is necessary, to approach someone from the right angle to get what they want. In British and American politics there is a special way of moving to envelope someone. Buying someone off in America and England is not simply a matter of "Here's twenty thousand rubles for you; now in exchange for that you do such-and-such." Subversion is a more subtle political game.

In Fefer's testimony it says that during the preparations for the U.S. trip, Epshteyn, Mikhoels, and I often discussed our goals for the trip, and that we had decided to use every opportunity to establish strong contact with elements hostile to the USSR and with representatives of Jewish capital in the United States in order to enlist their support in the upcoming battle against Soviet power. From this part of Fefer's testimony and from the indictment, it sounds as if when I gave instructions to Mikhoels and Fefer, I told them, "Get in touch with bourgeois elements there so that they will help us in the struggle against the Soviet Union." This fabrication is unworthy of a Soviet person. Further on in the indictment there is an even more curious accusation: "Believing that the best way to get help from reactionary Jewish circles in the United States in the fight against the Communist Party and the Soviet government might be to pass on to them classified information about the USSR, Mikhoels and Fefer, with Lozovsky's assistance, put together secret materials about Soviet industry prior to their departure and took it with them to America." And on page 33 of the indictment it says even more decisively that Lozovsky "supplied Mikhoels and Fefer with classified material about the state of industry, the economy, and cultural life in the USSR for transmission to the Americans."

Providing classified material to anyone is a crime punishable by death. How does the investigation know that these materials contained classified information? Did an investigator read these materials or not? I cannot imagine that the investigators have asked for the death penalty without first reading these materials. So that means these materials must exist somewhere. But they are not in the case materials.

In answer to my question about where this material is, Fefer replied that a copy had been kept in the files of the Jewish Anti-Fascist Committee, which had been confiscated during a search. Which means that the investigators have these materials. Do I have the right to examine what sort of materials these are? Do I, a simple Soviet citizen who is not a member of the Central Committee, have the right to know for what I am being executed? How can it say in the indictment that the materials were classified when these materials are not included in the forty-two volumes? How can such things be hidden? How can such things be hidden at all? Heads may roll over this matter. Not only my head, but the heads of those near and dear to me and a number of heads belonging to people present here. What is this—

the Soviet method of investigation? To accuse a person of espionage and then conceal from him and from the court the material for which he is supposed to be executed? I find this situation completely unacceptable.

And so, a Central Committee member and deputy minister of foreign affairs is accused of supplying two people with espionage materials during the war. Even had I wanted to engage in such activity, why would I transmit something through these people? After all, there is an American Embassy in Moscow that is simply swarming with intelligence officers. Would I have gotten in touch with a poet and an actor if I had wanted to engage in espionage? The doorman at the People's Commissariat of Finances would not do such a thing, let alone the deputy minister of foreign affairs, an old revolutionary and a veteran of the underground. All of this is nonsense.

I also forgot to say that when I was instructing Mikhoels and Fefer, I told them, "Don't have any conversations without the consul or the ambassador present, and consult with Moscow to ask about all important questions." In the indictment it says that they had a meeting with Weizmann. In his testimony Fefer has already related how they were allowed to meet with Weizmann. There was a telegram about that signed by Comrade Molotov. What is more, they received a telegram from Comrade Molotov with instructions to meet with Rosenberg to discuss the conditions under which the Soviet Union would accept aid proposed by the Joint. But in all of the testimonies and in the indictment the meeting with Rosenberg is described as criminal. Where is the crime here? Not only did they have the right to act as they did, but as Soviet people they were obligated to go and talk with a leader of the Joint, because the issue under discussion was assistance to the Soviet Union in the war against fascism.

Presiding Officer: So they were given a telegram with permission to meet with Weizmann, but they were able to make their own decisions about other meetings?

Lozovsky: They also received a telegram from Moscow about meeting a leader of the Joint.

Presiding Officer: And who were they allowed to meet with on their own?

Lozovsky: With whomever they might indicate, but only with the agreement of the ambassador and the consul. They were required to get the approval of the ambassador and Consul Kisselev and to request an interpreter from him as well. These were the instructions—not a step to be taken without the consul's permission and without an official interpreter. And the consul handled it in the following way: if it was a simple matter, then he gave permission himself and provided an interpreter, and if it was more complicated, then he would ask Moscow, that meant Comrade Molotov.

Presiding Officer: Were they supposed to speak at rallies?

Lozovsky: Yes, to talk about the struggle against fascism. I know that they spoke a great deal, at around three hundred rallies. The groups they addressed were not only Jewish.

But they traveled with firm instructions not to hold any conversations or negotiations without an official representative of the Soviet Union present, with everything under that person's control.

Presiding Officer: You mean, with an interpreter present?

Lozovsky: Not only an interpreter. For example, they were invited to meet with Mayor La Guardia of New York, a Democrat* and a friend of Roosevelt's. They went to see him along with Consul Kisselev. We received reports from the ambassador and from our consul in New York that went to the party leadership. It was clear from these reports that both the ambassador and the consul considered the work Mikhoels and Fefer were doing in the United States positive and beneficial. Money was starting to flow in. People were starting to turn against the enemies of the Soviet Union. The U.S. bourgeoisie was allied with us against Hitler, and Roosevelt—who represented the interests of American imperialism—believed that an alliance with the USSR was more advantageous than one with Hitlerite Germany. Mass rallies and meetings of our delegates with artists, poets, and other members of the intelligentsia were benefiting the USSR. They were in many cities, and what is interesting is that more and more people kept flowing in to hear their speeches about the Soviet Union and the Red Army's fight. Not only Jewish workers, but Poles, Italians, and Americans came, too.

When their stay abroad began to stretch out, I told Comrade Molotov that it was time to cut the lengthy visit short. After my conversation with Comrade Molotov I sent a telegram, which I signed in my capacity as deputy minister of foreign affairs, saying that they should hurry home. They came back in early December 1943. Of course, they were ecstatic about their trip. It was their first trip abroad. Their pictures had been in the newspapers, they had talked with important people. When they returned, they called me, and I told them that I was busy during the day, but because I wanted to talk with them at length, I invited them to my home in the evening. Fefer and Mikhoels were in my apartment and spent three hours telling me about their impressions.

Incidentally, they told me something that touched me emotionally and that was extremely interesting in the political sense. I don't recall what city this was in, but our consul had helped to organize a large gathering of White émigrés whose national feelings had moved them to find out what was going on in Russia. I remember that among them were not ordinary Whites, but people like Prince Meshchersky and Prince Putyatin. At a gathering of those who yesterday had been our enemies and who were still vacillating old anti-Semites, Mikhoels, a Jew and an actor, spoke in Russian

*Lozovsky was mistaken about La Guardia's party affiliation; he was a Republican.

about the Soviet people's struggle against Hitlerite Germany. I asked
whether they had met with Russians and Ukrainians, people who passion-
ately follow our struggle. Then they informed me that Rosenberg had
promised material assistance from the Joint should Jews settle in the Crimea.

This was what the conversation was about when we met for the first
time. Then, as Fefer has already said—for some reason, once again this is
missing from his written testimony—Comrade Molotov saw both of them.
As Fefer said, he received them with open arms. Here, for some reason, the
words "received with open arms" mean nationalism. Comrade Molotov
spent two hours talking with them. They discussed two plans with him
(and once again this is not in the records of Fefer's testimony): they talked
about the possibility of settling Jews in the Volga Germans' territory or in
northern Crimea. About the first option Comrade Molotov said that the
Volga Germans' territory was purely agricultural land and that it was unlikely that Jewish resettlement there would work. About the Crimea he
said, "Well, why don't you write a memorandum addressed to me and to
Comrade Stalin, and we'll see."

Comrade Molotov said, "We'll see." What does it mean when a high-
ranking government official says, "We'll see"? Does it mean approval? Of
course it doesn't. He, the government official, knows full well that there is
a group of people who make decisions on these things. What conclusion
did Mikhoels draw from this? Well, Bergelson said here that he knew from
something that Mikhoels had said that Comrade Molotov approved of the
plan of settling Jews in the Crimea. I asked Yuzefovich what he knew about
conversations about the Crimea, and he said that he had heard at the committee that Comrade Molotov approved of settling Jews in the Crimea.
And if you ask the others (and I will ask them), you will see that a dishonest campaign of demagoguery was waged about how Comrade Molotov
had a positive attitude toward the question. This information was spread
by Fefer, on the one hand, and by Mikhoels, on the other. They were the
ones who assured the others that once Comrade Molotov had "promised"
something, this meant that the question was almost resolved, and if it
wasn't resolved, then in any case it was moving along well. I believe that
this was a dishonest attitude toward government leaders and the party on
the part of Mikhoels and Fefer. They need to understand that when a person in such a position says "We'll see," that really means, "We'll see, we'll
think it over, we'll weigh the matter," but under no circumstances is it a
promise to resolve an issue favorably.

Presiding Officer: And you did not express your opinion to them before
Rosenberg made his promise? That if Jews settled in the Crimea, the Joint
would provide material assistance?

Lozovsky: When they told me for the first time that Rosenberg had promised
material assistance from the Joint should Jews settle in the Crimea, I told

them that if material assistance was provided, that would be great. Why did I say this? Because up until then we had not turned down material assistance from the Americans. Of course, when Americans, large capitalists, provided assistance, they were expecting a twenty-kopeck return on every five they invested. And anyone who doesn't understand that, doesn't understand the first thing about politics.

Had we ever refused assistance because we were afraid of it? I remember the ARA—the American Administration for Aid to Russia—headed by Herbert Hoover, one of our most ardent enemies.* When this organization proposed assistance, Comrade Lenin said (this was during the famine in 1921), "Even a mangy sheep gives a tuft or two of wool." We also accepted money from the Joint to organize settlements in the Crimea, and then we expelled the Joint representatives from the Soviet Union.

Did we take money for Birobidzhan? Yes. From private sources? No. The Soviet government allowed the money to be accepted, and it was only in 1951–1952 that Birobidzhan was forbidden to accept money from AMBIJAN. We took money and did what we needed to do, not what they wanted.

I cannot say who was involved in drafting the letter about the Crimea. I know that three people came to see me about it: Mikhoels, Epshteyn, and Fefer. I told them at the time that this matter looked very difficult to me from the practical standpoint because Jews were all urbanites, and the Crimea had to be settled in two to three years, which would mean transferring entire kolkhozes there. It would take fifty to sixty years to settle Jews in the Crimea, which would not do the Soviet Union any good. But because I had no objections in principle to settling Jews in the Crimea or elsewhere, I looked at their draft, and all I said was, "Why do you write about the sufferings of the Jews? That's well known. Why are you padding the letter? Cut the poetry and leave in your arguments about resettlement." On the whole, I had my doubts about how this would be carried out in a practical sense, but I had no political doubts about it. I saw no nationalism in it, and no plans against the Soviet Union. Besides, I told them that they didn't have the right to write on behalf of the Jewish Anti-Fascist Committee, because the question raised went beyond the committee's jurisdiction and its mission. But as Soviet citizens, they were free to send their proposal to the Soviet government on their own behalf.

It says rather naively in the indictment that "they demanded of the Soviet Union that the Crimea be handed over to the Jews." This is hard even to read. In actual fact, what they did was to apply to the Soviet government, as advised by Comrade Molotov, with a proposal that was rejected, based on what considerations I do not know. I repeat that I did not see in this any far-reaching hostile plan or anything like that.

---

*The American Relief Administration supplied significant relief supplies to the Ukraine following a severe famine in 1921–1923.

Presiding Officer: Did you say to them, "Jews, I wish you success"?

Lozovsky: This is fiction. These are writers and poets. They are given to all sorts of flights of fancy.

Presiding Officer: But that letter contains slander against the party, the state, and other peoples of our country.

Lozovsky: I did not edit every line of the letter.

Presiding Officer: But you said you did.

Lozovsky: I told them to get rid of certain phrases. I recognize that there are quite a number of nationalistic phrases in the letter, but the nationalism there does not consist of their desire to write and publish books in Yiddish; you can write in any language.

Presiding Officer: That's correct.

Lozovsky: The nationalistic character of the letter is contained in the fact that the very problem and resolution of the Jewish question is turned inside out. The October Revolution resolved the Jewish question, because it gave equal rights to all people, and for that phrase I bear full political responsibility. I believe that nationalism consists not of settling Jews in one or another part of the USSR. That is not nationalism. The nationalism is in the phrasing, in the sum total of the letter, as if the Jews in the Soviet Union have no rights. This is virulent nationalism. I let that slip through, and for that I bear political responsibility.

Presiding Officer: You should have thrown out their letter and made a move to expel them from the party after committing such an act of hostile slander. What kind of Bolshevik are you, if you believe that Jews in our country, in the USSR, do not have equal rights? That is slander.

Lozovsky: Yes, I bear full political responsibility for not counseling them not to send the letter, but I could not forbid them once Comrade Molotov had suggested that they write it. They received an answer, probably from Comrade Molotov's secretariat. Let Fefer tell about that—I don't know. I know that they received a negative response, but when it came, I cannot say. The letter was submitted around February 1944, but probably at that time the government was in no position to take the matter up right away.

Presiding Officer: From whom did you learn that the proposal had been turned down?

Lozovsky: One of them called me up on the telephone and said that they had gotten a negative reply. I hung up the receiver. What else is there to say? After they had placed such hopes in that letter and received a refusal, they whispered and mourned among themselves.

Presiding Officer: They being who?

Lozovsky: Fefer, Mikhoels, and Epshteyn, who was still around at the time. I don't know what Epshteyn's role was, but in any case this triumvirate, having told some of their closest friends about the successful advancement of their idea, now went through some internal regret and distress. They did not confide in me about this question. No one came to me or said anything about it. And that pretty much settled the Crimea question.

[The presiding officer declared a recess at 4:25 P.M. At 6:50 P.M., the court continued the session.]

Shtern: My name keeps being cited as belonging to a well-known and zealous nationalist. It has even been said that Lozovsky knew me long ago as a person with anti-Soviet sentiments, and I am struck by this. Solomon Abramovich Lozovsky and I met in 1944, I believe it was. I never saw him before that. And so I would like to ask him how it was and from whom that he knew me to be a nationalist long before we ever met?

Presiding Officer: He has already stated that he did not know you to be a nationalist and that he simply gave incorrect testimony about that.

Shtern: Another question. Has Lozovsky heard about a letter that I sent to Comrade Stalin?

Lozovsky: First of all, I state categorically to the Military Collegium of the USSR Supreme Court that I never heard of, and no one ever spoke to me about, Shtern's anti-Soviet views. If this is in my testimony, it is a lie, and I will speak separately to the question of why I signed it. I know nothing about nationalistic or anti-Soviet views on her part. It was Shcherbakov's initiative to include her on the presidium of the Jewish Anti-Fascist Committee as a woman academician, for we don't have all that many women academicians.

Second point. I don't remember what month it was, but in 1944, Shtern came to talk to me about how she should respond to letters she was receiving from scientists in various countries. At the time I told her that she should not send any letters herself, that all replies should be sent only through the Academy of Sciences. Because she was not a party member, I didn't tell her where these letters would be examined and by whom outside of the Academy of Sciences. During this conversation she informed me that she had written a letter to Comrade Stalin about the high rate of turnover and burnout at the upper managerial levels, and she had suggested a number of approaches for combating this phenomenon and helping people to stay on longer.

Shtern: Yes, that is correct.

Fefer: There was a question here about how we learned that the plan to settle the Crimea was not resolved in a positive manner. I remember that in the middle of 1944, Epshteyn called me and said that I had to go see Lazar Moiseyevich Kaganovich right away. He called in three of us: Mikhoels, Epshteyn, and me. There was a very long conversation, two hours or more. Lazar Moiseyevich tore into our memorandum about the Crimea from a strictly practical standpoint. He said that it was impractical, that Jews would not go to the Crimea, that they would all return to where they had come from, and that only actors and poets could have come up with such an idea. Frankly, Lozovsky and I did not have any nationalistic conversations.

Presiding Officer: Rosenberg told you that you needed to wrest the Crimea away?

Fefer: That is a freewheeling version. The investigator and I edited it that way together, but in fact the conversation was about settling Jews in the Crimea and about how the Joint would provide assistance if we started settling Jews in the Crimea.

Presiding Officer: But you said, "Rosenberg told us directly that the Crimea meant not only the Black Sea. It was also Turkey and the Balkan peninsula."

Fefer: He said that when he was in the Crimea, he saw the Black Sea, that the Crimea was in a very nice place on the shores of the Black Sea, with Turkey right nearby, and the Balkan peninsula, and that it was a very prominent place for a Jewish republic.

Presiding Officer: And he did not mean it in the sense that the Crimea would be a beachhead?

Fefer: No, at the time my brain was not working along those lines.

Presiding Officer: Further on you said that "even without him we understood the significance of the Crimea."

Fefer: That, too, was a phrase which I came up with.

Presiding Officer: You also testified that after you assured Rosenberg that you were going to fight for the Crimea, he said that you could count not only on material assistance from America, but on what other kind of assistance? Did such a conversation take place?

Fefer: There was no conversation about assistance being not only material. I deny this. There was a conversation about the Crimea being on the Black Sea.

[The presiding officer asked Fefer with whom they had consulted in the Soviet Union about the Crimea letter.]

Fefer: I know, for example, that he consulted with Zemlyachka and Zhemchuzhina.

Presiding Officer: Mikhoels?

Fefer: Yes, I even remember Zhemchuzhina's reply, and there are others who know it as well.

Bergelson: I know. Mikhoels told me.

Fefer: She said, "You can live wherever you like, but you need to have your own house and roof."

Lozovsky: Today Fefer has given a completely new version of his testimony about the Crimea. If one gives new versions every day, the resulting confusion is just extraordinary. First of all, he testified that the conversation with Rosenberg took place in the presence of the consul and an interpreter. It is quite clear that if they talked about something criminal, then the interpreter would have told the appropriate people. I believe that Fefer's testimony, from which this whole case begins, is the sheerest fantasy.

Fefer: The case began from Hofshteyn's testimony.

Lozovsky: I don't know. I was arrested two weeks after Fefer's testimony about a beachhead. And now it comes out, based on the words of the same Fefer, that there was no conversation with Rosenberg about how the Americans wanted to use the settlement of Jews in the Crimea for their own imperialistic purposes, and that they would support us in seizing the Crimea. From Fefer's testimony that he gave earlier, it follows that they promised to fight for the Crimea. Who? These two musketeers—Fefer and Mikhoels— were going to fight for the Crimea against Soviet power? Again, this is slanderous fiction. And who concocted it? Fefer himself, and this has served as the basis for the entire trial—it was the starting point of all the accusations and indictments, including those of treason. And today Fefer's testimony leads to something quite different. But I, for one, cannot be responsible for all the things that Fefer has woven out of whole cloth, testimony that he is now changing.

A final question remains—and this is in regard to the letter. I told how that went. I really did have it. I have nothing to add to that. I have no doubt that sending the letter to the government, even that, which reeks of something very nasty, was not criminal.

Presiding Officer: Defendant Hofshteyn, would you like to say something about the Crimea?

Hofshteyn: I was arrested in Kiev. There was not a single word about the Crimea during my interrogations. I was asked about Mikhoels at one point, but I was not questioned about the work of the committee. The first person to talk to me about the Crimea was investigator Lebedev in Moscow.

Presiding Officer: That was on January 5, 1949. And Fefer gave testimony about that on January 11, 1949, and that is why he asserts that you were supposedly the primary source of all the Crimea testimony.

Hofshteyn: I didn't even know that a note had been submitted to the government. I didn't know that Kvitko had been sent to the Crimea on business.

Presiding Officer: Now let us move on to the accusation about the committee sending classified information to America. Volume 32 contains a statement by the expert commission testifying to the fact that the requests that came from the United States were in fact intelligence related. More precisely, the replies to these requests must have contained state secrets.

The second conclusion in this statement is that in the requests that the committee sent to its correspondents and directors in Birobidzhan, there were orders to send materials containing state secrets. And, finally, the third part, in which it states that the Jewish Anti-Fascist Committee had systematic espionage contacts with American reactionaries by means of which it sent articles containing translated information about agriculture and industry, which were Soviet state secrets. You are accused of contributing to all of this activity of the Jewish Anti-Fascist Committee.

[Lozovsky recounted the procedures at the Sovinformburo for sending informational materials to foreign agencies and press organizations. Further on, the circumstances surrounding Goldberg's stay in the Soviet Union were studied: who the trip was organized by and whether materials containing state secrets were given to Goldberg.]

Lozovsky: When Mikhoels and Fefer returned from the United States and reported to me and then to Comrade Molotov, they visited Shcherbakov as well, and they told us that Goldberg had worked actively in the United States to help the Soviet Union during the entire duration of the war. You know yourselves that during the war years we were in contact with people who spoke out in favor of the Soviet Union. This contact was not for purposes of espionage, of course. Here, as soon as you say the word "contact," people think you must mean espionage contact. I will tell later on how they met with Goldberg and how I met with them.

[Lozovsky told the court that Goldberg was given materials about England's colonial policy. By Lozovsky's request, this material was prepared at an institute that was part of the Foreign Policy Department of the Central Committee.]

Lozovsky: Komarov even showed me Suslov's signature. When I got this material from Pukhlov, I leafed through it. What could the institute write about English imperialism that was new? Was our attitude toward British imperialism really a secret? Our newspapers had been covering the question for thirty years.

Presiding Officer: You passed material to a foreigner that would familiarize imperialist countries with the degree of our information on England's colonial policy. There are certain matters that we try not to discuss openly.

Lozovsky: I will address that now. Let's say that I committed the following crime: I ordered these materials from the institute, they sent them to me, and I passed them on to a foreigner. But the investigator had the material. If this material is classified, then why isn't it included in the material evidence of the case? Colonel Komarov promised to give me this material to read, but only showed it to me.

Presiding Officer: Did he read various excerpts to you?

Lozovsky: Yes. I laughed at that. He promised that I would see all of these materials. Over a period of three years, I asked the investigation ten times to let me see what sort of secret materials these were. I am, after all, answering for that with my head. Colonel Komarov may have already been made a general by this time, because three years have passed. But you can still ask him for this material, and I'm sure that if there were even one line there of a classified nature, that material would be here. What does this mean? It means that you can sentence anyone to death and hide the materials from the court. I ask you, Is this really a Soviet method for carrying out an investigation? Is it really a Soviet way to treat a person who gave fifty years of his life to revolutionary and communist work? I stand accused of espionage, and I want the court to study these materials.

Presiding Officer: Defendant Lozovsky, spies do not always keep a copy for themselves when they pass on material. Usually classified material is passed on secretly.

Lozovsky: Yes, that's just the point. It's very peculiar how we had this whole thing worked out. As indicated in the indictment, we pass on classified material and retain copies in the files. Then along come employees from the State Security Ministry and take everything away. How can I be accused of such nonsense? If I wanted to pass top-secret information, then, with my many years of experience as a conspirator in the underground, do you think I really would have left copies for the State Security Ministry to find? That is just out-and-out stupidity.

At the witness confrontation with Teumin I asked her where the copies were, and she replied that she didn't know. But I know where the copies are. At the investigative division of the State Security Ministry are copies of everything that Teumin passed along.

On that basis I believe that the accusation that I passed on classified information of some kind and that I, a senior functionary and Central Committee member, established some kind of espionage tie with some kind of American journalist behind the government and the party's back—this is all fabrication whose meaning and purpose you will understand when I am done with my testimony.

Finishing up with this so-called espionage contact, I would like to shed light on one more question. We had a practice that when anyone came from abroad to do something of use to the Soviet Union, the appropriate organization would arrange a reception. Depending on the status of the individual and the circumstances, among other things, the reception would be lavish or modest. If you look at the Slavic committee's budget, you will see that it organized many more such receptions than the other committees did.

Presiding Officer: Who organized Goldberg's reception?

Lozovsky: All I know is that I gave permission for money to be spent on his reception.

Presiding Officer: How much?

Lozovsky: Probably around fifty to sixty thousand [rubles]. I released funds for the reception, and the communists on the Jewish Anti-Fascist Committee were supposed to decide themselves how and what to do. Other committees organized this sort of reception as well. It was politically necessary, and we did it.

Now about Novick. It says in the indictment that I worked and worked to get permission for the spy Novick to enter the country. He came in the autumn of 1946, when I no longer had anything to do with the Jewish Anti-Fascist Committee. During my seven years at the People's Commissariat of Foreign Affairs I had nothing to do with issuing entry visas for the USSR.

Foster,* the chairman of the American Communist Party (he is a friend of mine), a laborer and an old metalworker, told me during meetings we had at congresses that Novick was the editor of their communist newspaper, a reliable fellow, and that he was doing a great job in the United States fighting for the Soviet Union.

Presiding Officer: Was Novick the editor of the communist newspaper the *Daily Worker?*

Lozovsky: The American Communist Party had several press organs, including the *Daily Worker* and the *Morgen Freiheit,* a Yiddish-language communist newspaper. There are a huge number of Jews there who emigrated from various countries, especially Russia. So he comes to Moscow as the editor of a communist newspaper, asks to meet with me (I was the head of the Sovinformburo), and of course I receive him. I received every bourgeois bastard, so how could I not receive the editor of a communist newspaper when he came? Why? The people who wrote the indictment assert that I received the spies Novick and Goldberg. I wonder when the Ministry of State Security found out that they were spies? If they knew before they got here, then why did they admit them into the USSR? It all depended on them, after all. And if they admitted them here, then that means they didn't know anything, but they were obligated to know more about those matters than I did.

During my time at the Sovinformburo, I met with I don't know how many hundreds of journalists. Chinese, French, Japanese, American, British, and others all came to see me, but the instant that American Jews arrived, I slip up. It's enough to make a hen burst out laughing. In addition to that, when Novick arrived, I no longer had anything to do with the committee. And who gave forty thousand for his reception? Suslov. So is he a Jewish nationalist, too? That's hard to imagine.

So neither the Central Committee nor the State Security Ministry nor I had any reason to suspect him. If Fefer maintains that Novick was "prowling" around the Soviet Union gathering top-secret information, then that is

---

*William Z. Foster (1881–1961) was a leader of the American Communist Party from the early 1920s until several years before his death in 1961. See his book *Toward Soviet America* (New York, 1932).

slander. I personally don't know Novick, but there are people who have known him for decades and know his work. It would seem that the State Security Ministry found out about their harmful activity after they left. Why am I being accused of not knowing this sooner? What, did I have a better staff than the State Security Ministry? Did I have representatives all over the world?

Presiding Officer: Fefer, is your testimony that I read out correct?

Fefer: No, it is fabricated.

Lozovsky: There will be many other fabrications in Fefer's testimony. The expert commission established that there was nationalism in a number of articles in *Eynikayt,* but what is strange is that the examination of the newspaper took place in mid-1947, not earlier than and not at the same time as the study of the Jewish Anti-Fascist Committee's work. This is explained by the fact that Alexandrov headed the Central Committee's Department of Agitation and Propaganda until the middle of 1947, and naturally he did not want some commission to come in and look over whatever he was responsible for.

Presiding Officer: This is your supposition.

Lozovsky: This is not a supposition. This was in fact the case. I believe that Alexandrov is an unscrupulous person. I have been in prison for forty months now, and I have no idea what is happening in the world. I don't know what has become of Alexandrov in that time, but I am sure that sooner or later he will be expelled from the party. I am deeply convinced that such a person cannot be in the party, for the party does not tolerate such people.*

I would like to direct the attention of the court to the fact that when the expert commission gives its conclusions concerning *Eynikayt,* it cites the date and issue of the newspaper that allows us to determine when the article was written. When the expert commission concludes that a state secret was divulged in articles sent abroad by the Jewish Anti-Fascist Committee, the dates of such articles are absent. Why are there no dates? Why doesn't it say when such-and-such an article, which contained a state secret, was sent to America by the Jewish Anti-Fascist Committee? What kind of strange silence is this? It is extremely strange to me that these dates are missing when each article had a certificate indicating the person who wrote it, the country, the press outlet to which the article was sent, the date when it was sent, and signed with three signatures. Don't you find it strange that it is precisely the most important documents that lack not only a certificate, but a date as well? After all, a copy of each article stayed in the files with a

---

*Lozovsky was prescient in his evaluation of Alexandrov. In 1955, under Khrushchev, he was fired from all official posts for establishing a brothel for the party and intellectual elite. See Arkady Vaksberg, *Stalin Against the Jews* (New York, 1994), p. 135.

certificate. What sort of espionage organizers are these, anyway, who leave copies?

Presiding Officer: And what do you have to say about the expert commission's conclusions about the classified nature of these materials?

Lozovsky: About forty to fifty articles were prepared over the committee's seven-year period of operations from April 1942 until the end of November 1948. Fifty articles were found for that seven-year period, that would mean seven articles a year. Would an espionage center really operate like this?

All of these articles can be divided into several categories. These fifty articles include some that clearly have to do with intelligence-gathering, and there are articles that bear the inscription "Not for publication."

Presiding Officer: Are you talking now about how the expert commission described them, or is this your opinion?

Lozovsky: This is my opinion. For example, I believe that the article about nonferrous metallurgy was harmful, despite the fact that it was published in *Krasny Flot* (Red Navy). Someone wormed himself into *Krasny Flot* and let that article through, and then it was picked up by the staff of the Jewish Anti-Fascist Committee, where this clearly harmful piece was sent off, but the first person responsible is the editor of *Krasny Flot*.

I also consider the article "On Listening to a Speech by Molotov" to have been damaging. And the expert commission states that the figures got garbled and that Comrade Molotov's speech did not have this information in it. I don't know when this article was sent, but I consider it sabotage, espionage, call it what you like.

Presiding Officer: Do you admit that some of the articles really did divulge state secrets?

Lozovsky: Yes. But I cannot say which ones. But it would be wrong to conclude from that that what you have here is an espionage center. It's wrong. It is no espionage center, but simply a case of materials slipping through, which, although they were harmful, slipped through in small numbers only.

Presiding Officer: Let us move on to the question of the expert conclusions regarding nationalistic propaganda. The experts certify that the Jewish Anti-Fascist Committee not only conducted nationalistic propaganda, but became a nationalistic center, and engaged in activities that were outside its mandate. In its conclusion the expert commission states as follows: "Based on analysis of the documents provided to us, we have come to the conclusion that they bear witness to the fact that the former directors of the Jewish Anti-Fascist Committee engaged in propaganda of nationalistic ideas on a broad scale. This found expression in the following ways: In public oral statements, articles, and other literary works, the former leaders of the

Jewish Anti-Fascist Committee espoused and spread the idea of nationalistic distinctness and isolationism" (vol. 33, p. 48).

Lozovsky: I remember that the expert commission drew three conclusions
based on the analysis of 122 documents. It is clear that some of these 122
documents are from *Eynikayt,* which was run by someone else, and they
have nothing to do with me. Forty to fifty articles, at any rate, went
through the Jewish Anti-Fascist Committee, and some of them were sent
abroad during the period when the Jewish Anti-Fascist Committee was no
longer part of the Sovinformburo system. Were these articles nationalistic?
Yes, they definitely were. I have read some excerpts. Their absurdity would
jump out at any Soviet reader. There are excerpts from Markish's nationalistic poems and Fefer's works, and articles that are socialist in form but nationalistic in content. I answer politically or criminally for the fact that the
Jewish Anti-Fascist Committee let such nationalistic articles through while
it was a part of the Sovinformburo system. But I state with full responsibility that these articles were not examined by me.

The question may arise, Why did we allow through, at Soviet expense,
the articles of Imam Hodzhi, who preached the struggle against fascism
based on the Koran? But it was necessary, and we did it.

Assessing the expert conclusions and allowing for the possibility that all
122 articles were sent abroad during the time when I was involved, I believe that this is an insignificant part of what went abroad. What is far
more terrible is all of their nationalistic quirks and tendencies, their attempts to go beyond the framework of tasks set for them. That is not only
a violation of Soviet instructions, but also an attempt to create a center to
represent all the Jews of the Soviet Union. It says here that they preached
the idea of classlessness, but even in Mikhoels I did not see classlessness.
They called him his lordship, but I think that he was a bohemian, not a
lord, who went without socks because he drank everything away. Perhaps
they expressed these attempts behind the back of their own presidium. This
is that very underground in question, that is, the illegal, anti-Soviet attempts to turn the Jewish Anti-Fascist Committee into an organization that
allegedly represented all the Jews of the Soviet Union, although no one had
empowered them to do this, no ordinary Jews from the shtetl, of whom
there are no small number in the Soviet Union.

Presiding Officer: And now, a question about *The Black Book.*

Lozovsky: They arranged the publication of *The Black Book.* Why that was
necessary and how it all came about I will recount. Why didn't they write a
memorandum about it when they got the idea of writing the book before
they left? While they were traveling to the United States, the question
would have been resolved, and I would have answered them by telegram.
But what they did was to arrive in the United States, talk with Goldberg,
and send a telegram from there, saying that the Americans were proposing

to publish *The Black Book*. You see what kind of scheme this was. They telegraphed here, saying that it was the Americans' proposal and that they were sort of on the sidelines, when in fact this was something that Fefer and Mikhoels had discussed and arranged among themselves even before the trip. This follows from Fefer's testimony.

Presiding Officer: During the preliminary investigation you were presented with the expert conclusion on *The Black Book*, that it was nationalistic in character, and you agreed with this.

Lozovsky: Let me tell you what I agreed with. When we received the telegram with the proposal about *The Black Book*, we knew only one thing, and that was that it was supposed to include material about Hitler's atrocities in Europe, and in this way the material should serve in the fight against fascism. I reported to Shcherbakov about the proposal. Shcherbakov decided that if such material could be gathered jointly and directed against Hitler, then it must be done. I was of the same opinion, and I answer for that. I responded, giving Mikhoels and Fefer permission to publish such a book, with the Jewish Anti-Fascist Committee and the American Committee of Jewish Artists and Writers doing it together. We were convinced that this was the Americans' proposal when in fact, as was revealed here, Mikhoels and Fefer themselves promoted the idea to the Americans.

The staff of the Jewish Anti-Fascist Committee began gathering material, and from the very beginning there was a fight. A fight not about the quality of materials, but on two fronts. Ehrenburg wanted to publish one *Black Book* in Russian in the USSR and another one in English and Yiddish in the United States. I objected to this and said that I didn't want to publish the book in the USSR, for the USSR had its own organizations, and *The Black Book* should be published in English in the United States. Then things got so mixed up that I had to form a special commission with Bregman as the chairman and the following people as members: Yuzefovich, Severin, Sheinin, Borodin, Troyanovsky, and others. Why were these the people on the commission? Because the material was in Yiddish, Russian, and English. When the commission reread all of the material, it informed me that there were a lot of things that were better left unpublished. Meanwhile Epshteyn had already sent off part of the material. I prohibited publication of this material until it had been examined by the commission.*

At the end of 1945 all of this material was set in type, and the printer's plates of the English-language version were sent for us to look over. So what happened? The commission, having looked through the material (the English text), sent the proof sheets to the United States. The book contained a foreword by Einstein in which our commission discovered Zionistic tenden-

*Alexander Troyanovsky (1882–1955) was the first Soviet ambassador to the United States. For further information on the *Black Book* commission, see Rubenstein, *Tangled Loyalties,* pp. 216–217.

cies and a number of issues about the history of the Jewish people, starting from the destruction of Jerusalem. This material had nothing to do with combating fascism. I had to send telegrams to make sure that this text was not included. An answer came back saying that Einstein had agreed to remove his foreword. The tone was along the lines that if the people in Moscow didn't want this kind of foreword, then it could be removed.*

The commission introduced several corrections into the text. Teumin said here during her testimony that Severin had doubts and he felt that this material was nationalistic. Severin didn't say anything at the time. This is a very recent fantasy. He is a very good Bolshevik and a good comrade. If he had told me, "We have doubts," I would have put a stop to sending the material, but he didn't say anything like this to me. After Borodin's and Troyanovsky's conclusion, a telegram was sent with permission to publish the book. It was printed in early 1946. By this time it was perfectly clear that the Nuremberg trials were going to take place, and our task was to send thousands of copies of this book about fascist atrocities to Nuremberg. I believe that the book, which contained in condensed form descriptions of all of the atrocities committed by the Hitlerites, should be at the Nuremberg trials because thousands of journalists were there, and this would focus world attention on the atrocities committed by the fascists. There were thousands of people there, and thousands of copies of the book were distributed.

A bit about the book itself. The book has serious nationalistic tendencies, and the expert commission did not place the emphasis where it should have when it gave its general conclusions. There is a large excerpt from the book cited there, in which it says that the Jews contributed a great deal to the advancement of science and industry in Germany, but the Hitlerites exterminated them all the same. I don't think we really need to be concerned about the German Jews who were exterminated. I should point out that the asphyxiating gas was invented by a Jewish professor named Haber.† This is no great honor for him, and the Hitlerites hanged him later on. *The Black Book* really did play a big role during the Nuremberg trials. Is that really nationalism? No, it is a fist in the face of those seated in the dock. We cleaned the book up, but perhaps some paragraphs and places containing a hint of nationalism remained. Besides, nationalism is not always reactionary. In a colonial country nationalism can even be revolutionary, and Comrade Lenin said that we would support it. Nationalism in tsarist Rus-

---

*See Albert Einstein, "Unpublished Preface to a *Black Book*," in his *Out of My Later Years* (New York, 1950), pp. 258–259.

†Fritz Haber (1868–1934) was a physical chemist and the recipient of the Nobel Prize in chemistry in 1918 for synthesizing ammonia from hydrogen and nitrogen. During World War I, he helped to develop chlorine and mustard gas. Although Haber disavowed his Jewish origins, he was subject to anti-Semitic harassment after Hitler's accession to power in 1933. Haber left Germany for Switzerland, where he died in 1934. Lozovsky was wrong when he asserted that the Germans executed him. For a comprehensive portrait of Haber, see Fritz Stern, *Einstein's German World* (Princeton, N.J., 1999).

sia was revolutionary, but in our country nationalism is without a doubt counterrevolutionary. But we must approach the nationalism in *The Black Book* from the historical standpoint of the Nuremberg trials. And here I have to say that from that standpoint, *The Black Book* was useful for the Soviet Union. But when the Central Committee prohibited publication of this book in the USSR, this was also the right thing to do, because Soviet people did not need such a book. In our country all peoples endured suffering from the Hitlerites' invasion.

Presiding Officer: What else do you have to say about *The Black Book?*

Lozovsky: I would like to clarify one point that has somehow been overlooked here. Apart from *The Black Book,* which was published in the United States and brought over specially by plane and distributed in Nuremberg, there was an attempt to publish *The Black Book* in Russian. Ehrenburg was the editor of this book. The book that Ehrenburg wanted to publish (Russian writers and Jewish ones who wrote in Russian were involved in it) contained descriptions of atrocities and was also supposed to reflect how Soviet people perceived these atrocities. I didn't read this book and wasn't all that interested in it. But Ehrenburg told me about it. Ehrenburg came up with the project.

[On May 31 at 8:25 P.M., the presiding officer announced a recess. On June 2 at 11:10 A.M., the judicial proceedings resumed.]

Presiding Officer: Defendant Lozovsky, the court has no further questions for you. What else would you like to say to the court?

Lozovsky: I have several things to add.

Presiding Officer: Please go ahead.

Lozovsky: It seems to me that Goldberg is the central figure in all of this, because the meeting with him qualifies as espionage. But what is the result of everything that happened? A man arrived, I had a meeting with him during which I supposedly passed along classified materials, and suddenly upon his return to the United States, he writes a book in which he expresses favorable views about Soviet policy and criticizes U.S. policy. So the money spent on this person was not wasted, was it?

Presiding Officer: Are you referring to Goldberg's pamphlet entitled "The Soviet Union, Enemy or Friend?"*

Lozovsky: I think that the investigation should have instructed the expert commission to give its conclusions about this pamphlet and testify about whether or not it was hostile.

I made a cursory reading of these forty-two volumes. There is a strange phenomenon in that everyone, not simply those present here in court, but those who testified as witnesses and were tried separately from this group,

---

*B. Z. Goldberg, *Sovetn-Farband: Faynot oder fraynot?* (New York, 1947).

talks a great deal about me. Everyone knows a great many varied details about me. I can cite the example of Shimeliovich, with whom I did not meet, with whom I did not even speak on the phone, and yet ten pages of his testimony are devoted to me. Where did this unanimity about my role in the Jewish Anti-Fascist Committee's activity come from? Let me explain. For Mikhoels, Fefer, and Epshteyn it was extremely important to convince others that they were being protected by prominent people. An enormous number of rumors of all sorts grew out of this, including statements by Mikhoels that he was friendly with Zhemchuzhina.

To say that Comrade Molotov's wife was their protector, on the one hand, and that, on the other, the deputy minister of foreign affairs needed to raise his prestige among Jews in order to show that they were not acting on their own but were protected by people trusted by the Central Committee and the government, was unscrupulous political game playing at its worst, and Mikhoels played the whole thing brilliantly. This is why there is an outward unanimity to all of the witness testimony about me, and it comes from the rumors sown by Mikhoels. As a result, it came to seem that I was the soul, the leader, the moving force.

When I read the third volume of Fefer's "collected works," I understood what it was all about. Fefer's testimony touches on about a hundred people unknown to me and whom he keeps on slandering, but he says not a word about himself. In my testimony I slandered myself and two women. What I said about these two women was untrue. I am referring to Lina Shtern and Polina Molotova [Zhemchuzhina].

Fefer clearly slandered a lot of people, and I have information about this. For example, Marshak asked to translate Fefer's poem, and in his statement Marshak is also vilified.

Fefer testified about Ehrenburg, who was never involved in specifically Jewish matters, yet Ehrenburg was vilified, too.

What is the political significance of all this? I will be completely candid. There is a very carefully thought-out criminal intention here to draw as many people as possible into the ranks of the accused and then go out with a bang, to draw in as many people as possible, so that it leaks out abroad through the Israeli Embassy or Mission.

Presiding Officer: Explain to the court the following: During the investigation you pled guilty to engaging in anti-Soviet activity. So why are you now repudiating everything, even though other defendants, especially Fefer, have confirmed your testimony?

Lozovsky: If you believe Fefer. I declare that Fefer is doing all of this in order to launch a campaign abroad against the Soviet government through the agency of the Israeli Mission vis-à-vis the closure of the Jewish Anti-Fascist Committee and *Eynikayt*. That is the political meaning of all this.

Presiding Officer: What did you sign the interrogation record for?

Lozovsky: Let me explain why I signed. Because over the course of eight nocturnal interrogations Colonel Komarov kept telling me over and over again that Jews are low, dirty people, that all Jews are lousy bastards, that all opposition to the party consisted of Jews, that Jews all over the Soviet Union are conducting an anti-Soviet whisper campaign, and that the Jews want to annihilate all of the Russians. This is what Colonel Komarov told me. I ask you, What sort of language is this? Is this fitting language for a Soviet person, a Soviet functionary?

Presiding Officer: So this is why you started slandering everyone? It doesn't make sense.

Lozovsky: I signed things that were stupid and senseless because I knew that they would go to highly placed government offices and people who, when they read all of this absurdity, would understand either that Lozovsky had gone mad or that there was something absurd here.

Presiding Officer: You are faced with an accusation, and you need to either confess to it or deny it and then prove your innocence. Your present explanations are unsatisfactory.

Lozovsky: I was completely stunned by Komarov's statement that Jews want to wipe out all the Russians. Further on he said that I should confess to all the accusations; otherwise he would hand me over to his investigators. Then he used a lot of obscenities that could not be entered into the stenographic report, and then he said that they would leave me to rot in a dark, cold cell and beat me with rubber nightsticks so badly that I wouldn't be able to sit down. Then I said that death would be better than such torture, to which they answered that they would not let me die right away, that I would die slowly.

Presiding Officer: And you got scared?

Lozovsky: No, I didn't get scared. Then Komarov started asking who among the senior people in Moscow had Jewish wives. I answered that I did not collect that kind of information. He told me that no one in the government was untouchable. The necessity arose, so we arrested Polina Semyonovna Molotova. Then he started demanding that I give testimony about my supposed contacts with Kaganovich and Mikhoels, although I had already proven to him dozens of times that I did not meet with them and that I was not close to them. Then I decided that it would be better for me to say something incriminating about myself and sign everything that they put in the record and then tell in court how the deputy director of the investigative division for especially important cases, Colonel Komarov, was conducting the investigation, and what sort of un-Soviet actions he was permitting. That is why I signed such a record. You say that this is inconsistent. It is very consistent; I had no other choice. On March 25, 1950, I was given the two first volumes to read, where the accused included Zhemchuzhina,

Sorkin,* Kotlyar, Halkin, and eleven other people, who were subsequently removed from the case, leaving only the fifteen who are here in the courtroom. After I read through the materials, I was taken to a room where Major General of Justice Nikolaev was seated. I was given a paper to sign saying that I had no statements to make. Nikolaev did not ask me about anything then, and I left thinking that if Nikolaev, who usually confirmed the extension of arrest, was occupied with that matter, then I could ask to see him. I submitted such an application to that effect through the investigator.

Presiding Officer: But why didn't you tell Nikolaev yourself about that when you were in his office?

Lozovsky: Komarov was sitting there.

Presiding Officer: Well, that should not have inhibited you.

Lozovsky: I wanted to live until the court convened and inform the court about everything. If I could have seen a senior person from the prosecutors' office face to face, I would have told him everything. But Komarov called me in and said that I had nothing to say to Nikolaev. So I had no opportunity to talk with anyone. Now that I have told you everything, you will see that starting with this record that I signed, the volume of testimony kept growing and growing, at least about the Crimea. Of course you can say that this is inconsistent, but what could I do, given the situation I was in?

Presiding Officer: It is still not clear why you didn't say anything about this, even to the people from the prosecutor's office, and now you are telling the court.

Lozovsky: Because the investigator is not here in the court, and all of my words are being recorded as I say them and not the way the investigators want them. If I had been able to write to Comrade Stalin or someone from the Central Committee, I would have set forth everything, but I did not have the opportunity.

I will tell you what else I did. I had a witness confrontation with Polina Semyonovna Molotova. The investigator asked me whether I knew her. I responded that I had known her for about twenty years, that she had been a candidate for membership on the Central Committee, and that besides that, we had met at various receptions which Comrade Molotov attended with his wife. "What do you know about Polina Molotova?" I answered that I didn't know anything in particular about her, but that Mikhoels had told me that she was interested in the Jewish theater and Jewish refugees from Poland. I thought that at the witness confrontation I would have to say something which seemed plausible to the investigator and absolutely

---

*Grigory Sorkin headed the photo information department of the Sovinformburo. He was sentenced to twenty-five years of imprisonment by a special conference of the MGB on September 14, 1949.

implausible to the party leadership. I said that I had asked her to remind Comrade Molotov about a letter which the Jewish Anti-Fascist Committee had sent to Comrade Molotov. I don't remember for sure what the letter was about. I think it was about complaints coming from various parts of the country. There had been such a letter. My statement seemed truthful to the investigation team, but if Comrade Molotov had read my testimony, he would have laughed out loud. Why would I go to Polina with a request like that when I was Comrade Molotov's deputy?

Presiding Officer: We don't need all of these details.

Lozovsky: What do you mean, you don't need them?

Presiding Officer: When you talk about yourself, you bring up issues that are not germane.

Lozovsky: I am talking about myself because this way of going along with the investigator by giving absurd testimony is something that I came up with myself.

Presiding Officer: You came up with a great many things, and now you are sweeping it all aside with great ease.

Lozovsky: It is not easy; it is very difficult. I had no other way to survive until the court proceedings except to sign that testimony. I incriminated myself and no one else, and I knew ten times more people than, say, Fefer did. I was asked about everyone, What do you know about whether Bregman and Yuzefovich are party members? I would say that I didn't know anything. If I had known, I would have written about it sooner. I had the right to incriminate myself, but I felt that it was morally unacceptable to incriminate other people. I have told you everything, Citizen Judges, and you will of course determine what is correct in these accusations and what are lies.

By the nature of the work I did, by the nature of my activities, through my duties at the Central Committee, I was involved with bourgeois circles and bourgeois newspapers all over the world: Yiddish ones, American ones, English ones, French ones. Why are you singling out the Yiddish newspapers and dealing with them separately?

Presiding Officer: Because you are accused of being a Jewish nationalist and maintaining ties with bourgeois Jewish reactionaries and not American or British ones. You were involved in hiring nonparty staffers at the Sovinformburo. Tell us what percentage of them were Jews and what their ratio was to the total number of employees.

Lozovsky: I did not do that kind of calculation. I never felt drawn to Jews and never denied that I was a Jew. A person who denies his nationality is a bastard.

Presiding Officer: No one is accusing you or any of the others seated here of being a Jew. That is not why you are here. You are here for carrying out anti-Soviet work.

Lozovsky: I am saying that I did not conduct any anti-Soviet work. I say that to a Soviet court. I say that to communists. I did not ask anyone whether or not he was a Jew. If I needed a good translator, I would take Talmy because he translates from four languages. Why should I hire some schoolgirl who is going to confuse me when I need a translator to dictate directly to a typist or to a stenographer? Take the translator Feinberg—he translated Lenin. That's more important than translating some article. Really, that is why three-quarters of the translators were Jews.

Presiding Officer: What else can you say?

Lozovsky: I don't wish to enumerate point by point the accusations I am facing now. I want to say the following: You don't have to make any allowances for my age or anything. I don't need any mitigating factors to be taken into account. If the court finds that even a single line of the accusation is confirmed, if you are even 5 percent certain that I committed treason and betrayed the Motherland, the party, and the government one-half of 1 percent, then I deserve to be executed.

[At 12:30 P.M., the presiding officer announced a recess. At 1:45 P.M., the judicial session was resumed.

Then Fefer asked the court to give him an opportunity to respond to Lozovsky. In a far-reaching statement, he again tried to demonstrate Lozovsky's direct involvement in drawing up the letter about the Crimea and his responsibility for passing on materials to Goldberg.]

Fefer: More about *The Black Book*. From Solomon Lozovsky's testimony it is apparent that the Sovinformburo was somewhat more involved in *The Black Book* than the entire presidium of the Jewish Anti-Fascist Committee was. There was so much confusion there that there were even several commissions. It would seem that *The Black Book* was a minor episode in the accusations that have been presented against us, but here suddenly a new version of events has been concocted according to which Mikhoels and I planned this all out in advance and then arranged matters with Goldberg, and Goldberg sent a telegram. We talked about *The Black Book* as a way of acting on a whole number of different issues, but as far as actually creating *The Black Book* goes, it was not initiated by us. The files contain a telegram signed by Epshteyn, Sholem Asch, and Goldberg, and there are minutes from a session of the Jewish Anti-Fascist Committee. The telegram has a stamp that reads "A.N."—that was Lozovsky's seal to indicate that he had read the telegram. The date of the telegram and the minutes indicate that the idea of creating *The Black Book* emerged before we left for the United States, and I think that the committee staff members in Kuibyshev remember those conversations well.

[The defendants had no questions. On June 2 at 2:25 P.M., the presiding officer announced a recess. Lozovsky's testimony was at an end. This part of the trial had lasted almost six days.]

BORIS SHIMELIOVICH

Boris Shimeliovich had impeccable revolutionary credentials: although he was a member of the Bund for five months, he joined the Bolsheviks in 1920. His older brother Julius had died during the Civil War, in January 1919, fighting on behalf of the revolution. Julius's story took on legendary proportions. Years later, in 1931, Moscow's State Jewish Theater produced a popular play about him. Entitled *Four Days*, it portrays a group of heroic Bolsheviks in Vilna who are betrayed by the Bund and the Polish Socialist Party. Under siege by White forces, the Bolsheviks, among them the doomed Julius, commit suicide rather than allow themselves to be captured. The play was written by the Yiddish playwright M. Daniel, whose real name was Daniel Meerovich. One of the historical ironies associated with the secret trial was that the playwright's son, Yuli Daniel, was arrested in the fall of 1965 for sending short stories to the West for publication. His trial the following February alongside the writer Andrei Sinyavsky sparked unprecedented protests within Moscow intellectual circles and led directly to the emergence of the Soviet human rights movement. Yuli Daniel was named for Julius Shimeliovich.

Boris Shimeliovich—like his brother Julius—remained a stubborn and principled believer in Communism. After joining the party, he was asked to help coordinate the work of the Joint Distribution Committee in the distribution of food packages among the starving in the Ukraine; this was in the early 1920s, when a severe famine ravaged parts of the Ukraine in the wake of the Civil War. In recognition of his work, President Kalinin himself presented Shimeliovich with government awards. As the longtime medical director of the prestigious Botkin Hospital in Moscow, he supervised the treatment of party and government leaders as well as foreign dignitaries, a responsibility that only someone with the complete trust of the Kremlin could have enjoyed. Alone among the defendants, Shimeliovich refused to confess to any crime throughout his interrogation, even after savage beatings.

[On June 2 at 7:00 P.M. the judicial session resumed.]

Presiding Officer: Defendant Shimeliovich, testify to the court.

Shimeliovich: Citizen Chairman of the Court, may I add something to Lozovsky's statement from this morning?

Presiding Officer: Perhaps you will do this in the course of your testimony?

Shimeliovich: What I want to say is, in my view, extremely important for the court, for Lozovsky stated that during the investigation I gave ten pages of testimony about him. From this, Lozovsky concludes that this is Mikhoels's unscrupulous political maneuvering. I declare before the court that during the three years and four months of the preliminary investigation, I did not sign any testimony about Lozovsky except for one page, and what I did sign constituted only one page. And apart from that, during that whole time, three years and four months, I was not asked about Lozovsky. To the testimony that fit onto approximately a single page, Ryumin added several words—namely, that Lozovsky was the chief criminal. I found out six weeks later that I had signed it. I am now declaring that I signed this report while I was in a difficult emotional state and unclear of mind. So ten pages of testimony about Lozovsky over my signature simply do not exist.

I did not and do not plead guilty to any thoughts or actions or to any crimes against the party or the government. Still, I should add that when I signed the final statement upon the completion of the investigation (I think that was on March 26, 1952), I asked investigator Strugov and the prosecutor Captain Kozhura to include in the report that I was not pleading guilty and had not pled guilty. For a fairly long time prosecutor Kozhura refused this request of mine, alluding to the fact that in my testimony during the preliminary investigation it was sufficiently clear that I had not pled guilty. It says in the indictment that Shimeliovich, in addition to his own confession, was unmasked by witnesses.

Presiding Officer: But still, during the preliminary investigation you gave testimony about the Jewish Anti-Fascist Committee's nationalistic activity, did you not?

Shimeliovich: I would rather not talk about that at the beginning of my testimony, but since you have raised the issue, I will tell you. I never uttered the words that are written in the initial record of my interrogation dated March 1949 and signed by me. This testimony was put together by investigator Ryumin and someone else without me present. Lozovsky was threatened with beatings and other things, and he decided, as he put it, to apologize to Shtern for slandering her, and he implicated himself and perhaps someone else, intending later on to repudiate everything in court. I did not go that route. I argued for three years and four months, and insofar as it is possible, I will keep arguing with the investigators and, if need be, with the prosecutor. If Lozovsky was merely threatened, then I must state, regretfully, at the outset of my testimony that for one month (January–February 1949) I received approximately eighty to one hundred blows a day, so altogether I think I was hit about two thousand times. I was subjected to corporal punishment on numerous occasions, but you will not find an investigator who will tell you that I changed my testimony under these circumstances. No, I said what I knew, and never, not standing, not sitting, not lying down, did I utter what is written in the interrogation records. Why did I sign them? The record dated March 1949 I signed while I was confused and in a very difficult emotional state. It was only six weeks later that I found out that I had signed that interrogation record. This was when investigator Ryumin read out excerpts to me from this record during an interrogation.

Presiding Officer: So are you entering a grievance against investigator Ryumin?

Shimeliovich: Ryumin personally did not touch me, but he said that he had seen me earlier. Where could he have seen me earlier, except during the floggings when, besides him, there were seven other people who participated directly in beating me? The secretary to the minister—a colonel in civilian dress—was there.

Presiding Officer: What minister?

Shimeliovich: State Security Minister Abakumov. Dissatisfied with my responses—I gave the same responses that I had given during the first interrogations by the investigators—he said, "Give him a deadly beating." The word "beating" I heard from him during the first meeting, and Ryumin was present. After this Ryumin was very gracious toward me for a month and heard out my testimony, the same testimony I had previously given to Shishkov. Ryumin listened to all of this attentively and recorded it. Once during an inopportune moment Ryumin called me in and said, "Sign the interrogation record." He gave it to me to read one page at a time. When I had finished, I said that I had never given such testimony, to which he responded: "The party Central Committee has made a special decision about your case. You will not evade moral responsibility." Furthermore, Ryumin told me that things would get easier for me if I signed that record, and he even showed me a key to the safe and said that no one would ever read the record. Ryumin told me on numerous occasions that he had saved me, that he had gotten me out of a terrible situation, and that I should be grateful to him for that. This was the state I was in at the time.

Presiding Officer: So, when Ryumin started conducting the investigation, he took no physical measures against you?

Shimeliovich: Right. But my answers to him were the same ones I had given previously to investigator Shishkov. And suddenly he called me in and told me to sign the record. We sat there for probably around six hours, and I signed, but I repeat that my mind was clouded from what I had endured. I believed that this was not the full course of treatment, because investigator Shishkov said to me, "You see, I'm doing everything I promised you I would. If you are in such a condition that you cannot walk to the interrogations, we will carry you in on a stretcher, and we will beat you and beat you some more."

Six weeks later, when I was myself again, I said only what I am repeating here, and that is this: Lozovsky ran all of the anti-fascist committees the same way he did the Jewish committee, and he bears full responsibility for the activity of the latter.

Presiding Officer: Now testify about the essence of the accusations that you face. During the preliminary investigation when you gave your life story, you testified that you had been in the Bund.

Shimeliovich: I was in the Bund for five months.

Presiding Officer: When?

Shimeliovich: I will tell you. It had to do with the environment I grew up in and my upbringing. I'll begin with my life story.

I was born on December 3, 1892. My father was at first a sexton at a synagogue in Riga. My father's duties included opening up the synagogue, keeping it clean, handing out prayer books, serving the congregants, and being the last one out. My mother was a housewife, and although she lived and died in bourgeois Latvia, she was a special pensioner of Russia, and she received a pension for her older son Julius, an underground revolutionary who was killed by the Whites on January 2, 1919.

I kept in my desk documentation that my father worked as a sexton in a synagogue and documentation from the city authorities that my mother received a pension, and these documents were confiscated when I was arrested. There was also a bank passbook, where I kept money to send to my mother in Latvia. Why am I going into this here? Because during the second round of my interrogation I testified for several evenings under Ryumin's orders about my relatives, both living and dead. I told him that my older brother Yakov and his wife had been murdered in occupied territory. Julius had perished in the underground. My brother Isaac had trained with a watchmaker, and then gone to the New World when he was forty. I was not in touch with him. I said that my father had worked as a sexton at a synagogue and that my mother had received a pension. But the investigator said that there is no such word as "sexton," and he wrote that I could not remember what my father did.

Presiding Officer: It says here that your father worked in a synagogue.

Shimeliovich: But it also says that I don't know, that I don't remember what he did. I remember very well and do not want to insult my parents' memory, because it appears from something that I signed that I am a son who doesn't remember. I do not want to be the sort of son to my parents who doesn't remember, and I state that my father was a sexton in a synagogue.

I should also add something about the influences on me when I was growing up. I slept in a bed with my older brother Julius. I knew that he belonged to some kind of organization. Vasya Ulrich* often came to see him.

*Vasily Ulrich (1890–1951), a Soviet judge, presided over many of the most notorious purge trials of the Stalin era.

Once there was a search that lasted six hours, after which Julius was arrested. At the time I did not belong to any organization, but I always followed my brother's instructions; it meant nothing to me to go up to the synagogue balcony where the women sat and throw down proclamations.

Presiding Officer: Did you live in Riga at the time?

Shimeliovich: Yes. This was in 1908–1909.

Presiding Officer: In your testimony you say: "I was a member of the Bund until 1920."

Shimeliovich: I was a member of the Bund from approximately November 1919 until April 1, 1920. I have held a party membership card since April 1, 1920.

Presiding Officer: So you joined the party in April 1920?

Shimeliovich: Yes, I had been in the Bund for about five months.

Presiding Officer: When did you first meet Mikhoels?

Shimeliovich: In the interrogation record that Ryumin drew up, it says that Mikhoels and I grew up together.

Presiding Officer: But that report contains no testimony about how you and Mikhoels met. When did you become acquainted?

Shimeliovich: I think that we got to know each other better when the first revolutionary play was produced at the Jewish Theater and *Pravda* published a prominent review of it. This was a play about Julius and the last four days of his life. Mikhoels played Julius.

Presiding Officer: When was this?

Shimeliovich: Around 1934.

Zuskin: It was in 1931.

Shimeliovich: Mikhoels played Julius. I already knew him.

Presiding Officer: So you met him in Moscow in 1931?

Shimeliovich: Yes, I used to go to the Jewish Theater, and I knew about Mikhoels and maybe even said hello and we shook hands, but we grew closer when the war started.

Presiding Officer: Was he ever in your home? Were you in his home?

Shimeliovich: He was in my home about three times, but this was after he got back from the United States. I heard that Mikhoels drank, but during all the time I knew him I never saw him drunk. I was in his home as well. I would stop by for fifteen or twenty minutes when I was in town or when he wasn't feeling well. I was also in his office at the theater. I saw Jews there waiting to meet with Mikhoels. I felt very warm toward him. I imagine he felt the same about me.

Presiding Officer: Did you talk about politics with him? Did you talk with him about the situation of the Jews?

Shimeliovich: No, he never raised questions about Jewish culture or how to settle Jews when I was around.

Presiding Officer: But testimony about Mikhoels being a Jewish nationalist has been a recurring theme in this case. You were friends with him over a long period of time. Did he really never talk with you about anything having to do with Jews?

Shimeliovich: I am telling what happened. In my presence he didn't talk about these questions. Mikhoels knew that my children did not know Yiddish. My son is a party member, and my daughter was a first-year student in college when I was arrested. Once when I went to see Mikhoels, he told me that Yiddish schools had been closed in Byelorussia.

Presiding Officer: In what year was this?

Shimeliovich: In 1936–1937, and he said it with sorrow. I remember saying to him, "Well, my children don't know Yiddish, and I am not involved with Yiddish literature. What can I tell you? The issue, after all, is not that they closed the schools, but whether it is clear why they were closed." I remembered this conversation and told Ryumin about it. Ryumin then rephrased it as if Mikhoels had said that the Yiddish schools were closed, and that was why it was necessary to fight the Soviet government and the party. This is a lie, invented by Ryumin.

Presiding Officer: And did you talk about other things—for example, the theater?

Shimeliovich: We talked about various plays being produced. He recalled Markish. It was not by chance that I asked Markish about seeing him with a navy knife, but that isn't the point. Mikhoels once asked me about Markish. He said, "You know, Boris, I find it unsettling that the Yiddish writer Markish was discharged from the navy for some impropriety." There were several discussions of Fefer's verse. I had not read Fefer's works, but I should say that Mikhoels had an extremely low opinion of Fefer's poetry.

Presiding Officer: How so?

Shimeliovich: He did not speak about nationalistic content. What he said was that the quality of his poetry was not high. Mikhoels talked to me about an unprincipled clash between Epshteyn and Markish. He said that they were unprincipled and that it was a disgrace to hear the way they dragged each other through the mud. More than once he asked how I was coping with difficulties at the hospital.

Presiding Officer: Were there any nationalistic conversations?

Shimeliovich: No, Mikhoels did not hold any nationalistic conversations with me.

Presiding Officer: But the accused have said during interrogations that Fefer was Mikhoels's main adviser on work at the committee and that Shimeliovich was a second adviser on nationalistic issues. How can it be that people observed your behavior, your friendship with Mikhoels, knew you and him as nationalists, and now suddenly you tell us something different?

Shimeliovich: No one among those present here said in answer to any of my questions that they heard any anti-Soviet or nationalistic statements from me. Fefer, when you asked him twice who he felt were nationalists, named Mikhoels, Epshteyn, Markish, and Bergelson, but he did not name me.

An hour and a half after I was arrested, I was received by the minister of state security in the presence of his secretary, a colonel.

When I entered the minister's office, he said, "Look at this nasty character." Then the secretary-colonel said to me, "You are Mikhoels's number one consultant." Later I read in Fefer's testimony that I was Mikhoels's number one consultant. But it seems that this testimony of Fefer's was given on January 11, 1949, and I was in the minister's office on January 3.

Presiding Officer: So your testimony is correct where, in response to the investigator's question about who recommended you for the committee, you said that it was Mikhoels?

Shimeliovich: Yes, it's correct. Yesterday we discussed my conversations with Mikhoels. There were no criminal conversations, but there were conversations that might interest the Supreme Court. He told me about an audience at the Kremlin and told me about two other visits to him by Lazar Kaganovich. I mention this because this issue was touched upon by Fefer, that they visited him and had a conversation with him. Mikhoels informed me that they were there more than once, not just once, as Fefer has said here.

Presiding Officer: We'll get to that.

Shimeliovich: Mikhoels also talked to me about incidents of anti-Semitism.

Presiding Officer: When were these conversations?

Shimeliovich: These conversations took place more than once.

Presiding Officer: These questions in your conversations were touched upon repeatedly.

Shimeliovich: Yes, I told him that I had encountered anti-Semitism at the People's Commissariat of Health. I told him what had to be done in such cases.

Presiding Officer: When did these conversations take place?

Shimeliovich: During the last years of his life, around 1946–1947.

Presiding Officer: Mikhoels was not a member of the party, and because in his eyes you were an old communist, he evidently came to you often on political questions, to have all sorts of doubts of his explained and cleared up. The defendants here have said that you were an adviser to Mikhoels. Adviser in this context is, of course, a relative term, but the defendants observing your relationship say that Mikhoels came to you most often for advice and was closer to you than to all of the others.

Shimeliovich: I told the court myself that he was close to me and that we were friendly.

Presiding Officer: What do you think, were there nationalists on the committee?

Shimeliovich: During my time on the committee and while in attendance at presidium sessions, I personally did not hear discussions of any nationalistic questions or hear any nationalistic statements made. But I should say that Bregman and I sometimes said that Markish "smelled" of nationalism.

Presiding Officer: You mean you heard him speak?

Shimeliovich: Yes, and I should add that he spoke with unbelievable pathos, and sometimes I didn't understand the content of his speeches. He spoke with such pathos that one experienced strong emotions and at the same time did not understand. And when he spoke about the Jewish people, he always used images from history. This was what Bregman and I based our feeling on when we said that Markish gave off an "odor" of nationalism.

Presiding Officer: So you considered Markish a nationalist?

Shimeliovich: No. If I had had information that Markish was a nationalist— and in our circumstances a nationalist is not only someone who is not a friend of the Soviet Union, but an opponent of the Soviet Union—then I would probably have exposed him. But I knew nothing about Markish being a nationalist. Maybe he is lucky that I did not read his published verse.

Presiding Officer: And did you talk with Mikhoels about the creation of the committee itself?

Shimeliovich: I said yesterday that I talked with him after the committee was created about how various distinguished scientists had called me to ask why there was no doctor's signature on the appeal.

Presiding Officer: And who told you about the fact that you had been included on the committee?

Shimeliovich: I have already said that Mikhoels told me this.

Presiding Officer: So the conversation between you about the very fact that the committee was being organized did take place. Mikhoels expressed to you his satisfaction and talked about the committee's prospective work—is that the case?

Shimeliovich: Yes, he was pleased not only that the Jewish Anti-Fascist Committee had been created at that time, but that there were other committees as well. Mikhoels said that the committee's mission was to mobilize Jews in the fight against fascism. Mikhoels did not speak with me about any other tasks, such as, for example, resolving issues having to do with the fate of the Jews or Jewish culture, past or future.

Presiding Officer: Then you had no grounds for friendship. Defendant Fefer and others confirm that Mikhoels was a convinced nationalist but you were a communist, so what did you have in common? If he was a nationalist and you were opposed to nationalism, then what kind of friendship could you have?

Shimeliovich: Everyone knows who Mikhoels was. He was a People's Artist of the USSR. He was sent to the United States on business. That is a sign of great trust.

Presiding Officer: And did you meet with them when they came back from the United States?

Shimeliovich: Yes, I saw Mikhoels.

Presiding Officer: Did he tell you about how Jewish reactionary circles in America had consented to help in the nationalistic work that the committee was doing?

Shimeliovich: No.

Presiding Officer: Well then, what did he talk to you about?

Shimeliovich: He told us that a special committee had been created in the United States to receive them. The committee included representatives of various groups, including reactionary ones, and his and Fefer's task was to gain as much sympathy as possible for the Soviet Union from among a wide spectrum of Jewish groups and from those who were influential in government circles. He told me that the *Forverts* was part of the yellow press and that unfortunately it was run by Lieber, Tamm, and Abramovich, former leaders of the Mensheviks in Russia, who had been conducting and were conducting a frenzied campaign against the Soviet Union. He told me about negotiations with the Joint, although I cannot say that he named Rosenberg specifically. I should add that even if he had mentioned that name, it would have meant nothing to me. Weizmann's name also meant nothing to me, because starting in 1922 and up through the creation of the Jewish Anti-Fascist Committee I had been removed from Jewish questions, from the Jewish masses, and from Yiddish writers, although I cannot say that I am completely assimilated.

[After questions about Shimeliovich's conversations with Mikhoels concerning the latter's trip to the United States, the chairman moved on to clarify when Shimeliovich had written the memorandum to the government about the Crimea. Shimeliovich insisted that it had been written in late 1945 or early 1946, not on February 12, 1944, as stated in the investigation materials.]

Presiding Officer (showing the memorandum): Tell us, Shimeliovich, are you the author of this document?

Shimeliovich: I read it.

Presiding Officer: I am asking you, Are you the author? Surely you can simply answer this question, can't you?

Shimeliovich: Yes. Perhaps not in its entirety, but I am the author.

Presiding Officer: What do you mean, perhaps not in its entirety? Was this document taken from you?

Shimeliovich: Apparently from my safe.

Presiding Officer: Then let's examine this memorandum, and you will see that it could not have been written in 1946. (He reads out the memorandum.) What right did you have to speak on behalf of all the Jews? Anti-Semitism in the Soviet Union, it follows from your memorandum, is more oppressive than the destruction of over four million Jews by the Germans. Judging from all the information available, this document was drawn up around 1943–1944, because, as you say, the people were awaiting liberation from Hitlerism, and the session that you mention was in late 1943 or early 1944. What is the purpose of your pointless arguing, Shimeliovich?

Shimeliovich: I just say what I know today.

Presiding Officer: You even speak of combating anti-Semitism at the government level. Here is your first demand: "We must gain dominance over our leaders."

Shimeliovich: I said that various individual leaders must be gotten under control, but not at the level of the whole government, of course.

Presiding Officer: How is it that your Mikhoels did not tell you that he, Epshteyn, and Fefer had signed the memorandum and sent it to the government?

Shimeliovich: I handed a draft of the memorandum to Mikhoels, and about five to seven days later he told me that Lozovsky had rejected my memorandum because it was emotional. We did not talk any more about it. I did not ask Mikhoels any more about how to settle Jews, and he said nothing to me about the Crimea, and nothing to me about the fact that the government and the Central Committee had refused to resolve the Crimea question. I was also unaware that a similar memorandum had been sent to Comrade Stalin.

Presiding Officer: So, you are asserting that Mikhoels sent his memorandum in 1946 rather than in 1944?

Shimeliovich: I am not asserting that at all.

Presiding Officer: Let's take a look at this document. It is pure nationalism through and through. In it you write: "The Jewish people are proud in the knowledge that the most sinister force in the history of humanity's existence (Hitlerite Germany) chose them for complete extermination, for this means that the Nazis see great danger to themselves in the high intellectual level of the Jewish masses and their incompatibility with them" (vol. 40, p. 325). So it seems to mean that since there were Jews, that is why Hitler conquered countries. This is one thing.

Further on you say that "the Jews who were evacuated from the western regions, not knowing Russian or the local language, were cut off not only from their own Jewish culture, but from the general sociopolitical life of the country." And then you emphasize that "there is no getting around the indisputable fact that as a result of the war, anti-Semitism is finding fertile soil in many extremely highly placed institutions, thanks especially to the political short-sightedness, lack of culture, and at times stupidity of individual leading bureaucrats, and that in this case anti-Semitism takes the form of the open, rude, and shameless firing of Jews from various positions. At times all of this creates an especially painful mood among a fairly significant part of the Jewish intelligentsia and among the broad Jewish masses. Anti-Semitism in the USSR, in one's own homeland, often has a more oppressive effect upon various strata of Jews than the extermination of four million Jews by the Germans and the death of their friends and loved ones." What right did you have to speak on behalf of a million and a half Jews?

Shimeliovich: Hitlerite Germany set itself the goal of destroying all the Jews and therefore in my memorandum the first task mentioned is peace among all of humanity and the destruction of fascism. I can confirm today, too, that the first goal of Hitlerite fascism was to exterminate all of the Jews. Now, about the Jews being proud in such knowledge, I heard a similar expression in the Hall of Columns at the third rally in 1944 when Ehrenburg spoke. He said, "I am proud that I belong to the Jewish people, which Hitler selected for total extermination."

Presiding Officer: But you wrote that the Jewish people are proud in the knowledge that Hitler selected them for total extermination—that is, you are speaking in the name of the Jewish people and are emphasizing their exceptional nature. And that amounts to nationalism.

Further, where did you get information that anti-Semitism is flourishing in many highly placed institutions? What does "highly placed" mean?

Shimeliovich: Let me explain. I personally have never experienced anti-Semitism. Before 1942 I never heard anything from anyone about anti-Semitism. Sometime in 1942 various acquaintances of mine, Jewish doctors, started telling me that there were manifestations of anti-Semitism among people in charge of health care. The thing is that former People's Commissar for Health Care Miterev* had committed a great act of political stupidity. Over a period of two and a half months he had removed all of the Jews from the editorial boards of the medical journals. In addition, there were individual cases of anti-Semitism in the Academy of Medical Sciences. I

---

*Georgy Miterev (1890–1971) was appointed people's commissar for health care of the Russian Federation in June 1939. He soon became minister of health care of the USSR, serving until 1947. Between 1954 and 1971 he served as chairman of the executive committee of the Union of Red Cross and Red Crescent Societies. Lina Shtern's objections to Miterev's crude anti-Semitic methods in 1943 apparently led to his being reprimanded.

wrote a letter about all of this to Malenkov and was summoned to the Central Committee. So I referred to all of this in my memorandum as well.

Presiding Officer: Tell us, Shimeliovich, what right did you have, given one instance of improper behavior on Miterev's part, to write that in many extremely highly placed institutions there is an element of anti-Semitism?

Shimeliovich: The People's Commissariat of Health Care is a highly placed institution. The Academy of Medical Sciences is as well. I cannot recall now what other institutions there were, but I do recall . . .

Presiding Officer: However, you state slanderously that anti-Semitism occurs in many government institutions.

Shimeliovich: I was not a slanderer.

Presiding Officer: So you assert that you see nothing nationalistic in this document of yours about the Crimea?

Shimeliovich: At the time I was writing that document, I saw nothing nationalistic in it because individual directors could commit certain acts of anti-Semitism owing to their poor managerial skills. Manifestations of anti-Semitism evoke a very painful feeling among particular Jews and strata of the Soviet people.

Presiding Officer: And Kvitko's trip to the Crimea—did this really fall within the functions of the presidium of the Jewish Anti-Fascist Committee?

Shimeliovich: The question of Kvitko's trip to the Crimea was not discussed at a presidium session. Is this within the purview of the committee? I believe that if there is a need to write about something in *Eynikayt,* then any Yiddish writer who is a correspondent for that newspaper could be dispatched to do necessary reporting.

Presiding Officer: But Kvitko was sent to the Crimea in order to study the situation of the Jews there and then send a document to the People's Commissariat of Agriculture. Is this really a committee function?

Shimeliovich: Kvitko testified here that he informed the members of the Jewish Anti-Fascist Committee of his trip at a presidium session. In his report he said that there were discussions among some groups of Jews about how Jewish settlements in the Crimea (here I should add that I did not know that there were Jewish settlements in the Crimea) would be put on the same level as the German ones, that is to say, that the Jewish settlements, like the German ones, would not be rebuilt. Now, this is a political question. In addition, Kvitko said that in a number of schools the atmosphere was very bad, the relationships between children were very poor, and he mentioned a particular word that Russian children used to taunt Jewish children, and said that there were even cases of Jews being beaten up by Russians. This is what I got from his report.

I recall that Mikhoels suggested that the government be informed, Andreyev in particular. A commission was elected right away, consisting of

Mikhoels, Gubelman, Kvitko, and Shimeliovich. I should point out that Kvitko's memorandum was not mentioned at any presidium session. And I don't remember when he sent this memorandum to Andreyev's attention. Perhaps it was when we were at Benediktov's. While we were in Andreyev's office, we were told that Benediktov would see us. Kvitko was a bit late, but when he arrived, I immediately signed the accompanying letter. Benediktov received us. Mikhoels spoke, Gubelman spoke, and so did Kvitko and I. I did not touch upon resettlement of the Jews, saying merely that I wanted to direct attention to a report about how there was anti-Semitism among schoolchildren and that this indicated that the same spirit reigned among their parents. We then asked Benediktov to verify the incidents that we had described and take measures to eliminate this sort of thing if they were confirmed. Benediktov said that he would do so and that, if necessary, the appropriate measures would be taken.

Presiding Officer: Now answer my question: What conversations did you have and with whom about Mikhoels's death? You once stated during the investigation that there were conversations about how he had been killed in an act of premeditated murder, and in connection with that you talked about investigator Sheinin. What the court would like to know is, how did these conversations start?

Shimeliovich: On the first evening of my arrest, when investigator Shishkov spoke with me, he said, "Well, well, now tell us who killed Mikhoels?" And then immediately he mentioned names.

Presiding Officer: I am asking you what conversations you had about the causes of Mikhoels's death. With whom? Who told you that he did not die as the result of an accident but was killed in a premeditated manner? The court is not interested in what Shishkov said to you.

Shimeliovich: I did not speak with anyone about the premeditated murder of Mikhoels. During the state funeral, I heard conversations about how he had supposedly been killed by Banderites* and how investigator Sheinin from the office of the public prosecutor had gone there. In Fefer's testimony it says that during the funeral there was a woman who stood by Mikhoels's body in the theater for six hours (I will not mention her name, for she is sufficiently well known to the court), who told Fefer that Mikhoels had not died from a car accident, but that the cause was completely different, and that supposedly he, Fefer, had told other people about this, mentioning my name, among others.[†]

*Banderites were the followers of Stepan Bandera (1909–1959), a Ukrainian nationalist who helped to proclaim the establishment of an independent Ukrainian state on June 30, 1941, a week after the Nazi invasion. Because he refused to rescind the proclamation, he was arrested by the Germans and interned in Sachsenhausen concentration camp. He survived the war, but was assassinated by a KGB agent in Munich on October 15, 1959.

[†]He is referring to Polina Zhemchuzhina. It is unlikely that she stayed at the funeral for Mikhoels for six hours.

I should add the following: I stood for several hours in the theater where the state funeral was held, but I did not see the woman mentioned. I became acquainted with her in 1948. I think that if she had been there, we would have been introduced. Neither during those days nor later did Fefer ever mention that she had been there for six hours. It was only from his testimony that I learned that, and that she was friendly to Mikhoels and that he also held her in the highest regard. Fefer never told me that she told him of any other reasons for Mikhoels's death.

Presiding Officer: Fefer, what happened?

Fefer: I wasn't even at the theater at that time. Zuskin testified about the meeting with her. Shimeliovich is all mixed up. This is his fantasy.

Presiding Officer: Have you read Greenberg's testimony? In volume 27, page 273, there is an interrogation record for Greenberg dated March 1, 1948. You know Zakhar Grigorievich Greenberg; prior to his arrest he was a senior research fellow at the World Literature Institute of the Soviet Academy of Sciences and a party member since 1930. On March 1, 1948—that is, a year before you were arrested—he gave testimony about the Jewish Anti-Fascist Committee's nationalistic activity and about Mikhoels's, Fefer's, and Lozovsky's roles in this nationalistic activity. He also said that Shimeliovich played a prominent role among the nationalists, saying the following: "Pursuing this goal (nationalistic activity), Mikhoels pulled in like-minded people onto the Jewish Anti-Fascist Committee, including Isaac Solomonovich Fefer, Peretz Davidovich Markish, the Yiddish poet Leyb Moiseyevich Kvitko, Academician Lina Solomonovna Shtern, Medical Director of the Botkin Hospital Boris Abramovich Shimeliovich" (vol. 27, p. 284). You see, he calls you one of the leaders of the nationalistic activity that the committee conducted.

Shimeliovich: I must state to you in full awareness of what I am saying that I read Greenberg's testimony in the volumes that were shown to me, but I do not recall his mentioning me.

Presiding Officer: Well, apparently you overlooked it. True, in his testimony, Greenberg cites Fefer and Mikhoels, saying that he knows about you from what they said. Greenberg himself was a member of the Jewish Anti-Fascist Committee.

Shimeliovich: I did not know that Greenberg was a member of the Jewish Anti-Fascist Committee.

Presiding Officer: He says: "In 1942 I was elected to the plenum of the Jewish Anti-Fascist Committee and soon became convinced that this committee was an organization hostile to Soviet power" (vol. 27, p. 281).

Shimeliovich: In 1952, in one of the volumes I saw a list of committee members for the first time, and in particular, I was extremely surprised that Professor Vovsi, with whom I had worked, was a member of the Jewish Anti-Fascist Committee. I think that if he was a member of the committee, he would have told me. How Professor Vovsi's name ended up on the committee membership list, which I saw only in 1952, is something that you should ask Fefer.

I know nothing about Greenberg. Fefer has said more than once here in court in response to your questions that it was only while he was in prison that he realized that the committee's work was nationalistic, that that became clear to him only here. But then how could he have said to Greenberg back then that the committee's work was nationalistic, if he, Fefer, did not come to that conclusion until he was here? And along with that, how could Fefer have then assessed my activity at the Jewish Anti-Fascist Committee as nationalistic? I have nothing more to say about Greenberg's testimony.

Presiding Officer: Tell us, Shimeliovich, do you consider yourself responsible for the committee's nationalistic activity?

Shimeliovich: Prior to the trial I didn't know about that. Now, after many people have spoken, including Fefer, I am convinced that there was conspiratorial work being carried out at the committee by several presidium members.

Presiding Officer: By whom?

Shimeliovich: I have come to be convinced from the statements by and answers to questions posed to Fefer that he was a nationalist all the time before he was in prison. He says that all his life he was opposed to assimilation. What does it mean to be against assimilation in our Soviet conditions? It means to struggle against the Soviet government. I can understand it in no other way.

Presiding Officer: You really did not know prior to your arrest that he was a nationalist?

Shimeliovich: I did not know him to be a nationalist.

Presiding Officer: You said yesterday that his poem "I Am a Jew" was nationalistic. Was this really the only nationalistic poem he wrote?

Shimeliovich: As I've already told you, I first read this poem when I was studying the expert commission's report, that is to say, in 1952, and it is perfectly clear to me that this poem is nationalistic.

Presiding Officer: The court has no other questions for you.

Shimeliovich: May I provide an explanation about Fefer's testimony?

Presiding Officer: Please go ahead.

Shimeliovich: I don't think that Fefer had such a bad three years in prison, and there is no reason for his memory to fail him. For that reason Fefer should have easily remembered that he came to see me with Mikhoels prior to leaving for the United States, without my inviting him. Fefer says that Vovsi and Zaslavsky were with me at the time. I deny that and state that neither Vovsi nor Zaslavsky was with me prior to Fefer's and Mikhoels's departure. There was no lunch and no tea. The entire conversation lasted no more than ten to fifteen minutes. Fefer has already implicated a lot of people in this case, even people who had nothing to do with the Jewish Anti-Fascist Committee. The story about Vovsi and Zaslavsky coming to see me is a lie.

When he spoke here, Markish said that a poet is often captive to poetry. That's a very bad thing, when the poet becomes a captive to poetry, and I don't know, Fefer, who you were captive to, but much of what you say here is lies.

Presiding Officer: What else do you have to say to the court? Your answers to the court are clear enough.

Shimeliovich: Here in court Fefer at first did not talk about me as a nationalist, but when you asked him about this and read out to him his testimony about there being almost no Russian employees at Botkin Hospital, he immediately stated that he had heard this from Mikhoels. For Fefer's information, several days after his statement I gave the chairman of the court a list of names of people in managerial positions at Botkin Hospital. It is apparent from this list that there were only forty-five or forty-seven department heads, of whom about thirty-six were Russian. There were over forty senior nurses at the hospital, and a senior nurse in the hospital is the main assistant to the department head, of whom only two were Jewish. Of eight doctors bearing the rank Honored Doctor of the Republic, there were six Russians and two Jews.

Presiding Officer: Defendant Shimeliovich, do have anything to add to your testimony?

Shimeliovich: Yes, I would like permission to give information about the minutes of the Jewish Anti-Fascist Committee sessions. Fefer said in the end that the question of sending congratulations to Weizmann was not discussed at a session. If the question was not discussed at the presidium, then why does the first item in the minutes from that session concern the congratulations to Weizmann?

Presiding Officer: Fefer, was this question discussed?

Fefer: The text of the congratulatory message was read aloud at the presidium, but since it had been approved by the Central Committee, there was no discussion of it.

Shimeliovich: I would like to say a few words about the fact that in the interrogation record dated March 11, 1949, the investigator wrote that I said certain things about Lina Solomonovna Shtern. For three and a half years I stood firm on the point that I was at that presidium session when the question of sending a telegram to trade unionists in England protesting anti-Jewish pogroms in England was discussed. Clearly such a telegram would have been approved in advance. Lina Shtern did not say what she is reported to have said in those minutes. I know this for certain. She asked twice, "Has it really been verified that there were pogroms there?" It is clear from the way this question was posed that political understanding was lacking, but for three and half years I said to all of the investigators, including Ryumin, that it was not the case that Lina Shtern said that "we should take a look and see where the pogroms are really taking place," meaning that they were happening not there, but right here in the USSR.

Presiding Officer: So you are now denying this testimony of yours about Shtern?

Shimeliovich: Ryumin wrote this. I talked with him about it, and he said that her statement was not political. To this I responded to him that she should have known that the telegram had been approved by the Central Committee.

Presiding Officer: What telegram?

Shimeliovich: The telegram of protest. I told Ryumin, "Write down my testimony about how Lina Shtern spoke at that session twice and asked, 'Is it true that there were really pogroms there?' I will sign that." And because that is in the interrogation record, it was written by Ryumin that same night. I cannot do what Lozovsky does, who said bad things about Lina Shtern and then apologized here. I did not slander anyone. I did not utter a single lie, and said only what was true and repeated it for the entire three years and four months of the investigation, and am talking about it during the court session.

Presiding Officer: What else can you say?

Shimeliovich: Mikhoels and Fefer accused me of not hiring Fefer's daughter [Dora Fefer] to work at Botkin Hospital. This is in fact true—I didn't hire her as a doctor at Botkin Hospital. We had a rule that no doctor with less than two years of experience could be hired at Botkin Hospital. Fefer's daughter was a doctor, but she had just graduated, and she was turned down for a job at the hospital.

Presiding Officer: After that you had a quarrel with Fefer?

Shimeliovich: Our relationship changed. He stopped calling me.

Presiding Officer: What year was this?

Shimeliovich: This was in 1946.

Presiding Officer: What else can you tell us?

Shimeliovich: I want to say that during my entire long life, I have never been against the party, neither in my soul nor in my thoughts. I never had any such ideas. And when Ryumin told me on March 11, 1949, that I was morally responsible for all the activity of the Jewish Anti-Fascist Committee, I replied to him that if moral responsibility consists of my being arrested and receiving corporal punishment, then I don't understand. He did not respond to that at all. Investigator Strugov told me that if I behaved well, and if I gave testimony, the court would take my good behavior into account.

Presiding Officer: The investigator could not have said that.

Shimeliovich: The party gave me all that was possible. I had everything, I was given the honorary degree of Distinguished Doctor of the Republic. The hospital was awarded the Order of Lenin. Shvernik* himself presented me with the Order of the Great Patriotic War, and [President] Mikhail Ivanovich Kalinin presented me with the Order of the Red Banner of Labor. In the thirty years during which I worked in the Soviet health care system, no one had a bad word to say about my work.

I ask that the court not consider any of my achievements over thirty years working in the health care field, if, after the party gave me everything, and after I was in the party for twenty-nine years and a member of the Moscow City Council for twenty-five years, I committed a transgression against the party. If the court finds me guilty of a crime against the party, then let it sentence me to death.

[With this Shimeliovich's testimony ended. At 7:48 P.M. on June 4, 1952, the presiding officer announced a recess. At 8:20 P.M. the judicial session was resumed.]

SOLOMON BREGMAN

Solomon Bregman became a Bolshevik activist in 1912 at the age of seventeen. Prior to joining the JAC, he held a number of prominent government positions, including deputy minister of state control for the Russian Federation. As the court testimony makes clear, Bregman was assigned to the JAC presidium in 1944 in order to enforce party discipline. He soon proved to be an earnest informer by providing denunciations of committee members to his party superiors. It was Bregman, for example, who denounced Peretz Markish in November 1944 after Markish complained at a meeting of the JAC presidium that Jews were not being allowed to register in their former towns and "that the Jews are once again in a ghetto." Bregman informed Lozovsky that Markish's speech "was alarmist and politically harmful." As for Mikhoels, "who was chairing the session," he "failed [to speak] out about it."[†] For political reasons,

---

*Nikolai Shvernik (1888–1970), longtime party leader, was chairman of the Presidium of the Supreme Soviet of the Russian Federation from 1944 to 1946 and chairman of the Supreme Soviet of the USSR from 1946 to 1953. In effect, he succeeded Kalinin as president of the country.

†RGASPI, f. 17, op. 125, d. 246, l. 204.

Bregman was often ready to compromise other JAC members. In March 1945, when *The Black Book* project and Ilya Ehrenburg's contribution were under serious review, Bregman advised that Ehrenburg's manuscript displayed "literariness" and lacked "principal facts."* Given his role at the JAC, it must have been a complete and unexpected surprise to the regime when Bregman turned out to be one of only four defendants to plead innocent to all charges at the outset of the trial.

Five weeks into the trial, on June 16, Bregman collapsed into a coma; soon thereafter, the court separated his case from that of the rest of the defendants. Bregman died on January 23, 1953.

Presiding Officer: Defendant Bregman, testify to the court, to what do you plead guilty?

Bregman: In spite of the fact that I have stated and state that according to the articles presented to me, 58-1a; 58-10, part 2; and 58-11 of the Criminal Code of the Russian Federation, I do not plead guilty, I believe it necessary to state to the court that I consider myself guilty of consenting to join the presidium of the Jewish Anti-Fascist Committee unbeknownst to the Central Committee. But I thought that in making me this offer, Lozovsky was acting with the knowledge of the Central Committee.

   I am also guilty of believing Lozovsky, of believing that he would take the measures necessary to improve the work of the Jewish Anti-Fascist Committee, which I was dissatisfied with.

   My third area of guilt consists of the fact that I should have gone to the Central Committee somewhat earlier to inform them of things going wrong at the Jewish Anti-Fascist Committee, but I went somewhat later than I should have.

Presiding Officer: For exactly what purpose should you have gone to the Central Committee earlier but ended up going later?

Bregman: Well, here is the situation. I told Lozovsky repeatedly (and I went to see him not twice, as he says here, but about twenty times) about troubling aspects of the committee's work. I saw that most of the work was being done without the involvement of the presidium members who came less often. As a member of the presidium, I saw that Mikhoels, Fefer, and others were ignoring me and other comrades, and that they were consulting with the editors more than they did with us.

Presiding Officer: Who were these others?

---

*State Archive of the Russian Federation (hereafter GARF), f. 8114, op. 1, d. 1054, ll. 305–306 from the minutes of the JAC Presidium of March 13, 1945.

Bregman: Kheifets, Goldberg, Halkin, and someone else—I don't remember.

Presiding Officer: Levin?*

Bregman: I don't remember. But judging from Fefer's statement, these people had the right to make final decisions about sending correspondence outside the country.

Presiding Officer: I would like to clarify what issue you feel you were late in bringing to the attention of the Central Committee.

Bregman: That I had noticed manifestations of nationalistic tendencies, above all in *Eynikayt*.

Presiding Officer: So it follows from your testimony that Lozovsky knew that you had nationalistic sentiments, and that was why he referred you to the committee.

Bregman: When Lozovsky summoned me to the Sovinformburo and started asking me how I would regard becoming a member of the Jewish Anti-Fascist Committee, he did not conduct any kind of agitation or propaganda as he did so. He did not try to persuade me, but said simply that it was a matter worth thinking about, that there were several anti-fascist committees, including a Jewish one, which lacked sufficient coordination between the members, writers, and poets, and since I had a fair amount of experience in civic and political work, I would be of use there. I did not ask Lozovsky anything particular about the Jewish Anti-Fascist Committee. The whole conversation lasted no more than twenty or thirty minutes. He also asked whether I knew any old Bolsheviks who, like me, could be brought onto the Jewish Anti-Fascist Committee.

Presiding Officer: You testified during the investigation that Lozovsky sent you to the Jewish Anti-Fascist Committee to make the nationalistic activity at the committee more inconspicuous, more concealed.

Bregman: Lozovsky did not say a single word about nationalistic manifestations in the work of the Jewish Anti-Fascist Committee. He said that there was a quarrel going on between Mikhoels, Fefer, and Epshteyn, and in fact many people knew about it.

Presiding Officer: It is clear from your testimony that Lozovsky was the ideological inspiration behind all of the committee's hostile activity.

Bregman: When I was arrested and learned from the investigator what the Jewish Anti-Fascist Committee actually was, that it was nationalistic and that it was a center for espionage and that the heads of the Sovinformburo knew that, I stated at the time that only a secret enemy could behave in that fashion. If I had known all of this earlier, before the investigation, I would of course have gone to the Central Committee and given a statement about everything.

*Naum Levin (1908–1950) was a Yiddish journalist and senior editor at the JAC. He was arrested in September 1949 and executed on November 23, 1950.

When I did go to the Jewish Anti-Fascist Committee, I discovered abnormalities there. I knew a bit of Yiddish, but I couldn't read the language well. I started reading *Eynikayt* with difficulty and saw how sessions were held at the committee, and I saw that from an organizational and political standpoint there was chaos there. The session minutes were abysmally recorded. There were no agendas drawn up, no work plan, and the minutes were not circulated to the presidium members. It reminded me of how the village councils operated back in 1919, when I often ran into this kind of thing.

Presiding Officer: And who was the secretary of the Jewish Anti-Fascist Committee at the time?

Bregman: Epshteyn, and later Fefer. The presidium sessions were also quite disorderly. One member of the presidium would attend, another one would not, one person would stroll in, someone else would not show up. Shimeliovich said here that one presidium member, Academician Frumkin, never came to any sessions.

Then I started to notice a tolerance for nationalistic shortcomings. Specifically, I remember a presidium session during which either Lurye* or Kvitko gave a report about a trip to the Crimea. When it was said that Jewish areas were being renamed and given Russian names (for example, Stalindorf [the name of the district in Yiddish] became Stalin District), Markish stood up and, in his usual temperamental way, expressed his outrage, saying, "The Stalinist Constitution is crumbling. The foundations of Stalinism are crumbling! Why was Stalindorf renamed? Someone needs to go talk to Comrade Stalin about this!"

I spoke then and said that Markish was incorrect from a political point of view. But neither Fefer nor Epshteyn nor Mikhoels said a word to him, from which I concluded that they were favorably and patiently disposed toward Markish. A day or two later I told Lozovsky about this and said that I found it dismaying. Later, when I read *Eynikayt,* I noticed that on the first page there were a lot of articles about Birobidzhan. I told them that Birobidzhan had its own newspaper. What was the point of making *Eynikayt* into a regional newspaper? as I explained to Zhits† and Lozovsky. But what I should have done was not tell him, but go to the Central Committee, because he had evidently forgotten that he was a member of the Central Committee. I also wrote three articles for *Eynikayt,* and I am ready to take full responsibility for their political content. They were about political work with the masses in the countryside and about the goals of the trade unions. I believed that it would have been wrong not to cover these issues in the paper.

---

*Noyekh Lurye (1886–1960) was a Soviet Yiddish writer and critic. During World War II he became a member of the JAC.

†Gershon Zhits (1903–1954) was editor in chief of *Eynikayt* after the death of Shakhno Epshteyn. He was arrested in 1949 and died in Butyrsky prison hospital on October 8, 1954.

There was another time, this was in 1945 by now, when Epshteyn reported on the committee's work. I spoke out quite sharply at that presidium session, in contrast to the others. And I said that positions at the Jewish Anti-Fascist Committee had been turned into sinecures for certain
Jewish writers, and that the Jewish Anti-Fascist Committee's work should
be folded in with the work being done in the Yiddish Writers' Section.
Someone was writing for a foreign audience—what and to whom we, the
members of the presidium, did not know.

Presiding Officer: Why did you go to Lozovsky when he behaved like a diplomat at that session? The question should have been raised elsewhere.

Bregman: I went to the Central Committee Section in 1946 and on April 7,
1947, and said there what I considered it necessary to say, those facts which
I knew. Shumeiko will not deny this. Mainly, I asked him to get me out of
the musty atmosphere of the Jewish Anti-Fascist Committee, where I could
not work. I agree with you, Citizen Chairman, that I made a big political
mistake when I kept agreeing with Lozovsky on this matter. I told him that
I would go to Zhdanov and raise the question of strengthening the committee because I believed that neither Mikhoels nor Fefer should be allowed to remain in the leadership.

Presiding Officer: Why?

Bregman: First of all, I saw manifestations of nationalism in the committee's
work, as well as in *Eynikayt.*

Presiding Officer: During the investigation (vol. 5, p. 95) you said that your
first hostile act was your involvement in discussing the letter to the government about the Crimea.

Bregman: This was a fatal mistake. It is quite clear to the court that these discussions were going on long before I came to the committee. The investigator stated that I participated in such discussions. But he was dishonest with
me in this regard. He should have shown me the interrogation record, but
he didn't. I had no involvement in the Crimea question and could not have
had any involvement at presidium sessions.

Presiding Officer: How were you involved in the publication of *The Black
Book?* Are you familiar with the conclusions of the expert commission on
The Black Book? The expert commission recognizes that it is a nationalis-
tic document and you were involved in putting it together.

Bregman: A curious thing happened with *The Black Book* several years after I
came on the committee. Those of us members who came in on an occasional basis and did not have specific duties on the committee presidium
were isolated from its day-to-day work. When I was at the Sovinformburo
talking to Lozovsky, and at the committee too, I often heard conversations
about *The Black Book* and about how there was some kind of fight going
on among the writers because of it. I had the impression that *The Black
Book* was connected to the Nuremberg trials and that the committee was

actively involved. I told Lozovsky that I had heard that there was some kind of incomprehensible bickering going on between Ehrenburg and Grossman but that I didn't know what it was about. And later I learned that Ehrenburg and Grossman had received tens of thousands of rubles for the materials they had written for *The Black Book*.* Lozovsky asked me how I felt about creating a commission at the Sovinformburo to examine materials for *The Black Book*. I consented to look through the materials.

Presiding Officer: You keep saying all the time that you were up to your ears in work, right?

Bregman: I am speaking now of civic duties. I was not overloaded with them, but as far as my job went, I had plenty to do. I saw that this proposal involved substantial work, because a member of the Central Committee and head of the Sovinformburo had recommended me to head the commission. He wasn't in a position to compel me to do it, since I was not subordinate to him. I agreed to it, for I felt all along that I was doing something valuable. A commission was set up that included me, Yuzefovich, Sheinin, Borodin, Grossman (who was not much involved), and Milshtein from the Forestry Ministry. Sheinin recommended him because there was a feeling that other people besides writers should be involved in this. For three weeks there was no order confirming that the commission had been established, but we worked hard, around the clock. Each member took on a specific section of the book to look through. There was a great deal of material, and we met after we had read the material and exchanged thoughts about it. But when we finally completed the work, we did not hand in any written report.

We did reach the conclusion, especially after Grossman wrote about Auschwitz and Maidanek, that Ehrenburg's and Grossman's materials were far better—more thoughtfully assembled and more substantial in the political sense. Besides, in the material from the Jewish Anti-Fascist Committee, there were a number of places where, from a political standpoint, there were distortions of reality. It even stated that individual Ukrainians and Belorussians participated with the Germans in annihilating the Jews, whereas Grossman's material emphasized the opposite, that no small number of incidents were cited of Ukrainian and Belorussian citizens saving and hiding Jews.[†]

I reported to Lozovsky about this and said that now all of the material

---

*No documents or other evidence have been found to corroborate that there was a dispute over money connected to *The Black Book* project.

†*Neizvestnaya Chyornaya Kniga* (The Unknown Black Book) was published by Yad Vashem and GARF in 1993. In 1945 the *Black Book* commission removed material from Ehrenburg and Grossman's compilation that documented collaboration by Soviet citizens in the massacre of Jews. Ehrenburg expressed his chagrin over this censorship but was powerless to change it. He later arranged for much of the material that he had collected to be transferred to Yad Vashem in Jerusalem. The volume *Neizvestnaya Chyornaya Kniga* includes a good deal of this material.

needed to be carefully edited and checked at the appropriate government bodies, and then it could be sent to the appropriate places.

Presiding Officer: And what were the appropriate places?

Bregman: Those places where the Sovinformburo decided it should be sent.

Presiding Officer: And did you really not know that the material was being prepared for America?

Bregman: Lozovsky and other members of the commission told me that this material had to do with the Nuremberg trials.

Presiding Officer: Since you looked through this book and studied its contents, it follows from that that you were an accomplice to the nationalistic character of the book.

Bregman: My assignment was quite narrow—to study this material.

Presiding Officer: If you were opposed to the contents of this book, you should have stated that it was nationalistic.

Bregman: If I had been assigned to do that, then I of course would have looked upon this material with a different eye. Now, you can frame the question any way you like. That is why it now appears that I am politically responsible for the fact that Lozovsky let me down. When Lozovsky called me in to see him, there was a quarrel over money between Grossman and Ehrenburg, on the one hand, and between the committee and the writers, on the other, but I still felt that we were doing something useful. After our commission looked through the materials, an editorial board was set up, but I did not get involved in this, and, characteristically, I didn't even know that I had been included on this editorial board. But I should add that I do not regret that. After this, I told Lozovsky that the material required further editing from the literary and political standpoint, for Ehrenburg and Grossman were only writers and could have allowed some inaccuracies to creep in. But there was no proposal on my part to send the materials to America.

What am I guilty of? I am guilty of the fact that this material is nationalistic, which the investigator emphasized. The investigator said to me the following: "You see one side of the question, that the Jews had more victims than anyone else and that other nationalities had fewer victims, so there should be more attention paid to the Jews. *The Black Book* was a consequence of all of this, and that is why you made your proposal to send materials for it to America." I am stating here, as I did to the investigator, that I did not make such a proposal. It would be, at the very least, ludicrous to point out that it was the commission that decided where to send this material.*

---

*In the fall of 1944, Andrei Gromyko requested the JAC to send material on Nazi atrocities to New York. The JAC responded by sending hundreds of pages of documents that Ehrenburg had compiled. He was not informed of this request and was furious when he learned that it had been carried out.

Lozovsky: Allow me to say a few words about Bregman's testimony. He said that Epshteyn told him that *The Black Book* was being prepared for the Nuremberg trials. In July 1945, during the Potsdam Conference, Epshteyn did not know, and actually no one in the world yet knew, that the Nuremberg trials would take place, so Epshteyn could not have said that this book was being prepared for the Nuremberg trials.

Presiding Officer: Defendant Lozovsky, the court has a question for you. In the case materials (vol. 37, p. 200) there is a copy of Mikhoels and Epshteyn's memorandum to Comrade Molotov about how packages should be distributed.

Lozovsky: From the Jewish Anti-Fascist Committee?

Presiding Officer: Yes. It is dated October 28, 1944.* The memorandum indicates that Mikhoels and Epshteyn framed the issue as follows: that these gifts should go only to Jews and that they should be distributed through Jewish organizations both in the capital and at points around the country. The memorandum contains an instruction to Krutikov, Mikhoels, and Epshteyn which says: "I request that the People's Commissariat of State Control check into this with all possible care and speed." At the end it says, "I feel it necessary to say that the Jewish Anti-Fascist Committee was not set up to handle these matters, and the committee apparently does not have a fully accurate understanding of its functions."

Lozovsky: This was Comrade Molotov's observation.

Presiding Officer: Did you know about this?

Lozovsky: I did. Jewish organizations in the United States raised money, bought things, and sent them to the Soviet Union through the Red Cross.

Presiding Officer: Did they really not consult with you when they wrote this document?

Lozovsky: No. On such matters as these they went to Comrades Kalinin and Molotov.

Presiding Officer: They went around you?

Lozovsky: They had the right to go to their government directly. They are all Soviet citizens, but I explained to them repeatedly that they shouldn't get involved in these matters. In spite of that, they systematically went beyond the mandate of the Jewish Anti-Fascist Committee, and we had pretty sharp exchanges over it.

Presiding Officer (to Bregman): Your name is mentioned by the expert commission in connection with a discussion within the presidium of the Jewish Anti-Fascist Committee about the State of Israel and about a demonstration organized to mark the arrival in the USSR of Israeli Ambassador Golda Meyerson. You participated in the discussion of this question, which

---

*The correspondence with Molotov can be found in Redlich, *War, Holocaust and Stalinism*, pp. 248–249.

characterized the nationalistic line of the committee. This is also recorded in the minutes of the Jewish Anti-Fascist Committee session on October 21, 1948.

Bregman: I cannot recall now what took place at that session. But there is nothing surprising in the fact that among people from various walks of life there were many puzzling questions about what was going on in Palestine. I was also asked a number of questions about that. In all likelihood the discussion at the session was about how Ambassador Meyerson was going to be received. Sheinin, I, and other members of the Jewish Anti-Fascist Committee were very indignant that such a nationalistic demonstration could take place in a synagogue in the center of the capital.

Presiding Officer: All of the committee's activity was a preparation for this demonstration. *Eynikayt,* with all of its nationalistic ideas, also played a part in laying the groundwork for this sort of demonstration. Here in the case materials (vol. 34, p. 57) are the minutes of the October 21, 1948, session of the Jewish Anti-Fascist Committee at which the events in Palestine were discussed*—Slepak's report.[†] And your statement is here as well (he reads out vol. 34, p. 63).

Bregman: There was a lot of discussion following this report. I didn't see the minutes, and I can't say whether the statements are recorded correctly. The impression one gets from reading my statement as recorded in the minutes is that I was sort of cautiously attempting to conceal what was happening, that I was aware of and supported Zionist activity, that I supported *Eynikayt* and its position on the demonstration. In fact, I knew nothing about that work. In conclusion, I consider it necessary once again to emphasize that I plead guilty to being too patient for too long with Lozovsky's assurances. This placed me in a very difficult situation.

Presiding Officer: What assurances?

Bregman: Assurances that the appropriate measures would be taken to prevent manifestations of nationalism in the committee's work and to improve organizational work. I believe that Lozovsky's comments made here, that the newspaper was run by a division of the Central Committee, are incorrect. *Eynikayt* was an organ of the Jewish Anti-Fascist Committee, its most fundamental division, so it is wrong to brush it aside. The propaganda section of the Central Committee could have examined the work that was going on there, of course, but that would not have relieved the leadership of the Jewish Anti-Fascist Committee, the Sovinformburo, and Lozovsky in particular, from responsibility. I also believe that in spite of the fact that I

---

*The JAC minutes of October 21, 1948 can be found in ibid., pp. 404–408.

[†]Solomon Slepak (1893–1978) had a long, complicated history as a veteran Bolshevik. See Chaim Potok, *The Gates of September: Chronicles of the Slepak Family* (New York, 1996). His son Vladimir became a well-known Jewish refusenik in Moscow in the 1970s and 1980s.

was on the Jewish Anti-Fascist Committee, I did not engage in any espionage, did not attend any illegal gatherings (in some people's testimony it says that there were various gatherings). You have heard from the testimony of the members of the Jewish Anti-Fascist Committee seated here that they did not even say everything in front of us—when the additional members of the presidium were present. For that reason I hope that the court will take this into account and draw the appropriate conclusions. If, of course, the court believes that mere membership of the presidium of the Jewish Anti-Fascist Committee, the fact that I was considered a member of the presidium, is enough to be indicted on all points, then that, of course, is for the court to decide. But it seems to me that even though I have been through a great deal emotionally during the investigation, I do not feel guilty either as a nationalist or as a spy for the benefit of America. I was never a nationalist or an American spy and have no plans to become either one.

[At 4 P.M., the presiding officer announced a recess in the proceedings.

On the same day, June 6, a closed judicial session was held. It began late in the evening. At 8:50 P.M., the chairman, Lieutenant General of Justice Cheptsov, announced that defendant Fefer had requested a closed session, that is, without the other defendants present. At this session, Fefer repudiated his testimony and confessed that he was an agent of the MGB under the pseudonym Zorin.]

Statements by Isaac Fefer and Joseph Yuzefovich in Closed Judicial Session

[Fefer testified that in 1943, immediately upon his arrival in the United States, he was summoned by General Zarubin, an MGB officer at the Soviet Embassy. Zarubin proposed that he coordinate all of his actions with him and maintain constant contact with him and his colleague Klarin. Fefer also related that he had given the MGB detailed reports about his activity. Fefer reported the following facts, which revealed the secret mechanism of how the trial was prepared and how the role he was given was prepared as well.]

Fefer: In court I gave confused testimony because even after I "signed" article 206, I was called in by the MGB and warned that I must give the court the same testimony that I had given during the preliminary investigation. And on the night of my arrest Abakumov told me that if I did not provide a full confession in my testimony, then I would be beaten. So I grew frightened, which was the reason why I gave incorrect testimony during the preliminary investigation and then partially confirmed it in court.

I did not plead guilty in court to espionage. My testimony about Goldberg being an enemy of the Soviet Union and a spy was pure fabrication.

I tried to deny this, but because I feared that Abakumov's and Likhachev's threats would be carried out, I started signing the interrogation records that the investigator drew up in my absence. I said the whole time during the investigation that I didn't believe that Goldberg was a spy and that there was nothing to confirm this.

[Fefer gave the same assessment of the alleged espionage contacts with Rosenberg. Further on Fefer turned to other subjects.]

Fefer: I spoke of this during the investigation, but I was told that my arguments had no basis, and they persisted in demanding that I give names of the comrades who were in charge, who allegedly helped us on the question of creating a Jewish republic in the Crimea. I was forced to name Lozovsky as the person who read our memorandum addressed to Comrades Stalin and Molotov.

Then Abakumov demanded that I tell him about Kaganovich and his attitude toward the Crimea question. He asked about Mekhlis and whether it was true that the Americans had summoned him to America.

Likhachev asked about our conversation with Comrade Molotov concerning the creation of a Jewish republic in the Crimea and about his attitude toward this question, saying that Abakumov himself would interrogate me about this in detail.

During a subsequent interrogation Abakumov told me that at an interrogation in which a Central Committee representative was involved, I should confirm that I had seen Zhemchuzhina at the synagogue in Moscow.

I was so mixed up that at the witness confrontation with Zhemchuzhina at the Central Committee I confirmed that I had seen her at the synagogue, although that had not actually happened.

Abakumov gave me this order in Likhachev's presence.

Another of the investigators' fabrications was the statement that Zhemchuzhina, supposedly in a conversation with me, accused Comrade Stalin of having a hostile attitude toward Jews. With Zhemchuzhina, with whom, incidentally, I never talked at all, I did not have any conversation like this, nor did I with anyone else, either.

[Fefer confirmed once again that he had been threatened with physical punishments, and he again denied the charges against him.]

Fefer: Investigator Likhachev said to me during the preliminary investigation: "If we arrested you, that means we will find a crime. We will 'beat out' of you everything that we need." And this is in fact what happened. I am not a criminal, but being terribly frightened, I fabricated testimony against myself and others. . . . The charges facing us members of the Jewish Anti-Fascist Committee—in particular, the charge of espionage, of sending classified materials to America, allegedly in accordance with our agreement with reactionaries—is not based on any proof at all. It is built on sand. And it could be no other way, because none of this ever happened. I have nothing more to add to my testimony.

[At 9:10 P.M., the presiding officer announced that the judicial session was over.

Twenty minutes later the next closed judicial session of the Military Collegium of the USSR Supreme Court took place with the same group of participants.

This time Yuzefovich gave testimony about the statement that he had made in court. He reported that back in 1938 he had signed a document for the State Security agencies in which he pledged that he would collaborate with them. His task included clarifying the sentiments of Soviet Yiddish writers. Yuzefovich said that insofar as these people had suspected something, they had not held incriminating conversations in his presence, so he had been unable to provide the MGB with any compromising information about them. Later Yuzefovich stated that "in late 1938 I requested that I be released from the commitment that I had signed, since all of my attempts to provide any information had been unsuccessful, and I was let go." His concluding remarks follow.]

Yuzefovich: At the very beginning of the investigation I gave truthful testimony and told the investigators that I did not feel I had committed any crime.

   I also said that I knew nothing about any crimes committed by Lozovsky. After this, Minister of State Security Abakumov summoned me and said that if I did not confess, then he would transfer me to Lefortovo prison, where I would be beaten. They had already been working me over and softening me up for several days before that. I answered Abakumov with a refusal, and then I was transferred to Lefortovo prison, where they started beating me with a rubber truncheon and trampling me when I fell. Because of this I decided to sign any testimony whatsoever just to make it to the trial. I think that in the Soviet Union the court can set everything right. I have nothing more to add to my testimony.

[At 9:55 P.M., the closed judicial session ended. The next session began on June 7 at 12:45 P.M.]

Testimony by the Defendants

SOLOMON BREGMAN CONTINUED

Presiding Officer: Who among the defendants has questions for defendant Bregman?

Lozovsky: I do, but first of all I would like to add a point of information. Bregman spoke here about how I deceived and tricked him and how I forgot that I was a member of the Central Committee. And you, Citizen Chairman, cited several lines from Sheinin's testimony that speak of how he was in my office with Bregman and how I told them that they had gotten onto the presidium in order to cover up the nationalistic line of the Jewish Anti-Fascist Committee.

In connection with this I would like to state the following: I called Bregman in to see me in late June or early July 1944—I don't remember precisely when—having arranged that in advance with Shcherbakov, and I told Bregman that Shcherbakov had instructed me to talk with him. I told him what the committee stood for and that we needed to find a group of Bolsheviks, because in its operations the committee kept getting involved with things which were beyond its responsibilities and functions. He gave me several names, the only one of which I recognized was Gubelman, but I did not know him well, and I had never laid eyes on the others, Brikker* and Sheinin. I gave these names to Shcherbakov, and he told me that I could speak with them. After this I called in all four of them, not only Bregman, and told them the same thing I had told Bregman earlier. You can imagine what I said to those four people: "Go to the committee! Help camouflage its nationalistic work! Be more cautious in implementing nationalistic policies!" I know why the investigator wrote it. Let Sheinin himself explain why he signed it, but anyone with any common sense can see that there's not an ounce of truth in it.

The second thing has to do with my deceiving Bregman about *The Black Book*. How could he not know what *The Black Book* was for? How could he, the chairman of the commission, not know that? I immediately adopted a number of proposals from the commission about omitting several chapters. There are two long telegrams that were sent to the Artists' Union about what needed to be taken out. This was done on the basis of the commission's proposals. Two Russians were brought onto the commission, Troyanovsky and Severin, so that they could look over the materials as well. After the draft of the book came back with the Americans' changes added to it, printed in English, I again gave it to Troyanovsky and Borodin (who knew English) so that they could have a final say about whether there was anything unacceptable there. In this connection another telegram went out about how a number of other parts needed to be removed. This is why I state that if Bregman didn't see anything in that book, then he should say that he was guilty of an oversight.

Third, Bregman never talked to me about *Eynikayt*. He himself said here that he read Yiddish with difficulty. Bregman talked with me about other things: about how the presidium of the Jewish Anti-Fascist Committee was organized undemocratically, how disorder reigned there. But that's why he and the others were sent there, to create some order.

Bregman said that I displayed a particular predilection for the Jewish Anti-Fascist Committee. This committee was one of sixteen departments of

*V. Brikker was president of the Film Workers' Union. After he became a member of the JAC in 1944, he was appointed to the presidium.

the Sovinformburo, and apart from the Sovinformburo I was responsible for twenty Latin American countries and all of the Far East. If I did have a predilection for the Jewish committee, still, I never attended its banquets, whereas I did attend the Slavic committee banquets. General Gundorov* and Colonel Mochalov can confirm this. I was there because they received dignitaries, and I attended these banquets in my capacity as deputy foreign minister.

Bregman was a member of the presidium of the Jewish Anti-Fascist Committee for four years and four months from July 1944 until the end of 1948. During those four years and four months the committee was still a part of the Sovinformburo for two years, and during the other two years and four months it was outside the Sovinformburo system and was directly subordinate to the Foreign Policy Department of the Central Committee. Bregman said here that he spoke to me several times about the squabbles going on at the Jewish Anti-Fascist Committee, and he said that I didn't do anything about his complaints. But he knows where Old Square is located. He is known at the Central Committee. All the secretaries, including Comrade Stalin, the party leader, know him. He could have written to any of them that he had seen things, that he had gone to Lozovsky, who said and did nothing about it. Bregman said that in 1948 he was in Shumeiko's office. Is once in two years enough? It seems to me that if Shumeiko didn't do anything, then Bregman should have written to the Central Committee secretary and complained about me and about everyone else. So in connection with this I would like to know when and where Bregman found out that I was a secret enemy of the party (that is what it says in the investigation reports, and he signed them). And did he know, when he took the assignment from me to go and work as a presidium member at the Jewish Anti-Fascist Committee, that I was an enemy of the party, or did the investigator prompt him to say that and he simply signed it?

Presiding Officer: Defendant Bregman, do you understand the question?

Bregman: Yes. As to the question of whether I myself knew that Lozovsky was a secret enemy of the party or whether the investigator urged that on me, I can say the following: No one prompted me to say that. I came to that conclusion after I learned during the investigation that the Jewish Anti-Fascist Committee had been transformed into a center for espionage and nationalism, and since Lozovsky ran this organization without any intermediaries, Lozovsky should have been responsible for all the committee's operations. On this basis I told the investigator that only a secret enemy of the party could have allowed such behavior and such an attitude toward the organization. But I never drew or stated the conclusion that Lozovsky was always a secret enemy of the party.

*Alexander Gundorov (1895–1973) was a lieutenant general of engineering troops. He served as chairman of the Anti-Fascist All-Slav Committee.

[On June 7 at 2:10 P.M., the presiding officer announced a recess. At 2:45 P.M., the judicial session resumed. It began with the testimony of Talmy.]

LEON TALMY

Leon Talmy embodied a variety of twentieth-century Jewish enthusiasms. Born in the small Belorussian town of Lyakhovichi, Talmy—his real name was Leyzer Talmovitsky—was the second of seven brothers and three sisters. In 1912, Talmy and his younger brother Isaac emigrated to the United States in order to spare Isaac the privilege of serving in the tsar's army. They traveled to Sioux City, Iowa, and then to Chicago, where relatives of theirs had settled earlier. But Talmy grew tired of life in the American Midwest and made his way to New York to pursue a career as a journalist working within Yiddish socialist circles. New York, too, proved to be a way station, for with the triumph of the October Revolution, Talmy needed to see for himself how the Bolsheviks were beginning to transform Russia. He returned in 1917 and stayed for four years, witnessing the turmoil of the Civil War and establishing contact with the Comintern. In 1921, Talmy married Sonia Rosenberg in Kiev before leaving for America, eventually embarking on a boat from Bremen to New York. This time, however, Talmy was not a young, greenhorn refugee; on instructions from the Comintern, he was hoping to establish a pro-Soviet communist party in the United States.

Back in New York, Talmy soon befriended the well-known figure William Z. Foster; together they helped to found the American Communist Party. At the same time, Talmy resumed his career as a journalist, using his visit to Soviet Russia as the basis for numerous articles, particularly in the *Morgen Freiheit* and the *Nation* magazine; the latter, beginning in the 1920s, maintained a decades-long infatuation with the Soviet Union. Talmy wrote about Soviet culture and industrial development and about Yiddish literature and may have been the first to translate verses by Vladimir Mayakovsky into English for an American publication. Talmy, in fact, was prominent enough in New York to host Mayakovsky during the poet's visit to the United States in 1924; Talmy's only child, Vladimir, was born earlier that year, and Mayakovsky rocked the baby in his arms. The following year, another prominent Soviet poet (and the husband of Isadora Duncan), Sergei Esenin, also came to New York, where Talmy again played a role in showing him the city.*

*Vladimir Talmy (son of Leon Talmy), interview with author, North Potomac, Md., 1997.

As Talmy's articles make clear, there can be no doubt of his enthusiastic support for the Soviet experiment. In Moscow and Petrograd, he insisted, "no two [newspapers] are quite alike in character. Each one . . . has its distinct individuality, which makes it easier to distinguish between two newspapers in collectivist communist Russia than in individualist America."* When he wrote about "Jews under the Soviet regime" in 1923, he focused entirely on official efforts in Belorussia and the Ukraine to provide resources for Jews to rebuild their communities after pogroms. Most notably, Talmy emphasized efforts to settle Jews on land where they could lead productive lives after centuries of being forbidden to engage in a broad range of professions. He also had praise for the "first State Jewish Theater in history," the Moscow theater that Solomon Mikhoels would lead for so many years before his murder in January 1948. In the same article, Talmy also praised the efforts of the American Jewish Joint Distribution Committee for its generous efforts in Russia, providing famine relief and training in handicrafts and agriculture.† Little could Talmy imagine how his destiny would be tied to the death of Mikhoels and the slander of the "Joint" by Stalin's appointed interrogators.

Among Talmy's articles in the 1920s, however, none expressed his full faith, as a Jew, in revolution more vividly than "Yiddish Literature: A Product of Revolt." Here Talmy gave full expression to his romantic hope in a socialist utopia, where Yiddish literature would be able to establish itself "as the vigorous artistic expression of the new life begotten by the revolution." Suddenly, Lenin's triumph had thrust Jews into the center of European politics. "The Jewish masses," Talmy wrote, "were shot out of their inertia and forced as active participants into the very midst of world history. The new Jewish personality which was hammered out in these struggles merged itself with the group—not of the passive herd, but a group determined to fight for the mastery of life, for the possession of the world, determined to conquer and build life anew."‡ But the revolution that Talmy was celebrating did not mark the rebirth of Yiddish literature. It marked the beginning of a tragic chapter whose climax would overtake him as well.

Talmy's commitment to the regime involved more than political or

---

*Leon Talmy, "The Soviet Press," *The Nation*, November 7, 1923, p. 519.
†Leon Talmy, "Jews Under the Soviet Regime," *The Nation*, November 7, 1923, p. 533.
‡Leon Talmy, "Yiddish Literature: A Product of Revolt," *The Nation*, August 8, 1923, p. 139.

cultural enthusiasms. By the mid-1920s he was heavily involved in ICOR (in 1925 he became executive secretary), an organization established by pro-Soviet American Jews to promote the agricultural settlement of Jews on Soviet territory. In 1928, when the regime announced the creation of a Jewish autonomous district in Birobidzhan, ICOR, and Talmy personally, became a mainstay of the project.

In 1929, together with another émigré (and later fellow defendant), Ilya Vatenberg, Talmy helped to organize a scientific expedition to Birobidzhan. He successfully recruited Franklin Harris, a distinguished agronomist and president of Brigham Young University, in Utah. They traveled together across the Soviet Union to Birobidzhan, where they spent two months evaluating the territory for agricultural development. Talmy and his colleagues explored hundreds of square miles on horseback with the hope of confirming its future prospects. Their trip was often strenuous and demanding, requiring them to contend with heavy rains and swarms of mosquitoes. During their visit, they met with prominent Soviet officials, including Alexei Rykov, chairman of the Council of Ministers, and with leaders of Jewish colonization efforts. After leaving the Soviet Union, they met with Jewish community leaders in Germany, France, and England. Upon returning to the United States, Harris maintained his enthusiasm for the project. On the way from New York to Utah by train, he stopped in Boston, Baltimore, Philadelphia, Chicago, and other cities to speak about Birobidzhan and encourage support for its development. His audiences, which most often met in synagogues, numbered in the hundreds and frequently included acknowledged leaders of the community, like Julius Rosenwald, head of Sears, Roebuck in Chicago. Harris kept in touch with Talmy for a time and always regarded his trip to Birobidzhan as a highlight of his professional career.* Talmy, soon after his return to America, wrote about the trip in the *Morgen Freiheit* and provided a more extensive account in a Yiddish-language book called *On Virgin Soil.*†

*Franklin Harris (1884–1960), president of Brigham Young University from 1921 to 1945, was the author of several books on agriculture and more than six hundred scientific papers, bulletins, and articles. Two diaries have been preserved about the 1929 expedition to Birobidzhan, one by Harris himself and a second, more expansive version, which he dictated to his secretary Kiefer B. Sauls. Some correspondence between Harris and Leon Talmy is also available. I am indebted to Russ Taylor of the Special Collections and Manuscripts Division of the Harold B. Lee Library of Brigham Young University in Provo, Utah, and to Janet Jensen, the granddaughter of Dr. Harris, for their generous assistance to my research efforts.

†Leon Talmy, *Af royer erd* (On Virgin Soil) (New York, 1931).

Talmy's life changed abruptly once more. In 1930 his wife, Sonia, went to Detroit to recruit Ford engineers for an automobile plant in the Soviet city of Nizhny Novgorod. Like her husband, she was a convinced communist, and in 1931 she took their American-born son with her to Russia to provide further assistance to these American workers. The following year Talmy joined his family in Nizhny Novgorod; then all three moved to Moscow, where he became a translator in a publishing house. His skills soon brought him prestigious assignments; for example, he was asked to render the works of Lenin and Stalin into English. In the 1930s the party trusted him. A decade later, that trust dissolved.

Presiding Officer: Defendant Talmy, testify to the court, to what do you plead guilty?

Talmy: I do not plead guilty to the crimes attributed to me in the indictment. I did not commit the crimes attributed to me in the indictment, and I did not carry out any espionage against the Soviet Union to aid America or any other country. I was never involved in a Jewish nationalistic underground, and never in my life did I carry out hostile activity against the Communist Party and the Soviet government, as stated in the wording of the indictment.

Presiding Officer: And what about the spirit of the indictment?

Talmy: I have already said that I do not plead guilty to any of the crimes attributed to me. I will testify later about how all of that is nothing but words with no proof to corroborate them. I ask that before I move on to biographical information, I be allowed to make several statements. I made these statements to the investigators, including the public prosecutor Colonel Prikhodko in the presence of an investigator while signing a document concerning the end of the investigation. At the time they said that I could make these statements to the court. On the first day, when I was served with the indictment, I filed an appeal about the inclusion in the case materials of my own handwritten testimony, on which the interrogation records dated September 7, 26, and 28, 1950, were based. The thing is that these reports contain testimony that I gave to the investigator Lieutenant Colonel Artemov. He told me that I could give either written or oral testimony, and I chose to give written testimony. I first wrote fifty-three pages, and then I wrote an additional ten to fifteen pages, and then the investigator told me that this was not enough, so I wrote an additional twenty-three pages. In a word, all of my handwritten testimony took up between ninety and one hundred pages. The thing is that the investigator put them into a question-and-answer format in the records dated September 1950.

Presiding Officer: Do you mean the interrogation record that was done with prosecutor Novikov present?

Talmy: Prosecutor Novikov did not really interrogate me. In my presence he dictated to a stenographer questions and answers from my testimony, which I had given earlier. True, at the time I did not understand what was happening, and when I was shown the records later on, I didn't understand why I was supposed to sign them. In fact, this was not a transcript of the interrogation, because he himself had dictated the whole record to a stenographer without asking me any questions and without hearing out my answers, except for two or three. In general, I would like to say that my testimony was recorded in a distorted manner; it either greatly exaggerates my role in the committee's activity or distorts it. I did not think about this at the time, and it was only later that I began pointing out this exaggerated testimony.

I would like to tell the court why I experienced such a flash of insight and how I reexamined my assessment of all of these matters. This happened because in late July 1950, after fourteen months of nocturnal interrogations and illness, Lieutenant Colonel Artemov, who was handling my case, gave me Comrade Lenin's and Comrade Stalin's statements about the national question and specifically how it applied to the Jewish question. And although I was already familiar with many of these statements, in particular about the assimilation of the Jews, they now appeared different to me. Before I had not understood, cut off as I was from the Jewish question. After I read what Lieutenant Colonel Artemov had given me, I asked him not to summon me for a while and give me a chance to think. I felt that the scales had fallen from my eyes. It became clear to me that all of this work in the Soviet Union in the area of Jewish culture, which had been carried out under the banner of Soviet power and supposedly with the Central Committee's consent, was in fact wrong. Evidently, some group of Jewish nationalists, who had wormed their way into senior positions, had misled the Soviet government and party organs. It became clear to me that the whole policy of building Jewish schools, museums, and vocational training institutes was, at its root, flawed and wrong. It was clear to everyone who had anything to do with Jewish culture that it was absolutely wrong to place all the emphasis on the Yiddish language. It was wrong to think that world culture in its entirety should be only in Yiddish. There was no need for everything to be in Yiddish for the Jewish people to develop their culture.

Presiding Officer: During the investigation (vol. 21, p. 24) you testified as follows: "We studied the entire territory of Birobidzhan in detail, familiarized ourselves with the type of soil there, with agriculture, climatic conditions, industrial capabilities, and the conditions in which people lived. Upon our return to the United States, we published a book in Yiddish and English in which we described in detail all that we had managed to learn about Birobidzhan."

Talmy: That is absolutely correct, but I would like to say that we were in Birobidzhan for five weeks. This area, thirty-five thousand square kilometers
[13,500 square miles], still has uninhabited parts. In this five-week period
we covered more than a thousand kilometers [620 miles] on foot, on trac-
tors, and on horseback. But we could not study the whole area in that period of time. My book *On Virgin Soil* describes very clearly what the expedition to Birobidzhan did. I wrote the book *On Virgin Soil* with the
feelings of a communist, with a feeling of love and respect for the Soviet
Union.

Presiding Officer: You say that you wrote this book with the feeling of a communist. But this is not apparent from the expert commission's conclusions.
"In his book *On Virgin Soil,* Talmy deals with Soviet reality from hostile
anti-Soviet positions. Under the guise of 'objectivism' he gives a slanderous
picture of life in the Soviet Far East and of Soviet people that has nothing in
common with reality."

Defendant Talmy, what else can you say about the expert commission's
conclusions?

Talmy: I have already cited a number of examples to show how tendentiously
the commission's report was drawn up. Even the indictment does not accuse me of having written the book from an anti-Soviet point of view, although the author of the indictment was not too concerned about providing an underpinning of more substantial proof for all of the allegations
made against me.

Presiding Officer: But you said directly that you do not deny the commission's
conclusions. And no one forced you to sign those interrogation records, did
they?

Talmy: In general, I did not sign anything under coercion. I want to say that if
I had been arrested as a communist in a bourgeois country, then I would
have known how to behave. In that case I would have known that there
was an enemy facing me and that I should behave with him as I would with
an enemy, and I would have had the fortitude not to give him any testimony. But when I faced a Soviet investigator, although he stated that I was
an enemy, I did not look upon him as an enemy, but as a Soviet person. I
have to say that in this situation I didn't know how to behave. After the
first week of interrogation, when Lieutenant Colonel Kuzmishin started
handling my case, he showed me the indictment and wrote a report in
which the first question was "Do you plead guilty to the charges made
against you?" I answered that I did not plead guilty to these charges. He
didn't write this down but instead noted that I pled guilty to being a member of the petit bourgeois nationalistic party Fareynikte in 1917. I told him
that I did not plead guilty at all. He quoted me a passage from Gorky saying that if an enemy doesn't surrender, then he should be destroyed. I
started to object that it was not yet proven that I was an enemy, but he

replied that since I had been arrested, that already meant that I was an enemy. He also informed me that I had no right to tell him what to write and what not to write in the interrogation records, and that I could object only when I believed that the investigator was wrong.

The investigator who told me this signed as the director of the MGB investigation division for especially important cases. How could I not believe him? After all, this was a Soviet man saying this, who had been invested with the trust of Soviet power. In addition, I should tell you about the psychological aspect to things introduced by Lieutenant Colonel Artemov when he gave me a selection of statements on the Jewish question by Comrades Lenin and Stalin to read, after which I reevaluated certain facts. I felt grateful to him for giving me this selection to read. It was his way of acknowledging that I was a Soviet person and that I could speak with him in the same language.

During an investigation, the investigator is the only live person you associate with. He's a Soviet person, and you don't feel like arguing with him over every word. After all, I thought, I will be judged by my actions, not by my words.

Presiding Officer: Why did you sign testimony that was wrong?

Talmy: I didn't feel like arguing over every word. I had already been in solitary confinement for twenty-nine months.

Presiding Officer: It's all true. If it weren't true, you shouldn't have signed.

Talmy: There is some truth here, but I didn't accentuate anti-Soviet statements, and the testimony about that is exaggerated. Because Bergelson had read the book, he translated it to the investigator. I would like to ask him whether I correctly conveyed various quotations in my testimony to the court.

Presiding Officer: Bergelson, do you consider Talmy's testimony on his book *On Virgin Soil* to be correct?

Bergelson: It is correct in a certain way. The main thing is that Talmy helped foreigners inspect everything there was in Birobidzhan. From the point of view of this court, it seemed to me that such things should not have been done—foreigners should not have been brought to Birobidzhan.

Talmy: If you read the book objectively, without a preconceived opinion, then you would see right away that there is nothing anti-Soviet, nationalistic, or classified in it, and there is nothing that reveals any state secrets. So I believe that in the commission's conclusions the book is discredited absolutely without basis, and white is presented as black.

I want to know whether Vatenberg recalls that the book was first published in 1930 in the *Morgen Freiheit*. Would it have been possible to publish an anti-Soviet book in the *Morgen Freiheit* back then?

Vatenberg: In response to the first question, articles about the trip to Birobidzhan were printed in the *Morgen Freiheit,* but I cannot say that they were in the same form as was later described in the book. The *Morgen Freiheit* was and is a communist paper, published by the Central Committee of the American Communist Party, and, clearly, an anti-Soviet book could not have been printed there. To the contrary, I think that these articles of Talmy's had a positive effect, as did the book, in refuting all attacks on the Soviet Union about resettling Jews to Birobidzhan.

Talmy: I think that that about settles the question of my book. So, I found a job at the *Morgen Freiheit,* where Olgin* was editor in chief, and the managing editor was Novick, who, at the time, was traveling around Europe. I had to handle his responsibilities. This lasted a year or a year and a half. And this whole time I kept raising the question of being allowed to go back to the Soviet Union.

Presiding Officer: With whom did you raise this question?

Talmy: With the Communist Party.

Presiding Officer: Did you raise the question officially?

Talmy: Yes. Completely officially. First of all, even after eleven years in America, I just couldn't get acclimated and never felt at home there. Besides, I had never had any thoughts of staying in America for good. I felt at home there only when I was among communists.

Presiding Officer: During the preliminary investigation you said that you arrived in the Soviet Union with hostile assignments.

Talmy: That's not true.

Presiding Officer: How can it not be true? Here is your testimony (vol. 22, p. 14): "Upon leaving America, I received from the Jewish nationalistic organization ICOR an assignment to be its representative on the presidium of OZET [Society for the Settlement of Jewish Toilers on the Land]. My accomplice in nationalistic work at ICOR, the Jewish nationalist Vatenberg, received a similar assignment upon leaving America. He arrived in the USSR in 1933, about half a year after I did."

The investigator informed you about Vatenberg and asked a question. "We arrested your accomplice Vatenberg, and during an interrogation on May 26, 1949, he testified that he arrived in the Soviet Union with assignments to carry out espionage that he had received from Almazov,[†] the gen-

---

*Moissaye Olgin (Moses Joseph Novomisky) (1878–1939) came to the United States in 1914. He had been arrested in Russia as a member of the Bund. He later became a member of the Central Committee of the American Communist Party. He served as an American correspondent for *Pravda* and as editor of the *Morgen Freiheit* from 1922 until his death in 1939. It was Olgin who first blamed the Hebron riots on British imperialism and then on the Jews.

[†]Sol Almazov (1888?–1979) (Sol Pearl) was a longtime contributor to the *Morgen Freiheit*. Born in the Ukraine, he came to the United States in 1922.

eral secretary of ICOR. Did Almazov give you an assignment?" To this
question you answered, "Yes." You were asked, "What did it consist of?"
What can you say about this?

Talmy: This "yes" does not have to do with receiving a similar assignment to
carry out espionage. It has to do with receiving an assignment to be ICOR's
representative at OZET. Almazov gave me an assignment similar to the one
he gave Vatenberg, but that doesn't mean that I received an assignment to
carry out espionage. In addition to this, I received some other instructions
that I didn't turn down. Olgin, the editor of the *Morgen Freiheit,* and the
Jewish Bureau of the Central Committee of the American Communist
Party asked me to write for the communist *Morgen Freiheit* from the Soviet
Union. I promised to do so, because I knew that it was very important for
this newspaper to show that it was the only newspaper in the United States
that had the right to have a correspondent in the Soviet Union. This was
useful for its work, and I agreed to it. The investigator described this assignment as "nationalistic and a form of espionage."

Presiding Officer: Defendant Talmy, where did you work before the war?

Talmy: For five years I worked as head of the English section of the Foreign
Languages Publishing House. By this time the major works of Marxism-
Leninism had come out in English for the first time—Marx-Engels and a
twelve-volume collection of Lenin's and Stalin's writings. They came out
during the period when I was heading the publishing house. I translated
and edited them myself. During my tenure there, a number of works were
published by government assignment—for example, the transcripts of the
Metro-Vickers trial of 1933, the trial of Zinoviev in 1936 and then
Bukharin's in 1938, and a whole series of similar transcripts.* I had to
spend forty hours working at the printer's. The publication of these transcripts was organized so that a day or two after a trial ended, a book in English was already prepared and could be sent wherever needed.

Presiding Officer: When and by whose recommendation did you start working at the Sovinformburo?

Talmy: In 1941, when the war started, I enlisted in the home guard, on July 2,
came to the assembly place, was entered as a member of a unit, and was ordered to show up on a certain day to be sent to the front. When I came with
my knapsack and all of the things I needed to the assembly place, I and others were then told, "Go back to work. You will be told when you need to
come." That was around July 10.

   Around July 12, the director of the publishing house summoned me and
said there had been a call from the Sovinformburo with a request that I and

---

*The Metro-Vickers trial involved eighteen defendants, including six British citizens who
were accused of "wrecking" electric power stations. Several defendants were actually acquitted. The trial of Grigory Zinoviev (1883–1936), a close associate of Lenin's, was held in
August 1936. The trial of Nikolai Bukharin (1889–1938) took place in March 1938.

two other employees go to see Lozovsky. The three of us went. When we arrived at the Central Committee, I was directed to a room where I found my old acquaintance Rokotov. At one time he had been the editor of the magazine *Inostrannaya Literatura* (Foreign Literature) and had edited English publications. He said to me, "We have recommended you for a job at the Sovinformburo." As he explained to me, the Union of Soviet Writers was forming a propaganda bureau as part of the Sovinformburo, which would send articles by well-known Soviet writers to the English-language press, and I was supposed to translate them. Because this was a more important job, directly related to the war, I agreed. Then I was directed to Lozovsky's office. There were several people there, including Litvakov's wife. There was a small meeting about how to organize this translation office. And I started to work at the Sovinformburo around July 16, 1941.

[Talmy gave the following testimony about his work at the Jewish Anti-Fascist Committee.]

Talmy: Sometimes we were invited to banquets and meetings, and our activity at the committee, specifically mine, was limited to this. Kvitko said here that I never talked about committee affairs. This is confirmed by the fact that Epshteyn, who was the person closest to me, never came to me to discuss committee affairs. He always went to Shimeliovich instead. In general, I did not play any role at the committee, and in addition, on February 15, 1942, I left Kuibyshev and went to work at the Sovinformburo in Moscow. At the time, Lozovsky was in Kuibyshev, where the committee was as well. In Moscow my immediate boss was Kruzhkov. During that period I didn't have any ties to the committee.

Lozovsky: So what happened was that part of the Sovinformburo staff returned to Moscow. At the time, Shcherbakov was in Moscow and I was in Kuibyshev. I was constantly receiving telegrams from Moscow ordering me to send translators, and that was why in February, Talmy was sent to Moscow, where he worked until we came back.

Presiding Officer: How long did Talmy work in Moscow?

Lozovsky: He worked there from February 1942 until the end of August 1943.

Talmy: It was during this period that I first participated in the Jewish Anti-Fascist Committee's activity—it was at the third plenum. I do not want to hide anything from the court, and so I should tell you that on the eve of Fefer's departure for America, I had a brief conversation with him. Fefer arrived in Moscow, and I think he brought me a letter from Vatenberg, with whom I was friendly. And when Fefer gave me the letter and said that he was going to America, he asked my advice about how to conduct himself in America. He asked me about this because I had lived there. First, I had heard that Mikhoels liked to drink, and I warned Fefer that there were a lot of enemies in America who would use every slipup for their own purposes.

The second piece of advice had to do with the following: I warned Fefer that people would try to strike up an acquaintance with him and he should be fearful of this. People like Levit [Leivick]* and Opatoshu would turn up, who, I emphasized, were irreconcilable enemies of the Soviet Union and who would try to use Yiddish literature as a way of hooking up with our delegation in order to derive some benefit for themselves. I said the same thing about Nadel [Nadir], a former *Morgen Freiheit* employee.

Presiding Officer: Defendant Fefer, did such a conversation take place?

Fefer: I don't remember exactly whether there was a conversation about Nadel [Nadir], because I think that he died before our trip. As to Levit [Leivick] and Opatoshu, Talmy did indeed warn me about them. But I didn't need these warnings, for I had always been in open conflict with them in the press, and we had spoken out against them in the *Morgen Freiheit*. As it was, our delegation was under the consulate's strict control.

Talmy: So my activity at the committee was limited to a speech at the third plenum of the Jewish Anti-Fascist Committee. Fefer gave a report on his trip to America. The report was given in a half-joking tone. Epshteyn asked me to speak, and I spoke. I said a few words.

Presiding Officer: And what can you say about the expert commission's conclusions about the nationalistic propaganda conducted by the Jewish Anti-Fascist Committee?

Talmy: When I read the expert commission's conclusions, I said that they were correct. I can confirm from my own experience that I believed, and believe today, that the very publication of *Eynikayt* was a nationalistic act. A newspaper is not only a collective agitator, but a collective organizer. Who and what did *Eynikayt* want to organize, and in whose name? You start thinking about this, and you realize that something fraudulent was going on. There was a regular section in *Eynikayt* describing the life of Jews abroad. Why should Soviet Jews be especially interested in the life of Jews abroad? What do they need it for? That in and of itself is nationalism.

Presiding Officer: And what did you go to synagogue for?

Talmy: I haven't been inside a synagogue for forty-five years.

Presiding Officer: But the case materials contain information about attendance by members of the Jewish Anti-Fascist Committee at a memorial service for victims of fascism?

Talmy: The attendance of members of the Jewish Anti-Fascist Committee at the memorial service was a manifestation of nationalism, but I was not there. I have not been in a synagogue at all since I was twelve years old.

---

*H. Leivick (Leyvik Halpern) (1888–1962), a poet and a playwright, is best known as the author of *The Golem* (1920). He and Moyshe Nadir quit the *Morgen Freiheit* in 1929 in protest over its pro-Arab coverage of the Hebron riots in Palestine. Fefer and other Jewish communists regularly attacked them.

Presiding Officer: So you were not there. And what was the demonstration that was organized for Meyerson's arrival?

Talmy: I heard that when Meyerson arrived at the synagogue, she was welcomed, and some people even kissed the hem of her dress. Later I talked about this with Vatenberg, because I was surprised and wondered where such a zealous manifestation of nationalism came from in the thirty-third year of the revolution. I was amazed—What do Soviet Jews have in common with the State of Israel? It is a tribe that is alien to us. We don't even have a common language. So when I thought over all of this once again, now already in prison, in order to understand where this burst of nationalism, this anti-Soviet demonstration, came from, I concluded that the Jewish Anti-Fascist Committee had become a sort of center around which nationalistic sentiments of the Jewish masses crystallized. And *Eynikayt* was one of the links organizing this nationalistic chain.

My subsequent thinking brought me to another source for the appearance of this nationalism. Bergelson has already said here that the Jewish religion is a crudely nationalistic religion, that it is entirely constructed upon the fact that the Jews are supposed to hope for the return of Palestine to them as the territory for their state. When the State of Israel did not yet exist, this was of no particular significance. But when the State of Israel became a reality, and Jews who are believers repeat every day that today we are here, but tomorrow we will be in the State of Israel (that is what the prayer says), this is of great significance. So when a representative of that state comes to them, they see in that person a messiah, and this is where such a nationalistic demonstration comes from.

Presiding Officer: Defendant Talmy, the court has no questions for you.

Talmy: Allow me to add something.

Presiding Officer: Please go ahead.

Talmy: I must emphasize once again that I had very little to do with the Yiddish Writers' Section. I was there three or four times. I do not take any particular credit for this, but I have not been interested in Yiddish literature since 1933. Vatenberg can confirm that he asked me why I didn't read Yiddish literature. I replied that I didn't read it because I felt it had no connection with the people. Why wasn't Hebrew a reality in the Soviet Union? Because it is not a language that live people speak. It's kind of artificial and lifeless, and this repelled me from Yiddish literature, all the more so because I was interested in a wide range of other things. True, I did purchase individual works, but I glanced through them in a superficial way.

Then I want to explain my passivity at the Jewish Anti-Fascist Committee, and this passivity can be easily checked upon and established. All that time, I worked at the Sovinformburo, and I should tell the court that I was let go from my job at the Sovinformburo on April 22, 1948. This happened when I learned that my son had been arrested in Berlin. I, of course, informed my boss, Troyanovsky, of this right away, and after a bit of time had passed, I was let go from my job.

Presiding Officer: In your testimony during the investigation you spoke of the staff of the Sovinformburo as being overgrown, about disorder in its work, and so on. Is this correct? Repeat it.

Talmy: I considered the way the Sovinformburo's leadership organized the work to be wrong. I believe that the mad rush to send as many articles abroad as possible caused quality to suffer in a number of cases. I did not consider this a great achievement. I should say that although I was not a Party member, I felt as if I were a Communist Party member, and so I considered it my obligation to state that this policy was wrong.

I should also say that the release from my job at the Sovinformburo on April 22, 1948, was a completely open act of self-protection on the part of Troyanovsky, because not only did I not stop receiving work, but they gave me very important assignments. The first project I got after I was let go was to check and translate Stalin's biography into English. This work was assigned to me, I did it, and I think I did it well, especially since Troyanovsky told me later that Heikin [Halkin] received a reprimand from the party for mistakes I found in a translation he had done earlier. I was also assigned to translate a report by Lysenko.*

And in the last months before my arrest I translated an article by a member of the Central Committee of the Chinese Communist Party, "Wang Xizhi," on the national question. This was an article directed against Tito's clique.† It was published first in *Pravda,* and I was assigned to translate it into English. I found a political mistake in *Pravda.* I called Troyanovsky's attention to it, and he agreed with me. There was a subheading that read, "The world is divided into those nations which are oppressed and those which oppress." I went to Troyanovsky and said, "How can someone say that, when there is the Soviet Union, where there are neither oppressors nor oppressed?" So it turns out that even in *Pravda* mistakes like that slip through. With Troyanovsky's permission I translated this part simply as follows: "Oppressed and oppressing nations." I cite this in order to show that if I had had nationalistic thoughts, I would not have noticed such a mistake. I was assigned to translate the magazine *The USSR Under Construction* into English. I translated one issue and did not have time to do any more.

---

*Trofim Lysenko (1898–1976) was a Soviet biologist, long favored by Stalin, who advanced a fraudulent theory of genetics that acquired traits can be inherited.

†Tito (Josip Broz) (1892–1980) was prime minister of Yugoslavia from 1945 to 1953 and president from 1953 to 1980. He had been in the resistance against the Germans during World War II. Under his leadership, Yugoslavia asserted its ideological and political independence from Stalin. The Chinese name was rendered phonetically in the original, and attempts to identify the member referred to have not so far been sucessful.

I also want to say that when I arrived in the Soviet Union in 1932–1933, it was the first time after long years of wandering that I felt I had found a homeland. I said that when I left for America in 1921, I was guided by nationalistic motives, and I cannot reproduce now how it was at that time, but of course these sentiments were there.

I was drawn to Jewish ways of life and Jewish ways of doing things, which were concentrated in New York City. But when I left there in 1932, this way of life repelled me; I couldn't take it any more. When I came to the Soviet Union, I felt that I was a member of the enormous Soviet people, and this was enough for me. I got wrapped up in my work, and everything that I do, as a rule I do wholeheartedly. I always get completely wrapped up in my work, and for that reason I have never felt free and unoccupied. I had no time for other goals. Of course, I went to the theater, to the Yiddish Section for literary evenings, but I did this infrequently. I was more interested in what was happening in Spain and China than in these Jewish affairs.

I would also like to say that my family, which is essentially my wife's family, her brothers, sisters, brothers-in-law, and sisters-in-law, were all, each and every one of them, party members or members of the Komsomol. And on top of that, the national makeup of this family was such that it included Ukrainians, Jews, and Russians. They were all friendly with one another.

I was friends with Vatenberg and his wife, Khayke Vatenberg. You can ask them whether during the entire period of our friendship they ever heard from me any statements of anti-Soviet views.

Presiding Officer: But I have already read out to you Khayke Vatenberg's testimony about that.

Talmy: If she testifies honestly, then she will repudiate it.

Presiding Officer: Why should she repudiate her testimony?

Talmy: I cannot say, but I know one thing, that I never made anti-Soviet statements. To the contrary, she complained in a narrow-minded way, which I sharply condemned. In December 1947, for example, after the ration system was eliminated, there were interruptions in deliveries of white bread, and many people complained about this, in particular Khayke Vatenberg. I told her then that I had just come from Nikitsky Gates, where I had seen people carrying white bread, so she was wrong to complain. Then Khayke Vatenberg said to me, "You don't have to stand in line, so you see everything through rose-colored glasses." Since I couldn't stand small-minded conversations, I yelled at her, and that ended the conversation.

My son was arrested in late 1947, and when I found out about it in February 1948, I did not demonstrate any mistrust and did not permit myself any conversations against Soviet justice.

Presiding Officer: And what was he arrested for?

Talmy: I don't know for sure.

Presiding Officer: There is information in the case materials.

Talmy: There is also his incorrect testimony about me. He could not have known that I was a Zionist or that I had been in the Bund, but he testifies about that. My son worked in the Economics Directorate of the Soviet Military Administration and received extremely favorable reviews there. Rudenko himself (a general), under whose direction he worked, gave excellent reviews of his work. I know that he was supposedly arrested for meeting with Americans.

Presiding Officer: He gave them some kind of information.

Talmy: He did not give any information. I was told at the military prosecutor's office that he was being accused under article 58-1b, and then the court changed the accusation to 58-10, part 2, and some other articles as well.

Presiding Officer: That means anti-Soviet conversations.

Talmy: That's not the point. He could not have had any anti-Soviet conversations. They found a book by that bastard Viktor Kravchenko in his room. And it seems to me that this was the main reason for his arrest.

Presiding Officer: So he was convicted for possession of counterrevolutionary literature.

Talmy: I am convinced that this book served as the grounds for his arrest. Out of foolishness he could not find the Soviet dignity in himself to refuse that book when presented with it. Why couldn't he refuse it? Because those foreigners told him that in the Soviet Union people are not allowed to read literature freely, and in order to prove the opposite, he agreed to take that book. It seems to me that this is the reason he was convicted. What that bastard deserved to have happen, happened instead to my son. I do not consider my son to be anti-Soviet or a criminal, although he received severe punishment. I did not condemn the Soviet justice system to anyone, and no one knew the true reason for my son's arrest. Troyanovsky, Vatenberg, and his wife were the only people whom I told that he had been arrested, and although I believed that my son had been arrested by mistake, I never once expressed indignation against Soviet power. To the contrary, I always expressed certainty that the Soviet justice system would correct this mistake.

I planned to have a meeting with my son to find out what was going on. I knew that he would tell me the whole truth and not lie. I wanted to collect all the material in order to know how to approach the authorities about rehabilitating my son. I had already purchased a ticket on the express train to Siberia, but I was arrested the next day. Then my apartment was searched. I had all sorts of notes, observations, and a journal which I kept having to do with my son's arrest. In this journal I recorded my thoughts, and all of this was examined and checked, as were letters I had received from my son, and they found nothing anti-Soviet in any of this. If anything anti-Soviet had been found, it would have turned up in the case materials.

I believe that I didn't protect my son and that I bear a large part of the guilt for what happened to him. When he came to Moscow in 1947 and said that some Americans had given him a gift and that he, not wishing to be beholden to them, wanted to give them something more valuable, instead of condemning that, I found nothing wrong in it. I found in it rather a wonderful expression of Soviet patriotism and a desire to show the Americans that we could give gifts far more beautiful and valuable than theirs. I went to a store at 10 Stanislavsky Street, which sold handicrafts, and chose several items made of ivory—a cigar case and some pipes. I paid over a thousand rubles for these things. My son gave them to the Americans. I wrote about this to the court when the case was being studied.

Presiding Officer: Instead of telling your son not to take gifts from these Americans, you pushed him to get involved with them.

Talmy: Yes, it seems that I myself pushed him into it.

Presiding Officer: In addition to 58-10, part 2, your son is accused of divulging state secrets.

Talmy: Yes. But the expert commission later found that no state secrets had been divulged.

Presiding Officer: In general, what you are saying is that in spite of the fact that your son was unjustly convicted, you did not condemn what happened.

Talmy: I never did. And I accused no one. There is one other important thing that I should recount, and that is why I received Novick and met with him. After all, he is a foreigner. I explained this to the prosecutor by saying that I believed that if in any way I gave Novick reason to feel that I was afraid to meet with him at that time, when there was a wave of slander about the "Iron Curtain," then that would have caused even more slander against the Soviet Union. After all, a person was coming whom I had known for twenty-five years. I believed it was my Soviet duty to meet with him.

Simonov wrote a play called *The Russian Question,** which tells about how a journalist named Smith comes to Moscow and how, because he met with Soviet people in the Soviet Union and spoke freely with them, he wrote a book favorable to the Soviet Union. So this play shows that it is possible to meet with foreigners. Our situation would have been strange if we had believed that all a Soviet person had to do was to meet with a foreigner to immediately cease being a Soviet person. My book *On Virgin Soil* tells how Soviet people spoke to foreigners with genuine dignity in 1929, and this should have been even more the case in 1949. We are stronger than all of these foreigners in every way, and we have nothing to fear from contacts with them.

---

*Konstantin Simonov's play can be found in Simonov, *Pyesy* (Plays) (Moscow, 1950), pp. 325–406.

I should add that in May 1949 a representative of the *Morgen Freiheit* came to Moscow again, to the Soviet Union, an artist well known in America, the cartoonist Grote [Gropper].* On May 2 or 3 he called me on the phone and said that at the moment he had a great deal of work and that he would be leaving on business in a few days. I asked him how long he would be in Moscow. He replied that he would soon be leaving for Leningrad and that he had come by invitation of VOKS [All-Union Society for Cultural Ties]. I didn't want to meet with him, because I felt that it was not good to meet with a foreigner, especially one from America, and at a time when we knew that the communist Zaltsman had not been given a visa to enter the USSR. I told Vatenberg at the time that when it was hard for Americans to get visas to come for an antiwar conference, one should deal with a person who had received a visa with extreme caution. This was why I didn't want to meet with Grote [Gropper]. In the end I didn't meet with him.

[On June 9 at 6:45 P.M., Vatenberg's testimony began.]

ILYA VATENBERG

Ilya Vatenberg and his wife, Khayke, were close friends of Leon and Sonia Talmy from their days together in New York. Ilya Vatenberg was born outside the Russian Empire, in the city of Stanislav, in Galicia, a province of the Austro-Hungarian Empire. As a young man, he was active in the left-wing Jewish movement Po'alei tsion (Workers of Zion), which had branches in Central and Eastern Europe, as well as in the United States. Like the Bund, Po'alei tsion advocated a socialist revolution on behalf of the working class and cultural autonomy for oppressed minorities, including the Jews, but unlike the Bund, Po'alei tsion also supported emigration to Palestine. Vatenberg was active in Europe and then in America, where his family emigrated in the early part of the century.

By the mid-1920s, Vatenberg had transferred his allegiance to the Bolsheviks and joined the American Communist Party. Like Leon Talmy, he was active in ICOR and visited Russia twice, in 1926 and 1929. Vatenberg was also an attorney; he graduated from Columbia Law School in 1926 at the age of thirty-nine under the name Elias Watenberg. He soon

---

*William Gropper (1897–1979) was a caricaturist associated with the *Morgen Freiheit* and many other radical and mainstream periodicals in New York. He was a leading figure among the social realist artists. His visit to the Warsaw Ghetto in 1948 deeply affected him and his work.

went to work for Amtorg, the Soviet trade agency that served as the
principal representative of Soviet interests in the United States until
diplomatic relations were established between the two countries in
1934. By then, Vatenberg had emigrated to the Soviet Union, reaching
Moscow to stay in 1933.

Presiding Officer: Defendant Vatenberg, do you plead guilty, and to what?

Vatenberg: I plead guilty to working for the Jewish Anti-Fascist Committee
for several months in 1942 and to writing a nationalistic article that was
broadcast on the radio to the United States. I also confess to being aware of
the nature of the articles sent by the Jewish Anti-Fascist Committee when it
was first in existence, and I knew to which bourgeois, reactionary press
outlets, agencies, and newspapers the committee was sending its material. I
do not plead guilty to espionage or hostile conspiracy.

Presiding Officer: Tell us briefly your life history.

Vatenberg: I was born in Austro-Hungary, in the province of Galicia, into a
poor Jewish family. My father was a woodcutter, and then a shipping receiver and a quality inspector, before emigrating to America, where he
worked in a garment factory fourteen hours a day, bent over a sewing machine. Only at the end of his life, when he was nearly seventy, did he become a real estate broker. In America I have a brother who is a lawyer and
a sister who is married to the manager of a movie theater.

[At the presiding officer's suggestion, Vatenberg recounted his whole life
story and told about his participation in the socialist movement in Galicia.
Embarking on the path of revolutionary struggle early in life, Vatenberg became a prominent figure in the Jewish socialist workers' party, Po'alei tsion.]

Vatenberg: I was in ICOR until 1927, when I was transferred by decree of the
Central Committee of the American Communist Party to a completely different sort of job—to a workers' housing cooperative. The political situation, as well as the housing situation and the situation in the party, had
grown quite complicated, and the party believed that fresh blood was
needed there. I was sent there. What happened was that a group of party
workers who were running this cooperative believed that Communism
could be achieved through cooperation while avoiding the class struggle
and revolution. And because, on top of this, they were also vegetarians, at
the summer camp cafeteria, which had been set up for workers who were
cooperative members, they had hung a large banner that read, "From veg-
etarianism to Communism." So, in a word, things had gotten quite complicated however you looked at it, and the party decided to transfer me
there to straighten things out.

At the OZET Congress, the Crimea question was the most pressing issue. A group of delegates led by Larin* presented a plan to drain the Sivash swamps and join this region to the northern Crimea in order to settle Jews there to create an autonomous Jewish republic. Even if draining the swamps would slow down settlement, a Jewish republic would be created nonetheless. Most people said that what was important was to settle as many Jews there as possible, to get them out of the situation they were in as quickly as possible and accustom them to physical labor.

Presiding Officer: Defendant Vatenberg, in 1926 you were in the Soviet Union, so why did you need to come back again in 1929?

Vatenberg: In 1929 there was a lot of discussion in the American press and within bourgeois society against setting aside the territory of Birobidzhan for Jewish settlement. The attacks on this plan were quite outlandish. People were saying that it shouldn't be done because there were Ussurian tigers there, and bears, that there was permafrost, that because it was Siberia it was not an appropriate place for resettlement, and that the Soviet government wanted to send Soviet Jews there on purpose so that they would be on the front lines in case of a Japanese attack. But there were also people in America who were vacillating on the issue, and our task was to prove to them that Soviet policy was correct. Of course, a Soviet government decree was all that ICOR needed. Those elements that were vacillating said after they heard our statements, "This is all true, but you haven't been there. Maybe there really is permafrost, so that it will be impossible to till the land there; maybe it's true that there is nothing but taiga, swamps, lakes, and water. What is the point in sending Jews there?" In order to convince those who were vacillating, in order to head off these attacks and prove that this was all slander, our commission was created. I don't remember whose initiative it was. The party agreed to it. The pay for this trip was good. For example, Professor Harris received five thousand dollars; others also received large amounts.

Presiding Officer: But did you get money here as well, in the USSR?

Vatenberg: We didn't get any money in the USSR. I personally was not included on the ICOR commission. Originally the commission consisted of three American experts, and I should add here that Harris is prominent and highly respected in his field in America. He is the president of a university in one of the southern states, and that is a very conservative part of the country.

Presiding Officer: And what nationality is he—Jewish?

*Yuri Larin (Mikhail Lurye) (1882–1932) was a leading party intellectual and an advocate for Jewish agricultural settlements in the Crimea. His daughter Anna Larina married Nikolai Bukharin in 1934. After Bukharin's arrest, she spent many years in prison and labor camps.

Vatenberg: The commission report was published in Yiddish and English in New York, and ICOR circulated it to everyone who requested it. The report could have been used by American, Japanese, and other intelligence services, because ICOR sent it to any organization as soon as it asked, but that doesn't mean that it contained classified material. I did not say that. I requested that the investigator include the commission report in the case materials. I have it on a bookshelf in my Moscow apartment. The investigator revealed a tendency that I, as a lawyer, do not approve of, of replacing material evidence with witness testimony about that material evidence. What is the testimony needed for if the commission report is available?

Presiding Officer: Where is this report?

Vatenberg: In my bookcase at home. When I received the indictment here, I asked the investigator to include the commission report in the case materials. I said to the investigator: "What is the point of us speculating here and squabbling. It would be better to take the report and append it to the case materials. Can I really remember what was written there twenty-five years ago?" In the Register of 1945, it says that it has retroactive authority, and so the register can be applied to the report. We need to take the register and see whether the information in the report falls under the prohibition, but for some reason the investigator saw fit to limit himself to my testimony and not to what was in the report. We did not consider it classified information. When I came here in 1926 and 1929, it did not even occur to me to gather that sort of information, that is, information that was not for public release. We gathered information of interest to the Soviet Union, for what needed to be released to the outside world, and if it had been secret, I would never have done that. My motto was to gather only what was needed and useful for the Soviet Union.

The investigation feels that because I met with Morris, who was "a member of the executive committee of ICOR," and talked about Birobidzhan, I indirectly passed on information to him. Allow me to explain. First of all, Morris was not a member of the executive committee of ICOR. He lived in the USSR and worked at the State Jewelry Trade Office.

Presiding Officer: During the investigation you said that you informed Morris on all issues relating to Birobidzhan. And you also said, "In conversations with Morris I also stated that the question of interest to us having to do with creation of a state within the USSR was moving forward very badly, and in connection with that I expressed to him my dissatisfaction with Soviet government policy" (vol. 19, p. 74). This interrogation report is dated February 18, 1949.

Vatenberg: I do not confirm that, because it is not true. I never expressed dissatisfaction with Soviet government policy. I had a conversation with him only once, but the content of the conversation was what I have already testified to. I also met with Budish* in 1937 and with Novick in 1936. I told them the same thing, that there were no great successes yet. It says in the indictment that I gave them information that was of interest to them. I told them what was happening in Birobidzhan, but I did not forward any information about Birobidzhan to the United States.

Presiding Officer: In the interrogation record dated May 26 (vol. 19, p. 140) it says, "Budish, like Novick, was interested not only in information about Birobidzhan, but also in receiving detailed classified information about the economic situation in the USSR. It was through all of these people that I passed on to the Americans the information that I had obtained."

Vatenberg: This interrogation record is an artfully woven tissue of truths and untruths, and the untruths begin with the first word on the first page in the upper right-hand corner.

Presiding Officer: What, are you repudiating your signature? That's what is here in the corner.

Vatenberg: In the corner it says "transcript." That I deny, and that can be checked, because the notebooks have been preserved. Was there ever such a transcript? I state that there were no such questions and answers. This interrogation record was brought to me on May 26. I read over those thirty-six pages and signed them over a period of forty minutes. It was like a nightmare. On the fourth page of that interrogation record it says that "I was not active in Po'alei tsion," and I said that that was absurd, because I was a member of the Central Committee. The investigator needed this so that it would appear in the interrogation record that I was denying something, since the next page contained an exposure, and I state again that everything was typed up in advance, and there were no such questions and answers as the ones given there.

Presiding Officer: But do you attest to your signature?

Vatenberg: I will say that I signed while clear of mind and memory, I signed this consciously, and I knew that I was signing my own sentence. And I will tell you why. Fairly quickly, at the start of the investigation, I mastered several rules having to do with how investigations are conducted.

The investigator does not record everything that the arrested person says, and in addition to that, he interprets his or her testimony in a completely different way from the way the testimony was given.

He interprets it as follows: "Anything that serves to protect the arrested person is not written in the interrogation record. The only thing of interest is a confession of guilt. If you have anything to say in your own defense, you can tell the court about it." If you take any fact and tear it out of its set-

---

*Jacob Budish (1886–1966) was a longtime member of the American Communist Party. He became executive vice president of AMBIJAN after World War II, when the organization merged with ICOR.

ting and present it in denuded form, it can look like an image reflected in a distorting mirror. But this contradicts all laws of dialectics. What you get is not a fact, but a distortion of a fact, and the investigator takes only facts that have been torn from their context of reality. The investigator says: "I am not your secretary." So he does not write what I say. This is also true. Everything should be expressed concisely, in literate form. But he interprets it in the following way: "I do not take down what you are saying." He doesn't write what I say, but writes what pleases him to strengthen an accusation.

And here is another rule: "Don't dare to challenge a question; questions are none of your business." But then you get questions like this: "It is known that in 1929 you engaged in espionage in Birobidzhan. Clarify. What was it you were doing?" I, of course, respond that I was not engaged in espionage, but did such-and-such. Then I see in the interrogation record that the beginning of my testimony is not there. I can't repudiate it. He wrote what I said, but not all of it. There was an interrogation record that had nothing to do with me, and suddenly there is a question such as this one: "And as an American intelligence agent, you were apparently interested in this question?" I respond, "You know that I am not an American intelligence agent," but as regards whether or not I was interested in certain information, I answer nonetheless, and this is recorded, cut off from the first half of the answer. In connection with this I said to him, "The first prosecutor will return the case to you for further investigation. If you have information that I am an American intelligence agent, although there is no trace in all of the case materials that I was recruited or that I did anything, the case will be returned to you for further investigation. How can you write that I am an agent when you have no information to that effect?" And I told him this after signing the 206th article: "Cross it out," I said. "The case will be returned to you anyway." I state that there are no interrogation records in the case that are properly drawn up.

Next. From the first day I was told, "You are a criminal. People who are innocent do not get arrested here." So, if this was the sort of case it was, I would have to spend time in prison. I had no great desire to do this, but the only way out of prison was through the camps. There was no other way out. Well, if that's the way things were, then the case had to be speeded up, and the investigator repeated every day, "You are drawing out the investigation. It needs to be finished up." There was an interrogation record dated the 29th, and he said sign it and let's finish up. It is over three years now since I signed that interrogation record, which was supposed to end the case.

And one more thing. Of course I could have fought and repudiated everything—the only way of fighting that remains. But I will tell you openly that I am no coward, either physically or morally. There's a completely different question here: Who are you going to fight? How I envied revolutionaries who stood up to the tsarist guards or the American police. You can look at my notes—I said this to the investigator three years before Talmy spoke of that here.

Presiding Officer: One must tell the truth everywhere and hide it from the enemy.

Vatenberg: There is no abstract truth. Truth is determined by class, and because truth is determined by class, then you think that maybe he really is right.

Presiding Officer: And if he really is right, then what is the point of your repudiating your testimony in court?

Vatenberg: Maybe he really is right. You have to take another look at your life. I left off saying that I had absolutely no desire to fight the investigation, because on the whole, I don't know the truth. I know class truth, and the front ranks of humanity are the bearer of class truth. I was faced with a representative of that body which, by directive of the Soviet Union, stood guard over the laws of the revolution. This is why one has to review and reevaluate one's life, and that requires a few landmarks. The investigator gave me such a landmark.

At the very beginning of the investigation I objected to the idea that I was engaged in espionage. He insisted that these were trips made for the purpose of espionage—especially that the conversations with Novick and the information that I passed on to him were classified. I presented arguments about how it was impossible that I could be a spy without malicious intent. He said, "Forget all your jurisprudence, which gave you the idea that an accusation based on paragraph 58-1a requires malicious intent, whereas other articles—specifically, the one about espionage—do not require malicious intent." If he had said that to someone ignorant of jurisprudence, that person would not have believed it, but I, as a lawyer, believed it. Then, if it was enough for a Soviet person to talk with a spy and give him some kind of information, even the most harmless, and if he didn't even know that he was a spy, even if he had no intention of passing on classified information, still the mere fact of his talking with a spy made a Soviet person guilty of the crime described in article 58-1. Since that was the way it was, I pled guilty to engaging in espionage, and then everything went smoothly, and since I had assumed responsibility for the most serious crime, treason, the rest was of no significance for me. So I signed the interrogation records.

Then, after I signed article 206 the first time, I went to Major General of Justice Nikolaev and requested that he allow me to ask him a question. "Please go ahead," he said, "but it is strange that you make this request after signing." In the presence of that same investigator I asked him whether it was true that according to Soviet law, malicious intent was not required under article 58-1. He replied that this was one of the main conditions for determining guilt for this crime. I thanked him. After the second stage of the investigation began, twenty months later, I took the first opportunity, which did not arise until the fall of 1951, and told prosecutor Novikov (this interrogation record is not in the case materials) and then prosecutor Prikhodko as well, that I did not plead guilty to espionage and that all the testimony from 1949 in which I pled guilty to espionage in whatever form, I was repudiating, removing, and not confirming. And I am making the same statement to the court today. I had been led astray. I do not know whether purposely or not.

Presiding Officer: But in the interrogation record dated February 23, 1950, you again confirm that you and Novick were linked by the espionage you both engaged in.

Vatenberg: That was before February 26, when I signed article 206.

Presiding Officer: And when Epshteyn came from Moscow, did he talk to you about the tasks of the Jewish Anti-Fascist Committee?

Vatenberg: He told me that the Central Committee assigned the Jewish Anti-Fascist Committee the task of launching a broad propaganda campaign abroad about the Soviet Union.

Presiding Officer: What position did he offer you?

Vatenberg: Executive assistant. I worked in this position as a staff member for around five to six weeks; then I fell ill and was checked into the hospital. When I returned, I renewed my ties to the committee on a contract basis, and then I left there altogether. So I was in a staff position for perhaps five or six weeks—that is, from early June until the first week of July.

Presiding Officer: And then what did you do, and when did your link with the Jewish Anti-Fascist Committee come to an end?

Vatenberg: At the beginning of my testimony I said that I understood the nature of the materials being sent abroad at that time, and knew exactly where these materials were being sent. How was I informed about the nature of the materials? It was not because they were given to me to correct and clean up. What happened was that most of the materials were sent by telegraph. To do this they needed to be translated into English. The only translator there was Ostrovskaya. She translated, and Epshteyn looked over what she did. Epshteyn's knowledge of English was not extensive, and Ostrovskaya was concerned that she might make a mistake. So it was necessary that someone else go over the translations. This had been set up in Moscow very well. Not only did they have particularly good translators there, but there was also an editorial control board, where the Russian text was compared to the English translation. Then the head of the translation bureau looked over the text, and it was only after this that the articles were sent out with the approval of the head of the translation bureau. So there was a very good system of control.

In this way, I was informed for a period of a month and a half to two months about the nature of the Jewish Anti-Fascist Committee materials. I should say that during that period, although they contained some exaggerations about Jews, which was characteristic of Epshteyn's style, there was still no nationalism during that period. Perhaps there was, but I did not see it.

Presiding Officer: Now, as regards the makeup of the committee. You said that Epshteyn and Lozovsky were the most important members of the committee and that there was a whole group of nationalists gathered around the committee, such as Bergelson, Kvitko, Fefer, and Yuzefovich, who was Lozovsky's confidant. And now you are saying that you did not see any nationalism there.

Vatenberg: I do not confirm this testimony in this form.

Presiding Officer: What about Talmy?

Vatenberg: He belongs to another category. I am talking now about Yiddish writers. I did not consider then, nor do I consider now, that Talmy was a nationalist. But it is quite possible that he experienced some nationalistic regression during the war. I underwent something similar myself.

Presiding Officer: What form did it take?

Vatenberg: That is very hard to describe. Every war is an upheaval and stirs up various feelings. There are various germs in the air during such a period. During this war, for example, there were nationalistic germs in circulation among certain groups of Jews.

Presiding Officer: How do you explain this?

Vatenberg: First of all, I think it is owing to the cruel and bestial policy which Hitler carried out and which reminded many Jews that they were Jews. Ehrenburg said in this context that Hitler reminded him that his mother's name was Hannah.

Presiding Officer: What nationalistic regression did you and Talmy have?

Vatenberg: I can cite an example which perhaps means nothing, but perhaps does add up to something. This was in 1943–1944, most likely in 1943. I became sick, and the doctors were unable to diagnose what was wrong with me. They suggested calling in Bykhovskaya, the head of the neuropathological branch at Botkin Hospital. This was a mutual acquaintance of ours. The day she came to see me was the very same day when the government decree was issued about awarding the Stalin Prizes to people in the sciences and arts. She looked down the list of recipients and noted that 28 to 30 percent of the last names were Jewish. And just five minutes before that, she had been telling me that that day, or maybe it was the previous day, she had been walking down Gorky Street with Lina Solomonovna Shtern, and Shtern had been telling her that all the Jewish employees had been let go from the editorial board of a medical journal. Bykhovskaya said that tears were running down Shtern's face when she told her this.

Presiding Officer: This was in 1943?

Vatenberg: In late 1943 or early 1944. Then I said to Bykhovskaya: "Several minutes ago you were telling me about manifestations of anti-Semitism, and now you are saying joyfully that about 30 percent of the Stalin Prize recipients were Jewish. These people included engineers, scientists, mechanics, and designers. How can you talk about anti-Semitism?"

Presiding Officer: So Bykhovskaya displayed nationalism, and what about you?

Vatenberg: That same evening Talmy came to my apartment and said (as always he and I exchanged opinions first, and then sat down to a game of chess): "Today I saw a list of the laureates and counted that about 30 percent of them were Jews." There was a whiff of nationalism in this calculation, and I should say that I had this, too. There was some nationalistic regression in this. True, it was eliminated quickly, but nonetheless a germ of nationalism really did exist.

Presiding Officer: In you and in Talmy?

Vatenberg: Yes, in me and in Talmy.

Presiding Officer: And so this germ existed until recently?

Vatenberg: Lately I have been far removed from that.

Presiding Officer: Perhaps it was not manifested externally, but existed in your soul?

Vatenberg: I find it very hard to evaluate this objectively. Perhaps it did exist somewhere in my soul. All I can say with certainty is that I rid myself of it completely here in prison.

Presiding Officer: Why is it that if you did have such a germ in you, you don't regard the first period of work at the committee as nationalistic? After all, Markish, Kvitko, Bergelson, and Hofshteyn joined the committee at that time—nationalists, as you characterized them, which means that the type of articles, the orientation of the work, everything, would have had a nationalistic orientation?

Vatenberg: To write articles, you had to have writers.

Presiding Officer: What do you know about Mikhoels and Fefer's trip abroad? What assignments did they get there?

Vatenberg: I cannot say what assignments they got. I was never friendly with Fefer, but neither were we enemies. We had a decent relationship. When he came back from America, he met Ostrovskaya at the committee building and said that he brought many greetings for her and me. She came home and told me to speak with Fefer and find out when it would be all right to stop by and see him. On a Sunday soon after that, we stopped by to see Fefer (this was the only time we went to Fefer's apartment). We stayed there for a fairly long time, maybe two hours, and he spoke in detail about his meetings in America, whom he'd met with and what conversations he'd had. He told us about his meeting with Weizmann—he may have forgotten, with the passage of time, but he told me that Weizmann had come to their hotel, whereas here he said that it was in a restaurant, but that is not of great significance—and about their conversation. He told us the same things that he recounted here. He spoke about his conversation with Rosenberg and said approximately the same things that he said here.

Presiding Officer: You said that in conversation with Mikhoels and Fefer, Rosenberg raised a question that had long concerned the Jewish masses—about creating a Jewish republic in the Crimea—and demanded that this problem be raised in the Soviet Union through the Jewish Anti-Fascist Committee.

Vatenberg: He could not have demanded this. I think that the question of creating a Jewish republic was of very little concern to him. But the Crimea was of importance to them because the Joint had invested a lot of money there, and they felt that they had lost face over that issue, for the Soviet Union had even made a good gesture and returned part of the money.

Fefer told me that Rosenberg had asked him how the Crimea situation was going, and stated that if settlement started up again, the Joint would be ready to renew its assistance, but he didn't talk about the Black Sea, Turkey, or the Balkan peninsula. During the investigation I became convinced that the conversation with Rosenberg as described in the indictment in Fefer's first testimony didn't take place, although Fefer said in his testimony that Rosenberg made a statement that the Crimea meant the Black Sea, Turkey, and the Balkan peninsula.

Maybe when he was speaking with me, Fefer misinterpreted the meaning of Rosenberg's remark. He told me that when they talked about California, Rosenberg said that California fell short of the Crimea in many ways, because the Crimea meant the Black Sea, and that if you took a close look, you could even see Turkey. I don't take this conversation seriously. If that conversation had been serious, then probably Fefer would have told me about it. True, I was never particularly close to Fefer, but even so, he should have told me. He told me about conversations with Budish, Novick, Einstein, and Charlie Chaplin. He told me about a conversation concerning assistance from the Joint, and if that conversation about the Crimea had been genuinely serious, he would have said so. One can't help but have some doubts about the internal logic of such a conversation. If you add to that the fact that this conversation took place in the presence of an interpreter from the consulate, then there is no doubt that it did not take place. If this conversation really had taken place in a serious form with an interpreter present, then the latter would have reported it to the appropriate parties, especially if Rosenberg had spoken about aid from the American government. I know Rosenberg by reputation. He is an adroit lawyer with ties to the most highly placed financial circles in the United States, and an inveterate politician.

Two people come from the Soviet Union. Rosenberg knows full well that if people are sent from the Soviet Union, these people must be communists and, even more than that, intelligence agents. Rosenberg himself has never displayed an interest in Yiddish literature and didn't know Yiddish, and suddenly two people come and he tells them such serious things, reveals such serious cards. Where is the logic in all of this?

Presiding Officer: Logic suggests, as you testified, that when they came back from America, the committee was completely transformed into an organization that acted according to orders from America and carried out their assignments, and then the Crimea issue was raised.

Vatenberg: That phrasing is not mine. The word "orders" is not mine. But it is hard to believe that the committee worked on these questions at the demand or request of these clients in America. Budish, Goldberg, and Novick are not Rosenberg.

Presiding Officer: When and from whom did you find out about the Crimea question?

Vatenberg: From Epshteyn. One day I stopped by the committee. Epshteyn greeted me with a smile and said that he, Mikhoels, and Fefer had been to see Comrade Molotov and that they had raised the Crimea question there, and supposedly Comrade Molotov had told them that they should write a memorandum about it. This sort of answer, according to Epshteyn, was meant to convey that Comrade Molotov did not have a negative attitude about it. Moreover, Epshteyn stated that "the ministerial portfolios were now being distributed," and he had been offered the post of chairman of the council of ministers of this Jewish republic. That was a joke, of course. I did not give it any significance at all, because we were speaking in jest. Then Epshteyn told me that a memorandum on the Crimea would be drafted. I would like to touch again on the moment when Epshteyn and I were evacuated from Moscow and we were traveling in the same train car. He touched on the problem of the Volga German Republic. I replied that there was a Jewish autonomous region, but if the possibility of moving existed, then let those who wished move. On the whole, I felt that all of these projects were part of a general mania for harebrained and impractical schemes.

Presiding Officer: And what should we make of the fact that commissions were sent to study the situation of the Jews, such as, for example, Kvitko's trip to the Crimea, while someone else was sent to the Ukraine? Questions were being raised in the government about Jews being offended somewhere, about the issue of packages. What is all this, in your view?

Vatenberg: Let's break this down and go over it point by point. There is nothing wrong with Kvitko's making a trip to the Crimea as a committee correspondent in order to then write a feature article for the foreign press. But the fact that after he got back, there was an uproar, and they went to the People's Commissariat of Land Management—this is another matter altogether and is not within the committee's jurisdiction. I always believed that the committee should not do anything except send materials. It was a propaganda office. I was against creating the presidium. But when I told Epshteyn about this, he said to me, "What, are you smarter than the Central Committee?" He always liked referring to the Central Committee. According to my interpretation, any other sort of work was not within the committee's jurisdiction.

[During the preliminary investigation, Vatenberg, in the course of describing his relationships with Hofshteyn, said that Hofshteyn had spoken against the assimilation of the Jews, and from these conversations, it was clear to Vatenberg that Hofshteyn regretted that he did not live in Palestine. The court obtained more information about this testimony from Vatenberg.]

Vatenberg: That I confirm. That's true.

Presiding Officer: But you testified that it was quite possible that such conversations did occur between you and Hofshteyn. Hofshteyn knew of your nationalistic sentiments, so he was not shy about talking with you about these subjects.

Vatenberg: That is not my answer, but the creative work of the investigator, although I didn't argue with him and signed the interrogation record.

Presiding Officer: But in 1942–1943 you said that he had nationalistic conversations with you?

Vatenberg: He was in Kuibyshev once. I met him on the street, and we talked for about ten minutes. In general, I never knew him well.

Presiding Officer: All the more so. You don't know each other well, and suddenly in 1942–1943 he has a conversation with you on nationalistic topics and expresses regret that he does not live in Palestine.

Vatenberg: He didn't say that directly, but I got the impression that he longed for Palestine.

Presiding Officer: This is a flagrantly anti-Soviet conversation, if someone is talking and thinking about Palestine, and not about his homeland. And you said that he talked with you this way because he trusted you and because you yourself had nationalistic sentiments.

Vatenberg: Why he trusted me, I don't know.

Presiding Officer: You also stated that you pled partially guilty (vol. 2, p. 288) to disseminating nationalistic ideas.

Vatenberg: All ideas of nationalism go against party policy.

Presiding Officer: Repeat what you consider yourself guilty of.

Vatenberg: I was of the opinion, which I spoke of yesterday, that in spite of deep ideological differences between Jews in the USSR and the United States, we nonetheless had something in common, and that is this: the Yiddish language and a progressive cultural heritage. This commonality between the Jews of the USSR and the United States is based on a commonality of language. I now consider this to be a nationalistic concept, so I consider all of the expert commission's findings on the issue of nationalism correct.

Presiding Officer: What questions do the defendants have for defendant Vatenberg?

[There were only a few questions for Vatenberg. They showed that Vatenberg was close only to Talmy, and that he had a nodding acquaintance with most of the remaining defendants. Vatenberg had not met or talked with them.]

Fefer: Did the Yiddish literature of the Soviet Union have an influence—there are a number of its leaders and creators here—did it have a positive influence on the working people of the United States and on any writers?

Vatenberg: To that I must reply in the affirmative. I must confirm that under the influence of Soviet Yiddish literature, a whole group of writers, poets, novelists, and essayists in the United States developed their art. The influence of Soviet Yiddish writers on the Jewish intelligentsia was also significant. Their works were read with great interest.

Fefer: During our conversation with you in my apartment, when you and Khayke Semyonovna were there, did you feel how thrilled I was with the Americans? Or did I tell you about the opposition with which the Jewish reactionary press received us, and about how we had to overcome these difficulties and struggle with them?

Vatenberg: You described various difficulties that you had to overcome, especially at the *Forverts,* and certain Yiddish bourgeois writers who tried to do harm to you and your work.

Fefer: Did you read my articles in *Eynikayt?*

Vatenberg: On the whole, yes.

Fefer: Did you read the article about the State of Israel, targeted against warmongers and Jewish reactionaries in America?

Vatenberg: Yes, I read it. There was one article either about the State of Israel or about our attitude toward Jews in the State of Israel, and I got the impression from that article that incorrect phrasing had slipped in and that there was something nationalistic in it. But for the most part your articles were correct.

[After the defendants finished their questions to Vatenberg, his testimony was completed at 12:15 P.M. on June 11. After a two-hour recess the court began to examine his wife, Khayke Vatenberg-Ostrovskaya.]

KHAYKE VATENBERG-OSTROVSKAYA

Khayke Vatenberg-Ostrovskaya met her husband, Ilya Vatenberg, in New York. She had emigrated from the Ukraine to America with her mother and several siblings in 1914. She finished her high school education in New York and later served as secretary for a number of civic organizations, including a union made up of Jewish workers. Vatenberg-Ostrovskaya shared her husband's political views and willingly emigrated back to the Soviet Union in 1933.

Two years later, Vatenberg-Ostrovskaya received an unusual assignment. She was sent to the United States on a secret mission by the Defense Ministry and stayed there for three months. "At that time I was trusted," she reminded her judges. During the war, she was a translator for the Sovinformburo. Now she was being held responsible for the articles she had been asked to translate from Russian into English and for having "anti-Soviet" discussions with people like Paul Novick, who, the court claimed, were American agents.

Presiding Officer: Defendant Vatenberg-Ostrovskaya, testify to the court, to what do you plead guilty?

Vatenberg-Ostrovskaya: I plead guilty in part to the fact that I, while working on the Jewish Anti-Fascist Committee, translated articles that, according to the expert commission, were nationalistic in character. To what degree I bear responsibility as a translator, I do not know. The court will judge. In the list of articles and materials marked as revealing military secrets, I do not find any of the articles that I translated, except an article about Birobidzhan whose name I do not remember.

Presiding Officer: Who wrote the article?

Vatenberg-Ostrovskaya: I don't remember that, either. It is no accident that my materials are not there. Because most of the articles that the Anti-Fascist Committee sent were in Yiddish for the Yiddish press, there was no need to translate them. There was a time when materials were sent by telegraph, and then they were translated into English. In addition to that, I was not the only one who translated materials for the Anti-Fascist Committee; there were other translators at the Sovinformburo.

Presiding Officer: And were you alone at the committee?

Vatenberg-Ostrovskaya: At the committee I was considered the only staff translator, but I did not work at the committee itself; I did not have a desk there. I received the articles to be translated at the Sovinformburo. I would also like to add that all of the articles were examined by the Soviet censor.

Presiding Officer: What censor?

Vatenberg-Ostrovskaya: The Soviet censor's office, which was part of the Sovinformburo, and after 1946, when the translation bureau for the Anti-Fascist Committees was organized, the materials were again looked at by the editorial control board, after which they were sent to the Glavlit censor.

Presiding Officer: What do you plead guilty to?

Vatenberg-Ostrovskaya: That I translated materials which were nationalistic in character. I never hesitated about it.

Presiding Officer: So you deny that there was classified information in those articles that you translated, but there were articles that were nationalistic in character?

Vatenberg-Ostrovskaya: I never analyzed them. I deny the accusation that I translated classified materials by order of Mikhoels, Epshteyn, and Fefer and that I had contacts for the purpose of espionage with Davis and Novick and that I was an active nationalist.

Presiding Officer: When did you emigrate? You were born in 1901 into the family of a sexton in a synagogue?

Vatenberg-Ostrovskaya: No. My father was a ritual slaughterer. The investigator was completely unable to understand what this meant, and asked another investigator, and ended up writing that my father was a synagogue sexton. A slaughterer is someone who slaughters cattle at a slaughterhouse. I was born several months after my father died in the city of Zvenigorod. My father died leaving seven children, and we lived with my grandfather, who supported us. My mother left the two older boys, who were fifteen and eleven, in Zvenigorod, and taking the five little ones with her, she moved to our paternal grandfather's in the shtetl of Rogachev, Volynsk province, where we lived until we left for America in 1914.

Presiding Officer: A slaughterer is a religious officer. Jews buy the meat of cattle that has been killed by a slaughterer—is that right?

Vatenberg-Ostrovskaya: Yes, it is called kosher meat.

Presiding Officer: And what—does that mean that prayers are said as the cattle are slaughtered?

Vatenberg-Ostrovskaya: Yes, absolutely.

[Vatenberg-Ostrovskaya's family moved to America before the revolution. There she was an administrative worker in a number of civic organizations, including the Jewish Workers' Union. Speaking of her work as a translator at the Sovinformburo, Vatenberg-Ostrovskaya gave the following testimony.]

Vatenberg-Ostrovskaya: I remember well that during the final years at the translation bureau, 90 percent of the materials were from the Slavic and the youth committees. The Jewish committee at that time sent us about eight to ten articles a month for translation because they had started sending materials in Yiddish to the Yiddish press. It would be very easy to check the books to see whether I am telling the truth. Take the logbook for the translation bureau for the final years and look at it. And there was another translator working there, too. I thought the system of work was a good one. That is why I said here that when I reviewed the list of articles for the Jewish Anti-Fascist Committee which is in the case materials, I did not find nationalistic articles or articles containing classified information among them.

Solomon Lozovsky said here that the article about nonferrous metals, which was published in the newspaper *Krasny Flot,* contained obviously classified information. I don't know about that. Frankly, if I had been given that article, I would have translated it; I didn't know that one is not supposed to write about nonferrous metals. Since the article passed the Glavlit censor, I didn't need to know that. I am saying that those articles that were sent for translation, absolutely all of them, had the seal and the signature of Glavlit. If they hadn't, no one would have agreed to translate them.

Presiding Officer: Fefer, what sort of censorship and control was there?

Fefer: I knew little about that question until I started working directly at the committee. Ostrovskaya was more familiar with how things worked. When I started working, I got in touch with Sadchenko, the head of Glavlit, and he and I agreed that not a single committee article would be sent to the foreign press without Glavlit checking it in advance. We had little money for sending material by telegraph, and for the most part we sent correspondence by mail. When we split off from the Sovinformburo, the Foreign Policy Department of the party Central Committee created an editorial control board.

Presiding Officer: Is Ostrovskaya's statement true that the number of articles to be translated dropped significantly because you started sending them in Yiddish?

Fefer: It made sense to translate articles into English when we were sending them by telegraph. But recently we had been deprived of hard currency for sending items by telegraph, and we had to send articles by other channels, but how this happened, from a technical standpoint, I do not know.

Presiding Officer: What do you mean, you didn't know? You confessed that you supplied the Americans with classified information, didn't you?

Fefer: I never confessed to that. I didn't have any conversations about sending classified information, and I didn't make any arrangements with anyone about that.

Presiding Officer: Were articles sent in Yiddish?

Fefer: Yes, they were sent in Yiddish as well. I confirm that the stamp and approval of Glavlit were on all the materials, and it is quite surprising to me that there is not any information about the articles included in the case materials. I don't know whether all of these articles were sent, for many were rejected.

Presiding Officer (to Vatenberg-Ostrovskaya): During the preliminary investigation, when you were interrogated, you confessed that you were guilty of orally conveying classified information during meetings with foreigners in Moscow (vol. 25, p. 24).

Vatenberg-Ostrovskaya: During the whole time of the investigation I did not confirm that. I did not have any conversations with foreigners on matters which were classified, and I do not believe that the figures which I mentioned were state secrets.

Presiding Officer: Why is it that during the preliminary investigation you understood this information to be classified, while now you find that it is not?

Vatenberg-Ostrovskaya: It was a very difficult investigation, and I was forced to sign that interrogation record, as well as the record dated June 20.

Presiding Officer: But as regards Novick, you confessed not in one record, but in many of them?

Vatenberg-Ostrovskaya: At the time when the investigation was being conducted by Lieutenant Colonel Tsvetaev, it was so difficult that after that I had a great fear of investigators in general and signed interrogation records that I considered to be complete lies. I refused repeatedly. I did not want to sign such records, but the road to the special punishment cell was familiar enough to me. I had no other way out. I was forced to sign those interrogation records.

Presiding Officer: You said that in Moscow when Novick came to your apartment, you made anti-Soviet, slanderous fabrications about discrimination against Jews in the USSR.

Vatenberg-Ostrovskaya: I did not say such words in the presence of the investigator. He repeatedly prompted me that this was written in my husband's interrogation record. I denied it the whole time and refused to sign the record, but in the end I was forced to sign it. I am now denying it categorically.

Presiding Officer: You testified that Novick was told that there was discrimination in this country and that Lina Shtern had written a complaint about it. For his part, Novick expressed to you his hostile views regarding the Soviet Union, stating that he, as well as others in America, were dissatisfied with the fact that in 1939 the Soviet Union had concluded a treaty with Germany and also with the Soviet government's punitive policy, specifically in regard to London and his wife (he reads vol. 25, p. 26).*

*This is a reference to Noah and Miril (Mary) London. Born in tsarist Russia, in the Pale of Settlement, they immigrated separately to America. They were both active in American Jewish socialism and garment unionism; they were married in New York in 1915. They were also founding members of the American Communist Party, in whose Jewish section Noah London played a leading role in its early years. He studied civil engineering at Cooper Union,

Vatenberg-Ostrovskaya: I will tell you what Novick said to me about London.

Presiding Officer: You testified that he was outraged by London's arrest in 1938 and by the repression of his wife, Mary, and asked you to pass on twelve hundred rubles to Mary London.

Vatenberg-Ostrovskaya: That is the only part that is true. I did indeed take that money and pass it on to Mary London. As to the treaty, I spoke about it to the investigator, but he wrote down something completely different from what I said. Novick said that after the treaty with Germany was signed, he had to work very hard at the *Daily Worker* and the *Morgen Freiheit.* He had to write a lot of articles to fend off attacks by the yellow press. He said that he and others sat up nights explaining the meaning of this treaty. Those are my words that I conveyed to the investigator, but it says something completely different in the interrogation record.

Presiding Officer: But did you make corrections in the interrogation record and sign the record with your own hand?

Vatenberg-Ostrovskaya: I made corrections on one page only. Then I started having hallucinations, and I signed that record without reading it, in five minutes. I think that the investigator would confirm that.

Presiding Officer: And how did your husband, Vatenberg, pass on figures and other secret data to Novick?

Vatenberg-Ostrovskaya: None of those who are present here gave secret data to Novick. We had a general conversation.

Presiding Officer: But that conversation with Novick, on the tram, on the bus—he was collecting information?

Vatenberg-Ostrovskaya: That is all a lie.

Presiding Officer: Where did the investigator get that from?

---

then worked on construction of the New York subway system and the Holland tunnel project. He was the first labor editor of the *Morgen Freiheit,* which was edited by Paul Novick for most of its existence. Noah London was also the founder and first president of the United Workers Cooperative Colony Association—the famous "coops" housing project in the Bronx. He was succeeded in this post by Ilya Vatenberg. The Londons moved to the Soviet Union in 1926. Noah became a prominent Soviet industrial manager, most notably of water projects in the Ukraine. He also participated in the expedition to Birobidjan in 1929 with Leon Talmy and Ilya Vatenberg. (He is mentioned in the diaries of Franklin S. Harris, the president of Brigham Young University, who led the expedition.) Miril London worked as a chemist and was also active alongside her husband in supporting Jewish settlement in Birobidjan. Noah London was arrested in October 1937 and accused of committing sabotage and espionage at the Donbass water trust, which he had earlier directed; he was executed on December 9. Miril was sentenced to seven years in the gulag as the wife of a "traitor." She survived her term but is believed to have committed suicide in the winter of 1949–1950. (I would like to acknowledge the assistance of John Holmes, the great-nephew of Noah London, who researched the lives of Noah and Miril London for his doctoral dissertation in European history at the University of California, Berkeley.)

Vatenberg-Ostrovskaya: I don't know. He said: "Your husband testified such-and-such, and I said, "Maybe my husband has gone crazy, but I never heard any anti-Soviet conversations from Novick." I knew Novick before my arrest as a member of the American Communist Party, editor of the *Morgen Freiheit*, and a dedicated communist, and I repeat that I see no material that would disprove that view of him.

Presiding Officer: During the entire investigation you stated that you and Novick had conversations on nationalistic topics, like discrimination and assimilation.

Vatenberg-Ostrovskaya: No such conversations ever took place.

The second time I saw Davis was in July 1945. When I went into Epshteyn's office, I heard Epshteyn saying, "There cannot be any anti-Semitism in our country."

Presiding Officer: Vatenberg-Ostrovskaya, did you talk with your husband about the causes of Mikhoels's death?

Vatenberg-Ostrovskaya: Approximately several days before I was arrested, Reiman told me about this, saying that her acquaintance Mokrichev believed that the MGB was guilty of Mikhoels's death. I understood this in a completely different way, not as it is written here. I told my husband, and he said, "You understand what you are saying? I forbid you to meet with Reiman. That is a lie and slander."

Presiding Officer: Why did you repeat that?

Vatenberg-Ostrovskaya: I understand that I should have informed the MGB about this. It was several days before I was arrested. I didn't tell anyone else about it. It was during a period when my husband and I had just finished some very important work, and I really thought at the time that the MGB should be told.

Presiding Officer: You also testified that Talmy and his wife, Sophia [in English she was called Sonia] Abramovna, were at your apartment and expressed anti-Soviet views and held anti-Soviet conversations.

Vatenberg-Ostrovskaya: I will now tell you what I testified to the investigator and what actually happened. Talmy, his wife, and my friend Leikind did come to our apartment once. I said in conversation that several Jewish professors had been fired from Moscow University. Talmy got very worked up when he heard this, leaping up and saying that this was slander and lies, and he left the room. Talmy's wife, who is a calmer person, said that there was no way that this could be true and that even if some petty tyrant had done this, the party committee existed in order to take care of such things. I told the investigator about this case, and the investigator put it down in the following way: that we had conversations about Jewish assimilation.

Presiding Officer: Enemies started rumors, and you spread these rumors.

Vatenberg-Ostrovskaya: I heard that, was confused, and tried to clarify the issue among those close to me.

Presiding Officer: If Talmy got so upset that he even left the room, that means that you confirmed it.

Vatenberg-Ostrovskaya: I explained these rumors very calmly. I understand that such things are impermissible, but they do happen, and I committed a mistake by repeating these rumors. Another example: I heard that Bykhovskaya had said that Lina Shtern had written to the government about several such cases. I believed that if Shtern wrote to the government about this, then she was doing the right thing.

Presiding Officer: When Novick returned from his travels around the Ukraine and other places, did you see him?

Vatenberg-Ostrovskaya: No, he described the destruction of Kiev and how eighty thousand Jews had been killed at Babi Yar. He told about how people were living in cramped conditions since many buildings had been destroyed.

Presiding Officer: And he did not tell you about how Jews were being prevented from returning to the Ukraine?

Vatenberg-Ostrovskaya: He never said that, and I don't mean just in my presence. I don't believe that Novick said such things to anyone. I know Novick; he is a communist, and he could not have said such things.

Presiding Officer: Did you correspond with your brother?

Vatenberg-Ostrovskaya: Yes, I corresponded with my brother, received packages, and corresponded with my sister. The investigator told me, "We know that you wrote good letters."

Presiding Officer: How did he know?

Vatenberg-Ostrovskaya: I don't know.

Presiding Officer: What did you write?

Vatenberg-Ostrovskaya: I wrote about how I felt in the Soviet Union. My sister suffers from the same illness that I do, diabetes. I wrote about the advantages here in the USSR, about how I was a patient in the hospital and received medicines, and my sister's husband is a workingman, and medical treatment there is very expensive.

Presiding Officer: Regarding Yuzefovich: during the investigation (p.135, vol. 25) you testified about your contacts with Yuzefovich. What anti-Soviet conversations did you have with him?

Vatenberg-Ostrovskaya: The investigator said to me, "How long have you known Yuzefovich?" I said, "I've known his wife since 1931 and him since 1940." He wrote that I had known Yuzefovich since 1931, when, in fact, I did not meet him until 1940. That is number one. Number two: The investigator stated that he was a rabid nationalist. I said that I was not aware of that. I don't know Yuzefovich to be a nationalist now. The investigator asked, "What anti-Soviet conversations did you have with Yuzefovich?" I answered that I myself had never had such conversations and had never heard anything anti-Soviet from Yuzefovich. Those were my words to the investigator. And in the interrogation record dated June 20 it says that I testified that Yuzefovich is a rabid nationalist. In my presence Yuzefovich never made any anti-Soviet fabrications. I kept telling this to the investigator, and I confirm those words now. The investigator would say to me, "Your testimony—my interpretations." I consider that wrong.

[Vatenberg-Ostrovskaya's testimony, which started after lunch on June 11, continued until the evening of the same day. At 8:00 P.M., the presiding officer declared a recess. At 8:40 P.M., the court session resumed.]

Presiding Officer: Defendant Vatenberg-Ostrovskaya, what else would you like to say to the court?

Vatenberg-Ostrovskaya: I want to say that I never translated material that expressed any nationalism. I never saw the heroism of the Jews being played up in them. I felt that since material about Soviet Jews was being sent, that was the way it was supposed to be, because the material had been reviewed by the censor. I myself never collected material and didn't write articles, and I don't understand what form my active nationalism could have assumed.

Here in the indictment it mentions the committee's espionage activity. But I knew nothing about the committee's work. I only knew the material that the committee needed to be translated, and did not know that the committee was engaged in espionage. The material was intended as Soviet propaganda, and if some material containing state secrets slipped through, I did not suspect it. The expert commission indicates that there was such material, and I have to believe the commission. That is all I can say.

[Without announcing a recess, the court moved on to Zuskin's testimony.]

BENJAMIN ZUSKIN

Benjamin Zuskin was the greatest actor of his time on the Soviet Yiddish stage. Born in the shtetl of Panevezhis, near the Lithuanian border with Prussia (the town was known as Ponevezh in Yiddish and was famous for its yeshivahs), Zuskin initially studied at the Ural Mining Institute and then at the Moscow Mining Academy. But in 1920 he learned that a studio was opening in Moscow to train actors for a new Yiddish theater. Zuskin immediately dropped his studies to pursue his dream. He was married by then to Rachel Holland, who was from another shtetl in Lithuania. After their daughter, Tamara, was born in 1921, her mother took the baby to Lithuania. The couple's marriage was already shaky, but soon after Rachel arrived in Lithuania, the border with Soviet Russia was closed—Lithuania was an independent country between 1920 and 1940—and Zuskin did not see his daughter again until 1928, when the State Jewish Theater company passed through Lithuania on the way to Paris. In the 1930s, Tamara moved to Moscow to live with her father and attend a Russian high school.*

Zuskin quickly became the theater's leading actor, his name closely associated with that of Solomon Mikhoels. In his court testimony, Zuskin tried to explain their relationship. On stage, they complemented one another, as in the troupe's famous production of *King Lear* with Mikhoels as Lear and Zuskin as the Fool. Mikhoels once observed about that production: "We do not play two roles. We play together a single role, only two sides of it."† They even lived in the same Moscow apartment building near Pushkin Square around the corner from the theater; Zuskin lived on the fourth floor, Mikhoels a floor below. They were constantly in touch throughout the day, calling each other on the telephone, amusing their children by pretending to be clowns or peasants worried about the harvest. During German air raids on Moscow in 1941, Zuskin and Mikhoels sat together on the roof of the State Jewish Theater, determined to prevent a fire from destroying the building.‡

But there was tension between the two men. Zuskin was nine years younger than Mikhoels. He was also a pure actor, whereas Mikhoels combined his acting career with the responsibilities of artistic director, along with the role of a visible and highly regarded public figure. Mikhoels, after all, became a member of the Moscow City Council in 1939, and he took those responsibilities seriously. Zuskin, too, was an elected official—a deputy to a district council—but he spent most meetings playing chess in the corner with another indifferent member. Although Zuskin adored Mikhoels, their relationship was not one of equals, and in spite of their intimate and long-standing friendship, they both acknowledged the inequality. Mikhoels, for example, used the familiar pronoun "*ty*" when he spoke to Zuskin, while Zuskin always addressed Mikhoels with the more formal "*vy*," an unusual linguistic im-

---

*Tamara Platt (daughter of Benjamin Zuskin), interview with author by telephone, 1998.

†Jeffrey Veidlinger, *The Moscow State Yiddish Theater: Jewish Culture on the Soviet Stage* (Bloomington, Ind., 2000), p. 144.

‡Ethel Kovenskaya, "In Memory of a Great Actor" (in Russian), *Evreysky Komerton* (The Jewish Tuning Fork), p. 14, supplement to *Novosti Nedelyi* (News of the Week), April 22, 1999.

balance for two adults who otherwise worked and lived with such an intimate connection. For Zuskin, it felt as if he were dealing with two separate people: Mikhoels the actor, director, and man of the theater and Vovsi, the deputy to the Moscow City Council and, later, chairman of the Jewish Anti-Fascist Committee.

The famous Polish Jewish actress Ida Kaminska took refuge in Moscow during the war and saw for herself how Mikhoels relished his renown. "Mikhoels sat in his dressing room like an emperor, surrounded by young actresses. One of them fanned him, another served coffee, a third asked him what he wanted. Everyone fawned over him," she wrote in her memoir. "I don't recall anyone dancing around a prima donna the way they crowded around Mikhoels."* It was this Vovsi that Zuskin had difficulty tolerating. "Vovsi is no Solomon Mikhoels," Zuskin once said in front of his family in a rare but telling display of exasperation.†

Zuskin, in spite of his close relationship with Mikhoels, had very little contact with the JAC. As he made clear to his interrogators, he wrote only three articles for the foreign press—two obituaries about individuals associated with the theater and an article marking the eight hundredth anniversary of the founding of Moscow.

Presiding Officer: Defendant Zuskin, to what do you plead guilty?

Zuskin: As a member of the Jewish Anti-Fascist Committee, I bear responsibility for its activity. And insofar as it has been acknowledged and proved by irrefutable information that the Jewish Anti-Fascist Committee conducted anti-Soviet hostile activity, that means that I bear responsibility for this as well. The degree of my guilt will be determined by the court.

Presiding Officer: Tell us about your activity.

Zuskin: Above all, I direct the court's attention to the fact that in three and a half years of investigation it has not been determined who Mikhoels was and who Zuskin was. In the investigation materials it says that Mikhoels headed the Jewish Theater, and after his death Zuskin.

Presiding Officer: That is exactly what we are determining here. So you confess that you, as a member of the Jewish Anti-Fascist Committee, carried out anti-Soviet work.

---

*Ida Kaminska, *My Life, My Theater* (New York, 1973), p. 134.

†Tamara Platt, interview with author, 1998. I am also indebted to Alla Zuskin-Perelman, whom I interviewed in Tel Aviv in 1998.

Zuskin: As a member of the presidium, I bear responsibility for the committee's activity, but the court will determine what work I carried out. I do not plead guilty to nationalistic activity or to espionage.

Presiding Officer: An accusation was presented to you on January 11, 1949. To the question "Do you plead guilty to treason, to conducting anti-Soviet nationalistic activity?" you said, "Yes, I confess that I held sentiments against Soviet power and was in contact with a nationalistic underground."

Zuskin: Allow me to state that I repudiate this testimony of mine, which I signed with my own hand. I will cite two examples of what happened during the investigation. Several days after my arrest I was called in by Minister of State Security Abakumov, and he asked me a number of questions. When I was arrested I knew nothing about the work the committee was doing. He asked me about one person, and I told him what I knew. A day later, at the Central Committee building, there was a witness confrontation in Shkiryatov's office with a person whose social position was well known to me. I want to say why I am repudiating all of the testimony that is recorded in the interrogation record and signed by me.

At the witness confrontation, Minister of State Security Abakumov, Shkiryatov, that person, and I were present. I said everything that I knew about that person, although he refuted it all. The minister then told me, "You conducted yourself honorably during that interrogation."

Next example. At the witness confrontation with Persov, Rassypninsky turned to me and said that this person was an object of interest of the investigative agencies and that by order of the minister he was asking me x,y, and z, and then he said that I was deserving of trust. Since then I have spent three and a half years in prison, and I have implored, I have begged to have a witness confrontation with the members of the presidium. Finally I was given a witness confrontation with Fefer, who said that I was not an active member, but that I was to some degree guilty. I have been in prison for three and a half years. I have been presented with the indictment. It is a terrible indictment, but I have not been given witness confrontations at which I would be able to prove my innocence.

I worked in the theater, the cinema, and even at an MGB club, and I produced the performance given by the border guards' ensemble. I was a deputy to a local Moscow Soviet in a district named after Comrade Stalin starting in 1932, and then I was elected deputy a second time. There you have it, my entire life.

Fedoseyev's testimony as a witness is mentioned in the case materials. Fedoseyev is deputy director of the dramatic theater of the All-Union Committee on the Arts, and in this testimony he calls me an enemy of the people. I learned of this on the eve of the trial. How can it be that the investigative organs have such a statement from a highly placed person who knew me as an actor for many years and who knows under what conditions I became the artistic director of the State Jewish Theater, and then I am not granted a witness confrontation with him? I would like to ask Fefer a question.

Presiding Officer: Please, go ahead.

Zuskin: Fefer, tell me, please, how many years have you and I known each other?

Fefer: A quarter-century.

Zuskin: What kind of relationship do we have?

Fefer: A good one. There was no personal friendship between us, but I had warm feelings toward you, and I think you felt the same about me.

Zuskin: Have I been in your home in Moscow?

Fefer: No.

Zuskin: Was I an active member of the presidium?

Presiding Officer: He has already testified about that.

Zuskin: Did I receive any assignments from the Jewish Anti-Fascist Committee?

Fefer: A couple of times you were asked to write articles about actors in the theater, which you did.

Zuskin: Did I draw up any letters and documents for the Jewish Anti-Fascist Committee?

Fefer: No.

Zuskin: Did you conduct any negotiations with me concerning committee matters?

Fefer: No.

Zuskin: It says in the indictment that as an active nationalist, defendant Zuskin conducted hostile activity against the Soviet Union.

Presiding Officer: We will get to that. Now tell the court, did you know Mikhoels for a long time?

Zuskin: Twenty-six years.

Presiding Officer: Since 1921, as you said during the investigation, owing to your joint work in the Moscow Jewish Theater?

Zuskin: Yes.

Presiding Officer: Did you consider him an indisputable authority?

Zuskin: At first, yes, but from December 21, 1939, until the end of his life there was bickering between us.

Presiding Officer: You described Mikhoels as a great egoist, someone who loved ringing phrases and glory. Is this true?

Zuskin: I think that I will take Mikhoels apart not to bring glory to myself, but to tell the truth about this person. In court the talk is of Mikhoels, but I knew Vovsi, and there is a colossal difference between Mikhoels and Vovsi. Vovsi brought me to the point where I was contemplating suicide. Why did I ask Fefer questions? Because since 1939 I have not spoken with Mikhoels, I mean with Vovsi. I spoke with Mikhoels only because I was involved in the theater. Now, this is interesting. Zuskin—Mikhoels. When long before the war I went to the district military committee, I was received by the district military commander; he looked at my military card, read it, and said, "Why does it have just the name Zuskin here? Where is Mikhoels's name?" These two names were so closely linked in the indictment as well, and at the same time no one gave any testimony about Zuskin. I kept waiting for people to mention Mikhoels and then Zuskin would follow, but no, that didn't happen.

Presiding Officer: This means that you were closely connected with him.

Zuskin: In matters having to do with the stage.

Presiding Officer: During the investigation you testified: "Falling under the influence of Mikhoels, I absorbed his nationalistic, anti-Soviet sentiments, and finally I myself went sliding down the path of hostile activity" (vol. 23, p. 53).

Zuskin: Yes, I gave this testimony, because certain investigators told me that they didn't believe me.

Presiding Officer: But you just told us that the investigation team trusted you.

Zuskin: I am not going to ask for any special treatment from the court. I am relating my life, and you should judge me not by the interrogation records, but by my deeds.

Presiding Officer: One cannot ignore such testimony. The task of the court is to verify this testimony of yours.

Zuskin: All of my testimony is false.

Presiding Officer: However, when other defendants unmasked you here and spoke of your nationalistic activity, about the theater's repertoire, and about your role in that theater, you didn't ask any questions of anyone and did not state that they were wrong.

Zuskin: Believe me, the doctor knows the condition I am in. I have days when I am incapable of uttering a single word. And you asked that questions be formulated precisely, something that I am not always capable of.

I would like to give just one piece of information. Granovsky was the artistic director of the Jewish Theater for ten years, whereas Mikhoels was the artistic director for nineteen years. Altogether, they were artistic directors for twenty-nine years, but I was the artistic director for only a few months. Who determined what the repertoire would be, who was responsible for it? Did I have anything to do with it? I did not, because I was an actor. Granovsky was exclusively involved in the work of the Jewish Theater. In addition, Litvakov was the ideological director of the theater for seventeen years. In three years the investigation could have determined what Zuskin's role in the theater was, but this was not done, although I requested that it be done.

Presiding Officer: You said yourself in conversation with Mikhoels that Jewish culture was being stifled in the Soviet Union.

Zuskin: I deny this, because I didn't say anything about that to him. Let those present here confirm whether or not I spoke with any one of them on anti-Soviet topics.

Presiding Officer: Perhaps you yourself did not express hostile, anti-Soviet sentiments, but as this case has unfolded it has become clear that as a member of the presidium, you supported its hostile activity, because not once did you object to its political line. Who recommended you to the committee?

Zuskin: I don't know. No, I don't know how to make speeches. I can only play a role; I can read what is already written.

On October 15, 1941, I was evacuated to Tashkent together with the theater company, and from that time until October 3, 1943, I remained there. So I had nothing to do with the committee's activity until I returned to Moscow, and until the third rally I had absolutely no idea that I had anything to do with the committee.

Presiding Officer: When and how did you find out about that?

Zuskin: I received an invitation to the third Jewish Anti-Fascist Committee rally at the Hall of Columns in the House of Unions.

Presiding Officer: Did you speak there?

Zuskin: No, I gave no speeches whatsoever. Then Epshteyn said to me, "Come to 10 Kropotkin Street. There's going to be a plenum of the Jewish Anti-Fascist Committee, and you are a member of it." I said to him, "Why wasn't I informed of this earlier?" After all, in Tashkent there was a whole group of people who went to the second plenum, and I knew about that.

Presiding Officer: You said that you consulted with Lozovsky on all important issues.

Zuskin: It was no coincidence that Lozovsky was called *gabbai,* which is Yiddish for an elder in the Jewish community. The same goes for Vovsi, but not for Mikhoels. But I spoke with Lozovsky once in my life and said a total of five or six words to him. This was on October 3, 1943, on the opening day of the season. *Tevye the Dairyman* was playing, the last play Mikhoels acted in. The ticket taker came up to me and said, "Solomon Mikhailovich requests that you go to Lozovsky and tell him that Mikhoels has invited him to stop in and see him." I went over to him and said, "Solomon Abramovich, Solomon Mikhailovich invites you and your wife backstage." Then I accompanied them backstage. That was my whole acquaintance with Lozovsky.

Presiding Officer: And where does the term *gabbai* come from?

Zuskin: I'll explain. Sometimes we had rehearsals in Mikhoels's office. During one of these rehearsals Mikhoels got a phone call, and during the conversation Mikhoels imitated Lozovsky's voice so exactly, saying, "Well, what does our *gabbai* have to say about it?" that we were all struck. Mikhoels always said that meeting with Lozovsky gave him an unpleasant feeling, because Mikhoels always addressed Lozovsky formally by his first name and patronymic, and Lozovsky called him by his last name. This was terribly unpleasant to Mikhoels. And it seems to me that Mikhoels never had particular respect for Lozovsky when he came to the theater.

I didn't know that in 1946 the committee came under the jurisdiction of the Central Committee. I was leading a completely different life. Committee affairs were of no interest to me, and I fended off this obligation like some kind of burden. I attended committee meetings very rarely, and people were so accustomed to this that often when the secretary informed me of the committee meetings, she expressed her complete certainty that I would not attend. When I was arrested, they couldn't get anything out of me, because I didn't know anything, so they read other people's testimony to me.

Presiding Officer: Whose testimony did they read to you?

Zuskin: Lozovsky's.

Presiding Officer: How could they read Lozovsky's testimony to you when he was arrested a month after you were? When were you arrested?

Zuskin: On December 24, 1948.

Presiding Officer: And that same day you gave the testimony we are talking about now. In that testimony you confessed to being a nationalist and described the committee's nationalistic activity. This is your interrogation record.

Zuskin: I was prompted to say all of that. For example, there is testimony about the Crimea, but only here did I learn that the Crimea question was an issue in January 1944; until April 11, 1944, I didn't know what was going on in the committee at all. Why did I give testimony about the Crimea? Because I was brought to the interrogation in a complete stupor wearing a hospital gown. I was arrested in the hospital where I was being treated. My illness was such that I had been in a deep sleep for an extended period of time. I was arrested while I was asleep, and it was only in the morning when

I woke up that I saw that I was in a cell and learned that I had been arrested.

During the interrogation they said to me that I was a "state criminal" and demanded testimony about my crimes. I replied that if the Ministry of State Security had arrested me, that meant there was a reason for it. It was stated to me that the investigation team knew everything and that I should tell everything. I replied that I didn't know why I had been arrested. Then the investigator began reading me someone's testimony and asked whether I had heard anything about Lozovsky at the committee meetings. I said that I had heard such a name, and then in my stupor "told" the investigator about the Crimea, when I really had no understanding about it whatsoever.

Presiding Officer: When did Mikhoels describe his trip, his meetings, and the assignments that the Americans had given him?

Zuskin: I don't know anything about that. I thought that since I was being arrested, that meant there would be a trial, and the court would figure things out. And as to my specific case, I would like to request that the specific crimes that I have committed be spelled out for me.

Presiding Officer: Tell us about your testimony.

Zuskin: What did I find out about his American intelligence work? I found out that he met there with Chaplin, with actors, and with Albert Einstein. I found out about this when he came back and told about it.

Presiding Officer: I am asking you, How did you get information about the details of Fefer and Mikhoels's trip to America and about their meetings with Weizmann and Goldberg?

Zuskin: Mikhoels reported on his trip at a session of the Jewish Anti-Fascist Committee, and I was at that session. I attended sessions rarely.

Presiding Officer: I am asking you for the last time about Mikhoels and Fefer's trip to America. Give us your testimony.

Zuskin: I personally knew nothing about what Mikhoels did in America.

Presiding Officer: Tell us, what sort of receptions were held at the theater, and is your testimony true, that "after these receptions which lasted for hours, Mikhoels would grow extremely furious"? He (reads) "used to curse the Soviet government, which was supposedly oppressing the Jewish population" (vol. 23, p. 60).

Zuskin: As soon as Mikhoels returned from America, people immediately began appearing at the theater. They sat waiting, as at a dentist's office. I was indifferent to the whole thing, but once I was going to a show, and I saw Mikhoels emerging, looking pale, and he literally sat on the stairs (he loved it when people pitied him) and said to me, "Where are you going so early?" "What do you mean, early," I replied. "It's 5:30, and the show is at 7:30." "Is it really 5:30 already?" Mikhoels said. "I haven't eaten anything yet. These Jews are tormenting me. Somebody can't get into school, someone can't get a job." I said, "Is that really your business?" He was, after all, a member of the Moscow City Council. Mikhoels replied to me that the committee could handle these matters. I said, "Who gave the committee the right to handle such questions? However, if you feel that the committee should be dealing with them, then let these people go to the committee."

Presiding Officer: You stated that he was extremely furious and used to curse the Soviet government, which was supposedly oppressing Jews.

Zuskin: He started receiving more and more people. They began to interfere with our work, and there were even some who opened the doors to the auditorium and watched our rehearsals. I told Mikhoels once that if he did not stop receiving these people, then I would go to the appropriate office and make it clear that this kind of activity was interfering with our work.

Presiding Officer: They went backstage?

Zuskin: His office was backstage close to us.

Presiding Officer: And who referred them to the theater—the committee?

Zuskin: I don't know.

Presiding Officer: Why didn't they go to his apartment?

Zuskin: If only I knew. He received them in the morning and after rehearsals. Epshteyn came often, and that is why in 1946 we did not stage a single new production.

Presiding Officer: But why did you just look on? You were the deputy?

Zuskin: I was an actor.

Presiding Officer: But who was Mikhoels's deputy?

Zuskin: No one. I was appointed after he died.

Presiding Officer: You yourself wrote articles?

Zuskin: I wrote from time to time. The case materials contain two articles of mine, from which it is possible to conclude that.

Presiding Officer: You say that you wrote articles that were flagrantly slanderous and nationalistic in character?

Zuskin: I am not a journalist. What did I write about? On January 24, 1948, Shteiman, a Distinguished Artist of the Republic, died. I wrote a brief article about him, just a few warm words. What could be nationalistic about this article?

Presiding Officer: I don't know. I'm asking you. You yourself testified to this effect, but now you are repudiating your own words. And what other articles did you write?

Zuskin: There was another performer who died in August.

Presiding Officer: So you wrote only obituaries?

Zuskin: No. Three performers from our collective, along with several actors from other theaters, were awarded the title of Distinguished Artist in connection with the eight hundredth anniversary of the founding of Moscow. One of them was a watchmaker, while two of them were tailors.

Presiding Officer: So you wrote only on theatrical topics?

Zuskin: Exclusively.

Presiding Officer: What was nationalistic and slanderous in these articles?

Zuskin: Absolutely nothing. I said to the investigator, "If you don't believe me, take an article and read it." He said, "What, am I going to read all of your articles over and over!" I was asked to write an article for the *Morgen Freiheit* as a way to send greetings to some actors in New York. How could I not write when people were weeping with joy that they had been awarded the title of Distinguished Artist?

Presiding Officer: And the other articles you wrote, those that contained nationalistic attitudes and classified information?

Zuskin: How could I have written such things? And what do I have to do with those subjects? Was I collecting information? What, am I a journalist, a reporter?

[Zuskin asked the court to hear his life story. For more than an hour Zuskin told about his life, his path as an artist, and the development of the Jewish theater. Then he summarized his testimony in the court session.]

Zuskin: If you will allow me, I will tell you what I plead guilty to in the indictment.

I confirm what is written in the indictment where Markish's testimony about the theater is cited. But I do not plead guilty to the repertoire, which I objected to and because of which Mikhoels and I had words.

I categorically deny, first of all, that I was an accomplice of Mikhoels and Fefer. Second, I did not carry out any hostile work against the Communist Party and the Soviet Union. By the way, in America, Mikhoels was called a professor and not an actor, while being an actor is my life. Would I really carry out espionage for accursed America, where a person is ashamed to call himself an actor?

In the indictment it says that Mikhoels and Epshteyn, by agreement with Lozovsky, brought a number of people onto the committee in 1942, including me, and thereby organized the backbone of a nationalistic group that helped Mikhoels, Epshteyn, and Fefer carry out anti-Soviet activity. In 1942 I was in Tashkent, where I lived until October 1943. No one informed me that I had been assigned to the committee, and no one sent me any materials. I was not aware of the appeal to brother Jews, but my signature is there. I completely reject the accusation that I provided a basis for nationalism or that they used me in any way to carry out anti-Soviet work. What do I accuse myself of? Of being politically immature. That sitting at certain presidium sessions at which I never spoke or participated in the discussions, I trusted those who were in charge. These people were old communists, senior people with years of experience in the party and work in the public sphere. In trusting them, I felt that everything that took place at the committee was being checked. I remember Gubelman once asking whether things were being sent that were prohibited. They assured him that everything was being checked.

Bergelson: Who checked?

Zuskin: I cannot say who. My memory is poor. I don't trust my memory. I have barely slept in four years. I trusted those people and lost my vigilance. I trusted Epshteyn and Fefer too much, and Lozovsky, who was running the committee and was in charge of it for all intents and purposes until 1946, and Bregman, the deputy minister of state control, and Gubelman. In the presence of such mammoth figures, I knew my place. I am an actor and am guilty of concentrating all of my activity on my work as an actor. I came to the committee and was an extra. These questions did not trouble me, and I didn't know that such terrible things were going on. Let the defendants say whether I was assigned to write any articles about the economy of the USSR. No. Did I make even a single anti-Soviet statement during the whole time I was present at the sessions? No.

I am guilty of not going to meetings when I was a member of the presidium of the Jewish Anti-Fascist Committee in 1947. After that, at one of the sessions Fefer noted that "we should congratulate Zuskin, who has recently displayed more activism." What did my activism consist of? I never spoke up during the discussions, and they did not report on what was going on. Fefer confirmed that I never spoke with him about committee matters. About Mikhoels I have already spoken, and I did not speak with all those seated here. I have been asked whether I provided active support for the nationalistic work and the espionage conducted by the committee. I saw Goldberg at the theater only. I did not attend the dinners. Kvitko says that Mikhoels wanted to take charge of the Yiddish Writers' Section. I request that you ask Kvitko whether I attended even one meeting of this section when it was being run by Markish and Kvitko. And I stand accused of carrying out activity hostile to Soviet power outside of the theater.

I never compromised Soviet art. While an active member of the Actors' Club for a number of years, I never demonstrated anti-Soviet leanings. I was a deputy to the local Soviet. How could I allow myself to do something against the country that made a man out of me! Who would I have been, the son of a tailor, whose father dreamed of giving him an education? And now I hold the rank of People's Artist of the Russian Federation and Distinguished Artist of the Uzbek Republic. I am a Stalin Prize Laureate and an associate professor at the Moscow School of Theatrical Arts. For what purpose would I carry out any activity against that Motherland to which I shall be devoted until I draw my last breath!

I stand before a Soviet court, and may this Soviet court issue the severest penalty against me. That shall not affect me, for life itself is a heavy burden to me now. All I wanted was to live until the day when I could prove to a court that I am not guilty of anything, and even if I receive the most severe punishment—execution—I will be satisfied. I do not need life. For me, a stay in prison is more terrible than death. I wanted only one thing—to live until that minute when I would face the court and tell the whole truth.

Presiding Officer: Get to the point.

Zuskin: I do not value life. All that I want is for you to be convinced that I did not carry out any hostile activity in my work at the theater or at the committee.

Now I would like to speak about Mikhoels's funeral. Many of those present here have spoken about details of Mikhoels's passing, but everyone got these facts garbled. I can introduce some clarity into these issues because I know the whole story of Mikhoels's death. Everyone who spoke of it here spoke inaccurately.

Presiding Officer: What can you say?

Zuskin: I would like to give some information on that question. Markish spoke here about a letter from Mikhoels that I read to him. This was in 1946, when the twenty-fifth anniversary of my career was being celebrated. After the show, as the audience was leaving, I was summoned onto the stage, and the collective congratulated me in an understated but warm way. When I returned home, I saw a large basket of flowers with a letter inside. I was told that Mikhoels had sent it. This serves as still additional evidence that Mikhoels didn't speak with me but rather sent me a letter. The letter said the following: "Zuska!"—This is what he called me when he was feeling kindly toward me—"One way or another, whether you want it or not, you must take my place in the theater. Mikhoels." I showed this letter to Markish.

Presiding Officer: What year was that?

Zuskin: That was in 1946. This is all preliminary to the main story, to refute Fefer's contention that I and others spread rumors that Mikhoels had been murdered.

Later, when we were getting ready for the thirtieth anniversary of the October Revolution, at three in the morning, when everyone had already left and I was planning to leave as well, Mikhoels told me to stay. I stayed. He invited me into his office, and with a theatrical gesture worthy of King Lear he gestured for me to sit in his chair. "Soon you will be sitting in this place." I told him that that was the seat I least wished to occupy. Then Mikhoels took an anonymous letter from his pocket and read it to me. The contents of this letter were as follows: "You kike scum, you have flown so high that it is painful to see; may your head not go flying off as well." He showed me this letter, and I told no one about it, not even my own wife. After this, Mikhoels tore up the letter and threw it out. This was in my presence. That's how things were before 1948.

I didn't know that Mikhoels had left for Minsk, and the only explanation I could find for his absence at the theater was that some important visitor had come. This often happened. On January 11 the director of the theater called me in and said that Mikhoels had called from Minsk and asked me, Zuskin, to keep careful track of how things were going for the upcoming production, for important people would be attending. The director told me that Mikhoels would be back in Moscow on the 14th.

On the morning of the 13th we started the rehearsal, and suddenly we heard a terrible cry in Mikhoels's office. The director was talking on the phone and was asking in a terrible voice, "Who? What? Died! Both? Mikhoels? Who is this?" We went running into the office, and he told us that workers had been heading to work at seven in the morning, and they had discovered two corpses in a snowbank, which turned out to be Golubov* and Mikhoels. Then the director called various government offices and learned that both of them had died as the result of an automobile accident. That's exactly what was said.

Various rumors were going around here—How could this have happened? There must be something wrong—but none of us had any doubt about what we had been told. On the morning of the 14th a coffin containing Mikhoels's body arrived in Moscow. Just before this, there was a call from Academician Zbarsky,† who had been friendly with Mikhoels. He said that someone should call him as soon as the coffin with the body arrived at the theater, because he wanted to see what condition the body was in and whether there could be an open coffin for people to pay their last respects. And at eleven o'clock, as soon as the body arrived, Academician Zbarsky, Vovsi (Mikhoels's first cousin), and the artist Tishler‡ all came to the theater.

When the zinc-sealed coffin was opened, there were five of us around the coffin. We saw the broken nose and one large bruise on the left cheek. Then Academician Zbarsky informed me that he was going to take the corpse to his institute, where he would work on the face so that the body could be displayed. At six o'clock Academician Zbarsky came with his assistants and brought the coffin with Mikhoels's body. They put the coffin on a pedestal, turned on all of the spotlights, and created a setting in which to present him. They worked over him for another half an hour and then said that the public could now pay their last respects.

A great many people came to say good-bye. Kvitko was wrong when he said that all of this was organized by the Jewish Anti-Fascist Committee

*Vladimir Golubov-Potapov (1908–1948) was a prominent Moscow theater critic. He accompanied Mikhoels to Minsk and shared his fate; their bodies were found together.

†Boris Zbarsky (1885–1954) was a member of the Academy of Medical Sciences and participated in the embalming of Lenin's body; he also helped to prepare the body of Mikhoels for the state funeral. See Ilya Zbarsky and Samuel Hutchinson, *Lenin's Embalmers* (London, 1998), for an account of Boris Zbarsky's life and career.

‡Alexander Tishler (1898–1980), a prominent artist, was associated with the State Jewish Theater for many years.

and the theater. There was a special funeral commission created by the Arts Committee that contained leading people from Moscow theaters. The funeral expenses were covered by the state. They buried the actor Mikhoels and not Vovsi. The theater community buried him, and among hundreds of wreaths there were four Yiddish ones. Barsova and Kozlovsky were in the honor guard.* Gundorov and Suprun spoke during the funeral, whereas Fefer was the only one to speak on the committee's behalf, and he spoke in Russian. I also had to say a few words on the theater's behalf; otherwise, it would have been awkward. Fadeyev, Zubov,† and others spoke. There were many Russians there. The girls' school across from the theater attended in full.

When Zbarsky came to the funeral, he told me that Mikhoels's death had definitely been the result of an automobile accident, and he explained to me that one arm was broken and then there was that bruise on his cheek. This had happened as a result of one car crashing into another, and both of them had gone flying off to the side, so they had died as a result of the impact. And then he told me that he had died painlessly. If he had received immediate assistance, maybe something could have been done, but he had frozen to death because he lay for several hours in the snow. After Zbarsky told me that Mikhoels had died as the result of an automobile accident, could I have possibly said that he had been murdered, even though here it has even been said that I spread rumors about his murder?

Presiding Officer: Zuskin, have you finished your testimony?

Zuskin: No, allow me to add more.

Presiding Officer: Go ahead, only please be brief.

Zuskin: I was describing how people were paying their final respects to Mikhoels. While I stood by the coffin, Mikhoels's family and members of the theater were standing there. A girl came over to me then, someone who worked at the theater, and she said that a "certain person" whom we knew was standing there. I went over and suggested to this "certain person" that we cross over to the other side because there were a lot of people on this side. This "certain person" expressed condolences to the members of the theater and then asked this question: "Tell me, do you know under what circumstances Mikhoels died?" I said, "We received special notification." "Do you think it is all so simple?" At the same time there was some sort of hysterical outburst by the coffin. This "certain person" said, "You go and see what is happening there." I went over. Some girl had fainted. As the girl was being brought around, I returned to the place where this "certain person" was standing. But there was now no one there.

*Valeria Barsova (Vladimirova) (1892–1967) was an opera singer. Ivan Kozlovsky (1900–1993) was an opera singer at the Bolshoi Theater.

†Konstantin Zubov (1888–1956) was a prominent Moscow actor and frequent recipient of the Stalin Prize.

Presiding Officer: Here, read all this about yourself and say whether or not this testimony is true. (Gives him material to read.)

Zuskin: No.

Presiding Officer: So it is incorrect?

Zuskin: No. I went over to where that "certain person" was standing, and there was no one there any more. In this interrogation record it says that this person supposedly said that Mikhoels's death was the authorities' fault, and the investigators wanted it to say "Soviet authorities."

Presiding Officer: There is no such expression here. Here's what it says (he reads): "I understood from all that was said that Mikhoels's death was the result of premeditated murder."

Zuskin: I want to finish. Fefer came over to me at this time, and I told him that I thought that both of them had been drunk. Fefer stated that he had had dinner with Mikhoels, and Mikhoels hadn't had a drop of vodka, anticipating a reception at the Central Committee. This was what happened. How could I talk about a murder? This troubled me a great deal.

Presiding Officer (gives Zuskin the case materials to read): Is this paragraph recorded correctly or not?

Zuskin: In the last sentence after the word "simple," there should be a period and not a question mark. Perhaps the court is interested in how I happened to be in the synagogue?

I was at the concert tour office, and a Russian girl, a singer, said to me that they were going to a concert in a synagogue where Alexandrovich was going to sing. I had never been to a synagogue in Moscow. When I came to the synagogue, I saw Kozlovsky, Reizen, and Utesov.* There was a real concert there. I did not get the ticket from the Jewish Anti-Fascist Committee. Alexandrovich finished singing, then I disappeared. In the synagogue Kvitko and Utesov sat next to me.

[After the court exhausted its questions to Zuskin, the defendants asked questions. Bergelson asked Zuskin to tell what he considered nationalistic about plays of his produced at the theater. Zuskin repudiated this type of accusation as it related to Bergelson's plays.]

Shimeliovich: Tell us, Zuskin, did you ever hear in Moscow or Tashkent or another city any comment about, or are you aware of any aspects of, my behavior that would discredit me as a Soviet citizen and a party member?

Zuskin: Never. I hardly know you.

Shimeliovich: Now that you have answered the questions I asked you, can I conclude, not knowing the reasons why you signed your testimony during the preliminary investigation, that the testimony which you signed during

---

*Mark Reizen (1895–1992) was a renowned Soviet opera singer. Leonid Utesov (1895–1982) was an actor and director who was famous for directing a jazz ensemble.

the preliminary investigation regarding me, Shimeliovich, is not true, that for some reason or another you slandered me?

Zuskin: Yes.

Shimeliovich: Do you remember how many times the productions *Tevye the Dairyman* and *Two Hundred Thousand* were performed?

Zuskin: Two Hundred Thousand was performed between three and four hundred times, and *Tevye the Dairyman* many fewer times, but I don't remember how many.

Shimeliovich: Do you feel that these productions which I have just asked about evoked in the audience feelings of regret for the golden past, or did they show the hopelessness of the Jews' situation?

Zuskin: The play *Two Hundred Thousand* was produced in 1923 and was formalistic in form. It showed class stratification among the Jewish population. It showed how the wealthy wear masks that are similar to each other, and the workers' joie de vivre was shown along with that. This play is similar to Molière's *Le Bourgeois Gentilhomme*. As regards the play *Tevye the Dairyman*, I should say that after Mikhoels received a much-deserved rebuke from Lazar Moiseyevich [Kaganovich], a different production of it was done. Tevye the Dairyman is a strong person who, in spite of all of life's storms, comes through unbowed.

Presiding Officer: And why did Lazar Moiseyevich criticize Mikhoels?

Zuskin: He directed Mikhoels's attention to the fact that he was portraying Jews in such an ugly light. In 1938, when this play was produced, it already looked different.

Markish: Tell us what you found to be nationalistic in my dramatic works, and can you remember how nationalism was demonstrated in those roles that you played in my works?

Zuskin: I cannot say anything about those two plays that I mentioned. I can comment on the play *Kol Nidre*.

Markish: So you are talking about *Kol Nidre*. Are you conveying your own thoughts or those of Mikhoels?

Zuskin: I heard a reading of this play once, and it seemed to me that it was nationalistic.

Markish: Can you cite even one small part of this play that reveals nationalistic attitudes?

Zuskin: Mikhoels made absolutely clear to me that this play was nationalistic.

Markish: When did he say that—when I was reading the play or after I left?

Zuskin: Mikhoels said it during one of the rehearsals when you were not there.

Fefer: In your last testimony you said that the Jewish Anti-Fascist Committee had been transformed by Dobrushin, Mikhoels, Fefer, and Markish into a center for espionage?

Zuskin: I deny that.

Fefer: You also testified that instead of engaging in propaganda, the Jewish Anti-Fascist Committee sent out classified information. Did you learn of this from the forty-two volumes?

Zuskin: All that I had to say about that was unknown to me prior to my arrest.

[With this, Zuskin's testimony concluded. Without interrupting the session, the court proceeded to Shtern's testimony.]

LINA SHTERN

At the time of her arrest, Lina Shtern was a world-renowned scientist. She was born near Kaunas, Lithuania, in 1875. Her father was a successful merchant who sold Russian grain to Germany. Her grandfather was a rabbi; he helped to raise her, and, as Shtern defiantly told her interrogators, she also studied Talmud with him. As a young woman, she was educated in Switzerland, where she graduated from medical school in 1903. Her dream was to become a practicing physician; the same year she traveled to Moscow to stand for an examination for a Russian medical license, a test she duly passed.

Shtern embarked on her scientific career at a propitious moment in history, for it was in 1903 that Marie Curie received the Nobel Prize in physics. Throughout Shtern's life, she, too, was a pioneering woman in science. In 1904, Shtern accepted an invitation to return to Geneva University to conduct research in physiology; she became the school's first female full professor in science and one of the few in all of Europe. In 1939 she would become the first woman to be elected to full membership in the prestigious Soviet Academy of Sciences. That was soon followed by election to the Academy of Medical Sciences, making her a "double academician."

During Shtern's three decades in Switzerland, she was drawn to Russian émigré circles. She was particularly close to Yekaterina Peshkova, the wife of Maxim Gorky, and to the family of Georgy Plekhanov, the founder of Russian Marxism and the principal mentor of Vladimir Lenin. She also knew many Russian students, among them Boris Zbarsky, who attended her lectures on biochemistry at a time when the field was not yet recognized as a separate, scientific discipline. Zbarsky later returned to Moscow, where he became a famous professor. In 1924 he helped to prepare Lenin's corpse for the mausoleum, and for many years afterward he supervised the laboratory that continued to "treat" Lenin's remains. In 1923 it was Zbarsky who came to Geneva and invited Shtern to consider moving to Moscow to head the physiology department of the Second Moscow University, a position she accepted in March 1925.*

Lina Shtern made several significant contributions to the study of human physiology and to medical research. Her pioneering work on the hematoencephalic barrier—the frontier between the blood and the cerebrospinal fluid around the brain—was particularly noteworthy; she received the Stalin Prize for her research in 1943. Her discoveries also had a direct impact on the treatment of wounded soldiers. Many with head wounds were not responding to ordinary antibiotic treatment until Shtern understood the need to inject medications directly through the cranium. Her work saved the lives of thousands of soldiers and earned her substantial prestige. In 1943 she wrote to Molotov with a request for a car, and in spite of severe wartime shortages, she received a car and a chauffeur, which helped her to visit field hospitals at the front.[†]

Shtern also used her innovative techniques for the application of streptomycin, an antibiotic that was discovered in the United States during World War II. Shtern received an unauthorized sample through her brother Bruno, who was a businessman in the United States. Using this sample, Shtern was the first doctor successfully to treat tubercular meningitis employing an intercranial injection of streptomycin; this procedure impressed Selman Waksman, the American discoverer of streptomycin, who had been born near Kiev and who visited Moscow in 1946. Waksman was awarded the Nobel Prize in medicine in 1952 for his discovery, the same year Lina Shtern faced a Soviet court.[‡]

Shtern proved to be a refreshing presence on the Jewish Anti-Fascist Committee—perhaps because of her many years in Western Europe or

*See Ya. Rossin and B. V. Malkin, *Lina Solomonovna Shtern* (in Russian) (Moscow, 1987), for a history of Shtern's life and career. Because the book was written in the 1980s, the authors could not address her arrest and exile or other aspects of her career that were deemed politically or ideologically sensitive.

†RGASPI, f. 82, op. 2, del. 1471, l. 160. The date of the letter was December 21, 1943. Molotov wrote a note across her letter, "It is necessary to arrange a car."

‡I am indebted to Ed Skipworth of the Special Collections and University Archives of Rutgers University Libraries in New Brunswick, N.J., for his assistance.

perhaps because of her innate intelligence and lack of fear. In 1943, for example, Shtern received a directive to dismiss two Jewish employees at the *Bulletin of Experimental Biology and Medicine,* of which she was editor in chief. Asking for an explanation, she was told that a Central Committee resolution called for a severe reduction in the number of Jews among visible medical workers. Shtern could not believe that such a decision had been made. She wrote to Stalin, who received her letter and assigned Malenkov to deal with her. Malenkov must have been stunned by Shtern's direct and honest manner. She told him that persecution of Jews was "being carried out by an enemy, and that possibly even within the Central Committee there were people who were giving such directives." In response, Malenkov blamed such incidents on "spy-saboteurs" sent by the Nazis, and reassured Shtern that the editorial board of her journal could remain as it was.*

Shtern behaved with equally penetrating naïveté at the JAC. At one presidium meeting in October 1945, when Fefer was discussing new functions that the committee should assume now that the war was over, including "assignments inside the country," Stern interrupted him with a question. "Here we are talking about work for our committee inside the country. I don't completely understand," she said. "We are an anti-fascist committee. Does this mean that fascism exists inside the country?" Fefer, like Malenkov before him, must have been nonplussed. He could say only that perhaps the committee would have to change its name.†

Presiding Officer: Defendant Shtern, testify to the court, to what do you plead guilty?

Shtern: I have to say that I felt quite differently about myself before the trial than I do today. At the beginning I considered myself guilty, but today I cannot consider myself guilty. I considered myself guilty of the fact that while I was a party member and an academician I agreed to be a member of the presidium. I should have taken my responsibilities more seriously and inquired more deeply into the matters being handled there, but the fact that I was indifferent to this does not diminish my guilt. After I familiarized myself with the contents of those forty-two volumes, I concluded that very terrible things had gone on there, and I thought that I really was guilty of treating those matters very lightly.

---

*For further details about Shtern's response to anti-Semitism in 1943, see Kostyrchenko, *Out of the Red Shadows,* p. 71.

†GARF, f. 8114, op. 1, del. 1053, l. 41 from the minutes of the JAC Presidium, October 23, 1945.

Sitting here in court, I have concluded that I cannot accuse myself of this, especially since even if I had delved more deeply into all of this, I would not have understood the full extent of the criminality, and therefore nothing would have changed there. I also think that there is much more contained in these volumes than actually took place there.

I am guilty of allowing myself to be in a suspect position. Caesar's wife is above suspicion and, perhaps it needs to be said, should be above suspicion. The same can be said of a Soviet academician and party member if his behavior arouses suspicion. Even before I became familiar in court with the accusations directed against the committee, I told myself that I should consider myself guilty in the same way that a sentry would be guilty for falling asleep at his post. Called as I was to become a member of the presidium, I am the same as that sentry who should not fall asleep at his post; and if he does happen to fall asleep, then he deserves a particular punishment. I am that sentry who fell asleep at his post. As a party member, I should have taken an interest and not been satisfied with what I heard from other people that everything was going well. I should have checked on one or another action. I am not an investigator, but a scientific researcher. When it comes to science, I accept nothing on faith, but check everything. In the field of science I have the satisfaction of knowing that I have not done one experiment or published one work (and it is fifty years since I began my first scientific activity) that could be cast in doubt, because before I ever published or said anything, I checked everything very carefully. And I blame myself for that.

Why is it that in science, in my work, I have been so strict and so careful, and here I took my work as a presidium member so lightly? But I don't see what I could have done, even if I had carefully inquired into that activity. How I should evaluate my life depends on that.

As regards the nationalism issue, I listened very attentively. Nationalism on the one hand, and cosmopolitanism on the other—I am, after all, being accused of both.

Presiding Officer: You are accusing yourself of that.

Shtern: I have to say that what you were told about how the investigation went (I have never lied in my entire life) was true; it happened as they said. This investigation is not an investigation, it is a case of the court being led astray and deluded. I will be blunt; at times I express myself very bluntly. Things are so confused here that . . .

Presiding Officer: Who is confusing things—during either the investigation or the trial?

Shtern: That is the point, that the court could have resolved things in two or three days. I studied those forty-two volumes—I'm used to working after all, figuring things out, and reading. But this work really is beyond anyone's strength.

Presiding Officer: When did you become a member of the presidium?

Shtern: I was informed that I had been elected to the presidium in the spring of 1944.

Presiding Officer: While before that you were a member of the committee?

Shtern: Perhaps I was listed as a committee member, but I didn't know it.

Presiding Officer: During the preliminary investigation you said that you became a member of the committee in 1944. This was shortly after the meeting at the Hall of Columns. And when was the last time you were at the committee?

Shtern: In 1947, when I spoke at a meeting about sending a protest about pogroms in England. I believe this was in October. In general, I didn't attend the Jewish Anti-Fascist Committee in 1947. I was at the sessions maybe twice. I was a member of all of the anti-fascist committees: I was a member of the Anti-Fascist Committee of Soviet Scientists, the Women's Anti-Fascist Committee, the Youth Committee—in a word, of all the antifascist committees. I was very active in the Anti-Fascist Committee of Scientists.

Presiding Officer: Did you participate at the sessions of all the committees?

Shtern: Yes. I was very active. This was just after the beginning of the war. I spoke often then, because I was also a member of the International Organization of University Women and the International Committee, which fought for peace and freedom. And so, in light of my contacts with international organizations, I was invited to speak in English, French, and German. I also was very active with the Soviet scientists. I organized two committees: one committee in Alma-Ata, where I was evacuated at one point, and a branch of that committee in Omsk, where a department of the Second Medical Institute was located, of which I was the head.

Presiding Officer: Tell us, Shtern, did you attend the session of the Jewish Anti-Fascist Committee when the report about the partisans was given?

Shtern: As I recall, I was at the session when someone complained that . . .

Presiding Officer: Jews were not being accepted into the Belorussian detachments?

Shtern: Yes. Here I heard about the impression that report left on several defendants, but that was not the meaning that I ascribed to it at all. I know that the same presentation can strike different people in different ways.

Presiding Officer: Is your testimony correct that discrimination against the Jews in the Soviet Union was discussed at one of the presidium sessions, and you insisted that the group should write to government institutions about it?

Shtern: That did take place, and I will tell you about the letter. I appealed to Comrade Stalin, and the letter had certain consequences. At that session, I spoke about the fact that if a person is turned down for something, they should not think that it was an offense against the Jews, that it was discrimination, that it was coming from higher up, as I had a strong basis for saying that this was the individual handiwork of the person who insulted you.

This is considered anti-Soviet activity on my part, because nothing else can be found in the materials besides this. I want to say that from the day I came to the Soviet Union, I have not had my rights infringed in the slightest. It's harder for me to express myself in Russian than in the language I was used to speaking before.

Presiding Officer: And what language is that?

Shtern: French.

Presiding Officer: You testified that at the session about the thirtieth anniversary of the October Revolution, when the agenda was under discussion, you spoke out from nationalistic positions. You demanded that the committee write more articles, and were indignant over the fact that our press downplays the role of the Jews (vol. 10, p. 83). "At that session I again raised the issue of supposed discrimination against Jews and demanded that the committee raise this question with government bodies."

Shtern: That's not quite how it was.

Presiding Officer: But you confessed during the investigation that you spoke, making nationalistic proposals regarding discrimination against the Jews in the USSR. Do you confirm that?

Shtern: I deny that. I am sufficiently grown up to change my opinion.

Presiding Officer: Why do you change your opinion?

Shtern: Because it doesn't correspond to what I think.

Presiding Officer: Were you interrogated about *Eynikayt?*

Shtern: I never read it and never wrote for it. Maybe it would have been useful if I had read it and written something for it, but I don't write in that language.

Presiding Officer: Regarding Jewish pogroms in England, that was at a session in 1947. You testified during the preliminary investigation: "When I was approached to sign a protest against the Jewish pogroms, I refused." You were asked why. "Because the information about this was unconvincing to me. I also said that I knew various things about pogroms in England, but that didn't mean such things were not taking place in our country, in the Soviet Union."

Shtern: This is not my testimony.

Presiding Officer: Your signature is here. This is the interrogation record dated January 30, 1952 (vol. 10, p. 96).

Shtern: No, that is not the case. I said at the time that we needed to verify whether such pogroms were taking place. I'm not used to signing without verifying. This is what had happened. They were discussing a plan to write a protest about Jewish pogroms in England. I didn't know anything about these incidents, although they said that it had been written about in our press. Then someone said that I had committed a political mistake, because if they were supposedly planning to write a protest or some kind of an appeal, then that was already approved on high and was practically a governmental directive. So that's what I didn't understand. Besides, I know England pretty well. I know how people live there, and it seemed to me that there was no basis for talking about Jewish pogroms there.

Presiding Officer: But fascists were operating there, weren't they?

Shtern: It depends where. If two merchants had an argument somewhere in some little town and one of them happened to be a Jew and his shop windows got broken, can you really call that a pogrom?

Presiding Officer: Fefer, explain what happened.

Fefer: There was an item in *Pravda* about Jewish pogroms that had taken place in England. Greater detail was given in *Trud*. When I read about this, I called Shumeiko and asked whether it made sense to latch onto this and make an issue out of it and write a protest about it in order to expose the Labour government under which such things were taking place. Shumeiko said he would call me after he had sought advice. Some time later, Shumeiko called and said that I should go ahead with the protest. I wrote it, filling two or three pages, and gave it to the Foreign Policy Department of the Central Committee.

The appeal was read at the Foreign Policy Department, and they decided that this was a necessary initiative, and they told me to call the presidium together and put forward this protest. It was also proposed that there be prominent people on the presidium, such as Academician Shtern, Marshak, and Ehrenburg. Mikhoels was the one who informed me about this proposal. The session went as usual. All present spoke out and joined the protest. I remember Shtern's question "In general, is this correct?"

Presiding Officer: Bregman, explain what happened.

Bregman: Shtern's words were, "Before we write a protest, we need to see where the pogroms are taking place." I interpreted her remark to mean that she was equivocating and misrepresenting her point for a political purpose.

Fefer: Words can be understood in a variety of ways, but I do not remember the same words as Bregman does. When Shtern had doubts about whether pogroms were taking place in England, I felt there was some disloyalty on her part. I said that there had been dispatches in *Pravda* and *Trud,* and that such a fact was unpleasant, and that this could take place in England, for Oswald Mosley had a following there and this was completely possible. It should be noted that Shtern's remark provoked a reaction, and that she acted very unpleasantly.

Presiding Officer: You are familiar with the expert commission's findings. Have you studied the expert commission's report on espionage in regard to the case?

Shtern: I have not read it.

Presiding Officer: But are you familiar with the reports about nationalistic activity? Your name is mentioned there.

Shtern: It says that I gave Americans a collection of scientific publications.

Presiding Officer: That has to do with your contact with foreigners, but now the question is about nationalistic propaganda work that you carried out. Did you speak out and make nationalistic statements at committee sessions?

Shtern: I cannot imagine such a thing. I still do not know whether or not I am a nationalist. Maybe I am a nationalist. I should explain how I feel about this question.

Presiding Officer: At the committee session when the agenda was under discussion a question about the article "What Soviet Power Has Done for the Jews" came up. This was in connection with the thirtieth anniversary of the October Revolution. In your statement you said that someone should write an article on a different subject, namely, "What the Jews Have Done for Soviet Power."

Shtern: That was tendentiously put.

Presiding Officer: But this was taken from the minutes of the committee presidium session.

Shtern: How do I see nationalism and the national question? I believe that the Jewish national question does not exist. I cannot imagine a nation without territory. Even in the Soviet Union there are no Jews living on their own territory. If we are talking about the Armenians who live in Armenia, then that makes sense. But I have no concept of a Jewish nation.

Presiding Officer: I am asking you a question, and you are lecturing me about the Jews. I am asking you a question. You make nationalistic statements about how it is not the Soviet people but the Jews who should be written about in the newspaper, and how the Jews need to be put forward and overemphasized. You look at everything from the viewpoint of what it will give the Jews—not What did Soviet power give the Jews? but What did the Jews give Soviet power?

Shtern: Everything depends on the context in which it is presented. If you want to give me the opportunity to explain my attitude about this question, I will do so. When I came to the Soviet Union, it did not occur to me that I should note when recording my nationality that I was a Jew.* In that space

*The internal Soviet passport system was instituted on December 27, 1932. At the age of

I always wrote "Soviet." I took Soviet citizenship—what does that have to do with being a Jew? I never wrote that. Then I was told that I had to do that. Well, since they said that this is what I had to do, I started to write "Jew." But that means nothing, because I would never have denied my origins. I was not offended by this, of course. They talk about Armenians, Uzbeks, and others, too.

Presiding Officer: We are talking about a specific document that contains your words.

Shtern: Those cannot be my words recorded here because I didn't talk about that.

Presiding Officer: They were recorded not in the interrogation record, but in the minutes of the Jewish Anti-Fascist Committee presidium session.

Shtern: I will explain where this comes from. Even if I were asked today whether I am a Jewish nationalist, I would not be able to answer such a question. It is taken as a crime, whereas in reality it is not a crime at all. Why is it a disgrace to talk about Jews?

Presiding Officer: And how does it look that you regard everything in terms of what it will do for the Jews?

Shtern: I don't look at it that way. If that is what's written there, then it was simply a joke. I have something of the French way about me, and I said that to defuse the atmosphere.

Presiding Officer: So these were your words: "What will this do for the Jews?"

Let's move on. When there was a report about partisans at the committee on August 30, 1944, you asked the question "How did the liberated population of Minsk greet the families of Jews who were returning from partisan detachments? Were they housed and provided with employment, and was there any information about what they were doing?" To which came the answer "The mood in the city is not good. There have been many incidents of anti-Semitism on the part of the local population."

The expert commission writes about this that Shtern expressed the nationalistic positions of the committee and its leaders with extreme cynicism, saying, "There has already been enough said and written about what the Germans have done. Now it is important for us to establish the attitudes of those people with whom we are going to have to live. It's important to have the names of those people who are now getting off scot-free."

Shtern: I would like to point out something here. I know a professor who was a city burgomaster during the German occupation. Then, of course, he and

---

sixteen each citizen was required to apply for a passport and declare his or her nationality based on the nationality of the parents. In a mixed marriage, the individual had the right to choose one of the nationalities. In the Soviet Union, to be a Jew was to be a member of a particular nationality.

others like him were exposed. But I said that there are also people who were able to get off scot-free, and one needs to be cautious with them, because they are the ones who sow evil deeds around them.

I know how well the people of the Ukraine and Belorussia treated the Jews. For example, I have a niece, and when the Germans appeared in Minsk, she left there with her child in her arms and with her ill mother. She told me about how her neighbors helped her and how people carried her child. And when she returned to Minsk, she encountered the same good treatment.

Presiding Officer: You keep making statements all the time about how Jews are being offended by other people and how much is required of them. I will read out your statement made at a presidium session in October 1947. You say, "Finally, it is time for us."

Shtern: I talked about how we needed to say what Soviet power had given the Jews. I saw how every factory and organization wrote about its achievements during the thirty years of Soviet power. If it was necessary to write separately about the Jews, then I felt that it would be much more correct to talk about what the Jews had achieved in these thirty years. If millions of people had previously had nothing, now these people had everything, had become professors, generals, that is, they had achieved the highest level of culture, and Soviet power had given them all of this. It was wonderful. Soviet power had given something to everyone. There wasn't a single person who hadn't gotten something from Soviet power. And I framed the question as "What did the Jews give Soviet power?" in order to show how they had repaid the concern for them.

Presiding Officer: Defendant Shtern, not so long ago—on March 11, 1952—you were interrogated by the prosecutor. At the time you were presented with an indictment which said that you committed the crimes described in article 58-1a, treason; article 58-10, part 2—anti-Soviet, nationalistic activity; and article 58-11—being a member of this counterrevolutionary organization. You answered that you understood the essence of the accusation and that you, as a member of the presidium starting in 1944, pled guilty to participating in its hostile work, managed by Mikhoels, Fefer, Kvitko, and their other accomplices. And at sessions of the committee presidium, you had spoken of alleged infringements of Jews' rights occurring in the USSR. "Among my friends I stated nationalistic views about the need to preserve the Hebrew language and culture. I sent a letter addressed to the head of the Soviet government about supposed discrimination against the Jews" (vol. 10, p. 52). Is this testimony correct?

Shtern: What can I say? Of course I don't consider myself guilty of any of the three counts. I never committed treason, I never distributed any information, and I never committed slander. What is there here that requires any particular discussion or argumentation?

Presiding Officer: I ask specifically: Do you plead guilty to demanding during your statements at the sessions of the committee presidium that the leaders raise with the government the question of defending Jews who were allegedly being subjected to discrimination?

Shtern: I said that the government must be informed of the way things were being interpreted. I believe that there was no need to defend anyone here, but those who were spreading these rumors needed a good slap.

Presiding Officer: The committee was supposed to be carrying out counter-propaganda, and if there were isolated incidents of anti-Semitism—let's say that Zuskin was insulted for being a Jew—then he had recourse, there are criminal laws—article 59-7—according to which anyone who insults the national feelings of another is responsible for committing criminal actions. And what is the purpose of discussing these questions? You stand accused of conducting nationalistic activity because the committee became the center of all of this.

Shtern: Only once at the presidium was the question raised, that a whole series of complaints had been received about discrimination against the Jews.

Presiding Officer: And who raised this question at the presidium?

Shtern: I don't remember; after all, I didn't know most members of the presidium. When this concern was raised, I said that since these complaints were coming in, the government needed to be informed that such events were occurring. In addition, I did not doubt for a minute that such things were happening, though perhaps not in the form they were described. For example, let's say a Jew was not admitted to college or was fired from a job. Instead of saying that this was done because he did not have the proper qualifications, he would say that this happened because he was a Jew.

Presiding Officer: And are you really unaware of cases when Russians were fired or Ukrainians, Belorussians, were expelled from the party or put on trial?

Shtern: The thing is, up until 1943 I never heard anything that would indicate that distinctions were being made between Jews and non-Jews. In 1943, this was in the spring, a colleague approached me: Professor Shtor. The chancellor of Moscow State University had suggested to him that he retire and had said in addition to that, that his situation would not change, he would still have his laboratory and his salary, but he shouldn't head the department. Shtor asked, "What's the reason for this?" The chancellor responded that it was awkward for the Lomonosov Institute to have a Jew heading a department, and pointed to a number of other people who had already been relieved of their posts.

Since Shtor had previously worked for me at the institute, he decided that I would hire him back, but I told him that he should ignore the incident and not retire. But the thing is that the chancellor explained to him that there was supposedly a decree. I said that this couldn't be, and he shouldn't pay it any mind. If he wanted to let him go, let him do so; he still had the right to appeal his action.

Presiding Officer: So you deny that you made such a statement?

Shtern: I repeat that my statement was in regard to the letter that I spoke of yesterday.

Presiding Officer: What letter?

Shtern: The letter that I wrote to Comrade Stalin. I want to recount another notable case. I was editor in chief of a medical journal that was published for many years. The editorial board had two employees, that is, two secretaries, with non-Russian last names. I was called in and told that these two secretaries must be replaced. This was in 1943. "Why?" I asked. "They must be replaced," I was told, and nothing else was said. I disagreed. They told me, "You are a member of the party, and if you learn the reason, you will neither protest nor disagree. There is a decree stating that the number of Jews on the editorial board must be reduced. You see," I was told, "Hitler is dropping leaflets saying that there are Jews everywhere in the USSR, and this degrades the culture of the Russian people."

Presiding Officer: Who said this?

Shtern: Academician Sergeyev.

Presiding Officer: Who is he?

Shtern: He is a full member of the Academy of Medical Sciences and the director of an institute. He also said that there was a decree requiring a reduction in the number of Jews in managerial positions, that almost 90 percent of the head doctors were Jewish. I said that if that was the approach, then I should be removed, too, for my last name was not Russian, either. He responded that I was too well known abroad, so this would not affect me. I said that I could not agree with such a proposal and that I needed to think about it.

The same evening I met Emelian Yaroslavsky* at some meeting of the academy (he was an academician), and I asked if there was such a decree. His eyes grew large, and he said that there was nothing of the kind and that the appropriate people should be informed of this, and then he immediately told me that the best thing would be for me to write a letter to Comrade Stalin. After some time had passed, I was called into the Central Committee secretariat. Comrades Malenkov and Shatalin† were there. Comrade Malenkov was very solicitous of me and said that Comrade Stalin had given him my letter and suggested that he have a talk with me. We talked for two

---

*Emilyan Yaroslavsky (Miney Gubelman) (1878–1943) was a longtime party activist close to Stalin. From 1931 on, he served as chairman of the All-Union Society of Old Bolsheviks.

†Nikolai Shatalin (1904–1984) was a veteran staff member of the Central Committee.

hours. I told him that I didn't doubt for a minute that this was the work of a hostile hand and that it was even possible that people had appeared on the staff of the Central Committee who were giving these orders.

Malenkov told me that all sorts of spies and saboteurs were planted around the USSR now and that this was possible. He also had very hard things to say about Sergeyev. And he told me that I had conducted myself as I should have, and that the editorial board should be reconstituted as it had been before. And indeed, after this conversation everything ceased immediately. Shimeliovich was right when he said that Mitirev was severely rebuked. I believe that I fulfilled my duty as a Soviet citizen and a party member.

Presiding Officer: But why did you need to raise this question before the committee presidium?

Shtern: I know how people are. If a person starts complaining, he doesn't stop at that. He tells his friends and family and in doing so causes great harm. This side of things is far more dangerous than talking openly about it. There are people who harm the interests of the state by taking cover under party and government directives. I believe that I was fulfilling my duty by speaking about this openly.

Presiding Officer: It says in your testimony that among your friends you expressed nationalistic views. Is this the case?

Shtern: I am not an advocate of the Hebrew language. I am from the Baltic region. In our family we always spoke German.

Presiding Officer: Did you testify to the prosecutor that in this country the achievements of Western science are ignored?

Shtern: I have always been of the opinion, and continue to hold the opinion, that when a scientific question is being studied, its history must be discussed. I can write my scientific papers only on the basis of work previously done in the same area.

Presiding Officer: But you said that our science lags behind Western science. That is another matter altogether.

Shtern: There are problems in science that are resolved simultaneously, not only in our country, but in England, France, and other places. We scientists must not be satisfied with what is being done in one place. I cannot imagine science developing in only one country. I do not deny the achievements in scientific thought in our country. We have achievements, but all of those achievements have a history. If we take the issue of atomic energy, it is based on the work of Mendeleyev* and his periodic table. This is the foundation of our chemistry, but we must not ignore what is being done else-

---

*Dmitry Mendeleyev (1834–1907) was a prominent Russian chemist. He devised the periodic table of chemical elements.

where. I am a person who lacks a strong grasp of political issues, but for fifty years I have worked in science, and I believe that we must not shut ourselves off from anyone. I said this to my colleagues.

Presiding Officer: At an interrogation on February 10, 1949 (vol. 9, p. 73), you said that science is outside politics. Is this testimony correct?

Shtern: I believe that science should truly stand outside politics. I said that science knows no borders and has no homeland; only art has a homeland. If one takes any scientific problem and follows its development, can one really say that science has a homeland or can betray its homeland? And what abstract and nonabstract science are I do not know.

Presiding Officer: So, in your view, this testimony is incorrectly recorded?

Shtern: Yes, it is incorrectly recorded.

Presiding Officer: And the idea of abstract world science?

Shtern: I don't know what is being called abstract science. I am very glad that I can speak here before you. If you want to know, it is very important for me to understand what and who I am. I considered myself an honest person, direct, but perhaps I am not that way at all. There are very many subjects here which I do not understand at all.

Presiding Officer: This is what has to be examined. Tell us, what about your testimony about how you took up a hostile stance when you arrived in the Soviet Union and established that there was a great deal here that was alien to you, because you were raised abroad under different conditions, and, in addition, were dissatisfied with the fact that your work at first did not meet with approval.

Shtern: In Geneva I had everything and more, but I left everything behind without hesitation, left in order to work in the Soviet Union. Every year I made business trips abroad and had the opportunity to remain there, but I did not do that.

Presiding Officer: What was the last year you were abroad?

Shtern: 1935. I had the opportunity to go in 1936 as well, but I turned it down. I had so many opportunities to go abroad again. An apartment and a department chairmanship were held for me for five years because they thought I would come back. Of course I have no regrets; I did the right thing in coming here.

[Next the court looked at various meetings Shtern had had with foreign scientists—with Tripp, the information attaché from the British Embassy, and with a prominent microbiologist, Professor Madd,* and with others. And al-

---

*This is a reference to Stuart Mudd (not Madd), a professor of microbiology at the University of Pennsylvania. He was also president of the American-Soviet Medical Society between 1945 and 1947. In 1946, Professor Mudd visited Moscow.

though Shtern confirmed that the conversations with Tripp and Madd were quite scientific—specifically, about the medical applications of streptomycin, of which, incidentally, British scientists had given her twelve hundred grams [forty-two ounces]—the chairman, summarizing these episodes in the indictment, referred to her party membership.]

Presiding Officer: At this time you had already been a communist for around ten years and should have known about vigilance and caution. After all, we live encircled by capitalists, and you mustn't be so trusting of people.

Shtern: If I were not trusting, I wouldn't be sitting here, but I don't regret that I was trusting. Today I face the court, and I understand that every incorrect or careless word of mine could turn out to be harmful to me, but I would like to think that my openness will not cause me any harm. I am a very trusting person, and I don't regret that. I have had the luck to know some very good people. I have had the luck and opportunity to see the very best people of our country. Abroad, in Geneva, for example, my friends were also the very best people. In this regard I am a pretty fortunate person. These people subsequently played important roles in our country. I want to say that if there were no such people among my friends, I would have looked on life differently. You are absolutely right that I was very trusting toward all people. And if I live, that will be a very good lesson for me in the future.

Presiding Officer: The court has no questions for you.

Shtern: I would like to tell the court who I am.

Presiding Officer: We are very familiar with your biography.

Shtern: No, I didn't write it down.

Presiding Officer: We know that you are from the family of a merchant, that you studied in Geneva and received your higher education there, and that you then engaged in scientific work. In 1925, at the recommendation of Academician Bakh,* you came here and started working at the Academy of Sciences. No one is holding that work against you.

Shtern: It is very important to me to tell about myself so that you know who you are dealing with. I may be the product of a bourgeois family, but that does not mean that I have to be hostile to Soviet power.

Presiding Officer: Go ahead. Only please tell us, do you confirm the testimony that you gave during the investigation?

Shtern: No, none of it.

Presiding Officer: Why?

Shtern: Because there is not a single word there that is mine.

---

*Alexei Bakh (1857–1946) was a prominent biochemist and a mentor to Lina Shtern.

Presiding Officer: So how did you come to sign it?

Shtern: I'll tell you what happened. When I was brought here, I was in a great state of confusion. It was on the seventh floor, and I was met in a strange fashion. There were a lot of people in the room; there were colonels and generals seated there. I was immediately asked from where I had come to the USSR, who sent me, and who my masters were. It sounded as though I had come to the Soviet Union as an intelligence agent and saboteur. I was taken aback. I asked, "What masters? What assignments?" Then two days later I was called in to see the minister. He asked me, "Do you know Zhemchuzhina?" I said, "Yes, I know her." He asked, "What is the nature of your relationship?" I said that I had met her at a reception for Madame Churchill and then met her once when she came to the institute. I was asked why I had spoken with her and why she came to see me. I replied that I had just gotten to know her, just as I might have gotten to know many other people. The minister said, "You think about it, and in a few days tell me everything, make a clean breast of it, and if you tell me everything, then you can go back to your work." I waited for a summons, but I didn't see him again. I was very distressed, for my work had been going wonderfully. Take my work with streptomycin. I had saved thousands of people. And prior to my arrest I had received many letters of gratitude.

Presiding Officer: So you admitted your guilt?

Shtern: Where?

Presiding Officer: During the preliminary investigation.

Shtern: I did not plead guilty to anything, but signed the interrogation record in order to leave here.

Presiding Officer: How could you leave here when you yourself signed testimony that you had conducted anti-Soviet activity?

Shtern: I wanted to have the opportunity to talk with the minister. I should say that I had the unshakable impression that they were trying to find a crime that would fit me. If I did have anti-Soviet tendencies, what would have made me come here and stay? Every year I went abroad on business and had so many opportunities to stay there. What do you think it was that drew me here? Why did I leave the surroundings in which I was raised? It was certainly not in order to live better here. I had enough of everything. I was not seeking glory. I had that, too. Perhaps this is not proper, but I will have to speak about myself. I am told that when three physiologists were named, I was always among them. Why did I come to the Soviet Union? Because I believed that a better world was being created here, and I had every reason to believe that, because I knew the best people in Geneva.

Presiding Officer: During the preliminary investigation you testified that you conducted anti-Soviet activity. How does this go with your ambitions?

Shtern: If you follow the course of the investigation, how do you explain the fact that three times now I have been transferred from the internal prison to Lefortovo for not wanting to sign the novel the investigator wrote?

Presiding Officer: Well, there's a prison there and a prison here. What's the difference?

Shtern: Over there was the anteroom to hell. You can go there sometime and see what goes on. I am not complaining that I was in solitary confinement. It's better to be alone than in bad company. When I signed the longest of the interrogation records, I saw that it was a stew concocted from several interrogations. I sat there for three weeks, and I was called in here once. That was in early February, and after I spent ten days here and nothing came of it, I was taken back there again. The floor there is cement, the heating in the cell is bad, the casement windows are small and not always open, and I couldn't eat the food. How long can a person sit? After all, I didn't want to die. I don't want to die today either, because I still have not done everything for science that I should. I consider what I've done in the Soviet Union in terms of curing people to be some of the most important work of the past decade.

[At 10:25 P.M., the chairman interrupted Shtern's testimony and announced a recess, ending the court session on Thursday, June 12, 1952. The next session did not take place until two weeks later, on June 26. Before resuming Shtern's testimony, the court moved on to a closed-session examination of the results of the expert commission's work.]

Experts' Testimony in Closed Judicial Session, June 26

[On June 26, 1952, at 12:30 P.M., two experts, Alexei Soldatov-Fedotov and Leonid Olshansky, came to the court session. Another expert, P. M. Kisel, did not appear because he was on vacation.

The chairman identified the experts, who gave the following testimony about themselves:]

Fedotov: I, Alexei Maximovich Soldatov-Fedotov, member of the Communist Party, have had higher education and graduated with a degree in literature. I have worked at Glavlit since 1947, and at the present time am the deputy director of department 5 of Glavlit.

Olshansky: I, Leonid Petrovich Olshansky, a member of the Communist Party since 1919, have had higher education and work as deputy director of inspection at the USSR Ministry of Armaments. My job is to establish the level of secrecy for documents and different types of information.

[The experts gave answers to the court's questions.]

Question: Does the expert commission confirm its findings on the case (dated January 30, 1952), which it gave on the documents enumerated in points

1–78 of the decree issued by the assistant director of the investigative division for especially important cases of the MGB dated January 18, 1952?

Fedotov: Yes, we confirm the findings of our expert commission that we gave on January 30, 1952.

Question: Did the commission familiarize itself with the original documents indicated in points 1–78 of the decree mentioned, or did the commission receive for examination copies of these documents and excerpts therefrom, which are appended as material evidence to the case in question?

Fedotov: We had in our possession copies of the documents that are appended to our conclusions in the case in question. While working with these materials, it did not even occur to us to wonder where the original documents are kept, because we believed that we should give our conclusions based on the materials provided to us by the agencies conducting the preliminary investigation.

Question: Were the files and warrants of the Jewish Anti-Fascist Committee that related to the abovementioned documents provided to the expert commission, and did the commission approve the original identifying papers of these documents? In the affirmative case, why didn't the expert commission append these identifying papers to the case?

Fedotov: The original Jewish Anti-Fascist Committee cases and files were not in the commission's possession. There were no identifying papers with the copies of the materials provided to us.

Question: Did the commission establish which of the documents they studied had been sent abroad?

Fedotov: The investigative agencies did not pose this question to the commission, and in studying the materials we were of the opinion that all of these materials had been sent abroad. We are also unable to say what systems and procedures were used at the Jewish Anti-Fascist Committee in sending these documents.

We know that according to current procedure, all materials that are sent abroad are supposed to be carefully reviewed by the censor. In this case it is difficult for me to say whether or not these materials went through the censor. If the commission knew while reaching its conclusions that all of these materials had gone through the censor according to established procedure, I am certain that we would have had a different attitude toward them. We believed that these materials were sent abroad using some other means, without going through the censor.

Question: Did the commission determine from the identifying documentation the names of the Glavlit censors and other responsible parties who gave permission to send the documents abroad?

Fedotov: Since each of us on the commission believed that all of the Jewish Anti-Fascist Committee materials were sent abroad by an unofficial route via some kind of secret channels, the issue of identifying who the censors were who checked this material did not come up. In addition, there were no identifying papers accompanying the documents, which would have indicated that these documents were sent abroad through official means after appropriate review by the censors.

Question: Why is it that when the commission was determining the degree of secrecy of the information in the Jewish Anti-Fascist Committee articles, it was guided by the register of publications from 1945, and not the one from 1948? Was the Register of 1945 in effect during the period when the commission was working?

Fedotov: We were guided by the Register of 1945 because that register directly determined whether or not various information could be published in the open press, and the Council of Ministers register published in 1948 was less specific as to this question. Starting in 1948, the Register of 1945 ceased to be valid.

Question: On the basis of what information did the commission conclude that the requests and letters to the Jewish Anti-Fascist Committee from America were from the representatives of reactionary circles rather than progressive ones?

Fedotov: This idea was formulated by Kisel, and we agreed with him. Now we cannot confirm that these requests came from reactionary circles in America and England, for we do not have precise information about this.

Question: What was guiding the commission when it concluded that while they were in America, Mikhoels and Fefer made a commitment to provide the Americans with state secrets?

Fedotov: We came to this conclusion after we familiarized ourselves with an excerpt from a memorandum saying that Mikhoels and Fefer had committed themselves to sending information about the Jewish autonomous region to America—specifically, information about the population, industry, and cultural institutions. We believed that anything requested from abroad could only be material containing state secrets.

On the basis of this document we concluded that such activity by Fefer and Mikhoels was espionage. I should say that on this question we went beyond the mandate we had been given in making findings about espionage and economic espionage.

Question: Tell the court what procedures you used in working with the Jewish Anti-Fascist Committee materials.

Fedotov: We were called into the investigative division of the MGB and asked to answer questions after we had studied the documents in the case.

I, Soldatov-Fedotov, and Kisel worked together the whole time, and Olshansky became involved in the work at the end, when the commission's report was almost completely written.

During our work of studying these materials Olshansky and I did not once meet. I met him for the first time here in court.

On the basis of our study of the materials provided to us by the investigators we drew our conclusions on the case. The author or, rather, the editor of the conclusions was Kisel.

In regard to certain documents we entered a stipulation in our conclusions that any information included in various articles was not a state secret if it had been previously published in the official Soviet press. We included such a stipulation because we did not have the opportunity to determine whether or not information had been published previously, for we did not have at our disposal official information indicating which of the articles placed by the Jewish Anti-Fascist Committee had figured previously in the official Soviet press and which had not. We informed the investigators of this, in response to which we were told that this had nothing to do with the case.

[Expert Olshansky responded to a question from the chairman.]

Olshansky: I took part in the commission's work at the very end. The date January 30, 1952, on the investigator's decree bringing me onto the case in an expert capacity is not correct. I signed the document about bringing me on in the capacity of an expert at the same time as the expert commission conclusions were signed. Indeed, when I got down to work, the expert commission's conclusions had already been almost completely written by expert Kisel. This was about three to four days prior to the end of our work.

Question: Were the following articles published in *Eynikayt:* "New Tasks for Soviet Industry" by D. Dneprov; "The Construction of a Mighty Phosphorite Mine Is Completed in the Distant Mountains of Kazakhstan" by A. Havin; "Listening to Comrade Molotov's Report" by Shcheglov; "The First Fruits of Peaceful Labor" by S. Solomonov; and "In New Conditions" by D. Reiser? Were the articles mentioned here sent abroad? If the answer is in the affirmative, can the expert commission say which of the Glavlit censors and which of the senior staff at the Jewish Anti-Fascist Committee allowed these articles to be sent and published and what time period they are from, and indicate specifically in what way these articles contain state secrets?

Olshansky: The expert commission cannot say whether these articles were sent abroad or printed in *Eynikayt,* because the investigators did not set the task of determining this. The commission believes the following about information contained in these articles:

a) The Dneprov article indicates that military plants were converting to peaceful production and, in addition to that, gives the plant locations;
b) Havin's article "In the Distant Mountains of Kazakhstan" reveals that there are phosphorite reserves in Kazakhstan;

    c) Shcheglov's article "Listening to Comrade Molotov's Report" contains
       general information about industry in the USSR. Shcheglov's allusions
       to the Soviet press go beyond the area the commission was studying;

    d) Similar information of a broad sort is contained in Solomonov's article
       "The First Fruits of Peaceful Labor" and Reiser's article "In New Con-
       ditions."

Taking as its guide the 1945 register of information that can be openly
printed, the commission believes that similar information can be published
only with Glavlit's permission. It was not part of the commission's task to
determine whether or not such permission was given.

As to our conclusion in regard to Zabelshinsky's article "Nonferrous
Metals," I can say that although it was published in the newspaper *Krasny
Flot,* we concluded that sending this article abroad did constitute divulging
a state secret. The Register of 1945 establishes a special procedure for publishing information about industry and railroad transport. Such information can be published only with permission from someone authorized by
the Council of Ministers. It was on this basis that we gave our conclusions
about these sorts of articles, specifically Yuzefovich's article, which refers
to construction of new railroad lines.

In addition I want to say that if among the articles we studied there are
articles that passed the Glavlit censor, then mention of them must be removed from our conclusions. We knew nothing about that side of the case.

Question: Was the commission guided by the Register of 1945 by its own decision or by order of the investigators?

Olshansky: The assistant director of the MGB investigative division for especially important cases, Lieutenant Colonel Grishaev, told us right away
that in assessing the degree of secrecy of the material given us we should use
the Register of 1945. The Register of 1945 was the only one that brought
together all issues having to do with the materials published in print. In
fact, this register was not a register of materials containing state secrets, but
indicated what information was forbidden to be published. The commission did not raise with the investigators the issue of applying the Register of
1948.

Question: What else can the expert commission add to its testimony?

Olshansky: Here in court we have come to the conclusion that the findings
that we gave during the preliminary investigation are incomplete and limited. It seems that because we did not understand our task, or our rights
and obligations in studying the materials and issuing conclusions, the expert commission did not request from the investigators that it be provided
with all the necessary materials to provide complete and correct conclusions. We believe that if we were given copies of particular documents to review, that meant that was the way it was supposed to be.

In making our conclusions we believed that all of these materials escaped the oversight of Glavlit and were sent abroad by a secret means. For that reason we did not find out the names of the censors and the editors responsible for sending them.

It is possible to conclude that under the current system of press control, systematic publication in newspapers and magazines of articles containing secret information cannot take place. Perhaps one individual article was published, but that would have been an isolated mistake. The commission has nothing more to add to its testimony.

[At 2:30 P.M., a recess was announced. It was proposed to the experts that they give written responses to the court's questions. At 7:45 P.M., the court session resumed. On behalf of the commission, Soldatov-Fedotov read out written answers to the court's questions.

After listening to the experts the court determined as follows: "The expert commission's written replies to the questions shall be included in the criminal case materials against Fefer et al." At 8:30 P.M. the chairman declared the court session over.]

Experts' Testimony in Closed Judicial Session, June 27

[On June 27, 1952, at 12:30 P.M. a new closed-court session began. As the court had determined, expert Sophia Godovskaya appeared in closed session. A second expert, A. M. Figelman, did not come to the court session, because he was on vacation. The chairman identified Godovskaya, who testified about herself as follows:]

Godovskaya: I, Sophia Yakovlevna Godovskaya, a member of the Communist Party since 1927, have had higher education and work as a senior bibliographer of books and manuscripts at the All-Union Book Archive. I have a good knowledge of Yiddish.

[Then Godovskaya answered the court's questions.]

Question: Does the expert confirm her conclusion that the book *On Virgin Soil* gives only a slanderous and distorted picture of the life of Soviet people in the Far East, or does the book portray positive aspects of Soviet reality?

Godovskaya: At the very beginning, the book *On Virgin Soil* does not adopt a slanderous orientation, but further on the contents of the book contain slander against Soviet reality. For example, Talmy describes the city of Khabarovsk as lacking in amenities and poorly built, blaming its residents for this. In another episode, Talmy describes Russian and Korean villages and compares them to the disadvantage of the Russian village. Talmy writes that conditions in the Russian village are far worse than in the Korean, although it has existed for only three to four years. I perceived this episode as emphasizing a negligent attitude toward their own amenities on the part of

Russian-Soviet citizens. Maybe someone else would have perceived this episode differently, but I personally understood it as I have already testified. I told the investigator about my doubts concerning the correctness of my conclusion about this episode. I feel that it was irresponsible for me to come to such a conclusion about this book after working with it for only three or four days. I believe it would make more sense to do a complete translation of this book so that the court itself could objectively study its contents.

Question: Does the expert confirm that the book *On Virgin Soil* contains information which constitutes state secrets?

Godovskaya: In Talmy's book *On Virgin Soil* there are several episodes that in our opinion were state secrets at the time—for example, the description of gold mines and of the Soviet gunboat moorings during the conflict at the Chinese Eastern Railroad,* of the sawmill and of the growth of industry in Birobidzhan. We responded to all of these facts on pages 10–12 of the expert commission's conclusions.

[A recess was announced at 1:25 P.M. After the recess, at 2:35 P.M., Godovskaya read out written responses to the court's questions. Regarding the divulging of state secrets, the written answer was as follows:]

Godovskaya: The book contains facts (which we cite on pp. 10–12) that in our opinion constituted, at the time, state secrets. Facts other than those cited are not to be found here. It may be that the facts we have cited are not state secrets, either.

[At 2:45 P.M. a recess was announced. Ten minutes later, at 2:55 P.M., the closed court session was resumed. The secretary reported that witness Pukhlov was now in attendance. The chairman confirmed the identity of witness Pukhlov, who testified about himself as follows:]

Pukhlov: I, Nikolai Nikolaevich Pukhlov, was born in 1912. I have been a member of the Communist Party since 1929. I have had higher education. I used to work as the director of Scientific Research Institute 205 and currently work at the Central Committee of the Communist Party.

[Pukhlov responded to the court's questions.]

Presiding Officer: Witness Pukhlov, tell the court what you know concerning the compilation of materials about England's colonial policy at Institute 205, which you forwarded to the Sovinformburo at Lozovsky's request and which he then sent abroad.

Pukhlov: In 1946, Comrade Panyushkin called me and said that an informational review of the foreign press and of radio broadcasts about England's

---

*The Chinese Eastern Railroad is a section of the Trans-Siberian Railroad that was built in the 1890s on Chinese Manchurian territory by the tsarist regime as a shortcut to Vladivostok. Russian troops were initially permitted to guard the rail line. Stalin sold the line to the Japanese after they captured the territory in the 1930s. The testimony here is referring to minor skirmishes between Soviet and Chinese troops in the Far East.

colonial policy needed to be put together. Panyushkin said that this material would have to be sent to Lozovsky at the Sovinformburo to be passed along to some progressive foreign journalist. Comrade Panyushkin explained that most of the materials should be selected from the English press and radio broadcasts in order to use English materials as a stick to beat England with.

In 1949, at the request of Mikhail Andreyevich [Suslov], I sent him a copy of this document from the institute, and he in turn sent it on to former Minister of State Security Abakumov. Then this material was returned to the Central Committee of the Communist Party, where it was placed in an archive. In March 1952 I again sought it out in the archive and sent it to the office of Comrade Ignatiev, where it is now.

In the Central Committee there is a copy of the accompanying letter with which this material was sent to Comrade Ignatiev. I considered this material secret because it was prepared at a secret institute, and there would have been a real scandal had it become known after it was published abroad that the material had been prepared in an organization that was subordinate to the Central Committee. But I don't consider the contents of this document to constitute state secrets, because it was compiled on the basis of articles previously published in the foreign press and in English radio broadcasts.

[The chairman read out an excerpt from Pukhlov's interrogation record (vol. 31, pp. 1–4).]

Pukhlov: I think my testimony in this interrogation record in which I assess the degree of secrecy of this material concerning England's colonial policy is deleted, and that the material was compiled at Comrade Panyushkin's order.

[Further on, the witness answered another question.]

Pukhlov: During the preliminary investigation I was interrogated twice, but this was drawn up in one report taking up both sides of five or six pages. I don't know why only a copy is appended to the case or, rather, an excerpt from the interrogation record, rather than the original record. I did not touch on any other questions, except my suspicion about there being too close a tie between Gelinder, former director of Institute 205, and Yuzefovich. Both times the conversations with the investigator were about this material on England's colonial policy.

[At 5:10 P.M. the chairman announced the court session to be over.]

Experts' Testimony in Closed Judicial Session, June 28

[On Saturday, June 28, 1952, at 1:10 P.M., the next closed court session began. Experts Lukin, Vladykin, and Yevgenov appeared at the court session. The chairman confirmed the experts' identity, and they testified about themselves as follows:]

Lukin: I, Yuri Borisovich Lukin, deputy director of the literary and art department at the editorial offices of *Pravda,* have had higher education, having graduated from the literature department of the School of Anthropology at Moscow State University in 1929. I am not a party member.

Vladykin: I, Grigory Ivanovich Vladykin, the chairman of the foreign commission of the Union of Soviet Writers, am a literary critic, a doctor of philosophy, and a member of the Communist Party.

Yevgenov: I, Semyon Vladimirovich Yevgenov, deputy managing secretary of the Union of Soviet Writers, am a member of the editorial board of *Druzhba Narodov* (Friendship of Peoples), and a critic. I did not complete my higher education, and I have been a member of the Communist Party since 1931.

[Expert V. R. Shcherbin did not appear at the court session, because he was on vacation. The experts responded to the court's questions. Yevgenov described how the commission had operated.]

Yevgenov: All members of the commission started studying materials from the Jewish Anti-Fascist Committee on the same day: January 20, 1952. This was officially confirmed on February 13, 1952. At first we were called into the MGB, where Lieutenant Colonel Grishaev gave us an assignment orally, and then two and a half to three weeks later this was drawn up in a report. We all worked together, approximately nine hours a day, except for Sunday. Expert Shcherbin spent less time working than the others owing to the heavy workload at his main job.

The investigators offered us a large quantity of documents to study, some of which we were unable to use because we felt it impossible to include them in our report as being nationalistic.

In our work we made use of the classics of Marxism-Leninism on the national question and especially on the Jewish question. The experts also studied Ehrenburg's article "In Regard to a Certain Letter." In total, the commission worked for over a month.

Question: Did the commission work with the original documents indicated in points 1–122 of the decree mentioned, or were the experts given for examination copies of these documents and excerpts from them, which were appended to the case materials as material evidence?

Yevgenov: Almost all of the articles and other documents of the Jewish Anti-Fascist Committee were given to the expert commission in the form of copies. Some of them we selected for inclusion in the report, and they have now been appended to the case materials as material evidence.

Question: Were original cases, files, and warrants of the Jewish Anti-Fascist Committee regarding the abovementioned documents put at the disposal of the commission, and did the commission confirm these documents' identifying papers, and if so, why didn't the commission append these identifying papers to the documents?

Yevgenov: The commission had no original files at its disposal. We believed that since the copies had the signatures of MGB employees on them, these documents were official.

Question: Who else besides the editors of *Eynikayt* and the leaders of the Jewish Anti-Fascist Committee should be held responsible for placing nationalistic articles in *Eynikayt?*

Vladykin: First of all, since the Jewish Anti-Fascist Committee was under the Sovinformburo, its director, Lozovsky, should bear responsibility for this. In addition, the Glavlit censors who checked these articles and the Central Committee workers who followed what was published in that newspaper should bear responsibility.

Yevgenov: It should also be said that of all the materials given us, we set aside only those that, in our opinion, were nationalistic, but there were also many good articles there that were Soviet in content.

Question: Could the speeches at the official Jewish Anti-Fascist Committee meetings be considered nationalistic?

Vladykin: We know from the investigators that the reason that the Jewish Anti-Fascist Committee was disbanded was the nationalistic character of its activity. Having reviewed and studied the texts of speeches made at the meetings of the Jewish Anti-Fascist Committee, we found nationalistic statements in them.

We believe that there needs to be propaganda urging Jews the world over to unite in the struggle against fascism, but not from a Zionist position. Nonetheless, the Jewish Anti-Fascist Committee was slipping into such a position.

In addition, I want to say that we did not know that our expert commission's conclusion that statements in rallies and articles, including those published in our press, were nationalistic would be used against the leaders of the Jewish Anti-Fascist Committee as an accusation in criminal proceedings.

Question: On what did the expert commission base its conclusion that the nationalistic activity of the Jewish Anti-Fascist Committee was carried out with Lozovsky's support (vol. 33, p. 60)?

Yevgenov: We stated repeatedly to Lieutenant Colonel Grishaev that we could not shed any significant light on Lozovsky's connection with the Jewish Anti-Fascist Committee. We drew this conclusion on the basis of the fact that in the documents of the Jewish Anti-Fascist Committee, even after 1946, there are allusions to help from Lozovsky in the work of the Jewish Anti-Fascist Committee and to his approval on various questions.

Lukin (added the following to Yevgenov's and Vladykin's testimony): I want to say that during the time when we worked with the Jewish Anti-Fascist Committee materials it should have occurred to us to ask how nationalistic propaganda could have taken place right before everyone's eyes.

I think that one article or sentence in an article might not have led the censor to think that there was something troubling in all of the Jewish Anti-Fascist Committee's work if he had not previously been sensitized to such material. But when we the experts received this mass of documents, because we were already prepared to look for something troubling in them, the nationalistic character of these materials made a disheartening impression on us.

Question: In the expert commission's opinion, who turned the Jewish Anti-Fascist Committee into a center of nationalistic activity among Jews, and why does the expert commission believe that the Jewish Anti-Fascist Committee was such a center (vol. 33, p. 33)?

Yevgenov: The question of which crime was involved and what the personal responsibility of each member of the Jewish Anti-Fascist Committee was, was not raised before the expert commission. In our conclusions we mentioned only those members of the presidium of the Jewish Anti-Fascist Committee who were most actively involved in nationalistic activity. For example, we mentioned the names of Shtern, Shimeliovich, and others, using as a basis the nationalistic statements made at the sessions of the Jewish Anti-Fascist Committee presidium.

The facts that the expert commission had about how the Jewish Anti-Fascist Committee began handling questions outside its competence—for example, the reevacuation of Jews to the Ukraine and the Crimea, appeals on various economic problems and problems of everyday life, and, finally, the question of creating a Jewish republic in the Crimea—gave us the basis to conclude that the Jewish Anti-Fascist Committee had become a nationalistic center. This is additionally confirmed by the fact that when the State of Israel was organized, the Jewish Anti-Fascist Committee raised a lot of nationalistic hullabaloo around this, up to and including a radio broadcast.

Vladykin: I would also like to emphasize Shimeliovich's remark during the discussion of a letter to Comrade Suslov in which he said that the phrase about "a mood of increased nationalism" should be struck from this letter. In addition, there are elements of duplicity in how the Jewish Anti-Fascist Committee handled the question of creating a Jewish republic in the Crimea, settling Polish Jews there, and rejecting Birobidzhan.

Question: What else does the expert commission have to add to its testimony?

Yevgenov: Seeing that the Jewish Anti-Fascist Committee was sending its authorized correspondents to all corners of the Soviet Union, who distributed money and packages from America to Jews only, and that the leaders of the

Jewish Anti-Fascist Committee were involved in the question of organizing a Jewish republic in the Crimea, we came away with the conviction that the Jewish Anti-Fascist Committee was stirring up nationalistic sentiments among Jews in the USSR. Abroad, people had already begun to consider it an official Jewish organization. On this basis we believe that, objectively speaking, the Jewish Anti-Fascist Committee had turned into a nationalistic center that stood up for the rights of the Jews which were supposedly being infringed on. And this was indeed how it was perceived by the backward part of the Jewish population.

In assessing the activity of the leaders of the Jewish Anti-Fascist Committee as nationalists, one can say that at the first stage, Mikhoels and Shimeliovich played a special role in this—he was Mikhoels's closest friend—and then, at the second stage, Epshteyn and Fefer. Later figures included Shtern, a congenital cosmopolitan, and Markish, although he barely participated in the committee's work; his unpublished verses about Mikhoels's death are flagrantly nationalistic and Zionist in character.

Perhaps if the questions had been framed for us by the investigators in the same way as they have been framed here in court, our conclusion would have been fuller. But while we were writing the expert commission report we periodically gave it to the investigative division of the MGB for them to review, and apparently they were satisfied by it.

[Later, experts Yevgenov, Vladykin, and Lukin stated that they could add nothing else to their testimony. At 4:10 P.M., the chairman announced the court session to be over.

On July 2, 1952, at 12:20 P.M., the court session resumed.]

Presiding Officer: The Military Collegium of the Supreme Court of the USSR, having studied the defendants' appeals filed by them during the judicial investigation, has determined to leave the appeals unsatisfied. (He reads out the determination of the Military Collegium of the Supreme Court of the USSR dated July 2, 1952.)

Determination Regarding the Defendants' Petitions

Supreme Court of the USSR

July 2, 1952   Moscow
Decision #SP 0065/522

Military Collegium of the Supreme Court of the USSR
MEMBERS   Chairman, Lieutenant General of Justice CHEPTSOV
                         Major General of Justice ZARYANOV and
                         Major General of Justice DMITRIEV

Having studied the appeals filed during the court proceedings by the defendants:

a) Fefer, Markish, Bergelson, Kvitko, Shtern, Talmy, Shimeliovich, and Zuskin—to include in the case materials literary works written by them (poetry, long poems, stories, and articles) that would present them in a positive light;

b) Kvitko—for the court to question the following witnesses: K. Chukovsky, V. Smirnova, S. Mikhalkov, K. Piskunova, E. Mitskevich, P. G. Tychina, and E. Blaginina, who know him through their work together and can give favorable character references for him and favorable reviews of his poetry;

c) Lozovsky—to include in the case materials various documents sent to the American press that do not contain secret information

and taking into consideration the fact that the literary works referred to in the appeal are not directly related to the accusations, whereas Kvitko's appeal for the court to question witnesses cannot be granted, because the witnesses named above were not questioned about the accusations brought against Kvitko and can only give their reactions to his literary work,

the Military Collegium of the Supreme Court of the USSR, seeing no basis for granting the abovementioned appeals,

Has Decided:

to dismiss the appeals of defendants Fefer, Markish, Bergelson, Kvitko, Shtern, Talmy, Shimeliovich, Zuskin, and Lozovsky.

Valid when accompanied by the necessary signatures.

Hereby certified:

Court Secretary of the Military Collegium

Senior Lieutenant (signature) AFANASIEV

[Then the chairman resumed Shtern's interrogation, which had been interrupted on June 12.]

Testimony by the Defendants

LINA SHTERN CONTINUED

Presiding Officer: Defendant Shtern, at the last session you gave testimony about yourself. Your interrogation was finished, and the court had no more questions for you. What would you like to add to your testimony?

Shtern: I would like to say that I waited for this trial with great impatience and feared that I would not live to see it. I did not want to die accused of the accusations that have been brought against me. And since I had no hope that I would live to see it, I wrote my autobiography, in which I recorded in short form my fairly long life. Since I am alive, I would like to recount it briefly.

Presiding Officer: I ask that you recount it briefly because the court is already aware of your life story.

[Shtern's account of her life took up the entire morning session of the court, more than an hour and a half. It was the story of a young girl from a Jewish family in the Baltic region who received her higher education in Geneva and remained at the university to do scientific research. In the 1920s she was invited to work in the Soviet Union. Her scientific research received recognition. She was appointed director of the Institute of Physiology and elected a full member of the Academy of Sciences.]

Shtern: When I came to the Soviet Union, I promised myself that I would dedicate my whole life to science, and my scientific work was recognized. It is a great joy for me that I was able to contribute something. My opponents will disappear. I will disappear. That's not important, but what I have done will remain. Still, I would not like to depart this life with that disgraceful stain that is on me now.

My cellmate told me that I would end up signing everything during the investigation, no matter what. And indeed there were moments when it seemed to me that I was going out of my mind, capable of uttering slander about myself and others.

Presiding Officer: But for the month and a half you have been in court, you feel well.

Shtern: I feel well.

Presiding Officer: So why did you feel bad then?

Shtern: But what is the point of talking about that? I can tell you how testimony is created. In each interrogation record it says, "The interrogation record has been written correctly using my words, and I have read it," but this is not the truth. During the three and a half years I was in prison, interrogation went on for three of those years. There were days when I was interrogated twice. After you've spent an entire night under interrogation, you come to your cell in the morning, and you're not allowed to sleep or even to sit down. I felt that things were going badly and that I might go out of my mind. And crazy people are not responsible for anything.

I repudiate all of my testimony presented here. I have never been an anti-Soviet person. From the time I arrived in Moscow, I swore that I would give all my strength to science, and I have done that. I wanted nothing for myself and had no other ambitions. I am not at all like other women. Everything in life came easily for me, but I sought nothing in terms of personal interests. I had only one desire, and that was to leave something good and useful behind. That is what I wanted. I've been that way since I was a child. When I was very young, I dreamed of being a heroine and wanted to sacrifice my life. This was long ago. But later, I realized that it was entirely unnecessary to sacrifice my life for the sake of nothing, that I needed to use my life for a good and useful cause.

If the court decides that I can be useful, perhaps I will still have time to do something useful. During this short recess in the proceedings I went through everything in my mind and did not find a single misdeed that would justify characterizing me as a traitor or a slanderer. I have never slandered anyone, I have lived honestly, but I am guilty of proving one thing in my scientific work while acting differently in my life—I looked at certain things frivolously. In my work, my scientific work, I relied on the principles of Marxism-Leninism. My research papers were published, so they were considered useful.

Presiding Officer: Have you finished your testimony?

Shtern: Yes, although there is much more that I would still like to say.

[At 2:00 P.M., the chairman announced a recess. At 2:30 P.M., the court session was resumed.]

ADDITIONAL TESTIMONY

Presiding Officer: Defendant Fefer, what do you have to add to your testimony?

Fefer: I ask you to take note of the following facts.

During the case there has been a story going around that after Mikhoels and Fefer returned from America, a special network of correspondents was created in order to collect classified information about the Soviet Union and send it abroad to satisfy the interests of reactionary American circles. I want to cite a number of facts that refute the assertion in the indictment that Mikhoels and I instructed the correspondents in this network.

First of all, nothing was ever said about collecting secret information. We asked them to collect material and write articles about industrial enterprises. I want to direct the court's attention to the fact that Mikhoels never gave instructions, did not work with the correspondents, and did not meet with them. As for Epshteyn and me, we really did give instructions that they write about industrial enterprises in accordance with directives from Shcherbakov and Lozovsky—that is, to do what the committee was created for—but we had no network of correspondents, neither when the committee was created nor after we returned from America. The committee became much more active after our return, but that had less to do with our return from America than with the move to Moscow, where there were other opportunities.

I have already informed the court that the story about the creation of a correspondents' network was not true. There was no network of correspondents. Committee members, journalists, and writers made trips to various places. We were provided with five thousand rubles a year for this, and you can't go far on that.

After Mikhoels's and my trip to America, interest there in the Soviet Union grew because we spoke at rallies attended by tens of thousands of people. These rallies were used as a propaganda platform for the achievements of the Soviet Union. Correspondents for the Jewish Anti-Fascist Committee wrote no fewer than three hundred to four hundred articles, which are now being held by the investigative division of the MGB. These people figured in the investigation, but not a single one of these three hundred to four hundred articles is in the forty-two volumes. What is the explanation for this?

If a group really was organized to gather classified materials, then at least some of these articles should have been included in the case documents as material evidence of such an important accusation: that the Jewish Anti-Fascist Committee became a center of espionage.

We wrote a great deal about Birobidzhan because at the time there was a lot of interest in Birobidzhan in the Jewish press abroad. It was no accident that the committee paid particular attention to Birobidzhan, because the reactionary press in America was conducting a systematic propaganda campaign against Birobidzhan to prove that this was a bluff, that nothing was being done there, and that Jews were not going there. Our articles took aim at our enemies. The experts, and specifically one of the directors of Glavlit, Fedotov-Soldatov, knows what is allowed to be published and what is not. I confirm that not a single article was sent without the permission of Glavlit or the editorial control board of the Central Committee.

The experts, and specifically the director of the register department of Glavlit, Fedotov-Soldatov, approached this serious assignment irresponsibly and carelessly. But there are some things that are completely monstrous. I ask that you take volume 32 and look at page 112, which contains a letter from the *Morgen Freiheit*. On the basis of this letter the expert commission concludes that reactionary circles in the United States demanded classified information and that we sent it. Is this really honest on the part of the experts? The reactionary circles are Novick and the *Morgen Freiheit,* an organ of the American Communist Party. I looked carefully at these documents and am convinced that the experts took a tendentious approach when they issued their conclusions.

Is it really a disgrace to help an orphanage in Stalingrad where the children of the heroes of Stalingrad live? Does receiving assistance from AMBIJAN foster a dependence by the Jewish Anti-Fascist Committee on AMBIJAN? Yet the expert commission regards this as a large payment to the employees of the Anti-Fascist Committee for sending secret information. This is certainly a strange thing.

There has been talk here of food packages. I forgot to say that I assigned the technical secretary of the Jewish Anti-Fascist Committee to receive these packages and send them to children's nurseries. Receipts from the nurseries are in the case materials. Can this really be considered a payment from reactionary circles?

On page 11 of the report it says, "During Mikhoels and Fefer's stay in the United States, they received an assignment to collect information about industry and culture in the Soviet Union and send it to America." But it did not say there that we agreed to send secret information. And further on, the expert commission concludes that we sent secret information. Where does this conclusion come from? The commission acted unconscionably. We were given the task of sending as many articles as possible about the Soviet Union to America, and the more we sent, the more we were praised. The information we sent could have done nothing but good. And Fedotov-Soldatov, apparently knowing that the leaders of the Jewish Anti-Fascist Committee were under arrest, now believes that he needs to blame them for everything. He says that in 1943 we sent classified information to America. But this was before Novick's letter, which we received in 1948.

We received requests from various countries—the United States, Argentina, Cuba, Brazil, Mexico, Poland, and Romania—but we did not respond affirmatively to all the questions. Could articles about the economic, agricultural, and cultural achievements of the Soviet Union contain only classified information and not truth?

We had very many articles devoted to the struggle against warmongers, against the remnants of fascism, against Bundist reaction, Trotskyites, and Zionist reactionaries. All of this was aimed at routing the enemy, not harming the Soviet Union. This is why I consider the expert commission's conclusions false and unscrupulous. Fedotov-Soldatov has forgotten his duties as an expert. He has forgotten that he should approach the case objectively, especially since he is one of the directors of Glavlit.

I am coming to the conclusion that the document was drawn up tendentiously, with a lack of objectivity. The absence of dates, identifying documents, and press reviews—these conclusions are absurd. It is unethical to present the *Morgen Freiheit* as a representative of anti-Soviet circles.

Fedotov-Soldatov's report is an example of spy mania or a desire to confuse Soviet courts.

I would like to turn your attention to a number of facts about our contacts in the United States. We did have contacts—that is true. There are photographs to show that we met with various people. Yes, we met, but what is important is the ends to which we put these meetings. I want to say that we used these connections in the interests of the Soviet Union.

Let me say a few words about Weizmann. I am stating to the court that we used Weizmann so that prominent Americans would join the Reception Committee for our delegation. Without this meeting, such people would not have joined, but then they spoke out in favor of uniting all forces against fascism. Before the meeting with Weizmann, a number of prominent figures did not want to participate in the work that our embassy was carrying out, and after the meeting with him they got involved.

We concluded an agreement with Rosenberg that was in the interests of the Soviet government.

We used Landau,* director of the Jewish Telegraphic Agency, in the interests of the Soviet Union; he sent our articles to three hundred Jewish newspapers around the world.

Goldberg we also used in the interests of the Soviet Union; he subsequently wrote a book against the Soviet Union's enemies and organized various events and rallies.

We also used Stephen Wise, and he spoke against Trotsky at one rally. There is a photograph of me shaking hands with Stephen Wise. What do these two have in common? you might ask. I was shaking his hand after his speech. We also used Sholem Asch during our stay in America. This most prominent writer, a modern Yiddish legend, became a staff member at the *Morgen Freiheit*. (And we were told that there was a great deal of interest in having Asch on the staff of the *Morgen Freiheit*.) We went to see him at his estate, and Kisselev went with us. I learned that Asch loved to cook, and together he and I put on white aprons and prepared meat patties. Three days later Asch had a letter in the *Morgen Freiheit* in which he said that he was going to be on the staff of the *Morgen Freiheit* because it was the most honest and truthful newspaper in America.

We used Einstein as well. We were interested in having him speak at our rally. For this purpose a microphone was set up in his apartment, and he spoke on the radio. He spoke about the victories of the Soviet Union and how everyone should help the Soviet Union.

Telma, who sent watches, is mentioned here in *Eynikayt*. It is thanks to Telma that two million sets of clothing were collected for Soviet citizens who were victims of the fascists. This was how we used Telma. When were in London, we used Sir Montagu,† a huge manufacturer, whose clothing is worn by almost 25 percent of the English. We were interested in getting something from him. He was at a conference of manufacturers in London. And when we were already back home, about two hundred bales of clothing arrived addressed to "The Red Cross, Mikhoels and Fefer."

[The court attempted to clarify how the information on the Baltic region had been passed on to Goldberg and whether Fefer had been present when it happened.]

Presiding Officer: Defendant Teumin, what do you have to add to your testimony?

Teumin: I ask the court to review the information about the Baltic region. Lozovsky said here that the investigators had this information. If I could have

---

*Jacob Landau (1892–1952) was a prominent journalist and publisher. He established the Jewish Telegraphic Agency in New York in 1940.

†This is a reference to Sir Ivor Goldsmid Samuel Montagu (1894–1984). He came from a prominent British Jewish family and joined the Communist Party, becoming active in the Soviet-inspired peace movement after the war.

it to examine, I would be able to recall exactly where I got the material for it. I got the material for that information from articles by government leaders of those republics. They provided articles for the newspapers, which included very detailed information about rebuilding industry and culture. In late 1947, here in Moscow, a book entitled *Soviet Estonia* came out. It was edited by the chairman of Gosplan* and passed the censor. Of course, there can be no comparison between what was contained in this book and what was in my two pages of information.

Member of the Court: During the preliminary investigation you testified that you had anti-Soviet conversations with Mikhoels and Fefer, did you not?

Teumin: No, never. I personally did not participate in such conversations. My testimony says that I heard such conversations. That is correct; there were three such instances. I have already testified to the court in detail about that.

Member of the Court: But there were anti-Soviet conversations?

Teumin: There were conversations, but not in such a form. I was guilty in that I should have responded in some way, but I kept silent, neither supporting nor objecting. And since I didn't react to these conversations, that means I, too, was infected with these sentiments.

Member of the Court: During the preliminary investigation you testified the opposite.

Teumin: The interrogation record was brought to me already prepared. In this sense I slandered myself. For three and a half years I lived with that nightmarish feeling that I was considered a spy and had provided direct help to spies. My whole life contradicts all of this. I was not concerned with Jewish problems, I was concerned with Baltic problems—those were the issues that constituted my life. Members of the Lithuanian, Latvian, and Estonian governments considered me to be competent in questions having to do with the Baltic region and its culture. I did not engage in any anti-Soviet matters or conversations.

Member of the Court: Defendant Fefer, was there such a conversation?

Fefer: I deny any conversations with Teumin aimed against the Soviet government. Teumin and I barely know each other. How could I tell her my sentiments, even had I had any like these?

Presiding Officer: Defendant Teumin, in the indictment you are accused of engaging in espionage and being an active nationalist, while in 1946 you passed along classified materials to Goldberg. Tell us, did you, under Lozovsky's orders, review and correct articles for the Jewish Anti-Fascist

---

*Gosplan was the office of state planning that controlled all aspects of Soviet economic policy for decades.

Committee that were sent to America? Have you been interrogated about this?

Teumin: I was never asked such a question during the investigation, and you will not find such information in an interrogation record, because I did not examine or proofread a single article. When I read this in the indictment, I was simply astonished. After all, it had been firmly established that I had nothing to do with the Jewish Anti-Fascist Committee, except for providing it with organizational and technical assistance in planning a rally. Lozovsky and my direct supervisors can confirm this.

[A recess was announced. At 4:35 P.M., the session was resumed.]

Presiding Officer: Defendant Markish, have you anything to add to your testimony?

Markish: It was said here that Markish smacks of nationalism. Some kind of nationalistic sentiment, it was said. But when all is said and done, nationalism is not an abstraction; it is flesh, it is action.

Lozovsky recalled that I said that he did not receive me well when I was visiting him with a book. He said that he was chatting with a member of the Writers' Union who said that I smacked of nationalism. I don't want to ask Lozovsky any questions. I was with him for all of three and a half minutes. When did he have time to consult about me and turn me down about the book? All I want to say is that at that time, in 1938, my book was already being put together, and its publication was set to coincide with the elections to the Supreme Soviet. The book was called *A Citizen's Voice*. At the same time, my books *Dawn over the Dnieper* and *The Way of the People* were being translated. People are asking whether Yevgenov engaged in a crime when he published my three books, knowing that I smacked of nationalism.

Shimeliovich: I do not know Markish to be a nationalist, but Bregman told me that he gives off an odor of nationalism. But he himself had not seen me for ten years. We had not met in ten years, and he wasn't interested in Yiddish literature. He said that Markish gave him the book and he put it on the shelf.

Markish: I gave him the book not in Yiddish, but in Russian, and even so, he put it on the shelf. Without knowing, seeing, or meeting someone, how can he say that, how can he talk that way about someone!

We are facing the court; we must think over every word. I ask, What is this nationalistic odor in my books, in which there is nothing nationalistic?

I am not going to talk about Bergelson's statements about how I gesticulate, but my gesticulation is not covered anywhere in the criminal code. Is that really nationalism?

Zuskin says that in my plays in which he acted, he did not see any nationalism (and he played a regional committee secretary and a kolkhoz worker), but those plays that were not accepted for production had some nationalistic tendencies. How can he make such thoughtless statements?

The piece received expressions of gratitude from the Arts Committee, and Mikhoels didn't accept it because I had already given it to a theater in the Ukraine. Mikhoels, who was a duplicitous person, told me that it was a wonderful play, that people had waited for it for twenty years, and he called my home and congratulated my wife on my writing such a play. But two days later he said that we could not portray people like the ones in the play.

I am not talking about Fefer, because his testimony requires so little commentary that I do not want to spend time on it.

A few words about the Yiddish Writers' Section. Fefer said in his testimony that the section had become kind of nationalistic. I should say that the section was not carrying out any program of work. I was the secretary for a very short period of time. Why did Fefer call this a sect? He lived in Kiev and didn't know what was happening with us. And neither did Kvitko, Bergelson, or Epshteyn, whom I saw very little, while I hardly ever met with Fefer—none of them can say that this is a sect. It was nothing of the kind, and I ask the court to believe me.

They themselves, having caused Jews to return to national topics and a national culture, didn't know what sort of culture this was. They defended culture in the synagogue, the culture of Chobrutsky. They artificially tore Soviet Yiddish literature out of the healthy flow of Soviet culture and herded it into the cattle car. This is a result of that criminal misunderstanding of the revolution's laws, a misunderstanding of the perspective and the course of history.

Talmy said here that he had nothing in common with Yiddish literature, and asks Vatenberg, "Did I speak Yiddish with my son?" Vatenberg answers, "No." Then Shimeliovich speaks and asks whether he spoke about the Jewish people. He is answered—no.

I am ashamed to hear such things. One might think that Yiddish is forbidden here in the Soviet Union. The question is not whether one can write in Yiddish, not whether one can write about the Jews of the shtetl. The question is how to write. I hope that Soviet culture will hand Yiddish over to history. This language helped the people sing and cry. It gave them everything during their difficult years, when they lived cut off from Russia in the Pale of Settlement.

Presiding Officer: What else do you want to add?

Markish: I want to say a few more words about my poem "To a Jewish Warrior." The accusation against me came into being as a direct result of this poem. It was unlawful for me to write this poem. I wrote a lot at that time. I wrote about Zoya Kosmodemyanskaya,* about the Panfilovites,† about

---

*Zoya Kosmodemyanskaya (1923–1941) was a high school student and member of the Komsomol involved in a partisan unit in the first months of World War II. Captured and tortured by the Nazis, she refused to divulge information and was executed.

†Panfilovites were a group of twenty-eight soldiers in a famous Red Army division that

heroic themes in general, and I did not want the Jewish soldier to lag behind his brother and friend, the Russian, who walks shoulder to shoulder
with him toward victory. I didn't want it to be said of the Jewish soldier
that he serves in a commissariat in Tashkent.

Russian nature inspired me with its inimitable beauty, as it would any
Soviet poet, and I would not surrender that to anyone. If a writer in America whom I've never heard of wrote that in Markish one feels the broad
sweep of Russia, I have every right to allow myself to think that I am a full-
blooded son of Russia.

I stand now before the court as before a supreme conscience. I say that
no literary merit will mitigate or remove guilt from me, but at the same
time, no slander will replace the truth, because slanderers do not notice the
weakness of their slander. We do not have, and cannot have, guilty parties
without guilt, and for that reason I say that if over the thirty years of my activity with the spoken word or in a book, the court finds a line infected with
nationalism, may the hand of the law come down on me with all its cruelty.

Presiding Officer: Defendant Yuzefovich, what else can you add to your testimony?

Yuzefovich: Here in court I have checked and read through the expert commission's conclusions regarding espionage, and it turns out that half of all
the articles that are the subject of conclusions are spoken of with all sorts of
"if"'s; specifically, the commission states that if these facts had not been
previously published in the press, then they were not for publication. The
only article that does not have an "if" attached to it is the one from the
newspaper *Krasny Flot*. The author of this article could have indicated
where he found the facts cited in this article. And Glavlit could have given
exhaustive explanations about how such an article could have been published. It seems to me that it is no accident that there is not a single Glavlit employee in the dock, because they are the ones who have the right
to decide whether or not to release a particular article into the light of day.
I asked the editor of the newspaper *Trud* to give me an evaluation of the
article "The Great Exploit of the Working Class." My appeal was not
granted.

Lieutenant Colonel Grishaev explained to me that neither the editor of
Trud nor the editor of *Pravda* could be competent in the question of what
can and cannot be made public. That requires knowledge of special instructions, registers, and orders. I should say that it is not clear to me why I
was turned down. By law I have the right to choose one or another person
for the expert commission. Why my proposal to include the head of Glavlit

---

helped to defend Moscow against the Nazis in the fall of 1941. Although vastly outnum-
bered and outgunned, the group was said to have fought off numerous German tanks at the
cost of heavy casualties. The commander of the division, Major General Ivan Panfilov
(1893–1941), fell in battle on November 19, 1941, in a separate encounter with the enemy.

was turned down I do not know. I have much evidence showing the whole senseless and bankrupt nature of the expert commission's conclusions.

Presiding Officer: On espionage?

Yuzefovich: Yes.

Presiding Officer: In the indictment it indicates that in 1945 [actually, 1946], Yuzefovich gave Goldberg secret material about Soviet industry and transportation.

Yuzefovich: I have already said, and now repeat, that I did not give any such material.

Presiding Officer: And what materials did you pass on to Eagan?

Yuzefovich: In accordance with Lozovsky's orders, I gave several copies of articles about trade unions that had already been published in the communist and trade union press in a number of countries; that is, they had already passed through the censor's office.

Presiding Officer: During the preliminary investigation you yourself pled guilty to this, did you not?

Yuzefovich: When I received the material from Institute 205 that Lozovsky had assigned me to give to Goldberg, I was supposed to get a paper from Lozovsky, which Lozovsky in turn was supposed to get from someone higher up, which "permitted" this document to be transmitted.

Presiding Officer: And did Lozovsky have this permission?

Yuzefovich: I cannot say. I can say only the following, that this material that was transmitted to Goldberg was supposed to be used by him to help and not to harm the Soviet Union.

Presiding Officer: But it had to be handed on with the permission of the Central Committee, did it not?

Yuzefovich: This was an oversight on my part.

Presiding Officer: And what is the specific nature of your guilt?

Yuzefovich: I was negligent in not surmising that I needed to get something on paper, and did not play it safe.

Presiding Officer: So the only thing you plead guilty to is not playing it safe?

Yuzefovich: To be perfectly honest, yes. I was negligent, and I confess to that. I believed that if a member of the Central Committee of the Party, a deputy minister of foreign affairs, speaks with the director of Institute 205 in my presence and explains to him what the material was and what it was needed for, then I could find nothing wrong with that.

Presiding Officer: What else do you plead guilty to?

Yuzefovich: That I trusted Grossman's material.

Presiding Officer: What material of Grossman's?

Yuzefovich: For *The Black Book.* When the material was being discussed, I spoke out and sharply criticized a section of the book called "The Minsk Ghetto." I was later thanked for this. When I was told that this material had been approved and passed on by Glavlit and I received orders from Lozovsky to give permission for the book to be published, I decided that this was necessary for the Nuremberg trials, and signed a telegram to that effect.

Fefer said that I spoke out in favor of building a monument to Jewish victims of the war. If you look at volume 33, page 273, it will be clear whether or not this is true.

I am sixty-two years old, and my whole life and all my work have been on view. I never deceived the Soviet Motherland, and I served it as I could, insofar as my abilities would allow. But I cannot tolerate the idea, it is completely preposterous and absurd, that I engaged in espionage or did nationalistic work.

I also cannot accept the idea that Lozovsky, Bergelson, Kvitko, and Vatenberg were spies. I think that there is a dreadful accumulation of absurd accusations, while for me personally, I want to assure the court, whatever decision it makes, that there is no force (even if I am not acquitted) that would compel me to become imbued with anti-Soviet sentiments. For three and a half years, no matter who my cellmates were, I did not utter a word about the investigation or about my case, and no matter what fate awaits me, I will always be true to the party and the Soviet Motherland.

[At 6:10 P.M., the chairman announced a recess. On July 3, 1952, at 12:30 P.M., the court session resumed.]

Presiding Officer: Defendant Lozovsky, what would you like to add to your testimony? I ask you to keep in mind that we are talking only about supplementary material now.

Lozovsky: The indictment as it relates to me is fundamentally flawed. It does not withstand criticism either from a political or from a legal point of view. Moreover, it contradicts truth, logic, and common sense, to which the following points testify. The dozens of volumes lying before you are built on the notion that I, a nationalist, supposedly sent Fefer and Mikhoels abroad at my own initiative, and they established criminal ties so that American Jews would help us struggle against the Communist Party and Soviet power.

By the way, it is not clear from these materials, but it is from oral testimony, and there are documents about this, that the connection with Rosenberg was established by orders from Comrade Molotov, the minister of foreign affairs and deputy chairman of the Soviet Council of Ministers. Further, it is known that the meeting with Weizmann took place with the embassy's permission and was sanctioned by a telegram from Comrade Molotov.

It is also known that Stephen Wise and others spoke in defense of the Soviet Union, making appeals to raise funds for the Soviet Union. What, do these speeches in defense of the Soviet Union and negotiations conducted at Comrade Molotov's orders constitute criminal ties?

I have already said that I was in Kuibyshev at the time when telegrams came from Moscow, from Comrade Molotov. What were the delegates, who went with the Central Committee's approval and without objections from the NKVD and the NKGB, supposed to do? Were they not supposed to listen to Comrade Molotov, not supposed to listen to the Soviet government? This is the Achilles heel of the indictment and all of those forty-two volumes of case materials.

But it seemed to the compilers of the indictment that Mikhoels's and Fefer's entering into a conspiracy with the Jewish bourgeoisie on my orders was not enough. So in order to increase the seriousness of the crime, the second page of the indictment contains the following assertion: that the Jewish Anti-Fascist Committee became a center for espionage and nationalistic activity, directed by reactionary circles in the United States, and that I and my accomplices, of whom more later, had a direct conspiracy with representatives of American reactionary circles. I have to ask, Where did American reactionary circles originate? Where did they spring from? This is from newspapers dated 1952, not 1943.

When Mikhoels and Fefer were in the United States, it was during Roosevelt's administration, and we were allies. Of course, Roosevelt was pursuing his own goals, but we were allied with him. At that time, reactionary circles meant fascist American circles who were against Roosevelt and the Soviet Union. Reactionary circles at that time meant those gangs that were agitating against us in favor of Germany. This was what reactionary circles in the United States meant. Neither Rosenberg nor Stephen Wise belonged to those circles. A significant majority of people were then with Roosevelt, even if a minority, for its own imperialistic aims, was against him and for Germany.

And what does "reactionary circles" mean in the United States in 1952? It means Truman, it means General Deane, who was the military attaché here and who later wrote a book against the Soviet Union.* It is those fascist and semi-fascist elements who are running things in Italy, Greece, and Turkey and who are providing aid to SS generals in the Western zones. It is those fascist and semi-fascist elements who are trying to subjugate Korea, and if they haven't, you understand why.

What right did the investigator have to apply the arrangement of forces

---

*General John Russell Deane (1896–1982) arrived in Moscow in October 1943 to participate in the Conference of Foreign Ministers. He stayed on as head of the U.S. Military Mission to the USSR until October 1945. See his book *The Strange Alliance: The Story of Our Efforts at Wartime Co-operation with Russia* (New York, 1947).

in 1952 to the arrangement of forces in 1943? What does this mean—with what circles in the United States was I involved, and why? Let them name even one name. This is nowhere to be found in any of the volumes; there is not a word about it, although twenty-five investigators conducted the investigation. Is that really correct from a political point of view? Does it really withstand criticism from a legal standpoint? Or have we ceased to be Marxists, ceased to understand what is happening in the world? Is that why someone can concoct the things written here, can write "reactionary circles in the United States," "Roosevelt," "Rosenberg," as if they are all one gang?

Comrade Lenin said that one must understand that in the political life of the bourgeoisie certain disagreements arise, and whoever does not understand this understands nothing in politics.

A children's expression seems appropriate here: "They are turning a fly into an elephant and then selling the tusks for ivory." And they are demanding the heads of fifteen people in exchange for this ivory, including my head, which has done a thing or two for the revolutionary movement and for the struggle against right-wingers and numerous other enemies of the party and the Soviet Union.

I didn't have the opportunity to copy out everything that was written about the Crimea. In fact, everything started with the Crimea, as Fefer has explained here, and ended with me wanting to sell the Crimea as a beachhead. That is how it is put in the indictment. If we copy out all of these comments about the Crimea, then we will see how they grow and grow. It all began with Fefer's testimony that Rosenberg said the Crimea means the Black Sea, the Balkan peninsula, and Turkey, although Fefer subsequently stated that Rosenberg did not say that, and that this was the investigator's choice of words.

In the course of the other interrogations, this phrase began to take on a life of its own. Each investigator added something until finally the Crimea was covered with such a furry growth that it turned into a monster. And that's how we got a beachhead. Where did it come from? Why? On what basis? Someone supposedly reported that the American government had gotten involved in the matter. That means Roosevelt. I have to remind you that in the fall of 1943, Roosevelt met with Comrade Stalin in Teheran. I dare to assure you that I know more than all of the investigators put together about what was discussed in Teheran, and I should say that nothing was said there about the Crimea. In 1945, Roosevelt flew to the Crimea with a large group of intelligence agents in numerous airplanes. He did not fly in to see either Fefer or Mikhoels, or to worry about settling Jews in the Crimea, but to see about more serious matters. What is the point of taking this phrase, which smells of blood, and making it more pointed? What could Hofshteyn, Vatenberg-Ostrovskaya, or Zuskin, as well as a whole number of distinguished people, pass along? What do they understand about this matter, and why has this phrase been so highly polished? It's because the investigators conspired among themselves, some added something, others a bit more, until finally Lozovsky wanted to sell the Crimea to American reactionaries. When you take a closer look at these phrases, it is apparent that it was not those under arrest who came up with them. What could Shtern have said on this question? She understands nothing about this matter, and incidentally, all of them—Markish and Zuskin—have all become quite the specialists in international affairs.

Presiding Officer: You have to speak about things that you have not already given the court, but all of this you have already said.

Lozovsky: This is my closing statement, perhaps the last statement of my life.

Presiding Officer: No, you will still have a last word.

Lozovsky: I want to say something new. I don't know a great deal about Soviet criminal law, but I don't think that there is a paragraph in the legal code stating that material evidence may be replaced by an investigator's nonmaterial creations. There are documents; they are in the investigative division. Why are they missing here?

To prove that I was supposedly the organizer and the ideological and political inspiration for espionage, forty articles are cited. But the person who should answer for an article placed in a newspaper is the director of the organization that publishes it. So if an article that is clearly unacceptable is published in *Krasny Flot,* then the people who are responsible for that are the minister and the editor of the newspaper *Krasny Flot,* the censor, the head of the department, and the author. What do I have to do with it? We had a rule that any article printed in the newspaper could be clipped and sent abroad. I am asking, Why weren't those people brought to justice? Why aren't they here in the seat of "honor"? Because they aren't guilty? So why am I guilty? These forty articles out of twenty thousand are the sole basis for the accusation of espionage; there is nothing else.

And the final claim from this whole espionage saga is that I personally received Goldberg and supposedly established contact to carry out espionage with him. I received hundreds of correspondents from every country, men and women, old and young. And is Goldberg really a representative of reactionary circles in the United States? That is nonsense. Reactionary circles in the United States have many more serious representatives.

The presidium of the Jewish Anti-Fascist Committee as a center of espionage—this contradicts the experience of the Cheka, the GPU, the NKVD, and the MGB. It is such nonsense that it contradicts all the experience of our struggle against counterrevolution. There may have been members of the presidium who were engaged in espionage, but to say that the entire presidium engaged in it—that is political nonsense and contradicts common sense.

Of course, if Fefer asserts that he was engaged in espionage, that is his affair. I absolutely cannot forget the testimony which the investigator came up with and which Bregman signed, that I allegedly hinted in a conversation with him that anti-Semitism in our country was coming from "on high." This is wrong, both politically and theoretically, as is Shimeliovich's assertion in the draft of his letter that manifestations of anti-Semitism result from a lack of culture. This is wrong. In feudal-capitalist countries, in tsarist Russia, anti-Semitism spread from the top down, from the government and the church. In the Soviet Union manifestations of anti-Semitism cannot come either from the bottom—from workers and kolkhoz members—or from above, from the government and the party. Various individual manifestations of anti-Semitism are a channel for counterrevolution, although in the Soviet Union this line could lead to sad results for the people who conduct it.

I understood that my assignment was to conduct a propaganda campaign abroad. I met with various journalists—some wrote one thing, others wrote another—but it was clear that our job was to present propaganda in the right way. And when the question was put of publishing books favorable to the Soviet Union, I did everything possible to heed this. I considered it a positive thing if a journalist returning to his home country wrote a favorable book about the Soviet Union. If my successor Ponomarev takes the opposite point of view, that is his business. But I always held the opinion that any sort of propaganda favorable to the Soviet Union was a good thing. If one proceeds from the premise that any kind of information constitutes espionage, if making our work go more energetically constitutes espionage, if contact with journalists who write favorably about the Soviet Union is also espionage and a form of contact between spies, if the slogan "Jewish unity in the struggle against fascism" constitutes nationalism, if it was proven that the material which Mikhoels and Fefer took to America was classified, if there was proof of my nationalism, if my criminal link with reactionary circles in the United States were really proved, then the indictment would not contradict my activity. I believe that there are neither grounds nor material evidence for that. Nationalism on my part has not been proved; there is no evidence of it. The investigation reports are too similar to each other in their phrasing. The investigators will not succeed in dressing Lozovsky in the dog collar of an agent of reactionary American circles. The investigators will not succeed in herding me into a nationalistic bedbug-infested hole. You would be better off to think about the entire purpose of my testimony.

My last three comments. In all of the interrogation records and indictments, Lozovsky figures along with his accomplices. Who are these accomplices? There is Zuskin, whom I met once in thirty years, when he informed me that Mikhoels wanted me to see him. Vatenberg-Ostrovskaya is another such accomplice, with whom I didn't even have a conversation. Hofshteyn is another such accomplice, who in 1942 came to see me on business and did not stay longer than three minutes. Another such accomplice is Ilya Semyonovich Vatenberg, who reported to me in 1942 about Epshteyn. And Shimeliovich is another such accomplice. What is this?

Presiding Officer: But you knew Epshteyn, Fefer, and Mikhoels. You supervised everyone, didn't you?

Lozovsky: I knew them, as I did others. I didn't even know that Shtern was a party member, and in my testimony I spoke of her as being unaffiliated with the party. Teumin, a Sovinformburo employee, is such an accomplice as well. If one considers them my accomplices, then I had a much larger number of such "accomplices." I had known Fefer very superficially since 1942 and then more closely starting in 1945, when he came to see me along with Mikhoels. I have known Yuzefovich more closely since 1917. Is he also an accomplice? I knew Epshteyn, who worked at the MGB. Where is all of this from? Where is the evidence? There is no evidence. If previously there was some hint that Lozovsky the nationalist was connected with nationalists in the United States, then now there is nothing to support this.

So, it is not proved that I had accomplices. It is not proved that I engaged in espionage. It is not proved that I was a nationalist. By the way, the indictment states very boldly that I was an enemy of the party from 1919. Moreover, it says here that I was already an enemy of Soviet power when the Jewish Anti-Fascist Committee was created, ready at the first opportunity to intensify subversive work against the Communist Party and the Soviet state. Twenty-two years passed from December 1919 to December 1941, when the Jewish Anti-Fascist Committee arose in embryonic form. What subversive work was I doing, and why was it necessary to wait until the war started and the committee was created in order to engage in subversive work? Where is the evidence? Aside from two or three meetings with Bergelson in 1938 and two meetings with Nusinov and Markish there is nothing.

If the court has not asked me, has not attempted to get information out of me, about what I was doing at the All-Union Central Council of Trade Unions, how I struggled with right-wingers, what I was doing in the Comintern, why I traveled abroad, then the court apparently has no doubt that during these twenty-two years I was not engaged in subversive work. And was there really a need to create the Jewish Anti-Fascist Committee during the war in order to take up subversive work?

There is nothing logical here, there is no common sense here, there is no political sense or any other kind of sense here. How did these forty-two volumes come to be? How did it happen that all of these twenty-five investigators traveled along the same path? It's because the trial requires a target, it needs a representative, it needs some sort of a name, because the director of the investigation—the deputy director of the investigative division for especially important cases, Colonel Komarov—held a very strange view, which I would like to repeat to you. He told me that the Jews are a despicable nation, that the Jews are scoundrels, bastards, and good-for-nothings, that the entire opposition consisted of Jews, that all Jews are spitting on Soviet power, and that the Jews want to annihilate every Russian. That is what Colonel Komarov told me. And naturally, if he held such a view, then he was capable of writing whatever he pleased. And this is the soil in which the tree of forty-two volumes took root, those volumes which lie before you and in which there is not a word of truth about me.

Here is my conclusion. I said everything in my testimony. and I tell you now and repeat it with all the blood of my weakened heart: I am not guilty of nationalism, of treason, or of betraying the government.

[At 1:30 P.M. the chairman announced a recess. At 2:15 P.M. the session resumed.]

Presiding Officer: Defendant Kvitko, can you add anything new to your testimony?

Kvitko: The first charge of the indictment has absolutely no basis in reality from start to finish. I did not commit any action that could have served as the grounds for such an accusation. I do not have hope that the court will believe my words, although my words are true. No small number of liars have passed before the court. But I hope that the court will verify facts I have cited and interrogate witnesses and find out the truth about me, the Bolshevik truth, the people's truth, confirmed by the October Revolution. Although formally I was not a member of the party of Lenin and Stalin until 1941, nonetheless, spiritually, I have considered myself a Bolshevik since the beginning of the October Revolution. For that reason, I have to bear responsibility for my actions throughout this entire period, like any party member.

I am accused of collaborating with the bourgeois press while abroad. A conference for writers of children's literature was held, including Kornei Chukovsky. They also familiarized themselves with my work in this field and acknowledged it to be Soviet and quite timely. At the same time, when certain Jews were lamenting the assimilation of the Jewish masses, I devoted myself fully to translating literary works into Russian. So I lost hundreds of readers in Yiddish and gained thousands in Russian. Thus I drew closer to the great Russian culture. My poem "A Letter to Voroshilov" was included in a school textbook.

During my presentation at that conference on children's literature the following happened. Politburo member Andreyev arrived, he was greeted with a standing ovation, then he suggested that the conference be resumed. At the end of the conference I read a new poem—a lullaby about how Comrade Stalin helps all Soviet people when they are threatened with danger.

Many facts and a great deal of evidence confirm how devoted I was with all my soul to the party and the Soviet state. During my stay abroad I carried out secret assignments to benefit the Soviet Union. The indictment cannot present a single fact to state that I battled against the party. There are no such facts and there cannot be. In my literary works I expressed opinions and feelings that were peace-loving and favored friendship among peoples, while I condemned nationalistic, hostile views. The works dating to 1919 prove this. All of my works engender in the hearts of children a feeling of love toward the party and selfless devotion to the Motherland and toward her great cause. Soviet critics have acclaimed my works "Letter to Voroshilov," "Lullaby," and others as patriotic. All of the abovementioned facts prove that the first charge of the indictment is based on nothing whatsoever and cannot be true.

The second charge of the indictment concerns a conspiracy with Mikhoels, Fefer, and Epshteyn. I have already spoken of how there was none, but I didn't cite any facts or reasons, and now I would like to do so. The accusation of being in a conspiracy with Fefer and Epshteyn to use the Jewish Anti-Fascist Committee for criminal purposes is not true and can be refuted by the following facts. I met with Mikhoels quite rarely before the committee was formed, as I did during its existence. I was no devotee of his theater and never had heart-to-heart, friendly, or official conversations with him. We had a deep antipathy toward each other, and Fefer should have acknowledged in court that Mikhoels never consulted with me.

Fefer and I were openly hostile toward each other from the time I returned home to Russia in 1925 until 1936. After the government put a stop to Fefer's and others' lording it over everyone in matters of Yiddish literature in the Ukraine, our open hostility turned into ever-present mistrust and hostility toward each other. After 1935 I was in Moscow more often, involved in translating my works, while Fefer lived in Kiev. So I did not see him. We did not have any frank face-to-face conversations, no conversations about politics or talks about Jewish subjects, because I considered him of little interest as a poet, and a weak playwright, and he probably held the same opinions about me. I did not consider him a competitor of mine, but I did consider him to be a treacherous person, capable of malicious things, a careerist, a climber, and a money-grubber. When I saw him in Kuibyshev, I immediately had the thought that I should keep my distance from him, and in spite of Epshteyn's exhortations, I fled Kuibyshev.

The higher-ups in the Jewish Anti-Fascist Committee did not consider me suitable for the ideological and political work of the committee and did not share their plans with me. My secretary position was a sinecure. They needed me in the position either because my name was better known to Soviet readers than Fefer's and Epshteyn's or in order to control Markish, with whom they were quarreling. But it is not out of the question that Shcherbakov recommended me, and they would have had to take that into account. One thing is clear—I was not part of a conspiracy with them and I was not involved in or even aware of any criminal doings. This accusation does not correspond to the facts.

I also do not plead guilty to the third charge of the indictment regarding assigning correspondents to do espionage. The whole system of practical work at the Jewish Anti-Fascist Committee refutes this accusation. Assignments to send material were given to the correspondents by either the executive secretary or the managing editor, at first Epshteyn, then Fefer, and no one else. This accusation is based on false testimony given by mercenary people and has nothing in common with the truth.

The fourth charge in the indictment states that I traveled to the Crimea to collect information about the economic situation in the region. This is not true. To gather that sort of information one must be knowledgeable about economic questions or be a seasoned journalist. Everyone knows that I did not possess such knowledge or qualities. I argued at length with the investigator to prove to him how ludicrous this assertion was. Furthermore, do several Jewish settlements around Dzhankoy really constitute a region? All of my meetings were with Russians. At that time there were hardly any Jewish settlers. They had been evacuated, and the only Jews in the settlements were those whose Russian neighbors had saved them from the fascists. I stayed with Russians in the settlements. I gathered information about fascist atrocities from Russians. It was impossible to conduct interviews with those Jews who were there because they had still not recovered from what they had suffered, seen, and been through when their families, including children and the elderly, were thrown alive into wells.

I will recount exactly how my mission to the Jewish settlement in the Crimea took place. In Simferopol I went to the regional committee, where Tyulyaev received me. He received me warmly and said that I needed to find out about the fascists' atrocities in the settlements themselves. He promised to help me. I showed him letters that had been sent to the Jewish Anti-Fascist Committee from the editorial offices of the central newspapers, from *Pravda*, *Izvestia*, and others. The letters had been written by evacuated settlers, asking for advice about how to get information about people who had been left behind under the Germans and also about returning to the places where they had lived before. At the time I didn't even know that the government had made a decision to settle a special contingent of people in the Crimea. Tyulyaev said that he himself had had many similar letters, but that he was now busy resettling people from the Kursk and Voronezh regions, and after that he would start dealing with the return of Jews.

When I returned to Moscow, I reported orally on all of this to the members of the presidium at a presidium session. There were no written reports. I cited many examples of Russians and Ukrainians who had saved Jews. Those seated here can testify to this. I recounted stories about wells and pits where the fascists had thrown the elderly and children alive, about the execution of Russians in Yevpatoria, and of the oppressive mood among the Jews who remained. Clearly these people's psyches had been damaged, and normal life had not been reestablished. It was also possible that fascist agents still remained, trying to create all sorts of disturbances.

I am asserting that I personally did not under any circumstances, either orally or in print, or by means of conspiracies, or any other kind of actions, ever commit those crimes against the Motherland that are being ascribed to me. The facts on the basis of which crimes are being attributed to me do not exist. The accusation is based on the false testimony of certain mercenary, dishonest people and on my mistakes, whose nature cannot serve as the basis for such heinous accusations. I consider myself an honest person, devoted with all my soul to the cause of Leninism-Stalinism, and I find tragic the accusation that I committed treason. In the interests of clarifying the truth about me and my activity, I ask that the facts I have cited be verified, that my books be studied and witnesses be questioned. I ask that you study the reviews of my work in the Russian press. I ask that you question witnesses who knew my work firsthand, such as Chukovsky, Vera Vasilievna Smirnova, Mikhalkov, Piskunova, Blaginina, Dmitrievskaya, and Yevgeny Petrovich Mitskevich, who can talk about my work while I was in Germany, and Pavlo Grigorievich Tychina.*

Presiding Officer: In answer to a question from the court you said at the beginning of the trial that you plead guilty in part. To what do you plead guilty in part?

Kvitko: I say the same thing now. I believed, and believe today, in the accusation against the Jewish Anti-Fascist Committee: that it brought harm to the Soviet government. On what basis do I say this? On the basis of the expert commission's findings and on the basis of the investigation materials. And since the committee caused harm, and since I worked there as well, that means that responsibility for a portion of this harm falls on me. I cannot phrase it as it is in the code of law.

Presiding Officer: You are accused of high treason.

Kvitko: That is not true and did not happen.

Presiding Officer: Defendant Bergelson, have you anything to add to your testimony?

Bergelson: I do.

Presiding Officer: You said that you plead guilty in part. To what do you plead guilty?

Bergelson: I plead guilty, as I have already said, in part. Since the committee's work went beyond the framework of its officially assigned duties, and since

---

*Sergei Mikhalkov (1913–) is a writer particularly well known for his children's verses; he also wrote the words to the Soviet national anthem. Elena Blaginina (1903–1989) wrote poetry for children and translated works by Kvitko into Russian. Pavlo Tychina (1891–1967) was a Ukrainian poet and political figure.

all of these facts are nationalistic in nature, as is already well known, I, too, as a member of the committee, am also a party to this.

Presiding Officer: Do you confess that you conducted nationalistic activity and engaged in espionage?

Bergelson: No, I did not engage in any espionage, and I had nothing to do with classified materials and did not know about them prior to my arrest. I did not plead guilty to that, nor do I do so now.

I was a professional writer, and from the very beginning of my literary career I strove to master the craft. That means nothing other than striving to reveal the truth of life, and I am telling the truth when I say that I had no ill feelings toward the Bolsheviks in the first years of the revolution. When I say that I found the Bolsheviks to be highly attractive, I am telling the truth, because Bolsheviks, people who are raised in the Bolshevik spirit, bring their truth directly out into the open, and for a writer this is a gift.

The evidence that I had no ill feelings toward the Bolsheviks lies in the fact that as soon as I settled abroad, I took pen in hand and started writing favorable things about the Bolsheviks. These books were printed in the Soviet Union both when I was abroad and now. I wrote two articles against the members of the Yevsektsiya. I said that they were not real Bolsheviks, that they were late and would not catch up with the revolution. I spoke out against Kamenev and Zinoviev, who were members of the Politburo. They are all enemies of the people, they are no longer among the living, but the investigation is accusing me of writing against Soviet power.

While abroad, I saw all that was wrong with the capitalist world, fell in love with the Soviet Union, began reading the classics of Marxism-Leninism, and gradually changed my views. That is what makes me a person: that I have brains. It was much harder for me to come around to the ideas of the Soviet Union than it was for others, but I came around nonetheless. I am speaking of the reasons why I was detained so long abroad. I had the opportunity to remain abroad, had I been an enemy of the Soviet Union, but I did not. All of these facts can be verified, and I have every reason to believe that they have been. Everyone who is popular abroad was not and could not have been hidden from the vigilant eye of the GPU. From 1926 until 1934 I, a person who had supposedly fled from the Soviet Union six times, was permitted to leave five times, and I was not such an ordinary man that no one would pay attention to me. There were items in the press in Moscow, Kharkhov, Kiev, and Odessa about each of my returns, and in August 1931 there was an item about my return in *Izvestia,* which means that the GPU knew who was coming, and they allowed me to go abroad again. And in 1934 I was issued a Soviet passport with their permission. This was not done for people who struggled against Soviet power and against the party starting from the very founding of the Soviet state.

As for my nationalism, I would like to say that the essence of the nationalism that remains in me is that I was extremely attached to the Yiddish language as an instrument. I have worked in the language for twenty-eight years, and I love it, although it has many shortcomings. I know that I do not have long to live, but I love it like a son who loves his mother. I genuinely envy Russian authors because the Russian language is much richer.

My arrival in the USSR came at the same time that the Amur region was being set aside for Jewish settlers and declared a Jewish autonomous region. I regarded this as a desire on the part of the party and the Soviet government to give Jewish working people the opportunity to establish a feature of nationhood that they lacked—a shared territory. Once the government found this to be necessary, that meant it was a good thing. Is there nationalism in this? Let the court determine that. But I am telling the truth, that this corresponded with my desires. I was in Birobidzhan three or four times, and I came to love this little piece of the Soviet Union very much, sang its praises in quite a number of my works, told about its people, and praised not only Jews, at that.

But I felt that language was not the whole point, but rather it was a question of political systems. It's hard to move from one political system to another. That requires a lot of time. I am saying all of this so that my "nationalism" will be clear to the court. I wanted the Jews to make the transition from one way of life to another, not in some large city like Leningrad, Kiev, or Odessa, but in their own little corner. Let the court decide whether this looks like an attempt to fight assimilation.

Even before I arrived in Kuibyshev, I headed the art and literature section of *Eynikayt*. By the time I came to Kuibyshev, material had already begun coming in, but I didn't edit it or have anything to do with it. In Kuibyshev I was doing completely different work. Seven people oversaw this work, or rather were involved in it—at the Jewish Anti-Fascist Committee and at *Eynikayt*. Epshteyn was executive secretary, Vatenberg was a consultant, Kvitko was Epshteyn's assistant for radio broadcasts, Halkin selected material to be sent to Moscow, Orland was the editor in chief of the Jewish Anti-Fascist Committee, Fefer was Epshteyn's assistant at *Eynikayt*, and I headed the art and literature section. Mikhoels would come by only rarely. Epshteyn himself would go to see Lozovsky, taking only his deputies with him, and since I headed the art and literature section, there was no reason for me to go there, so I was not taken along. I wrote no letters to any correspondents, and I gave no instructions about gathering information. Lozovsky said that I was the one who gave *Eynikayt* its nationalistic character. To put it more accurately, he said that one of the people who gave *Eynikayt* its nationalistic character was Bergelson.

Lozovsky: I didn't read *Eynikayt*. I had nothing to do with it, as the court knows quite well.

Bergelson: In his testimony Lozovsky said that the Jewish Anti-Fascist Committee spread propaganda about the exceptional nature of the Jewish people. At one of the presidium sessions, Yuzefovich said that life in the USSR needed to be presented through a Jewish prism. Epshteyn said and did the same thing. From the very start they established this type of activity for the Jewish Anti-Fascist Committee as a whole, as well as for *Eynikayt* specifically. Epshteyn said that communist workers and workers in America or other countries who were sympathetic to the Soviet Union did not need Jewish Anti-Fascist Committee materials, that the main focus of propaganda should be Jewish petit bourgeois elements who read Yiddish newspapers hostile to the Soviet Union. Epshteyn adjusted the paper to the level of these masses. He said that the only way to get their attention was by presenting the achievements of Jews in the Soviet Union and the destruction of the Jews by the fascists. There was no way that Lozovsky could not have known about all of this, and as is apparent, this was a generally held point of view, based on the idea that petit bourgeois Jewish elements abroad were not interested in how various peoples lived in the Soviet Union.

In addition, I am accused in the indictment of going to Kiev in 1947 with the intention of carrying out espionage. In 1947 the Jewish Anti-Fascist Committee sent me to Kiev (it was the only business trip I made during the entire time) in order to study the work of the Office of Jewish Culture of the Ukrainian Academy of Sciences and write an article about it.* Surely everyone understands that an organization that collects folklore, folk songs, and language research cannot be an object of interest for espionage.

In the indictment I am accused of giving Goldberg and Novick information about Birobidzhan while they were in the USSR, but it doesn't say what information.

When I went to Goldberg's room at the National Hotel after dinner to pay him a return visit, I discovered that he had several issues of *Eynikayt* lying about in his room. There were frequent items about Birobidzhan in that paper. I saw that Goldberg was displeased about something. Without even offering me his hand, he said, "Tell me, what sort of Jews are going to Birobidzhan?" I thought a moment and said, "The Jews who are going are people quite capable of productive labor." After that he did not speak about Birobidzhan with me any more. This is all of the information that I gave to Goldberg.

In regard to Novick. Starting in 1928, I knew Novick as an honorable and devoted communist who worked almost every day for twenty-five years using the pages of the *Morgen Freiheit* to sincerely and energetically fight off slanderous attacks on the Soviet Union. I knew him as a communist and a hard worker, ready to give his whole life to see the communist movement in the United States succeed. Birobidzhan was of interest to Novick as a means to attract the attention of the United States and sympathy for Jewish laborers and for the Soviet Union. Since these masses in the

---

*The Office of Jewish Culture of the Ukrainian Academy of Sciences was closed in 1948.

United States were suffering from growing anti-Semitism, by showing them the nationality policy of the Communist Party, the *Morgen Freiheit* was inspiring them with some hope. Novick was with me in Birobidzhan at one time and had really no idea of all the things going on there.*

[At 6:10 P.M., the chairman announced a recess. On July 9, 1952, at 1:20 P.M., the court session resumed.]

Presiding Officer: Defendant Hofshteyn, do you have anything to add to your testimony?

Hofshteyn: I will not take advantage of your attention. I have never been an enemy of the Soviet Union. In the indictment it says that I was not only a member of the committee but held a leadership position, and that I was an enemy of Soviet power and the party. I want to say that I cannot plead guilty to these accusations, and I think that the court will give me the opportunity to live out the rest of my days in freedom among my family members so that I might serve the workers with the most painstaking labor.

Presiding Officer: Defendant Ilya Vatenberg, what do you have to add to the court proceedings?

Vatenberg: I would like to add several details about my party activity in the United States because this is mentioned in the indictment. One. For a number of years during the second half of the 1920s, I wrote regular political commentary and articles for the Yiddish communist newspaper the *Morgen Freiheit,* in which from a communist position I waged fierce battle against Zionism and Jewish nationalism in all of its manifestations. Two. In ICOR during that same period I spoke out repeatedly, orally and in print, against the Jewish bourgeois organizations Joint and Agro-Joint, exposing the reactionary essence of these organizations and their subversive work. Three. I constantly waged a consistent struggle against nationalistic attempts by Jewish nationalists in the United States, and they considered me their main enemy. Four. All of this happened in full view of Jews in the United States and other countries and is known to many of those seated here. Epshteyn knew about it as well.

So when he hired me to work at the Jewish Anti-Fascist Committee, he was not hiring a Jewish nationalist. To the contrary, he was hiring a communist whom he had known through my many years' work in the United States.

Now, in regard to the indictment. I am accused of participation in the Jewish Anti-Fascist Committee's nationalistic activity and espionage and, beyond that, of personally carrying out espionage.

I have shown and, I hope, proven to the court that my entire contact with the committee was limited to a five- to six-week period in 1942 when I was employed as a consultant and carried out routine assignments, none of

*Their meeting in Birobidzhan probably took place in 1936.

which were criminal in nature. That was all. Thus, I did not participate in any way in any of the principal crimes mentioned in the indictment, including espionage, nationalistic activity, or the Crimea venture.

On page 31 of the indictment it says that Vatenberg has been exposed as having committed crimes through personal confessions, through the testimony of his accomplices who were convicted earlier, through the testimony of witnesses, through the expert commission's conclusions, through material evidence, and through documents. We need to go into this deeply and figure out how it relates to each of the defendants. I was unable to do this, but on the basis of the material that I did examine, I can state that there is nothing, literally nothing, in the documents, the material evidence, the experts' findings, or the testimony of so-called accomplices who were convicted earlier that would prove my guilt. What remains? There remains the testimony of witnesses and personal confessions. Let us look at the witnesses' testimony. In my case, the materials contain testimony from four witnesses: Zuskin, Bergelson, Fefer, and Talmy.

As regards Zuskin's testimony, he testified to the immaterial fact that he saw me in Mikhoels's reception room, and then here in court he repudiated this testimony. So this testimony can be considered immaterial.

As to Bergelson's testimony, he testified that he met me at literary events and in private situations and that he held conversations with me from which he formed the impression that I was a nationalist, but this accusation is unproven.

Talmy's testimony about how I gave classified information to Novick relates to my personal espionage, but this testimony is not confirmed by any evidence, either.

As regards Fefer's testimony, he said, first of all, that I left the committee in early 1943. Thus he confirmed my testimony and not the investigators' assertion. Fefer testified that I wrote some articles on international topics, and in saying so he confirmed what I said here, and not the investigators' conclusions. Fefer spoke about how Epshteyn said that I am known in America and that I know America, but there is nothing scandalous in that. Finally, Fefer told about the appeal to a *Landsmanshaft*,* which I confessed to drafting.

So here is my conclusion. There is nothing in the witness testimony to confirm my participation or collaboration in any of the three principal crimes mentioned in the indictment—that is, the Crimea conspiracy, the gathering of classified information, or the plot to carry out nationalistic activity through practical work. What is left? My personal confessions remain. I have to say, Citizen Chairman, that I am far from taking a frivolous attitude toward personal confessions; I acknowledge that they carry a good

---

*Landsmanshaft, or "hometown society," refers to an organization of immigrants from the same town in Eastern Europe.

deal of weight and must be taken seriously. However, they are not irrefutable or unrefuted facts. They are not absolute proof—that is what the
supervisory investigation is for, and the court exists to compare and put
various facts together in order to see the extent to which testimony from
the preliminary investigation reflects reality.

I have already spoken of my testimony from the time of the preliminary
investigation. I have to say that the testimony which I gave during the preliminary investigation is refuted by my testimony in court and refuted by
what is and is not in these forty-two volumes, because not one of these volumes confirms that I participated in espionage for the committee, or that I
participated in nationalistic activity for the committee, or that I was involved in the Crimea question. On the contrary, I have proven and other
witnesses have proven that I was an opponent of that scheme, have proven
that I was opposed to Jewish topics and fought to write about other subjects. My testimony is confirmed by Talmy, Yuzefovich, and Fefer, who,
here in this court, confirmed the testimony that I have given. Thus I have
proven my innocence. So I am declaring in summary that nothing material
remains of that accusation on the third main charge, that Vatenberg was an
enemy of the Soviet Union. The accusation against me is not proven.

As for my personal espionage, it is the third charge that is under discussion here. It has to do with the trip to Birobidzhan in 1929. I am not going
to speak about 1926, when I was at the OZET Congress. I will touch on the
trip to Birobidzhan in 1929. During this trip I studied the settlers' living
conditions and observed how they were adjusting to their new life. I was interested in the benefits the Soviet government was providing to Birobidzhan. I visited three collective farms, and that was it, as far as my work
was concerned. The accusation states that this was done in order to gather
classified information. But that is not proven. And incidentally, as a coun-
terweight to that I can cite Talmy's book, which makes it clear that our
work had nothing to do with espionage or anti-Soviet activity. This book
proves that Talmy and I were interested only in what I am talking about
now, and it refutes the accusation.

Almazov's so-called hostile assignment is being presented as an indication of my guilt—I have already spoken about that. In the language of the
indictment, this was an assignment from reactionary circles in the United
States to commit espionage, but in fact this was a request from the general
secretary of ICOR, a Soviet friendship organization and an organization
run by the American Communist Party. His request to me was that from
time to time I provide information about successes in construction in Birobidzhan.

In the indictment it says that along with information about Birobidzhan
I provided information about the activity of a nationalistic underground in
the USSR and forwarded this information to the United States. This unsub-
stantiated assertion in the indictment—something that, incidentally, one

encounters with some regularity in these documents, which were compiled within four or five days after forty months of investigation—is an indication of how hastily all of this was done. Nowhere in all of the case materials is it apparent or proven that I was the kind of person described here. The assertion contained in these documents has no ground beneath it.

I will not say anything here about Novick. I will sing no songs of praise to Novick because the MGB considers him a spy. I allow that even if it is impossible to prove that he is a spy, based on considerations of state security, the fact that it has been officially announced means that it must be taken into account. But to bring me to justice for complicity in espionage, the accusation must prove that I knew or—given a reasonable degree of vigilance—should have known that Novick was a spy and an American intelligence agent. But that is not there. On the contrary, I saw that he received an entry visa, that he got help in traveling freely around the country and gathering information, so the security organs trusted him. How could it be demanded of me that I not talk with him and not facilitate the task assigned him by the Communist Party when he came here, when I knew him to be a communist? So I am declaring that these three cases of personal espionage mentioned in the indictment are not proven.

To what do I plead guilty? I pled guilty to writing in a single article that Jews in the USSR and the United States, although they have some fundamental differences in ideology, have several things in common, specifically the Yiddish language and a progressive cultural heritage. I now find elements of nationalism in this phrasing. I have to say that the concepts of nationalism and cosmopolitanism were mutually exclusive. They were completely opposite concepts. Today, however, everything has gotten confused. Today, when American imperialism presents itself under the slogan of worldwide domination, when Churchill speaks under the slogan "the United States of Europe," everything looks different.

In view of all of these considerations I ask the Military Collegium to take into account that the indictment as it relates to me is not proven and therefore to draw the appropriate conclusions.

I also have to say that during the investigation and in court I said nothing prejudicial about Talmy, and he was wrong in saying that I allegedly said something prejudicial about him. There is only one phrase in the interrogation record that has caused me many sleepless nights. It says that Talmy met the October Revolution with hostility, but these were not my words. I said "with a wait-and-see attitude," and then after long arguments with the investigator I agreed to the word "negatively," and in the end the investigator wrote "with hostility." I want to say that I know nothing prejudicial about Talmy. I know that he is a very honorable, dedicated, and uncompromising Soviet patriot.

And finally, a few words about my testimony regarding Vatenberg-Ostrovskaya, which the presiding officer read out to me here. I will not go into how this testimony came into being, but I have to say that it is in the language of the investigators and recorded from the investigators' viewpoint. To this I also have to add that in the thirty years I have known Ostrovskaya, I have not heard from her a single disloyal word about the Soviet Union. On the contrary, she has always demonstrated the greatest devotion to Soviet power and to the Soviet Union.

[At 2:20 P.M., the chairman announced a recess. After an hour, the court session was resumed.

The chairman read out the Military Collegium's decision to separate the materials on Solomon Leontevich Bregman from the case and cease the judicial proceedings against him because of his illness. Bregman had collapsed during the trial in the middle of June and had been transferred to a prison infirmary, where he would die on January 23, 1953.]

Presiding Officer: Defendant Shimeliovich, what can you add to the judicial proceedings?

Shimeliovich: In 1952 I had the opportunity to study the forty-two volumes of the preliminary investigation. Over a period of two months I have had the opportunity to attend all of the sessions of the Military Collegium, where I have experienced a calm situation for the very first time in three and a half years. And I would like to ask myself a question in the presence of the Military Collegium.

Were secrets kept from me at the Jewish Anti-Fascist Committee as a former member of the committee presidium? I reply, "Yes, secrets were kept from me, and to quite a great extent." I will permit myself to dwell on this and enumerate some things.

I learned in court that the galleys for *The Black Book* had been received from the United States. I learned in 1952, when I was presented with a decree stating that the book would be subjected to a study by a commission of experts, that *The Black Book* had been published in 1946. I learned in court about the receipt of *The Black Book*. I learned in court that the Jewish Anti-Fascist Committee had been subjected to a five-month inspection by the Central Committee. I learned in court about discussions with Panyushkin and Suslov about closing down the committee. I learned in 1952 about the resolution by Comrade Molotov and People's Commissar for State Control of the Russian Federation Popov about distributing gifts to the population. I learned in court that Shkiryatov had called Kvitko and Fefer in to see him. I learned in 1952 that Goldberg was the editor of a reactionary newspaper. I learned in 1952 from a telegram sent by Goldberg and appended to the case materials about Goldberg's conversation with Kalinin, in which Kalinin allegedly said to Goldberg that now there was an autonomous region called Birobidzhan, and later it would be an autonomous republic as well. Until 1952 I did not know about the memorandum to Comrade Stalin concerning the Crimea that had been signed by

Mikhoels, Fefer, and Epshteyn, nor did I see its contents until this year. I learned only in 1952 about Comrade Molotov's refusal on this question and whether this refusal was oral or in writing. I can cite many such facts.

The question arises, Why were things kept secret from me? I am speaking only about myself because you would be unlikely to find someone in Moscow who does not respect me as a party member, as a Soviet man, as someone having a fundamental Bolshevik persistence. They concealed their activity from me because they knew that I would definitely interfere and try to prevent their carrying out such things.

It has been said here that the question of Israel was discussed in the presidium. That session took place on October 21, 1948, whereas on October 1, 1948, I left for Kislovodsk with my wife and my doctor, and on October 21 I was at the Dzherzhinsky Sanatorium, so I could not have been at that session on October 21. I am not familiar with Slepak's report on Israel, and I don't know what is recorded in the session minutes. Kvitko has already said that one cannot rely on the Jewish Anti-Fascist Committee minutes, and Bregman said that once he was at a presidium session where Shimeliovich spoke, and then he was horrified when he read the record of my presentation in the minutes. The citizen member of the Military Collegium asked Fefer several times whether I had raised at presidium sessions the question of broadening the functions of the Jewish Anti-Fascist Committee, and although Fefer said that the broadening of functions was merely a brief episode, I have to say that I never raised the question of broadening the functions of the Jewish Anti-Fascist Committee. I was speaking only of broadening counterpropaganda and propaganda work, and if it says in the presidium session minutes that I spoke about broadening the committee's functions to include more work in the area of defending Jews' rights, then there is as much truth in that section as there is snow right now in Moscow and the surrounding area.

Further, as to my meeting with Goldberg and Novick, I deny what was said about me, namely, that I kissed them. That did not take place. Neither Yuzefovich nor Bregman confirmed that. Who could have seen it? Only the investigator could have seen this, and he ascribes this to me. And the words "a good Jewish soul" are insufficient for an accusation, because these words mean nothing.

Presiding Officer: Defendant Zuskin, do you have anything to add to your testimony? I ask you not to repeat yourself, but to say that which you have not already said and the court does not know.

Zuskin: I will be very specific and say only what I said during my extremely tumultuous and garrulous testimony to the court on June 11 and 12. I made use of the recesses in the court session to try and recall the testimony of all the interrogated defendants and to analyze the indictment in the most painstaking way possible. I read every page of it many times and noticed a strange circumstance in regard to myself. The indictment takes up forty-five pages. On all forty-five pages my name—Zuskin—is mentioned six times, four times on page 1 and twice where it says that, together with Mikhoels, I turned the theater into a center of espionage activity directed by American reactionary circles. Fourteen of the accused are specifically mentioned by name—those who assisted in gathering secret materials. All fourteen defendants being tried in this case are mentioned as participants in nationalistic activity except for me, Zuskin.

I attended official committee sessions, I repeat, official sessions, and that I did rarely, for the issues of the Jewish Anti-Fascist Committee did not interest me, my heart was not in them. In all the volumes of investigation materials there is nothing said specifically about my personal work at the Jewish Anti-Fascist Committee, nor is there anything about that in the forty-five pages of the indictment. This is apparent from the testimony of the other defendants as well, who did not mention my name once in connection with the Jewish Anti-Fascist Committee's work. Defendant Fefer was the only one who, alluding to what Mikhoels had said, described me as a convinced nationalist, but without having any serious basis for this. I simply cannot understand why the investigators have not specifically described my personal criminal activity at the Jewish Anti-Fascist Committee. Mikhoels and Epshteyn have died, but Fefer is here, and he testified at a witness confrontation that he never gave me any assignment for the Jewish Anti-Fascist Committee, and in court he confirmed this testimony of his.

Mikhoels believed that the Yiddish theater was above all a Jewish theater, and that the public should find something there that was not available in other theaters. I told him that the Jewish theater was above all a Soviet theater in Yiddish. This is the formula that I wanted to tell of here.

I would like to dwell for a moment on the witness testimony of Fedoseyev, who considers the play *The Ghetto Uprising,** produced in 1947, when Mikhoels was still alive, to be a vile work. After this, Mikhoels lived for another year. If Fedoseyev criticizes the play, then why, when he saw it while Mikhoels was still alive, didn't he demand to have the play removed from the repertoire?

In conclusion I can say that there is no way that I can plead guilty to the baseless, vague accusation presented against me. I did not participate actively in the work. I saw only what took place at the sessions, so for that reason I cannot bear full responsibility for what went on in the committee.

**The Ghetto Uprising* was written by Peretz Markish. In the fall of 1946, M. Shcherbakov, director of the personnel department of the Central Committee, sent a memorandum to Alexei Kuznetsov, secretary of the Central Committee, in which he criticized Markish's play for displaying nationalistic tendencies and for implying that the Jews could be free only in a land of their own. The memorandum was dated October 7, 1946. See Redlich, *War, Holocaust and Stalinism,* pp. 417–421.

To a certain degree, of course, the shadow falls on me as well. This is what I can plead guilty to. I looked at the entire indictment very carefully and found not a single fact to indicate that I should be faced with such a terrible accusation. I now hope and believe that the court will make a just decision as regards my work at the Jewish Anti-Fascist Committee.

[At 8:20 P.M., the chairman announced a recess.

On July 10, 1952, at 1:45 P.M., the court session was resumed.]

Presiding Officer: Defendant Talmy, do you have anything to add to your testimony?

Talmy: My nationalism dates for the most part to the period before the October Revolution, to the time when the Jewish masses, among whom I lived, were oppressed both in tsarist Russia and in other countries. My nationalism came from the interests of the toiling Jewish masses. True, I understood these interests incorrectly, but nonetheless, that is how I understood them. Again, this was not a crime, but I would say rather a delusion. In any case, there was nothing chauvinistic in my nationalism, no propaganda about the exclusive or chosen nature of the Jewish people. To the contrary, I also struggled against that.

[Later, Talmy recounted in detail his activity in the United States as a member of the American Communist Party in the 1920s.]

Presiding Officer: Defendant Vatenberg-Ostrovskaya, what do you have to add to your testimony?

Vatenberg-Ostrovskaya: I would like to add that I do not deny that perhaps there was a lack of caution on my part, but there was no intention to pass along any sort of secret information. I confirm that I never heard anti-Soviet statements from Novick. During the preliminary investigation I said that I told Novick that at one time Jews returning from evacuation had to live in cramped living quarters, but this was interpreted by the investigators to mean that Jews were not given apartments and that they were oppressed.

I need to say that I had an especially hard time during the investigation. I was interrogated with a rubber cudgel lying on the table. Because I was on the staff of the committee, the investigator believed that I should have known everything, and the threats from him were never-ending. They threatened me constantly with terrible beatings, saying that they would make a cripple out of me. Lozovsky said here that this did not scare him, but it frightened me terribly. I was in a sort of frenzy. Every day and night I heard from the investigator that I was going to be beaten, and beaten terribly. In my fevered imagination I constantly heard the screams of my husband, whom they were supposedly beating; I was driven to such a psychological state that I started looking for crimes and agreeing with the investigator and coming up with incomprehensible things about myself.

I have wanted to say the following. None of my work at the committee had anything criminal about it, and all of the translations were done for

Glavlit. I didn't receive from the committee leaders any work or any articles to translate. I sometimes heard conversations about how Jews were being fired from their jobs somewhere or other, how somebody didn't have an apartment. That I did hear, but I never regarded it as discrimination against the Jews by the government. Many outrages committed against Jews in the provinces I took to be wrong actions by local leaders, and I thought that the government was unaware of these things. My only mistake was in not refuting such conversations instead of listening to them in silence. But I never concluded from this that Jews were enduring any kind of oppression by the government. So, that part of the June 20 interrogation record is wrong where it says that I allegedly told Shlesberg that the government was trying to consign Mikhoels's memory to oblivion simply because he was a Jew. That is wrong. I never had such a conversation.

Everything in the interrogation records is made up and distorted. Friendships are attributed to me of which I had absolutely no idea. I was told that I knew Léon Blum.* I didn't know him. The investigator told me, "Sign it anyway," and I signed it because at the time it made no difference to me. Nor did I know Anna Louisa Strong.† I saw her once at a publishing house. Although I can describe what she looks like, I was never acquainted with her. And the last interrogation record in 1949 about my friendships in America is simply not true.

In 1947, when an MGB agent came to see me and expressed a desire to have a list of the people I knew in America who could be useful to the MGB, I gave him a list. They were people in the arts, sciences, literature, and business. I had known these people fifteen years earlier. Some of them may have passed away by this time, but nonetheless I provided the list. On the list were such people as the Columbia professor Kuntz,‡ a close friend of ours and of others. The MGB agent told me that these people might be used for good ends. All of these people whom I knew and whose names I gave were ultimately described as my Zionist contacts, which was not true.

It seems to me that in 1935 the People's Commissariat of Defense deemed it necessary to send me on a secret trip to America, an assignment which indicates that at that time I was trusted. I underwent a security check, and my trip to America was made possible. Exactly three months later I returned from this secret trip having fulfilled the assignment, for which I received official recognition.

---

*Léon Blum (1872–1950), a French socialist political figure and leader of the Popular Front, was prime minister of France three times: 1936–1937, 1938, and 1946–1947.

†Anna Louise Strong (1885–1970) was a radical American journalist. She first visited the Soviet Union in 1921 and stayed for two years. She later visited China, but had to flee, with Mikhail Borodin, in 1927. In 1930 she founded the English-language *Moscow Daily News*. She was arrested in February 1949, accused of spying, and expelled from the country.

‡Charles Kuntz was chairman of ICOR. He spoke Russian and is believed to have been a sociologist and agriculturist at Columbia University.

Presiding Officer: Defendant Shtern, what do you have to add to your testimony?

Shtern: The committee's work did not interest me, although I didn't think that any kind of hostile work was going on there. I looked on it as some sort of charitable organization, a small-scale organization of the kind that existed before the revolution. But I should have approached this question differently, and if I had faced this question head-on, maybe I would have spotted something there.

I deny that there were any sort of nationalistic, anti-Soviet statements on my part. I did not utter a single anti-Soviet syllable. I have doubts about the accuracy of the minutes from the sessions of the Jewish Anti-Fascist Committee, for they do not reflect what I wanted to say.

I knew how we were seen abroad. Abroad, people say all the time that Soviet citizens are not allowed to meet with foreigners. I wanted to show that this wasn't true. I said to foreign scientists of my acquaintance, "Please do drop by if you'd like to," not because they interested me, but because I wanted to show that they were wrong. Some Swiss people came, including the husband of a friend of mine who was a secretary at the embassy. I met him at an official reception. He came over to me and said, "I have greetings for you, but I couldn't make up my mind to come and see you because I've been told that Soviets are forbidden to meet with foreigners, and I didn't want to get you in trouble." Then he added that he was being followed. I said that none of that was true. "Please come see me tomorrow if you'd like to at the institute, and you'll see that no one will be following you." I didn't invite him to my apartment because the conditions there were not suitable.

Presiding Officer: He told you that he was being followed?

Shtern: Yes. He said that it seemed to him that he was being followed.

Presiding Officer: What else would you like to say?

Shtern: I repeat once again that I did not pass along any secret information to anyone. There is no way anyone could say that I informed Madd of anything. Madd is a prominent bacteriologist, but he was not interested in the scientific work that I was doing. American scientists are generally quite limited. They know only their own area of science and aren't interested in anything else. I learned from him what was important to me, that is, an erroneous opinion that one should give a large dose of streptomycin at the start of treatment. What he said was important to me. It confirmed what I thought. As for Lesley, I didn't talk with him about anything having to do with science.

Presiding Officer: Why did Madd come?

Shtern: He was invited by Oparin* under the aegis of VOKS. They were Oparin's guests.

---

*Alexander Oparin (1894–1980) was a biochemist famous for his work on the origins of life.

Presiding Officer: What made you meet with them when you were in different areas of science?

Shtern: When Madd and Lesley came, they informed me by phone that they brought greetings from my brother. I was very interested in meeting with them because I knew that they worked in medicine, and I also wanted to hear about my brother.*

    Now about Tripp. She is the press attaché at a foreign embassy, but she was also a member of the same society of which I am a member, the International League of University Women. I did not pass along any information to her.

[At 3:15 P.M., the chairman announced a recess.]

Determination to Separate Solomon Bregman's Case

Determination

July 9, 1952   Moscow

MILITARY COLLEGIUM OF THE SUPREME COURT OF THE USSR

MEMBERS:

CHAIRMAN	Lieutenant General of Justice CHEPTSOV
MEMBERS	Major General of Justice ZARYANOV
	Major General of Justice DMITRIEV

Having discussed the question of the possibility of further consideration of the case of Solomon Leontevich Bregman, accused under articles 58-1a; 58-10, part 2; and 58-11 of the Criminal Code of the Russian Federation, in connection with the findings received from the doctor regarding the extremely serious illness afflicting Bregman, who is currently unconscious, in consequence of which he cannot attend the judicial session and testify,

Based on the above, the Military Collegium of the Supreme Court of the USSR

Has Decided:

to halt consideration of the criminal case of the accused Solomon Leontevich Bregman until he has recovered.

Investigative materials on Bregman's case shall be separated from the general case into a separate legal proceeding.

Valid when accompanied by the necessary signatures.

Hereby certified:

Secretary of the Military Collegium of the Supreme Court of the USSR

    Senior Lieutenant   (signature)   AFANASIEV

---

*Her brother Bruno Shtern (Stern) lived in the United States.

Statement by Isaac Fefer in Closed Judicial Session

[At 8:10 P.M. on July 10 the chairman announced that defendant Fefer had been brought to the court session. In response to the chairman's questions, Fefer stated that he could not "consider himself a nationalist" and that he considered the poem "I Am a Jew" "a mistake."]

Fefer: In court I spoke of various individual, nationalistic errors committed by Markish and other Yiddish poets and writers, but I knew nothing about their nationalism as a crime. All that I knew about them I told the MGB, and the court can check on this.

Part of my testimony that I gave during the preliminary investigation about the nationalism of certain people is correct, and part is not. I confirm my testimony about Kagan. As to the testimony about Sheinin (the prosecutor), it is correct only in regard to the nationalistic contents of the play *Eliss,* but I talked about this based only on what Mikhoels had said. I cannot confirm my testimony in regard to Sheinin's role at the Nuremberg trials. In general, the interrogation about him was conducted under duress.

During the entire investigation I gave honest factual information about all the cases of which I knew when nationalism was manifested by various people. But later, all of my testimony was cast in a different light by the investigators' editing. Usually I signed interrogation records drawn up in advance by the investigator.

As regards Epshteyn, my testimony is correct for the most part. I wrote about him to the MGB, saying that his remarks sounded to me as if they were disloyal to Soviet power.

Etinger was very interested in the fate of the State of Israel and was very dissatisfied that the Soviet government was not doing much in this area. In addition, he expressed dissatisfaction over the fact that Lysenko's work and teachings received wide distribution in the Soviet Union. Epshteyn was the one who introduced me to Etinger.

In court, especially on the first day, May 8, I tried to stick to the testimony I had given during the preliminary investigation. This happened because three days earlier I had been summoned to the investigative division of the MGB for a witness confrontation with Zbarsky, and then Kuzmin, at first in the presence of Zhirukhin and then in the presence of Konyakhin, warned me that I should give the same testimony in court that I had given during the investigation.

I spoke in court about my nationalism under the effect of the conversation with Kuzmin because I didn't want to end up like Shimeliovich.

[On other questions Fefer testified:]

The Jewish Anti-Fascist Committee was not a nationalistic center, although there were individual mistakes in the work done there. Questions having to do with settling the Jews were Mikhoels's personal concern, and this had nothing to do with the activity of the Jewish Anti-Fascist Committee presidium. The presidium members were selected, not on the basis of nationalistic considerations, but on the basis of how well known various people were. So, for example, Zbarsky, Tankilovich,* and Zaslavsky were nominated for the chairmanship.

For the most part, broadening of the Jewish Anti-Fascist Committee's functions took place before 1945 and came down to writing several letters to the Central Committee and the government, but this was back before I became executive secretary.

The Jewish Anti-Fascist Committee had nothing to do with the publishing house Der emes, the State Jewish Theater, or the Office of Jewish Culture of the Ukrainian Academy of Sciences, which also refutes the title of "nationalistic center" that has been attributed to the Jewish Anti-Fascist Committee.

The findings of the expert commission in regard to *Eynikayt* I consider to be wrong, because I reject the idea that a newspaper as hostile as the one described by the commission could possibly have existed within the USSR in plain view of everyone.

I would also like to say that there were and are nationalistic sentiments among Jews, and they were especially strong in 1948, when the State of Israel was founded, and I have informed the MGB about all of that. So, for example, there was a case when the engineer Rogachevsky came by to see me at the Jewish Anti-Fascist Committee. He started telling me that a group of Jewish engineers had been meeting at his apartment to discuss alleged discrimination against Jews in the USSR in order to write a letter about this to the government. Rogachevsky invited me to come over as well. I, of course, refused, and then informed Marchukov at the MGB about it. The next time he came to see me, Rogachevsky informed me that he had initiated the organization of a volunteer division to be sent to Israel and gave me a written statement about it with a request that I pass it on. I conveyed the statement to the MGB.

Again I say to the court that all of my testimony about the nationalism of various people is true for the most part but has been exaggerated by the investigators. I have nothing else to add to my testimony.

[At 9:00 P.M., the chairman declared the closed court session over. On July 11, 1952, at 12:45 P.M., the trial proceedings resumed.]

The Defendants' Final Statements

[The chairman declared the trial of the case to be over and offered each defendant the opportunity to make a final statement.]

---

*Abram Tankilovich was a member of the JAC presidium. In 1949 he was among twenty-two Jews from a Moscow subway construction company who were accused of embezzlement and arrested. See RGASPI, f. 17, op. 119, del. 1024, ll. 74–77, for further information on this case.

Fefer: Citizen Chairman and Citizen Judges! I have already told the court all that I know about this case. I want to assure you that in my life and work I have never been a bird of passage. My life is closely intertwined with my creative work. In fact, my first literary work was a poem about Budyonny's* cavalry. My entire life and literary work have been connected with the Communist Party. My works were always published in communist newspapers and magazines in various capitalist countries. In my articles I always wrote that the achievements of Jews in the Soviet Union were the result of implementing Comrade Stalin's teachings on the national question and the great example of the Russian people. In the course of thirty years I had the good fortune to extol the heroic labor of the Soviet people, and I wrote more about Russia and the Ukraine than I did about Jews, for which some people even faulted me. I ask the court to take into consideration all that I have said and not deprive me of the opportunity to serve the Soviet people until my last breath.

Teumin: I want to say to the court that when I gave Goldberg the information about the Baltic republics, I thought that I was doing something useful for the Soviet Union. I wanted to use Goldberg to spread propaganda about the achievements of the Soviet Union as I had previously used many other foreign correspondents and journalists. I always tried to use every way possible to carry out the tasks assigned to me by the party. In the episode with Goldberg I displayed political short-sightedness and swallowed the bait of an American spy and intelligence agent.

My work was my only joy in life, and I was proud of this. I still have hope that I will be able to atone for this mistake of mine through further honorable work.

Second, I am guilty of not rebutting Fefer's and Mikhoels's nationalistic conversations on three occasions, but I state that I myself was never a nationalist. I ask that the court take all of this into account when making its decision about me.

Markish: Citizen Chairman and Citizen Judges! I know full well that robbery starts not when the thief breaks into the safe, but much earlier, and nationalism starts not with open propaganda about racial superiority, but rather with thoughtless flaunting of one's own putative superiority. Large crimes begin with small actions. I did not commit even such small actions. I want to say to the court that my whole life and my literary work and activity have been a battle against backwardness in literature. I have been called a troublemaker, and in America I was sharply criticized for this. All of my books were brimming with this struggle. I was a rank-and-file soldier among Soviet writers and a correspondent for *Pravda* and *Izvestia.*

---

*Semyon Budyonny (1883–1973) was a Red Army commander during the Civil War. Isaac Babel's experiences in Budyonny's cavalry brigade formed the basis of Babel's famous short story collection *Red Cavalry.*

In 1934 at the First Congress of Soviet Writers I read a poem of mine in which I said that there was no longer any point in writing about the "shtetl Jew," for which I was sharply criticized. During the thirty years in which the first generation of Soviet writers has been active many mistakes have been made, but nonetheless we headed firmly toward the summits of Communism. The current generation of Soviet writers is working with the next millennium in mind, and this work could not be without mistakes. This is why I say that if my works are not good now, then I am proud that they will serve as fertilizer for future Soviet Homers. Soviet culture in the future will not be able to toss aside my small brick that I have contributed to the great construction of Communism.

This in fact explains why my name is hardly mentioned in connection with the activity of the Jewish Anti-Fascist Committee, for I had nothing to do with it. A tragic misunderstanding has occurred: that I share responsibility for the activity of the Jewish Anti-Fascist Committee. During the first round of the investigation, I was not included among the people responsible for the activity of the Jewish Anti-Fascist Committee and was accused only of reviewing non-Soviet books favorably.

While in prison I did not feel I had committed any crime, and it was easy for me, even though I was longing for my family. I figured out what all of the mistakes were that I could possibly have committed. If I made a mistake in the poem "To a Jewish Warrior," it could have become a terrible sin, but thanks to the Jewish Anti-Fascist Committee, it did not. Have I really not atoned for my mistakes by spending three and a half years in prison?

Colonel Nosov told me that they would sentence only the leaders, and I would be released. Back in 1950, Ryumin told me that I could already begin planning a new book, and I was terribly surprised when I saw my name on the list of leaders of the Jewish Anti-Fascist Committee, for I had, in fact, been a bone in their throats. I do not want to talk about the indictment because the fact that my name appears there is a sheer misunderstanding.

I want to request that the court give me the opportunity to give all the energy and love that I have for the Soviet people to them as I did over the course of thirty years of creative activity. I want to write now in the language of Comrades Lenin and Stalin with a new awareness. Citizen Judges, I want to say that slander has not broken me. I believe that the party, the government, and the Soviet people will themselves find my words useful, which will give me further opportunity to serve our Soviet Motherland.

Yuzefovich: I ask the court in deciding my fate to consider that it has become clear in the court that I didn't participate in any sort of conspiracy with shrewd American business operators. I ask you to take into account the fact that I did not convey any classified materials to anyone. I passed along material from Institute 205, carrying out Lozovsky's instructions, and I committed the blunder of not obtaining written permission. For that I should be held responsible according to party procedure. I believe that for participating in the selection of materials for *The Black Book,* I should also be held responsible according to party procedure. In court it has also been established that I was not involved in drafting the memorandum about the Crimea. I believe that it has become clear in court that I entertained no nationalistic thoughts or sentiments and that I also spoke out against such a thing. I ask that you take into account that in court all the defendants have repudiated the testimony they gave during the preliminary investigation concerning my statements about party and government leaders.

It never occurred to me that hostile work could be going on at the Jewish Anti-Fascist Committee, for its activity was overseen by the Central Committee. This is why I can say to the Military Collegium and to the party with absolute confidence that I am not guilty of the crimes of which I am accused. I ask the court to take into account the fact that for thirty years I served the party and the government faithfully and honorably and had nothing to do with Jewish organizations.

I never deceived the party or engaged in treacherous behavior. I was not involved in any anti-party groups and always upheld the party line. I may have committed a mistake of some kind or demonstrated short-sightedness, but I could not have betrayed the party or the Motherland. This is a monstrous accusation. My conscience before the party and the Motherland is clear. If the Military Collegium doubts my honesty and my innocence for even a moment, then I ask that the death penalty be applied to me.

Lozovsky: From my testimony the court knows everything about me except for nine-tenths of my activity in the All-Union Central Council of Trade Unions, Profintern, and Comintern. I consider it proven that the accusation leveled against me has nothing to corroborate it. I am convinced that the Military Collegium will correctly assess the forty-two volumes composed by the fifteen witnesses and thirty-five investigators and will expose the slander in a way befitting the party. All the testimony against me has been refuted in court by those same people who signed it during the preliminary investigation.

The only document that is the primary battering ram of the accusation is the letter to Comrades Molotov and Stalin about settling Jews in the Crimea. This letter contains hints of nationalism in it, but since it was not written for publication, I did not believe that it required careful editing.

The expert commission's findings on espionage are very strangely put together. Nothing in the materials selected indicates or confirms that they were sent abroad or indicates who was responsible. These materials were selected by Ponomarev and Alexandrov in order to blacken my name, but the commission's approach to their evaluation was very superficial. On the basis of this conclusion one is moved to ask, "In whose name did Lozovsky do all of this?" There are only two possible motives: a desire for material gain or an ideology held in common with American bourgeois circles. In the course of the investigation the first motive was immediately ruled out, and nothing was found to confirm the second.

I think the Americans would have been willing to pay dearly for an agent such as myself, but they won't live so long, and neither will those who are slandering me now. In confirmation of this I want to point out that on the basis of my articles, foreign parties and trade unions studied Leninist tactics and programs of action. I could cite a number of examples of my activity in this area. So, for example, during World War II the general secretary of the American Communist Party swerved from the correct line and advanced a theory of "progressive American imperialism." But in spite of this he remained a friend of the USSR, and at Comrade Stalin's direction I spent eight evenings in conversation with this person. Subsequently Ponomarev tried to use the fact that Lozovsky had spoken with someone who had been expelled from the party.

I have said everything and request no favors. I need either complete rehabilitation or death. I have given my entire life for the cause of the party and do not wish to be a parasite. If the court finds me guilty of anything at all, then I would ask for the opportunity to appeal to the government to substitute execution for punishment. But should anything come to light indicating that I was innocent, then I ask that I be posthumously readmitted to the ranks of the party and that the information about my rehabilitation be published in the newspapers.

[At 1:50 P.M. the chairman announced a recess. At 2:45 the judicial session was resumed.]

Kvitko: Citizen Chairman and Citizen Judges! For decades I spoke before joyous audiences of children who wore the necktie of the Young Pioneers, and extolled the good fortune of being a Soviet citizen. I now end my life by speaking before the Supreme Court of the Soviet people, accused of the most serious crimes. This fabricated accusation has come crashing down on me and caused me dreadful agonies. Why is it that my every word here in court is soaked in tears? Because the dreadful accusation of treason is unbearable to me, a Soviet citizen.

There would not have been such lengthy conversations and repetitions as have taken place here in court had I been shown the specific materials that, according to the statement in the indictment, I transmitted abroad as a spy, and the documents that confirmed that I waged a struggle against the party. During the preliminary investigation I was told that the accusation of espionage against me had been removed, but then I saw my name once again in the indictment among the names of a number of others accused of such serious crimes. But no one has ever heard a critical word from me about the party or the government. You can be certain that if there were anything of the sort, it would definitely have been introduced in court. But I was known as a dedicated Soviet man, and none of the defendants seated here could have shared their criminal designs with me.

For a long time in prison I tried to identify my crime, but I could not. It is asked why I needed to let happiness slip from my hands by committing

treason against the Motherland, which has given me everything, then fling-
ing myself into the embrace of the imperialists. But I have nothing in common with them. I have never been a member of any anti-party group. I have
never had contacts with Zionists, and all of my statements, poems, and articles were in favor of party policy.

The Soviet Union has given me everything. Materially I was well provided for and never pursued money. My family and I lived modestly and
needed nothing fancy. What reasons could have compelled me to commit
treason? There were no reasons for that, just as there was in fact no treason. If the investigators are accusing me of something, I want them to present material evidence. If they are trying to assert that I wanted to exchange
the honorable title of Soviet writer and poet for the title American spy, then
let them present proof of that. While my mind is not yet completely
clouded, I believe that to be accused of treason, one must first commit an
act of treason.

I ask that it be indicated specifically what secret documents I transmitted
abroad. There is no such information in the case materials because no such
event ever really took place.

Perhaps I am a bad worker or generally a bad person who must be isolated from society, and that is why I am faced with grave accusations. I state
to the court that I am not guilty of anything, not of espionage nor of nationalism. I made various mistakes, but there was no malicious intent. I feel
that I have offended the Motherland, but I have not committed any crime.
The entire accusation is a dreadful lie of embittered slanderers.

What a great pleasure it was to help raise and educate Soviet children in
the spirit of Leninism. I know for sure that if artistic work is not steeped
in our modern ideas, then it quickly wilts, because although I am in prison,
in my soul I feel myself to be among the family of the great Soviet people. I
have not ceased to maintain contact with children in my mind, so while in
prison I have created a new collection of poems, called *Toward the Sun*.*
The party is my family and my faith, and no one can ever take that great
strength of a communist away from me.

I ask that the court take into consideration that there is no documentary
evidence in the indictment of my supposedly hostile activity against the
party and the Soviet government, and there is no proof of any criminal tie
with Mikhoels and Fefer. I also ask that you take into account that there is
no evidence that I instructed correspondents of the Jewish Anti-Fascist
Committee to gather classified material or that I myself traveled to the
Crimea for that purpose. There is also no proof that I transmitted secret information about the USSR to Goldberg. I believe that all of these accusations have fallen away completely during the process of the judicial proceedings. It seems to me that we exchanged roles with the investigators,

*Kvitko's volume of verse *K Solntsu* appeared in 1948.

because they are required to make accusations based on facts, and I, a poet, to create literary works. But it has turned out the other way around.

I need to state that I knew the defendants here so slightly that I can barely recall whether I had any conversations with any of them. Although I was not their accomplice, that does not mean that I do not confess to part of the responsibility for the scandalous practices of the Jewish Anti-Fascist Committee. If the court confirms the experts' findings, then I ask that you take into account that although I do not relieve myself of responsibility for the activity of the Jewish Anti-Fascist Committee, I do not feel that I am guilty of a crime. I did not commit treason and do not plead guilty to a single one of the five accusations facing me. Realizing with pain that I could not have been alert, I ask the party's forgiveness and ask to atone for my guilt with my work.

It is easier for me to be in prison on Soviet soil than "free" in any capitalist country. I am a citizen of the Soviet Union, and my Motherland is the Motherland of those geniuses of the party and of humanity Comrades Lenin and Stalin. I believe that I cannot be accused of such grave crimes without evidence. I hope that my arguments will be perceived by the court as they should be. I ask the court to return me to the honest labor of the great Soviet people.

Bergelson: I am not a poet, and I want to say simply that I never engaged in hostile activity against the party and the Soviet government. I have already spoken of this in court, and I repeat it now. I was not the backbone of the Jewish Anti-Fascist Committee, for there wasn't one, and I didn't know about any hostile conspiracy. I knew that the committee had been created to mobilize all people in the struggle against fascism. There is no evidence that I personally gathered or transmitted any classified materials abroad or gave anyone assignments to gather materials of that sort, but I feel my guilt and would like to speak of it to the Supreme Court of the USSR.

I looked very lightly on the fact that I had been brought onto the presidium of the Jewish Anti-Fascist Committee. I knew that Epshteyn had drawn up the list of presidium members. He included names there that would sound impressive abroad so that no one there could say that the Jewish Anti-Fascist Committee was a political organization. The fact that my nomination was confirmed by the Central Committee was an expression of great responsibility and trust in me in connection with the materials sent abroad by the Jewish Anti-Fascist Committee. I should have followed the activity of the Jewish Anti-Fascist Committee, but I didn't do that while the committee was doing other things. For that reason I turned out not to be a real Soviet man and did not live up to the trust of the party and the government, although I personally participated in a minimal way in the activity of the Jewish Anti-Fascist Committee. There were old party members at the Jewish Anti-Fascist Committee who also slipped up as I did. I feel that herein lies my guilt.

I ask you, Citizen Chairman and Citizen Judges, to take my whole life under consideration, and although I did not attain the level of a real Soviet man, to take into account that my starting point was somewhere back in the Middle Ages. My literary activity received very high marks in the USSR as well as abroad. I was compared with Gorky and Flaubert. I was compared with the great Russian authors whom I studied and whom I love. I gave my entire gift as a writer to the working masses and not to those rich people from whom I came. I ask the court to take note of the fact that not one of the Yiddish writers of my age has entered the ranks of Soviet literature—such writers as Sholem Asch, Bialik, and Nomberg.* I am the only one of that entire generation of writers who accepted the ideas of Comrades Lenin and Stalin and devoted the last thirty years to Soviet themes. I was headed toward attaining the level of a real Soviet man, but did not quite reach it, and of that I am guilty. I am guilty that I did not attain the level of vigilance inherent in a Soviet man. I ask the Supreme Court to give me, an older Yiddish writer, the opportunity to expend my strength for the good of the people and attain the level of a Soviet man.

Hofshteyn: I have already stated my request to the court as an addition to the court proceedings.

Vatenberg: Citizen Judges! Everything bearing on the case materials has already been said. I would only like to direct the judges' attention to the circumstance that all the case materials directly prove my innocence and that the accusations are based only on my personal testimony which I gave during the preliminary investigation and which I have completely repudiated. I gave this testimony under pressure owing to a confluence of circumstances during the preliminary investigation. I do not want to reveal these reasons completely, and should the court find it possible to believe me, then I ask that it acquit me.

If the court finds me guilty, then I ask it to take into account that since 1921 I have followed the line of Comrades Lenin and Stalin in the ranks of the Communist Party. Since 1929 I have honorably served the interests of the Soviet Union in the area of foreign trade, where I saved hundreds of thousands of rubles in Soviet hard currency, and then for nine years I gave all of my strength, working in the area of ideology. I also ask that you take into account that I chose the Soviet Union as my Motherland when I was already an adult, and I have had no reason to betray this Motherland.

If the court finds me guilty, then I ask that my contributions and the period of my preliminary confinement be taken into account during sentencing. Although I don't know what I should be punished for, if the court believes that I have not been sufficiently punished, then I ask that the punishment meted out be one that will permit me to use my knowledge in a

---

*Hersh Dovid Nomberg (1876–1927) was a prominent Yiddish prose writer in Warsaw early in the century. He supported Jewish agricultural settlements in the Soviet Union.

domestic setting. And I also ask, should my wife be convicted, that we be allowed to bear our punishment together.

I would also like to say that the interrogation record of my interrogation dated May 26, 1949, was not a transcript. I understood later why this interrogation record was needed. Before the interrogation I was told that Talmy had already been arrested and pled guilty to all the charges presented to him, but then I saw that he was arrested on the basis of my testimony. I say to the court that this testimony of mine about Talmy is incorrect. I also say to the court that I am not guilty of espionage or of nationalism.

Shimeliovich: I have already had the opportunity to say everything to the court during the trial. I only want to note certain issues. During the entire period of the preliminary investigation I did not once have to think about what I needed to say to the investigator. I said only what I knew. Here in court the question of conversations about replacing eighteen editors of medical journals was looked into. I need to say that at that time I believed that they should be replaced, but that it needed to be done very carefully.

During the court session I transmitted to the chairman of the court nine copies of my statements to the government that I wrote during the investigation, and now I am certain that they will reach the Central Committee. Two words about the Crimea. It has been established here that I had nothing to do with sending the memorandum about the Crimea. Epshteyn told me that this was done by orders from "on high." The case materials contain a memorandum about the Crimea, allegedly written by me in February 1944. But this cannot be true, because the date indicated does not correspond to the memorandum's contents. In addition to all that has been said, I ask the court to go to the appropriate bodies and request that corporal punishment be forbidden in prison. And also wean certain MGB employees from the notion that the investigative division is the holy of holies and make them understand that the holiest thing we have is the party.

I ask that the prison administration no longer be made dependent on the investigative division. I would ask that certain investigators be forbidden from studying the classics of Marxism-Leninism during interrogations. On the basis of what I have said in court I would request that certain MGB employees be brought to justice.

I never pled guilty during the preliminary investigation. Not once has a thought of mine cast a shadow on the party or even on the MGB as a whole. But such a shadow has fallen on particular people among the employees of the MGB, including Abakumov, and I ask that the strictest measures be taken in regard to them. My conscience is clear, and it has always been principled and in line with the party, and those people from the MGB were unable to break me. I want to emphasize again that nothing in the indictment has survived this trial. All that was "obtained" during the preliminary investigation was dictated by the investigators themselves, including Ryumin.

The last thirty years of my life were very good because I never relied on particular people, but only on the party, which always pushed me forward.

When there is talk about some kind of contact of mine with Goldberg and Novick, to refute that, it is enough to point out that during my eighteen years working in the hospital, there were many employees of foreign embassies and other foreigners there, but I never received any reprimands from the MGB. I loved my hospital very much, and it is unlikely that anyone else would love it as I have. In addition, I carried out various MGB assignments better than others did. On the basis of all that has been said I request that the case against me be dropped owing to lies and lack of evidence and that I be released from being under guard. I also request that I be given the opportunity once again to live within the family of Soviet party members and resume my work at Botkin Hospital.

Zuskin: Citizen Judges of the Military Collegium! In my final statement I would like to say a bit about my life. I was eighteen when the Great October Revolution took place. At that time I was not burdened by any nationalistic views. After the revolution I became a full and equal citizen of the USSR, and up to this day I have not tainted this high title in any way. I ended up in the State Jewish Theater completely by chance, and that then became my life's tragedy. I have not yet told the court that when investigator Pogrebnoy informed me about the closing of the Jewish theater, I told him that this was the right thing to do. I had already seen that this was necessary, and envisioned my future on the stage of the Russian theater and in the movies. In conclusion I want to say to the court that I feel that my conscience is clear before the party and the Soviet people. I have done nothing hostile or malicious. If the Military Collegium believes me and returns my freedom to me, I promise to prove my devotion to the party, the Soviet government, and the people through honest labor.

Talmy: I stated at the very beginning of the trial that I was not pleading guilty, and I now believe that this has been proven. When I analyze my thoughts and feelings, I find no bitterness in them. There is only pain over the fate of my son, whom I failed to shield, and pain for my wife, who has been branded the mother of one convicted man and the wife of another under arrest. I do not regard the time I have spent in prison as wasted. In that time I have become more conscious and experienced. In that time I have written several works, which I transmitted to the court and which are not lacking in a certain literary and political merit. They reflect my feelings and thoughts. For a Soviet man the measure of his value is his usefulness to society. I have no reason to blush for my thirty years of labor prior to being arrested. I also need to say that although I was not an enemy of and committed no crimes against the Motherland, the party, and the Soviet government, I did make various mistakes for which I should be punished. I request that the period of preliminary confinement prior to the trial be considered punishment for that. I hope that the sentence will be one that will allow me to be included in the tireless work of the Soviet people, to use all of my strength and make a contribution to the cause of building Communism.

Vatenberg-Ostrovskaya: I hope that the court believes that I was not involved in any kind of espionage with Novick. The fact that I conveyed information to him showed a lack of caution, but it was not espionage.

I had absolutely nothing to do with the Jewish Anti-Fascist Committee, and I think that I have succeeded in proving that. I never had any nationalistic sentiments. I left America and came to the Soviet Union because it was emotionally difficult to live over there. I have never regretted leaving that life. My desire was to work in a socialist state. Since 1934 I have labored honestly in the Soviet Union and found complete satisfaction in my work. Perhaps there were various instances when I entertained narrow-minded sentiments, but not anti-Soviet ones.

If the court still finds me guilty, I request that I be given the opportunity to serve out my punishment with my husband. I would also like to tell the court that all of my so-called testimony during the preliminary investigation was a figment of the investigator's imagination and is not true.

Shtern: I want to give the court an explanation of my attitude toward Western culture. I want to say that I never kowtowed to Western culture and science, but I did feel great gratitude and respect toward those scientists for all that I received from them as my teachers. This does not diminish the respect that I feel toward the leaders of the Soviet government and the party. I will always be grateful to them for all that they have given me. If, in the old days, Russians had to turn to the West for knowledge, now the center of science has shifted eastward, but I believe that this does not mean that we should refuse the opportunity to assimilate those scientific discoveries that are made there. Soviet science is the most modern science, it stands above Western science, but it would not be cringing servility to use the scientific achievements of bourgeois science. The cosmopolitanism of which I am accused is, from my point of view, internationalism. Our science develops according to the laws of Marxism-Leninism, and this is its fundamental difference from bourgeois science. I want to request that the court give me the opportunity to use my half-century of experience to resolve those scientific problems that I was working on.

My arrest has caused the Soviet Union far more harm than all the activity of the Jewish Anti-Fascist Committee because it has provided the opportunity to discredit my work and destroy all that has been achieved. I consider this work to be a new page in medicine and do not believe I have the right to carry into the grave with me all that I know. It seems to me that my work is very important for the people. My second area of work, treating heart ailments, is already almost complete. And my third project is the development of valuable medicinal preparations. I do not consider myself guilty, and again I request that I be given the opportunity to continue my work together with my colleagues. Should the court determine that I am guilty, I request the opportunity to meet with the secretary of the party organization at the institute where I worked for twenty-nine years in order to instruct him as to the direction further work should take. I only ask that the court not find me guilty of treason and of deceiving the party and the Soviet government. My work is important to me, and to do good work I need to have complete rehabilitation and trust in me reestablished so that I may continue serving the people and our Motherland. I consider my Motherland to be not only the territory of the Soviet Union, but the territory of the new democratic republics as well.

[At 5:50 P.M., the court withdrew to the deliberation room for sentencing.
On July 18, 1952, at noon, the chairman opened the court session and announced the Military Collegium's sentence in the case and clarified the rights of the convicted to appeal to the Presidium of the Supreme Soviet of the USSR for a pardon. At 1:05 P.M., the court session was closed.]

| *Presiding Officer* | (signature) | A. CHEPTSOV |
| *Secretary* | (signature) | AFANASIEV |

The Sentence

In the Name of the Union of Soviet Socialist Republics
The Military Collegium of the Supreme Court of the USSR

MEMBERS:
CHAIRMAN General Lieutenant of Justice CHEPTSOV
MEMBERS Major General of Justice DMITRIEV
  Major General of Justice ZARYANOV
WITH SECRETARY Senior Lieutenant M. AFANASIEV

in a closed deliberation in Moscow, from July 11 to July 18, 1952, has studied the case of the accused:

1. Lozovsky, Solomon Abramovich, born in 1878, from the village of Danilovka, Dnepropetrovsk region, Jewish, a citizen of the USSR, married, higher education uncompleted, expelled from the Communist Party in 1949, former director of the Sovinformburo;

2. Fefer, Isaac Solomonovich, born in 1900, from the shtetl of Shpola, Kiev region, Jewish, a citizen of the USSR, married, higher education uncompleted, member of the Communist Party since 1919, a Yiddish poet, secretary of the Jewish Anti-Fascist Committee;

3. Yuzefovich, Joseph Sigizmundovich, born in 1890, from the city of Warsaw, Jewish, a citizen of the USSR, married, with higher education, a member of the Communist Party since 1917, former researcher at the Institute of History of the Soviet Academy of Sciences;

4. Shimeliovich, Boris Abramovich, born in 1892, from the city of Riga, Jewish, a citizen of the USSR, married, with higher education, a member of the Communist Party since 1920, former medical director of Botkin Clinical Hospital;

5. Kvitko, Leyb Moiseyevich, born in 1890, from the village of Goloskovo, Odessa region, Jewish, a citizen of the USSR, married, schooled at home, a member of the Communist Party since 1941, a poet, a member of the Soviet Writers' Union;

6. Markish, Peretz Davidovich, born in 1895, from the city of Polonnoye, formerly Volynsk province, currently Zhitomir region, Jewish, a citizen of the USSR, married, self-educated, a member of the Communist Party since 1939, a poet;

7. Bergelson, David Rafailovich, born in 1882 [actually, 1884], from the shtetl of Sarna, Kiev province, currently Vinnitsa region, Jewish, a citizen of the USSR, married, schooled at home, not a party member, a poet;

8. Hofshteyn, David Naumovich, born in 1889, from the shtetl of Korostyshev, Kiev region, Jewish, a citizen of the USSR, married, with higher education, a member of the Communist Party since 1940, a poet;

9. Zuskin, Benjamin Lvovich, born in 1899, from the city of Panevezhis, Lithuanian Soviet Socialist Republic, Jewish, a citizen of the USSR, married, higher education uncompleted, not a party member, performer and artistic director of the State Jewish Theater;

10. Shtern, Lina Solomonovna, born in 1878, from the city of Liepaya, Latvian Soviet Socialist Republic,* Jewish, a citizen of the USSR, unmarried, a member of the Communist Party since 1938, former director of the Institute of Physiology of the Soviet Academy of Medical Sciences, head of the physiology department of the Second Moscow Medical Institute, full member of the Soviet Academy of Sciences and the Soviet Academy of Medical Sciences;

11. Talmy, Leon Yakovlevich, born in 1893, from the shtetl of Lyakhovichi, Baranovichi region, Jewish, a citizen of the USSR, married, not a party member (but a former member of the American Communist Party), higher education uncompleted, prior to arrest a journalist and translator at the Sovinformburo;

12. Vatenberg, Ilya Semyonovich, born in 1887, from the city of Stanislav, Jewish, a citizen of the USSR, married, not a party a member, has advanced legal education, prior to arrest was senior control editor of the State Publishing House of Literature in Foreign Languages;

13. Teumin, Emilia Isaacovna, born in 1905, from the city of Bern (Switzerland), Jewish, citizen of the USSR, unmarried, with higher education, member of the Communist Party since 1927, prior to arrest was deputy editor

---

*The court is mistaken here; Lina Shtern was actually born in Lithuania in 1875.

of the *Diplomatic Dictionary,* former editor of the International Division of the Sovinformburo;

14. Vatenberg-Ostrovskaya, Khayke Semyonovna, born in 1901, from the village of Zvenigorodka, Kiev region, Jewish, a citizen of the USSR, married, higher education uncompleted, not a party member, prior to arrest was a translator at the State Publishing House of Literature in Foreign Languages, former translator at the Jewish Anti-Fascist Committee—

all accused of committing the crimes covered by articles 58-1a; 58-10, part 2; and 58-11 of the Criminal Code of the Russian Federation.

The preliminary investigation and the court proceedings have established that to mobilize the Jewish population abroad in the struggle against fascism and to publicize the achievements of the USSR in the foreign press, the Jewish Anti-Fascist Committee was founded in April 1942 under the aegis of the Soviet Information Bureau.

Lozovsky, being a clandestine enemy of the Communist Party who had spoken out against the party line repeatedly in the past and twice been expelled from the party for this, as the deputy director of the Sovinformburo used the organization of the Jewish Anti-Fascist Committee to unite Jewish nationalists to struggle against the national policy of the party and the Soviet state.

As the immediate supervisor of the Jewish Anti-Fascist Committee, Lozovsky hired Mikhoels to be chairman of the Jewish Anti-Fascist Committee and Epshteyn (both deceased) to be the executive secretary. They were both ardent Jewish nationalists, who with Lozovsky's knowledge and consent, in order to conduct anti-Soviet nationalistic activity, in turn hired as members of the presidium of the Jewish Anti-Fascist Committee prominent Jewish nationalists—the Yiddish poet Fefer, a former Bundist who had in the past repeatedly spoken out in his works as a nationalist; the Yiddish poets Kvitko and Markish and the Yiddish writer Bergelson, who greeted the Great October Socialist Revolution with hostility and in 1920–1921 fled abroad, where in their works they slandered Soviet reality and the national policy of the Communist Party and the Soviet government and after their return to the USSR again spoke out expressing nationalistic views in their works; Shtern, who came from an alien class background and immigrated to the USSR from abroad in 1925; Shimeliovich, a former Bundist; Yuzefovich, in 1917–1919 one of the leaders of the Russian Social-Democratic Workers' Party (internationalist); and Zuskin.

Furthermore, with the knowledge and consent of Lozovsky, the following people were made members of the Jewish Anti-Fascist Committee: the Yiddish poet Hofshteyn, a Zionist who lived abroad from 1925–1927* and published nationalistic works in Palestine in the reactionary Jewish press; Talmy, who was actively involved in 1917–1920 in the work of Jewish nationalistic orga-

---

*The court is mistaken here; Hofshteyn returned to the USSR from Palestine in the spring of 1926.

nizations in the Ukraine and fled to the United States in 1921, becoming an American citizen and continuing nationalistic activity there; and Vatenberg, who from 1905 through 1924 was one of the leaders of the Jewish nationalistic party Po'alei tsion, first in Austria and then in the United States.

This group of participants not only allowed Lozovsky and his like-minded confederates to carry out hostile nationalistic activity under the banner of the Jewish Anti-Fascist Committee among Jews in the USSR, but also created conditions for the establishment of criminal ties with Jewish nationalistic circles in the United States and other countries, for most of the directors of the Jewish Anti-Fascist Committee were known abroad as Jewish nationalists.

Soon after the Jewish Anti-Fascist Committee was organized, its directors, under the cover of carrying out the tasks assigned to the committee, began to unfurl a program of nationalistic activity and established contact with Jewish nationalistic organizations in America. They began sending information to these organizations about the economy of the USSR, as well as slanderous information about the situation of Jews in the USSR, expecting in this way to obtain material aid from Jewish bourgeois circles and enlist their support in carrying out nationalistic activity in the USSR.

In May 1943, Lozovsky, under the pretext of intensifying propaganda about the achievements of the USSR and about the struggle with fascism, obtained permission for Mikhoels and Fefer to go to the United States. He assigned them to establish personal contact with Jewish nationalistic circles in the United States in a struggle against the Soviet state. Before they left for America, Mikhoels and Fefer, at Lozovsky's instruction, collected a number of materials about industry in the USSR, which they conveyed to the Americans. While in the United States, Mikhoels and Fefer established ties with representatives of Jewish nationalists—with the millionaire Rosenberg, with Budish, with the Zionist leader Weizmann, and with others to whom they provided slanderous information about the situation of Jews in the USSR. In conversations with these nationalists, Mikhoels and Fefer agreed to intensify nationalistic activity in the USSR, while Rosenberg demanded of Mikhoels and Fefer that in exchange for material aid they would arrange for the Soviet government to settle Jews in the Crimea and create a Jewish republic there, in which, as Rosenberg stated, American Jews had an interest not only as Jews but as Americans. Along with this, Mikhoels and Fefer agreed with Jewish nationalists in the United States to send broad information about the Soviet economy on a regular basis.

Upon their return to the USSR in late 1943, Mikhoels and Fefer informed Lozovsky and their other confederates about the criminal conspiracy with Jewish nationalists in the United States. Carrying out Rosenberg's assignment, Mikhoels, Fefer, Epshteyn, and Shimeliovich, with the knowledge and consent of their accomplices, drafted a letter to the Soviet government in which they raised the question of settling Jews in the Crimea and creating a Jewish republic there. This letter was edited by Lozovsky before it was sent to the government. In the letter, Lozovsky and his accomplices slandered the national policy of the Communist Party and the Soviet government, asserting that anti-Semitism was supposedly flourishing in the USSR, that the Jewish population in the USSR was not being "properly settled," that the "Jewish question" was not resolved, and that the Jewish masses of "all the countries of the world" would provide material assistance in building a Jewish republic.

At the same time that this was taking place, the Jewish Anti-Fascist Committee leaders Mikhoels, Epshteyn, Fefer, and their accomplices, with Lozovsky's knowledge, broadened their activity in gathering and sending to the United States information about the economy of the USSR. For this purpose Fefer and others brought on as correspondents Yiddish writers and journalists with nationalistic sentiments who were living in Moscow and other cities of the USSR. These correspondents, who were carrying out instructions from leaders of the Jewish Anti-Fascist Committee, visited various industrial sites, newly constructed buildings, and scientific institutions and under the pretense of studying the life and work of Jews gathered classified information about the work of these organizations.

In addition, in order to gather such information in various parts of the USSR, leading members of the Jewish Anti-Fascist Committee—Hofshteyn, Bergelson, Kvitko, and others—traveled around the country.

The findings of the expert commission about this case have established that a significant portion of the materials sent to the United States by the leaders of the Jewish Anti-Fascist Committee were secret and contained state secrets.

During their stay in the USSR from 1943–1946,* the American journalists Goldberg and Novick, who were Jewish nationalists, were provided by Lozovsky and Fefer with broad opportunities to gather information of interest to them. Lozovsky arranged for intelligence agent Goldberg to receive secret materials about the Soviet economy and the economies of Latvia, Lithuania, and Estonia and also secret materials that Lozovsky received from Scientific Research Institute 205 about British foreign policy. Furthermore, Lozovsky assigned Fefer to accompany Goldberg to the Baltic region and to the Ukraine, where Goldberg, with Fefer's assistance, contacted local Jewish nationalists and through them also received secret information about the economy and culture of the Soviet Union.

In pursuit of the criminal goal of struggling against the national policy of the party and the Soviet government, Lozovsky, Fefer, Yuzefovich, Shimeliovich, Kvitko, Markish, Bergelson, Hofshteyn, Shtern, Zuskin, Talmy, and I. Vatenberg, at the direction of Jewish nationalistic circles in the United States, launched a broad campaign of propaganda among the Jewish population in the USSR and abroad, using for these purposes the newspaper *Eynikayt*—which had been created under the aegis of the Jewish Anti-Fascist Committee—the

---

*The court is mistaken here; Goldberg and Novick visited the Soviet Union in 1946, after the war was over.

publishing house Der emes, Yiddish literary anthologies, the Jewish theater, and the Office of Jewish Culture of the Ukrainian Academy of Sciences.

In their public remarks, in articles in *Eynikayt,* and in other literary works, the leaders of the Jewish Anti-Fascist Committee spread the notion that the Jews as a nation are separate and different and the false thesis of the exceptional nature of the Jewish people as a people who displayed supposedly exceptional heroism in the struggle against fascism and who supposedly had made exceptional contributions in labor and science.

Idealizing the distant past, they extolled biblical images in a nationalistic spirit and spread the idea of a "fraternal" unity of Jews the world over transcending class and based solely on "shared blood," in doing so joining ranks with bourgeois nationalists in the United States, Palestine, and other countries.

By means of their propaganda, the leaders of the Jewish Anti-Fascist Committee aroused nationalistic and Zionist sentiments among the Jewish population and spread slanderous rumors that anti-Semitism was supposedly flourishing in the USSR.

A vivid example of how the leaders of the Jewish Anti-Fascist Committee joined ranks with Jewish nationalists in the United States in their nationalistic activity was the publication in 1946 of the so-called *Black Book,* which was carried out jointly with Jewish nationalists in the United States and Palestine at the behest of the Jewish Anti-Fascist Committee with Lozovsky's consent. In this book the Jews are set off in a category separate and opposed to other peoples; the contribution of the Jews to world civilization is exaggerated; attention is paid exclusively to the losses borne by the Jews during the Second World War; and the idea is presented that fascism supposedly represented a threat to the Jews alone, and not to all peoples and to world civilization.

As a result of the anti-Soviet work carried out by Lozovsky, Fefer, and their accomplices, nationalistic elements among the Jews began turning to the Jewish Anti-Fascist Committee with requests to send them to Palestine, to organize volunteer military units to fight on the side of the State of Israel, together with a great number of slanderous complaints about the infringement of Jews' rights allegedly taking place in various parts of the country. On the basis of these complaints, the leaders of the Jewish Anti-Fascist Committee—Fefer and others—sent letters to various government organizations demanding that measures be taken to protect the Jews.

Broadening the functions of the Jewish Anti-Fascist Committee without permission, its leaders engaged in getting housing and jobs for Jewish settlers sent to Birobidzhan and for Jews returning from evacuation, and finding employment for Jews in the formerly occupied parts of the Ukraine and the Crimea.

All of these criminal anti-Soviet activities by the leaders of the Jewish Anti-Fascist Committee attest to the fact that the Jewish Anti-Fascist Committee was transformed into a center of nationalistic activity and espionage.

The court proceedings have established that the main organizers and leaders of this criminal anti-Soviet activity were Lozovsky and Fefer, while defendants Yuzefovich, Shimeliovich, Kvitko, Bergelson, Markish, Hofshteyn, Zuskin, Talmy, Shtern, and I. Vatenberg not only knew about the criminal activity being carried out at the Jewish Anti-Fascist Committee, but were actively involved in it themselves.

Thus, defendant Shimeliovich spoke repeatedly at sessions of the Jewish Anti-Fascist Committee presidium in favor of broadening the nationalistic activity of the Jewish Anti-Fascist Committee inside as well as beyond the borders of the USSR, and spoke slanderously about discrimination against Jews allegedly occurring in the USSR. Shimeliovich was one of the authors of the letter to the government about organizing a Jewish republic in the Crimea that was written at the behest of American Jewish nationalists.

Defendant Bergelson, the scion of a prominent merchant family and a convinced Jewish nationalist, carried out nationalistic activity starting in 1918 and was a member of the Central Committee of the Jewish nationalistic organization the Kultur lige, while in 1921, being hostile to Soviet power, he fled abroad, where over a number of years he collaborated with the Jewish reactionary press, publishing anti-Soviet, nationalistic articles. Returning to the USSR in 1934, he continued his nationalistic activity. In addition to active involvement in the anti-Soviet work of the presidium of the Jewish Anti-Fascist Committee, he personally wrote a number of articles in which he spread the idea that the Jews as a people are set apart, special, and exceptional and the idea of the unity of Jews the world over transcending class, and he extolled biblical images.

In meetings with American intelligence agent Goldberg, he provided him with information about Birobidzhan.

Defendant Kvitko, upon returning to the USSR in 1925 after fleeing abroad, joined up with a nationalistic Jewish literary group in the city of Kharkov called Boi (Construction), headed by Trotskyites.

As deputy executive secretary of the Jewish Anti-Fascist Committee when it was first formed, he entered into a criminal conspiracy with the nationalists Mikhoels, Epshteyn, and Fefer, aiding them in gathering materials about the economy of the USSR for transmittal to the United States.

In 1944, carrying out the criminal instructions of the leaders of the Jewish Anti-Fascist Committee, he went to the Crimea to gather information about the economic situation in the region and the situation of the Jewish population. He was one of those who initiated raising the question with the government of alleged discrimination against the Jewish population in the Crimea.

He spoke repeatedly at sessions of the Jewish Anti-Fascist Committee presidium, demanding that the committee's nationalistic activity be broadened.

In 1946 he established personal contact with the American intelligence officer Goldberg, whom he informed on the state of affairs in the Soviet Writers'

Union and to whom he gave permission to publish a Soviet-American literary annual.

Defendant Markish, upon his return in 1926 to the USSR from abroad, where he had been in touch with Jewish nationalists and collaborated with the Jewish nationalistic press, continued his anti-Soviet activity in the USSR. While living in the city of Kharkov in 1927, he was in contact with the Jewish nationalistic literary group Boi, and in 1940 he maintained criminal links with a group of Jewish nationalists operating in Minsk.

While a member of the presidium of the Jewish Anti-Fascist Committee, he spread in his articles and poems the idea of the unity of Jews the world over regardless of class and extolled biblical images.

In 1945 [actually, 1946] he had several meetings with the American intelligence agent Goldberg, to whom he passed on information about the sentiments of Yiddish writers in the USSR.

Defendant Hofshteyn, a convinced Zionist, participated actively in the anti-Soviet activity of Jewish nationalistic organizations during the Civil War and slandered Soviet power in his literary works.

In 1925 he fled from the USSR to Germany and then to Palestine where he collaborated with the reactionary Jewish press. Returning from Palestine to Kiev in 1927 [actually, 1926], he continued to conduct nationalistic activity among the Jewish population in the Ukraine. As an active member of the Jewish Anti-Fascist Committee and its representative in the Ukraine, he was involved in anti-Soviet activity with a number of Jewish nationalists and with religious Jewish communal organizations in Kiev and Lvov. In 1946 he established criminal ties with the American intelligence agent Goldberg, who came to Kiev and whom he assisted in gathering information of interest to Goldberg, and he passed on to him slanderous fabrications about the life of Jews in the Ukraine.

Defendant Yuzefovich in 1944 passed to the American intelligence agent Eagan secret information about the work of Soviet trade unions, while in 1945 [actually, 1946] at Lozovsky's orders, he established ties with the American intelligence officer Goldberg and passed secret material to him about Soviet industry, transportation, and culture. Also, on Lozovsky's instruction he passed to Goldberg secret material from Institute 205 about British foreign policy.

As a member of the presidium of the Jewish Anti-Fascist Committee, defendant Shtern repeatedly made anti-Soviet nationalistic speeches at presidium sessions. In 1945 and in 1946 she established ties with a number of foreigners living in Moscow, and informed the Americans Madd and Lesley about scientific problems being worked on by Soviet scientists. She also informed press attaché Tripp of the British Embassy about research at an institute of the Soviet Academy of Sciences of which she was director.

As a member of the presidium of the Jewish Anti-Fascist Committee and at the same time a leading actor at the Moscow Jewish Theater, which, as established by the case materials, was one of the nationalistic propaganda branches of the Jewish Anti-Fascist Committee, defendant Zuskin, together with Mikhoels, produced plays at the theater that extolled ancient Jewish ways, shtetl traditions, and daily life and presented the Jewish people as tragic and doomed, thereby arousing nationalistic feelings among their Jewish viewers. He also sent a number of nationalistic articles to America about the state of the arts in the USSR.

Over a long period of time, defendant Talmy conducted nationalistic activity. While living in America from 1913 through 1917, he was a member of a reactionary Jewish party of social-territorialists, editor of the party's central organ, and then secretary of the central committee of this party. Arriving in the USSR, in Kiev, in 1917, he participated actively in the work of Jewish nationalistic organizations. Fleeing in 1921 from the USSR to America, where he became an American citizen, he continued to carry out anti-Soviet activity there. Arriving in the USSR in 1929 as a tourist along with other Americans, he contacted Jewish nationalists and with their help gathered information about Birobidzhan.

Arriving in the USSR in 1932 for permanent residence, he carried out the instructions of Jewish nationalists in the United States, and established ties with Jewish nationalists in Moscow. While a member of the Jewish Anti-Fascist Committee, he participated in nationalistic activity. In 1946, during a meeting with the American journalist Novick, he provided him with information about the Soviet economy and slanderous information about the lives of Jews in the USSR.

Defendant Vatenberg, while living abroad from 1905 through 1924, conducted nationalistic activity as one of the leaders of the Jewish party Po'alei tsion, first in Austria and then in America. Joining the American Communist Party in 1924, he got involved in a factional struggle with the leadership of the central committee. In 1926–1929 he came as a tourist to the USSR, where he established ties with Jewish nationalists and with their help collected information about Birobidzhan.

Arriving for permanent residence in the USSR in 1933, he once again established ties with Jewish nationalists who were carrying out anti-Soviet activity in the USSR. As a member of the Jewish Anti-Fascist Committee, he was involved in conducting nationalistic activity at the Jewish Anti-Fascist Committee. In 1946, he met with the American journalist Novick and provided him with information about the Soviet economy and slanderous fabrications about the lives of Jews in the USSR.

Defendant Vatenberg-Ostrovskaya, holding nationalistic sentiments and working as a translator at the Jewish Anti-Fascist Committee, knew about the nationalistic activity of the leaders of the Jewish Anti-Fascist Committee and on instructions from them translated from Yiddish into English materials containing state secrets which were sent to the United States. In 1945–1946, meeting with the Americans Novick and Davis in Moscow, she provided them with information about Jews living in Birobidzhan and in the Soviet Central Asian republics.

Defendant Teumin, while working in the Sovinformburo as editor of the Scandinavian division, met frequently with Mikhoels and Fefer and shared their anti-Soviet nationalistic views, and in 1945 [actually, 1946], under assignment by Lozovsky, she gathered secret materials about the economies of the Lithuanian, Latvian, and Estonian Soviet Socialist Republics and personally avoided the censor while passing them on to the American intelligence agent Goldberg.

On the basis of the aforementioned, the Military Collegium of the Supreme Court of the USSR finds Lozovsky, Fefer, Bergelson, Yuzefovich, Shimeliovich, Markish, Zuskin, Kvitko, Shtern, Hofshteyn, Teumin, Vatenberg, I., Talmy, L., and Vatenberg-Ostrovskaya guilty of committing the crimes referred to in articles 58-1a; 58-10, part 2; and 58-11 of the Criminal Code of the Russian Federation. Guided by articles 319 and 320 of the Code of Criminal Procedure of the Russian Federation, the Military Collegium of the Supreme Court of the USSR

Has Sentenced:

> Lozovsky, Solomon Abramovich,
>
> Fefer, Isaac Solomonovich,
>
> Bergelson, David Rafailovich,
>
> Yuzefovich, Joseph Sigizmundovich,
>
> Shimeliovich, Boris Abramovich,
>
> Markish, Peretz Davidovich,
>
> Zuskin, Benjamin Lvovich,
>
> Kvitko, Leyb Moiseyevich,
>
> Hofshteyn, David Naumovich,
>
> Teumin, Emilia Isaacovna,
>
> Vatenberg, Ilya Semyonovich,
>
> Talmy, Leon Yakovlevich, and
>
> Vatenberg-Ostrovskaya, Khayke Semyonovna,

on the basis of article 58-1a of the Criminal Code of the Russian Federation to the severest measure of punishment for the crimes committed by them jointly: execution by firing squad, with all of their property to be confiscated.

Shtern, Lina Solomonovna, for her role in the crimes committed on the basis of article 58-1a of the Criminal Code of the Russian Federation and article 51 of the Criminal Code of the Russian Federation, is to be confined in a correctional labor camp for a period of three years and six months, to be deprived of her rights for three years, without the confiscation of her property, and after this period of confinement has been completed, on the basis of article 35 of the Criminal Code of the Russian Federation the convict Shtern shall be sent to a remote area for five years.

The period of preliminary confinement shall be applied toward convict Shtern's period of confinement, to be counted starting on January 28, 1949.

The Military Collegium has decided to deprive the following people of their medals, as follows:

Lozovsky—For the Defense of Moscow, In Memory of Moscow's Eight-hundredth Anniversary;

Fefer—two medals For Valiant Labor During the Great Patriotic War, 1941–1945;

Bergelson—For Valiant Labor During the Great Patriotic War, 1941–1945;

Yuzefovich—For Valiant Labor During the Great Patriotic War, 1941–1945, and In Memory of Moscow's Eight-hundredth Anniversary;

Shimeliovich—For Victory over Germany During the Great Patriotic War, 1941–1945; For Defense of Moscow; For Valiant Labor During the Great Patriotic War, 1941–1945; and In Memory of Moscow's Eight-hundredth Anniversary;

Markish—For Victory over Germany During the Great Patriotic War, 1941–1945, and For Valiant Labor During the Great Patriotic War, 1941–1945;

Zuskin—For Valiant Labor During the Great Patriotic War, 1941–1945;

Kvitko—For Valiant Labor During the Great Patriotic War, 1941–1945;

Hofshteyn—For Valiant Labor During the Great Patriotic War, 1941–1945;

Teumin—For Valiant Labor During the Great Patriotic War, 1941–1945, and In Memory of Moscow's Eight-hundredth Anniversary;

Vatenberg, I.—In Memory of Moscow's Eight-hundredth Anniversary;

Talmy—For Valiant Labor During the Great Patriotic War, 1941–1945;

Vatenberg-Ostrovskaya—For Valiant Labor During the Great Patriotic War, 1941–1945, and

Shtern—For Valiant Labor During the Great Patriotic War, 1941–1945, and In Memory of Moscow's Eight-hundredth Anniversary;

and to petition the Presidium of the Supreme Soviet of the USSR to deprive the following people of these decorations:

Lozovsky—Order of Lenin and Order of the Great Patriotic War, First Degree;

Fefer—Badge of Honor;

Shimeliovich—Order of the Red Banner of Labor and Order of the Great Patriotic War, First Degree;

Markish—Order of Lenin;

Zuskin—Order of the Red Banner of Labor;

Kvitko—Order of the Red Banner of Labor;

Hofshteyn—Badge of Honor;

Teumin—Badge of Honor; and

Shtern—Order of the Red Banner of Labor and Order of the Red Star.

The sentence is final and not subject to appeal.

Valid when accompanied by the proper signatures.

Hereby certified:

Court Secretary of the Military Collegium

Senior Lieutenant   (signature) AFANASIEV

PART TWO

The Resolution:
Post-Trial Documents

Certificate That the Sentence Was Carried Out,
August 12, 1952

CERTIFICATE

The sentence of the Military Collegium of the Supreme Court of the USSR of July 18, 1952, regarding Solomon Abramovich Lozovsky, born in 1878, from the village of Danilovka, Dnepropetrovsk region, and condemned to the severest measure of punishment, execution, was carried out on August 12, 1952.

Director of the
Third Division of
Sector 1 of Department A of the
MGB USSR   Colonel (signature) VOROBYOV

[Similar certificates about the carrying out on August 12, 1952, of the sentence of the Military Collegium of the Supreme Court of the USSR are available for I. Fefer, L. Kvitko, P. Markish, V. Zuskin, L. Talmy, B. Shimeliovich, D. Bergelson, D. Hofshteyn, I. Vatenberg, C. Vatenberg-Ostrovskaya, E. Teumin, and I. Yuzefovich.]

Death Certificate for Solomon Bregman, January 23, 1953

REPORT

On January 23, 1953, at 12:05 P.M., inmate Solomon Leontevich Bregman died. He was born in 1895 and had been in the Butyrsky Prison infirmary since June 16, 1952, due to a decompensated mitral valve defect with manifestations of cardial asthma, hypertension, arteriosclerosis, fibrosis of the pulmonary tissue, and a secondary contracted kidney. Inmate Bregman's death was accompanied by a drop in cardiovascular activity.

Doctor (signature) SMIRNOVA

January 23, 1953

Round seal   Authentic copy: (signature) GROMOVA

Determination to Cease Solomon Bregman's Prosecution, June 3, 1953

DECISION OF THE JUDICIAL SESSION OF THE MILITARY COLLEGIUM OF THE USSR

The Military Collegium of the Supreme Court of the USSR

MEMBERS:
CHAIRMAN   General Lieutenant of Justice CHEPTSOV
MEMBERS   Major General of Justice DMITRIEV and
                Major General of Justice ZARYANOV
WITH SECRETARY Senior Lieutenant M. AFANASIEV,

without participation by representatives of the state prosecutor's office or the defense, in a closed judicial session on June 3, 1953, in Moscow considered the case of Solomon Leontevich Bregman, born in 1895, from the city of Zlynka, from a merchant family, Jewish, with secondary education, a former member of the Communist Party since 1912, former deputy minister of state control of the Russian Federation—accused of committing crimes detailed in articles 58-1a; 58-1, part 2; and 58-11 of the Criminal Code of the Russian Federation,

Has Established:

Solomon Leontevich Bregman was tried by the Military Collegium of the Supreme Court of the USSR for crimes he had committed. Defendant Bregman fell ill during the trial and was placed in an infirmary for treatment, and consideration of his case by the Military Collegium of the Supreme Court of the USSR was suspended on July 9, 1952.

According to information provided to the Military Collegium by the Butyrsky Prison infirmary, the condition of defendant Solomon Leontevich Bregman's health during the entire time that he was in the infirmary ruled out the possibility of considering the case and the accusations brought against Bregman in judicial session.

According to information in the court's possession and provided by the Butyrsky Prison infirmary, the MVD has learned that defendant Bregman died on January 23, 1953, which is also confirmed by a document certifying that an autopsy of the corpse took place on January 26, 1953.

On the basis of the above and guided by articles 319 and 320 of the Code of Criminal Procedure of the Russian Federation, the Military Collegium of the Supreme Court of the USSR

Has Decided:

to close the criminal case of Solomon Bregman based on point 1, article 4, of the Code of Criminal Procedure of the Russian Federation and cease further criminal litigation thereof.

Presiding Officer	(signature)	CHEPTSOV
Member	(signature)	DMITRIEV
	(signature)	ZARYANOV

Determination to Annul the Sentence and Terminate the Case of Lozovsky et al., November 22, 1955

SUPREME COURT OF THE USSR

Decision #0065/52

The Military Collegium of the Supreme Court of the USSR

CONSISTING OF
PRESIDING OFFICER Chairman of the Supreme Court
of the USSR A. VOLIN
AND MEMBERS Colonel of Justice G. KOVALENKO and
Colonel of Justice I. DASHIN

having considered in a session on November 22, 1955, the conclusions of the General Prosecutor of the USSR on the sentencing by the Military Collegium of the Supreme Court of the USSR during the week of July 11–18, 1952, which resulted in the conviction of:

1. Solomon Abramovich Lozovsky, born in 1878, from the village of Danilovka, Dnepropetrovsk region;

2. Isaac Solomonovich Fefer, born in 1900, from the shtetl of Shpola, Kiev region;

3. Joseph Sigizmundovich Yuzefovich, born in 1890, from the city of Warsaw;

4. Boris Abramovich Shimeliovich, born in 1892, from the city of Riga;

5. Leyb Moiseyevich Kvitko, born in 1890, from the village of Goloskovo, Odessa region;

6. Peretz Davidovich Markish, born in 1895, from the city of Polonnoye, Zhitomir region;

7. David Rafailovich Bergelson, born in 1882, from the shtetl of Sarna, Vinnitsa region;

8. David Naumovich Hofshteyn, born in 1889, from the shtetl of Korostyshev, Kiev region;

9. Benjamin Lvovich Zuskin, born in 1899, from the city of Panevezhis, Lithuanian SSR;

10. Leon Yakovlevich Talmy, born in 1893, from the shtetl of Lyakhovichi, Baranovichi region;

11. Ilya Semyonovich Vatenberg, born in 1887, from the city of Stanislav;

12. Emilia Isaacovna Teumin, born in 1905, from the city of Bern (Switzerland);

13. Khayke Semyonovna Vatenberg-Ostrovskaya, born in 1901, from the village of Zvenigorodka, Kiev region,

all thirteen under articles 58-1a; 58-10, part 2; and 58-11 of the Criminal Code of the Russian Federation and on the basis of article 58-1a of the Criminal Code of the Russian Federation—to the severest measure of criminal punishment—the execution of each, with all property to be confiscated;

14. Lina Solomonovna Shtern, born in 1878, from the city of Liepaya, Latvian SSR,

under article 58-1a; 58-10, part 2; and 58-11 of the Criminal Code of the Russian Federation on the basis of article 58-1a of the Criminal Code of the Russian Federation, applying article 51 of the Criminal Code on confinement in a correctional labor camp for a period of three years and six months with loss of rights for three years, without the confiscation of property, to be followed by exile, according to article 35 of the Criminal Code of the Russian Federation, in a remote area of the USSR for a period of five years. The convicted persons are to be deprived of government awards.

Having listened to Comrade G. Ye. Kovalenko's report and the findings of the Deputy General Prosecutor of the USSR, State Counselor of Justice First Class Comrade P. V. Baranov, repealing the sentencing and halting the case of Lozovsky and the others owing to the absence of counterrevolutionary crime,

Has Established:

[Omitted here is a summary of the accusations drawn up in the sentence of the Military Collegium of the Supreme Court of the USSR drawn up between July 11 and July 18, 1952.]

The General Prosecutor of the USSR in his findings requests that the sentence of the Military Collegium of the Supreme Court of the USSR dated July 11–18, 1952, in reference to S. Lozovsky, I. Fefer, J. Yuzefovich, B. Shimeliovich, L. Kvitko, P. Markish, D. Bergelson, D. Hofshteyn, V. Zuskin, L. Shtern, L. Talmy, I. Vatenberg, E. Teumin, and C. Vatenberg-Ostrovskaya and also the decision of the Military Collegium dated June 3, 1953, in regard to S. Bregman be repealed, owing to newly discovered circumstances, and that their case be closed in accordance with criminal procedure for the following reasons.

As established in a new investigation conducted by the prosecutor's office of the USSR in accordance with articles 373–378 of the Code of Criminal Procedure of the Russian Federation, the basis for arresting Fefer and Shimeliovich and for starting the case of the former directors of the Jewish Anti-Fascist Committee was the testimony of Goldshtein and Greenberg, who had been arrested earlier. Goldshtein was arrested on December 19, 1947, on the orders of Abakumov without the prosecutor's approval. After he was arrested, investigator Sorokin, former Deputy Director of the MGB Investigative Division for Especially Important Cases Likhachev, and Komarov on the orders of Abakumov began to solicit testimony from Goldshtein about the espionage and nationalistic activity he had supposedly conducted, even though there was no information about this in the state security organs.

In connection with the fact that Goldshtein denied his guilt for a long period of time, Sorokin and Komarov, again on the orders of Abakumov, subjected Goldshtein to beatings and in this way forced him to sign an interrogation record, which they fabricated together with Broverman, who worked in Abakumov's secretariat, that stated that Goldshtein knew, based on conversations with Greenberg and then through personal contact with the directors of the Jewish Anti-Fascist Committee, that Lozovsky, Fefer, Markish, and others, using the Jewish Anti-Fascist Committee as a cover, were engaged in allegedly anti-Soviet nationalistic activity and were in close touch with reactionary Jewish circles abroad, and were engaging in espionage.

On the basis of this falsified testimony of Goldshtein's, Greenberg was arrested on December 28, 1947, and during interrogations with Likhachev, after denying his guilt over a long period of time, signed a work composed by Likhachev, an "interrogation record," which confirmed Goldshtein's testimony about the active anti-Soviet activity allegedly conducted by Lozovsky, Fefer, and others and their criminal contact with American intelligence.

Former Deputy Director of the MGB Investigative Division for Especially Important Cases Komarov, in his handwritten testimony dated June 15–22, 1953, stated the following:

"In 1948, Goldshtein's case was handled in the investigative division. He was a former researcher at an institute of the Soviet Academy of Sciences. I was involved in his interrogation. After Goldshtein had been interrogated several times, Abakumov stated that Goldshtein was interested in the personal life of the leader of the Soviet government and his family, not on his own initiative but because foreign intelligence services were behind his activity. We had no materials about this. Nonetheless, Goldshtein was now interrogated with all this in mind. At first he did not confess to this accusation, but after he was beaten on Abakumov's orders, Goldshtein gave testimony. Abakumov did not express his attitude toward Goldshtein's testimony, stating only that he could not keep Goldshtein's testimony to himself and was required to report about it to the appropriate government bodies.

"So, as a result of Goldshtein's unverified testimony obtained via beatings, Greenberg was arrested, and his testimony served as the beginning of the well-known case against the Jewish Anti-Fascist Committee" (vol. 1, p. 36, of the inspection materials).

As is apparent from Greenberg's statement addressed to Likhachev, which he wrote during the investigation, he did not plead guilty, and the testimony about his criminal activity and the activity of Fefer, Lozovsky, and others was obtained by Likhachev using deception and promises to release Greenberg from detention.

In his statement dated April 19, 1949, Greenberg wrote to Likhachev: "Four months ago you announced officially to me that my case was finished and that I would soon be released, but unfortunately that is not what has happened. I have been confined for sixteen months, and my strength is ebbing" (vol. 3, p. 41, of the inspection materials).

Greenberg's interrogation record containing descriptions of the criminal activity of Lozovsky, Fefer, and others, is dated December 17, 1948—that is exactly four months before Greenberg wrote the statement mentioned above. Greenberg died on December 22, 1949 (vol. 1, pp. 50, 70, and 73, of the inspection materials).

So it is established beyond any doubt by the materials obtained during the new investigation that Lozovsky, Fefer, and others were arrested on the basis of Goldshtein's and Greenberg's testimony, which was falsified by Abakumov and his accomplices.

During the preliminary investigation all of the accused, except for Shimeliovich, pled guilty and gave detailed testimony about the criminal, anti-Soviet activity allegedly carried out by the Jewish Anti-Fascist Committee. However, during the trial before the Military Collegium, which lasted from May 8 through July 18, 1952, only Fefer initially pled guilty and exposed the others. At the end of the trial, however, Fefer requested to have a closed session, during which, in the absence of the other defendants, he repudiated his testimony and stated that he was an MGB agent under the pseudonym Zorin and was acting under the orders of representatives of those organs (record of the trial proceedings, vol. 8, pp. 1–3, 68–69).

In addition, during this same closed judicial session Fefer stated: "On the night of my arrest Abakumov told me that if I did not confess during my testimony, they would beat me. So I grew frightened, which was the reason that I gave incorrect testimony during the preliminary investigation."

A review has been conducted which has established that Fefer did in fact collaborate with the MGB. It has also been established that Fefer was called in by Abakumov and was interrogated in his office for thirty-five minutes. However, this summons of Fefer by Abakumov was not recorded in a report (vol. 1, p. 74, and vol. 2, p. 125 of the inspection materials).

Fefer also told the court that after article 206 of the Criminal Code of the Russian Federation had been carried out, investigator Kuzmin summoned him and demanded that he, Fefer, confirm all of the testimony in court that he had given during the preliminary investigation.

In the course of the investigation it has been established that former MGB employees who carried out the criminal orders of Abakumov did in fact subject those under arrest to beatings and torture and systematically deprived them of sleep, in this way compelling them to sign interrogation records that had been falsified by the investigators.

Former employees of the MGB investigative division for especially important cases, Ryumin, Komarov, Likhachev, Kuzmin, and others, confirmed that illegal methods were used during the investigation of those under arrest in this case.

From Fefer's explanations in court and also from the materials acquired during the additional investigation, it is clear that the investigators were aware that Fefer's meetings with the leaders of Jewish circles in the United States took place with the approval of Soviet representatives in America, who gave Fefer high marks for the work he did in the United States.

Lozovsky, Fefer, Yuzefovich, and other senior people at the Jewish Anti-Fascist Committee were accused of establishing criminal contact in 1943–1946 [actually, 1946] with American intelligence agents Goldberg and Novick and transmitting to them secret information about the economy and culture of the USSR, including secret material from Institute 205 about British foreign policy. The former director of Institute 205, Pukhlov, who was questioned during the trial, testified that at Lozovsky's request the institute did in fact prepare and transmit to Lozovsky material about British foreign policy. This material, according to Pukhlov's testimony, was compiled from information published in the British press and contained no secret information.

The investigative organs were also aware that Goldberg and Novick were progressive activists in the United States and that they had been investigated at the hands of American intelligence organizations for their pro-Soviet activity. It is clear from the information acquired during the additional investigation in 1955 that Novick was a veteran of the workers' movement, had been a member of the American Communist Party since 1921, and at present is the editor in chief of the American communist newspaper the *Morgen Freiheit*. From this same information it is clear that after returning from his trip to the USSR, Goldberg published several objective articles in the American press about the lives of Jews in the Soviet Union (vol. 1, pp. 79–80, of the inspection materials).

Two rounds of study by expert commissions were carried out on the case of Lozovsky and others: one in order to establish the degree of secrecy of the materials transmitted by the members of the Jewish Anti-Fascist Committee for publication in the foreign press and another to establish the nationalistic character of their literary works. As established by this review, these studies were conducted in a nonobjective fashion and with flagrant violations of the law. Interrogated during an additional investigation, the experts testified that their examinations were conducted under the direct control of the investigators, and the influence of the investigators on the experts was so strong that in a number of instances they drew conclusions that in no way followed from the documents which they had studied (vol. 1, pp. 270–273, 280–287, of the inspection materials).

In the course of the new investigation conducted in 1955, it has been established that the secret information indicated in the expert findings from 1951 did not constitute state secrets (vol. 2, pp. 58–62, of the additional investigation materials).

As proof of the guilt of Lozovsky, Fefer, and others, copies of interrogation records of people arrested in other cases were appended to this case—those of Kheifets, Tokar, Belenky, Sheinin, Sorkin, and others. As established by this examination, these people repudiated their testimony, and at the present time their cases are closed. Others who repudiated their testimony include Strongin, Halkin, Kagan, Drukker, and Bakhmutsky;* copies of interrogation records for them are included in the case materials of Lozovsky and the others.

There are indications in the case materials, noted in the findings of the General Prosecutor of the USSR as well, that certain people among the condemned in this case took on functions that were uncharacteristic for them while working at the Jewish Anti-Fascist Committee: in the name of the committee they got involved in resolving job placement issues for people of Jewish nationality and filed appeals to release Jewish prisoners from camps, and in various literary works, letters, and conversations at times permitted themselves comments of a nationalistic nature.

Using all of this, Abakumov and his accomplices inflated this activity by the leaders of the Jewish Anti-Fascist Committee into a case of state counterrevolutionary crime, although the information that served as the basis for the accusations against Lozovsky and the others of such grave crimes as treason, espionage, and other counterrevolutionary crimes was not to be found in the materials for this case.

Having considered the case materials and the additional investigation materials, and agreeing with the arguments cited in the conclusions of the General Prosecutor of the USSR, and finding that the case of Lozovsky and the others was falsified by former MGB employees, enemies of the people Abakumov, Ryumin, Komarov, Likhachev (sentenced by the Military Collegium to execution), and others, owing to which the sentencing of Lozovsky and the others is subject to repeal, and their case is closed because of an absence of counterrevolutionary crime, the Military Collegium of the Supreme Court of the USSR, guided by articles 373, point 3 and article 378, of the Criminal Code of the Russian Federation,

Has Decided:

to repeal the sentence of the Military Collegium of the Supreme Court of the USSR dated July 11–18, 1952, concerning Solomon Abramovich Lozovsky, Isaac Solomonovich Fefer, Joseph Sigizmundovich Yuzefovich, Boris Abramovich Shimeliovich, Leyb Moiseyevich Kvitko, Peretz Davidovich Markish, David Rafailovich Bergelson, David Naumovich Hofshteyn, Benjamin Lvovich Zuskin, Lina Solomonovna Shtern, Leon Yakovlevich Talmy, Ilya Semy-

---

*Alexander Bakhmutsky (1911–1961) was a government official in Moscow when he transferred to Birobidzhan in 1943 to become first secretary of the regional party committee. He was arrested in August 1949, sentenced in 1952 to twenty-five years of imprisonment, and released in 1956.

onovich Vatenberg, Emilia Isaacovna Teumin, and Khayke Semyonovna Vatenberg-Ostrovskaya, and also the decision of the Military Collegium dated July 3, 1953, concerning Solomon Leontevich Bregman, and to close their case based on article 4, point 5, of the Code of Criminal Procedure of the Russian Federation because there was no substance to the charges against them.*

Valid when accompanied by the necessary signatures.

Hereby certified:

Court Secretary of the Military Collegium

Captain   (signature) AFANASIEV

---

*This decision "closed" the case; it did not "rehabilitate" the defendants.

Notes

1. Natalia Vovsi-Mikhoels, *Moy Otets Solomon Mikhoels* (My Father Solomon Mikhoels) (Moscow, 1997), p. 204.

2. Arkady Vaksberg, *Stalin Against the Jews* (New York, 1994), p. 182.

3. Ibid., p. 173.

4. The veteran writer Alexander Borshchagovsky examined the forty-two volumes of investigation records for his book *Obvinyaetsa Krov* (Accused by Blood) (Moscow, 1994); the historian Gennadi Kostyrchenko gained access to a great deal of material about official Soviet anti-Semitism for his book *Out of the Red Shadows: Anti-Semitism in Stalin's Russia* (Amherst, N.Y., 1995), originally published in Moscow as *V Plenu u Krasnogo Faraona* (1994); and the Israeli scholar Shimon Redlich unearthed hundreds of documents relating to the case for his book *War, Holocaust and Stalinism: A Documented History of the Jewish Anti-Fascist Committee in the USSR* (Luxembourg, 1995). It is also worth noting a documentary film about the period, *Grand Concert of the People,* by Semyon Aronovich (Moscow, 1991).

5. Boris Sandler, "Waiting for Israel to Stand Up for Yiddish," *Forward,* January 29, 1999, p. 4. See also Arye Leyb Pilowsky, "Yiddish and Yiddish Literature in Eretz Israel, 1907–1948," Ph.D. dissertation, Hebrew University in Jerusalem, 1980.

6. Cited in Zvi Gitelman, *Jewish Nationality and Soviet Politics: The Jewish Sections of the CPSU, 1917–1930* (Princeton, N.J., 1972), pp. 471–472. The letter was dated November 25, 1929.

7. Cited in Khone Shmeruk, "Der Nister's 'Under a Fence': Tribulations of a Soviet Yiddish Symbolist," in Uriel Weinrich, ed., *The Field of Yiddish,* 2d collection (London, 1965), p. 285.

8. See Gennadi Estraikh, *Soviet Yiddish: Language Planning and Linguistic Development* (Oxford, 1999), for an incisive review of Soviet Yiddish culture.

9. See Yehoshua A. Gilboa, *The Black Years of Soviet Jewry, 1939–1953* (Boston, 1971), pp. 25–26, for details about the fate of Zelig Akselrod.

10. David Lederman, *Fun yener zayt forhang* (From the Other Side of the Curtain) (Buenos Aires, 1960), p. 108.

11. Peretz Markish, *Poeme vegn stalinen* (Poem About Stalin), *Sovetish literatur almanakh* (Soviet Literary Almanac) (Moscow, 1940), pp. 7–118.

12. Russian State Archive of Social and Political History (hereafter RGASPI), f. 17, op. 125, d. 35, ll. 62–65. The letter is dated August 16, 1941. A full translation can be found in Redlich, *War, Holocaust and Stalinism,* pp. 173–174.

13. Redlich, *War, Holocaust and Stalinism,* pp. 177–183, for excerpts from several speeches at the rally. The speeches were also widely quoted in the Soviet press; see *Pravda,* August 25, 1941, pp. 3–4; *Izvestia,* August 26, 1941, p. 3.

14. See Shimon Redlich, *Propaganda and Nationalism in Wartime Russia, 1941–1948,* East European Monographs no. 108 (Boulder, Colo.: East European Quarterly, 1982), p. 22.

15. See Redlich, *War, Holocaust and Stalinism,* pp. 167–171, about the fate of Erlich and Alter.

16. Epshteyn had a long and sinister history within the party. Before the revolution, he had been an active member of the Bund, living in Austria, Switzerland, and, for several years, in the United States, before returning to Russia in 1917. He joined the Communist Party in 1919, then went back to New York in 1921 and resumed his career as a journalist and editor in leftist Yiddish circles before returning once again to Moscow. He often traveled on assignments from the party and by the 1930s was deeply involved with Soviet intelligence and security agencies. In one notorious episode in 1937, Epshteyn helped Soviet agents abduct Juliet Stuart Poyntz, a leading member of the American Communist Party, who was suspected of writing anti-Soviet memoirs. Epshteyn's appointment as executive secretary of the JAC in 1942 reflected the Kremlin's faith in his absolute loyalty. See Redlich, *Propaganda and Nationalism in Wartime Russia,* pp. 83–85 and 203 nn. 29, 31, 32, and 33, for further information on Epshteyn's history.

17. Redlich, *War, Holocaust and Stalinism,* pp. 196–197. Jews in Palestine also responded to the appeal with generous enthusiasm. During the war, they "raised funds for ambulances that were driven to Iran and handed over to Soviet army units." See Nehemiah Levanon, "Israel's Role in the Campaign," in Murray Friedman and Albert D. Chernin, eds., *A Second Exodus: The American Movement to Free Soviet Jews* (Hanover, N.H., 1999), p. 70.

18. Redlich, *War, Holocaust and Stalinism,* p. 186.

19. Ibid., p. 190.

20. Joseph Leftwich, ed., *An Anthology of Modern Yiddish Literature* (The Hague, 1974), pp. 321–324; the translation is by Thomas Bird. The poem was originally published in *Eynikayt,* December 27, 1942, p. 3.

21. *Farmest* (Struggle), no. 1, 1934, pp. 196–197, cited in Chone Shmeruk, "Yiddish Literature in the U.S.S.R.," in Lionel Kochan, ed., *The Jews in Soviet Russia Since 1917,* 3d ed. (Oxford, 1978), p. 267.

22. Redlich, *War, Holocaust and Stalinism,* p. 75.

23. B. Z. Goldberg, *The Jewish Problem in the Soviet Union* (New York, 1961), p. 144.

24. Dr. Tamara Platt (daughter of Benjamin Zuskin), interview with author by telephone, 1998.

25. *New York Times,* February 26, 1943, p. 5; March 4, 1943, p. 3.

26. Eugene Orenstein, interview with author, Montreal, 1999. His father was among the furriers who made the coats and inscribed their names on the inside lining. Years later, when he understood Stalin's ruthlessness toward the Jews, he regretted working on the gift. In her memoirs, Natalia Vovsi-Mikhoels refers to the three coats. See Vovsi-Mikhoels, *Moy Otets Solomon Mikhoels,* p. 214.

27. Letter from Marc Chagall to Joseph Opatoshu, July 24, 1943, cited in Benjamin Harshav, *The Life of Marc Chagall: A Documentary Narrative* (in manuscript).

28. Irving Howe, Ruth R. Wisse, and Khone Shmeruk, eds., *The Penguin Book of Modern Yiddish Verse* (New York, 1987), p. 529. Alexander Pomerantz mentions his talk with Fefer in *The Jewish Book Annual,* vol. 15 (New York, 1957), pp. 14–26.

29. Susan Josephs, "The Chagall File," *Art News*, May 1999, pp. 158–161.

30. This account of the visit by Mikhoels and Fefer to North America draws from Redlich, *Propaganda and Nationalism in Wartime Russia*, pp. 115–125. See also *Voina i Rabochy Klass* (War and the Working Class), no. 3, 1944 (February 1, 1944), pp. 27–31, for an account by Mikhoels and Fefer themselves.

31. *Eynikayt*, February 5, 1948, p. 3.

32. Mordechai Altshuler, Yitshak Arad, and Shmuel Krakowski, eds., *Sovietskie Yevrei Pishut Ilye Erenburgu* (Soviet Jews Write to Ilya Ehrenburg) (Jerusalem, 1993), pp. 159–160. For further information on *The Black Book,* see Joshua Rubenstein, *Tangled Loyalties: The Life and Times of Ilya Ehrenburg* (Tuscaloosa, Ala., 1999), pp. 212–217; Redlich, *War, Holocaust and Stalinism*, pp. 347–371; Ilya Altman, "Toward the History of *The Black Book,*" in Aharon Weiss, ed., *Yad Vashem Studies* 21 (Jerusalem, 1991). In English, the fullest version is Ilya Ehrenburg and Vasily Grossman, eds., *The Black Book* (New York, 1981). In Russian, the most complete edition is *Chyornaya Kniga* (The Black Book) (Vilnius, 1993); this volume was edited by Irina Ehrenburg, the late daughter of Ilya Ehrenburg.

33. See Yehuda Bauer, *My Brother's Keeper: A History of the American Jewish Joint Distribution Committee, 1929–1939* (Philadelphia, 1974), pp. 57–104, for a history of the Agro-Joint project; and James N. Rosenberg, *On the Steppes: A Russian Diary* (New York, 1927), for an account of his visit to the Soviet Union in 1926. See also Shimon Redlich, "The 'Crimean Affair,'" *Jews and Jewish Topics,* Fall 1990, pp. 55–65, for a close analysis of this episode.

34. Memorandum by Joseph C. Hyman dated September 21, 1943, p. 2. Similar sentiments were repeated by James Rosenberg when he summarized his discussions with Mikhoels and Fefer in a memorandum of May 18, 1944, p. 2. Archive of the American Jewish Joint Distribution Committee in New York, Folder USSR General, 1942–1945, no. 1056.

35. Many close observers of this episode, including Alexander Borshchagovsky, believe that raising the question of a Jewish republic in the Crimea was a provocation on the part of Fefer and Epshteyn in their roles as MGB provocateurs. According to this account, they persuaded Mikhoels to join them, knowing that the regime had no intention of granting such a request and would use it against the JAC in due course. See Borshchagovsky, *Obvinyaetsa Krov,* pp. 134–135.

36. Redlich, *War, Holocaust and Stalinism,* p. 266. One former Soviet intelligence agent, the late Pavel Sudoplatov, claimed that Stalin was seriously considering the establishment of a Jewish republic in the Crimea before Mikhoels and Fefer left for America "as a probe of Western intentions to give us substantial economic aid after the war." See Pavel and Anatoli Sudoplatov, with Jerrold L. and Leona P. Schecter, *Special Tasks: The Memoirs of An Unwanted Witness—A Soviet Spymaster* (Boston, 1994), p. 287. If Sudoplatov's claim is correct, then Mikhoels would have had all the more reason to believe that the project would reach fruition.

37. On September 28, 1944, p. 4, *Eynikayt* carried an announcement that Kvitko would speak two days later in Moscow about his trip to the Crimea.

38. Marina Yuzefovich (daughter of Joseph Yuzefovich), interview with author, Rehovot, Israel, 1998. In the 1980s, when the regime began allowing relatives of the JAC members to examine the trial proceedings, one prosecutor hesitated to show Marina Yuzefovich the stenographic record. He did not know if she understood that she had been adopted, and out of humanitarian motives he did not want her to learn about this for the first time from her father's testimony.

39. David Hofshteyn, *Ikh gleyb* (*Milkhome lider*) (I Believe: War Poems) (Moscow, 1944), p. 50, cited in Mordechai Altshuler, "Anti-Semitism in Ukraine in 1944," *Jews in Eastern Europe,* Winter 1993, p. 44.

40. Ilya Ehrenburg, *Derevo* (Tree) (Moscow, 1946), pp. 45–46.

41. Center for Judaic Studies Library, University of Pennsylvania, Philadelphia, B. Z. Goldberg papers, Box 69. The letter was dated November 8, 1944.

42. David Bergelson, "About to Burst," *Eynikayt*, August 15, 1942, p. 2, cited in an unpublished paper about *Eynikayt* by Edward Portnoy, p. 18.

43. "Brotherly Greeting to the Jews in Palestine and Great Britain," *Eynikayt*, September 5, 1942, p. 4, cited in Portnoy's paper about *Eynikayt*, p. 19.

44. Shakhno Epshteyn, "Rebirth of a People," *Eynikayt*, November 4, 1944, p. 4, cited in Portnoy's paper about *Eynikayt*, pp. 24–25.

45. Letter from V. Kruzhkov to Alexander Shcherbakov, May 11, 1943, in Redlich, *War, Holocaust and Stalinism*, p. 285; letter from Epshteyn to Shcherbakov, November 23, 1943, in ibid., p. 289.

46. Minutes of the JAC Presidium, October 24, 1944, in State Archive of the Russian Federation (hereafter GARF), f. 8114, op. 1, d. 1064, ll. 122–123.

47. RGASPI, f. 17, op. 125, d. 211, ll. 25–26, l. 28. The letter was dated April 16, 1943.

48. From the minutes of the Sovinformburo concerning the JAC, May 22, 1945, in Redlich, *War, Holocaust and Stalinism*, p. 292.

49. RGASPI, f. 17, op. 125, d. 246, ll. 184–1840b. See also Redlich, *War, Holocaust and Stalinism*, pp. 248–249, for the letter to Molotov on October 28, 1944, and his response the next day.

50. Redlich, *War, Holocaust and Stalinism*, p. 414. Three years earlier, on April 7, 1943, Ehrenburg was already being criticized in a secret report from a party official for "citing the necessity of struggling against anti-Semitism." RGASPI, f. 17, op. 125, d. 158, l. 31; and Redlich, *War, Holocaust and Stalinism*, p. 215.

51. From the minutes of a Sovinformburo meeting on May 22, 1945, in Redlich, *War, Holocaust and Stalinism*, p. 294.

52. See N. K. Petrova, *Antifashistkie Komitety v SSSR, 1941–1945* (The Anti-Fascist Committees in the USSR, 1941–1945) (Moscow, 1999), pp. 258–266, for the postwar fate of each of the committees.

53. RGASPI, f. 17, op. 125, del. 459, l. 33.

54. There was a good deal of correspondence between the JAC and various Western Jewish organizations, particularly the World Jewish Congress. See Redlich, *War, Holocaust and Stalinism*, pp. 314–346.

55. Center for Judaic Studies Library, University of Pennsylvania, Philadelphia, B. Z. Goldberg papers, Box 70.

56. Kostyrchenko, *Out of the Red Shadows*, p. 78.

57. Redlich, *Propaganda and Nationalism in Wartime Russia*, pp. 154 and 217 n. 25.

58. Letter of Mikhoels and Fefer to Suslov, June 21, 1946, in RGASPI, f. 17, op. 128, del. 76, ll. 4–5.

59. Goldberg, *Jewish Problem in the Soviet Union*, pp. 59, 63, 59.

60. Goldberg, "Ten Years Later," *Israel Horizons*, vol. 10, no. 8, October 1962, p. 14.

61. Erich Goldhagen, interview with author, Cambridge, Mass., 1997.

62. Letter to Mikhoels and Fefer, October 17, 1946, in Center for Judaic Studies Library, University of Pennsylvania, Philadelphia, B. Z. Goldberg papers, Box 69.

63. Statement by the National Council of American-Soviet Friendship, February 22, 1948, in Center for Judaic Studies Library, University of Pennsylvania, Philadelphia, B. Z. Goldberg papers, Box 70.

64. See RGASPI, f. 17, op. 128, del. 76, l. 29, for the letter of Mikhoels and Shpiegelglas to Zhdanov, July 31, 1946; and RGASPI, f. 17, op. 128, del. 76, l. 30, for the note from Suslov to Zhdanov.

65. Paul Novick, *Yidn in birobidzhan* (Jews in Birobidzhan) (New York, 1937), p. 1, in Archives of the YIVO Institute for Jewish Research, New York, Paul Novick Files, envelope 17.

66. Paul Novick, interview with Shimon Redlich, May 20, 1976, p. 5, of the Hebrew Uni-

versity, Institute of Contemporary Jewry, Oral History Department, in the Archives of the YIVO Institute for Jewish Research, New York, Paul Novick Files, envelope 223.

67. For their letter, dated September 16, 1946, see RGASPI, f. 17, op. 128, del. 868, l. 79.

68. RGASPI, f. 17, op. 128, del. 76, ll. 53–530b. The note is dated October 1, 1946. A week earlier, on September 24, 1946, Novick had asked Mikhoels and Fefer to secure permission for him to visit Birobidzhan; see RGASPI, f. 17, op. 128, del. 76, ll. 54–59.

69. See Paul Novick, *Eyrope tvishn milkhome un sholem* (Europe Between War and Peace) (New York, 1948), pp. 268–270, 262–263, and 322–325, cited in Nora Levin, *The Jews in the Soviet Union Since 1917*, vol. 2 (New York, 1988), pp. 904–906, for an account of his visit to the Soviet Union in 1946.

70. Paul Novick, interview with Shimon Redlich, May 20, 1976, p. 9, of the Hebrew University, Institute of Contemporary Jewry, Oral History Department, in the Archives of the YIVO Institute for Jewish Research, New York, Paul Novick Files, envelope 223.

71. Shirley Novick (widow of Paul Novick), interview with author, New York, 1996.

72. Redlich, *War, Holocaust and Stalinism*, p. 425. The report was dated November 19, 1946. A secret review of the JAC's activity, and particularly of publications that had been sent abroad, was prepared on October 16, 1946. It roundly condemned the JAC on a number of counts: several correspondents had exaggerated the role of individual Jews during World War II; the JAC had failed to mention one Soviet film in its dispatches while praising a series of American films; JAC leaders had overstepped their responsibilities by appealing to Soviet officials on behalf of individual Soviet Jews and in defense of Polish Jews after anti-Semitic incidents in Cracow and elsewhere; and, finally, the "Joint" was identified as an organization that engaged in "espionage" and "anti-Soviet, subversive work." This secret review may well have been the basis for Suslov's report to Stalin and other members of the Central Committee. Many of the accusations were later repeated in the indictment against the defendants in the 1952 trial. RGASPI, f. 17, op. 128, del. 1057, ll. 92–114; the review was written by N. L. Norovkov.

73. Cited in Kostyrchenko, *Out of the Red Shadows*, p. 14.

74. Vladimir Lenin, "The Position of the Bund in the Party," in Lenin, *Collected Works*, vol. 6: *January 1902–August 1903* (Moscow, 1961), p. 100.

75. Writing in 1913, Stalin defined a nation "as a historically constituted, stable community of people, formed on the basis of a common language, territory, economic life and psychological make-up manifested in a common culture." Joseph Stalin, *Marxism and the National Question* (London, 1936), p. 8. Because the Jews did not have a territory of their own, it was natural for Stalinists to deny them the status of a "nation."

76. Strobe Talbot, ed., *Khrushchev Remembers* (Boston, 1970), p. 263.

77. Stalin's statement to the Jewish Telegraphic Agency, dated January 12, 1931, was widely reported; see *New York Times,* January 15, 1931, p. 9. It was not prominently cited in the Soviet press until November 1936, when Molotov mentioned it in a speech. See Solomon M. Schwarz, *Anti-Semitism in the Soviet Union* (New York, 1952), p. 100.

78. Cited in Gitelman, *Jewish Nationality and Soviet Politics*, p. 431.

79. Richard Pipes, *Russia Under the Bolshevik Regime* (New York, 1995), p. 281.

80. David Ortenberg, *1943* (Moscow, 1991), p. 399.

81. Irina Ehrenburg, interview with author, Moscow, 1991. See also Irina Ehrenburg, *Razluka. Vospominaniya. Dnevnik* (The Separation. Memoirs. A Diary.) (Israel, 1998), privately published by her daughter Faina Paleyeva.

82. Svetlana Alliluyeva, *Twenty Letters to a Friend* (New York, 1967), p. 181.

83. Svetlana Alliluyeva, *Only One Year* (New York, 1969), p. 152.

84. Davis Strassler, "The Dictator Feared the Actor," *Jerusalem Post,* August 14, 1992, p. 1.

85. Marina Raskin (granddaughter of David Bergelson), interview with author by telephone, 1999.

86. From the minutes of the JAC Presidium, October 5, 1947, in GARF, f. 8114, op. 1, del. 1053, ll. 203–204.

87. Grigory Kheifets had a long history of work within Soviet intelligence circles before being designated consul in San Francisco, where he was involved in atomic espionage during World War II. See Sudoplatov, *Special Tasks,* pp. 174–176; note also Sudoplatov's hightly tendentious and questionable account of Kheifets's contacts with Robert Oppenheimer.

88. Marina Raskin, interview with author by telephone, 1999.

89. Jeffrey Veidlinger, *The Moscow State Yiddish Theater: Jewish Culture on the Soviet Stage* (Bloomington, Ind., 2000), p. 136.

90. Mikhoels's performance in King Lear was widely hailed. In April 1935, the famous British theater director Gordon Craig was in Moscow and saw the production. Craig had requested a seat in the theater "from which he could get up and leave when he deemed it necessary." But he was riveted by Mikhoels and "understood that one does not walk out of such a production." See Ya. Grinvald, *Mikhoels* (Moscow, 1948), p. 62.

91. Nadezhda Mandelstam, *Hope Against Hope* (New York, 1970), p. 300.

92. Kostyrchenko, *Out of the Red Shadows,* pp. 23, 51.

93. Cited in Tatyana Tsarevskaya, "Krimskaya Alternativa Birobidzhanu i Palestinu" (The Crimean Alternative to Birobidzhan and Palestine), *Otechestvennaya Istoriya* (History of the Fatherland), no. 2, 1999, p. 124. The document cited is a secret police report of communications between Mikhoels and his colleagues on the JAC.

94. Shimon Kipnis, "A kristal vaz funem erd fun Babi Yar" (A Crystal Vase Filled With Earth From Babi Yar), *Di naye prese* (The New Press), September 29, 1973, cited in Levin, *Jews in the Soviet Union Since 1917,* vol. 1, pp. 421–422.

95. From the minutes of the JAC Presidium, October 23, 1945, in GARF, f. 8114, op. 1, d. 1053, l. 94.

96. Abraham Sutzkever, "Mit shloyme mikhoels" (With Solomon Mikhoels), *Di goldene keyt* (The Golden Chain), vol. 43, 1962, p. 165, cited in Levin, *Jews in the Soviet Union Since 1917,* vol. 1, p. 390.

97. Vovsi-Mikhoels, *Moy Otets Solomon Mikhoels,* pp. 191–192. Already in 1946, officials were alarmed by the willingness of Soviet Jews to voice pro-Zionist sympathies. On July 17, 1946, V. Lutsky, a specialist on the Arab world, presented a lecture in Moscow on the Palestinian problem. Afterward, based on the two hundred questions and comments submitted to him in writing, Lutsky complained to the Central Committee that there was a "nationalistic mood among Jews." In his report, he made note of questions about Zionism, Palestine, and anti-Semitism. One person wondered why the JAC had not condemned a pogrom in Poland. Others asked why the committee was silent about the situation in Palestine. Another asked about the use of Hebrew there. See RGASPI, f. 17, op. 128, del. 1057, ll. 115–136.

98. Alliluyeva, *Only One Year,* p. 153.

99. See Kostyrchenko, *Out of the Red Shadows,* pp. 79–88, for further details of the plot against Mikhoels.

100. Redlich, *War, Holocaust and Stalinism,* pp. 384–385.

101. Ibid., p. 401.

102. Ibid., pp. 390–392.

103. Mordechai Namir, *Shlihut bi-Moskva* (Mission to Moscow) (Tel Aviv, 1971), p. 49.

104. Redlich, *War, Holocaust and Stalinism,* p. 464.

105. Alliluyeva, *Twenty Letters to a Friend,* p. 196.

106. Robert Weinberg, *Stalin's Forgotten Zion: Birobidzhan and the Making of a Soviet Jewish Homeland—an Illustrated History, 1928–1996* (Berkeley, 1998), pp. 82–83. See also Israel Emiot, *The Birobidzhan Affair: A Yiddish Writer in Siberia* (Philadelphia, 1981).

107. RGASPI, f. 17, op. 116, del. 415, l. 3. The meeting took place on February 3, 1949.

Four months later, on May 27, Anatoly Sofronov, an executive member of the Writers' Union, sent a letter to the Central Committee describing the poverty of a number of Yiddish writers in Moscow; they were asking to go to Birobidzhan, hoping work would be available for them there. RGASPI, f. 17, op. 132, del. 224. While Sofronov was a notorious anti-Semite, he directed his attacks against Russian writers of Jewish origin within the Writers' Union; those who wrote in Yiddish were of less concern to him.

108. See Kostyrchenko, *Out of the Red Shadows*, pp. 100–101.

109. David Hofshteyn and Feige Hofshteyn, *Izbranniye. Stikhotvoreniya. Pisma. S Lyubovyu i Bolyu o Davidye Hofshteyne* ([David Hofshteyn,] Selected Poems. Letters. [Feige Hofshteyn,] With Love and Pain About David Hofshteyn) (Jerusalem, 1997), p. 73.

110. Vovsi-Mikhoels, *Moy Otets Solomon Mikhoels,* p. 216.

111. Dora Fefer (daughter of Itsik Fefer), interview with author, Moscow, 1997.

112. Marlen Korallov, interview with author, Moscow, 1997.

113. Tamara Platt, interview with author by telephone, 1998; Alla Zuskin-Perelman (daughter of Benjamin Zuskin), interview with author, Tel Aviv, 1998.

114. Vladimir Shamberg (grandson of Solomon Lozovsky), interview with author, Cambridge, Mass., 1997.

115. Kostyrchenko, *Out of the Red Shadows,* pp. 37–38.

116. Ibid., p. 116.

117. Letter from Faina Sivachinskaia to the author, December 9, 1997.

118. Vladimir Talmy (son of Leon Talmy), interview with author, North Potomac, Md., 1997.

119. Namir, *Shlihut bi-Moskva,* pp. 83–91.

120. See Kostyrchenko, *Out of the Red Shadows,* pp. 119–123, for further details about the case against Zhemchuzhina. See also Albert Resis, *Molotov Remembers: Inside Kremlin Politics—Conversations with Felix Chuev* (Chicago, 1993), pp. 323–325, for Molotov's reminiscences of his wife's arrest.

121. Three months after seeing Fadeyev in New York, the Yiddish writer and editor Nakhmen Mayzl wrote to Fadeyev in Moscow asking for word on the fate of several Yiddish writers and publishing institutions; the letter was dated June 24, 1949. Center for Judaic Studies Library, University of Pennsylvania, Philadelphia, B. Z. Goldberg papers, Box 75. In March 1949 the *New York Times* reported on protests against the Waldorf Conference and the visit by Soviet delegates. The philosopher Sidney Hook helped to organize demonstrations by a group of prominent intellectuals associated with Americans for Intellectual Freedom who raised questions about the fate of numerous Soviet cultural figures, but there is no evidence that Hook knew about the rumors concerning the Yiddish writers. See *New York Times,* March 23, 1949, p. 26. I am also indebted to Dale Reed, who examined the Sidney Hook papers at the Hoover Institution Archives on my behalf.

122. Howard Fast, *Being Red* (Boston, 1990), pp. 206–207, 217–219; letter of Howard Fast to Paul Novick, September 5, 1957, in the Archives of the YIVO Institute for Jewish Research, New York, Paul Novick Files, envelope 55. For confirmation of Fast's account of his encounter with Fadeyev in Paris, see succeeding editions of Ehrenburg's memoirs. In 1967, Ehrenburg was permitted to relate how Fadeyev acknowledged that the questions of an unnamed American writer "tormented" him. *Lyudi, Gody, Zhizn* (People, Years, Life), in Ehrenburg, *Sobranie Sochinenie* (Collected Works), vol. 9 (Moscow, 1967), p. 596. Almost a quarter of a century later, when a more complete edition of the memoirs appeared in Moscow, Ehrenburg's text was restored, with Fadeyev acknowledging that it was Fast who had "tormented" him in Paris; see *Lyudi, Gody, Zhizn,* vol. 3 (Moscow, 1990), p. 122.

123. The letter was dated July 5, 1949. From Harshav, *Life of Marc Chagall.*

124. Paul Robeson, Jr., interview with author by telephone, 1997. "Zog nit keyn mol" was written by Hirsh Glik in the Vilna Ghetto. A compact disc recording of the concert was

released in 1995; see Paul Robeson, *The Legendary Moscow Concert,* recorded on June 14, 1949 (Fenix Entertainment, Burbank, Calif.). Robeson's remarks after his performance are not included.

125. Martin Bauml Duberman, *Paul Robeson* (New York, 1988), pp. 353–354; Paul Robeson, Jr., interview with author by telephone, 1997.

126. Howard Fast, *The Naked God* (New York, 1957), p. 131.

127. Rubenstein, *Tangled Loyalties,* p. 266. Later on, throughout the 1950s, rumors and accusations circulated in Jewish circles in the West that Ehrenburg had betrayed the defendants by testifying against them during their trial; such accusations were complete fabrications. See *Tangled Loyalties,* pp. 315–316.

128. *American Jewish Yearbook,* vol. 51 (New York, 1950), p. 337.

129. Borshchagovsky, *Obvinyaetsa Krov,* p. 238.

130. Marlen Korallov, interview with author, Moscow, 1997. Korallov, who is a leader of Memorial in Moscow, a human rights organization dedicated to documenting the crimes of the regime, particularly during the Stalin period, was held in the same cell as Hofshteyn for nine months.

131. See Vladimir Naumov's introduction to *Nepravedny Sud* (An Unjust Trial) (Moscow, 1994), p. 8.

132. Esther Markish, *The Long Return* (New York, 1978), p. 243.

133. Borshchagovsky, *Obvinyaetsa Krov,* p. 217.

134. Arrested in 1951, around the same time as Viktor Abakumov, Komarov appealed to Stalin on February 18, 1952, in a last-ditch attempt to save his own life. In the letter, Komarov repeated his animosity toward the Jews: "I especially hated Jewish nationalists and was merciless with them, seeing them as the most dangerous and wicked enemies. Because of my hatred for them, not only those under arrest but even former MGB employees of Jewish nationality considered me an anti-Semite and tried to compromise me before Abakumov." Borshchagovsky, *Obvinyaetsa Krov,* pp. 50–51.

135. Ibid., p. 108.

136. Nadezhda Aizenshtadt Bergelson (daughter of Miriam Aizenshtadt Zheleznova), interview with author, Moscow, 1997. For further information on the case of Miriam Aizenshtadt Zheleznova and Shmuel Persov, see Kostyrchenko, *Out of the Red Shadows,* pp. 134–136.

137. Borshchagovsky, *Obvinyaetsa Krov,* p. 257. In the post-Stalin novel *Going Under* (London, 1972), the dissident author Lydia Chukovskaya provides a portrait of Halkin after his release from prison.

138. See Kostyrchenko, *Out of the Red Shadows,* pp. 125–126, for further details on the fall of Abakumov.

139. See ibid., pp. 258–265, for further information on the case of Yakov Etinger.

140. Ibid., pp. 127–128.

141. See Harold J. Berman, "Introduction and Analysis," in Harold J. Berman and James W. Spindler, eds., *Soviet Criminal Law and Procedure: The RSFSR Codes,* 2d ed., (Cambridge, Mass., 1992), pp. 50–51, 56–57.

142. See Robert Conquest, *The Great Terror—A Reassessment* (New York, 1990), pp. 109–131, for his explanation of the role that confessions played within Stalin's system of judicial terror.

143. See Arkady Vaksberg, *Stalin Against the Jews* (New York, 1994), pp. 227–236, for the full text of Cheptsov's letter.

144. Meir Cotic, *The Prague Trial: The First Anti-Zionist Show Trial in the Communist Bloc* (New York, 1987), p. 144. Israel, in fact, did initiate a clandestine program in 1952 that was based in its embassies behind the Iron Curtain. The task of this Liaison Bureau "was to maintain contact with Jews in those countries; help them in every possible way; provide them with information; smuggle in Jewish cultural and religious material; explore the possibilities

for aliyah; and, in some cases, help Jews escape across borders." Levanon, "Israel's Role in the Campaign," p. 71. It is not known whether the activities of the Liaison Bureau were detected by Soviet intelligence before Stalin's death. If it had been, it would surely have provoked a sharp response. As it happens, an explosion in the courtyard of the Soviet embassy in Tel Aviv in February 1953 was used as a pretext for breaking off diplomatic relations with Israel. Relations were not resumed until the following July.

145. V. Malyshev, "Dnevnik Narkoma" (Diary of a People's Commissar), *Istochnik* (Source), no. 5, 1997, pp. 140–141.

146. *Pravda,* January 13, 1953, p. 1, carried a lead editorial, with further details carried in a TASS dispatch on p. 4.

147. See Rubenstein, *Tangled Loyalties,* pp. 268–276, for a full discussion of Ehrenburg's response to the Doctors' Plot. His letter to Stalin was found at the dictator's dacha in October 1953. See also Alexander Fursenko, "Konets Ery Stalina" (The End of the Stalin Era), *Zvezda* (Star), no. 12, 1999, pp. 178–179, which contains new information about this episode and Stalin's political maneuvers at the end of his life.

148. Fast, *The Naked God,* pp. 131–134. In the fall of 1955 the Soviet writer Boris Polevoy visited New York, where he saw Howard Fast. In answer to a question from Fast about the fate of Leyb Kvitko, Polevoy claimed that they were living in the same apartment building. Soon thereafter, Fast learned of Kvitko's execution. He subsequently wrote to Polevoy about their conversation. See ibid., pp. 186–195, for copies of their correspondence.

149. Leon Kristal, "5 Barimte yidishe shrayber in rusland dershosn in 1952, keyblt *forverts* korespondent" (Five Famous Yiddish Writers Executed in Russia in 1952), Forverts Correspondent Cables), *Forverts,* March 7, 1956, p. 1; "*Forverts* nayes vegn ermordete yidishe shrayber in rusland ruft aroys a sensatsiyi" (*Forverts* News About the Murdered Yiddish Writers in Russia Creates a Sensastion), *Forverts,* March 8, 1956, p. 1.

150. "Our Pain and Our Consolation" (in Yiddish), *Folks-shtime* (People's Voice), April 4, 1956, p. 2. The *Morgen Freiheit* followed up the news from Warsaw with several articles of its own; see the issues of April 10, April 11, and April 13, 1956.

151. Shirley Novick, interview with Edward Portnoy, New York, 1995.

152. Marina Raskin, interview with author by telephone, 1997. Both B. Z. Goldberg and Paul Novick were permitted to visit the Soviet Union separately in 1959. During his trip, Goldberg was able to learn a great deal about the fate of the JAC leadership and the Yiddish writers, even to the point of confirming, as he wrote in 1961, that both he and Novick "had figured in the plot . . . as [emissaries] of American imperialists." See Goldberg, *Jewish Problem in the Soviet Union,* p. 3.

Index

Abakumov, Viktor, 341; and Alliluyeva family, 39–40; arrest of, xv, 53–54; evidence falsified by, 44, 47, 411–412, 414; interrogation by, xiii, 51–52, 172, 235, 259–260, 261, 304, 412; and JAC members, 42, 43, 44, 45, 53–54

Afinogenov, Alexander, 185, 204

Agro-Joint, 19, 370

Akselrod, Zelig, 6, 136n

Aleichem, Sholem, 15, 26, 28, 89, 119, 127, 136, 176

Alexandrov, Georgy, 121, 137, 174, 185, 186, 189, 192, 206, 222

Alexandrovich, Mikhail, 93, 316

Aliger, Margarita, 18

Alliluyeva, Nadezhda, 46

Alliluyeva, Svetlana, 35, 39–40, 41

Alter, Viktor, 9–10, 14

AMBIJAN (American Birobidjan Committee), 29, 198, 214, 349

American Committee of Jewish Writers, Artists, and Scientists, 17, 27, 88n, 195–196, 208, 225

American Communist Party, 6, 189, 208; founding of, 264, 297–298n; on missing Jewish writers, 47–48; and *Morgen Freiheit*, 30, 85, 271, 272, 299, 413; Talmy, 264, 271, 272; Vatenberg, 280, 281

American Jewish Joint Distribution Committee. *See* Joint Distribution Committee

anti-fascist committees: creation of, 7, 103, 187–188, 199–200, 240; disbanding,
206; goals of, 7, 71, 174, 200, 240; information disseminated by, 190–191, 194; Lozovsky, 7, 187–188, 194, 199–200, 206; Shtern, 322. *See also* Jewish Anti-Fascist Committee

anti-Semitism: denial of, 6, 29, 49; in England, 87, 323–324; in France, 22; in government circles, 35, 38, 42, 48, 54, 98, 103, 242–244; of interrogators, xii–xiii, 52, 54, 61, 229; JAC efforts, 24, 32, 38, 86, 100–101, 103; nativization policy, 129; protests against, 17, 24, 297; quotas and restrictions, 31, 34, 37, 86, 113, 243, 289; of Stalin, xix, 2, 32–35, 40, 41, 61–62; trials and executions, 2, 55–64. *See also* Holocaust; Nazi atrocities

Asch, Sholem, 14, 16, 17, 48, 232, 351

assimilation, Jewish: dwindling Yiddish communities, 128, 134; and language, 32, 57, 92, 146–147, 148–149, 152, 156, 268; Lenin on, 32, 57, 146, 148; nativization policy, 129; resistance to, 57, 89, 92, 135, 197, 247; Stalin on, 32–33

Babel, Isaac, 131

Babi Yar, 21–22, 38, 300

Bakhmutsky, Alexander, 42, 414

Baranov, Leonid, 94

Benediktov, Ivan, 86, 245

Bergelson, David: accusations against, xvii–xviii, 132, 366–367, 395, 397, 399; arrest, 44, 50, 68, 132; awards, 68, 403;

BOOKS IN THE ANNALS OF COMMUNISM SERIES